A. 6/8

D1576362

CORPUS CHRISTI
BUTLER LIBRARY
COLLEGE

A — 5 — 3

A - 6

SELECT STATUTES, CASES
AND DOCUMENTS

SELECT STATUTES
CASES AND DOCUMENTS

TO ILLUSTRATE ENGLISH
CONSTITUTIONAL HISTORY, 1660–1832

WITH A SUPPLEMENT FROM 1832–1894

EDITED BY

C. GRANT ROBERTSON, M.A.

FELLOW OF ALL SOULS' COLLEGE, OXFORD
EXAMINER IN THE HONOUR SCHOOL OF MODERN HISTORY IN THE
UNIVERSITY OF OXFORD, 1901–1904

METHUEN & CO.
36 ESSEX STREET W.C.
LONDON

First Published in 1904

CORPUS CHRISTI
BUTLER LIBRARY
A.6/8
COLLEGE

TABLE OF CONTENTS

II
CASES

PREFACE

THE origin, purpose, and scope of this volume require a brief explanation. For the past few years, when lecturing in the Honour School of Modern History at Oxford on English Constitutional History from 1660 to the Great Reform Bill, I invariably found that both my classes and I laboured under the serious disadvantage of having no handy collection of *pièces justificatives* in the shape of selected original authorities for our subject, such as is at the disposal of teachers and students for the preceding periods of English history in the well-known *Select Charters* of Stubbs, and the similar volumes of Professor Prothero and Mr. Gardiner—with what profit to all concerned needs no proof here. A teacher's increasing experience of this disadvantage for the important epoch which opens with the Restoration of Charles II. has been reinforced by a three years' experience as an examiner in the Oxford Honour School of Modern History, a school which now numbers annually nearly two hundred candidates. If the student, in short, of English Constitutional History for the hundred and seventy years from 1660 —the period in which the bases of the constitution under which we live to-day were finally established—desire access to the most important statutes and documents, or to the text of the decisions in the leading cases in constitutional law, he has so far been compelled to seek them scattered in the ponderous collection of Parliamentary Statutes, in the still more voluminous and confusing mass of Law Reports, or piecemeal in various books not always to be found in his college library, and certainly not within the reach of a modest purse. Otherwise he must rest content with the quotations or paraphrases of the leading secondary authorities, or, worse still, the *ipse dixit* of the lecturer. The educational value of bringing the student face to face with the original authorities is a point that to-day requires no laboured proof; it is one of the truisms common to all places where history is seriously studied. Furthermore, I fancy that all teachers will agree on these two propositions : First, that even if the desire to undertake the hunt for a reference to original authorities given by a lecturer were present in the average student (which in nine cases out of ten it is not), the pressure on his time of other studies and interests under an ordinary university course would veto the attempt; and secondly, that most students not only require to be tempted to walk to the original founts, but that the fount itself must be in a reasonably accessible place, and its salutary waters must be presented to an artfully created thirst in a tolerably digestible form and in a vessel easily handled. This volume, then, is the outcome of the truth of these two conclusions. Since no such collection existed as I required for my own purposes as a lecturer, some years ago I set to work to make one for myself, utilising to the best of my powers a teacher's experience. I am ready frankly to admit that criticism of the selection, both on the grounds of what is included and what is omitted—to show that it is both arbitrary and incomplete—will be easy. The extended task of selection, indeed, would enable me to play very effectively the part of *advocatus diaboli* against the form of my own labours. On the other hand, I can but ask those who are disposed to criticise unfavourably to remember one or two things. (1) A very serious, I might say an insurmountable, difficulty has been the singular wealth and copiousness of the material at the compiler's disposal. Yet four hundred and fifty pages can only contain, after all, a certain number of words. Rigorous considerations of space have compelled me reluctantly to eliminate much of what I had carefully excerpted and intended to include. It would have been easy to compile two volumes, but the condition of the task, as I conceived it, required the material to be limited to a single volume, and that of a reasonable compass. (2) I have endeavoured to cover a period of one hundred and seventy-two years—years increasingly crowded with illustrative and important material. Professor Prothero's collection covers a period of sixty-five, Mr. Gardiner's of thirty-two years; and a glance at the shelves of any library which contains the Statutes and Law Reports (to mention no other possible sources) would show that parliamentary and legal activity, and parliamentary and legal draughtsmanship, have not gained in brevity or lost in the importance of their contents as the centuries advance; and as the constitution has increased in its fearful and wonderful complexity, so too have the necessity and means for illustrating it. (3) Many kind friends have freely offered me numerous suggestions—suggestions as varied and embarrassing, from their range, originality, number, and disinterestedness, as those which the modern Chancellor of the Exchequer receives on the eve of his budget. Had I carried out all these I should have finally constructed an admirable encyclopædia almost as bulky and costly as the sources from which it would have been derived. That I have not done so is not because I am not grateful for so much valuable advice, but simply because of the sheer impossibility of acting on it within the limits of the space at my command; and when I survey the material at the disposal of a compiler, and remember the suggestions acted upon and then reluctantly put aside, I confess to a legitimate surprise at my own moderation. (4) Let it then be pointed out at once that this collection does not pretend to illustrate documentarily the growth of the Cabinet system, of our financial system, nor the slow and elaborate evolution of the structure and working of the government of the Empire (save for the inclusion of two important legislative enactments on the government of India). Reflection, I think, will convince that the Cabinet system and the government of the Empire are each of them subjects requiring a volume a-piece for satisfactory treatment. Nor do the shifting conventions of the constitution, the spirit and essence of the government of the Sovereign in Parliament, the complex totality of varying and intangible nuances, understandings, unwritten rules, constitutional etiquette, lend themselves to satisfactory documentary illustration in the rigid black and white of textual authorities, save at great length and with copious explanation. Moreover, throughout the process of selection my desire, fortified by some experience, has been to treat adequately some important features rather than to attempt to treat scrappily and inadequately all.

The material in the following pages will be found to fall under three heads—Selected Statutes, Selected Cases, and an Appendix. As regards the statutes, I have endeavoured to give what seem to me the most important legislative enactments between 1660 and 1832. That the selection is more full for the period down to 1720 than for that immediately following will not, I think, surprise any student. The lull in the passing of great formative statutes after 1714 is a familiar commonplace in the authorities, and the very remarkable period of strenuous legislative reform which commenced some ten years before the Reform Bill, and continues for half a century after it, largely falls outside the chronological limits of the plan of this volume. I have not scrupled to modernise the spelling of the text, to supplement the punctuation if necessary, and to eliminate the necessary verbiage of the parliamentary draughtsman. But in the case of the more important statutes, such as the Bill of Rights or the Act of Settlement, the text is given entire; and in that of the Bill of Rights I thought it desirable to print the document as it appears in the statutes of the realm, so that students might have at least one example of a historic and epoch-making statute in its original form. In the text all omissions, even of intelligible verbiage, are indicated by printed dots . . .; where whole clauses are eliminated the fact is noted in brackets, and, if required, the substance of the omission epitomised, that the student may at least follow the scope of the whole statute. The notes throughout are of the briefest, save perhaps in the case of the Mutiny Act of 1689, where I have endeavoured to collate and summarise some forty subsequent enactments and extensions of the law, in the hope of showing as briefly as possible their constitutional import on, and connection with, the original statute, and to bring them into relation, through an ordered and instructive process of constitutional development, with the modern law. A reference to pp. 58–62 will perhaps explain both the object and the result. Where it seemed necessary or desirable, additional illustrative matter in the shape of Parliamentary Resolutions, Protests, or other documents has been appended to certain statutes—for example, the Test Act (p. 39), the Coronation Oath Act (p. 65), and so on. The connection of this additional matter with the statute will be, I trust, self-evident, and its value to the student, I hope, not less so. Throughout I have cited very sparingly from the Protests of the Peers, important as they are, partly because they are accessible as a whole to all in Thorold Rogers' scholarly collection of three volumes, partly because of their length. When given, the version has been taken from the printed text of the Lords Journals, and I have not thought myself entitled to borrow even with acknowledgment Thorold Rogers' laborious identification of the signatures. These, therefore, are given as they stand in the authoritative printed text; but a reference is always supplied to the pages of Rogers' edition, to which the student can easily turn for fuller information. The suggestions at the end of each statute as to leading secondary authorities, while new in a collection of this kind, have a two-fold object: (1) to save the space of explanatory matter as to the statute itself; (2) to help the student, rather than the teacher, to find authoritative comment on, and explanation of, the subject-matter of the document. Such references are easily extended to any length; it is only necessary to say here that they are not intended to be even a select bibliography. Their presence in the book, I was glad to find, was warmly approved of by several teachers of wide experience, and a preliminary key to the abbreviations is intended to make plain the symbols employed.

The second part of the volume consists of leading Cases in constitutional law, treated somewhat differently to the statutes. For reasons that will, I hope, be intelligible, each is prefaced by a brief introduction, limited to explaining as tersely and plainly as possible the facts and points necessary for understanding the excerpts given, and here, too, reference to the most helpful commentaries has been attempted. The excerpts which follow are severally original authorities, *i.e.* they are part of the texts on which a historical student would work if writing from first-hand evidence. Yearly experience strengthens my conviction that cases in constitutional law, which most historical students not unreasonably find in an epitome dry, unduly technical, frequently repulsive, can be made more attractive, and therefore more profitable in every way, if for the paraphrases of the text-book writer are substituted the salient parts of the authority itself; if, for example, in the famous cases connected with the name and cause of Wilkes the student can study the actual words of the judges who made both history, law, and liberty by their decisions. The principle on which these excerpts are framed will be most clearly seen by reference to the documents themselves; I will only remark here that the illustrative matter is not confined to purely judicial decisions. No apology, I take it, to-day is necessary for allotting in a volume of this kind, covering the years from 1660–1832, a considerable place to cases in constitutional law. The part played by the law courts in defining, extending, limiting, even creating constitutional law, machinery, and rights, is explained and justified in the leading authorities, and the argument need not be repeated. Certainly a student who had studied the period in question, and was ignorant of the leading cases, would have a very partial, unsatisfactory, and misleading knowledge of his subject, both as regards historical and philosophical principles and historical matters of fact. As to the actual selection made, I would simply remark: (1) That I have been guided in choosing from the wealth of illustrative material by the intrinsic and historic importance of the case itself, and also necessarily by the possibility of representing it satisfactorily within due limits; (2) that owing to the importance of Parliamentary Privilege and judicial decisions with regard to it, I have not scrupled to give it as full a representation as possible; (3) that at the risk of apparent inconsistency the chronological limits have been in this department slightly extended beyond 1832; (4) that no one regrets more than myself the omission of more illustrative cases, more especially on the law of Treason, particularly in the period between 1792 and 1820. But the length of these cases, and generally their highly technical, not to say their transient, character, made it impossible to include them within the limits at my disposal; (5) a glance at the Table of Contents will, I hope, make clear the principles on which I have acted, and some knowledge of constitutional history will perhaps help in answering why; (6) lastly, I cannot claim to be a trained lawyer, nor have I written nor selected for trained lawyers. Throughout this section in particular I have thought chiefly of the historical student and his more imperative needs, and have endeavoured both to choose and explain almost wholly in his interests. The cases selected, in fact, primarily and ultimately, are there because of their historical value and importance. In the later constitutional history it is inevitable that the student must from time to time deliberately trespass on the sacred and mysterious domains of law; but he has no intention of challenging established and jealously guarded rights. Modestly and rapidly he will return from his raids, having spoken with bated breath the language that makes those mysterious domains more mysterious, and invariably will protest his desire to do a minimum of damage to the property of the owners. At the same time, an editor confessedly working for historical students would indeed be pleased if the result of his trespasses were found useful also to students in schools of law in whose curriculum constitutional law necessarily and constitutional history indirectly have their due place.

The Appendix, which forms Part III., will be found to contain some material which could not conveniently be grouped under the first two parts. It also contains supplementary epitomes of some of the leading statutes since 1832. Their inclusion in this or any form was not, however, a feature of the volume as originally planned, since the Reform Bill had been chosen as the *terminus ad quem*. But several kind friends of weight and experience insistently urged me at least to extend in skeleton the story illustrated as far as 1832; and they dwelt on the necessity of continuing for the student

the reforms begun in 1827.   To have printed the full text of
the statutes which since 1832 have virtually given the British
race a new constitution was impossible by reason of their bulk
and their number, but I have endeavoured to meet the friendly
representations made by epitomising, as far as possible in the
language of the documents themselves, some of these great
formative statutes, in the hope that though the selection is
both somewhat incomplete and novel in form, it will prove of
use to those who have worked with the help of this volume
on the period from 1660–1832.   Briefly, then, as regards the
selection as a whole, my object may be stated thus.   In so
far as the student of constitutional history may reasonably
demand: What was the law that created or defined this or
that important power?   Upon what statutory authority is this
important right based?   In what way was this or that right
or power abolished, limited, extended?   For what reasons and
with what results were the judges called upon to decide this
or that great constitutional issue?   I have endeavoured to
supply him with an answer.

It only remains to thank all who have from time to time
assisted me with advice and suggestions, many pupils un-
consciously included.   That I do not more specifically mention
names is because when advice and suggestions have so often
been gratefully received, carefully weighed, and then not acted
on, I am anxious to relieve my friends of all responsibility.
Furthermore, my best thanks are due to Miss Prior, who
assisted me in the laborious task of copying no small portion
of the material.

C. G. R.

ALL SOULS' COLLEGE,
     May, 1904.

ABBREVIATIONS FOR AUTHORITIES CITED

Abbey and Overton, E.C. C. J. Abbey and J. H. Overton. The English Church in the Eighteenth Century. 2 vols.

Adolphus, H.E. J. Adolphus. History of England from the Accession of George III.

Anson, L.C. Sir W. R. Anson. Law and Custom of the Constitution. 2 vols.

A. and S., S.D. G. B. Adams and H. M. Stephens. Select Documents of English Constitutional History.

Broom, C.L. H. Broom. Constitutional Law.

C.J. Journals of the House of Commons, 1547–1832.

Cobbett, P.H. W. Cobbett. Parliamentary History of England. 48 vols.

Craik, C.S.H. A Century of Scottish History. 2 vols.

Dicey, L.C. A. V. Dicey. The Law of the Constitution.

Fowle, P.L. T. W. Fowle. The Poor Law (English Citizen Series).

Gardiner, C.D. S. R. Gardiner. The Constitutional Documents of the Puritan Revolution.

Gneist, E.C. H. R. Gneist. History of the English Constitution. Tr. P. Ashworth.

Gneist, S.G. Self-Government in England.

G. and H., S.S. H. Gee and W. J. Hardy. Documents Illustrative of English Church History.

Hallam, C.H. The Constitutional History of England. 3 vols.

Hansard, P.D. Parliamentary Debates, First, Second, and Third Series.

Hargrave, H.J.L. Sir M. Hale. The Jurisdiction of the Lords' House of Parliament. Ed. by F. Hargrave.

Hawkins, P.C. William Hawkins. A Treatise of the Pleas of the Crown. 2 vols.

Hill Burton, H.S. J. H. Burton. History of Scotland. 8 vols.

H.M.C.R. Historical Manuscripts Commission. XV. Reports, with Appendices.

Holdsworth, H.E.L. W. S. Holdsworth. A History of English Law. Vol. i.

Hunter, H.B.D. Sir W. W. Hunter. A History of British Dominion in India. 2 vols.

Ilbert, G.I. Sir C. P. Ilbert. The Government of India.

Lecky, H.E. W. H. Lecky. A History of England in the Eighteenth Century. 7 vols.

L.J. Journals of the House of Lords, 1547–1832.

L.Q.R.   Law Quarterly Review.

L.R.Q.B.D.   Law Reports, Queen's Bench Division.

Macaulay, H.E.   History of England. 2 vols.

Macqueen, A.J.L.   A Treatise on the Appellate Jurisdiction of the House of Lords and the Privy Council.

Mahon, H.E.   Mahon, Viscount. History of England from the Reign of Queen Anne. 7 vols.

Makower, C.H.E.   Felix Makower. Constitutional History of the Church of England.

May, C.H.E.   Sir T. E. May. Constitutional History of England. 3 vols.

May, P.P.   Law, Privileges, Proceedings, and Usage of Parliament.

Michael, E.G.   W. Michael. Englische Geschichte im 18 Jahrhundert. 1 vol.

Odgers, L. and S.   Odgers, W. B. A Digest of the Law of Libel and Slander.

Perry, H.C.E.   History of the Church of England. 3 vols.

Pike, H.L.   L. O. Pike. A Constitutional History of the House of Lords.

Porritt, U.H.C.   E. and A. E. Porritt. The Unreformed House of Commons. 2 vols.

Prothero, C.D.   Select Statutes and Constitutional Documents for the Reigns of Elizabeth and James I. Ed. G. W. Prothero.

Ranke, H.E.   History of England, principally in the Seventeenth Century, 6 vols. Eng. Translation.

Redlich and Hirst, E.L.G.   J. Redlich and F. W. Hirst. Local Government in England. 2 vols.

Rogers, P.L.   The Protests of the House of Lords. Ed. J. E. T. Rogers. 3 vols.

S.L.   The Statutes at Large. Ed. D. Pickering.

S.R.   The Statutes of the Realm, 1101–1713. 9 vols.

S.T.   The State Trials. Ed. Howell.

S.T.N.S.   The State Trials (New Series).

Stephen, H.C.L.   Sir J. F. Stephen. A History of the Criminal Law of England. 3 vols.

Stubbs, C.H.   The Constitutional History of England. 3 vols.

Taswell-Langmead, E.C.H.   English Constitutional History. 1 vol.

Todd, P.G.   Parliamentary Government in England. 2 vols. Ed. S. Walpole.

Walpole, H.E.   History of England from 1815. By Sir S. Walpole. 5 vols.

Wyon, H.G.B.   F. W. Wyon, History of Great Britain during the Reign of Anne. 2 vols.

I

STATUTES AND DOCUMENTS

I

THE ABOLITION OF FEUDAL TENURES

12 Charles II. Cap. 24, 1660.[1]

An act for taking away the Court of Wards and liveries, and tenures in capite, and by knights-service, and purveyance, and for settling a revenue upon his Majesty in lieu thereof.

Whereas it hath been found by former experience, That the courts of wards and liveries and tenures by knights-service, either of the king or others, or by knights-service *in capite*, or socage *in capite* of the King, and the consequents upon the same, have been much more burthensome . . . to the kingdom, than they have been beneficial to the King: And whereas since the intermission of the said Courts . . .[2] many persons have by will and otherwise made disposal of their lands held by knights-service, whereupon divers questions might possibly arise, unless some seasonable remedy be taken to prevent the same; Be it therefore enacted . . . That the court of wards and liveries, and all wardships, liveries, primer seisins and ousterlemains, values and forfeitures of marriages, by reason of any tenure of the King's Majesty, or of any other by knights-service, and all mean rates, and all other gifts, grants, changes incident or arising, for or by reason of wardships, liveries, primer seisins or ousterlemains, be taken away and discharged, . . . from the said twenty-fourth day of February one thousand six hundred forty-five; any law, statute, custom or usage to the contrary hereof in any wise notwithstanding; And that

---

[1] Repealed in part Stat. Law Revis. Act, 1863.   [2] Since 1645.

B

all fines for alienations, seizures and pardons for alienations, tenure by
homage, and all charges incident or arising, for or by reason of wardship, livery, primer seisin or ousterlemain, or tenure by knights-service,
escuage, and also *aid pur fille marier*, and *pur fair fitz chivalier*, all
other charges incident thereunto, be likewise taken away and discharged, from the said twenty-fourth day of February one thousand
six hundred forty and five; any law, statute, custom or usage to the
contrary hereof in any wise notwithstanding: And that all tenures by
knights-service of the King, or of any other person, and by knights-
service *in capite*, and by socage *in capite* of the King, and the fruits
and consequents thereof, happened . . . thereupon or thereby, be taken
away and discharged; any law, statute, custom or usage to the contrary
hereof in any wise notwithstanding; and that all tenures of any honours,
manors, lands, tenements or hereditaments, or any estate of any inheritance at the common law, held either of the King, or of any other
person or persons, bodies politic or corporate, are hereby enacted to be
turned into free and common socage, to all intents and purposes, from
the said twenty-fourth day of February one thousand six hundred
forty-five, and shall be so . . . deemed to be from the said day of
February one thousand six hundred forty-five, and forever thereafter,
turned into free and common socage; any law, statute, custom or
usage to the contrary hereof in any wise notwithstanding;

II. And that the same shall for ever hereafter stand and be discharged of all tenure by homage, escuage, voyages royal and charges
for the same, wardships incident to tenure by knights-service, and
values and forfeitures of marriage, and all other charges incident to
tenure by knights-service, and of and from *aide pur fille marier*, and
aide pur fair fitz chivalier; any law, statute, usage or custom to the
contrary in any wise notwithstanding: And that all conveyances and
devices of any manors, lands, tenements and hereditaments made since
the said twenty-fourth day of February, shall be expounded to be of
such effect, as if the said manors, lands, tenements and hereditaments
had been then held and continued to be holden in free and common
socage only ; any law, statute, custom or usage to the contrary hereof
in any wise notwithstanding.

III. And be it further ordained . . . That one act[1] . . . intituled,
An act for the establishment of the court of the King's wards ; and
also one act [2] . . . concerning the officers of the court of wards and
liveries, and every clause, article and matter in the said acts contained, shall from henceforth be . . . utterly void.

---

[1] 23 Hen. VIII. c. 6.   [2] 33 Hen. VIII. c. 22.

IV. And be it further enacted . . . That all tenures hereafter to be created by the King's Majesty, his heirs or successors, upon any gifts or grants of any manors, lands, tenements or hereditaments, of any estate of inheritance at the common law, shall be . . . in free and common socage only, and not by knights-service or *in capite*, and shall be discharged of all wardship, value and forfeiture of marriage, livery, primer seisin, ousterlemain, *aide pur fair fitz chivalier* and *pur file marrier;* any law, statute or reservation to the contrary thereof in any wise notwithstanding.

V. Provided nevertheless, . . . That this act, or anything herein contained shall not take away, . . . any rents certain, heriots or suits of court belonging or incident to any former tenure now taken away or altered by virtue of this act, or other services incident or belonging to tenure in common socage, due . . . to the King's Majesty, or mean lords, or other private person, or the fealty and distresses incident thereunto; and that such relief shall be paid in respect of such rents as is paid in case of a death of a tenant in common socage.

VI. Provided always, . . . That anything herein contained shall not take away . . . any fines for alienation due by particular customs of particular manners and places, other than fines for alienation of lands or tenements holden immediately of the King *in capite*.

VII. Provided also, . . . That this act, . . . shall not take away, . . . tenures in *frank-almoign*, or to subject them to any greater or other services than they now are; nor to alter or change any tenure by copy of court-roll, or any services incident thereunto; nor to take away the honorary services of grand serjeanty, other than of wardship, marriage, and value of forfeiture of marriage, escuage, voyages royal, and other changes incident to tenure by knights service; and other than *aide pur faire fitz chivalier*, and *aide pur fille marier*.

VIII. And be it further enacted . . . That where any person hath or shall have any child or children under the age of one and twenty years, and not married at the time of his death, that it shall be . . lawful to and for the father of such child or children, whether born at the time of the decease of the father, or at that time in *ventre sa mere*, or whether such father be within the age of one and twenty years, or of full age, by deed executed in his lifetime, or by his last will and testament in writing, in the presence of two or more credible witnesses, . . . to dispose of the custody and tuition of such child or children, for and during such time as he or they shall respectively remain under the age of one and twenty years, . . . to any person or persons in possession or remainder, other than popish recusants; and that such disposition of the custody of such child or children, . . . shall be good and effectual against all and every person or persons claiming the custody and tuition of such child or children as guardian in socage or otherwise : And that such person or persons to whom the custody of such child or children hath been . . . devised as aforesaid, shall . . . maintain an action of ravishment of ward or trespass, against any person or persons which shall wrongfully take away or detain such child or children, for the recovery of such child or children ; and shall and may recover damages for the same in the said action, for the use and benefit of such child or children.

.   .   .   .

(§§ IX., X., XI. deal with the lands of minors and all rights touching " titles of honours feudal.")

XII. And whereas by like experience it hath been found, That though divers, good, strict, and wholesome laws have been made in the times of sundry his Majesty's most noble progenitors, some extending so far as to life, for redress of the grievances and oppressions committed by persons employed for making provisions for the King's household, carriages, and other purveyance for his Majesty and his occasions ; yet divers oppressions have been still continued, and several counties have submitted themselves to sundry rates and taxes and compositions, to redeem themselves from such vexations and oppressions : And for as much as the lords and commons assembled in parliament do find that the said remedies are not fully effectual, and that no other remedy will be so effectual and just, as to take away the occasion thereof, especially if satisfaction and recompense shall be therefore made to his Majesty, his heirs and successors, which is hereby provided to his Majesty's good-liking and content ; his Majesty is therefore graciously pleased, That it may be enacted ; . . . That from henceforth no sum or sums of money, or other thing, shall be taken, raised, taxed, rated, imposed, paid, or levied, for or in regard of any provision, carriages, or purveyance for his Majesty, his heirs or successors.

XIII. And that henceforth no person or persons by any warrant, commission, or authority, under the Great Seal or otherwise, by colour of buying or making provision or purveyance for his Majesty or any Queen of England for the time being, or of any the children of any king or queen of England for the time being, or that shall be, or for his, their, or any of their household, shall take any timber, fuel, cattle, corn, grain, malt, hay, straw, victual, cart, carriage, or other thing whatsoever, of any the subjects of his Majesty, his heirs or successors, without the free and full consent of the owner or owners thereof had and obtained without menace or inforcement; nor shall summon, warn, take, use or require any of the said subjects, to furnish or find any horses, oxen, or other cattle, carts, ploughs, wains, or other carriages, for the use of his Majesty, his heirs or successors, or of any Queen of England, . . . for the carrying the goods of his Majesty, his heirs or successors, or the said Queens, or children, or any of them, without such full and free consent as aforesaid; any law, statute, custom, or usage to the contrary notwithstanding.

.   .   .   .

(§ XIV. forbids pre-emption claimed on behalf of the King, and awards Recompense to his Majesty for the court of wards and purveyances, as explained in the next section.)

XV. Be it therefore enacted . . . That there shall be paid unto the King's Majesty, his heirs and successors for ever hereafter, in recompense as aforesaid, the several rates, impositions, duties and charges hereinafter expressed. . . .

(§§ XVI.-LII. give elaborate details for the levying of the excise, the articles excisable, the powers, duties, and status of the excise officers, and the penalties for evading the duties and the method of procedure in the courts. § XLVI. provides for a principal office of excise to be erected in London.)

(See *Hallam*, C.H. ii. 313 ; *Ranke*, H.E. iii. 365–380 ; *Dowell*, History of Taxation, ii. ch. 2 ; *Cunningham*, English Industry and Commerce, ii. 221.)

II

THE ACT AGAINST TUMULTUOUS PETITIONING

13 Charles II. St. I. Cap. 5, 1661.

An Act against tumults and disorders, upon pretence of preparing or presenting public petitions, or other addresses to his Majesty or the parliament.

Whereas it hath been found by sad experience, that tumultuous and other disorderly soliciting and procuring of hands by private persons to petitions, complaints, remonstrances and declarations, and other addresses to the King, or to both or either houses of parliament, for alteration of matters established by law, redress of pretended grievances in church or state, or other public concernments, have been made use of to serve the ends of factious and seditious persons gotten into power, to the violation of the public peace, and have been a great means of the late unhappy wars, confusion and calamities in this nation ; for preventing the like mischief for the future,

II. Be it enacted . . . That no person or persons whatsoever shall from and after the first of August, one thousand six hundred and sixty one, solicit labour or procure the getting of hands, or other consent of any persons above the number of twenty or more, to any petition, complaint, remonstrance, declaration, or other address to the King, or both or either houses of parliament, for alteration of matters established by law in church or state, unless the matter thereof have been first consented unto and ordered by three or more justices of that county, or by the major part of the grand jury of the county. . . .

And that no person or persons whatsoever shall repair to his Majesty, or both or either of the houses of parliament, upon pretence of delivering or delivering any petition . . . accompanied with excessive number of people, nor at any one time with above the number of ten persons ; upon pain of incurring a penalty not exceeding the sum of one hundred pounds in money, and three months imprisonment . . .

Provided always, That this act, . . . shall not . . . extend to debar or hinder any person or persons, not exceeding the number of ten aforesaid, to prevent any public or private grievance or complaint to any member or members of parliament after his election . . . or to the King's majesty, for any remedy to be thereupon had ; nor to extend to any address whatsoever to his Majesty, by all or any of the members of both or either houses of parliament, during the sitting of parliament, but that they may enjoy their freedom of access to his Majesty, as heretofore hath been used.

(See *May*, P.P. ch. xx. ; *Hallam*, C.H. ii. xi. ; *Anson*, L.C. i. 343–348 ; *Porritt*, U.H.C. i. 574 *et seq.*)

RESOLUTION OF THE COMMONS IN 1669

(1) That it is an inherent right of every commoner in England to prepare and present Petitions to the House of Commons in case of grievances, and the House of Commons to receive the same.

(2) That it is an undoubted right and privilege of the Commons to judge and determine concerning the nature and matter of such petitions, how far they are fit or unfit to be received.

(See Parlt. Hist. iv. 432.)

(No better comment on these two resolutions and the Act cited above can be given than the treatment of "the Kentish Petition" of April 29, 1701. The Resolutions of the Commons are here given.)

RESOLUTIONS OF THE HOUSE OF COMMONS

A Petition from several Gentlemen of the County of Kent being offered to the House;

Ordered, That the said Petition be brought up to the Table.

And it was brought up accordingly.

And the House being informed, That several of the Gentlemen, who signed the said Petition, were at the Door, ready to own the same,

They were called in accordingly; viz.

Mr. William Colepeper, Mr. Thomas Colepeper, Mr. David Polhill, Mr. Justinian Champneys, and Mr. William Hamilton:

And they, at the Bar, owned the same Petition, and their Hands to the same.

And then they withdrew.

And the Petition was read, intituled, The humble Petition of the Gentlemen, Justices of the Peace, Grand Jury, and other Freeholders, at the General Quarter Sessions of the Peace, holden at Maidston, in Kent, the 29th Day of April, in the 13th Year of the Reign of our Sovereign Lord King William the Third, over England, etc.; setting forth, That they, deeply concerned at the dangerous Estate of this Kingdom, and of all Europe; and considering, that the Fate of them, and their Posterity, depends on the Wisdom of their Representatives in Parliament; think themselves bound in Duty humbly to lay before this Honourable House the Consequence, in this Conjuncture, of a speedy Resolution, and most sincere Endeavour, to answer the great Trust reposed in their said Representatives by the Country: And in regard that, from the Experience of all Ages, it is manifest no Nation can be great or happy without Union, they hope no Pretence whatsoever shall be able to create a Misunderstanding among ourselves, or the least Distrust of his Majesty, whose great Actions for this Nation are writ in the Hearts of his Subjects, and can never, without the blackest Ingratitude, be forgot: And praying, that this House will have Regard to the Voice of the People; that our Religion and Safety may be effectually provided for; that the loyal Addresses of this House may be turned into Bills of Supply; and that His Majesty may be enabled powerfully to assist his Allies, before it is too late.

Resolved, That the said Petition is scandalous, insolent, and seditious; tending to destroy the Constitution of Parliaments, and to subvert the established Government of this Realm.

Resolved, That Mr. William Colepeper is guilty of promoting the said Petition.

Resolved, That Mr. Thomas Colepeper is guilty of promoting the said Petition.

Resolved, That Mr. David Polhill is guilty of promoting the said Petition.

Resolved, That Mr. Justinian Chamneys is guilty of promoting the said Petition.

Resolved, That Mr. William Hamilton is guilty of promoting the said Petition.

Ordered, That the said Mr. William Colepeper be, for the said Offence, taken into the Custody of the Serjeant at Arms attending this House.

Ordered, That the said Mr. Thomas Colepeper be, for the said Offence, taken into the Custody of the Serjeant at Arms attending this House.

Ordered, That the said Mr. David Polhil be, for the said Offence, taken into the Custody of the Serjeant at Arms attending this House.

Ordered, That the said Mr. Justinian Champneys be, for the said Offence, taken into the Custody of the Serjeant at Arms attending this House.

Ordered, That the said Mr. William Hamilton be, for the said Offence, taken into the Custody of the Serjeant at Arms attending this House.

(C.J. xiii. 518.)

III

THE MILITIA ACT
13 Cha. II. St. I. Cap. 6, 1661.

An Act declaring the sole right of the Militia to be in the King, and for the present ordering and disposing the same.

Forasmuch as within all his Majesty's realms and dominions, the sole supreme government, command, and disposition of the militia, and of all forces by sea and land, and of all forts and places of strength, is, and by the laws of England ever was the undoubted right of his Majesty, and his royal predecessors, kings and queens of England; and that both, or either of the houses of parliament cannot, nor ought to pretend to the same; nor can nor lawfully may raise, or levy any war offensive or defensive against his Majesty, his heirs or lawful successors; and yet the contrary thereof hath of late years been practised almost to the ruin and destruction of this kingdom; and during the late usurped governments, many evil and rebellious principles have been distilled into the minds of the people of this kingdom, which unless prevented, may break forth to the disturbance of the peace and quietness thereof.

. . . .

(The other provisions of this Act, being purely temporary, are omitted.)

V. Provided, that neither this Act, nor any matter or thing therein contained, shall . . . extend to the giving or declaring of any power for the transporting of any the subjects of this realm, or any way compelling them to march out of this Kingdom otherwise than by the laws of England ought to be done. . . .

(The establishment of the militia as a constitutional force was determined by 13 and 14 Cha. II. c. 3 (1662) and 15 Cha. II. c. 4 (1663), the substantial clauses of which are appended.)

Be it therefore . . . enacted . . . That the King's most excellent Majesty . . . shall and may . . . issue forth several commissions of lieutenancy . . . to be his Majesty's lieutenants for the several and respective countries . . . which lieutenants shall have full power and authority to call together all such persons at such times, and to arm and array them in such manner, as is hereafter expressed and declared . . . and in case of insurrection, rebellion, or invasion, them to lead, conduct and employ . . . according as they shall . . . receive directions from his Majesty . . . and that the said respective lieutenants shall have power . . . to appoint and give commissions . . . always understood, That his Majesty, his heirs and successors, have power and authority to direct and order otherwise. . . .

That the said lieutenants . . . have hereby full power and authority to charge any person with horse, horseman, and arms, or with foot-soldier and arms, in the same country . . . where his, her or their estates lie, having respect unto . . . the proportions hereafter mentioned. . . .

(13 and 14 Cha. II. c. 3.)

Be it also enacted that every trooper or foot soldier at any time raised by virtue . . . of this present act, shall be subject to such exercise and duty . . . and shall accordingly upon like pains and penalties observe and keep all the respective orders and directions of the said act,[1] and of this present act, and shall suffer the same

[1] 13 and 14 Cha. II. c. 13.

penalties for committing any of the respective crimes and offences expressed in the said act. . . .

Provided always and be it enacted, That it shall be lawful to every person and persons that shall have any action or suit brought against him or them for anything done in execution of this or the said act, to plead the general issue, and to give the special matter in evidence; and if judgment shall be given for the defendant, or if the plaintiff shall become non-suit, . . . then he shall recover double costs. . . .

(15 Cha. II. c. 4.)

(See *Hallam*, C.H. iii. 262 *et seq.*; *Clode*, Military Forces of the Crown, i. ch. iii.; Manual of Military Law (ed. 1899), Introduction.)

IV

THE CORPORATION ACT.[1]   No. 1

13 Charles II. St. II. Cap. I., 1661.

An Act for the well-governing and regulating of Corporations.

Whereas questions are likely to arise concerning the validity of elections of magistrates, and other officers and members in corporations, as well in respect of removing some, as placing others, during the late troubles, contrary to the true intent and meaning of their charters and liberties : And to the end that the succession in such corporations may be most profitably perpetuated in the hands of persons well affected to his Majesty and the established government, it being too well known, that notwithstanding all his Majesty's endeavours, and unparalleled indulgence in pardoning all that is past, nevertheless many evil spirits are still working.[2]

II. Wherefore for prevention of the like mischief for the time to come, and for preservation of the public peace both in church and state, . . . That commissions shall, before the twentieth day of February next, be issued forth under the Great Seal of England, unto such persons as his Majesty shall appoint for the executing of the powers and authorities hereinafter expressed : And that all and every the . . . commissioners . . . shall . . . be commissioners respectively, for and within the several cities, corporations, and boroughs, and cinque ports, and their members, and other port towns within the kingdom of England, dominion of Wales, and town of Berwick upon Tweed, for which they shall be respectively nominated and appointed.

---

[1] Repealed as regards the oath and subscription by 5 Geo. I. c. 6, § 2.

[2] Repealed Stat. Law Rev. Act, 1863.

III. And be it further enacted . . . That no charter of any corporation, cities, towns, boroughs, cinque ports, and their members, and other port towns in England or Wales, or town of Berwick upon Tweed, shall at any time hereafter be avoided, for or by reason of any act or thing done, or omitted to be done, before the first day of this present parliament.

IV. And be it further enacted . . . That all persons who upon the four and twentieth day of December, one thousand six hundred sixty and one, shall be mayors, aldermen, recorders, bailiffs, town clerks, common council-men, and other persons then bearing any office or offices of magistracy, or places, or trusts, or other employment relating to or concerning the government of the said respective cities, corporations, and boroughs, and cinque ports, and their members, and other port towns, shall at any time before the five and twentieth day of March, one thousand six hundred sixty and three, . . . be required by the said respective commissioners, . . . to take the Oaths of Allegiance and Supremacy, and this oath following:

V. 'I, A. B. do declare and believe, That it is not lawful, upon any pretence whatsoever, to take arms against the King; and that I do abhor that traitorous position of taking arms by his authority against his person, or against those that are commissioned by him: So help me God.'

VI.[1] And also at the same time shall publicly subscribe, before the said commissioners or any three of them, this following declaration:

'I, A. B. do declare, That I hold that there lies no obligation upon me or any other person, from the oath commonly called, The solemn league and covenant, and that the same was in itself an unlawful oath, and imposed upon the subjects of this realm against the known laws and liberties of the kingdom.'

VII. And that all such of the said mayors and other the persons aforesaid, who shall refuse to take and subscribe the same oath . . . shall, . . . be by authority of this act (*ipso facto*) removed and displaced of and from the said offices and places respectively; and the said offices and places . . . shall be . . . void to all intents and purposes, as if the said respective persons were naturally dead.

VIII. And nevertheless, Be it further enacted, . . . That the said commissioners, or any five or more of them, shall have full power . . . by order and warrant . . . to displace or remove any of the persons aforesaid from the said respective offices and places, or trusts aforesaid, if the said commissioners, . . . shall deem it expedient for the

[1] Repealed by 5 Geo. I. c. 6, § 2.

public safety, although such persons shall have taken and subscribed, or be willing to take and subscribe, the said oaths and declaration.

. . . .

(§§ IX., X., XI. define in detail the powers and procedure of the Commissioners.)

XII. Provided also, . . . That from and after the expiration of the said commissions, no . . . persons shall for ever hereafter be placed, elected or chosen, in or to any the offices or places aforesaid, that shall not have, within one year next before such election or choice, taken the sacrament of the Lord's Supper, according to the rites of the Church of England; and that every such person . . . so placed, elected or chosen, shall likewise take the aforesaid three oaths, and subscribe the said declaration at the same time when the oath for the due execution of the said places and offices respectively shall be administered; and in default hereof, every such placing, election and choice, is hereby enacted and declared to be void.

XIII. Provided always, . . . That every person who shall be placed in any corporation by virtue of this act, shall upon his admission take the oath or oaths usually taken by the members of such corporation.

. . . .

(§§ XIV., XV. define further the powers of the Commissioners.
§ XVI exempts the reversions of offices in London from the operation of the Act.)

V

THE ACT OF UNIFORMITY
14 Charles II. Cap. IV., 1662.[1]

An act for the uniformity of public prayers, and administration of sacraments, and other rites and ceremonies: And for establishing the form of making, ordaining, and consecrating bishops, priests, and deacons, in the Church of England.

Whereas in the first year of the late Queen Elizabeth, there was one uniform order of common service and prayer, and of the administration of sacraments, rites, and ceremonies, in the Church of England, (agreeable to the Word of God, and usage of the primitive

---

[1] Commonly cited as 13 and 14 Cha. II. c. 4. Repealed as to so much as confirms any Act thereby repealed, 7 and 8 Vict. c. 102, § 1. Repealed as to so much whereby an Act therein repealed has been confirmed, 9 and 10 Vict. c. 59, § i. Repealed also in part by 28 and 29 Vict. c. 122, and Stat. Law Rev. Act, 1863.

church), compiled by the reverend bishops and clergy, set forth in one book, intituled, The Book of Common Prayer, and Administration of Sacraments, and other rites and ceremonies in the Church of England, and enjoined to be used by act of parliament, holden in the said first year of the said late queen, intituled, An act for the uniformity of common prayer and service in the church, and administration of the sacraments, very conformable to all good people desirous to live in christian conversation, and most profitable to the estate of this realm; upon the which the mercy, favour, and blessing of almighty God is in no wise so readily and plentifully found, as by common prayers, due using of the sacraments, and often preaching of the gospel, with devotion of the hearers; and yet this notwithstanding, a great number of people in divers parts of this realm, following their own sensuality, and living without knowledge and due fear of God, do wilfully and schismatically abstain and refuse to come to their parish churches, and other public places where common prayer, administration of the sacraments, and preaching of the Word of God is used upon the Sundays and other days ordained and appointed to be kept and observed as holy-days: And whereas by the great and scandalous neglect of ministers in using the said order or liturgy so set forth and enjoined as aforesaid, great mischiefs and inconveniences, during the times of the late unhappy troubles, have arisen and grown, and many people have been led into factions and schisms, to the great decay and scandal of the reformed religion of the Church of England, and to the hazard of many souls: For prevention thereof in time to come, for settling the peace of the church, and for allaying the present distempers which the indisposition of the time hath contracted, the King's Majesty, according to his declaration of the five and twentieth of October, one thousand six hundred and sixty, granted his commission under the Great Seal of England to several bishops and other divines, to review the Book of Common Prayer, and to prepare such alterations and additions as they thought fit to offer: And afterwards the convocations of both the provinces of Canterbury and York, being by his Majesty called and assembled, and now sitting, his Majesty hath been pleased to authorize and require the presidents of the said convocations, and other the bishops and clergy of the same, to review the said Book of Common Prayer, and the book of the form and manner of the making and consecrating of bishops, priests, and deacons; And that after mature consideration they should make such additions and alterations in the said books respectively, as to them should seem meet and convenient; and should exhibit and present the same to his Majesty in writing for his further allowance of confirmation : Since which time, upon full and mature deliberation, they the said presidents, bishops, and clergy, of both provinces, have accordingly reviewed the said books, and have made some alterations which they think fit to be inserted to the same ; and some additional prayers to the said Book of Common Prayer to be used upon proper and emergent occasions, and have exhibited and preferred the same unto his Majesty in writing, in one book, intituled, The Book of Common Prayer and administration of the sacraments, and other rites and ceremonies of the church, according to the use of the Church of England, together with the psalter, or psalms of David, pointed as they are to be sung or said in churches ; and the form or manner of making, ordaining, and consecrating, of bishops, priests, and deacons : All which his Majesty having duly considered, hath fully approved and allowed the same, and recommended to this present parliament, That the said Books of Common Prayer, and of the form of ordination and consecration of bishops, priests, and deacons, with the alterations and additions which have been so made and presented to his Majesty by the said convocations, be the book which shall be appointed to be used by all that officiate in all cathedral and collegiate churches and chapels, and in all chapels of colleges and halls in both the universities, and the colleges of Eaton and Winchester, and in all parish churches and chapels within the kingdom of England, dominion of Wales, and town of Berwick upon Tweed, and by all that make or consecrate bishops, priests, or deacons, in any of the said places, under such sanctions and penalties as the houses of parliament shall think fit.

II. Now in regard that nothing conduced more to the settling of the peace of this nation, (which is desired of all good men), nor to the honour of our religion, and the propagation thereof, than an universal agreement in the public worship of almighty God ; and to the intent that every person within this realm may certainly know the rule to which he is to conform in public worship, and administrations of sacraments, and other rites and ceremonies of the Church of England, and the manner how and by whom bishops, priests, and deacons, are and ought to be made, ordained, and consecrated ; be it enacted by the King's most excellent Majesty, by the advice and with the consent of the lords spiritual and temporal, and of the commons, in this present parliament assembled, and by the authority of the same, That all and singular ministers in any cathedral, collegiate or parish church or chapel, or other place of public worship within this realm of England, dominion of Wales, and town of

Berwick upon Tweed, shall be bound to say and use the Morning Prayer, Evening Prayer, celebration and administration of both the sacraments, and all other the public and common prayer, in such order and form as is mentioned in the said book annexed and joined to this present act, and intituled, The Book of Common Prayer and administration of the sacraments, and other rites and ceremonies of the church, according to the use of the Church of England; together with the psalter or psalms of David, pointed as they are to be sang or said in churches; and the form or manner of making, ordaining, and consecrating bishops, priests, and deacons: And that the morning and evening prayers therein contained shall, upon every Lord's day, and upon all other days and occasions, and at the times therein appointed, be openly and solemnly read by all and every minister or curate, in every church, chapel, or other place of public worship, within this realm of England and places aforesaid.

III. And to the end that uniformity in the public worship of God (which is so much desired) may be speedily effected, be it further enacted ... That every parson, vicar, or other minister whatsoever, who now hath or enjoyeth any ecclesiastical benefice or promotion within the realm of England or places aforesaid, shall, in the church, chapel, or place of public worship, belonging to his said benefit or promotion, upon some Lord's day before the feast of St. Bartholomew which shall be in the year of our Lord God one thousand six hundred and sixty and two, openly, publicly, and solemnly read the Morning and Evening Prayer appointed to be read by and according to the said Book of Common Prayer, at the times thereby appointed; and after such reading thereof, shall openly and publicly, before the congregation there assembled, declare his unfeigned assent and consent to the use of all things in the said book contained and prescribed, in these words, and no other:

IV. 'I, A. B. do here declare my unfeigned assent and consent to all and every thing contained and prescribed in and by the book, intituled, The Book of Common Prayer and administration of the sacraments, and other rites and ceremonies of the church, according to the use of the Church of England, together with the psalter or psalms of David, pointed as they are to be sung or said in churches; and the form or manner of making, ordaining, and consecrating of bishops, priests, and deacons.'

V. And that all and every such person, who shall (without some lawful impediment to be allowed and approved of by the ordinary of the peace) neglect or refuse to do the same within the time aforesaid, (or in case of such impediment, within one month after such impediment removed,) shall *ipso facto* be deprived of all his spiritual promotions: And that from thenceforth it shall be lawful to and for all patrons and donors of all and singular the said spiritual promotions, or any of them, according to their respective rights and titles, to present or collate to the same, as though the person or persons so offending or neglecting were dead.

VI. And . . . That every person who shall hereafter be preferred or collated, or put into any ecclesiastical benefice or promotion, within this realm of England or places aforesaid, shall, in the church, chapel, or place of public worship belonging to his said benefice or promotion, within two months next after that he shall be in actual possession of the said ecclesiastical benefice or promotion, upon some Lord's day, openly, publicly, and solemnly read the morning and evening prayers appointed to be read by and according to the said Book of Common Prayer, at the times thereby appointed; and after such reading thereof shall openly and publicly, before the congregation there assembled, declare his unfeigned assent and consent to the use of all things therein contained and prescribed, according to the form before appointed: And that all and every person who shall (without some lawful impediment to be allowed and approved by the ordinary of the place) neglect or refuse to do the same within the time aforesaid, (or in case of such impediment, within one month after such impediment removed) shall (ipso facto) be deprived of all his said ecclesiastical benefices and promotions: And that from thenceforth it shall and may be lawful to and for all patrons and donors of all and singular the said ecclesiastical benefices and promotions, or any of them, according to their respective rights and titles, to present or collate to the same, as though the person or persons so offending or neglecting were dead.

VII. And . . . That in all places where the proper incumbent of any parsonage or vicarage, or benefice with cure, doth reside on his living and keep a curate, the incumbent himself in person (not having some lawful impediment to be allowed by the ordinary of the place) shall once (at the least) in every month openly and publicly read the common prayers and service in and by the said book prescribed, and (if there be occasion) administer each of the sacraments and other rites of the church, in the parish church or chapel, of or belonging to the same parsonage, vicarage, or benefice, in such order, manner, and form, as in and by the said book is appointed; upon pain to be forfeit the sum of five pounds to the use of the poor of the parish for every offence, upon conviction by confession, or proof of two credible witnesses, upon oath, before two justices of the peace of the county, city or town corporate, where the offence shall be committed, (which oath the said justices are hereby impowered to administer) and in default of payment within ten days, to be levied by distress and sale of the goods and chattels of the offender, by the warrant of the said justices, by the churchwardens or overseers of the poor of the said parish, rendering surplusage to the party.

VIII.[1] And be it further enacted by the authority aforesaid, That every dean, canon, and prebendary of every cathedral or collegiate church, and all masters and other heads, fellows, chaplains, and tutors of or in any college, hall, house of learning or hospital, and every public professor and reader in either of the universities, and in every college elsewhere, and every parson, vicar, curate, lecturer, and every other person in holy orders, and every schoolmaster keeping any public or private school, and every person instructing or teaching any youth in any house or private family as a tutor or schoolmaster, who upon the first day of May, which shall be in the year of our Lord God one thousand six hundred sixty-two, or at any time thereafter, shall be incumbent or have possession of any deanery, canonry, prebend, mastership, headship, fellowship, professor's place or reader's place, parsonage, vicarage, or any other ecclesiastical dignity or promotion, or of any curate's place, lecture, or school, or shall instruct or teach any youth as tutor or schoolmaster, shall, before the feast day of St. Bartholomew, which shall be in the year of our Lord one thousand six hundred sixty-two, or at or before his or their respective admission to be incumbent or to have possession aforesaid, subscribe the declaration or acknowledgment following, *scilicet*,

IX. 'I, A. B. do declare, That it is not lawful, upon any pretence whatsoever to take arms against the king ; and that I do abhor that traitorous position of taking arms by his authority against his person, or against those that are commissionated by him ; and that I will conform to the liturgy of the Church of England, as it is now by law established : And I do declare that I do hold, there lies no obligation upon me or on any other person, from the oath commonly called, The solemn league and covenant, to endeavour any change or alteration of government either in church or state, and that the same was in itself an unlawful oath, and imposed upon the subjects of this realm against the known laws and liberties of this kingdom.'

X. Which said declaration and acknowledgment shall be subscribed by every one of the said masters and other heads, fellows, chaplains, and tutors of or in any college, hall, or house of learning,

---

[1] Repealed 28 and 29 Vict. c. 122, § 15.

C

and by every public professor and reader in either of the universities, before the Vice Chancellor of the respective universities for the time being, or his deputy : And the said declaration or acknowledgment shall be subscribed before the respective archbishop, bishop, or ordinary of the diocese, by every other person hereby enjoined to subscribe the same ; upon pain that all and every of the persons aforesaid failing in such subscription, shall lose and forfeit such respective deanery, canonry, prebend, mastership, headship, professor's place, reader's place, parsonage, vicarage, ecclesiastical dignity or promotion, curate's place, lecture and school, and shall be utterly disabled and (*ipso facto*) deprived of the same : And that every such respective deanery, canonry, prebend, mastership, headship, fellow-ship, professor's place, reader's place, parsonage, vicarage, ecclesiastical dignity or promotion, curate's place, lecture, and school, shall be void, as if such person so failing were naturally dead.

XI. And if any schoolmaster or other person, instructing or teaching youth in any private house or family as a tutor or school-master, shall instruct or teach any youth as a tutor or schoolmaster, before licence obtained from his respective archbishop, bishop, or ordinary of the diocese, according to the laws and statutes of this realm, (for which he shall pay twelve-pence only) and before such subscription and acknowledgment made as aforesaid ; then every such schoolmaster and other, instructing and teaching as aforesaid, shall, for the first offence, suffer three months imprisonment without bail or mainprize ; and for every second, and other such offence, shall suffer three months imprisonment without bail or mainprize ; and also forfeit to his Majesty the sum of five pounds : And after such subscription made, every such parson, vicar, curate, and lecturer, shall procure a certificate under the hand and seal of the respective archbishop, bishop or ordinary of the diocese, (who are hereby enjoined and required, upon demand, to make and deliver the same) and shall publicly and openly read the same, together with the declaration and acknowledgment aforesaid, upon some Lord's day within three months then next following, in his parish church where he is to officiate, in the presence of the congregation there assembled, in the time of divine service ; upon pain that every person failing therein shall lose such parsonage, vicarage, or benefice, curate's place, or lecturer's place respectively, and shall be utterly disabled, and *ipso facto* deprived of the same ; and that the said parsonage, vicarage, or benefice, curate's place or lecturer's place, shall be void as if he was naturally dead.

XII. Provided always, That from and after the twenty-fifth day of March, which shall be in the year of our Lord God one thousand six hundred eighty-two, there shall be omitted in the said declaration or acknowledgment so to be subscribed and read, these words following, scilicet:

'And I do declare, That I do hold there lies no obligation on me, or on any other person, from the oath commonly called, The solemn league and covenant, to endeavour any change or alteration of government either in church or state, and that the same was in itself an unlawful oath, and imposed upon the subjects of this realm against the known laws and liberties of this kingdom.'

So as none of the persons aforesaid shall from thenceforth be at all obliged to subscribe or read that part of the said declaration or acknowledgment.

XIII. Provided always, and be it enacted, That from and after the feast of St. Bartholomew, which shall be in the year of our Lord one thousand six hundred sixty and two, no person who is now incumbent, and in possession of any parsonage, vicarage, or benefice, and who is not already in holy orders by episcopal ordination, or shall not before the said feast day of St. Bartholomew be ordained priest or deacon, according to the form of episcopal ordination, shall have, hold, or enjoy the said parsonage, vicarage, benefice with cure, or other ecclesiastical promotion within this kingdom of England, or the dominion of Wales, or town of Berwick upon Tweed, but shall be utterly disabled, and (*ipso facto*) deprived of the same, and all his ecclesiastical promotions shall be void, as if he was naturally dead.

XIV. And be it further enacted by the authority aforesaid, That no person whatsoever shall thenceforth be capable to be admitted to any parsonage, vicarage, benefice, or other ecclesiastical promotion or dignity whatsoever, nor shall presume to consecrate and administer the Holy Sacrament of the Lord's Supper, before such time as he shall be ordained priest according to the form and manner in and by the said book prescribed, unless he have formerly been made priest by episcopal ordination; upon pain to forfeit for every offence the sum of one hundred pounds; one moiety thereof to the King's Majesty, the other moiety, thereof to be equally divided between the poor of the parish where the offence shall be committed; and such person or persons as shall sue for the same by action of debt, bill, plaint, or information, in any of his Majesty's Courts of record, wherein no essoin, protection, or wager of law shall be allowed, and to be disabled from taking or being admitted into the order of priest, by the space of one whole year then next following.

XV. Provided that the penalties in this act shall not extend to the foreigners or aliens of the foreign reformed churches allowed or to be allowed by the King's Majesty, his heirs or successors in England.

XVI. Provided always, That no title to confer or present by lapse, shall accrue by any avoidance or deprivation (*ipso facto*) by virtue of this statute, but after six months after notice of such avoidance or deprivation given by the ordinary to the patron, or such sentence of deprivation openly and publicly read in the parish church of the benefice, parsonage, or vicarage becoming void, or whereof the incumbent shall be deprived by virtue of this act.

XVII. And be it further enacted by the authority aforesaid, That no form or order of common prayers, administration of sacraments, rites or ceremonies, shall be openly used in any church, chapel or other public place of worship, or in any college or hall in either of the universities, the colleges of Westminster, Winchester, or Eaton, or any of them, other than what is prescribed and appointed to be used in and by the said book; and that the present governor or head of every college and hall in the said universities, and of the said colleges of Westminster, Winchester, and Eaton, within one month after the feast of St. Bartholomew, which shall be in the year of our Lord one thousand six hundred sixty and two; and every governor or head of any of the said colleges or halls hereafter to be elected or appointed, within one month next after his election or collation, and admission into the same government or headship, shall openly and publicly in the church, chapel, or other public place of the same college or hall, and in the presence of the fellows or scholars of the same, or the greater part of them then resident, subscribe unto the nine and thirty articles of religion, mentioned in the statute made in the thirteenth year of the reign of the late Queen Elizabeth, and unto the said book, and to the use of all the prayers, rites and ceremonies, forms and orders, in the said book prescribed and contained, according to the form aforesaid; and that all such governors or heads of the said colleges and halls, or any of them, as are or shall be in holy orders, shall once (at least) in every quarter of the year (not having a lawful impediment) openly and publicly read the Morning Prayer and service in and by the said book appointed to be read in the church, chapel, or other public place of the same college or hall; upon pain to lose, and be suspended of and from all the benefits and profits belonging to the same government or headship, by the space of six months, by the visitor or visitors of the same college or hall; and if any governor or head of any college or hall, suspended for not subscribing unto the said articles and book, or for not reading of the Morning Prayer and Service as aforesaid, shall not at or before the end of six months next after such suspension, subscribe unto the said articles and book, and declare his consent thereunto as aforesaid, or read the Morning Prayer and Service as aforesaid, then such government or headship shall be (*ipso facto*) void.

XVIII. Provided always, That it shall and may be lawful to use the Morning and Evening Prayer, and all other prayers and services prescribed in and by the said book, in the chapels or other public places of the respective colleges and halls in both the universities, in the colleges of Westminster, Winchester, and Eaton, and in the convocations of the clergies of either province, in Latin; anything in this act contained to the contrary notwithstanding.

XIX.[1] And be it further enacted by the authority aforesaid, That no person shall be or be received as a lecturer, or permitted, suffered, or allowed to preach as a lecturer, or to preach or read any sermon in any church, chapel, or other place of public worship, within this realm of England, or the dominion of Wales, and town of Berwick upon Tweed, unless he be first approved, and thereunto licenced by the archbishop of the province, or the bishop of the diocese, or (in case the see be void) by the guardian of the spiritualities, under his seal, and shall in the presence of the same archbishop or bishop, or guardian, read the nine and thirty articles of religion mentioned in the statute of the thirteenth year of the late Queen Elizabeth, with declaration of his unfeigned assent to the same; and that every person and persons, who now is, or hereafter shall be licenced, assigned, and appointed, or received as a lecturer, to preach upon any day of the week, in any church, chapel, or place of public worship within this realm of England, or places aforesaid, the first time he preacheth (before his sermon) shall openly, publicly, and solemnly read the common prayers and service in and by the said book appointed to be read for that time of the day, and then and there publicly and openly declare his assent unto, and approbation of, the said book, and to the use of all the prayers, rites, and ceremonies, forms and orders, therein contained and prescribed, according to the form before appointed in this act; And also shall upon the first lecture day of every month afterwards, so long as he continues lecturer or preacher there, at the place appointed for his said lecture or sermon, before his said lecture or sermon, openly, publicly, and solemnly read

---

[1] Repealed 28 and 29 Vict. c. 122, § 15.

the common prayers and service in and by the said book appointed to be read for that time of the day at which the said lecture or sermon is to be preached, and after such reading thereof shall openly and publicly, before the congregation there assembled, declare his unfeigned assent and consent unto, and approbation of, the said book, and to the use of all the prayers, rites, and ceremonies, forms and orders, therein contained and prescribed, according to the form aforesaid ; and that all and every such person and persons who shall neglect or refuse to do the same, shall from thenceforth be disabled to preach the said or any other lecture or sermon in the said or any other church, chapel, or place of public worship, until such time as he and they shall openly, publicly and solemnly read the common prayers and service appointed by the said book, and conform in all points to the things therein appointed and prescribed, according to the purport, true intent, and meaning of this act.

XX. Provided always, That if the said sermon or lecture be to be preached or read in any cathedral or collegiate church or chapel, it shall be sufficient for the said lecturer, openly at the time aforesaid, to declare his assent and consent to all things contained in the said book, according to the form aforesaid.

XXI. And be it further enacted by the authority aforesaid, That if any person who is by this act disabled to preach any lecture or sermon, shall, during the time that he shall continue and remain so disabled, preach any sermon or lecture ; that then for every such offence, the person and persons so offending shall suffer three months imprisonment in the common gaol without bail or mainprize ; and that any two justices of the peace of any county of this kingdom and places aforesaid, and the mayor or other chief magistrate of any city, or town corporate within the same, upon certificate from the ordinary of the place made to him or them of the offence committed, shall and are hereby required to commit the person or persons so offending, to the gaol of the same county, city, or town corporate accordingly.

XXII. Provided always, and be it further enacted by the authority aforesaid, That at all and every time and times when any sermon or lecture is to be preached, the common prayers and service in and by the said book appointed to be read for that time of the day, shall be openly, publicly, and solemnly read by some priest or deacon, in the church, chapel, or place of public worship, where the said sermon or lecture is to be preached, before such sermon or lecture be preached, and that the lecturer then to preach shall be present at the reading thereof.

XXIII. Provided nevertheless, That this act shall not extend to the university church in the universities of this realm, or either of them, when or at such times as any sermon or lecture is preached or read in the said churches, or any of them, for or as the public university sermon or lecture; but that the same sermons and lectures may be preached or read in such sort and manner as the same have been heretofore preached or read; this act, or anything herein contained to the contrary thereof in any wise notwithstanding.

XXIV. And be it further enacted by the authority aforesaid, That the several good laws and statutes of this realm, which have been formerly made, and are now in force, for the uniformity of prayer and administration of the sacraments, within this realm of England and places aforesaid, shall stand in full force and strength, to all intents and purposes whateoever, for the establishing and confirming the said book, intituled, The Book of Common Prayer and administration of the sacraments, and other rites and ceremonies of the church, according to the use of the Church of England; together with the psalter or psalms of David, pointed as they are to be sung or said in churches, and the form or manner of making, ordaining, and consecrating of bishops, priests, and deacons, herein before mentioned to be joined and annexed to this act; and shall be applied, practised, and put in use for the punishing of all offences contrary to the said laws, with relation to the book aforesaid and no other.

XXV. Provided always, and be it further enacted by the authority aforesaid, That in all those prayers, litanies, and collects, which do any way relate to the king, queen, or royal progeny, the names be altered and changed from time to time, and fitted to the present occasion, according to the direction of lawful authority.

XXVI. Provided also, and be it enacted by the authority aforesaid, That a true printed copy of the said book, intituled, The Book of Common Prayer and administration of the sacraments, and other rites and ceremonies of the church, according to the use of the Church of England, together with the psalter or psalms of David, pointed as they are to be sung or said in churches, and the form and manner of making, ordaining, and consecrating of bishops, priests, and deacons, shall at the costs and charges of the parishioners of every parish church and chapelry, cathedral church, college and hall, be attained and gotten before the feast-day of St. Bartholomew, in the year of our Lord one thousand six hundred sixty and two; upon pain of forfeiture of three pounds by the month, for so long time as they shall then after be unprovided thereof, by every parish or chapelry, cathedral church, college and hall, making default therein.

XXVII. Provided always, and be it enacted by the authority aforesaid, That the bishops of Hereford, St. David's, Asaph, Bangor, and Sandaff, and their successors, shall take such order among themselves, for the soul's health of the flocks committed to their charge within Wales, that the book hereunto annexed be duly and exactly translated into the British or Welsh tongue; and that the same so translated, and being by them, or any three of them at the least, viewed, perused and allowed, be imprinted to such number at least, so that one of the said books so translated and imprinted, may be had for every cathedral, collegiate and parish church, and chapel at ease, in the said respective dioceses and places in Wales, where the Welsh is commonly spoken or used, before the first day of May, one thousand six hundred sixty-five; and that from and after the imprinting and publishing of the said book so translated, the whole divine service shall be used and said by the ministers and curates throughout all Wales, within the said dioceses, where the Welsh tongue is commonly used, in the British or Welsh tongue, in such manner and form as is prescribed according to the book hereunto annexed to be used in the English tongue, differing nothing in any order or form from the said English book; for which book, so translated and imprinted, the churchwardens of every the said parishes shall pay out of the parish money in their hands for the use of the respective churches, and be allowed the same on their account; and that the said bishops and their successors, or any three of them at the least, shall set and appoint the price for which the said book shall be sold: And one other Book of Common Prayer in the English tongue shall be bought and had in every church throughout Wales, in which the Book of Common Prayer in Welsh is to be had by force of this act, before the first day of May, one thousand six hundred sixty and four, and the same books to remain in such convenient places within the said churches, that such as understand them may resort at all convenient times to read and peruse the same, and also such as do not understand the said language, may, by conferring both tongues together, the sooner attain to the knowledge of the English tongue; anything in this act to the contrary notwithstanding: And until printed copies of the said book so to be translated may be had and provided, the Form of Common Prayer, established by parliament before the making of this act, shall be used as formerly in such parts of Wales where the English tongue is not commonly understood.

XXVIII. And to the end that the true and perfect copies of this act, and the said book hereunto annexed, may be safely kept and perpetually preserved, and for the avoiding of all disputes for the time to come, be it therefore enacted by the authority aforesaid. That the respective deans and chapters of every cathedral or collegiate church within England and Wales shall, at their proper costs and charges, before the twenty-fifth day of December, one thousand six hundred sixty and two, obtain under the Great Seal of England a true and perfect printed copy of this act, and of the said book annexed hereunto, to be by the said deans and chapters and their successors, kept and preserved in safety for ever, and to be also produced and shewed forth in any court of record, as often as they shall be thereunto lawfully required; and also there shall be delivered true and perfect copies of this act, and of the same book, into the respective courts at Westminster, and into the Tower of London, to be kept and preserved for ever among the records of the said courts, and the records of the Tower, to be also produced and shewed forth in any court, as need shall require; which said books so to be exemplified under the Great Seal of England, shall be examined by such persons as the King's Majesty shall appoint, under the Great Seal of England, for that purpose, and shall be compared with the original book hereunto annexed, and shall have power to correct and amend in writing any error committed by the printer in the printing of the same book, or of any thing therein contained, and shall certify in writing under their hands and seals, or the hands and seals of any three of them, at the end of the same book, that they have examined and compared the same book, and find it to be a true and perfect copy; which said books, and every one of them, so exemplified under the Great Seal of England as aforesaid, shall be deemed, taken, adjudged and expounded to be good and available in the law, to all intents and purposes whatsoever, and shall be accounted as good records as this book itself hereunto annexed; any law or custom to the contrary in any wise notwithstanding.

XXIX. Provided also, that this act, nor any thing therein contained, shall not be prejudicial or hurtful unto the King's professor of the law within the university of Oxford, for or concerning the prebend of Shipton within the cathedral church of Sarum, united and annexed unto the place of the same king's professor for the time being by the late King James of blessed memory.

XXX. Provided always, That whereas the six and thirtieth article of the nine and thirty articles agreed upon by the archbishops and bishops of both provinces, and the whole clergy in the convocation holden at London in the year of our Lord one thousand five hundred sixty-two, for the avoiding of diversities of opinions, and for establishing of consent touching true religion, is in these words following, viz.

" That the Book of Consecration of archbishops and bishops, and ordaining of priests and deacons, lately set forth in the time of King Edward the Sixth, and confirmed at the same time by authority of parliament, doth contain all things necessary to such consecration and ordaining, neither hath it anything that of itself is superstitious and ungodly : And therefore whosoever are consecrated or ordered according to the rites of that book, since the second year of the aforenamed King Edward unto this time, or hereafter shall be consecrated or ordered according to the same rites, We decree all such to be rightly, orderly and lawfully consecrated and ordered ; "

XXXI. It be enacted, and be it therefore enacted by the authority aforesaid, That all subscriptions hereafter to be had or made unto the said articles by any deacon, priest or ecclesiastical person, or other person whatsoever, who by this act, or any other law now in force, is required to subscribe unto the said articles, shall be construed, and be taken to extend, and shall be applied (for and touching the said six and thirtieth article) unto the book containing the form and manner of making, ordaining, and consecrating of bishops, priests and deacons, in this act mentioned, in such sort and manner as the same did heretofore extend unto the book set forth in the time of King Edward the Sixth, mentioned in the said sixth and thirtieth article ; anything in the said article, or in any statute, act or canon heretofore had or made, to the contrary thereof in any wise notwithstanding.

XXXII. Provided also, That the Book of Common Prayer, and administration of the sacraments, and other rites and ceremonies of this Church of England, together with the form and manner of ordaining and consecrating bishops, priests and deacons, heretofore in use, and respectively established by act of parliament in the first and eighth years of Queen Elizabeth, shall be still used and observed in the Church of England, until the feast of St. Bartholomew, which shall be in the year of our Lord God one thousand six hundred sixty and two.

(This Act should be compared with the Acts of Uniformity and Supremacy, 1 Eliz. c. 1 and 1 Eliz. c. 2 (*Prothero*, C.D. pp. 1–20), and see *Hallam*, C.H. ii. xi.; *Perry*, H.C.E. ii. 349 ; *Ranke*, H.E. iii. 365–380 ; *Makower*, C.H.E. § 15; *Todd*, P.G. i. ch. x. ; *Gneist*, 639.)

VI

THE LICENSING ACT[1]

14 Charles II. Cap. 33, 1662.

An act for preventing the frequent abuses in printing seditious, treasonable and unlicensed books and pamphlets, and for regulating of printing and printing-presses.

Whereas the well government and regulating of printers and printing-presses is matter of public care, and of great concernment, especially considering, that by the general licentiousness of the late times, many evil-disposed persons have been encouraged to print and sell heretical, schismatical, blasphemous, seditious and treasonable books, pamphlets and papers, and still do continue such their unlawful and exorbitant practice, to the high dishonour of Almighty God, the endangering the peace of these kingdoms, and raising a disaffection to his most excellent Majesty and his government; for prevention whereof, no surer means can be advised, than by reducing and limiting the number of printing-presses, and by ordering and settling the said art or mystery of printing by act of parliament, in manner as herein after is expressed.

II. The King's most excellent Majesty, . . . doth ordain and enact, . . . That no person or persons whatsoever shall presume to print, or cause to be printed, either within this realm of England, or any other of his Majesty's dominions, or in parts beyond the seas, any heretical, seditious, schismatical or offensive books or pamphlets, wherein any doctrine or opinion shall be asserted or maintained, which is contrary to the Christian faith, or the doctrine or discipline of the Church of England, or which shall or may tend, or be to the scandal of religion, or the church, or the government or governors of the church, state or commonwealth, or of any corporation or particular person or persons whatsoever; nor shall import, publish, sell or disperse any such book or books, or pamphlets, nor shall cause . . . any such . . . to be bound, stitched, or sewed together.

III. And be it further ordained . . . That no private person or persons whatsoever shall at any time hereafter print or cause to be printed any book or pamphlet whatsoever, unless the same book and pamphlet, together with all and every the titles, epistles, prefaces,

---

[1] Commonly cited as 13 and 14 Cha. II. St. 2, c. 33. Finally repealed Stat. Law Rev. Act, 1863.

proems, preambles, introductions, tables, dedications, and other matters and things thereunto annexed, be first entered in the book of the register of the Company of Stationers in London, except acts of parliament, proclamations, and such other books and papers as shall be appointed to be printed by virtue of any warrant under the King's Majesty's sign-manual, or under the hand of one or both of his Majesty's principal Secretaries of State; and unless the same book and pamphlet, and also all and every said titles, epistles, prefaces, proems, preambles, introductions, tables, dedications, and other matters and things whatsoever thereunto annexed, or therewith to be imprinted, shall be first lawfully licensed and authorized to be printed by such person and persons only as shall be constituted and appointed to license the same, according to the direction and true meaning of this act herein after expressed, and by no other; (that is to say) That all books concerning the common laws of this realm, shall be printed by the special allowance of the Lord-Chancellor, or Lord Keeper of the Great Seal of England for the time being, the Lords Chief-Justices, and Lord Chief-Baron for the time being, . . . or one or more of their appointments; And that all books of history concerning the state of this realm, or other books concerning any affairs of state, shall be licensed by the principal Secretaries of State for the time being, or one of them, . . . And that all books to be imprinted concerning heraldry, titles of honour, and arms, or otherwise concerning the office of Earl-Marshal, shall be licensed by the Earl-Marshal for the time being or by his appointment, or in case there shall not then be an Earl-Marshal, shall be licensed by the three kings of arms, Garter, Clarencieux and Norroy, or any two of them, whereof Garter principal king of arms to be one; And that all other books to be imprinted or reprinted, whether of divinity, physick, philosophy, or whatsover other science or art, shall be first licensed and allowed by the Lord Archbishop of Canterbury, and Lord Bishop of London for the time being, or one of them, or by their or one of their appointments, or by either of the Chancellors, or Vice-Chancellors of either of the universities of this realm for the time being; provided always, that the said Chancellors, or Vice-Chancellors of either of the universities shall only license such books as are to be imprinted or reprinted within the limits of the said universities respectively, but not in London or elsewhere, not meddling either with books of common laws, or matters of state or government, nor any book or books, the right of printing whereof doth solely and properly belong to any particular person or persons, without his or their consent first obtained in that behalf.

IV. And be it enacted . . . That every person and persons who
. . . are, . . . authorized to license the imprinting of books, or re-
printing thereof with any additions or amendments, as aforesaid, shall
have one written copy of the same book or books which shall be so
licensed . . . with the titles, epistles, prefaces, tables, dedications,
and all other things whatsoever thereunto annexed; which said copy
shall be delivered by such licencer or licencers to the printer or
owner for the imprinting thereof, and shall be solely and entirely
returned by such priests or owner, after the imprinting thereof,
unto such licencer or licencers, to be kept in the public registries
of the said Lord Archbishop, or Lord Bishop of London respectively, or in the office of the Chancellor or Vice-Chancellor
of either of the said universities, or with the said Lord Chancellor
or Lord-Keeper of the Great-Seal for the time being, or Lord-Chief-
Justices, or Chief-Baron, or one of them, of all such books as
shall be licensed by them respectively; And if such book so to be
licensed shall be an English book, or of the English tongue, there
shall be two written copies thereof delivered to the licencer or
licencers (if he or they shall so require) one copy whereof so licenced
shall be delivered back to the said printer or owner, and the other
copy shall be reserved and kept as is aforesaid, to the end such
licencer or licencers may be secured, that the copy so licenced shall
not be altered without his or their privity; and upon the said copy
licenced to be imprinted, he or they who shall so licence the same,
shall testify under his or their hand or hands, that there is not anything in the same contained that is contrary to the Christian faith, or
the doctrine or discipline of the Church of England, or against the
state or government of this realm, or contrary to good life, or good
manners, or otherwise as the nature and subject of the work shall
require; which licence on approbation shall be printed in the beginning
of the same book, with the name or names of him or them that shall
authorize or licence the same, for a testimony of the allowance thereof.

. . . .

(§§ V.–IX. provide that books are to be imported to London only, and
not to be opened without permission of the Archbishop of Canterbury or his
deputy, and attaches penalties to violation of this; printers of books, under
penalty, are to put their names on their books; the persons who may sell
books are limited and placed under regulation; and no English books
printed abroad are, in the interests of the printing trade, to be imported
without special license.)

X. And be it further enacted . . . That no person or persons within
the city of London, or the liberties thereof, or elsewhere, shall erect
or cause to be erected any press or printing-house, nor shall knowingly

demise or let, or willingly suffer to be held or used any house, vault, cellar, or other room whatsoever, to or by any person or persons for a printing-house, . . . unless he or they who erect such press, or shall so knowingly demise or let such house, cellar, vault, or room, . . . shall first give notice to the master or wardens of the said Company of Stationers for the time being, of the erecting of such press. . . .

.   .   .   .

(§§ XI.-XIV. furnish detailed regulations as to the printing trade.)

XV. And for the better discovering of printing in corners without licence Be it further enacted . . . That one or more messengers of his Majesty's Chamber, by warrant under his Majesty's sign manual, or under the hand of one or more of his Majesty's principal Secretaries of State, or the Master and Wardens of the said Company of Stationers, or any one of them, shall have power and authority with a constable, to take unto them such assistance as they shall think needful, . . . to search all houses and shops where they shall know, or upon some probable reason suspect any books or papers to be printed, bound or stitched, especially printing-houses, booksellers' shops and warehouses, and bookbinders' houses and shops, and to view there what is imprinting, binding or stitching, and to examine whether the same be licensed, and to demand a sight of the said licence; and if the said book . . . shall not be licensed then to seize upon so much thereof, as shall be found imprinted, together with the several offenders, and to bring them before one or more justices of the peace, who are hereby . . . required to commit such offenders to prison, there to remain until they shall be tried and acquitted, or convicted and punished for the said offences : and in case the said searchers shall . . . find any book or books, . . . which they shall suspect to contain matters therein contrary to the doctrine or discipline of the Church of England, or against the state and government, then upon such suspicion to seize upon such book or books, . . . and to bring the same unto the said Lord Archbishop of Canterbury, and Lord Bishop of London . . . or to the Secretaries of State, . . . who shall take up such further course for the suppressing thereof, as to them or any of them shall seem fit.

.   .   .   .

(§ XVI. lays down the procedure of prosecution.)

XVII. And be it further enacted . . . That every printer shall reserve three printed copies of the best and largest paper of every book new printed, or reprinted by him with additions, and shall before any public vending of the said book bring them to the Master of the Company of Stationers, and deliver them to him, one whereof shall be delivered to the Keeper of his Majesty's Library, and the other two to be sent to the Vice-Chancellors of the two universities respectively, for the use of the public libraries of the said universities.

XVIII. Provided always, That nothing in this act contained shall . . . extend to the prejudice or infringing of any of the just rights and privileges of either of the two universities of this realm, touching and concerning the licensing or printing of books in either of the said universities.

XIX. Provided always, That no search shall at any time be made in the house or houses of any the peers of this realm, or of any other person or persons not being free of, or using any of the trades in this act before mentioned, but by special warrant from the King's Majesty, under his sign-manual, or under the hand of one or both of his Majesty's principal Secretaries of State, or for any other books than such as are in printing, or shall be printed after the tenth of June, 1662; anything in this act to the contrary thereof in any wise notwithstanding.

(§§ XX.-XXI. are special provisos for booksellers in London and in Westminster Hall.)

XXII. Provided also, That neither this act . . . shall extend to prejudice the just rights and privileges granted by his Majesty, or any of his royal predecessors, to any person or persons, under his Majesty's Great Seal, or otherwise, but that such person or persons may exercise and use such rights and privileges, as aforesaid, according to their respective grants; anything in this act to the contrary notwithstanding.

XXIII. Provided also, That neither this act, . . . shall extend to prohibit John Streater Stationer, from printing books and papers, but that he may still follow the art and mystery of printing, as if this act had never been made; anything therein to the contrary notwithstanding.

(§ XXIV. is a special proviso for York city, reserving the licensing right of the Archbishop of York.)

XXV. Provided, That this act shall continue and be in force for two years to commence from the tenth of June, one thousand six hundred and sixty and two, and no longer.

(The Act was continued by 16 Cha. II. c. 8, and for seven years from 1685 by 1 Ja. II. c. 17.)

(For the History of the Licensing Acts see *Macaulay*, H.E. ii. 409-417, 503-504; *Odgers*, L. and S. ch. 1 and 2; *Stephen*, H.C.L. ii. 298-396; *Dicey*, L.C. ch. vi.; *Ranke*, H.E.; *Hallam*, iii. 166 *et seq.; May*, C.H.E. ii. 239-382; *F. K. Hunt*, The Fourth Estate, *passim.* And see the cases cited, pp. 241, 242.)

VII

A TRIENNIAL ACT
16 Charles II. Cap. I., 1664.

An act for the assembling and holding of parliaments once in three years at the least; and for the repeal of an act, intituled, An act for the preventing of inconveniences happening by the long intermission of parliaments.

Whereas the act[1] made in the parliament begun at Westminster the third day of November, in the sixteenth year of the reign of our late sovereign lord King Charles, of blessed memory, intituled, An act for the preventing of inconveniences happening by the long intermission of parliaments, is in derogation of his Majesty's just rights and prerogative inherent to the imperial crown of this realm, for the calling and assembling of parliaments, and may be an occasion of manifold mischiefs and inconveniences, and much endanger the peace and safety of his Majesty, and all his liege people of the realm:

II. Be it therefore enacted . . . That the said act[2] . . . and all and every the articles, clauses, and things therein contained, . . . are hereby . . . declared to be null and void to all intents and purposes whatsoever, as if the said act had never been had or made; anything in the said act contained to the contrary in any wise notwithstanding.

III. And because by the ancient laws and statutes of this realm, made[3] in the reign of King Edward the third, parliaments are to be held very often; . . . be it declared and enacted . . . That hereafter the sitting and holding of parliaments shall not be intermitted or discontinued above three years at the most; but that within three years from and after the determination of this present parliament, and so from time to time within three years after the determination of any other parliament or parliaments, or if there be occasion more often, your Majesty, your heirs and successors, do issue out your writs for calling, assembling, and holding of another parliament, to the end there may be a frequent calling, assembling, and holding of parliaments once in three years at the least.

(*Hallam*, C.H. ii. 330 ; *Ranke*, H.E. iii. 417–464 ; and cp. The Triennial Act (16 Cha. I. c. i.) in *Gardiner*, C.D. p. 74.)

---

[1] 16 Cha. I. c. i. See *Gardiner*, C.D. p. 74.   [2] 16 Cha. I. c. i.
[3] 4 Edw. III. c. 14 ; 36 Edw. III. St. i. c. 10.

VIII

THE CORPORATION ACT. No. 2[1]
(THE FIVE MILE ACT)
17 Charles II. Cap. II., 1665.

An act for restraining Non-conformists from inhabiting in corporations.

Whereas divers parsons, vicars, curates, lecturers, and other persons in holy orders, have not declared their unfeigned assent and consent to the use of all things contained and prescribed in the Book of Common Prayer, and administration of the sacraments and other rites and ceremonies of the church, according to the use of the Church of England; or have not subscribed the declaration or acknowledgment contained in a certain act of parliament made in the fourteenth year of his Majesty's reign, and intituled, An act[2] for the uniformity of public prayers and administration of sacraments, . . . or any other subsequent act: And whereas they, or some of them, and divers other person and persons not ordained according to the form of the Church of England, and as have, since the act of oblivion, taken upon them to preach in unlawful assemblies, conventicles, or meetings, under colour or pretence of exercise of religion, contrary to the laws and statutes of this kingdom, have settled themselves in divers corporations in England, sometimes three or more of them in a place, thereby taking an opportunity to distil the poisonous principles of schism and rebellion into the hearts of his Majesty's subjects, to the great danger of the church and kingdom.

II. Be it therefore enacted . . . That the said parsons, vicars, curates, lecturers, and other persons in holy orders, or pretended holy orders, or pretending to holy orders, and all stipendaries and other persons who have been possessed of any ecclesiastical or spiritual promotion, and every of them, who have not declared their unfeigned assent and consent as aforesaid, and subscribed the declaration aforesaid, and shall not take and subscribe the oath following;

'I, A. B. do swear, That it is not lawful, upon any pretence whatsoever, to take arms against the King; and that I do abhor that traitorous position of taking arms by his authority against his person, or against those that are commissionated by him, in pursuance of such

---

[1] Repealed by 52 Geo. IV. c. 155, § 1.   See also p. 184 (for 9 Geo. IV. c. 17).
[2] 14 Cha. II. c. 4.

D

commissions; and that I will not at any time endeavour any alteration of government, either in church or state.'

III. And all such person and persons as shall take upon them to preach in any unlawful assembly, conventicle, or meeting, under colour or pretence of any exercise of religion, contrary to the laws and statutes of this kingdom, shall not at any time from and after the four and twentieth day of March which shall be in this present year of our Lord God one thousand six hundred sixty and five, unless only in passing upon the road, come or be within five miles of any city, or town corporate, or borough that sends burgesses to the parliament, within his Majesty's kingdom of England, principality of Wales, or of the town of Berwick upon Tweed, or within five miles of any parish, town, or place wherein he or they have since the Act of Oblivion [1] been parson, vicar, curate, stipendary, or lecturer, or taken upon them to preach in any unlawful assembly, conventicle, or meeting, under colour or pretence of any exercise of religion, contrary to the laws and statutes of this kingdom; before he or they have taken and subscribed the oath aforesaid, . . . in open court, (which said oath the said justices are hereby impowered there to administer;) upon forfeiture for every such offence the sum of forty pounds of lawful English money; the one third part thereof to his Majesty and his successors, the other third part to the use of the poor of the parish where the offence shall be committed, and the other third part thereof to such person or persons as shall or will sue for the same . . . wherein no essoin, protection, or wager of law, shall be allowed.

IV. Provided always, . . . That it shall not be lawful for any person or persons restrained from coming to any city, town corporate, borough, parish, town, or place, as aforesaid, or for any other person or persons as shall not first take and subscribe the said oath, and as shall not frequent divine service established by the laws of this kingdom, and carry him or herself reverently, decently, and orderly there, to teach any public or private school, or to take any boarders or tablers that are taught or instructed by him or herself, or any other; upon pain, for every such offence, to forfeit the sum of forty pounds, to be recovered and distributed as aforesaid.

V. Provided also, . . . That it shall be lawful for any two justices of the peace of the respective county, upon oath to them of any offence against this act, which oath they are hereby impowered to administer, to commit the offender for six months, without bail or mainprize, unless upon or before such commitment he shall, before

---

[1] 12 Cha. II. c. 11.

the said justices of the peace, swear and subscribe the aforesaid oath and declaration.

VI. Provided always, That if any person intended to be restrained by virtue of this act, shall without fraud or covin be served with any writ, *subpœna*, warrant, or other process, whereby his person and appearance is required, his obedience to such writ, *subpœna*, or process, shall not be construed an offence against this act.

(*Hallam*, C.H. ii. 329; *Ranke*, iii. 447; *Gneist*, E.C. 584; *Perry*, H.C.E. ch. xxvi.).

IX

THE SECOND CONVENTICLE ACT [1]
22 Charles II. Cap. 1, 1670.

An Act to prevent and suppress Seditious Conventicles.

I. For providing further and more speedy remedies against the growing and dangerous practices of seditious sectaries and other disloyal persons, who, under pretence of tender consciences, have or may at their meetings contrive insurrections (as late experience has shown), be it enacted . . . that if any person of the age of sixteen years or upwards, being a subject of this realm, at any time after the tenth day of May next shall be present at any assembly, conventicle, or meeting, under colour or pretence of any exercise of religion, in other manner than according to the liturgy and practice of the Church of England, in any place within the kingdom of England, dominion of Wales, or town of Berwick upon Tweed, at which conventicle, meeting or assembly there shall be five persons or more assembled together, over and above those of the same household, or if it be in a house where there is a family inhabiting, or if it be in a house, field, or place where there is no family inhabiting, then where any five persons or more are so assembled as aforesaid, it shall . . . be lawful . . . for any one or more justices of the peace of the county, limit, division, corporation, or liberty . . . and he and they are hereby required and enjoined, upon proof . . . made of such offence, either by confession of party or oath of two witnesses (which oath the said justice and justices of the peace, . . . are hereby . . . required to administer), or by notorious evidence and circumstance

[1] Repealed 52 Geo. III. c. 155, § 1.

of the fact, to make a record of every such offence . . . which record . . . shall, to all intents and purposes, be in law . . . a full and perfect conviction of every such offender for such offence ; and thereupon the said justice, justices and chief magistrate respectively shall impose, on every such offender, so convicted as aforesaid, a fine of five shillings for such first offence ; which record and conviction shall be certified . . . at the next quarter sessions of the peace for the county or place where the offence was committed.

II. And be it enacted further . . . that if such offender . . . shall, at any time, again commit the like offence or offences contrary to this Act, and be thereof, in manner aforesaid, convicted, then such offender . . . shall for every such offence incur the penalty of ten shillings; which fine and fines shall be levied by distress and sale. . . .

III. And be it further enacted . . . that every person who shall take upon him to preach or teach in any such meeting, assembly, or conventicle, and shall thereof be convicted as aforesaid, shall forfeit for every such first offence the sum of twenty pounds, to be levied in manner aforesaid upon his goods and chattels ; and if the said preacher or teacher . . . be a stranger, and his name and habitation not known, or is fled and cannot be found, or in the judgment of the justice, justices, or chief magistrates, . . . shall be thought unable to pay the same, the said justice, justices, or chief magistrate respectively are hereby empowered and required to levy the same, . . . upon the goods and chattels of any such persons who shall be present at the same conventicle ; anything in this or any other Act, law, or statute to the contrary notwithstanding ; and the money so levied to be disposed of in manner aforesaid : and if such offender . . . shall at any time again . . . be thereof convicted in manner aforesaid, then such offender so convicted . . . shall . . . incur the penalty of forty pounds, to be levied and disposed as aforesaid.

IV. And be it further enacted . . . that every person who shall wittingly and willingly suffer any such conventicle, meeting, or unlawful assembly aforesaid to be held in his or her house, outhouse, barn, yard, or backside, and be convicted thereof in manner aforesaid, shall forfeit the sum of twenty pounds, to be levied in manner aforesaid. . . :

And be it further enacted . . . that the justice, justices of the peace, and chief magistrate respectively, or the respective constables, headboroughs, and tithingmen, by warrant . . . shall and may, with what aid, force, and assistance they shall think fit, for the better execution of this Act, after refusal or denial to enter, break open

and enter into any house or other place where they shall be informed
any such conventicle as aforesaid is or shall be held, as well within
liberties as without, and take into their custody the persons there
unlawfully assembled, to the intent they may be proceeded against
according to this Act ; and that the lieutenants or deputy-lieutenants,
or any commissionated officer of the militia, or other of his majesty's
forces, with such troops or companies of horse and foot, and also the
sheriffs, and other magistrates and ministers of justice, or any of
them, jointly or severally, . . . with such other assistance as they
shall think meet, or can get in readiness with the soonest, on certificate . . . of any one justice of the peace or chief magistrate, of his
particular information or knowledge of such unlawful meeting or
conventicle held or to be held in their respective counties or places,
and that he, with such assistance as he can get together, is not able
to suppress and dissolve the same, . . . are hereby required and
enjoined to repair unto the place . . . and, by the best means they
can, to dissolve, dissipate, or prevent all such unlawful meetings, and
take into their custody such and so many of the said persons so
unlawfully assembled as they shall think fit, to the intent they may
be proceeded against according to this Act.

V. Provided always, that no dwelling house of any peer of this
realm, where he or his wife shall then be resident, shall be searched
by virtue of this Act, but by immediate warrant from his majesty,
under his sign manual, or in the presence of the lieutenant, or one
deputy-lieutenant, or two justices of the peace, whereof one to be
of the quorum of the same county or riding.

And be it enacted further . . . that if any constable, headborough,
tithingman, churchwarden, or overseer of the poor, who shall know
or be credibly informed of any such meetings or conventicles held
within his precincts, parish, or limits, and shall not give any information thereof to some justice of the peace or the chief magistrate, and
endeavour the conviction of the parties according to his duty, but such
constable, headborough, tithingman, churchwarden, overseers of the
poor, or person lawfully called in aid of the constable, headborough, or
any tithingham, shall wilfully and willingly omit the performance of
his duty . . . and be thereof convicted in manner aforesaid, he shall
forfeit for every such offence the sum of five pounds, to be levied
upon his goods and chattels, and disposed in manner aforesaid : and
that if any justice of the peace or chief magistrate shall wilfully
and wittingly omit the performance of his duty in the execution of
this Act, he shall forfeit the sum of one hundred pounds. . . .

VI. And be it further enacted . . . that if any person be at any time sued for putting in execution any of the powers contained in this Act, otherwise than upon appeal allowed by this Act, such person shall and may plead the general issue, and give the special matter in evidence; and if the plaintiff be nonsuited, or a verdict pass for the defendant, or if the plaintiff discontinue his action, or if, upon demurrer, judgment be given for the defendant, every such defendant shall have his full treble costs.

VII. And be it further enacted by the authority aforesaid, that this Act, and all clauses therein contained, shall be construed most largely and beneficially for the suppressing of conventicles, and for the justification and encouragement of all persons to be employed in the execution thereof: and that no record, warrant, or mittimus to be made by virtue of this Act or any proceedings thereupon, shall be reversed, avoided, or any way impeached by reason of any default in form. . . .

VIII. Provided also, that no person shall be punished for any offence against this Act, unless such offender be prosecuted for the same within three months after the offence committed; and that no person who shall be punished for any offence by virtue of this Act shall be punished for the same offence by virtue of any other Act or law whatsoever.

IX. . . . Provided, also, that no peer of this realm shall be attached or imprisoned by virtue of force of this Act; any thing, matter, or clause therein, to the contrary, notwithstanding. Provided also, that neither this Act, nor anything therein contained, shall extend to invalidate or avoid his majesty's supremacy in ecclesiastical affairs; but that his majesty and his heirs and successors may from time to time, and at all times hereafter, exercise and enjoy all powers and authorities in ecclesiastical affairs, as fully and as amply as himself or any of his predecessors have or might have done the same; anything in this Act notwithstanding.

(The First Conventicles Act, 16 Cha. II. c. 4, was re-enacted in a more permanent form by this Act. See *Hallam*, C.H. ii. 348 ; *Ranke*, H.E. 505 *et seq.*; *Perry*, H.C.E. ii. ch. 26 and 27; *Gneist*, E.C. 583.)

X

THE TEST ACT [1]

25 Charles II. Cap. II. 1673.

An Act for preventing dangers which may happen from popish recusants.

For preventing dangers which may happen from popish recusants, and quieting the minds of his Majesty's good subjects; be it enacted . . . That all and every person or persons, as well peers as commoners, that shall bear any office or offices civil or military, or shall receive any pay, salary, fee or wages, by reason of any patent or grant from his Majesty, or shall have command or place of trust from or under his Majesty, or from any of his Majesty's predecessors, or by his or their authority, or by authority derived from him or them, within the realm of England, dominion of Wales, or town of Berwick upon Tweed, or in his Majesty's navy, or in the several islands of Jersey and Guernsey, or shall be of the household, or in the service or employment of his Majesty, or of his Royal Highness the Duke of York, who shall inhabit, reside, or be within the city of London or Westminster, or within thirty miles distant from the same, on the first day of Easter term that shall be in the year of our Lord one thousand six hundred seventy-three, . . . all and every the said person and persons shall personally appear before the end of the said term, or of Trinity term next following, in his Majesty's high court of chancery, or in his Majesty's court of King's bench, and there in public and open court, between the hours of nine of the clock and twelve in the forenoon, take the several Oaths of Supremacy and Allegiance, (which Oath of Allegiance is contained in the Statute made in the third year of King James [2]), by law established; and during the time of the taking thereof, . . . all pleas and proceedings in the said respective courts shall cease; and that all and every . . . not having taken the said oaths in the said respective courts aforesaid, shall, on or before the first day of August, one thousand six hundred seventy-three, at the quarter sessions for that county or place where he or they shall be, inhabit, or reside on the twentieth day of May, take the said oaths in open court between the said hours of nine and twelve of the clock in the forenoon; and the said respective officers

---

[1] Repealed by 9 Geo. IV. c. 17.   See p. 184.
[2] 3 and 4 Ja. I. c. 4, § 9 (*Gardiner*, C.D. 258).

aforesaid shall also receive the Sacrament of the Lord's Supper, according to the usage of the Church of England, at or before the first day of August in the year of our Lord one thousand six hundred and seventy-three, in some parish church, upon some Lord's day, commonly called Sunday, immediately after divine service and sermon.

II. And be it further enacted . . . That all and every person or persons, . . . taken into any office or offices civil or military, or shall receive any pay, salary, fee, or wages, by reason of any patent or grant of his Majesty, or shall have command or place of trust from or under his Majesty, his heirs or successors, or by his or their authority, or by authority derived from him or them, within this realm of England, . . . or in his Majesty's navy, or in the several islands of Jersey and Guernsey, or that shall be admitted into any service or employment in his Majesty's or Royal Highness's household or family, after the first day of Easter term aforesaid, and shall inhabit, . . . within the cities of London or Westminster, or within thirty miles of the same, shall take the said oaths aforesaid in the said respective court or courts aforesaid, in the next term after such his or their admittance or admittances into the office or offices, employment or employments aforesaid, between the hours aforesaid, and no other, and the proceedings to cease as aforesaid. . . . And all and every such person . . . shall also receive the sacrament of the Lord's Supper, according to the usage of the Church of England, within three months after his or their admittance in or receiving their said authority and employment, in some public church upon some Lord's day, commonly called Sunday, immediately after divine service and sermon.

III. And every of the said persons . . . shall first deliver a certificate of such his receiving the said sacrament as aforesaid, under the hands of the respective minister and churchwarden, and shall then make proof of the truth thereof by two credible witnesses at the least, upon oath; all which shall be enquired of, and put upon record in the respective courts.

IV. And be it further enacted . . . That all . . . that do . . . refuse to take the said oaths and sacrament in the said courts and places, . . . shall be *ipso facto* adjudged uncapable and disabled in law, to all intents and purposes whatsoever, to have, occupy, or enjoy the said office or offices, employment, or employments, or any part of them, or any matter or thing aforesaid, or any profit or advantage appertaining to them, or any of them; and every such office and place, employment and employments, . . . is hereby adjudged void.

V. And be it further enacted, That all . . . that shall . . . refuse to take the said oaths or the sacrament as aforesaid, . . . and yet after such neglect or refusal shall execute any of the said offices or employments after the said times expired, . . . and being thereupon lawfully convicted, . . . every such person . . . shall be disabled from thenceforth to sue or use any action, bill, plaint, or information in course of law, or to prosecute any suit in any court of Equity, or to be guardian of any child, or executor or administrator of any person, or capable of any legacy or deed of gift, or to bear any office within this realm of England, dominion of Wales, or town of Berwick upon Tweed; and shall forfeit the sum of five hundred pounds. . . .

VI. And be it further enacted, . . . That the names of all and singular such persons and officers aforesaid, That . . . shall take the oaths aforesaid, shall be in the respective courts of Chancery and King's-bench, and the quarter sessions inrolled, . . . in rolls made and kept only for that intent and purpose, and for no other; the which rolls, as for the court of chancery, shall be publicly hung up in the office of the Petty-bag, and the roll for the King's-bench in the crown office of the said court, and in some public place in every quarter sessions, and there remain . . . for every one to resort to and look upon without fee or reward; and likewise none of the person or persons aforesaid, shall give or pay as any fee or reward to any officer or officers belonging to any of the courts as aforesaid, above the sum of twelve-pence for his or their entry of his or their taking of the said oaths as aforesaid.

VII. And further, That it shall and may be lawful to and for the respective courts aforesaid, to give and administer the said oaths aforesaid to the person or persons aforesaid, . . . and upon the due tender of any such person or persons to take the said oaths, the said courts are hereby required and enjoined to administer the same.

VIII. And be it farther enacted, That if any person or persons, not bred up by his or their parent or parents from their infancy in the popish religion, and professing themselves to be popish recusants, shall breed up, instruct, or educate his or their child or children, or suffer them to be instructed or educated in the popish religion, every such person being thereof convicted, shall be from thenceforth disabled of bearing any office or place of trust or profit in church or state : And all such children as shall be so brought up, instructed or educated, are and shall be hereby disabled of bearing any such office or place of trust or profit, until he and they shall be perfectly reconciled and converted to the Church of England, and shall take the Oaths of Supremacy and Allegiance aforesaid before the justices of the peace . . . and thereupon receive the sacrament of the Lord's Supper after the usage of the Church of England, and obtain a certificate thereof under the hands of two or more of the said justices of the peace.

IX. And be it further enacted . . . That at the same time when the persons concerned in this act shall take the aforesaid Oaths of Supremacy and Allegiance, they shall likewise make and subscribe this declaration following, under the same penalties and forfeitures as by this act is appointed ;

'I, A. B. do declare, That I do believe that there is not any transubstantiation in the sacrament of the Lord's Supper, or in the elements of Bread and Wine, at or after the consecration thereof by any person whatsoever.'

X. Of which subscription there shall be the like register kept, as of taking the oaths aforesaid.

.   .   .   .

(XI. exempts the peerage and certain officers, and requires " Popish officers" to appoint deputies who shall take the oath.

XII. provides that peers may take the oath in parliament.

XIII. A saving proviso for married women.

XIV. A person forfeiting under the Act may receive back his office on compliance with the statutory requirements.

XV. exempts non-commissioned officers in the navy who take the subscription.

XVI. exempts the pensions of the Earl of Bristol.

XVII. exempts constables, tithingmen, church wardens, and various private officers.)

(See *Hallam*, C.H. ii. ch. xii. ; *Perry*, H.C.E. ii. xxvii. ; *Ranke*, H.E. iii. 531–542 ; *Porritt*, U.H.C. i. 122–149.)

(The passing of " The Test Act" was in no small measure due to the issuing of The Declaration of Indulgence, which is here given, together with the resolutions of the House of Commons relating to it.)

THE DECLARATION OF INDULGENCE OF CHARLES II.

Our care and endeavours for the preservation of the rights and interests of the Church have been sufficiently manifested to the world by the whole course of our government, since our happy restoration, and by the many and frequent ways of coercion that we have used for reducing all erring or dissenting persons, and for com-

posing the unhappy differences in matters of religion, which we
found among our subjects upon our return. But it being evident
by the sad experience of twelve years, that there is very little fruit of
all those forcible courses, we think ourselves obliged to make use of
that supreme power in ecclesiastical matters, which is not only inherent
in us but hath been declared and recognized to be so by several
statutes and acts of parliament. And therefore we do now accordingly
issue out this our royal declaration, as well for the quieting the
minds of our good subjects in these points, for inviting strangers in
this conjuncture to come and live under us, and for the better encouragement of all to a cheerful following of their trades and callings,
from whence we hope, by the blessing of God, to have many good and
happy advantages to our government; as also for preventing for the
future the danger that might otherwise arise from private meetings
and seditious conventicles. And in the first place, we declare our
express resolution, meaning and intention to be, that the Church of
England be preserved, and remain entire in its doctrine, discipline,
and government, as it now stands established by law: and that this
be taken to be, as it is, the basis, rule and standard of the general
and public worship of God, and the orthodox conformable clergy
do receive and enjoy the revenues belonging thereunto; and that no
person, though of different opinion and persuasion, shall be exempt
from paying his tithes, or other dues whatsoever. And further, we
declare, that no person shall be capable of holding any benefice,
living, or ecclesiastical dignity or preferment of any kind in this
kingdom of England, who is not exactly conformable. We do in the
next place declare our will and pleasure to be, that the execution of
all and all manner of penal laws in matters ecclesiastical, against
whatsoever sort of non-conformists, or recusants, be immediately
suspended, and they are hereby suspended. And all judges of assize
and gaol-delivery sheriffs, justices of the peace, mayors, bailiffs, and
other officers whatsoever, whether ecclesiastical or civil, are to take
notice of it, and pay due obedience thereunto, and that there may
be no pretence for any of our subjects to continue their illegal
meetings and conventicles, we do declare, that we shall from time to
time allow a sufficient number of places, as shall be desired, in all
parts of this our kingdom, for the use of such as do not conform to
the Church of England, to meet and assemble in, in order to their
public worship and devotion; which places shall be open and free
to all persons. But to prevent such disorders and inconveniences as
may happen by this our indulgence, if not duly regulated, and that
they may be better protected by the civil magistrate, our express will

and pleasure is, that none of our subjects do presume to meet in any place, until such place be allowed, and the teacher of that congregation be approved by us. And lest any should apprehend that this our restriction should make our said allowance and approbation difficult to be obtained, we do further declare, that this our indulgence as to the allowance of public places of worship, and approbation of teachers, shall extend to all sorts of non-conformists and recusants, except the recusants of the Roman Catholic religion, to whom we shall no ways allow in public places of worship, but only indulge them in their share in the common exemption from the executing the penal laws, and the exercise of their worship in their private houses only. And if after this our clemency and indulgence, any of our subjects shall presume to abuse this liberty, and shall preach seditiously, or to the derogation of the doctrine, discipline, or government of the established church, or shall meet in places not allowed by us; we do hereby give them warning, and declare, we will proceed against them with all imaginable severity: and we will let them see, we can be as severe to punish such offenders, when so justly provoked, as we are indulgent to truly tender consciences.

RESOLUTIONS OF THE HOUSE OF COMMONS

The House then resumed the Debate of that Part of His Majesty's Speech, which relates to his Declaration of Indulgence to Dissenters. And the Declaration was read.

The Question being propounded, That penal Statutes, in Matters Ecclesiastical, cannot be suspended but by Act of Parliament;

The Question being put, That the Question be now put;

The House divided.

The Noes go forth.

Tellers,

Sir Thomas Lee,
Sir Trevor Williams, } For the Yeas, 168.

Sir Solomon Swale,
Mr. Collingwood, } For the Noes, 116.

And so it was resolved in the Affirmative.

The main Question being put, That penal Statutes, in Matters Ecclesiastical, cannot be suspended but by Act of Parliament;

It was resolved in the Affirmative.

Resolved, etc. That an humble Petition and Address, upon this Vote and the Debate of the House, be forthwith prepared and drawn up, to be presented to his Majesty; and that it be referred to . . . [names follow here] . . . to prepare and bring in the Petition and Address. . . .

(C.J. ix. 251.)

Mr. Powle reports from the Committee appointed to prepare and draw up a Petition and Address to his Majesty, the said Petition and Address: Which he read, in his Place; and after, delivered the same in at the Clerk's Table: And the same being again twice read, is as followeth; viz.

Most gracious Sovereign,

We your Majesty's most loyal and faithful Subjects, the Commons assembled in Parliament, do, in the first place, as in all Duty bound, return your Majesty our most humble and hearty Thanks for the many gracious Promises and Assurances which Your Majesty hath several times, during this present Parliament, given to us, that Your Majesty would secure and maintain unto us the true Reformed Protestant Religion, our Liberties, and Properties: Which most gracious Assurances Your Majesty hath, out of your great Goodness, been pleased to renew unto us more particularly, at the Opening of this present Session of Parliament.

And further we crave Leave humbly to represent, That we have, with all Duty and Expedition, taken into our Consideration several Parts of Your Majesty's last Speech to us, and withal the Declaration therein mentioned, for Indulgence to Dissenters, dated the Fifteenth of March last: And we find ourselves bound in Duty to inform Your Majesty, that penal Statutes, in Matters Ecclesiastical, cannot be suspended, but by Act of Parliament.

We therefore, the Knights, Citizens and Burgesses of Your Majesty's House of Commons, do most humbly beseech Your Majesty, that the said Laws may have their free Course, until it shall be otherwise provided for by Act of Parliament: And that Your Majesty would graciously be pleased to give such Directions herein, that no Apprehensions or Jealousies may remain in the Hearts of Your Majesty's good and faithful subjects.

Resolved, etc. That this House doth agree with the Committee in the Petition and Address by them drawn up to be presented to his Majesty.

(C.J. ix. 252.)

XI

THE HABEAS CORPUS AMENDMENT ACT[1]
31 Charles II. Cap. 2, 1679.

An act for the better securing the liberty of the subject, and for prevention of imprisonments beyond the seas.

Whereas great delays have been used by sheriffs, gaolers, and other officers, to whose custody any of the King's subjects have been committed for criminal or supposed criminal matters, in making returns of writs of Habeas Corpus to them directed, by standing out an Alias and Pluries Habeas Corpus, and sometimes more, and by other shifts to avoid their yielding obedience to such writs, contrary to their duty and the known laws of the land, whereby many of the King's subjects have been, and hereafter may be long detained in prison, in such cases where by law they are bailable, to their great charges and vexation;

II. For the prevention whereof, and the more speedy relief of all persons imprisoned for any such criminal or supposed criminal matters; be it enacted by the King's most excellent Majesty, by and with the advice and consent of the lords spiritual and temporal, and commons in this present parliament assembled, and by authority thereof, That whensoever any person or persons shall bring any Habeas Corpus directed unto any sheriff or sheriffs, gaoler, minister, or other person whatsoever, for any person in his or their custody, and the said writ shall be served upon the said officer, or left at the gaol or prison with any of the under officers, under keepers, or deputy of the said officers or keepers, that the said officer or officers, his or their under officers, under keepers, or deputies, shall, within three days after the service thereof as aforesaid, (unless the commitment aforesaid were for treason or felony, plainly or specially expressed in the warrant of commitment), upon payment or tender of the charges of bringing the said prisoner, to be ascertained by the judge or court that awarded the same, and indorsed upon the said writ, not exceeding twelvepence per mile, and upon security given by his own bond to pay the charges of carrying back the prisoner, if he shall be remanded by the court or judge to which he shall be brought according to the true intent of this present act, and that he will not

---

[1] Repealed in part by Stat. Law Rev. Act, 1863.

make any escape by the way, make return of such writ; and bring, or cause to be brought, the body of the party so committed or restrained, unto or before the Lord Chancellor, or Lord Keeper of the Great Seal of England for the time being, or the judges or barons of the said court from whence the said writ shall issue, or unto or before such other person or persons before whom the said writ is made returnable, according to the command thereof; and shall then likewise certify the true causes of his detainer or imprisonment, unless the commitment of the said party be in any place beyond the distance of twenty miles, from the place or places where such court or person is or shall be residing; and if beyond the distance of twenty miles, and not above one hundred miles, then within the space of ten days, and if beyond the distance of one hundred miles, then within the space of twenty days, after such delivery aforesaid, and not longer.

III. And to the intent that no sheriff, gaoler, or other officer, may pretend ignorance of the import of any such writ; be it enacted by the authority aforesaid, That all such writs shall be marked in this manner, *per statutum tricesimo primo Caroli secundi regis*, and shall be signed by the person that awards the same; and if any person or persons shall be or stand committed or detained as aforesaid, for any crime, unless for felony or treason plainly expressed in the warrant of commitment, in the vacation time, and out of term, it shall and may be lawful to and for the person or persons so committed or detained (other than persons convict or in execution by legal process) or any one on his or their behalf, to appeal or complain to the Lord Chancellor or Lord Keeper, or any one of His Majesty's justices, either of the one bench or of the other, or the barons of the exchequer of the degree of the coif; and the said Lord Chancellor, Lord Keeper, justices or barons, or any of them, upon view of the copy or copies of the warrant or warrants of commitment or detainer, or otherwise upon oath made that such copy or copies were denied to be given by such person or persons in whose custody the prisoner or prisoners is or are detained, are hereby authorized and required, upon request made in writing by such person or persons, or any on his, her or their behalf, attested and subscribed by two witnesses who were present at the delivery of the same, to award and grant a Habeas Corpus under the seal of such court whereof he shall then be one of the judges, to be directed to the officer or officers in whose custody the party so committed or detained shall be; returnable *immediate* before the said Lord Chancellor, or Lord Keeper, or such justice, baron, or any other justice or baron of the degree of the coif of any of the said courts; and upon service thereof as aforesaid, the officer or officers, his or their under officer or under officers, under keeper or under keepers, or their deputy, in whose custody the party is so committed or detained, shall, within the times respectively before limited, bring such prisoner or prisoners before the said Lord Chancellor or Lord Keeper, or such justices, barons, or one of them, before whom the said writ is made returnable, and in case of his absence, before any other of them, with the return of such writ, and the true causes of the commitment and detainer ; and thereupon, within two days after the party shall be brought before them, the said Lord Chancellor or Lord Keeper, or such justice or baron before whom the prisoner shall be brought as aforesaid, shall discharge the said prisoner from his imprisonment, taking his or their recognizance, with one or more surety or sureties, in any sum according to their discretions, having regard to the quality of the prisoner and nature of the offence, for his or their appearance in the Court of King's Bench the term following, or at the next assizes, sessions, or general gaol, delivery of and for such county, city, or place where the commitment was, or where the offence was committed, or in such other court where the said offence is properly cognizable, as the case shall require, and then shall certify the said writ with the return thereof, and the said recognizance or recognizances into the said court where such appearance is to be made ; unless it shall appear unto the said Lord Chancellor or Lord Keeper, or justice or justices, or baron or barons, that the party so committed is detained upon a legal process, order or warrant, out of some court that hath jurisdiction of criminal matters, or by some warrant signed and sealed with the hand and seal of any of the said justices or barons, or some justice or justices of the peace, for such matters or offences for the which by the law the prisoner is not bailable.

IV. Provided always, and be it enacted, That if any person shall have wilfully neglected by the space of two whole terms after his imprisonment, to pray a Habeas Corpus for his enlargement, such person so wilfully neglecting shall not have any Habeas Corpus to be granted in vacation time, in pursuance of this act.

V. And be it further enacted by the authority aforesaid, That if any officer or officers, his or their under officer or under officers, under keeper or under keepers, or deputy, shall neglect or refuse to make the returns aforesaid, or to bring the body or bodies of the prisoner or prisoners according to the command of the said writ, within the respective times aforesaid, or upon demand made by the prisoner or person in his behalf, shall refuse to deliver, or within the space of six hours after demand shall not deliver, to the person so demanding, a true copy of the warrant or warrants of commitment and detainer of such prisoner, which he and they are hereby required to deliver accordingly; all and every the head gaolers and keepers of such prison, and such other person in whose custody the prisoner shall be detained, shall for the first offence forfeit to the prisoner or party grieved, the sum of one hundred pounds; and for the second offence the sum of two hundred pounds, and shall and is hereby made incapable to hold or execute his said office; the said penalties to be recovered by the prisoner or party grieved, his executors or administrators, against such offender, his executors, or administrators, by any action of debt, suit, bill, plaint or information, in any of the King's courts at Westminster, wherein no essoin, protection, privilege, injunction, wager of law, or stay of prosecution by *Non vult ulterius prosequi*, or otherwise, shall be admitted or allowed, or any more than one importance; and any recovery or judgement at the suit of any party grieved, shall be a sufficient conviction for the first offence; and any after recovery or judgement at the suit of a party grieved for any offence after the first judgement, shall be a sufficient conviction to bring the officers or person within the said penalty for the second offence.

VI. And for the prevention of unjust vexation by reiterated commitments for the same offence; be it enacted by the authority aforesaid, That no person or persons which shall be delivered or set at large upon any Habeas Corpus, shall at any time hereafter be again imprisoned or committed for the same offence by any person or persons whatsoever, other than by the legal order and process of such court wherein he or they shall be bound by recognizance to appear, or other court having jurisdiction of the cause; and if any other person or persons shall knowingly, contrary to this act, recommit or imprison, or knowingly procure or cause to be recommitted or imprisoned, for the same offence or pretended offence, any person or persons delivered or set at large as aforesaid, or be knowingly aiding or assisting therein, then he or they shall forfeit to the prisoner or party grieved the sum of five hundred pounds; any colourable pretence or variation in the warrant or warrants of commitment, notwithstanding, to be recovered as aforesaid.

VII. Provided always, and be it further enacted, That if any person or persons shall be committed for high treason or felony, plainly and specially expressed in the warrant of commitment, upon his prayer or petition in open court the first week of the term, or the first day of the sessions of *Oyer* and *Terminer*, or general gaol-delivery, to be brought to his trial, shall not be indicted some time in

E

the next term, sessions of *Oyer* and *Terminer* or general gaol-delivery, after such commitment; it shall and may be lawful to and for the judges of the Court of King's Bench and justices of *Oyer* and *Terminer,* or general gaol-delivery, and they are hereby required, upon motion to them made in open court the last day of the term, sessions, gaol-delivery, either by the prisoner or any one in his behalf, to set at liberty the prisoner upon bail, unless it appear to the judges and justices upon oath made, that the witnesses for the King could not be produced the same term, sessions, or general gaol-delivery; and if any person or persons committed as aforesaid, upon his prayer or petition in open court the first week of the term or first day of the sessions of *Oyer* and *Terminer* and general gaol-delivery, to be brought to his trial, shall not be indicted and tried the second term, sessions of *Oyer* and *Terminer* or general gaol-delivery, after his commitment, or upon his trial shall be acquitted, he shall be discharged from his imprisonment.

VIII. Provided always, That nothing in this act shall extend to discharge out of prison any person charged in debt, or other action, or with process in any civil cause, but that after he shall be discharged of his imprisonment for such his criminal offence, he shall be kept in custody according to the law, for such other suit.

IX. Provided always, and be it enacted by the authority aforesaid, That if any person or persons, subjects of this realm, shall be committed to any prison, or in custody, of any officer or officers whatever for any criminal or supposed criminal matter, that the said person shall not be removed from the said prison and custody into the custody of any other officer or officers; unless it be by Habeas Corpus or some other legal writ; or where the prisoner is delivered to the constable or other inferior officer to carry such prisoner to some common gaol; or where any person is sent by order of any judge of assize or justice of the peace, to any common workhouse or house of correction; or where the prisoner is removed from one prison or place to another within the same county, in order to his or her trial in discharge of due course of law; or in case of sudden fire or infection, or other necessity; and if any person or persons shall, after such commitment aforesaid, make out and sign, or countersign any warrant or warrants for such removal aforesaid, contrary to this act; as well he that makes or signs, or countersigns such warrant or warrants, as the officer or officers that obey or execute the same, shall suffer and incur the pains and forfeitures in this act before mentioned, both for the first and second offence respectively, to be recovered in manner aforesaid by the party aggrieved.

X. Provided also, and be it further enacted by the authority aforesaid, That it shall and may be lawful to and for any prisoner and prisoners as aforesaid, to move and obtain his or their Habeas Corpus, as well out of the High Court of Chancery or Court of Exchequer, as out of the Courts of King's Bench or Common Pleas, or either of them ; and if the said Lord Chancellor or Lord Keeper, or any judge or judges, baron or barons for the time being of the degree of the coif, or any of the courts aforesaid, in the vacation time, upon view of the copy or copies of the warrant or warrants of commitment or detainer, or upon oath made that such copy or copies were denied as aforesaid, shall deny any writ of Habeas Corpus, by this act required to be granted, being moved for as aforesaid, they shall severally forfeit to the prisoner or party grieved the sum of five hundred pounds, to be recovered in manner aforesaid.

XI. And be it declared and enacted by the authority aforesaid, That an Habeas Corpus, according to the true intent and meaning of this act, may be directed and run into any county palatine, the cinque ports, or other privileged places within the kingdom of England, dominion of Wales, or town of Berwick-upon-Tweed, and the Islands of Jersey or Guernsey; any law or usage to the contrary notwithstanding.

XII. And for preventing illegal imprisonments in prisons beyond the seas, be it further enacted by the authority aforesaid, That no subjects of this realm that now is, or hereafter shall be an inhabitant or resident of this kingdom of England, dominion of Wales, or town of Berwick upon Tweed, shall or may be sent prisoner into Scotland, Ireland, Jersey, Guernsey, Tangier, or into other parts, garrisons, islands, or places beyond the seas, which are or at any time hereafter shall be within or without the dominions of His Majesty, his heirs or successors; and that every such imprisonment is hereby enacted and adjudged to be illegal; and that if any of the said subjects now is or hereafter shall be so imprisoned, every such person and persons so imprisoned, shall and may, for every such imprisonment, maintain, by virtue of this act, an action or actions of false imprisonment, in any of His Majesty's courts of record, against the person or persons by whom he or she shall be so committed, detained, imprisoned, sent prisoner, or transported, contrary to the true meaning of this act, and against all and any person or persons that shall frame, contrive, write, seal, or countersign any warrant or writing for such commitment, detainer, imprisonment, or transportation, or shall be advising, aiding, or assisting in the same, or any of them ; and the plaintiff in every such action shall have judgement to recover his treble costs, besides damages, which damages so to be given shall not be less than five hundred pounds; in which action, no delay, stay, or stop of proceeding by rule, order, or command, nor no injunction, protection, or privilege whatsoever, nor any more than one imparlance, shall be allowed, excepting such rule of the court wherein the action shall depend, made in open court, as shall be thought in justice necessary, for special cause to be expressed in the said rule; and the person or persons, who shall knowingly frame, contrive, write, seal, or countersign any warrant for such commitment, detainer, or transportation, or shall so commit, detain, imprison, or transport any person or persons contrary to this act, or be anyways advising, aiding, or assisting therein, being lawfully convicted thereof, shall be disabled from thenceforth to bear any office of trust or profit within the said realm of England, dominion of Wales, or town of Berwick upon Tweed, or any of the islands, territories, or dominions thereunto belonging; and shall incur and sustain the pains, penalties, and forfeitures limited, ordained, and provided, in and by the statute of provision and præmunire made in the sixteenth year of King Richard the Second; and be incapable of any pardon from the King, his heirs or successors, of the said forfeitures, losses, or disabilities, or any of them.

XIII. Provided always, That nothing in this act shall extend to give benefit to any person who shall by contract in writing agree with any merchant or owner of any plantation, or other person whatsoever, to be transported to any parts beyond the seas, and receive earnest upon such agreement, although that afterwards such person shall renounce such contract.

XIV. Provided always, and be it enacted, That if any person or persons, lawfully convicted of any felony, shall, in open court, pray to be transported beyond the seas, and the court shall think fit to leave him or them in prison for that purpose, such person or persons may be transported into any parts beyond the seas; this act, or anything therein contained to the contrary notwithstanding.

XV. Provided also, and be it enacted, That nothing herein contained shall be deemed, construed, or taken, to extend to the imprisonment of any person before the first day of June, one thousand six hundred seventy and nine, or to anything advised, procured, or otherwise done, relating to such imprisonment; anything herein contained to the contrary notwithstanding.

XVI. Provided also, That if any person or persons, at any time resiant in this realm, shall have committed any capital offence in Scotland or Ireland, or any of the islands, or foreign plantations of the King, his heirs or successors, where he or she ought to be tried for such offence, such person or persons may be sent to such place, there to receive such trial, in such manner as the same might have been used before the making of this act; anything herein contained to the contrary notwithstanding.

XVII. Provided also, and be it enacted, That no person or persons shall be sued, impleaded, molested, or troubled for any offence against this act, unless the party offending be sued, or impleaded for the same within two years at the most after such time wherein the offence shall be committed, in case the party grieved shall not be then in prison; and if he shall be in prison, then within the space of two years after the decease of the person imprisoned, or his or her delivery out of prison, which shall first happen.

XVIII. And, to the intent no person may avoid his trial at the assizes or general gaol delivery, by procuring his removal before the assizes, at such time as he cannot be brought back to receive his trial there, be it enacted, That, after the Assizes proclaimed for that county where the prisoner is detained, no person shall be removed from the common gaol upon any Habeas Corpus granted in pursuance of this act, but upon any such Habeas Corpus shall be brought before the judge of assize in open court, who is thereupon to do what to justice shall appertain.

XIX. Provided nevertheless, That, after the Assizes are ended, any person or persons detained, may have his or her Habeas Corpus according to the direction and intention of this act.

XX. And be it also enacted by the authority aforesaid, That if any information, suit, or action shall be brought or exhibited against any person or persons for any offence committed or to be committed against the form of this law, it shall be lawful for such defendants to plead the general issue, that they are not guilty, or that they owe nothing, and to give such special matter in evidence to the jury that shall try the same, which matter being pleaded had been good and sufficient matter in law to have discharged the said defendant or defendants against the said information, suit or action, and the said matter shall be then as available to him or them, to all intents and purposes, as if he or they had sufficiently pleaded, set forth, or alledged the same matter in bar or discharge of such information, suit, or action.

XXI. And because many times persons charged with petty treason or felony, or as accessories thereunto, are committed upon suspicion only, whereupon they are bailable, or not, according as the circumstances making out that suspicion are more or less weighty, which are best known to the justices of peace that committed the persons,

and have examinations before them, or to other justices of the peace
in the county; be it therefore enacted, That where any person shall
appear to be committed by any judge or justice of the peace, and
charged as accessory before the fact, to any petty treason or felony,
or upon suspicion thereof, or with suspicion of petty treason or
felony, which petty treason or felony shall be plainly and specially
expressed in the warrant of commitment, that such person shall not
be removed or bailed by virtue of this act, or in any other manner
than they might have been before the making of this act.

(See *Dicey*, L.C. iv. and v.; *Hallam*, C.H. ii. xii.; *Gneist*, E.C. xl.–xlv.;
Ranke, H.E. iv. 85 *et seq.; Macaulay*, H.E. ch. i.; *Hurd*, The Habeas
Corpus.)

A MODERN WRIT UNDER THE ACT

Victoria, by the grace of God, of the United Kingdom of Great
Britain and Ireland, Queen, defender of the faith, to the Keeper of
our gaol of   , at   , or his deputy, greeting.

We command you, that you have before us at Westminster Hall,
immediately after the receipt of this writ, the body of C. D., being
committed and detained in our prison under our custody (as is said),
together with the day and cause of the taking and detaining of the
said C. D., by whatever name the said C. D. be called in the same, to
undergo and receive all and singular such things as our Court shall
then and there consider of him in that behalf, and that you have
then there this writ.   Witness Thomas, Lord Denman, at Westminster, the   day of   , in the   year of our reign. By the
Court,   D.

THE RETURN TO THE WRIT

[Indorsed on the writ as follows] The execution of this writ
appears in a certain schedule hereunto annexed.

E. F. Keeper.

I, E. F. Keeper of her Majesty's gaol of   , at   , in the
writ to this schedule annexed named, do certify and return to our
Sovereign Lady, the Queen, that before the coming to me of the said
writ, (that is to say), on &c.   C. D. in the said writ also named, was
committed to my custody, by virtue of a certain warrant of commitment, the tenor of which is as follows : [here insert a copy of the
warrant].   And these are the causes of the detaining of the said
C. D., whose body I have here ready, as by the said writ I am
commanded.   E. F. Keeper.

(*Burns'* Justice of the Peace, ii. 947–948.)

XII

THE CONVENTION PARLIAMENT
1 Will. and Mary, Cap. I. 1689.

An Act for removing and preventing all Questions and Disputes concerning the Assembling and Sitting of this present Parliament.

For preventing all doubts and scruples which may in any wise arise concerning the meeting, sitting and proceeding of this present Parliament, be it declared and enacted . . .

II. That the Lords Spiritual and Temporal and Commons convened at Westminster, the two and twentieth day of January in the year of Our Lord one thousand six hundred eighty eight and there sitting on the thirteenth day of February following are the two Houses of Parliament, and so shall be and are hereby declared, enacted and adjudged to be to all intents, constructions and purposes whatsoever, notwithstanding any want of writ or writs of summons or any other defect of form or default whatsoever, as if they had been summoned according to the usual form, and that this present Act and all other Acts, to which the royal assent shall at any time be given before the next prorogation after the said thirteenth of February, shall be understood taken and adjudged in law to begin and commence upon the said thirteenth of February on which day their said Majesties at the request and by the advice of the Lords and Commons did accept the crown and royal dignity of King and Queen of England, France and Ireland and the dominions and territories thereunto belonging.

.   .   .   .

(III. repeals 30 Cha. II. c. 6.   IV. provides that the taking of the oaths prescribed by this Act shall be as effectual as taking the oaths prescribed by the Act repealed, and that future parliaments shall take the oaths prescribed by this Act.)

V. And it is hereby further enacted [1] . . . that the oaths above appointed by this Act to be taken in the stead and place of the oaths of allegiance and supremacy, shall be in the following words . . .

VI. "I, A. B. do sincerely promise and swear, that I will be faithful and bear true allegiance to their Majesties King William and Queen Mary, so help me God."

[1] See 1 Will. and Mar. c. 8, p. 69.

VII. "I, A. B. do swear, that I do, from my heart abhor, detest and abjure as impious and heretical, that damnable doctrine and position that princes excommunicated or deprived by the pope or any authority of the see of Rome may be deposed or murdered by their subjects or any other whatsoever ; and I do declare, that no foreign prince, person, prelate, state or potentate hath or ought to have any power, jurisdiction, superiority, pre-eminence or authority, ecclesiastical or spiritual, within this realm, so help me God."

VIII. Provided always and be it declared, that this present Parliament may be dissolved after the usual manner, as if the same had been summoned and called by writ.

(Note that 2 Will. and Mar. Cap. I. deals with the "Convention Parliament," saying, "We (the Lords Spiritual and temporal and Commons) do most humbly beseech your Majesties that . . . it be enacted . . . that all and singular the Acts made and enacted in the said (Convention) Parliament were and are laws and statutes of this kingdom, and as such ought to be reputed, taken and obeyed by all the people of this kingdom.")

(See *Ranke*, H.E. iv. 473 *et seq.* ; *Macaulay*, H.E. i. 654 *et seq.* ; *Hallam*, C.H. iii. 93 *et seq.* ; *Freeman*, Growth of the Eng. Constitution, ch. 2.)

THE LETTERS SUMMONING THE ASSEMBLY OF THE CONVENTION PARLIAMENT

I

SUMMONS TO THE ASSEMBLY, 1688

Whereas the Necessity of affairs do require speedy Advice, we do desire all such persons as have served as Knights, Citizens and Burgesses, in any of the Parliaments that were held during the reign of the late King Charles the Second, to meet us at St. James's upon Wednesday the six and twentieth of this Instant December, by Ten of the clock in the Morning, And we do likewise desire that the Lord Mayor and Court of Aldermen of the City of London would be present at the same time ; and that the Common Council would appoint Fifty of their number, to be there likewise, and hereof we desire them not to fail.

Given at St. James's, the three and twentieth day of December, 1688.

W. H. PRINCE OF ORANGE.

By his Highness' Special Command

C. HUGGENS.

(C.J. ix. 5.)

II

THE LETTERS FOR ELECTING OF MEMBERS FOR THE CONVENTION

Whereas the Lords Spiritual and Temporal, the Knights, Citizens and Burgesses, heretofore Members of the Commons House of Parliament, during the reign of Charles the Second, residing in and about the City of London, together with the Aldermen, and divers of the Common-Council of the said city, in this extraordinary conjuncture at our request, severally assembled, to advise as the best manner how to attain the Ends of our Declaration, in calling a free Parliament, for the Preservation of the Protestant Religion, and restoring the Rights and Liberties of the Kingdom, and Settling the same, that they may not be in danger of being again subverted, have advised and desired us to cause our Letters to be written and directed, for the Counties, to the Coroners of the respective Counties; and for the Universities, to the respective Vice-Chancellors; and for the Cities, Boroughs and Cinque-Ports, to the Chief Magistrate of each respective City, Borough and Cinque-Port; containing Directions for the choosing, in all such Counties, Cities, Universities, Boroughs and Cinque Ports, within Ten Days after the Receipt of the said respective Letters, such a Number of Persons to represent them, as from every such Place is or are of Right to be sent to Parliament; of which Elections, and the Times and Places thereof, the respective officers shall give Notice; the Notice for the intended Election, in the Counties, to be published in the Market-Towns within the respective Counties, by the space of Five Days, at the least, before the said Election; and for the Universities, Cities, Boroughs and Cinque-Ports, in every of them respectively, by the space of Three Days, at the least, before the said Election: The said Letters, and the Execution thereof, to be returned by such officer and officers who shall execute the same, to the Clerk of the Crown in the Court of Chancery, so as the Persons, so to be chosen, may meet and sit at Westminster the Two-and-Twentieth Day of January next.

We, heartily desiring the Performance of what we have in our Said Declaration expressed, in pursuance of the said Advice and Desire, have caused this our Letter to be written to you, to the Intent that you, truly and uprightly, without Favour or Affection to any Person, or in direct Practice or Proceeding, do and execute what of your Part ought to be done, according to the said advice, for the due execution thereof; the Elections to be made by such Persons only, as, according to the ancient Laws and Customs, of Right, ought to choose Members for Parliament; and that you cause a Return to be made, by Certificate under your Seal, of the Names of the Persons elected, annexed to this our Letter, to the said Clerk of the Crown, before the said Two-and-Twentieth Day of January.

Given at St. James's, the Nine and Twentieth Day of December, in the Year of our Lord 1688.

(C.J. ix. 7, 8.)

XIII

THE MUTINY ACT

1 Will. and Mar. Cap. 5, 1689

[The text printed below is that of the First Mutiny Act, the passages printed in brackets or appended in the notes being additions made between 1689 and 1832, to illustrate the growth of this important Statute. Only those additions which imply either a new principle or an important extension of the scope of the Act are noted. Purely administrative details, which run to great lengths in the later forms of the Statute, are passed over. See especially *Clode*, The Military Forces of the Crown, i. and appendices, and the same author's Military and Martial Law, ch. ii., and the introduction to the Manual of Military Law, ch. ii., by *Lord Thring*. Other authorities : *Ranke*, H.E. iv. 502–579 ; *Macaulay*, H.E. i. 674 *et seq.;* *Hallam*, C.H. iii. 149 ; *Dicey*, L.C. ch. ix.; *Stephen*, H.C.L. i. 204 *et seq.*]

An Act for punishing Officers and Soldiers who shall Mutiny or Desert their Majesties' Service [in England or Ireland][2] *(and for punishing false Musters)*[1] *(and for payment of (the Army and) Quarters).*[2]

Whereas, the raising or keeping a standing Army within this Kingdom in time of peace unless it be with the consent of Parliament is against law.[3] And whereas, it is judged necessary by their Majesties and this present Parliament That [during this time of danger][4] several ([5]) of the Forces which are now on foot should be continued and others raised for the safety of the Kingdom, for the Common Defence of the Protestant Religion and for (the reducing of Ireland)[6] (carrying on the War with France)[7] (the preservation of the liberties of Europe)[8] (a Guard[9] to his Majesty's Royal Person,

---

[1] Added 1 Will. and Mar. Sess. 2, c. 4. Omitted 13 and 14 Will. III. c. 2.

[2] Added 1 Anne, Stat. 2, c. 20.

[3] Bill of Rights (1 Will. and Mar. Sess. 2, c. 2).

[4] Omitted 13 and 14 Will. III. c. 2.

[5] " A number of troops, not exceeding 8,000 men " (12 Anne, c. 13), and henceforward the number is always specified.

[6] Omitted 13 and 14 Will. III. c. 2.

[7] 2 Will. and Mar. Sess. 2, c. 6.

[8] Inserted 13 and 14 Will. III. c. 2, and retained 1 Anne, Stat. 2, c. 20.

[9] Formula first adopted in 12 Anne, c. 13, the first Act passed in time of peace.

the safety of this Kingdom [and of suppressing this present Rebellion][10] and the Defence of her Majesty's Dominions beyond the seas) (the preservation of the Balance of Power in Europe).[11]

And, whereas, no man may be forejudged of Life or Limb,[12] or subjected (in time of peace)[13] to any kind of punishment (within this Realm)[14] by Martial Law, or in any other manner than by the judgment of his Peers, and according to the known and established Laws of this Realm.[15] Yet nevertheless it being requisite for retaining such forces as are or shall be raised during this exigence of Affairs in their duty an exact Discipline be observed. And that Soldiers who shall Mutiny or stir up Sedition or shall desert their Majesties' Service (within this Realm or the Kingdom of Ireland)[16] be brought to a more exemplary and speedy Punishment than the usual forms of Law will allow.

II. Be it therefore enacted by the King and Queen's most excellent Majesties by and with the Advice and Consent of the Lords Spiritual and Temporal and Commons in this present Parliament assembled, and by the authority of the same, That from and after the 12th day of April, A.D. 1689,[17] every person being in their Majesties' Service in the Army, and being mustered and in pay as Officer or Soldier, who shall at any time before the 10th day of November, A.D. 1689, excite, cause or join in any mutiny or sedition in the Army or shall desert Their Majesties' Service in the Army, shall suffer death or such other Punishment as by a Court-Martial shall be inflicted.

III. And it is hereby further enacted and declared, That Their Majesties or the General of their Army for the time being, may by virtue of this Act have full power and authority to grant Commissions to any Lieutenants General or other Officers, not under the degree of Colonels, from time to time to call and assemble Court-Martials for punishing such offences as aforesaid.

IV. And it is hereby further enacted and declared, That no Court-Martial which shall have power to inflict any punishment by

---

[10] Inserted 1 Geo. I. Stat. 2, c. 34.

[11] 13 Geo. I. c. 4.

[12] 25 Edw. III. Stat. 5, c. 1; 3 Cha. I. c. 1 (Petition of Right).

[13] 1 Will. and Mar. Sess. 2, c. 4.

[14] *Ib. st. cit.*

[15] Magna Carta, Art. 39 ; 25 Edw. III. St. 5, c. 1 ; 3 Cha. I. c. 1.

[16] 1 Anne, Stat. 2, c. 20. By 7 Anne, c. 4, "this realm" implies the extension of the Act to Scotland. See § 39 of the Act. But special provision for Scotch law is provided by 4 Geo. I. c. 4, § 19.

[17] The date is inserted annually in each Act.

virtue of this Act for the offences aforesaid shall consist of fewer than thirteen, whereof none to be under the degree of Captains.

V. Provided always, That no Field Officer be tried by other than Field Officers. And that such Court-Martial shall have power and authority to administer an oath to any witness in order to the examination or trial of the offences aforesaid.

VI. Provided always, That nothing in this Act contained shall extend or be construed to exempt any Officer or Soldier whatsoever from the ordinary process of Law.

VII. Provided always, That this Act, or anything therein contained, shall not extend or be any ways construed to extend to or concern any of the Militia Forces of this Kingdom.[18]

VIII. Provided also, That this Act shall continue and be in force until the said 10th day of November, A.D. 1689.

IX. Provided always, and be it enacted, That in all trials of offenders by Courts-Martial to be held by virtue of this Act, where the offence may be punished by Death, every officer present at such trial, before any proceeding be had thereupon, shall take an oath upon the Evangelists before the Court (and the Judge Advocate or his Deputy shall, and are hereby respectively authorized to administer the same) in these words, that is to say :—

"You shall well and truly try and determine according to your evidence now before you between Our Sovereign Lord and Lady the King and Queen's Majesties and the Prisoner to be tried,

So help you God."

X. And no sentence of Death shall be given against any offender in such case by any Court-Martial, unless nine of thirteen Officers present shall concur therein. And if there be a greater number of officers present, then the judgment shall pass by the concurrence of the greater part of them so sworn, and not otherwise ; and no Proceedings, Trial or Sentence of Death shall be had or given against any Offender, but between the hours of eight in the morning and one in the afternoon.

---

[18] The Militia were included by 47 Geo. III. c. 32, § 100, by which "all troops in Pay" under a commissioned officer in any of the Dominions of the Crown or in places " in possession of subjects of the Crown" are brought under the operation of the Act. The Volunteers and Yeomanry were organised by 44 Geo. III. c. 54 (1804). For various statutes dealing as occasion required with both and the reserve forces see *Clode, op. cit.*

(XI. [19] [20] [21] [22] [23] [24] [25] [26] [27] [28] [29] [30] [31])

[19] Clauses added here as to mustering. 1 Will. and Mar. Sess. 2, c. 4, and in subsequent Acts.

[20] 13 and 14 Will. III. c. 2, recites the Petition of Right and 31 Cha. II. c. i. § 32, and adds clauses as to power to billet soldiers.

[21] 13 and 14 Will. III. c. 2, § 24, extends the Act to Jersey and Guernsey, but as to payment and mustering only. The Channel Islands were not included till 30 Geo. II. c. 6 (1757).

[22] 13 and 14 Will. III. c. 2, § 33, extends the Act as to punishment of Mutineers and Deserters to Ireland.

[23] Correspondence with the enemy "out of England or upon the Sea" punishable as High Treason by 1 Anne, Stat. 2, c. 20, § 36.

[24] Power given to make articles of war, etc., "as might have been done by her Majesty's authority beyond the Seas in the Time of War before the making of this Act" by 1 Anne, Stat. 2, c. 20, § 39.

[25] The Marines whilst on shore to be under the Act by 1 Anne, Stat. 2, c. 20, § 46. They were furnished with a separate annual Act—the Marine Mutiny Act —28 Geo. II. c. 11.

[26] Power to plead the general issue for executing the Act by 1 Anne, Stat. 2, c. 20, § 52.

[27] No volunteer liable to Process. 1 Geo. I. Stat. 2, c. 34, Art. 47.

[28] Power to constitute Courts-Martial in any of the Crown's dominions beyond the seas or elsewhere beyond the seas by 12 Anne, c. 13.

[29] Power to make Articles of War and constitute Courts-Martial "as well *within* the Kingdoms of Great Britain and Ireland, as in any of his Majesty's dominions beyond the seas" (4 Geo. I. c. 4). [But Ireland was excluded between 1782 and 1801, a separate Mutiny Act being passed by the Irish Parliament.] This power was extended to include the army *without* the dominions, but the Articles of War for troops *without* the dominions of the Crown by 43 Geo. III. c. 20 still rested on prerogative.

[30] The British Army in India was brought under the Act by 26 and 27 Vict. c. 48 (1863).

[31] The Act and the *statutory* Articles of War were extended to troops *without* as well as *within* the dominions of the Crown by 53 Geo. III. c. 17, § 146, *i.e.* the *prerogative* Articles of War were now made *statutory*.

MODERN FORM
1 Edw. VII. Cap. 2, 1901.

An Act to provide, during Twelve Months, for the Discipline and Regulation of the Army.

Whereas . . . (as in preamble to Act of 1689 reciting clause of the Bill of Rights) a body of forces should be continued for the safety of the United Kingdom and the defence of the possessions of His Majesty's Crown . . . (number of forces specified) but *exclusive* of the numbers (in India) and whereas (Marines when not in the vessels of the Royal Navy included) and whereas no man can be forejudged (etc.) . . . and whereas the Army Act will expire (date specified) be it therefore enacted. . . . (Then follows the Army Act 44 and 45 Vict. c. 58, *i.e.* the Code of Military Law, which with any amendments required since its last enactment is then enacted for a certain period with specified dates.)

(The annual enactment of the Mutiny Bill occasioned at different times various Protests from dissentient peers. The Protest cited below has been selected because it sums up most tersely and completely the views of objectors, not merely in the Lords, but in the nation, views which have an important historical and constitutional value. See *Rogers*, P.L. i. 233, 238, 240, 241, 269, 322, 355, 356, 405, 413, 419, 431 ; ii. 19, 256.)

PROTEST

1st, Because the number of sixteen thousand three hundred and forty-seven men is declared necessary by this Bill; but it is not therein declared, nor are we able, any way, to satisfy ourselves from whence that necessity should arise, the Kingdom being now (God be praised) in full peace, without any just apprehensions, either of insurrections at home, or invasions from abroad.

2ndly, Because so numerous a force is near double to what hath ever been allowed within this Kingdom, by authority of Parliament, in times of public tranquillity ; and being, as we conceive, no ways necessary to support, may, we fear, endanger our constitution, which hath never yet been entirely subverted but by a standing army.

3rdly, Because the charge of keeping up so great a force ought not unnecessarily to be laid on the nation, already over-burthened with heavy debts; and this charge we conceive to be still more unnecessarily increased by the great number of officers now kept on the establishment in time of peace; a number far greater (in proportion to that of the soldiers commanded by them) than hath ever yet been thought requisite in times of actual war.

4thly, Because such a number of soldiers, dispersed in quarters throughout the Kingdom, may occasion great hardships, and become very grievous to the people; and thereby cause or increase their disaffection, and will, probably, ruin many of his Majesty's good subjects, on whom they shall be quartered, and who have been already by that means greatly impoverished.

5thly, Because such a standing army, dangerous in itself to a free people in time of peace, is, in our opinion, rendered yet more dangerous, by their being made subject to martial law, a law unknown to our constitution, destructive of our liberties, not endured by our ancestors, and never mentioned in any of our statutes, but in order to condemn it.

6thly, Because the officers and soldiers themselves, thus subjected to martial law, are thereby, upon their trials, divested of all those rights and privileges which render the people of this realm the envy of all other nations, and become liable to such hardships and punishments as the lenity and mercy of our known laws utterly disallow; and we cannot but think those persons best prepared, and most easily tempted to strip others of their rights, who have already lost their own.

7thly, Because a much larger jurisdiction is given to courts martial by this Bill, than, to us, seems necessary for maintaining discipline in the army, such jurisdiction extending not only to mutiny, desertion, breach of duty and disobedience to military commands, but also to all immoralities, and every instance of misbehaviour which may be committed by any officer or soldier towards any of his fellow-subjects; by which means the law of the land, in cases proper to be judged by that alone, may, by the summary method of proceedings in courts martial, be obstructed or superseded, and many grievous offences may remain unpunished.

8thly, Because the officer constituting a court martial, do at once supply the places of judges and jurymen, and ought therefore, as we conceive, to be sworn upon their trying any offence whatsoever; and yet it is provided by this Bill, that such officers shall be sworn upon their trying such offences only as are punishable by death; which provision we apprehend to be defective and unwarranted by any precedent, there being no instance within our knowledge, wherein the judges of any court, having cognisance of capital and lesser crimes, are under the obligation of an oath in respect of the one, and not of the other.

9thly, Because the Articles of War thought necessary to secure the discipline of the army, in many cases unprovided for by this Bill, ought, in our opinion, to have been inserted therein, in like manner as the Articles and Orders for regulating and governing the navy were enacted in the thirteenth year of King Charles II., to the end that due consideration might have been had by Parliament of the duty enjoined by each article to the soldiers, and of the measure of their punishment; whereas the sanction of Parliament is now given by this Bill to what they have had no opportunity to consider.

10thly, Because the clause in this Bill enabling his Majesty to establish Articles of War, and erect courts martial, with power to try and determine any offences to be specified in such Articles, and to inflict punishments for the same within this Kingdom in time of peace, doth (as we conceive) in all those instances, vest a sole legislative power in the Crown; which power, how safely soever it may be lodged with his present Majesty, and how tenderly soever it may be exercised by him, may yet prove of dangerous consequence, should it be drawn into precedent in future reigns.

.   .   .   .

(11th reason, dealing with recovery of debts and purely technical points of legal procedure, omitted.)

YORK	BOYLE	BINGLEY	WESTON
NORTHAMPTON	COMPTON	NORTH AND GREY	HEREFORD
STRAFFORD	POULETT	FOLEY	TREVOR
CHESTER	LICHFIELD	ILAY	OXFORD
SCARSDALE	BUTE	DARTMOUTH	ROCHESTER
BRISTOL	TADCASTER	MANSEL	ABINGDON.
GOWER	GUILFORD	MONTJOY	
GREENWICH	HARCOURT	BATHURST	

(L.J. February 24, 1718.   *Rogers*, P.L. i. 241 *et seq.*)

XIV

THE CORONATION OATH ACT ✓
1 Will. and Mar. Cap. 6, 1689.

An Act for establishing the coronation Oath.

I. Whereas by the law and ancient usage of this realm, the kings and queens thereof have taken a solemn oath upon the Evangelists at their respective coronations, to maintain the statutes, laws, and customs of the said realm, and all the people and inhabitants thereof, in their spiritual and civil rights and properties. But forasmuch as the oath itself on such occasion administered, hath heretofore been framed in doubtful words and expressions, with relation to ancient laws and constitutions at this time unknown : To the end thereof that one uniform oath may be in all times to come taken by the kings and queens of this realm, and to them respectively administered at the times of their and every of their coronation ; may it please your Majesties that it may be enacted ;

II. And be it enacted . . . That the oath herein mentioned, and hereafter expressed, shall and may be administered to their most excellent Majesties King William and Queen Mary, (whom God long preserve) at the time of their coronation in the presence of all persons that shall be then and there present at the solemnizing thereof, by the Archbishop of Canterbury, or the Archbishop of York, or either of them, or any other bishop of this realm, whom the King's Majesty shall thereunto appoint, and who shall be hereby thereunto respectively authorized ; which oath followeth and shall be administered in this manner, that is to say ;

(For the text of the Coronation Oath as here enacted see pp. 66–68.)

Then the king and queen shall kiss the Book.

IV. And be it further enacted, That the said oath shall be in like manner administered to every King or Queen that shall succeed to the Imperial Crown of this realm, at their respective coronations, by one of the archbishops or bishops of this realm of England, for the time being, to be thereunto appointed by such King or Queen respectively, and in the presence of all persons that shall be attending, assisting, or otherwise present at such their respective coronations ; any law, statute, or usage to the contrary notwithstanding.

(See *Wickham Legg*, Eng. Coronation Records. *Macaulay*, H.E. i. 712. For the Declaration against Transubstantiation see p. 82 and note.)

F

THE CORONATION OATH

1660.

Sir, will you grant and keep and by your oath confirm to the people of England the Laws and Customs to them granted by the Kings of England your lawful and religious predecessors: and namely the Laws, Customs and Franchises granted to the clergy by the glorious King St. Edward your predecessor, according to the laws of God, the true profession of the Gospel established in this Kingdom, and agreeing to the Prerogative of the Kings thereof, and the ancient Customs of the Realm?

King. I grant and promise to keep them.

Archbp. Sir, will you keep peace and godly agreement entirely according to your power both to God, the holy Church, the Clergy and the people?

King. I will keep it

1689.

(As prescribed by the Act 1 Will. and Mar. c. 6.)

Will you solemnly promise and swear to govern the people of this Kingdom of Great Britain and the dominions thereunto belonging according to the statutes in Parliament agreed on, and the respective laws and customs of the same?

King. I solemnly promise so to do.

1902.

Will you solemnly promise and swear to govern the People of this United Kingdom of Great Britain and Ireland, the Dominions thereto belonging, according to the Statutes in Parliament agreed on, and the respective Laws and customs of the same?

King. I solemnly promise so to do.

Archbp. Sir, will you to your power cause law justice and discretion in mercy and truth to be exercised in all your judgments?

King. I will.

Archbp. Sir, will you grant to hold and keep the Laws and rightful customs which the commonalty of this your Kingdom have: and will you defend and uphold them to the honour of God, so much as in you lieth?

King. I grant and promise so to do.

Our Lord and King, we beseech you to pardon and to grant and to preserve unto us and the churches committed to our charge all canonical privileges, and due law and justice, and to protect and defend us, as every good King in his Kingdom ought to be Protector and Defender of the Bishops and Churches under their Government.

Archbp. Will you to your power cause law and justice in mercy to be executed in all your judgments?

King. I will.

Archbp. Will you to the utmost of your power maintain the laws of God, the true profession of the Gospel, and the Protestant reformed religion established by law. And will you maintain and preserve inviolately the settlement of the Church of England and Ireland and the doctrine, worship, discipline and government thereof as by law established, within the Kingdoms of England and Ireland, the dominion of Wales, and the town of Berwick-upon-Tweed, and the territories thereto belonging. And will you preserve unto the bishops and clergy of England, and to the churches there committed to their charge, all such rights and privileges as by law do or

Will you to your power acuse Law and Justice, in Mercy, to be executed in all your Judgments?

King. I will.

Will you to the utmost of your power maintain the law of God, the true Profession of the Gospel, and the Protestant Reformed Religion established by Law? And will you maintain and preserve inviolately the settlement of the Church of England, and the Doctrine, Worship, Discipline, and Government thereof, as by Law established in England? And will you preserve unto the Bishops and Clergy of England and to the Church therein committed to their charge, all such Rights and Privileges, as by Law do or shall appertain to them, or any of them?

1660.

The King answereth. With a willing and devout heart I promise and grant you my pardon: and that I will preserve and maintain to you and the Churches committed to your charge all canonical privileges and due law and justice: and that I will be your Protector and Defender to my power by the assistance of God, as every good King in his Kingdom ought in right to protect and defend the Bishops and Churches under their Government.

The things which I have here promised I will perform and keep; so help me God, and the contents of this Book.

1689.

shall appertain unto them or any of them?

King. All this I promise to do.

The things which I have here before promised I will perform and keep, so help me God.

1902.

King. All this I promise to do.

The things which I have here before promised, I will perform and keep. So help me God.

(From the Form and Order of the Service in the Coronation of King Edward VII. and Queen Alexandra, 1902.)

XV

THE OATHS OF SUPREMACY AND ALLEGIANCE

1 Will. and Mar. Cap. 8, 1689 (1688).

An Act for the abrogating of the oaths of supremacy and allegiance, and appointing other oaths.

. . . .

(I. abrogates 1 Eliz. c. 1 ; 3 and 4 Ja. I. c. 4. II. abrogates the old oaths. III. provides how the new oaths are to be taken, and before whom. IV. and V., that all persons in office are to take the oath, on penalty, VI., of voiding the office.)

VII. And be it further enacted . . . That any archbishop, or bishop, or any other person now having any ecclesiastical dignity, benefice or promotion shall neglect or refuse to take the oaths by this act appointed . . . every such person . . . is . . . suspended from the execution of his . . . office by the space of six months . . . and if the said person . . . shall not within the said space of six months take the said oaths . . . then he . . . shall be ipso facto deprived of his . . . office, benefice, dignity and promotion ecclesiastical.

. . . .

(VIII. The same provided for "any person . . . now being master, governor, head or fellow of any college or hall, in either of the two universities, or of any other college, or master of any hospital or school, or professor of divinity, law, physic or other science in either of the said universities, or in the city of London. . . ."

IX. Penalties for refusal to take the oath on tender. A third refusal to do so shall bring the offenders under 30 Car. II. Stat. 2, c. 1, and he shall be deemed a "popish recusant convict." X. Land and sea officers to take the oath.)

XI. And be it further enacted, That the oath appointed by the statute made in the thirteenth and fourteenth year of King Charles the second,[1] . . . the form and words of which oath are in the same statute expressed; and also so much of a declaration prescribed in another act made in the same year, intituled, An act for the uniformity of public prayers,[2] . . . as is expressed in these words, (viz.)

'I A. B. declare, That it is not lawful upon any pretence whatsoever to take arms against the king ,and that I do abhor that traitorous position of taking arms by his authority against his person, or against those that are commissioners by him';

[1] 13 and 14 Cha. II. c. 3 (see p. 10).   [2] 13 and 14 Cha. II. c. 4 (see p. 12).

shall not from henceforth be required or enjoined, not any person suffer any forfeiture, penalty, or loss, by the not taking, subscribing or making the said oath, or the said recited part of the said declaration; the last fore-mentioned statutes, or any other law or statute to the contrary notwithstanding.

XII. And be it enacted, That the oaths that are intended and required to be taken by this act, are the oaths in these express words hereafter following; . . .

(For the terms of the oath see 1 Will. and Mar. c. 1, p. 55.)

XIII. And be it further enacted . . . That the names of all and singular such persons and officers aforesaid that do or shall, in the courts of Chancery and King's Bench, and the quarter sessions, take the oaths by this act required . . . shall be in the said respective courts of Chancery and King's Bench, and the quarter sessions, inrolled with the day and time of their taking the same, in rolls made and kept only for that intent and purpose, and for no other.

.   .   .   .

(XIV. and XV. Provision for members of Corporations and officers who could not take the abrogated oaths.   XVI. The King may allow to twelve of the nonjurant clergy subsistence.)

(See *Rogers*, P.L. i. 71, 72, 77; *Macaulay*, H.E. i. 704 *et seq.*, ii. 97 *et seq.*; *Lathbury*, The Non-Jurors; *Overton*, The Non-Jurors; Parlt. Hist. v.; *Perry*, H.C.E. iii. xxxv.)

XVI

THE TOLERATION ACT
1 Will. and Mar. Cap. 18, 1689.

An Act for exempting their Majesties Protestant Subjects, differing from the Church of England, from the Penalties of certain Laws.

Forasmuch as some ease to scrupulous consciences in the exercise of religion may be an effectual means to unite their Majesties' protestant subjects in interest and affection:

II. Be it enacted . . . That neither the statute made in the three and twentieth year of the reign of the late Queen Elizabeth, intituled An act to retain the Queen's Majesty's[1] subjects in their due obedience; nor the statute made in the twenty-ninth year of the

[1] 23 Eliz. c. 1 (*Prothero*, C.D. 74).

said Queen, intituled An act[2] for the more speedy and due execution
of certain branches of the statute made in the three and twentieth
year of the Queen's Majesty's reign, viz. the aforesaid act; nor that
branch or clause of a statute made in the first year of the reign of the
said Queen, intituled, An act[3] for the uniformity of common prayer
and service in the church, . . . by all persons, having no lawful or
reasonable excuse to be absent, are required to resort to their parish
church or chapel, or some usual place where the common prayer shall
be used, upon pain of punishment by the censures of the church, and
also upon pain that every person so offending shall forfeit for every
such offence twelve pence; nor the statute[4] made in the third year of
the reign of the late King James the first, intituled, An act for the
better discovering and repressing popish recusants; nor that other
statute[5] made in the same year, intituled An Act to prevent and avoid
dangers which may grow by popish recusants; nor any other law or
statute of this realm made against papists or popish recusants;
except the statute made in the five and twentieth year of King
Charles the second,[6] intituled, An act for preventing dangers which
may happen from popish recusants; and except also the statute[7]
made in the thirtieth year of the said King Charles the second,
intituled an Act for the more effectual preserving the King's person
and government, by disabling papists from sitting in either house of
parliament; shall be construed to extend to any person or persons
dissenting from the church of England, that shall take the oaths
mentioned in a statute[8] made by this present parliament, . . . and
that shall make and subscribe the declaration mentioned in a statute
made in the thirtieth year of the reign of King Charles the second,[9]
. . . which oaths and declaration the justices of peace at the general
sessions of the peace, . . . are hereby required to tender and
administer to such persons as shall offer themselves to take, make,
and subscribe the same, and thereof to keep a register : and likewise
none of the persons aforesaid shall give or pay, as any fee or reward,
to any officer or officers belonging to the court aforesaid, above the
sum of sixpence, nor that more than once, for his or their entry of
his taking the said oaths, and making and subscribing the said

2 28 and 29 Eliz. c. 6 (*Prothero*, C.D. 88).
3 1 Eliz. c. 2 (*Prothero*, p. 13).
4 3 and 4 Ja. I. c. 4 (*Prothero*, p. 256).
5 3 and 4 Ja. I. c. 5 (*Prothero*, p. 262).
6 25 Cha. II. c. 2 (see p. 39).
7 30 Cha. II. St. 2, c. i.
8 1 Will. and Mar. c. i. (see p. 55).
9 30 Cha. II. St. 2, c. i.

declaration; nor above the further sum of sixpence for any certificate of the same, to be made out and signed by the officer or officers of the said court.

III. And be it further enacted . . . That all . . . persons already convicted or prosecuted in order to conviction of recusancy, . . . grounded upon the aforesaid statutes, or any of them, that shall take the said oaths mentioned in the said statute[10] in this present parliament, and make and subscribe the declaration aforesaid, . . . and to be thence respectively certified into the Exchequer, shall be thenceforth exempted and discharged from all the penalties, seizures, forfeitures, judgements, and executions, incurred by force of any of the aforesaid statutes, without any composition, fee, or further charge whatsoever.

IV. And be it further enacted . . . That all . . . persons that shall . . . take the said Oaths, and make and subscribe the declaration aforesaid, shall not be liable to any pains, penalties, or forfeitures, mentioned in an act made in the five and thirtieth year of the reign of the late Queen Elizabeth[11] . . . nor an act[12] made in the two and twentieth year of the reign of the late King Charles the second, . . . nor shall any of the said persons be prosecuted in any ecclesiastical court, for or by reason of their nonconforming to the church of England.

V. Provided always, . . . That if any assembly of persons dissenting from the Church of England shall be had in any place for religious worship with the doors locked, barred, or bolted, during any time of such meeting together, all and every person or persons, which shall come to and be at such meeting, shall not receive any benefit from this law, but be liable to all the pain and penalties of all the aforesaid laws recited in this act, for such their meeting, notwithstanding his taking the oaths, and making and subscribing the declaration aforesaid.

VI. Provided always, That nothing herein contained shall . . . exempt any of the persons aforesaid from paying of tithes or other parochial duties, or any other duties to the church or minister, nor from any prosecution in any ecclesiastical court, or elsewhere for the same.

(Clause VII. allows officers "scrupling the oaths" to act by deputy.)

VIII. And be it further enacted, . . . That no person dissenting from the Church of England in holy orders, or pretended holy orders, or pretending to holy orders, nor any preacher or teacher of any con-

---

[10] 1 Will. and Mar. c. i.

[11] 35 Eliz. c. i.   [12] 22 Cha. II. c. 1 (see p. 35).

gregation of dissenting protestants, that shall make and subscribe the declaration aforesaid, and take the said oaths . . . and shall also declare his approbation of and subscribe the articles of religion mentioned in the statute [13] made in the thirteenth year of the reign of the late Queen Elizabeth, except the thirty-fourth, thirty-fifth, and thirty-sixth, and these words of the twentieth article, viz. [The church hath power to decree rites or ceremonies, and authority in controversies of faith, and yet] shall be liable to any of the pains or penalties mentioned in an act [14] made in the seventeenth year of the reign of King Charles the Second, . . . nor the penalties mentioned in the aforesaid act [15] made in the two and twentieth year of his said late Majesty's reign, for or by reason of such person's preaching at any meeting for the exercise of religion ; nor to the penalty of one hundred pounds mentioned in an act made in the thirteenth and fourteenth of King Charles the Second,[16] . . . for officiating in any congregation for the exercise of religion permitted and allowed by this act.

. . . .

(§ IX. The subscription to be registered.)

X. And whereas some dissenting protestants scruple the baptizing of infants ; be it enacted . . . That every person in pretended holy orders, or pretending to holy orders, or preacher, or teacher, that shall subscribe the aforesaid articles of religion, except before excepted, and also except part of the seven and twentieth article touching infant baptism and shall take the said oaths, and make and subscribe the declaration aforesaid, . . . every such person shall enjoy all the privileges, benefits, and advantages, which any other dissenting minister, as aforesaid, might have or enjoy by virtue of this act.

XI. And be it further enacted . . . That every teacher or preacher in holy orders, or pretended holy orders, that is a minister, preacher, or teacher of a congregation, that shall take the oaths herein required, and make and subscribe the declaration aforesaid, and also subscribe such of the aforesaid articles of the Church of England, as are required by this act, . . . shall be thenceforth exempted from serving upon any jury, or from being chosen or appointed to bear the office of churchwarden, overseer of the poor, or any other parochial or ward office, or other office in any hundred of any shire, city, town, parish, division, or wapentake.

. . . .

[13] 13 Eliz. c. 12, § i. (*Prothero*, p. 14).
[14] 17 Cha. II. c. 2 (see p. 33).   [15] 22 Cha. II. c. 1.
[16] 13 and 14 Cha. II. c. 4.

(§ XII. permits a justice of the peace to tender the oath and prescribes a penalty if the oath so tendered is not taken.)

XIII. [16] And whereas there are certain other persons, dissenters from the Church of England, who scruple the taking of any oath ; be it enacted by the authority aforesaid, That every such person shall make and subscribe the aforesaid declaration, and the declaration of fidelity following, viz.

'I A. B. do sincerely promise and solemnly declare before God and the world, that I will be true and faithful to King William and Queen Mary ; and I do solemnly profess and declare, That I do from my heart abhor, detest, and renounce, as impious and heretical, that damnable doctrine and position, That princes excommunicated or deprived by the Pope, or any authority of the see of Rome, may be deposed or murdered by their subjects, or any other whatsoever, and I do declare, that no foreign prince, person, prelate, state, or potentate hath, or ought to have, any power, jurisdiction, superiority, pre-eminence, or authority, ecclesiastical or spiritual, within this realm.'

And shall subscribe a profession of their christian belief in these words :

'I A. B. profess faith in God the Father, and in Jesus Christ His eternal Son, the true God, and in the Holy Spirit, one God blessed for evermore ; and do acknowledge the Holy Scriptures of the Old and New Testament to be given by divine inspiration.'

. . . .

(The remainder of the section exempts all who make the subscription from penalties prescribed by 5 Eliz. c. i.; 13 and 14 Car. II. c. 1.)

(§§ XIV. and XV. prescribe for " purging " after refusal of the oaths.)

XVI. Provided always, and it is the true intent and meaning of this act, That all the laws made and provided for the frequenting of divine service on the Lord's day, commonly called Sunday, shall be still in force, and executed against all persons that offend against the said laws, except such persons come to some congregation or assembly of religious worship, allowed or permitted by this act.

XVII. Provided always, . . . That neither this act, nor any clause, article, or thing herein contained, shall . . . extend to give any ease, benefit, or advantage to any papist or popish recusant whatsoever, or any person that shall deny in his preaching or writing the doctrine of the Blessed Trinity, as it is declared in the aforesaid articles of religion.

. . . .

[16] Altered as to Quakers by 8 Geo. I. c. 6.

(§ XVIII. prescribes penalties for disturbance of religious worship permitted by law.)

XIX. Provided always, That no congregation or assembly for religious worship shall be permitted or allowed by this act, until the place of such meeting shall be certified to the bishop of the diocese, or to the archdeacon of that archdeaconry, or to the justices of the peace at the general or quarter sessions of the peace for that county, city, or place in which such meeting shall be held and registered in the said bishop's or archdeacon's court respectively, or recorded at the said general or quarter sessions; the register or clerk of the peace whereof is hereby required to register the same, and to give certificate thereof to such person as shall demand the same, for which there shall be no greater fee nor reward taken than the sum of sixpence.

(*Macaulay*, i. 695 *et seq.*; *Hallam*, iii. 170; *Perry*, H.C.E. iii. xxxiv.)

XVII

THE BILL OF RIGHTS

1 Will. and Mar. Sess. 2, Cap. 2, 1689.

An Act declareing the Rights and Liberties of the Subject and Setleing the Succession of the Crowne.

I. Whereas the Lords Spirituall and Temporall and Commons assembled at Westminster lawfully fully and freely representing all the Estates of the People of this Realme did upon the thirteenth day of February in the year of our Lord one thousand six hundred eighty-eight present unto their Majesties then called and known by the Names and stile of William and Mary Prince and Princesse of Orange being present in their proper Persons a certain Declaration and Writeing made by the said Lords and Commons in the Words following viz.

Whereas the late King James the Second by the Assistance of diverse evill Councellors Judges and Ministers imployed by him did endeavour to subvert and extirpate the Protestant Religion and the Lawes and Liberties of this Kingdome.

By Assumeing and Excercising a Power of Dispensing with and suspending of Lawes and the Execution of Lawes without Consent of Parlyament.

By Committing and Prosecuting diverse Worthy Prelates for humbly Petitioning to bee excused from Concurring to the said Assumed Power.

By issueing and causeing to be executed a Commission under the Great Seale for Erecting a Court called the Court of Commissioners for Ecclesiasticall Causes.

By Levying Money for and to the use of the Crowne by Pretence of Prerogative for other time and in other manner then the same was granted by Parlyament.

By raising and keeping a Standing Army within this Kingdome in time of Peace without Consent of Parlyament and Quartering Soldiers contrary to Law.

By causing severall good Subjects being Protestants to be disarmed at the same time when Papists were both Armed and Imployed contrary to Law.

By Violating the Freedome of Election of Members to Serve in Parlyament.

By Prosecutions in the Court of Kings Bench for Matters and Causes cognizable onely in Parlyament and by diverse other Arbitrary and Illegal Courses.

And whereas of late yeares Partiall Corrupt and Unqualifyed Persons have been returned and served on Juryes in Tryalls and particularly diverse Jurors in Tryalls for High Treason which were not Freeholders.

And excessive Baile hath been required of Persons committed in Criminal Cases to elude the Benefitt of the Lawes made for the Liberty of the Subjects.

And excessive Fines have been imposed.

And illegall and cruell Punishments inflicted.

And severall Grants and Promises made of Fines or Forfeitures before any Conviction or Judgement against the Persons upon whome the same were to be levyed.

All which are utterly and directly contrary to the knowne Lawes and Statutes and Freedome of this Realme.

And whereas the said late King James the Second having abdicated the Government and the Throne being thereby vacant His Highnesse the Prince of Orange (whome it hath pleased Almighty God to make the glorious Instrument of Delivering this Kingdome from Popery and Arbitrary Power) did (by the advice of the Lords Spirituall and Temporall and diverse principall Persons of the Commons) cause Letters to be written to the Lords Spirituall and Temporall being Protestants and other Letters to the severall

Countyes Cityes Universities Burroughs and Cinque Ports for the choosing of such Persons to represent them as were of right to be sent to Parlyament to meete and sit at Westminster upon the two and twentyeth day of January in this yeare One thousand six hundred eighty and eight in order to such an Establishment as that their Religion Lawes and Liberties might not again be in danger of being Subverted, upon which Letters Elections haveing beene accordingly made.

And thereupon the said Lords Spirituall and Temporall and Commons pursuant to their respective Letters and Elections being now assembled in a full and free Representative of this Nation takeing into their most serious consideration the best Meanes for attaining the Ends aforesaid Doe in the first place (as their Auncestors in like case have usually done) for the Vindicating and Asserting their Auntient Rights and Liberties, Declare

That the pretended Power of Suspending of Laws or the Execution of Laws by Regall Authority without consent of Parlyament is illegall.

That the pretended Power of Dispensing with Laws or the Execution of Laws by Regall Authoritie as it hath beene assumed and excercised of late is illegall.

That the Commission for erecting the late Court of Commissioners for Ecclesiasticall Causes and all other Commissions and Courts of like Nature are Illegall and Pernicious.

That levying Money for or to the Use of the Croune by Pretence of Prerogative without Consent of Parlyament for longer time or in other Manner then the same is or shall be granted is Illegall.

That it is the Right of the Subjects to Petition the King and all Commitments and Prosecutions for such Petitioning are Illegall.

That the raising or keeping a Standing Army within the Kingdome in time of Peace unless it be with Consent of Parlyament is against Law.

That the Subjects which are Protestants may have Arms for their Defence suitable to their Conditions and as allowed by Law.

That Election of Members of Parlyament ought to be free.

That the Freedome of Speech and Debates or Proceedings in Parlyament ought not to be impeached or questioned in any Court or Place out of Parlyament.

That excessive Baile ought not to be required nor excessive Fines imposed nor cruell and unusuall Punishments inflicted.

That Jurors ought to be duely impannelled and returned and Jurors which passe upon Men in Trialls for High Treason ought to be Freeholders.

That all Grants and Promises of Fines and Forfeitures of Particular Persons before Conviction are illegall and void.

quiet
Parliaments

And that for Redresse of all Grievances and for the Amending strengthening and preserving of the Lawes Parlyaments ought to be held frequently.

And they doe Claime Demand and Insist upon all and singular the Premises as their undoubted Rights and Liberties and that noe Declarations Judgements Doeings or Proceedings to the Prejudice of the People in any of the said Premises ought in any wise to be drawne hereafter into Consequence or Example. To which Demand of their Rights they are particularly encouraged by the Declaration of his Highnesse the Prince of Orange as being the onely meanes for obtaining a full Redresse and Remedy therein. Having therefore an intire Confidence That his said Highnesse the Prince of Orange will perfect the Deliverance soe farr advanced by him and will still preserve them from the Violation of their Rights which they have here asserted and from all other Attempts upon their Religion Rights and Liberties. The said Lords Spirituall and Temporall and Commons assembled at Westminster doe Resolve That William and Mary Prince and Princesse of Orange be and be declared King and Queene of England France and Ireland and the Dominions thereunto belonging to hold the Crowne and Royall Dignity of the said Kingdomes and Dominions to them the said Prince and Princesse dureing their Lives and the Life of the Survivor of them And that the sole and full excercise of the Regall Power be onely in and executed by the said Prince of Orange in the Names of the said Prince and Princesse dureing their joynt Lives And after their Deceases the said Crowne and Royall Dignity of the said Kingdoms and Dominions to be to the Heires of the Body of the said Princesse And for Default of such Issue to the Princesse Anne of Denmark and the Heires of her Body And for Default of such Issue to the Heires of the Body of the said Prince of Orange. And the Lords Spirituall and Temporall and Commons doe pray the said Prince and Princesse to accept the same accordingly.

And that the Oaths hereafter mentioned be taken by all Persons of whome the Oaths of Allegiance and Supremacy might be required by Law instead of them And that the said Oaths of Allegiance and Supremacy be abrogated.

I A B doe sincerely promise and sweare That I will be faithfull and beare true Allegiance to their Majestyes King William and Queene Mary   Soe helpe me God.

I A B doe sweare That I doe from my Heart Abhor, Detest and Abjure as Impious and Hereticall this damnable Doctrine and Position That Princes Excommunicated or Deprived by the Pope or any

Authority of the See of Rome may be deposed or murdered by their Subjects or any other whatsoever. And I doe declare that noe Foreigne Prince Person Prelate, State or Potentate hath or ought to have any Jurisdiction Power Superiority Preeminence or Authority Ecclesiasticall or Spirituall within this Realme. So helpe me God.

Upon which their said Majestyes did accept the Crowne and Royall Dignity of the Kingdoms of England France and Ireland and the Dominions thereunto belonging according to the Resolution and Desire of the said Lords and Commons contained in the said Declaration. And thereupon their Majestyes were pleased That the said Lords Spirituall and Temporall and Commons being the two Houses of Parlyament should continue to sitt and with their Majestyes Royall Concurrence make effectual Provision for the Settlement of the Religion Lawes and Liberties of this Kingdome soe that the same for the future might not be in danger again of being subverted, To which the said Lords Spirituall and Temporall and Commons did agree and proceed to act accordingly. Now in pursuance of the Premisses the said Lords Spirituall and Temporall and Commons in Parlyament Assembled for the ratifying confirming and establishing the said Declaration and the Articles Clauses Matters and Things therein contained by the Force of a Lawe made in due Forme by Authority of Parlyament doe pray that it may be declared and enacted That all and singular the Rights and Liberties asserted and claimed in the said Declaration are the true auntient and indubitable Rights and Liberties of the People of this Kingdome and soe shall be esteemed allowed adjudged deemed and taken to be and that all and every the particulars aforesaid shall be firmly and strictly holden and observed as they are expressed in the said Declaration And all Officers and Ministers whatsoever shall serve their Majesties and their Successors according to the same in all times to come. And the said Lords Spirituall and Temporall and Commons seriously considering how it hath pleased Almighty God in his marvellous Providence and mercifull Goodness to this Nation to provide and preserve their said Majestyes Royall Persons most happily to Raigne over us upon the Throne of their Auncestors for which they render unto him from the bottome of their Hearts their humblest Thanks and Praises do truely firmly and assuredly and in the Sincerity of their Hearts thinke and doe hereby recognize acknowledge and declare That King James the Second having abdicated the Government and their Majestyes haveing accepted the Crowne and Royall Dignity as aforesaid Their said Majestyes did become were are and of right ought to be by the Lawes of this Realme our Soveraigne Liege

Lord and Lady King and Queen of England France and Ireland and
the Dominions thereunto belonging in and to whose Princely Persons
the Royall State Croune and Dignity of the said Realms with all
Honours Stiles Titles Regalities Prerogatives Powers Jurisdictions
and Authorities to the same belonging and appertaining are most
fully rightly and intirely invested incorporated united and annexed
And for preventing all Questions and Divisions in this Realme by
Reason of any pretended Titles to the Croune and for preserving
a Certainty in the Succession thereof in and upon which the Unity
Peace Tranquillity of this Nation doth under God wholly consist and
depend The said Lords Spirituall and Temporal and Commons doe
beseech there Majestyes That it may be enacted established and
declared That the Crowne and Regall Government of the said Kingdoms and Dominions with all and singular the Premisses thereunto
belonging and appertaining shall bee and continue to their said
Majestyes and the Survivor of them dureing their Lives and the
Life of the Survivor of them And that the intire perfect and full
Excercise of the Regall Power and Government be onely in and
executed by his Majestie in the Names of both their Majestyes dureing their joynt Lives and after their deceases the said Crowne and
Premisses shall be and remaine to the Heires of the Body of her
Majestie and for default of such Issue to her Royall Highnesse the
Princesse Anne of Denmarke and the Heires of her Body and for
default of such Issue to the Heires of the Body of his said Majestie
And thereunto the Lords Spirituall and Temporall and Commons doe
in the Name of all the People aforesaid most humbly and faithfully
submitt themselves their Heires and Posterities for ever and doe
faithfully promise that they will stand to maintaine and defend their
said Majestyes and also the Limitation and Succession of the Crowne
herein specified and maintained to the utmost of their Power with
their Lives and Estates against all Persons whatsoever that shall
attempt any thing to the contrary. And whereas it hath beene found
by Experience that it is inconsistent with the Safety and Welfare of
this Protestant Kingdome to be governed by a Popish Prince or by
any King or Queene marrying a Papist the said Lords Spirituall and
Temporall and Commons doe further pray that it may be enacted
That all and every person and persons that is are or shall be reconciled to or shall hold Communion with the See or Church of Rome
or shall professe the Popish Religion or shall marry a Papist shall be
excluded and be forever uncapable to inherit possesse or enjoy the
Crowne and Government of this Realme and Ireland and the
Dominions thereunto belonging or any part of the same or to have

use or excercise any Regall Power Authoritie or Jurisdiction within the same [And in all and every such Case or Cases the People of the Realmes shall be and are hereby absolved of their Allegiance] And the said Crowne and Government shall from time to time descend to and be enjoyed by such Person or Persons being Protestants as should have inherited and enjoyed the same in case the said person or persons soe reconciled holding Communion or Professing or Marrying as aforesaid were naturally dead [And that every King and Queen of this Realme who at any time hereafter shall come to and succeede in the Imperiall Crowne of this Kingdome shall on the first day of the meeting of the first Parlyament next after his or her comeing to the Crowne sitting in his or her Throne in the House of Peeres in the presence of the Lords and Commons therein assembled or at his or her Coronation before such person or persons who shall administer the Coronation Oath to him or her at the time of his or her takeing the said Oath (which shall first happen) make subscribe and audibly repeate the Declaration mentioned in the Statute[1] made in the Thirtieth yeare of the Raigne of King Charles the Second Entituled An Act for the more effectuall Preserving the Kings Person and Government by disabling Papists from sitting in either House of Parlyament But if it shall happen that such King or Queene upon his or her Succession to the Crowne shall be under the Age of twelve yeares then every such King or Queene shall make subscribe and audibly repeate the said Declaration at his or her Coronation or the first day of the meeting of the first Parlyament as aforesaid which shall first happen after such King or Queene shall have attained the said Age of twelve yeares.] All which their Majestyes are contented and pleased shall be declared enacted and established by authority of this present Parlyament and shall stand remaine and be the Law of this Realme for ever And the same are by their said Majestyes by and with the advice and Consent of the Lords Spirituall and Temporall and Commons in Parlyament assembled and by the Authority of the same declared enacted and established accordingly.

II. And be it further declared and enacted by the authority aforesaid That from and after this present Session of Parlyament noe Dispensation by Non obstante of or to any Statute or any part thereof shall be allowed but the same shall be held void and of noe Effect except a Dispensation be allowed of in such Statute and except in such Cases as shall be specially provided for by one or more Bill or Bills to be passed dureing this present Session of Parlyament.

[1] 30 Cha. II. Stat. 2, c. i. See the Declaration annexed, p. 32.

G

III. Provided that noe Charter or Grant or Pardon granted before the three and twentieth day of October in the yeare of our Lord one thousand six hundred eighty nine shall be anyways impeached or invalidated by this Act but that the same shall be and remaine of the same force and effect in Law and noe other then as if this Act had never been made.

(See *Macaulay*, H.E. i. 625 *et seq.*; *Hallam*, iii. 83 *et seq.*; *Anson*, L.C. ii. 32 and 63; *Gneist*, E.C. 611; *Rogers*, P.L. i. 90; and for the Military Clauses especially *Clode*, Military Forces, ch. v.)

THE
DECLARATION AGAINST TRANSUBSTANTIATION

I A. B. do solemnly and sincerely in the presence of God profess testify and declare that I do believe that in the sacrament of the Lord's Supper there is not any transubstantiation of the elements of bread and wine into the body and blood of Christ at or after the consecration thereof by any person whatsoever; and that the invocation or adoration of the Virgin Mary or any other saint, and the sacrifice of the mass as they are now used in the Church of Rome are superstitious and idolatrous, and I do solemnly in the presence of God profess testify and declare that I do make this declaration and every part thereof in the plain and ordinary sense of the words read unto me as they are commonly understood by English protestants without any evasion, equivocation or mental reservation whatsoever and without any dispensation already granted me for this purpose by the Pope or any other authority or person whatsoever, or without any hope of any such dispensation from any person or authority whatsoever or without thinking that I am or can be acquitted before God or man or absolved of this declaration or any part thereof although the Pope or any other person or persons or power whatsoever should dispense with or annul the same, or declare that it was null and void from the beginning.

(At the Coronation of Queen Anne the Declaration was inserted before the Coronation oath, and this was also done at the Coronations of George I and George II. From the Coronation of George III. till to-day the custom has been for the Sovereign to read the Declaration in the House of Lords. Strictly speaking, it is not part of the Coronation oath. A Bill to modify the Declaration was introduced into Parliament in 1901, but was not proceeded with. See Hansard, Fourth Series, vol. 100, and ref. under *Royal Declaration Bill.*)

XVIII

THE TRIENNIAL ACT
6 and 7 Will. and Mar. Cap. 2, 1695.

An Act for the frequent Meeting and Calling of Parliaments.[1]

I. Whereas by the ancient Laws and Statutes of this Kingdom frequent Parliaments ought to be held And whereas frequent and new Parliaments tend very much to the happy Union and good Agreement of King and People We Your Majesties' most loyal and obedient Subjects the Lords Spiritual and Temporal and Commons in this present Parliament assembled do most humbly beseech Your most excellent Majesties that it may be declared and enacted in this present Parliament and it is hereby declared and enacted by the King and Queens most excellent Majesties by and with the Advice and Consent of the Lords Spiritual and Temporal and Commons in this present Parliament assembled and by the authority of the same That from henceforth a Parliament shall be holden once in Three years at the least.

II. And be it further enacted by the authority aforesaid That within Three at the farthest from and after the Dissolution of this present Parliament and so from time to time for ever hereafter within Three years at the farthest from and after the determination of every other Parliament Legal Writs under the Great Seal shall be issued by directions of Your Majesties your Heirs and Successors for assembling and holding another new Parliament.

III. And be it further enacted by the authority aforesaid That from henceforth no Parliament whatsoever that shall at any time hereafter be called assembled or held shall have any continuance longer than for Three years only at the farthest to be accounted from the day on which by the Writs of Summons the said Parliament shall be appointed to meet.

IV. And be it further enacted by the authority aforesaid That this present Parliament shall cease and determine on the First day of November which shall be in the year of our Lord one thousand six hundred ninety six unless their Majesties shall think fit to dissolve it sooner.

(*Rogers*, P.L. i. 115 ; *Macaulay*, H.E. ii. 407 *et seq.; Hallam*, C.H. iii. 48.)

---

[1] Repealed by 1 Geo. I. Stat., 2 c. 38 (see p. 117).

XIX

THE TRIAL OF TREASONS ACT
7 and 8 Will. III., Cap. 3,[1] 1696.

An Act for regulating of Trials in Cases of Treason and Misprision of Treason.

I. Whereas nothing is more just and reasonable than that Persons prosecuted for High Treason and Misprision of Treason, whereby the Liberties, Lives, Honour, Estates, Blood and Posterity of the Subject may be lost and destroyed, should be justly and equally tried and that Persons accused as offenders therein should not be debarred of all just and equal Means for Defence of their Innocencies in such cases ; In order thereunto and for the better Regulation of Trials of Persons prosecuted for High Treason and Misprision of such Treason Be it enacted . . . That from and after the Five and twentieth Day of March in the Year of our Lord One thousand six hundred ninety six all and every Person and Persons whatsoever that shall be accused and indicted for High Treason whereby any Corruption of Blood may or shall be made . . . or for Misprision of such Treason, shall have a true Copy of the whole Indictment but not the Names of the Witnesses delivered unto them or any of them Five Days at the least before he or they shall be tried for the same, whereby to enable them and any of them respectively to advise with Counsel thereupon to plead and make their Defence his or their Attorney or Attorneys' Agent or Agents or any of them requiring the same and paying the Officer his reasonable Fees for writing thereof not exceeding Five Shillings for the Copy of such Indictment, And that every Person so accused and indicted arraigned or tried for any such Treason as aforesaid or for Misprision of such Treason from and after the said time shall be received and admitted to make his and their full Defence by Counsel learned in the Law and to make any Proof that he or they can produce by lawful Witness or Witnesses who shall then be upon Oath for his and their just Defence in that behalf, And in case any Persons or Persons so accused or indicted shall desire Counsel the Court before whom such Person or Persons shall be tried or some Judge of that Court shall and is hereby authorized and required

---

[1] See also 7 Anne, c. 21. Repealed in part 30 and 31 Vict. c. 59, and 51 and 52 Vict. c. 3.

immediately upon his or their request to assign to such Person or Persons such and so many Counsel, not exceeding Two, . . . to whom such Counsel shall have free access at all seasonable Hours Any Law or Usage to the Contrary notwithstanding.

II. And be it further enacted, That from and after the said [date] . . . no Person or Persons whatsoever shall be indicted, tried or attainted of High Treason whereby any Corruption of Blood may or shall be made . . . or of Misprision of such Treason but by and upon the Oaths and Testimony of Two lawful Witnesses either both of them to the same overt act or one of them to one and another of them to another overt act of the same Treason, unless the Party indicted and arraigned or tried shall willingly without Violence and in open Court confess the same or shall stand mute or refuse to plead, or in cases of High Treason shall peremptorily challenge above the Number of Thirty-five of the Jury, Any Law Statute or Usage to the contrary notwithstanding.

III. Provided always that any Person or Persons being indicted as aforesaid for any the Treasons or Misprisions of the Treasons aforesaid may be outlawed and thereby attainted of or for any of the said Offences of Treason or Misprision of Treason, And in cases of the High Treasons aforesaid whereby the Law after such Outlawry the Party outlawed may come in and be tried he shall upon such Trial have the Benefit of this Act.

IV. And be it further enacted . . . That if Two or more distinct Treasons of diverse Heads or Kinds shall be alleged in one Bill of Indictment, one Witness produced to prove one of the said Treasons and another Witness produced to prove another of the said Treasons shall not be deemed or taken to be Two Witnesses to the same Treason within the Meaning of this Act.

V. And to the intent that the Terror and Dread of such Criminal Accusations may in some reasonable time be removed, Be it further enacted . . . That from and after the said [date] . . . no Person or Persons whatsoever shall be indicted tried or prosecuted for any such Treason as aforesaid or for Misprision of such Treason that shall be committed or done within the Kingdom of England Dominion of Wales or Town of Berwick upon Tweed after the said [date] . . . unless the same Indictment be found by a Grand Jury within Three Years next after the Treason or Offence done and committed. And that no Person or Persons shall be prosecuted for any such Treason or Misprision of such Treason ocmmitted or done or to be committed or done within the Kingdom of England Dominion of Wales or Town of Berwick upon Tweed before the said [date] . . . unless he or they shall be indicted thereof within Three Years after the said Five and twentieth Day of March.

VI. Always provided and excepted that if any Person or Persons whatsoever shall be guilty of designing endeavouring or attempting any Assassination on the Body of the King by Poison or otherwise such Person or Persons may be prosecuted at any time notwithstanding the aforesaid Limitation ;

VII. And that all and every Person or Persons who shall be accused, indicted such or tried for Treason as aforesaid or for Misprision of such Treason after the said [date] shall have Copies of the Panel of the Jurors who are to try them, duly returned by the Sheriff and delivered unto them and every of them so accused and indicted respectively, Two Days at the least before he or they shall be tried for the same, And that all Persons so accused and indicted for any such Treason as aforesaid shall have the like Process of the Court where they shall be tried to compel their Witnesses to appear for them at any such Trial or Trials as is usually granted to compel Witnesses against them.

VIII. And be it further enacted, That no Evidence shall be admitted or given of any overt Act that is not expressly laid in the Indictment against any Person or Persons whatsoever.

IX. Provided also, . . . That no Indictment for any of the Offences aforesaid nor any Process or Return thereupon shall be quashed on the Motion of the Prisoner or his Counsel for miswriting misspelling false or improper Latin, unless Exception concerning the same be taken and made in the respective Court where such Trial shall be by the Prisoner or his Council assigned before any Evidence given in open Court upon such Indictment ; Nor shall any such miswriting, misspelling, false or improper Latin after the Conviction on such Indictment be any Cause to stay or arrest Judgement thereupon ; But nevertheless any Judgement given upon such Indictment shall and may be liable to be reversed upon a Writ of Error in the same manner and no other than as if this Act had not been made.

X. And whereas by the good Laws of this Kingdom in Cases of Trials of Commoners for their Lives a Jury of Twelve Freeholders must all agree in one Opinion before they can bring a Verdict either for Acquittal or Condemnation of the Prisoner. And whereas upon the Trials of Peers or Peeresses a Major Vote is sufficient either to acquit or condemn, Be it further enacted . . . That upon the Trial of any Peer or Peeress either for Treason or Misprision all the Peers who have a right to sit and vote in Parliament shall be duly summoned Twenty Days at least before every such Trial, And that every Peer

so summoned and appearing at such Trial shall vote in the Trial of
such Peer or Peeress so to be tried, every such Peer first taking the
Oaths mentioned in an Act of Parliament made in the First Year of
the Reign of King William and Queen Mary [1] . . . And also every
such Peer subscribing and audibly repeating the Declaration mentioned
in an Act[2] for the more effectual preserving the Kings Person and
Government by disabling Papists from sitting in either House of
Parliament and made in the Thirtieth Year of the Reign of the late
King Charles the Second.

XI. Provided always That neither this Act nor any thing therein
contained shall any ways extend or be construed to extend to any Impeachment or other Proceedings in Parliament in any Kind whatever.[3]

XII. Provided also That neither this Act nor any thing therein
contained shall any ways extend to any Indictment of High Treason
nor to any Proceedings thereupon for counterfeiting His Majesty's
Coin, His Great Seal or Privy Seal, His Sign Manual or Privy
Signet.[4]

(*Hallam*, C.H. iii. 150 *et seq.*; *Macaulay*, H.E. ii. 312 ; *Stephen*, H.C.L.
i. xi.)

XX

THE ACT OF SETTLEMENT
12 and 13 Will. III. Cap. 2,[5] 1701.

*An Act for the further Limitation of the Crown and better securing
the Rights and Liberties of the Subject.*

I. Whereas in the First Year of the Reign of Your Majesty and of
our late most gracious Sovereign Lady Queen Mary (of blessed
Memory) An Act of Parliament was made intituled An Act[6] for
declaring the Rights and Liberties of the Subject and for settling
the Succession of the Crown wherein it was (amongst other things)
enacted established and declared That the Crown and Regal Government of the Kingdoms of England France and Ireland and the
Dominions thereunto belonging should be and continue to Your

---

[1] Will. and Mar. c. 8 (see p. 69).
[2] 30 Cha. II. Stat. 2, c. i.   Repealed 34 and 35 Vict. c. 48.
[3] See 20 Geo. II. c. 30.
[4] See 2 and 3 Anne, c. 20, § 43.   Repealed 30 and 31 Vict. c. 59.
[5] Repealed in part 44 and 45 Vict. c. 59.
[6] 1 W. and M. Sess. 2, c. 2.

Majesty and the said late Queen during the joint Lives of Your
Majesty and the said Queen and to the Survivor And that after the
Decease of Your Majesty and of the said Queen the said Crown and
Regal Government should be and remain to the Heirs of the Body
of the said late Queen And for Default of such Issue to her Royal
Highness the Princess Ann of Denmark and the Heirs of her Body
And for Default of such Issue to the Heirs of the Body of Your
Majesty And it was thereby further enacted That all and every
Person and Persons that then were or afterwards should be reconciled
to or shall hold Communion with the See or Church of Rome or
should profess the Popish Religion or marry a Papist should be excluded and are by that Act made forever incapable to inherit possess
or enjoy the Crown and Government of this Realm and Ireland and
the Dominions thereunto belonging or any part of the same or to
have use or exercise any regal Power Authority or Jurisdiction within
the same And in all and every such Case or Cases the People of these
Realms shall be and are thereby absolved of their Allegiance And
that the said Crown and Government shall from time to time descend
to and be enjoyed by such Person or Persons being Protestants as
should have inherited and enjoyed the same in case the said Person or
Persons so reconciled holding Communion professing or marrying as
aforesaid were naturally dead; After the making of which Statute and
the Settlement therein contained Your Majesty's good Subjects who
were restored to the full and free Possession and Enjoyment of their
Religion Rights and Liberties by the Providence of God giving
Success to Your Majesty's just Undertakings and unwearied Endeavours for that Purpose had no greater temporal Felicity to hope
or wish for than to see a Royal Progeny descending from Your
Majesty to whom (under God) they owe their Tranquillity and whose
Ancestors have for many Years been principally Assertors of the
reformed Religion and the Liberties of Europe and from our said
most gracious Sovereign Lady whose Memory will always be precious
to the Subjects of these Realms; And it having since pleased Almighty
God to take away our said Sovereign Lady and also the most hopeful
Prince William Duke of Gloucester (the only Surviving Issue of Her
Royal Highness the Princess Ann of Denmark) to the unspeakable
Grief and Sorrow of Your Majesty and Your said good Subjects who
under such Losses being sensibly put in mind that it standeth wholly
in the Pleasure of Almighty God to prolong the Lives of Your Majesty
and of Her Royal Highness and to grant to Your Majesty or to Her
Royal Highness such Issue as may be inheritable to the Crown and
Regal Government aforesaid by the respective Limitations in the said

recited Act contained do constantly implore the Divine Mercy for
those Blessings; And Your Majesty's said Subjects having Daily Experience of Your Royal Care and Concern for the present and future
Welfare of these Kingdoms and particularly recommending from
Your Throne a further Provision to be made for the Succession of the
Crown in the Protestant Line for the Happiness of the Nation and
the Security of our Religion; And it being absolutely necessary for the
Safety Peace and Quiet of this Realm to obviate all Doubts and Con-
tentions in the same by reason of any pretended Titles to the Crown
and to maintain a Certainty in the succession thereof to which Your
Subjects may safely have Recourse for their Protection in case the
Limitations in the said recited Act should determine Therefore for a
further Provision of the Succession of the Crown in the Protestant
Line We Your Majesty's most dutiful and Loyal Subjects the Lords
Spiritual and Temporal and Commons in this present Parliament
assembled do beseech Your Majesty that it may be enacted and
declared and be it enacted and declared by the King's most Excellent
Majesty by and with the Advice and Consent of the Lords Spiritual
and Temporal and Commons in this present Parliament assembled and
by the Authority of the same That the most excellent Princess Sophia
Electress and Duchess Dowager of Hanover Daughter of the most
Excellent Princess Elizabeth late Queen of Bohemia Daughter of our
late Sovereign Lord King James the First of happy Memory be and is
hereby declared to be the next in Succession in the Protestant Line
to the Imperial Crown and Dignity to the said Realms of England
France and Ireland and of the Dominions thereunto belonging after
His Majesty and the Princess Ann of Denmark and in Default of
Issue of the said Princess Ann and of His Majesty respectively
and that from and after the Deceases of His said Majesty our now
Sovereign Lord and of Her Royal Highness the Princess Ann of
Denmark and for Default of Issue of the said Princess Ann and of
His Majesty respectively the Crown and Regal Government of the
said Kingdoms of England France and Ireland and of the Dominions
thereunto belonging with the Royal State and Dignity of the said
Realms and all the Honours Styles Titles Regalities Prerogatives Powers
Jurisdictions and Authorities to the same belonging and appertaining
shall be remain and continue to the said most Excellent Princess
Sophia and the Heirs of her Body being Protestants; And thereunto
the said Lords Spiritual and Temporal and Commons shall and will
in the Name of all the People of this Realm most humbly and faithfully submit themselves their Heirs and Posterities and do faithfully
promise That after the Deceases of His Majesty and Her Royal High-

ness and the failure of the Heirs of their respective Bodies to stand to maintain and defend the said Princess Sophia and the Heirs of her Body being Protestants according to the Limitation and Succession of the Crown in this Act specified and contained to the utmost of their Powers with their Lives and Estates against all Persons whatsoever that shall attempt anything to the contrary.

II. Provided always and it is hereby enacted That all and every Person and Persons who shall or may take or inherit the said Crown by virtue of the Limitation of this present Act and is are or shall be reconciled to or shall hold Communion with the See or Church of Rome or shall profess the Popish Religion or shall marry a Papist shall be subject to such Incapacities as in such Case or Cases are by the said recited Act provided enacted and established and that every King and Queen of this Realm who shall come to and succeed in the Imperial Crown by virtue of this Act shall have the Coronation Oath administered to him her or them at their respective Coronations according to the Act of Parliament[1] made in the First Year of the Reign of His Majesty and the said late Queen Mary intituled An Act for establishing the Coronation Oath and shall make subscribe and repeat the Declaration in the Act first above recited mentioned or referred to in the Manner and Form thereby prescribed.

III. And whereas it is requisite and necessary that some further Provision be made for securing our Religion Laws and Liberties from and after the Death of His Majesty and the Princess Ann of Denmark and in Default of Issue of the Body of the said Princess and of his Majesty respectively Be it enacted by the King's most excellent Majesty by and with the Advice and Consent of the Lords Spiritual and Temporal and Commons in Parliament assembled and by the Authority of the same

That whosoever shall hereafter come to the Possession of this Crown shall join in Communion with the Church of England as by Law established.

That in case the Crown and Imperial Dignity of this Realm shall hereafter come to any Person not being a Native of this Kingdom of England this Nation be not obliged to engage in any War for the Defence of any Dominions or Territories which do not belong to the Crown of England without the consent of Parliament.

That no Person who shall hereafter come to the possession of the Crown shall go out of the Dominions of England Scotland and Ireland without the consent of Parliament.[2]

---

[1] W. and M. Sess. 1 c. 6, (see p. 65).
[2] Repealed by 1 Geo. I. Stat. 2, c. 51.

That from and after the Time that the further Limitation by this Act all Matters [1] and Things relating to the well governing of this Kingdom which are properly cognizable in the Privy Council by the Laws and Customs of this Realm shall be transacted there and all Resolutions taken thereupon shall be signed by such of the Privy Council as shall advise and consent to the same.

That [2] after the said Limitation shall take Effect as aforesaid no Person born out of the Kingdoms of England Scotland or Ireland or the Dominions thereunto belonging (although he be naturalized and made a Denizen) (except such as are born of English parents) shall be capable to be of the Privy Council or a Member of either House of Parliament or to enjoy any Office or Place of Trust either Civil or Military or to have any Grant of Lands Tenements or Hereditaments from the Crown to himself or to any other or others in trust for him.

That no Person who has an Office or Place of Profit under the King or receives a Pension from the Crown shall be capable of serving as a Member of the House of Commons. [3]

That after the said Limitation shall take Effect as aforesaid Judges Commissions be made *Quam diu se bene Gesserint* and their Salaries ascertained and established but upon the Address of both Houses of Parliament it may be lawful to remove them.

That no Pardon under the Great Seal of England be pleadable to an Impeachment by the Commons in Parliament.

IV. And whereas the Laws of England are the Birthright of the People thereof and all the Kings and Queens who shall ascend the Throne of this Realm ought to administer the Goverment of the same according to the said Laws and all their Officers and Ministers ought to serve them respectively according to the same The said Lords Spiritual and Temporal and Commons do therefore further humbly pray That all the Laws and Statutes of this Realm for securing the established Religion and Rights and Liberties of the People thereof and all other Laws and Statutes of the same now in Force may be ratified and confirmed And the same are by His Majesty by and with the Advice and Consent of the said Lords Spiritual and Temporal and Commons and by Authority of the same ratified and confirmed accordingly.

(*Hallam*, C.H. iii. 179 ; *Rogers*, P.L. i. 161 ; *Ranke*, H.E. v. 226 *et seq.* ; and authorities for Bill of Rights.)

[1] Repealed by 4 and 5 Anne, c. 20, § 27.
[2] Repealed by 7 and 8 Vict. c. 66, and 33 Vict. c. 14, § 7.
Modified by 4 and 5 Anne, c. 20 ; 6 Anne, c. 7 ; 1 Geo. I. Stat. 2, c. 56.

XXI

THE ACT FOR THE UNION WITH SCOTLAND

5 Anne, Cap. 11,[1] 1706.

An Act for the Union of the Two Kingdoms of England and Scotland.

Most gracious Sovereign

Whereas Articles of Union were agreed on the Twenty-second Day of July in the Fifth Year of Your Majesty's Reign by the Commissioners nominated on Behalf of the Kingdom of England under Your Majesty's Great Seal of England bearing Date at Westminster the Tenth Day of April then last past in pursuance of an Act of Parliament made in England in the Third Year of Your Majesty's Reign and the Commissioners nominated on Behalf of the Kingdom of Scotland under Your Majesty's Great Seal of Scotland bearing Date the Twenty-second Day of February in the Fourth Year of Your Majesty's Reign in pursuance of the Fourth Act of the Third Session of the Present Parliament of Scotland to treat of and concerning an Union of the said Kingdoms; And whereas an Act hath passed in the Parliament of Scotland at Edinburgh the Sixteenth Day of January in the Fifth Year of Your Majesty's Reign wherein 'tis mentioned that the Estates of Parliament considering the said Articles of Union of the Two Kingdoms had agreed to and approved of the said Articles of Union with some Additions and Explanations and that Your Majesty with Advice and Consent of the Estates of Parliament for establishing the Protestant Religion and Presbyterian Church Government within the Kingdom of Scotland had passed in the same Session of Parliament an Act intituled Act for securing of the Protestant Religion and Presbyterian Church Government which by the Tenor thereof was appointed to be inserted in any Act ratifying the Treaty and expressly declared to be a fundamental and essential Condition of the said Treaty or Union in all Times coming, the Tenor of which Articles as ratified and approved of with Additions and Explanations by the said Act of Parliament of Scotland follows.

ARTICLE I. That the Two Kingdoms of England and Scotland shall upon the First Day of May which shall be in the Year one thousand seven hundred and seven and for ever after be united into

---

[1] Cited as 5 and 6 Anne, c. 8, in common printed editions. Repealed in part Stat. Law Rev. Act, 1867.

one Kingdom by the Name of Great Britain and that the Ensigns Armorial of the said United Kingdom be such as Her Majesty shall appoint and the Crosses of St. George and St. Andrew be conjoined in such Manner as Her Majesty shall think fit and used in all Flags Banners Standards and Ensigns both at Sea and Land.

ARTICLE II. That the Succession to the Monarchy of the United Kingdom of Great Britain and of the Dominions thereunto belonging after Her most Sacred Majesty and in Default of Issue of Her Majesty be remain and continue to the most Excellent Princess Sophia Electoress and Duchess Dowager of Hanover and the Heirs of Her Body being Protestants upon whom the Crown of England is settled by an Act of Parliament made in England in the Twelfth Year of the Reign of His late Majesty King William the Third intituled An Act for the further Limitation of the Crown and better securing the Rights and Liberties of the Subject; And that all Papists and Persons marrying Papists shall be excluded from and forever incapable to inherit possess or enjoy the Imperial Crown of Great Britain and the Dominions thereunto belonging or any part thereof and in every such case the Crown and Government shall from time to time descend to and be enjoyed by such Person being a Protestant as should have inherited and enjoyed the same in case such Papist or Person marrying a Papist was naturally dead according to the Provision for the Descent of the Crown of England made by another Act of Parliament in England in the First Year of the Reign of Their late Majesties King William and Queen Mary intituled An Act declaring the Rights and Liberties of the Subject and settling the Succession to the Crown.

ARTICLE III. That the United Kingdom of Great Britain be represented by One and the same Parliament to be styled the Parliament of Great Britain.

ARTICLE IV. That all the Subjects of the United Kingdom of Great Britain shall from and after the Union have full Freedom and Intercourse of Trade and Navigation to and from any Port or Place within the said United Kingdom and the Dominions and Plantations thereunto belonging and that there be a Communication of all other Rights Privileges and Advantages which do or may belong to the Subjects of either Kingdom except where it is otherwise expressly agreed in these Articles.

. . . .

(Article V. declares all Scotch ships to be British.)

ARTICLE VI. That all parts of the United Kingdom for ever from and after the Union shall have the same Allowances Encouragements and Drawbacks and be under the same Prohibitions Restrictions and Regulations of Trade and liable to the Same Customs and Duties on Import and Export, And that the Allowances Encouragements and Drawbacks Prohibitions Restrictions and Regulations of Trade and the Customs and Duties on Import and Export settled in England when the Union commences shall from and after the Union take place throughout the whole United Kingdom, excepting and reserving the Duties upon Export and Import of such particular Commodities from which any Persons the Subjects of either Kingdom are specially liberated and exempted by their Private Rights which after the Union are to remain safe and entire to them in all Respects as before the same. . . . [Scotch Cattle imported into England to be subject only to the same duties as English Cattle].

.   .   .   .

(Article VII. Scotland to be liable to the English Excise.
Article VIII. The Salt Duties.
Article IX. The Land Tax.
Articles X., XI., XII., XIII. "Stampt Vellum, Window Tax, Coals, Culm and Cynders and Malt.")

ARTICLE XIV. That the Kingdom of Scotland be not charged with any other Duties laid on by the Parliament of England before the Union except these consented to in this Treaty in regard it is agreed that all necessary Provision shall be made by the Parliament of Scotland for the Public Charge and Service of that Kingdom for the Year one thousand seven hundred and seven, Provided nevertheless that if the Parliament of England shall think fit to lay any further Impositions by way of Customs or such Excises with which by virtue of this Treaty Scotland is to be charged equally with England in such case Scotland shall be liable to the same Customs and Excises and have an Equivalent to be settled by the Parliament of Great Britain with this further Provision That any Malt to be made and consumed in that part of the United Kingdom now called Scotland shall not be charged with any Imposition on Malt during this present War. And seeing it cannot be supposed that the Parliament of Great Britain will ever lay any sort of Burthens upon the United Kingdom but what they shall find of Necessity at Time for the Preservation and Good of the Whole and with due regard to the Circumstances and Abilities of every part of the United Kingdom, therefore it is agreed that there be no further Exemption insisted upon for any part of the United Kingdom but that the Consideration of any Exemptions beyond what are already agreed on in this Treaty shall be left to the Determination of the Parliament of Great Britain.

.   .   .   .

(Article XV. deals with equivalents in duties as between the two kingdoms, and provides "That all the public debts of the Kingdom of Scotland, as shall be adjusted by this present parliament shall be paid, and that two thousand pounds per annum for the space of seven years shall be applied towards encouraging and promoting the manufacture of coarse wool.")

ARTICLE XVI. That from and after the Union the Coin shall be of the same Standard and Value throughout the United Kingdom as now in England and a Mint shall be continued in Scotland under the same Rules as the Mint in England and the present Officers of the Mint continued subject to such Regulations and Alterations as Her Majesty Her Heirs or Successors or the Parliament of Great Britain shall think fit.

ARTICLE XVII. That from and after the Union the same Weights and Measures shall be used throughout the United Kingdom, as are now established in England and Standards of Weights and Measures shall be kept by those Burghs in Scotland to whom the keeping the Standards of Weights and Measures now in use there does of Special Right belong. All which Standards shall be sent down to such respective Burghs from the Standards kept in the Exchequer at Westminster subject nevertheless to such Regulations as the Parliament of Great Britain shall think fit.

ARTICLE XVIII. That the Laws concerning Regulation of Trade Customs and such Excises to which Scotland is by Virtue of this Treaty to be liable be the same in Scotland from and after the Union as in England and that all other Laws in use within the Kingdom of Scotland do after the Union and notwithstanding thereof remain in the same Force as before (except such as are contrary to or inconsistent with this Treaty) but alterable by the Parliament of Great Britain with this Difference betwixt the Laws concerning public Right Policy and Civil Government and those which concern private Right that the Laws which concern public Right Policy and Civil Government may be made the same throughout the whole United Kingdom, But that no alteration be made in Laws which concern private Right except for evident Utility of the Subjects within Scotland.

ARTICLE XIX. That the Court of Session or College of Justice do after the Union and notwithstanding thereof remain in all Time coming within Scotland as it is now constituted by the Laws of that Kingdom and with the same Authority and Privileges as before the Union subject nevertheless to such Regulations for the better Administration of Justice as shall be made by the Parliament of Great

Britain and that hereafter none shall be named by Her Majesty or Her Royal Successors to be Ordinary Lords of Session but such who have served in the College of Justice as Advocates or Principal Clerks of Session for the Space of Five Years or as Writers to the Signet for the Space of Ten Years with this Provision that no Writer to the Signet be capable to be admitted a Lord of the Session unless he undergo a private and public Trial on the Civil Law before the Faculty of Advocates and be found by them qualified for the said Office Two years before he be named to be a Lord of the Session, yet so as the Qualifications made or to be made for capacitating Persons to be named Ordinary Lords of Session may be altered by the Parliament of Great Britain And that the Court of Justiciary do also after the Union and notwithstanding thereof remain in all Time coming within Scotland as it is now constituted by the Laws of that Kingdom and with the same Authority and Privileges as before the Union, subject nevertheless to such Regulations as shall be made by the Parliament of Great Britain and without Prejudice of other Rights of Justiciary; And that all Admiralty Jurisdictions be under the Lord High Admiral or Commissioners for the Admiralty of Great Britain for the Time being and that the Court of Admiralty now established in Scotland be continued and all Reviews Reductions or Suspensions of the Sentences in maritime Cases competent to the Jurisdiction of that Court remain in the same manner after the Union as now in Scotland until the Parliament of Great Britain shall make such Regulations and Alterations as shall be judged expedient for the whole United Kingdom, so as there be always continued in Scotland a Court of Admiralty such as in England for the Determination of all Maritime Cases relating to private Rights in Scotland competent to the Jurisdiction of the Admiralty Court subject nevertheless to such Regulations and Alterations as shall be thought proper to be made by the Parliament of Great Britain; And that the Heritable Rights of Admiralty and Vice Admiralties in Scotland be reserved to the respective Proprietors as Rights of Property subject nevertheless as to the manner of exercising such Heritable Rights to such Regulations and Alterations as shall be thought proper to be made by the Parliament of Great Britain And that all other Courts now being within the Kingdom of Scotland do remain but subject to Alterations by the Parliament of Great Britain and that all inferior Courts within the said Limits do remain subordinate as they are now to the Supreme Courts of Justice within the same in all Time coming, And that no Causes in Scotland be cognoscible by the Courts of Chancery Queen's Bench Common Pleas or in any other Court in Westminster

Hall and that the said Courts or any other of the like nature after the Union shall have no Power to cognosce, review or alter the Acts or Sentences of the Judicatures within Scotland or stop the Execution of the same; And that there be a Court of Exchequer in Scotland after the Union for deciding Questions concerning the Revenues of Customs and Excises there having the same Power and Authority in such Cases as the Court of Exchequer has in England and that the said Court of Exchequer in Scotland have Power of passing Signatures, Gifts, Tutories and in other Things as the Court of Exchequer at present in Scotland hath and that the Court of Exchequer that now is in Scotland do remain until a new Court of Exchequer be settled by the Parliament of Great Britain in Scotland after the Union ; And that after the Union the Queen's Majesty and Her Royal Successors may continue a Privy Council in Scotland for preserving of public Peace and Order until the Parliament of Great Britain shall think fit to alter it or establish any other effectual method for that End.

ARTICLE XX. That all Heritable Offices Superiorities Heritable Jurisdictions Offices for Life and Jurisdictions for Life be reserved to the owners thereof as Rights of Property in the same manner as they are now enjoyed by the Law of Scotland notwithstanding this Treaty.

ARTICLE XXI. That the Rights and Privileges of the Royal Burghs in Scotland as they now are do remain entire after the Union and notwithstanding thereof.

ARTICLE XXII. That by virtue of this Treaty of the Peers of Scotland at the Time of the Union Sixteen shall be the number to sit and vote in the House of Lords and Forty-five the number of the Representatives of Scotland in the House of Commons of the Parliament of Great Britain and that when Her Majesty Her Heirs or Successors shall declare her or their Pleasure for holding the First or any subsequent Parliament of Great Britain until the Parliament of Great Britain shall make further provision therein a Writ do issue under the Great Seal of the United Kingdom directed to the Privy Council of Scotland commanding them to cause Sixteen Peers who are to sit in the House of Lords to be summoned to Parliament and Forty-five Members to be elected to sit in the House of Commons of the Parliament of Great Britain according to the Agreement in this Treaty in such manner as by an Act of this present Session of the Parliament of Scotland is or shall be settled which Act is hereby declared to be as valid as if it were a Part of and ingrossed in this Treaty ; And that the Names of the Persons so summoned and elected shall be returned by the Privy Council of Scotland into the Court from whence the said Writ did issue ; And that if her Majesty

H

on or before the First Day of May next on which Day the Union is
to take place shall declare under the Great Seal of England that it is
expedient that the Lords of Parliament of England and Commons of
this present Parliament of England should be the Members of the
respective Houses of the First Parliament of Great Britain for and
on the Part of England then the said Lords of Parliament of England
and Commons of the present Parliament of England shall be the
Members of the respective Houses of the First Parliament of Great
Britain for and on the Part of England ; And Her Majesty may by
Her Royal Proclamation under the Great Seal of Great Britain
appoint the said First Parliament of Great Britain to meet at such
Time and Place as Her Majesty shall think fit which Time shall not
be less than Fifty Days after the Date of Such Proclamation and
the Time and Place of the Meeting of such Parliament being so
appointed a Writ shall be immediately issued under the Great Seal
of Great Britain directed to the Privy Council of Scotland for the
Summoning of the Sixteen Peers and for electing the Forty-five
Members by whom Scotland is to be represented in the Parliament
of Great Britain ; And the Lords of Parliament of England and the
Sixteen Peers of Scotland such Sixteen Peers being summoned and
returned in the Manner agreed in this Treaty and the Members of
the House of Commons of the said Parliament of England and the
Forty-five Members for Scotland Such Forty-five Members being
elected and returned in the Manner elected and agreed in this Treaty
shall assemble and meet respectively in the respective Houses of the
Parliament of Great Britain at such Time and Place as shall be so
appointed by Her Majesty and shall be the Two Houses of the First
Parliament of Great Britain and that Parliament may continue for
such time only as the present Parliament of England might have
continued if the Union of the Two Kingdoms had not been made
unless sooner dissolved by Her Majesty ; And that every one of the
Lords of Parliament of Great Britain and that every Member of the
House of Commons of the Parliament of Great Britain in the First
and all succeeding Parliaments of Great Britain until the Parliament
of Great Britain shall otherwise direct shall take the respective
Oaths appointed to be taken instead of the Oaths of Allegiance
and Supremacy by an Act of Parliament made in England in the
First Year of the Reign of the late King William and Queen Mary
intituled An Act for the abrogating of the Oaths of Supremacy
and Allegiance and appointing other Oaths and make subscribe and
audibly repeat the Declaration mentioned in an Act of Parliament
made in England in the Thirtieth Year of the Reign of King Charles

the Second intituled An Act for the more effectual preserving the Kings Person and Government by disabling Papists from sitting in either House of Parliament and shall take and subscribe the Oath mentioned in An Act of Parliament made in England in the First Year of Her Majesty's Reign intituled an Act to declare the Alterations in the Oath appointed to be taken by the Act intituled An Act for the further Security of his Majesty's Person and the Succession of the Crown in the Protestant Line and for extinguishing the Hopes of the pretended Prince of Wales and all other Pretenders and their open and secret Abettors and for declaring the Association to be determined at such Time and in such Manner as the Members of both Houses of Parliament of England are by the said respective Acts directed to take make subscribe the same upon the Penalties and Disabilities in the said respective Acts contained; And it is declared and agreed that these words This Realm The Crown of this Realm and the Queen of this Realm mentioned in the Oaths and Declaration contained in the aforesaid Acts which were intended to signify the Crown and Realm of England shall be understood of the Crown and Realm of Great Britain and in that sense the said Oaths and Declaration be taken and subscribed by the Members of both Houses of the Parliament of Great Britain.

ARTICLE XXIII. That the aforesaid Sixteen Peers mentioned in the last preceding Article to sit in the House of Lords of the Parliament of Great Britain shall have all Privileges of Parliament which the Peers of England now have and which they or any Peers of Great Britain shall have after the Union and particularly the Right of sitting upon the Trials of Peers; And in Case of the Trial of Any Peer in Time of Adjournment or Prorogation of Parliament the said Sixteen Peers shall be summoned in the same Manner and have the same Powers and Privileges at such Trial as any other Peers of Great Britain and that in Case any Trials of Peers shall hereafter happen when there is no Parliament in being the Sixteen Peers of Scotland who sat at the last preceding Parliament shall be summoned in the same Manner and have the same Powers and Privileges at such Trials as any other Peers of Great Britain and that all Peers of Scotland and their Successors to their Honours and Dignities shall from and after the Union be Peers of Great Britain and have Rank and Precedency next and immediately after the Peers of the like Orders and Degrees in England at the Time of the Union and before all Peers of Great Britain of the like Orders and Degrees who may be created after the Union and shall be tried as Peers of Great Britain and shall enjoy all Privileges of Peers as fully as the Peers of England do now or as they or any other Peers of Great Britain may hereafter enjoy the same except the Right and Privilege of sitting in the House of Lords and the Privileges depending thereon and particularly the Right of sitting upon the Trials of Peers.

ARTICLE XXIV. That from and after the Union there be one Great Seal for the United Kingdom of Great Britain which shall be different from the Great Seal now used in either Kingdom; And that the quartering the Arms and the Rank and Precedency of the Lyon King of Arms of the Kingdom of Scotland may as best suit the Union be left to Her Majesty; And that in the mean time the Great Seal of England be used as the Great Seal of the United Kingdom and that the Great Seal of the United Kingdom be used for sealing Writs to elect and summon the Parliament of Great Britain and for sealing all Treaties with Foreign Princes and States and all Public Acts Instruments and Orders of State which concern the whole United Kingdom; And in all other Matters relating to England as the Great Seal of England is now used and that a Seal in Scotland after the Union be always kept and made use of in all Things relating to private Rights or Grants which have usually passed the Great Seal of Scotland and which only concern Offices Grants Commissions and private Rights within that Kingdom and that until such Seal be appointed by Her Majesty the present Great Seal of Scotland shall be used for such purposes and that the Privy Seal Signet Casset Signer of the Justiciary Court Quarter Seal and Seals of Courts now used in Scotland be continued but that the said Seals be altered and adapted to the State of the Union as Her Majesty shall think fit and the said Seals and all of them and the Keepers of them shall be subject to such Regulations as the Parliament of Great Britain shall hereafter make; And that the Crown Sceptre and Sword of State the Records of Parliament and all other Records Rolls and Registers whatsoever both Public and Private General and Particular and Warrants thereof continue to be kept as they are within that Part of the United Kingdom now called Scotland and that they shall so remain in all Time coming notwithstanding the Union.

ARTICLE XXV. I. That all Laws and Statutes in either Kingdom so far as they are contrary to or inconsistent with the Terms of these Articles or any of them shall from and after the Union cease and become void and shall be so declared to be by the respective Parliaments of the said Kingdoms.

As by the said Articles of Union ratified and approved by the said Act of Parliament of Scotland Relation being thereunto had may appear.

II. And the Tenor of the aforesaid Act for securing the Protestant Religion and Presbyterian Church Governments within the Kingdom of Scotland is as follows.

Our Sovereign Lady and the Estates of Parliament considering that by the late Act of Parliament for a Treaty with England for an Union of both Kingdoms it is provided that the Commissioners for that Treaty should not treat of or concerning any Alteration of the Worship Discipline and Government of the Church of this Kingdom as now by Law established which Treaty being now reported to the Parliament and it being reasonable and necessary that the true Protestant Religion as presently professed within this Kingdom with the Worship Discipline and Government of this Church should be effectually and unalterably secured therefore Her Majesty with Advice and Consent of the said Estates of Parliament doth hereby establish and confirm the said true Protestant Religion and Worship Discipline and Government of this Church to continue without any alteration to the People of this Land in all succeeding Generations, and more especially Her Majesty with Advice and Consent aforesaid ratifies approves and for ever confirms the Fifth Act of the First Parliament of King William and Queen Mary intituled an Act ratifying the Confession of Faith and settling Presbyterian Church Government with all other Acts of Parliament relating thereto in Prosecution of the Declaration of the Estates of this Kingdom containing the Claim of Right bearing Date the Eleventh of April One thousand six hundred and eighty-nine ; And Her Majesty with Advice and Consent aforesaid expressly provides and declares that the foresaid true Protestant Religion contained in the abovementioned Confession of Faith with the Form and Purity of Worship presently in use within this Church and its Presbyterian Church Government and Discipline (that is to say) the Government of the Church by Kirk Sessions, Presbyteries, Provincial Synods and General Assemblies all established by the foresaid Acts of Parliament pursuant to the Claim of Right shall remain and continue unalterable and that the said Presbyterian Government shall be the only Government of the Church within the Kingdom of Scotland.

III. And further for the greater Security of the foresaid Protestant Religion and of the Worship Discipline and Government of this Church as above established Her Majesty with Advice and Consent foresaid statutes and ordains that the Universities and Colleges of Saint Andrews, Glasgow, Aberdeen, Edinburgh as now established by Law shall continue within this Kingdom for ever and that in all Time coming no Professors, Principals, Regents, Masters or

Others bearing Office in any University College or School within this Kingdom be capable or be admitted or allowed to continue in the Exercise of their said Functions but such as shall own and acknowledge the Civil Government in Manner prescribed or to be prescribed by the Acts of Parliament, as also that before or at their Admissions they do and shall acknowledge and profess and shall subscribe to the foresaid Confession of Faith as the Confession of their Faith and that they will practise and conform themselves to the Worship presently in use in this Church and submit themselves to the Government and Discipline thereof and never endeavour directly or indirectly the Prejudice or Subversion of the same and that before the respective Presbyteries of their Bounds by whatsoever Gift Presentation or Provision they may be thereto provided.

IV. And further Her Majesty with Advice aforesaid expressly declares and statutes that none of the Subjects of this Kingdom shall be liable to, but all and every one of them forever free of any Oath Test or Subscription within this Kingdom contrary to or inconsistent with the foresaid true Protestant Religion and Presbyterian Church Government Worship and Discipline as above established and that the same within the bounds of this Church and Kingdom shall never be imposed or required of them in any Sort; And lastly that after the Decease of Her present Majesty (whom God long preserve) the Sovereign succeeding to her in the Royal Government of the Kingdom of Great Britain shall in all Time coming at His or Her Accession to the Crown swear and subscribe that they shall inviolably maintain and preserve the foresaid Settlement of the True Protestant Religion with the Government Worship Discipline Right and Privileges of this Church as above established by the Laws of this Kingdom in Prosecution of the Claim of Right.

V. And it is hereby statute and ordained that this Act of Parliament with the Establishment therein contained shall be held and observed in all Time coming as a fundamental and essential condition of any Treaty or Union to be completed between the Two Kingdoms without any Alteration thereof or Derogation thereto in any Sort for ever; As also that this Act of Parliament and Settlement therein contained shall be insert and repeated in any Act of Parliament that shall pass for agreeing and concluding the foresaid Treaty or Union betwixt the Two Kingdoms and that the same shall be therein expressly declared to be a fundamental and essential Condition of the said Treaty or Union in all Time coming which Articles of Union and Act immediately above written Her Majesty with Advice and Consent aforesaid statutes enacts and ordains to be and continue in

all Time coming the sure and perpetual Foundation of a Complete
and Entire Union of the Two Kingdoms of Scotland and England
under the express Condition and Provision that this Approbation
and Ratification of the aforesaid Articles and Act shall be no ways
binding on this Kingdom until the said Articles and Act be ratified
approved and confirmed by Her Majesty with and by the Authority
of the Parliament of England as they are now agreed to approved
and confirmed by Her Majesty with and by the Authority of the
Parliament of Scotland, declaring nevertheless that the Parliament of
England may provide for the Security of the Church of England as
they think expedient to take place within the Bounds of the said
Kingdom of England and not derogating from the Security above
provided for establishing of the Church of Scotland within the
Bounds of this Kingdom as also the said Parliament of England may
extend the Additions and other Provisions contained in the Articles
of Union as above insert in Favour of the Subjects of Scotland to
and in Favour of the Subjects of England which shall not suspend
or derogate from the Force and Effect of this present Ratification in
the Parliament of Scotland.

VI. And lastly her Majesty enacts and declares that all Laws and
Statutes in this Kingdom so far as they are contrary to or inconsistent with the Terms of these Articles as above mentioned shall
from and after the union cease and become void.

.   .   .   .

(§ VII. recites 5 Anne, c. 5, an Act for securing the Church of England,
13 Eliz. c. 12, an Act for the ministers of the Church to be of sound
religion, and 13 and 14 Car. 2, c. 4, the Act of Uniformity, and re-
enacts them as regards the Church of England.)

VIII. And be it further enacted by the authority aforesaid, That
after the demise of her Majesty (whom God long preserve) the
Sovereign next succeeding to her Majesty in the royal government
of the Kingdom of Great Britain, and so for ever hereafter, every
King or Queen succeeding . . . at his or her Coronation, shall in the
presence of all persons who shall be attending . . . take and subscribe
an oath to maintain and preserve inviolably the said settlement of the
Church of England. . . .

IX. And be it further enacted by the authority aforesaid, That
this Act, and all and every the matters and things therein contained,
be, and shall be for ever holden and adjudged to be a fundamental
and essential part of any treaty of union to be concluded between
the said two Kingdoms. . . .

X. May it therefore please your most Excellent Majesty, that it may be enacted; and be it enacted by the Queen's most excellent Majesty, by and with the Advice and Consent of the Lords spiritual and Temporal, and Commons, in this present Parliament assembled, and by the Authority of the same, That all and every the said Articles of Union as ratified and approved by the said Act of Parliament of Scotland, as aforesaid, and herein before particularly mentioned and inserted; and also the said Act of Parliament of Scotland for establishing the Protestant Religion, and Presbyterian Church Government within that Kingdom, intituled, Act for securing the Protestant Religion, and Presbyterian Church Government, and every Clause, Matter and Thing in the said Articles and Act contained, shall be, and the said Articles and Act are hereby for ever ratified, approved, and confirmed.

XI. And it is hereby further enacted by the Authority aforesaid That the said Act passed in this present Session of Parliament intituled an Act for securing the Church of England as by Law established and all and every the Matters and Things therein contained and also the said Act of Parliament of Scotland intituled Act for securing the Protestant Religion and Presbyterian Church Government with the Establishment in the said Act shall for ever be held and adjudged to be and observed as fundamental and essential Conditions of the said Union and shall in all Times coming be taken to be and are hereby declared to be essential and fundamental Parts of the said Articles and Union and the said Articles of Union so as aforesaid ratified approved and confirmed by Act of Parliament of Scotland and by this present Act and the said Act passed in this present Session of Parliament intituled An Act for securing the Church of England as by Law established and also the said Act passed in the Parliament of Scotland intituled Act for securing the Protestant and Presbyterian Church Government are hereby enacted and ordained to be and continue in all Times coming the complete and entire Union of the Two Kingdoms of England and Scotland.

XII. And whereas since the passing the said Act in the Parliament of Scotland for ratifying the said Articles of Union one other Act intituled Act settling the manner of electing the Sixteen Peers and Forty-five Members to represent Scotland in the Parliament of Great Britain hath likewise passed in the said Parliament of Scotland at Edinburgh the Fifth Day of February One thousand seven hundred and seven the Tenor whereof follows.

Our Sovereign Lady considering that by the Twenty-Second Article of the Treaty of Union as the same is ratified by an Act passed in this Session of Parliament upon the Sixteenth of January last it is provided

That by virtue of the said Treaty of the Peers of Scotland at the
Time of the Union Sixteen shall be the Number to sit and vote in
the House of Lords and Forty-five the Number of the Representatives
of Scotland in the House of Commons of the Parliament of Great
Britain and that the said Sixteen Peers and Forty-five Members in
the House of Commons be named and chosen in such Manner as by
a subsequent Act in this present Session of Parliament in Scotland
should be settled, which Act is thereby declared to be as valid as if it
were a Part of and ingrossed in the said Treaty, Therefore Her
Majesty with Advice and Consent of the Estates of Parliament
statutes enacts and ordains that the said Sixteen Peers who shall
have Right to sit in the House of Peers in the Parliament of Great
Britain on the Part of Scotland by Virtue of this Treaty shall be
named by the said Peers of Scotland whom they represent their
Heirs or Successors to their Dignities and Honours out of their own
Number and that by open Election and Plurality of Voices of the
Peers present and of the Proxies for such as shall be absent the said
Proxies being Peers and producing a Mandate in Writing duly signed
before Witnesses and both the Constituent and Proxy being qualified
according to Law, declaring also that such Peers as are absent being
qualified as aforesaid may send to all such Meetings Lists of the Peers
whom they judge fittest validly signed by the said absent Peers which
shall be reckoned in the same Manner as if the Parties had been
present and given in the said List; and in Case of the Death or legal
Incapacity of any of the said Sixteen Peers that the aforesaid Peers
of Scotland shall nominate another of their own Number in the Place
of the said Peer or Peers in Manner before and after mentioned; And
that of the said Forty-five Representatives of Scotland in the House
of Commons in the Parliament of Great Britain Thirty shall be chosen
by the Shires and Stewartries and Fifteen by the Royal Burrows as
follows. . . .

(The remainder of the clause at great length prescribes in detail the
Representation of Scotland in the Imperial Parliament, and subjects electors and elected to the electoral laws of Scotland, together with the penal
clauses against Papists laid down in 8 and 9 Will. III. cap. 3 ; it also prescribes the regulations for the election of the representative peers.)

(XIII. re-enacts the Scottish Act settling the election of sixteen representative peers and forty-five members.)

(See Nos. 88 and 89 in *Gardiner*, Const. Doc.; *Hill Burton*, H.S. viii. *et
seq.; Hallam*, C.H. ch. xvii.; *Wyon*, Reign of Anne, i. 155 *et seq.; Mack-
innon*, The Union between Eng. and Scot. ; *Rogers*, P.L. i. 179–189 ;
Porritt, U.H.C. ii. 3–181.)

XXII

THE PLACE ACT (ANNE)
6 Anne, Cap. 41,[1] 1707.

. . . XXV. And be it further enacted . . . That no person, who shall have in his own name, or in the name of any person or persons in trust for him, or for his benefit, any new office or place of profit whatsoever under the crown, which at any time since the five and twentieth day of October, in the year of our Lord one thousand seven hundred and five, have been created or erected, or hereafter shall be created or erected, nor any person who shall be a commissioner or sub-commissioner of prizes, secretary, a receiver of the prizes, nor any comptroller of the accounts of the army, nor any commissioner of transports, nor any commissioner of the sick and wounded, nor any agent for any regiment, nor any commissioner for any wine licences, nor any governor or deputy governor of any of the plantations, nor any commissioners of the navy employed in any of the out-ports, nor any person having any pension from the crown during pleasure, shall be capable of being elected, or of sitting or voting as a member of the house of commons in any parliament, which shall be hereafter summoned and holden.

XXVI. Provided always, That if any person being chosen a member of the house of commons, shall accept of any office of profit from the crown, during such time as he shall continue a member, his election . . . is hereby declared to be void, and a new writ shall be issued for a new election, as if such person so accepting was naturally dead. Provided nevertheless, that such person shall be capable of being again elected, as if his place had not become void as aforesaid.

XXVII. Provided also . . . That in order to prevent for the future too great a number of commissioners to be appointed or constituted for the executing of any office, that no greater number of commissioners shall be made or constituted for the execution of any office, than have been employed in the execution of such respective office at some time before the first day of this present parliament.

XXVIII. Provided also, That nothing herein contained . . . be construed to extend to any member of the house of commons, being an officer in her Majesty's navy or army, who shall receive any new or other commission in the navy or army respectively.

[1] 6 Anne, c. 7, in common printed editions.

XXIX. And be it further enacted, That if any person hereby disabled, or declared to be incapable to sit or vote in any parliament hereafter to be holden, shall nevertheless be returned as a member to serve for any county, stewartry, city, town, or cinque port in any parliament, such election and return are hereby . . . declared to be void to all intents and purposes whatsoever; and if any person disabled or declared incapable . . . shall after the dissolution . . . of this present parliament presume to sit or vote as a member of the house of commons in any parliament . . . such person so sitting or voting shall forfeit the sum of five hundred pounds.. . . .

XXX. And be it further enacted . . . That every person disabled to be elected, . . . in the house of commons of any parliament of England, shall be disabled to be elected, or to sit or vote in the house of commons of any parliament of Great Britain.

(These famous disabling and enabling clauses form part of a Statute (since repealed) the first twenty-four sections of which deal with the Act of Settlement (11 and 12 W. III. c. 2) and provide for the government on the demise of the Sovereign, should the successor to the throne not be in England (cf. *Wyon, op. cit.*, i. 385). On the subject of the clauses cited above see *Todd*, P.G. ii. pt. iv. chs. 2 and 3; *Anson*, L.C. ii. ch. iv.; *Taswell-Langmead*, E.C.H. 712 *et seq.*; *Porritt*, U.H.C. i. 204–222 and 292–308.)

XXIII

THE OCCASIONAL CONFORMITY ACT
10 Anne, Cap. 6,[1] 1711.

An act for preserving the protestant religion, by better securing the Church of England, as by law established; and for confirming the toleration granted to protestant dissenters by an act, intituled, An act for exempting their Majesties' protestant subjects, dissenting from the Church of England, from the penalties of certain laws, and for supplying the defects thereof; and for the further securing the protestant succession, by requiring the practisers of the law in North Britain to take the oaths, and subscribe the declaration therein mentioned.

I.[2] Whereas an act[3] was made in the thirteenth year of the reign of the late King Charles the second, . . .[4] and another act was made

---

[1] The common printed edition, cap. 2.
[2] §§ I.–VI. repealed by 5 Geo. I. c. i.   The remainder virtually repealed.
[3] 13 Cha. II. St. 2, c. 1.   [4] 25 Cha. II. c. 2.

in the five and twentieth year of the reign of late King Charles the Second, . . . both which acts were made for the security of the Church of England as by law established : Now for the better securing the said Church, and quieting the minds of her Majesty's protestant subjects dissenting from the Church of England, and rendering them secure in the exercise of their religious worship, as also for the further strengthening of the provision already made for the security of the succession to the crown in the House of Hanover . . . Be it enacted by the Queen's most excellent majesty . . . That if any Person or Persons . . . either Peers or Commoners who have or shall have any office or offices Civil or Military or receive any Pay, Salary, Fee or Wages by reason of any Patent or grant from or under Her Majesty or any of Her Majesty's Predecessors or of Her Heirs or Successors . . . or if any Mayor, Alderman, Recorder, Bailiff, Town Clerk, Common Council Man or other Person bearing any office of Magistracy . . . who by the said recited acts . . . are obliged to receive the Sacrament of the Lord's Supper according to the rites and usage of the Church of England . . . shall at any time after their Admission into their respective offices . . . knowingly or willingly resort to or be present at any Conventicle, Assembly or Meeting . . . for the exercise of Religion in other Manner than according to the Liturgy and Practice of the Church of England . . . shall forfeit Forty Pounds to be recovered by Him or them that shall sue for the same . . . in any of her Majesty's Courts. . . .

II. And be it further enacted That every Person convicted . . . shall be disabled from thenceforth to hold such office . . . and shall be adjudged incapable to bear any office or employment whatsoever. . . .

III. Provided always and be it further enacted . . . That if any Person . . . who shall have been convicted . . . shall after such Conviction conform to the Church of England for the space of one year without having been present at any Conventicle, Assembly or Meeting . . . and receive the Sacrament of the Lord's Supper according to the Rites and Usage of the Church of England at least Three Times in the year every such Person shall be capable of the grant of any the offices or employments aforesaid.

. . . .

(§ IV. Such conforming persons to make oath of Conformity and that he has received the Sacrament. § V. limits Prosecution to three months. § VI. exempts offices of Inheritance from being made void, but requires a non-conforming Holder to appoint a Deputy.)

VII. And it is hereby further enacted . . . That the toleration granted to the protestant dissenters, by the act[1] made in the first year of the reign of King William and Queen Mary, . . . shall be, and is hereby ratified and confirmed, and that the same act shall at all times be inviolably observed for the exempting of such protestant dissenters as are thereby intended, from the pains and penalties therein mentioned.

VIII. And for rendering the said last-mentioned act more effectual according to the true intent and meaning thereof; Be it further enacted . . . That if any person dissenting from the Church of England, (not in holy orders, or pretended holy orders, or pretending to holy orders, nor any preacher or teacher of any congregation) who should have been entitled to the benefit of the said last-mentioned act, if such person had duly taken, made, and subscribed the oaths and declaration, or otherwise qualified him or herself, as required by the said act, and now is or shall be prosecuted upon or by virtue of any of the penal statutes, from which protestant dissenters are exempted by the said act, shall at any time during such prosecution, take, make, and subscribe the said oaths and declaration, or being of the people called Quakers, shall make and subscribe the aforesaid declaration, and also the declaration of fidelity, and subscribe the profession of their christian belief, according to the said act, or before any two of her Majesty's justices of the peace, (who are hereby required to take and return the same to the next quarter-sessions of the peace, to be there recorded) such person . . . is hereby entitled to the benefit of the said act, and shall be thenceforth exempted . . . from all the penalties and forfeitures incurred by force of any of the aforesaid penal statutes.

IX. And whereas it is or may be doubted whether a preacher or teacher of any congregation of dissenting protestants, duly in all respects qualified according to the said act, be allowed, . . . to officiate in any congregation in any county, other than that in which he so qualified himself, although in a congregation or place of meeting duly certified and registered as is required by the said act; Be it . . . enacted . . . That any such preacher or teacher, so duly qualified . . . is hereby allowed to officiate in any congregation, although the same be not in the county wherein he was so qualified; provided that the said congregation, or place of meeting, hath been before such officiating duly . . . registered . . . and such preacher or teacher shall, if required, produce a certificate of his having so qualified himself, under the hand of the clerk of the peace for the

[1] 1 W. and M. Sess. 1, c. 18.

county or place where he so qualified himself, which certificate such clerk of the peace is hereby required to make; and shall also before any justice of the peace of such county or place where he shall so officiate, make and subscribe such declaration, and take such oaths as are mentioned . . . if thereunto required.

X. And be it further enacted . . . That on or before the sixteenth day of June next, all advocates, writers to the signet, notaries public, and other members of the college of Justice, within . . . Scotland, . . . are hereby obliged to take and subscribe the oath appointed by the act [1] of the sixth year of her Majesty's reign, intituled, an Act for the better security of her Majesty's person and government, before the lords of session of the aforesaid part of her Majesty's kingdom; except such of the said persons who have already taken the same: And if any of the persons aforesaid do . . . refuse to take and subscribe the said oath, as aforesaid, such persons shall be *ipso facto* adjudged . . . disabled in law to . . . exercise in any manner his said employment or practice.

XI. And be it further enacted . . . That in all time coming no person . . . shall be admitted to the employment of advocate, writer to the signet, notary public, or any office belonging to the said college of Justice, until he . . . have taken and subscribed the aforesaid oath, in manner as is above directed.

(*Wyon*, H.G.B. i. 135 *et seq.;* ii. 335; *Perry*, H.C.E. 2; *Rogers*, P.L. i. 177.)

XXIV

THE SCHISM ACT [2]
13 Anne, Cap. 7,[3] 1713.

An Act to prevent the growth of schism and for the further security of the Churches of England and Ireland as by law established.

. . . [4] Be it enacted . . . That every person or persons who shall, . . . keep any public or private school or seminary, or teach and instruct any youth as tutor or schoolmaster, within that part of great Britain called England, the dominion of Wales, or town of Berwick upon Tweed, before such person or persons shall have subscribed

---

[1] 6 Anne, c. 14; 10 Anne, c. 32.
[2] Repealed by 5 Geo. I. c. 4.
[3] 12 Anne, St. 2, c. 7, in common printed editions.
[4] The preamble simply recites 13 and 14 Cha. II. c. 4.

so much of the said declaration and acknowledgement, as is before
recited, and shall have had and obtained a licence from the respective
archbishop, bishop, or ordinary of the place, under his seal of office
(for which the party shall pay one shilling, and no more over and
above the duties payable to Her Majesty for the same) and shall
be thereof lawfully convicted, upon an information, presentment
or indictment, in any of Her Majesty's courts of record at Westminster, or at the Assizes, or before justices of *Oyer* and *Terminer*,
shall . . . be committed to the common gaol . . . there to remain
without bail or mainprize for the space of three months, to commence from the time that such person or persons shall be received
into the said gaol.

II. Provided always, . . . That no licence shall be granted by any
archbishop, bishop, or ordinary, unless the person or persons who
shall sue for the same, shall produce a certificate of his or their
having received the sacrament according to the usage of the Church
of England, in some parish church, within the space of one year next
before the grant of such licence, under the hand of the minister and
one of the church-wardens of the said parish, nor until such person
or persons shall have taken or subscribed the oaths of allegiance and
supremacy, and abjuration, as appointed by law, and shall have made
and subscribed the declaration against transubstantiation, contained
in the act [1] . . . intituled, An act for preventing dangers which may
happen from popish recusants, before the said archbishop, bishop, or
ordinary ; which said oaths and declarations, the said archbishop,
bishop or ordinary, are hereby empowered to administer and receive ;
and such archbishops, bishops, and ordinaries, are required to file
such certificates, and keep an exact register of the same. . . .

III. And be it further enacted . . . That any person who shall
have obtained a licence, and subscribed the declarations, and taken
and subscribed the oaths, as above appointed, and shall at any time
after, during the time of his or their keeping any public or private
school or seminary, or instructing any youth as tutor or schoolmaster,
knowingly or willingly, resort to, . . . any conventicle, . . . within
England, Wales, or town of Berwick upon Tweed, for the exercise of
religion in any other manner than according to the liturgy and practice of the Church of England, or shall . . . be present at any meeting . . . although the liturgy be there used, where Her Majesty
(whom God long preserve) and the Elector of Brunswick, . . . shall
not there be prayed for in express words, according to the liturgy
of the Church of England, except where such particular offices of the

[1] 25 Cha. II. c. 2.

liturgy are used, wherein there are no express directions to pray for Her Majesty and the royal family, shall . . . thenceforth be incapable of keeping any public or private school or seminary, or instructing any youth as tutor or schoolmaster.

IV. And be it further enacted . . . That if any person licenced, as aforesaid, shall teach any other catechism than the catechism set forth in the book of common prayer, the licence of such person shall from thenceforth be void, and such person shall be liable to the penalties of this act.

V. And be further enacted . . . That it shall . . . be lawful, to and for the bishop of the diocese, or other proper ordinary, to cite any person or persons whatsoever, keeping school or seminary, or teaching without licence, as aforesaid, and to proceed against, and punish such person or persons by ecclesiastical censure, subject to such appeals as in cases of ordinary jurisdiction; this act or any other law to the contrary notwithstanding.

.   .   .   .

(§§ VI. and VII. provide that none shall be punished twice for the same offence.)

VIII. Provided always, That this act, . . . shall not extend, . . . to any tutor teaching or instructing youth in any college or hall, within either of the universities of . . . England, nor to any tutor who shall be employed by any nobleman or noblewoman, to teach his or her own children, grand-children or great-grand-children only, in his or her family; provided such tutor, . . . do in every respect qualify himself according to this act, except only in that of taking a licence from the bishop.

IX. Provided also, That the penalties in this act shall not extend to any foreigner, or alien of the foreign reformed churches, allowed, . . . by the Queen's Majesty, her heirs or successors, in England, for instructing or teaching any child or children of any such foreigner or alien only, as a tutor or schoolmaster.

X. Provided always, . . . That if any person who shall have been convicted, as aforesaid, . . . shall, after such conviction, conform to the Church of England, for the space of one year, . . . and receive the sacrament of the Lord's Supper according to the rites and usage of the Church of England at least three times in that year every such person or persons shall be again capable of having and using a licence to teach school, or to instruct youth as a tutor or schoolmaster, her or they also performing all that is made requisite thereunto by this act.

XI. Provided also, and be it further enacted, That every such person, so convicted, and afterwards conforming, . . . shall, at the next term after his being admitted to, . . . teach or instruct youth, as aforesaid, make oath in writing, in some one of Her Majesty's courts at Westminster, in public and open court, or at the next quarter sessions for that county or place where he shall reside, between the hours of nine and twelve in the forenoon, that he hath conformed to the Church of England for the space of one year before such his admission, without having been present at any conventicle, assembly or meeting, as aforesaid, and that he hath received the Sacrament of the Lord's Supper at least three times in the year, which oath shall be there enrolled and kept upon record.

XII. Provided always, That this act shall not extend, . . . to any person, who as a tutor, or schoolmaster, shall instruct youth in reading, writing, arithmetic, or any part of mathematical learning only, so far as such mathematical learning relates to navigation, or any mechanical art only, and so far as such reading, writing, arithmetic or mathematical learning shall be taught in the English tongue only.

(The first part of the clause recites the Act of Uniformity in the Irish Statutes,—17 and 18 Car. II.)

XIII. . . . Be it therefore enacted . . . That all . . . the remedies, provisions, and clauses, in and by this act . . . shall extend, . . . to Ireland, in as full and effectual manner, as if Ireland had been expressly named and mentioned in all and every the clauses in this act.

(*Perry*, H.C.E. iii. 145 ; *Wyon*, H.G.B. ii. 500 ; *Rogers*, P.L. i. 219.)

XXV

THE RIOT ACT

1 Geo. I. Stat. 2, Cap. 5, 1715.

An Act for preventing Tumults and Riotous Assemblies, and for the more speedy and effectual punishing the Rioters.

I. Whereas of late many rebellious Riots and Tumults have been in divers Parts of this Kingdom, to the Disturbance of the Public Peace, and the endangering of his Majesty's Person and Government, and the same are yet continued and fomented by Persons disaffected to his Majesty, presuming so to do, for that the Punishments provided by the Laws now in being are not adequate to such heinous

I

Offences; and by such Rioters his Majesty and his Administration
have been most maliciously and falsely traduced, with an Intent to
raise Divisions, and to alienate the Affections of the People from his
Majesty : Therefore for the preventing and suppressing of such Riots
and Tumults, and for the more speedy and effectual punishing the
offenders therein; Be it enacted ... That if any Persons to the Number
of twelve or more, being unlawfully, riotously, and tumultuously
assembled together, to the Disturbance of the Public Peace, at any
Time after the last Day of July, in the Year of Our Lord One
thousand seven hundred and fifteen, and being required or commanded by any one or more Justice or Justices of the Peace, or by
the Sheriff of the County, or his Under Sheriff, or by the Mayor,
Bailiff or Bailiffs, or other Head Officer, or Justice of the Peace of
any City or Town-corporate, where such Assembly shall be, by
Proclamation to be made in the King's Name, in the Form hereinafter directed, to disperse themselves and peaceably to depart to their
Habitations, or to their lawful Business, shall, to the Number of
twelve or more (notwithstanding such Proclamation made) unlawfully, riotously, and tumultuously remain or continue together by the
Space of one Hour after such Command or Request made by Proclamation, that then such continuing together to the Number of
twelve or more, after such Command or Request made by Proclamation, shall be adjudged Felony without Benefit of Clergy, and the
Offenders therein shall be adjudged Felons, and shall suffer Death as
in the case of Felony without Benefit of Clergy.

II.   And be it further enacted ... That the Order and Form of th
Proclamations that shall be made by the Authority of this Act, shal
be as hereafter followeth (that is to say) the Justice of the Peace, o
other Person authorized by this Act to make the said Proclamation
shall, among the said Rioters or as near to them as he can safel
come, with a loud Voice command, and cause to be commande
Silence to be, while Proclamation is making, and after that sha
openly, and with loud Voice make or cause to be made Proclamatio
in these Words, or like in Effect :

'Our Sovereign Lord the King chargeth and commandeth all Per
sons, being assembled to disperse themselves, and peaceably to depar
to their Habitations, or to their lawful Business, upon the Pains con
tained in the Act made in the First Year of King George, for preven
ing Tumults and riotous Assemblies.   'God save the King.'

And every such Justice and Justices of the Peace, Sheriff, Unde
sheriff, Mayor, Bailiff, and other Head-officer, aforesaid, within th

Limits of their respective Jurisdictions, are hereby authorized, impowered and required, on Notice or Knowledge of any such unlawful, riotous, and tumultuous Assembly, to resort to the Place where such unlawful, riotous and tumultuous Assemblies shall be, of persons to the Number of twelve or more, and there to make or cause to be made Proclamation in manner aforesaid.

III. And be it further enacted . . . That if such Persons so unlawfully, riotously, and tumultuously assembled, or twelve or more of them after Proclamation made in manner aforesaid, shall continue together and not disperse themselves within one Hour, That then it shall be . . . lawful to and for every Justice of the Peace, Sheriff, or Under-Sheriff of the County where such Assembly shall be, and also to and for every High or Petty-constable, and other Peace-officer within such County, and also to and for every Mayor, Justice of the Peace, Sheriff, or Bailiff, and other Head-officer, High or Petty-constable, and other Peace-officer of any City or Town-corporate where such Assembly shall be, and to and for such other Person and Persons as shall be commanded to be assisting unto any such Justice of the Peace, Sheriff or Under-Sheriff, Mayor, Bailiff, or other Head officer aforesaid, (who are hereby authorized and impowered to command all his Majesty's subjects of Age and Ability to be assisting to them therein) to seize and apprehend, and they are hereby required to seize and apprehend such Persons so unlawfully, riotously and tumultuously continuing together after Proclamation made, as aforesaid, and forthwith to carry the Persons so apprehended before one or more of His Majesty's Justices of the Peace of the County or Place where such Persons shall be so apprehended, in order to their being proceeded against for such their Offences according to law, and that if the Persons so unlawfully, riotously and tumultuously assembled, or any of them, shall happen to be killed, maimed or hurt, in the dispersing, seizing or apprehending, or endeavouring to disperse, seize or apprehend them, by reason of their resisting the Persons so dispersing, seizing or apprehending, or endeavouring to disperse, seize or apprehend them, that then every such Justice of the Peace, Sheriff, Under-sheriff, Mayor, Bailiff, Head-officer, High or Petty-constable, or other Peace-officer, and all and singular Persons, being aiding and assisting to them, or any of them, shall be free, discharged and indemnified, as well against the King's Majesty, his Heirs and Successors, as against all and every other Person and Persons, of, for, or concerning the killing, maiming, or hurting of any such Person or Persons so unlawfully, riotously and tumultuously assembled, that shall happen to be so killed, maimed, or hurt as aforesaid.

IV.[1] And be it further enacted . . . That if any Persons unlawfully, riotously and tumultuously assembled together, to the Disturbance of the Public Peace, shall unlawfully, and with Force demolish
or pull down, or begin to demolish or pull down any Church or
Chapel, or any Building for Religious Worship certified and registered
according to the Statute[2] made in the First Year of the Reign of the
late King William and Queen Mary, . . . or any Dwelling-house,
Barn, Stable or other Out-house, that then every such demolishing,
or pulling down, or beginning to demolish or pull down, shall be
adjudged Felony without Benefit of Clergy, and the offenders therein
shall be adjudged Felons, and shall suffer Death as in case of Felony
without Benefit of Clergy.

V. Provided always, . . . That if any Person or Persons do, or
shall, with Force and Arms, willingly and knowingly oppose, obstruct
or in any manner willfully and knowingly let, hinder, or hurt any
Person or Persons that shall begin to proclaim, or go to proclaim
according to the Proclamation hereby directed to be made, whereby
such Proclamation shall not be made, that then every such opposing
obstructing, letting, hindering or hurting such Person or Persons, so
beginning or going to make such Proclamation, as aforesaid, shall be
adjudged Felony without Benefit of Clergy, and the offenders therein
shall be adjudged Felons, and shall suffer Death as in case of Felony
without Benefit of Clergy ; and that also every such Person or Persons so being unlawfully, riotously and tumultuously assembled, to
the Number of Twelve, as aforesaid, or more, to whom Proclamation
should or ought to have been made if the same had not been hindered, as aforesaid, shall likewise, in case they or any of them, to the
Number of Twelve or more, shall continue together, and not disperse
themselves within one Hour after such Let or Hindrance so made
having Knowledge of such Let or Hindrance so made, shall be
adjudged Felons, and shall suffer Death as in case of Felony without
Benefit of Clergy.

·   ·   ·   ·   ·   ·   ·   ·

(VI. provides how damages shall be made good if a church or other
building shall be destroyed.

VII. The act to be read at every quarter session, leet, and law-day.

VIII.–X. deals with the executive officials in Scotland, and extends
to all places of religious worship tolerated by law.)

(*Dicey*, L.C. 284 and App. xii. ; *Mahon*, H.E. i. 195.)

[1] Repealed as to England, 7 and 8 Geo. IV. c. 24, § 1.
[2] 1 W. and M. Sess. 1, c. 18.

XXVI

THE SEPTENNIAL ACT[1]

1 Geo. I. Stat. 2, Cap. 38, 1716.

An Act[1] for enlarging the Time and Continuance of Parliaments, appointed by an Act made in the sixth year of the Reign of King William and Queen Mary, intituled, An Act for the frequent Meeting and Calling of Parliaments.

Whereas in and by an Act[1] of Parliament made in the sixth year of the Reign of their late Majesties King William and Queen Mary (of ever Blessed Memory) intituled, An Act for the frequent Meeting and Calling of Parliaments: It was among other Things enacted, That from thenceforth no Parliament whatsoever, that should at any Time then after be called, assembled or held, should have any continuance longer than for three years only at the farthest, to be accounted from the Day on which by the Writ of Summons the said Parliament should be appointed to meet: and whereas it hath been found by Experience, that the said clause hath proved very grievous and burthensome, by occasioning much greater and more continued Expenses in order to Elections of Members to serve in Parliament, and more violent and lasting heats and animosities among the Subjects of this Realm, than were ever known before the said Clause was enacted; and the said Provision, if it should continue, may probably at this juncture, when a restless and Popish Faction are designing and endeavouring to renew the Rebellion within this Kingdom, and an Invasion from abroad, be destructive to the Peace and Security of the Government; Be it enacted . . . That this present Parliament, and all Parliaments that shall at any Time hereafter be called, assembled or held, shall and may respectively have continuance for seven Years, and no longer, to be accounted from the Day on which by the Writ of Summons this present Parliament hath been, or any future Parliament shall be appointed to meet, unless this present, or any such Parliament hereafter to be summoned, shall be sooner dissolved by His Majesty, His Heirs or Successors.

(*Hallam,* C.H. iii. xvi. ; *Parlt. Hist.* vii. 292–379 ; *Dicey,* L.C. ; 42 seq.; *Michael,* E.G. i. 604 *et seq.; Mahon,* H.E. i. iv.)

[1] Repeals 6 W. and M. c. 2 (see p. 83).

(The subjoined Protest has both a great historic and constitutional interest, seeing that the Statute is still law. See *Lords Journals*, Ap. 14, 1716; *Rogers*, P.L. i. 228.)

Parliament Act 1911 5 yearly parliaments.

PROTEST

1st, Because, we conceive, that frequent and new Parliaments are required by the fundamental constitution of the Kingdom; and the practice thereof for many ages (which manifestly appears by our records) is a sufficient evidence and proof of this constitution.

2ndly, Because it is agreed, that the House of Commons must be chosen by the people, and when so chosen, they are truly the representatives of the people, which they cannot be so properly said to be, when continued for a longer time than that for which they were chosen; for after that time they are chosen by the Parliament, and not the people, who are thereby deprived of the only remedy which they have against those, who either do not understand, or through corruption, do wilfully betray the trust reposed in them; which remedy is, to choose better men in their places.

3rdly, Because the reasons given for this Bill, we conceive, were not sufficient to induce us to pass it, in subversion of so essential a part of our constitution.

1. For as to the argument, that this will encourage the princes and states of Europe to enter into alliances with us, we have not heard any one minister assert, that any one prince or state has asked, or so much as insinuated, that they wished such an alteration.

Nor is it reasonable to imagine it, for it cannot be expected, that any prince or state can rely upon a people to defend their liberties and interests, who shall be thought to have given up so great a part of their own; nor can it be prudent to wish such an experiment to be made, after the experience that Europe has had of the great things this nation has done for them, under the constitution which is now to be altered by this Bill.

But on the other hand they may be deterred from entering into measures with us, when they shall be informed by the preamble of this Bill, 'that the popish faction is so dangerous, as that it may be destructive to the peace and security of the Government,' and may apprehend from this Bill that the Government is so weak, as to want so extraordinary a provision for its safety; which seems to imply that the gentlemen of Britain are not to be trusted or relied upon, and that the good affections of the people are restrained to so small a number, as that of which the present House of Commons consists.

2. We conceive that this Bill is so far from preventing expenses and corruptions, that it will rather increase them; for the longer a Parliament is to last the more valuable to be purchased is a station in it, and the greater also is the danger of corrupting the members of it; for if ever there should be a Ministry who shall want a Parliament to screen them from the just resentment of the people, or from a discovery of their ill practices to the King, who cannot otherwise, or so truly, be informed of them, as by a free Parliament, it is so much the interest of such a Ministry to influence the elections (which by their authority, and the disposal of the public money, they, of all others, have the best means of doing) that it is to be feared they will be tempted, and not to fail to make use of them; and even when the members are chosen, they have greater opportunity of inducing very many to comply with them, than they could have, if not only the Sessions of Parliament, but the Parliament itself, were reduced to the ancient and primitive constitution and practice of frequent and new Parliaments; for as a good Ministry will neither practise nor need corruption, so it cannot be any Lord's intention to provide for the security of a bad one.

4thly, We conceive, that whatever reasons may induce the Lords to pass this Bill, to continue this Parliament for seven years, will be at least as strong, and may, by the conduct of the Ministry, be made much stronger, before the end of seven years, for continuing it still longer, and even to perpetuate it; which would be an express and absolute subversion of the third estate of the realm.

POULETT	ANGLESEY	GUILFORD	ASHBURNHAM
DARTMOUTH	BERKSHIRE	AYLESFORD	HEREFORD
SOMERSET	MONTJOY	OSBORNE	WHORLTON
SALISBURY	BRISTOL	CHESTER	ROCHESTER
BINGLEY	TREVOR	MANSEL	WESTON
SHREWSBURY	TADCASTER	GOWER	FOLEY
NOTTINGHAM	NORTHAMPTON	COMPTON	WILLOUGHBY DE
STRAFFORD	ABINGDON	BATHURST	BROKE.

XXVII

THE IRISH PARLIAMENT
6 Geo. I. Cap. 5, 1719.[1]

An act for the better securing the dependency of the Kingdom of Ireland upon the Crown of Great Britain.

Whereas the House of Lords of Ireland have of late, against law, assumed to themselves a power and jurisdiction to examine, correct and amend the judgments and decrees of the courts of justice in the kingdom of Ireland: Therefore for the better securing of the dependency of Ireland upon the Crown of Great Britain, May it please your most excellent Majesty that it may be declared, and be it declared . . . That the same kingdom of Ireland hath been, is, and of right ought to be subordinate unto and dependent upon the imperial Crown of Great Britain, as being inseparably united and annexed thereunto; and that the King's Majesty, by and with the advice and consent of the Lords spiritual and temporal, and commons of Great Britain in parliament assembled, had, hath, and of right ought to have full power and authority to make laws and statutes of sufficient force and validity to bind the kingdom and people of Ireland.

II. And be it further declared . . . That the House of Lords of Ireland have not, nor of right ought to have any jurisdiction to judge of, affirm or reverse any judgment, sentence or decree, given or made in any court within the said kingdom, and that all proceedings before the said House of Lords upon any such judgment, sentence, or decree, are, and are hereby declared to be utterly null and void to all intents and purposes whatsoever.

(*Lecky*, H.E. ii. 412 *et seq.*; *Froude*, Eng. in Ireland, i. 285 *et seq.*; *Hallam*, C.H. iii. xviii.; *Porritt*, U.H.C. ii. 424–449.)

(For the convenience of the student, 10 Hen. VII. c. 4 is annexed.)

---

[1] Repealed 22 Geo. III. c. 53 (see p. 144).

POYNING'S LAW
10 Hen. VII Cap. 4, 1495.

An Act that no Parliament be holden in this Land until the Acts be certified into England.

Item, at the request of the Commons of the land of Ireland, be it ordained, enacted and established, That at the next Parliament that there shall be holden by the King's Commandment and licence, wherein amongst other, the King's grace entendeth to have a general resumption of his whole revenues sith the last day of the reign of King Edward the Second, no Parliament be holden hereafter in the said land, but at such season as the King's lieutenant and counsaile there first do certifie the King, under the great seal of that land, the causes and considerations, and all such acts as them seemeth should pass in the same Parliament, and such causes, considerations, and acts affirmed by the King and his counsail to be good and expedient for the land, and his licence thereupon, as well in affirmation of the said causes and acts, as to summon the said Parliament under his great seal of England had and obtained ; that done, a Parliament to be had and holden after the form and effect afore rehearsed : and if any Parliament be holden in that land hereafter, contrary to the form and provision aforesaid, it be deemed void and of none effect in law.

(Irish Statutes, i. p. 44.)

XXVIII
THE PEERAGE BILL
1719.

Resolutions of the Lords in relation to the Peerage.

But after a debate that lasted till near seven of the clock in the evening by a majority of 83 votes against 30, their Lordships came to the following Resolutions, viz.

" 1. That in lieu of the 16 elective peers, to sit in this House on the part of Scotland, 25 peers to be declared by his majesty, shall have hereditary seats in parliament, and be the peers on the part of the peerage of Scotland.

2. That such 25 peers shall be declared by his majesty, before the next session of parliament.

3. That 9 of the said 25 shall be appointed by his majesty to have immediate right to such hereditary seats in parliament, subject to the qualifications requisite by the laws now in being.

4. That none of the remaining 16 so to be declared by his majesty, or their heirs, shall become sitting peers of the parliament of Great Britain until after the determination of this present parliament, except such are of the number of the sixteen peers now sitting in parliament on the part of Scotland, and their heirs.

5. That if any of the 25 peers so to be declared by his majesty, and their heirs shall fail, someone or other of the peers of Scotland shall be appointed by his majesty, his heirs and successors, to succeed to every such peer so failing; and every peer so appointed shall be one of the peers on the part of the peerage of Scotland, in the parliament of Great Britain, and so, *toties quoties*, as often as such failure shall happen.

6. That the hereditary right of sitting in Parliament, which shall accrue to the 25 peers of Scotland, to be declared by his majesty, shall be so limited as not to descend to females.

7. That the number of peers of Great Britain, on the part of England, shall not be enlarged, without precedent right, beyond six of what they are at present; but as any of the said present peers, or such six new peers, in case they be created, shall fail, their numbers may be supplied by new creations of commoners of Great Britain, born within the kingdom of Great Britain or Ireland, or any of the dominions thereunto belonging, or born of British parents, and so, *toties quoties*, as often as such failure shall happen.

8. That no person be at any time created by writ, nor any peerage granted by patent, for any longer estate than for the grantee, and the heirs male of his body.

9. That there be not any restraint upon the Crown, from creating any of the princes of the blood, peers of Great Britain, with right to sit in parliament.

10. That whenever those Lords now sitting in parliament, whose sons have been called by writ, shall die; then it shall be lawful for his majesty, his heirs and successors, to create a peer to supply the number so lessened.

11. That every creation of a Peer hereafter to be made, contrary to these Resolutions, shall be null and void to all intents and purposes."

The Peerage Bill brought in.] March 5th.

The Earl of Clarendon reported these Resolutions to the House, which being agreed to, the Judges were ordered to bring in a Bill thereupon; which they did accordingly on the 14th, when the said Bill was read the first, and ordered to be read a second time.

The Peerage Bill dropped.] March 16th.

The Lords having read this Bill a second time, three Scotch Lords petitioned to be heard by their counsel against the said Bill; but it being represented by some English peers that the Lords being sole judges of what relates to the Peerage, they could not allow their rights and privileges to be questioned and canvassed by lawyers; and having to that purpose cited a precedent, viz. the case of the late duke Hamilton, when he claimed a seat in that house as duke of Brandon, the said petition of the three Scotch Lords was rejected without dividing.

(*Cobbett*, Parlt. Hist. vii. 592.)

(The Bill was introduced into the House of Lords on November 25, 1719, and read a first time. On November 26 it was read a second time and committed. On November 27 it was in Committee; on November 28 it was passed through Committee and ordered to be ingrossed. It was read a third time on November 30. It was read a first time in the House of Commons on December 1. The second reading (203 against 158 votes) was deferred to December 18. And on that day the Bill was thrown out, after "a warm debate which lasted from one o'clock in the afternoon till near nine at night.")

(*Hallam*, iii. xvi.; *Pike*, H.L. 363 ; *Coxe*, Walpole, i. 116, ii. 170 *et seq.*; *Lecky*, H.E. i. 185 ; *Mahon*, H.E. i. 530.)

XXIX

ENGLISH IN THE LAW COURTS
4 Geo. II. Cap. 26, 1731.

An act that all proceedings in courts of justice within that part of Great Britain called England, and in the court of exchequer in Scotland, shall be in the English language.[1]

Whereas many and great mischiefs do frequently happen to the subjects of this kingdom from the proceedings in courts of justice being in an unknown language, those who are summoned and impleaded having no knowledge or understanding of what is alleged for or against them in the pleadings of their lawyers and attornies, who use a character not legible to any but persons practising the law ; to remedy these great mischiefs, and to protect the lives and fortunes of the subjects of that part of Great Britain called England, more effectually than heretofore, from the peril of being ensnared or brought

---

[1] It was extended to Wales by 6 Geo. II. c. 14.

in danger by forms and proceedings in courts of justice, in an unknown language, be it enacted. . . . That from and after the twenty-fifth day of March one thousand seven hundred and thirty three, all writs, processes and returns thereof, and proceedings thereon, and all pleadings, rules, orders, indictments, informations, inquisitions, presentments, verdicts, prohibitions, certificates and all patents, charters, pardons, commissions, records, judgments, statutes, recognizances, bonds, rolls, entries, fines and recoveries, and all proceedings relating thereunto, and all proceedings of courts leet, courts baron, and customary courts, and all copies thereof, and all proceedings whatsoever in any courts of justice within that part of Great Britain called England, and in the court of exchequer in Scotland, and which concern the law and administration of justice, shall be in the English tongue and language only, and not in Latin or French, or in any other tongue or language whatsoever, and shall be written in such a common legible hand and character, as the acts of parliament are usually ingrossed in, and the lines and words of the same to be written at least as close as the said acts usually are, and not in any hand commonly called *court hand*, and in words at length and not abbreviated, any law, custom or usage heretofore to the contrary thereof notwithstanding: And all and every person or persons offending against this act, shall for every such offence forfeit and pay the sum of fifty pounds to any person who shall sue for the same, by action of debt, bill, plaint or information, in any of his Majesty's courts of record in Westminster-hall, or court of exchequer in Scotland respectively, wherein no essoin, protection or wager of law, or more than one imparlance, shall be allowed.

II. And be it further enacted . . . That mistranslation, variation in form by reason of translation, misspelling or mistake in clerkship, or pleadings began or to be begun before the said twenty-fifth day of March one thousand seven hundred and thirty-three, being part in Latin and part in English, shall be no error, nor make void any proceedings by reason thereof; but that all manner of mistranslation, errors in form, misspellings, mistakes in clerkship, may at any time be amended, whether in paper or on record or otherwise, before or after judgment, upon payment of reasonable costs only.

III. Provided always, That nothing in this act, nor any thing herein contained, shall extend to certifying beyond the seas any case or proceedings in the court of admiralty; but that in such cases the commissions and proceedings may be certified in Latin as formerly they have been.

IV. And whereas several good and profitable laws have been enacted, to the intent that the parties in all manner of actions and demands might not be delayed and hindered from obtaining the effect of their suits, after issue tried and judgment given, by reason of any subtile, ignorant, or defective pleadings, nor for any defect in form, commonly called *Jeofails;* It is hereby enacted . . . That all and every statute and statute for the reformation and amending of the delays arising from any *Jeofails* whatsoever, shall and may extend to all and every form and forms, and to all proceedings in courts of justice (except in criminal cases) when the forms and proceedings are in English; and that all and every error and mistake whatsoever, which would or might be amended and remedied by any statute of Jeofails, if the proceedings had been in Latin, all such errors and mistakes of the same and like nature, when the forms are in English, shall be deemed, and are hereby declared to be amended and remedied by the statutes now in force for the amendment of any *Jeofails;* and this clause shall be taken and construed in all courts of justice in the most ample and beneficial manner, for the ease and benefit of the parties, and to prevent frivolous and vexatious delays.

XXX

A PLACE ACT
15 Geo. II. Cap. 22, 1742.

An act to exclude certain officers from being members of the House of Commons.

For further limiting or reducing the number of officers capable of sitting in the House of Commons, Be it enacted . . . That from and after the dissolution or other determination of this present parliament, no person who shall be commissioner of the Revenue in Ireland, or commissioners of the navy or victualling offices, nor any deputies or clerks in any of the said offices, or in any of the several offices following; that is to say, The office of Lord High Treasurer, or the Commissioners of the Treasury, or of the auditor of the receipt of his Majesty's Exchequer, or of the tellers of the Exchequer, or of the Chancellor of the Exchequer, or of the Lord High Admiral, or of the Commissioners of the Admiralty, or of the paymasters of the army, or of the navy, or of his Majesty's principal

Secretaries of State, or of the Commissioners of the Salt, or of the Commissioners of the Stamps, or of the Commissioners of Appeals, or of the Commissioners of Wine Licences, or of the Commissioners of Hackney Coaches, or of the Commissioners of Hawkers and Pedlars, nor any persons having any office, civil or military, within the Island of Minorca, or in Gibraltar, other than officers having commissions in any regiment there only, shall be capable of being elected, or of sitting or voting as a member of the House of Commons, in any parliament which shall be hereafter summoned and holden.

II. And be it further enacted . . . That if any person hereby disabled . . . shall nevertheless be returned as a member . . . such election and return are hereby enacted and declared to be void to all intents and purposes whatsoever: And if any person disabled and declared incapable . . . shall, . . . presume to sit or vote as a member of the House of Commons in any parliament to be hereafter summoned, such person so sitting or voting, shall forfeit the sum of twenty pounds for every day in which he shall sit or vote in the said House of Commons, to such person or persons who shall sue for the same in any of his Majesty's Courts at Westminster; . . . and shall from thenceforth be incapable of taking, holding, or enjoying any office of honour or profit under his Majesty, his heirs or successors.

III. Provided always, . . . That nothing in this act shall extend or be construed to extend, or relate to, or exclude the Treasurer or Comptroller of the Navy, the Secretaries of the Treasury, the Secretary to the Chancellor of the Exchequer, or Secretaries of the Admiralty, the Under Secretary to any of his Majesty's principal Secretaries of State, or the deputy paymaster of the army, or to exclude any person having or holding any office or employment for life, or for so long as he shall behave himself well in his office, anything herein contained to the contrary notwithstanding.

(*Lecky*, H.E. i. 447 ; *Porritt*, U.H.C. i. 204–222 ; *Anson*, L.C. i. v. 72–93.)

XXXI

AN ACT FOR THE PACIFICATION OF THE HIGHLANDS OF SCOTLAND
19 Geo. II. Cap. 39, 1746.[1]

An act for the more effectual disarming the Highlands in Scotland; and for the more effectually securing the peace of the said Highlands; and for the restraining the use of the Highland dress; and for further indemnifying such persons as have acted in defence of his Majesty's person and government, during the unnatural rebellion; and for indemnifying the judges and other officers of the Court of Justiciary in Scotland, for not performing the northern circuit in May one thousand seven hundred and forty-six; and for obliging the masters and teachers of private schools in Scotland, and chaplains tutors and governors of children or youth, to take the Oaths to his Majesty, his heirs and successors, and register the same.

Whereas by an act made in the first year of the reign of his late Majesty King George the First, of glorious memory, intituled, An act for the more effectual securing the peace of the Highlands in Scotland, it was enacted, That from and after the first day of November, which was in the year of our Lord one thousand seven hundred and sixteen, it should not be lawful for any person or persons (except such persons as are therein mentioned and described) . . . to have in his or their custody, use, or bear, broad sword or target, poignard, whinger, or durk, side pistol, gun, or other warlike weapon, otherwise than in the said act was directed, under certain penalties appointed by the said act; which act having by experience been found not sufficient to attain the ends therein proposed, was further enforced by an act made in the eleventh year of the reign of his late Majesty, intituled, An act for more effectual disarming the Highlands in that part of Great Britain called Scotland; and for the better securing the peace and quiet of that part of the kingdom : And whereas the said act . . . is now expired : And whereas many persons within the said bounds and shires still continue possessed of great quantities of arms, and there, with a great number of such persons, have lately raised and carried on a most audacious and wicked rebellion against

[1] Virtually repealed.

his Majesty, in favour of a popish pretender, and in prosecution
thereof did, in a traitorous and hostile manner, march into the
southern parts of this kingdom, took possession of several towns,
raised contributions upon the country, and committed many other
disorders, to the terror and great loss of his Majesty's faithful
subjects, until, by the blessing of God on his Majesty's arms, they
were subdued : Now for preventing rebellion and traitorous attempts
in time to come, and the other mischiefs arising from the possession
or use of arms, by lawless, wicked, and disaffected persons, inhabiting
within the several shires and bounds ; Be it enacted . . . That
from and after the first day of August, one thousand seven hundred
and forty-six, it shall be lawful for the respective Lords Lieutenants
of the several shires above recited, and for such other person or
persons as his Majesty, his heirs or successors, shall, by his or their
sign manual, from time to time, think fit to authorize and appoint,
in that behalf, to issue, . . . letters of summons in his Majesty's
name, and under his or their respective hands and seals, . . . thereby
commanding and requiring all and every person and persons therein
named, or inhabiting within the particular limits therein described,
to bring in and deliver up, at a certain day in such summons to be
prefixed, and at a certain place therein to be mentioned, all and
singular his and their arms and warlike weapons, unto such Lord
Lieutenant, or other person or persons appointed by his Majesty,
. . . and to be disposed of in such manner as his Majesty, his
heirs or successors shall appoint ; and if any person or persons,
in such summons mentioned by name, or inhabiting within the
limits therein described, shall, by the oaths of one or more credible
witness or witnesses, be convicted of having or bearing any arms, or
warlike weapons, after the day prefixed in such summons, before any
one or more of his Majesty's justices of the peace for the shire or
stewartry where such offender or offenders shall reside, or be apprehended, or before the judge ordinary, or such other person or persons
as his Majesty, his heirs or successors shall appoint, . . . every such
person or persons so convicted, shall forfeit the sum of fifteen pounds
sterling, and shall be committed to prison until payment of the said
sum ; and if any person or persons, convicted as aforesaid, shall refuse
or neglect to make payment of the foresaid sum of fifteen pounds
sterling, within the space of one calendar month from the date of
such conviction, it shall and may be lawful to any one or more of his
Majesty's justices of the peace, or to the judge ordinary of the place
where such offender or offenders is or are imprisoned, in case he or
they shall judge such offender or offenders fit to serve his Majesty as

a soldier or soldiers, to cause him or them to be delivered over . . .
to such officer or officers belonging to the forces of his Majesty, his
heirs or successors, who shall be appointed from time to time to
receive such men, to serve as soldiers in any of his Majesty's forces
in America; for which purpose the respective officers, who shall
receive such men, shall then cause the articles of war against mutiny
and desertion to be read to him or them in the presence of such
justices of the peace, or judge ordinary, who shall so deliver over
such men, who shall cause an entry or memorial thereof to be made,
together with the names of the persons so delivered over, with a
certificate thereof in writing, under his or their hands, to be delivered
to the officers appointed to receive such men; and from and after
reading of the said articles of war, every person so delivered over, to
such officer, to serve as a soldier as aforesaid, shall be deemed a listed
soldier to all intents and purposes, and shall be subject to the
discipline of war; and in case of desertion shall be punished as
a deserter; and in case such offender or offenders shall not be judged
fit to serve his Majesty as aforesaid, then he or they shall be imprisoned for the space of six calendar months, and also until he or
they shall give sufficient security for his or their good behaviour for
the space of two years from the giving thereof.

.   .   .   .

(§§ II., III., IV. prescribe penalties for concealing arms; when such
offender is fit to serve he shall serve as a soldier in America.)

V. And for the more effectual execution of this present act, be it
further enacted . . . That it shall be lawful to his Majesty, . . . to
authorize and appoint such persons as he or they shall think proper,
to execute all the powers and authorities by this act given to one or
more justice or justices of the peace, or to the judge ordinary.

.   .   .   .

(VI., VII., VIII. prescribe the conditions of the summons.
IX. empowers the appointment of persons to carry out the Act.
X.-XVI. prescribe the conditions of search, arrest, with penalties for
resistance.)

XVII. And be it further enacted . . . That from and after the
first day of August, one thousand seven hundred and forty-seven, no
man or boy within that part of Great Britain called Scotland, other
than such as shall be employed as officers and soldiers in his Majesty's
forces, shall, on any pretence whatsoever, wear or put on the clothes
commonly called Highland clothes (that is to say) the plaid, philibeg,
or little kilt, trowse, shoulder belts, or any part whatsoever of what
peculiarly belongs to the Highland garb; and that no tartan or party-

coloured plaid or stuff shall be used for great coats, or for upper coats ; and if such person shall presume, after the said first day of August, to wear or put on the aforesaid garments, or any part of them, every such person so offending, being thereof convicted . . . shall suffer imprisonment, without bail, during the space of six months, and no longer ; and being convicted for a second offence, before a court of justiciary, or at the circuits, shall be liable to be transported to any of his Majesty's plantations beyond the seas, there to remain for the space of seven years.

XVIII. And whereas by an act[1] made in this session of parliament, intituled, An act to indemnify, etc. . . . And whereas it is also reasonable that acts done for the public service, since the said thirtieth day of April, though not justifiable by the strict forms of law, should be justified by act of parliament ; Be it enacted . . . That all personal actions and suits, indictments and informations, which have been or shall be commenced or prosecuted, and all molestations, prosecutions, and proceedings, whatsoever, and judgments there upon, if any be, for or by reason of any act, matter, or thing advised, commanded, appointed, or done before the twenty-fifth day of July in the year of our Lord one thousand seven hundred and forty-six, in order to suppress the said unnatural rebellion, or for the preservation of the public peace, or for the safety or service of the government, shall be discharged and made void ; and that every person by whom such act, matter or thing shall have been so advised, commanded, appointed or done for the purposes aforesaid, or any of them, before the said five and twentieth day of July, shall be freed, acquitted, and indemnified, as well against the King's Majesty, his heirs and successors, as against all and every other person and persons, and that if any action or suit hath been or shall be commenced or prosecuted, within that part of Great Britain called England, against any person for any such act, matter or things so advised, commanded, appointed or done for the purposes aforesaid, or any of them, before the said twenty-fifth day of July, he or she may plead the general issue, and give this act and special matter in evidence ; and if the plaintiff or plaintiffs shall become non-suit, or forbear further prosecution, or suffer discontinuance ; or if a verdict pass against such plaintiff or plaintiffs, the defendant or defendants shall recover his, her, or their double costs. . . .

. . . .

(§§ XIX., XX. enact an indemnity for judges not performing the cir cuit courts, and for the disarming of certain parts of Dumbartonshire.)

[1] 19 Geo. II. c. 20.

XXI. And whereas it is of great importance to prevent the rising generation being educated in disaffected or rebellious principles, and although sufficient provision is already made by law for the due regulation of teachers in the four universities, and in the public schools authorized by law in the royal burghs and country parishes in Scotland, it is further necessary, that all persons who take upon them to officiate as masters or teachers in private schools, in that part of Great Britain called Scotland, should give evidence of their good affection to his Majesty's person and government; Be it therefore enacted . . . That from and after the first day of November in the year of our Lord one thousand seven hundred and forty-six, it shall not be lawful for any person in Scotland to keep a private school for teaching English, Latin, Greek, or any part of literature, or to officiate as a master or teacher in such school, or any school for literature, other than those in the universities, or established in the respective royal burghs, by public authority, or the parochial schools settled according to law, or the schools maintained by the society in Scotland for propagating christian knowledge, or by the general assemblies of the Church of Scotland, or committees thereof, upon the bounty granted by his Majesty, until the situation and description of such private school be first entered and registered in a book, which shall be provided and kept for that purpose by the clerks of the several shires, stewartries and burghs in Scotland, together with a certificate from the proper officer, of every such master and teacher having qualified himself by taking the oaths appointed by law to be taken by persons in offices of public trust in Scotland; and every such master and teacher of a private school shall be obliged, . . . to pray, or cause to be prayed for, in express words, his Majesty, his heirs and successors, by name, and for all the royal family; and if any person shall, . . . presume to enter upon, or exercise the function or office of a master or teacher of any such private school as shall not have been registered in manner herein directed, or without having first qualified himself, and caused the certificate to be registered as above-mentioned; or in case he shall neglect to pray for his Majesty by name, and all the royal family, or to cause them to be prayed for as hereby directed; or in case he shall resort to, or attend divine worship in any episcopal meeting-house not allowed by the law; every person so offending . . . shall, for the first offence, suffer imprisonment for the space of six months; and for the second or any subsequence offence, being thereof lawfully convicted before the court of justiciary, or in any of the circuit courts, shall be adjudged to be transported, and accordingly shall be transported to some of his Majesty's plantations in America for life; and in case any person adjudged to be so transported shall return into, or be found in Great Britain, then every such person shall suffer imprisonment for life.

XXII. And be it further enacted . . . That if any parent or guardian shall put a child or children under his care to any private school that shall not be registered according to the directions of this act, or whereof the principal master or teacher shall not have registered the certificate of his having qualified himself as herein directed, every such parent or guardian so offending, . . . shall, for the first offence, be liable to suffer imprisonment by the space of three months; and for the second or any subsequent offence, being thereof lawfully convicted before the court of justiciary, or in any of the circuit courts, shall suffer imprisonment for the space of two years from the date of such conviction. . . .

.   .   .   .

(§ XXIII. Chaplains and tutors in families to take the oath.)

XXIV. Provided always, That it shall be lawful for every chaplain, schoolmaster, governor, tutor, or teacher of youth, who is of the communion of the Church of Scotland, instead of the Oath of Abjuration appointed by law to be taken by persons in offices civil or military, to take the oath directed to be taken by preachers and expectants in divinity of the established Church of Scotland, by an act passed in the fifth year of the reign of King George the First, . . . and a certificate of his having taken that oath, shall, to all intents and purposes, be as valid and effectual, as the certificate of his having taken the Oath of Abjuration above mentioned, and he shall be as much deemed to have qualified himself according to law, as if he had taken the Abjuration appointed to be taken by persons in civil offices. . . .

.   .   .   .

(§ XXV. Penalties for persons keeping chaplains who have not qualified.)

XXVI. And for the better preventing any private schools from being held or maintained, or any chaplain in any family, or any governor, tutor, or teacher of any children or youth, from being employed or entertained contrary to the directions of this act, Be it further enacted, That the sheriffs of shires, and stewarts of stewartries and magistrates of burghs of Scotland, shall be obliged . . . to make diligent enquiry within their respective jurisdictions, concerning any offences . . . and cause the same, being the first offence, to be prosecuted before themselves; and in case of a second or subsequent offence, to give notice thereof, and of the evidence for providing the same, to his Majesty's advocate for the time being, who is hereby required to prosecute such second or subsequent offences before the court of justiciary, or at the circuit courts.

(*Lecky*, ii., 65. See *Rogers*, P.L. ii. 49, and the Act 20 Geo. II. c. 43, p. 133, abolishing the heritable jurisdictions in Scotland. *Craik*, C.S.H. i. 360.)

XXXII

THE ABOLITION OF HERITABLE JURISDICTIONS (SCOTLAND).

20 Geo. II. Cap.[1] 43, 1747.

An Act for taking away and abolishing the Heritable Jurisdictions in that part of Great Britain called Scotland; and for making satisfaction to the Proprietors thereof; and for restoring such Jurisdictions to the Crown; and for making more effectual provision for the administration of justice throughout that part of the United Kingdom, by the King's Courts and Judges there; and for obliging all persons acting as Procurators, Writers or Agents in the Law in Scotland to take the Oaths; and for rendering the Union of the Two Kingdoms more complete.

I. For remedying the inconveniences that have arisen and may arise from the multiplicity and extent of heritable jurisdictions in that part of Great Britain called Scotland, for making satisfaction to the proprietors thereof, for restoring to the crown the powers of jurisdiction originally and properly belonging thereto, according to the constitution, and for extending the influence, benefit and protection of the King's laws and courts of justice to all his Majesty's subjects in Scotland, and for rendering the union more complete, Be it enacted . . . that all heritable jurisdictions of justiciary, and all regalities and heritable baillieries, and all heritable constabularies, other than the office of high constable of Scotland, and all stewartries . . . and all sheriffships . . . belonging unto or possessed or claimed by any subject . . . and all jurisdictions, powers, authorities and privileges thereunto appurtenant . . . shall be and are hereby . . . totally dissolved and extinguished.

(II. The lands and rents to remain.)

[1] Repealed in part 1 and 2 Vict. c. 119 and Stat. Law. Rev. Act, 1867.

III. And be it further enacted . . . that all jurisdictions . . . belonging to any such justiciary, regalities, baillieries, constabularies, stewartries, sheriffships . . . shall . . . be vested in and exercised by the Court of Session, Court of Justiciary at Edinburgh, the judges in the several circuits, and the courts of the sheriffs and stewarts of shires and counties, and other of the King's courts in Scotland respectively. . . .

IV. And it is hereby further enacted . . . that . . . all sheriff-ships of any county or shire, and all stewartries not hereby before taken away . . . and all jurisdictions . . . thereunto belonging . . . shall be and are hereby resumed and annexed to the crown; and that the sheriffs and stewarts of such counties . . . respectively shall from henceforth be nominated and appointed by his Majesty, his heirs and successors.

. . . .

(V. No sheriffship to be granted for more than one year.

VI.-XVI. provide regulations for the decrees of the courts abolished by the Act.)

XVII. And whereas the jurisdiction in capital cases that was heretofore granted to many heritors . . . whose lands were erected by the crown into baronies or granted cum fossa et furca, or with power of pit and gallows, . . . hath been long discontinued . . . and whereas it is reasonable that some further regulations should be made relating to the jurisdiction of such barons who are infeofft cum curiis . . . be it enacted that . . . no heritor or proprietor of lands within Scotland . . . shall have, exercise or enjoy any jurisdiction in capital cases . . . or enjoy any jurisdiction in any criminal cause whatsoever (except in assaults and smaller crimes, nor in civil causes where the sum shall exceed 40*s.*)

. . . .

(XVIII.-XXV. provide regulations for the prisons and jurisdictions of the heritable jurisdictions left by the Act.)

XXVI. Provided always . . . that nothing in this Act shall extend . . . to take away . . . any jurisdiction or privilege by law vested in or competent to the corporation or community of any royal borough in Scotland. . . .

. . . .

(The remainder of the Act—XXVII.-XLIII.—deals with the proceedings and organisation of the courts to which the jurisdiction of the abolished courts are assigned.)

(See *Rogers*, P.L. ii. 49 and authorities cited p. 133.)

XXXIII

HARDWICKE'S MARRIAGE ACT
26 Geo. II. Cap. 33, 1753.[1]

An act for the better preventing of clandestine marriages.

Whereas great mischiefs and inconveniences have arisen from clandestine marriages ; for preventing thereof for the future, Be it enacted
. . . That from and after the twenty-fifth day of March in the year of
our Lord one thousand seven hundred and fifty-four, all banns of
matrimony shall be published in an audible manner in the parish
church, or some public chapel, in which public chapel banns of marriage have been usually published, of or belonging to such parish or
chapelry wherein the persons to be married shall dwell, according to
the form of words prescribed by the rubric prefixed to the office of
matrimony in the book of common prayer, upon three Sundays preceding the solemnization of marriage, during the time of morning
service, or of evening service (if there be no morning service in such
church or chapel upon any of those Sundays) immediately after the
second lesson : and whensoever it shall happen that the persons to be
married shall dwell in divers parishes or chapelries, the banns shall
in like manner be published in the church or chapel belonging to
such parish or chapelry wherein each of the said persons shall dwell ;
and where both or either of the persons to be married shall dwell in
any extraparochial place, (having no church or chapel wherein banns
have been usually published) then the banns shall in like manner be
published in the parish church or chapel belonging to some parish or
chapelry adjoining to such extraparochial place : and where banns
shall be published in any church or chapel belonging to any parish
adjoining to such extraparochial place, the parson, vicar, minister or
curate, publishing such banns, shall, in writing under his hand, certify
the publication thereof in such manner as if either of the persons to
be married dwelt in such adjoining parish ; and that all other rules
prescribed by the said rubric concerning the publication of banns, and
the solemnization of matrimony, and not hereby altered, shall be duly
observed ; and that in all cases where banns shall have been published, the marriage shall be solemnized in one of the parish churches

[1] Repealed 4 Geo. IV. c. 76, § 1.

or chapels where such banns have been published, and in no other place whatsoever.

II. Provided always, . . . That no parson, vicar, minister or curate shall be obliged to publish the banns of matrimony . . . unless the persons to be married shall, seven days at the least before . . . deliver or cause to be delivered to such parson, vicar, minister or curate, a notice in writing of their true christian and surnames, and of the house or houses of their respective abodes within such parish, chapelry or extraparochial place as aforesaid, and of the time during which they have dwelt, inhabited or lodged in such house or houses respectively.

III. Provided always, . . . That no parson, minister, vicar or curate solemnizing marriages after the twenty-fifth day of March one thousand seven hundred and fifty-four, between persons, both or one of whom shall be under the age of twenty-one years, after banns published, shall be punishable by ecclesiastical censures for solemnizing such marriages without consent of parents or guardians, whose consent is required by law, unless such parson, minister, vicar or curate shall have notice of the dissent of such parents or guardians ; and in case such parents or guardians, or one of them, shall openly and publicly declare, . . . at the time of the publication, his, her, or their dissent to such marriage, such publication of banns shall be absolutely void.

IV. . . . That no licence of marriage shall, from and after the said twenty-fifth day of March in the year one thousand seven hundred and fifty-four, be granted by any archbishop, bishop, or other ordinary or person having authority to grant such licences, to solemnize any marriage in any other church or chapel, than in the parish church or public chapel of or belonging to the parish or chapelry, within which the usual place of abode of one of the persons to be married shall have been for the space of four weeks immediately before the granting of such licence ; or where both or either of the parties to be married shall dwell in any extra parochial place, having no church or chapel wherein banns have been usually published, then in the parish church or chapel belonging to some parish or chapelry adjoining to such extra-parochial place, and in no other place whatsoever.

V. Provided always, . . . That all parishes where there shall be no parish church or chapel . . . may be deemed extraparochial places for the purposes of this act, but not for any other purpose.

VI. Provided always, That nothing herein before contained shall be construed to extend to deprive the Archbishop of Canterbury and

his successors, and his or their proper officers, of the right which
hath hitherto been used, in virtue of a certain statute[1] made in the
twenty-fifth year of the reign of the late King Henry the Eighth,
intituled, An act concerning Peter pence and dispensations ; of
granting special licences to marry at any convenient time or place.

VII. Provided always, . . . That . . . no surrogate deputed by
any ecclesiastical judge, who hath power to grant licences of marriage, shall grant any such licence before he hath taken an oath
before the said judge faithfully to execute his office, according to law,
to the best of his knowledge, and hath given security by his bond in
the sum of one hundred pounds to the bishop of the diocese, for the
due and faithful execution of his said office.

VIII. And whereas many persons do solemnize matrimony in
prisons and other places without publication of banns or licence of
marriage first had and obtained; therefore, for the prevention thereof,
Be it enacted, That if any person shall, . . . solemnize matrimony in
any other place than in a church or public chapel, . . . unless by
special licence from the Archbishop of Canterbury ; or shall solemnize
matrimony without publication of banns, unless licence of marriage
be first had and obtained from some person or persons having
authority to grant the same, every person knowingly and wilfully so
offending, and being lawfully convicted thereof, shall be deemed and
adjudged to be guilty of felony, and shall be transported to some of
His Majesty's plantations in America for the space of fourteen years,
. . . and all marriages solemnized from and after the twenty-fifth
day of March in the year one thousand seven hundred and fifty-four,
in any other place than a church or such public chapel, unless by
special licence as aforesaid, or that shall be solemnized without publication of banns, or licence of marriage from a person or persons
having authority to grant the same . . . shall be null and void to all
intents and purposes whatsoever.

(§§ IX., X. Prosecutions for such felony to be commenced within three
years ; proofs of the dwelling of persons in the parishes where banns are
published not necessary to the validity of such marriage.)

. . . .

XI. . . . That all marriages solemnized by licence, after the said
twenty-fifth day of March one thousand seven hundred and fifty-four,
where either of the parties, not being a widower or widow, shall be
under the age of twenty-one years, which shall be had without the
consent of the father . . . (if then living) . . . or if dead, of the

[1] 25 Hen. VIII. c. 3.

guardian or guardians . . . and in case there shall be no such guardian or guardians, then of the mother (if living and unmarried) or if there shall be no mother living and unmarried, then of a guardian or guardians of the person appointed by the court of Chancery; shall be absolutely null and void to all intents and purposes whatsoever.

XII. . . . Be it therefore enacted, That in case any such guardian or guardians, mother or mothers, or any of them, whose consent is made necessary as aforesaid, shall be *Non compos mentis*, or in parts beyond the seas, or shall refuse or with-hold his, her, or their consent to the marriage of any person, it shall and may be lawful, for any person desirous of marrying, in any of the before-mentioned cases, to apply by petition to the Lord Chancellor, Lord Keeper, or the Lords Commissioners of the Great Seal of Great Britain for the time being, who is and are hereby empowered to proceed upon such petition, in a summary way; and in case the marriage proposed shall upon examination appear to be proper, the said Lord Chancellor, Lord Keeper, or Lords Commissions of the Great Seal for the time being, shall judicially declare the same to be so by an order of court, and such order shall be deemed and taken to be as good and effectual to all intents and purposes, as if the guardian or guardians, or mother of the person so petitioning, had consented to such marriage.

. . . .

(§ XIII. No suit to be in the Ecclesiastical Court to compel a marriage *in facie ecclesiæ* by reason of any contract.)

XIV. And for preventing undue entries and abuses in registers of marriages; Be it enacted by the authority aforesaid, That . . . the churchwardens and chapelwardens of every parish or chapelry shall provide proper books of vellum, or good and durable paper, in which all marriages and banns of marriage respectively, there published or solemnized, shall be registered, . . . and all banns and marriages published or celebrated in any church or chapel, or within any such parish or chapelry, shall be respectively entered, registered, printed, or written . . . and shall be signed by the parson, minister or curate, or by some other person in his presence, and by his direction; and such entries shall be made as aforesaid, . . . and all books provided as aforesaid shall be deemed to belong to every such parish or chapel respectively, and shall be carefully kept and preserved for public use.

XV. And in order to preserve the evidence of marriages, and to make the proof thereof more certain and easy, and for the direction of ministers in the celebration of marriages and registering thereof,

Be it enacted, That . . . all marriages shall be solemnized in the presence of two or more credible witnesses, besides the minister who shall celebrate the same; and immediately after the celebration of every marriage an entry thereof shall be made in such register to be kept as aforesaid; in which entry or register it shall be expressed, That the said marriage was celebrated by banns or licence; and if both or either of the parties married by licence, be under age, with consent of the parents or guardians, as the case shall be; and shall be signed by the minister with his proper addition, and also by the parties married, and attested by such two witnesses; . . .

.   .   .   .

(§ XVI. Penalty of death for persons falsifying, forging, or destroying a licence or entry in the register.)

XVII. Provided always, That this act, or anything therein contained, shall not extend to the marriages of any of the royal family.[1]

XVIII. Provided likewise, That nothing in this act contained shall extend to that part of Great Britain called Scotland, nor to any marriages amongst the people called Quakers, or amongst the persons professing the Jewish religion, where both the parties to any such marriage shall be of the people called Quakers, or persons professing the Jewish religion respectively, nor to any marriages solemnized beyond the seas.

XIX. And be it further enacted . . . That this act shall be publicly read in all parish churches and public chapels, by the parson, vicar, minister or curate of the respective parishes or chapelries, on some Sunday immediately after morning prayer, or immediately after evening prayer, . . . in each of the months of September, October, November, and December, in the year of our Lord one thousand seven hundred and fifty-three, and afterwards at the same times, on four several Sundays in each year, . . . after the first day of January in the said year one thousand seven hundred and fifty-four.

(*Lecky*, H.E. i. 490 *et seq.*; *Harris*, Life of Hardwicke, ii. 484; *Abbey* and *Overton*, E.C. ii. 19.)

[1] See p. 141.

XXXIV

THE JUDGES AND THE DEMISE OF THE CROWN

1 Geo. III. Cap. 23, 1760.

An Act for rendering more effectual the provisions in an Act made in the twelfth and thirteenth years of the reign of his late majesty King William the Third . . . (i.e. The Act of Settlement) . . . relating to the commissions and salaries of judges.

(The preamble cites the Act of Settlement at length, and then resolves "to enable your Majesty to effectuate the wise, just and generous purposes of your royal heart.")

Be it enacted . . . That the commissions of judges for the time being, shall be, continue and remain, in full force, during their good behaviour, notwithstanding the demise of his Majesty (whom God long preserve) or of any of his heirs and successors; any law, usage or practice, to the contrary thereof in any wise notwithstanding.

II. Provided always, and be it enacted by the authority aforesaid, That it may be lawful for his Majesty, his heirs, and successors, to remove any judge or judges upon the address of both houses of parliament.

III. And be it enacted by the authority aforesaid, That such salaries as are settled upon judges for the time being, or any of them, by act of parliament, and also such salaries as have been or shall be granted by his Majesty, his heirs and successors . . . shall . . . be paid and payable . . . so long as the patents or commissions . . . shall continue and remain in force.

IV. And be it further enacted by the authority aforesaid, That such salaries of judges as are now or shall become payable out of the annual rent or sums granted for the support of his Majesty's household . . . shall . . . after the demise of his Majesty . . . be charged upon, and paid and payable out of, such of the duties or revenues granted for the uses of the civil government of his Majesty, . . . until some further or other provision be made by parliament for the expenses of the the civil government. . . .

XXXV

THE ROYAL MARRIAGE ACT
12 Geo. III. Cap. 2, 1772.

An act for the better regulating the future Marriages of the Royal Family.

Most gracious Sovereign,

Whereas your Majesty, from your paternal affection to your own family, and from your royal concern for the future welfare of your people, and the honour and dignity of your crown, was graciously pleased to recommend to your parliament to take into their serious consideration, Whether it might not be wise and expedient to supply the defect of the laws now in being, and, by some new provision, more effectually to guard the descendants of his late Majesty King George the second (other than the issue of princesses who have married or may hereafter marry into foreign families) from marrying without the approbation of your Majesty, your heirs or successors, first had and obtained; we have taken this weighty matter into our serious consideration: and being sensible that marriages in the royal family are of the highest importance to the state, and that therefore the kings of this realm have ever been entrusted with the care and approbation thereof; and being thoroughly convinced of the wisdom and expediency of what your Majesty has thought fit to recommend on this occasion, we, your Majesty's most dutiful and loyal subjects the lords spiritual and temporal, and commons, in this present parliament assembled, do humbly beseech your Majesty, that it may be enacted; . . . That no descendant of the body of his late Majesty King George the second, male or female, (other than the issue of princesses who have married, or may hereafter marry into foreign families) shall be capable of contracting matrimony without the previous consent of his Majesty, his heirs or successors, signified under the great seal, and declared in council (which consent, to preserve the memory thereof, is hereby directed to be set out in the licence and register of marriage, and to be entered in the books of the privy council); and that every marriage, or matrimonial contract, of any such descendant, without such consent first had and obtained, shall be null and void, to all intents and purposes whatsoever.

II. Provided always, . . . That in case any such descendant of the body of his late Majesty King George the second, being above the age of twenty-five years, shall persist in his or her resolution to contract a marriage disapproved of, or dissented from, by the King, his heirs or successors; that then such descendant, upon giving notice to the King's privy council, which notice is hereby directed to be entered in the books thereof, may at any time from the expiration of twelve calendar months after such notice given to the privy council as aforesaid, contract such marriage; and his or her marriage with the person before proposed, and rejected, may be duly solemnized, without the previous consent of his Majesty, his heirs or successors; and such marriage shall be good, as if this act had never been made, unless both houses of parliament shall before the expiration of the said twelve months, expressly declare their disapprobation of such intended marriage.

III. And be it further enacted . . . That every person who shall knowingly or wilfully presume to solemnize or to assist, or to be present at the celebration of any marriage with any such descendant, or at the his or her making any matrimonial contract, without such consent as aforesaid first had and obtained, except in the case above-mentioned, shall, being duly convicted thereof, incur and suffer the pains and penalties ordained and provided by the Statute of Provision and Premunire, made in the sixteenth year of the reign of Richard the second.

(*Lecky*, H.E. iii. 463; *Adolphus*, H.E. i. 538 *et seq.*)

XXXVI

THE PLACE ACT (BURKE'S)

22 Geo. III. Cap. 41, 1782.

An act for better securing the freedom of elections of members to serve in parliament, by disabling certain officers, employed in the collection or management of his Majesty's revenues, from giving their votes at such elections.

For the better securing the freedom of elections of members to serve in parliament, be it enacted. . . . That from and after the first day of August one thousand seven hundred and eighty-two, no commissioner, collector, supervisor, gauger, or other officer or person whatsoever, concerned or employed in the charging, collecting, levy-

ing, or managing the duties of excise, or any branch or part thereof;
nor any commissioner, collector, comptroller, searcher, or other officer
or person whatsoever, concerned or employed in the charging, collecting, levying or managing the customs, or any branch or part thereof;
nor any commissioner, officer, or other person concerned or employed
in collecting, receiving, or managing any of the duties on stamped
vellum, parchment, and paper, nor any person appointed by the commissioners for distributing of stamps; nor any commissioner, officer,
or other person employed in collecting, levying, or managing any of
the duties on salt; nor any surveyor, collector, comptroller, inspector,
officer, or other person employed in collecting, managing, or receiving
the duties on windows or houses; nor any postmaster, postmasters
general, or his or their deputy or deputies, or any person employed
by or under him or them in receiving, collecting or managing the
revenue of the Post Office, or any part thereof; nor any captain,
master, or mate of any ship, packet, or other vessel employed by or
under the postmaster or postmasters general in conveying the mail to
and from foreign ports, shall be capable, . . . of giving his vote for
the election of any knight of the shire, commissioner, citizen, burgess,
or baron, to serve in parliament . . . or for choosing any delegate in
whom the right of electing members to serve in parliament for that
part of Great Britain called Scotland, is vested: And if any person,
hereby made incapable of voting, as aforesaid, shall nevertheless presume to give his vote, during the time he shall hold, or within twelve
calendar months after he shall cease to hold or execute any of the
offices aforesaid, contrary to the true intent and meaning of this act,
such votes so given shall be held null and void . . . and every person
so offending shall forfeit the sum of one hundred pounds; one moiety
thereof to the informer, and the other moiety thereof to be immediately paid into the hands of the treasurer of the county, riding
or division, . . . and into the hands of the clerk of the justices of
the peace of the counties or stewartries in that part of Great Britain
called Scotland, . . . to be recovered, by any person that shall sue
for the same. . . .

II. Provided always, . . . That nothing in this act contained shall
extend or be construed to extend to any person or persons for or by
reason of his or their being a commissioner or commissioners of the
land tax, or for or by reason of his or their acting by or under
the appointment of such commissioners of the land tax, for the
purpose of assessing, levying, collecting, receiving, or managing the
land tax, or any other rates or duties already granted or imposed,

or which shall hereafter be granted or imposed, by authority of parliament.

III. Provided also, . . . That nothing in this act contained shall extend, or be construed to extend, to any office now held, or usually granted to be held, by letters patent for any estate of inheritance or freehold.

IV. Provided always, . . . by the authority aforesaid, That nothing herein contained shall extend to any person who shall resign his office or employment on or before the said first day of August, one thousand seven hundred and eighty-two.

V. Provided also, . . . That no person shall be liable to any forfeiture or penalty by this act laid or imposed, unless prosecution be commenced within twelve months after such penalty or forfeiture shall be incurred.

(*Burke's* Works, ii. 175 *et seq.*; *Adolphus*, H.E. iii. 475 *et seq.*; *Anson* L.C. i. 73–87 ; *Porritt*, U.H.C. i. 204–222.)

XXXVII

THE DECLARATORY ACT (IRELAND)
22 Geo. III. Cap. 53, 1782.

An act to repeal an act, made in the sixth year of the reign of his late Majesty King George the First, intituled, An act for the better securing the dependency of the kingdom of Ireland upon the crown of Great Britain.

Whereas an act was passed in the sixth year of the reign of his late Majesty King George the First, intituled, An act[1] for the better securing the dependency of the kingdom of Ireland upon the crown of Great Britain, may it please your most excellent Majesty that it may be enacted; and be it enacted . . . That from and after the passing of this act, the above-mentioned act, and the several matters and things therein contained, shall be, and is and are hereby repealed.

(*Lecky*, H.E. vi. 301 *et seq.*; *May*, C.H.E. iii. 299 *et seq.*; *Porritt*, U.H.C. ii. 424–448.)

[1] See p. 120.

XXXVIII

PITT'S INDIA ACT

24 Geo. III. Sess. 2, Cap. 25,[1] 1784.

An act for the better regulation and management of the affairs of the East India Company, and of the British possessions in India; and for establishing a court of judicature for the more speedy and effectual trial of persons accused of offences committed in the East Indies.

For the better government and security of the territorial possessions of this kingdom in the East Indies, be it enacted . . . That it shall and may be lawful to and for the King's Majesty, his heirs and successors, by any commission to be issued under the Great Seal of Great Britain, to nominate and appoint such persons, not exceeding six in number, . . . being of his Majesty's most honourable privy council, of whom one of his Majesty's principal secretaries of state for the time being, and the Chancellor of the exchequer for the time being, shall be two, to be, . . . commissioners for the affairs of India.

II. And be it further enacted . . . That any number not less than three of the said commissioners, shall form a board for executing the several powers which, by this or any other act, shall be vested in the commissioners aforesaid.

III. And be it further enacted, That the said secretary of state, and, in his absence, the said chancellor of the exchequer, and, in the absence of both of them, the senior of the said other commissioners, according to his rank in seniority of appointment, shall preside at, and be president of the said board; and that the said commissioners shall have, . . . the superintendence and control over all the British territorial possessions in the East Indies, and over the affairs of the united company of merchants trading thereto in manner herein after directed.

IV. And be it further enacted, That in case the ministers present at the said board shall at any time be equally divided in opinion, . . . the then president of the said board shall have two voices, or the casting vote.

.   .   .   .

[1] See also 21 and 22 Vict. c. 106, p. 442.

L

(V. Power to revoke commissions and make new ones.)

VI. And be it further enacted, That the said board shall be fully authorised and impowered, from time to time, to superintend, direct, and control, all acts, operations, and concerns which in any wise relate to the civil or military government or revenues of the British territorial possessions in the East Indies, in the manner herein after directed.

VII. And be it further enacted, That the said secretary of state for the time being shall nominate and appoint such secretaries, clerks, and other officers, as shall be necessary to attend upon the said board, who shall be subject to dismission at the pleasure of the said board; and that all proceedings whatsoever to be had by or before the said board shall be entered in proper books; and that the said secretaries, clerks, and other officers, shall be paid such salaries as his Majesty shall, by warrant under his sign manual, direct.

VIII. Provided always, . . . That the members of the said board, before they shall proceed to act in the execution of any of the powers or authorities . . . shall severally take and subscribe the following oath; (that is to say,)

'I, A. B. do faithfully promise and swear, That, as a commissioner or member of the board of affairs of India, I will give my best advice and assistance for the good government of the British possessions in the East Indies; and will execute the several powers and trusts reposed in me, according to the best of my skill and judgment, without favour or affection, prejudice or malice, to any person whatsoever.'

Which said oath any two of the members of the said board shall, . . . administer; and the said oath shall be entered by the said secretary amongst the acts of the board, and be duly subscribed and attested by the members thereof. . . .

IX. And be it further enacted, That the several secretaries, clerks and other officers or the said board, shall also take and subscribe before the said board, such oath of secrecy and office as the said board shall direct.

X. And for avoiding any doubt which may arise, whether the office or place of a commissioner of the said board for the affairs of India, or of a secretary to the said board, be within any of the provisions contained in an act of the sixth year of the reign of Queen Anne,[1] intituled, An act for the security of her Majesty

[1] 6 Anne, c. 7. See p. 106.

person and government, and of the succession of the crown of Great
Britain in the protestant line; or whether the appointment of any
such commissioner or secretary, being a member or members of the
House of Commons, shall vacate his or their seat or seats in that
house; be it further enacted . . . That the said respective offices,
. . . of a commissioner, or of the chief secretary of the said board for
the affairs of India, . . . shall not be deemed or taken to be within
the intent or purview of the said act . . . whereby to disqualify
. . . from voting as a member of the House of Commons nor shall
the appointment of any commissioner or chief secretary, . . . vacate
his or their seat or seats in the said house; anything contained in the
said act of the sixth year of Queen Anne, or in any other act, to the
contrary notwithstanding.

XI. . . . Be it further enacted, That all the members of the said
board shall, at all convenient times, have access to all papers and
muniments of the said united company, and shall be furnished with
such extracts or copies thereof, as they shall from time to time
require; and that the court of directors of the said united company
shall, and they are hereby required and directed, to deliver to the
said board copies of all minutes, orders, resolutions, and other proceedings, of all general and special courts of proprietors of the said
company, and of the said court of directors, as far as relate to the
civil or military government or revenues of the British territorial
possessions in the East Indies, within eight days after the holding of
such respective courts; and also copies of all dispatches which the
said directors, or any committee of the said directors, shall receive
from any of their servants in the East Indies, immediately after the
arrival thereof; and also copies of all letters, orders, and instructions
whatsoever relating to the civil or military government or revenues
of the British territorial possessions in the East Indies, proposed to
be sent or dispatched, by the said court of directors, or any committee
of the said directors, to any of the servants of the said company in
the East Indies; and that the said court of directors of the said
united company . . . are hereby required to pay due obedience to,
. . such orders and directions as they shall from time to time receive
from the said board, touching the civil or military government and
revenues of the British territorial possessions in the East Indies.

XII. And be it further enacted, That within fourteen days after
the receipt of such copies last mentioned, the said board shall return
the same to the said court of directors, with their approbation
thereof, subscribed by three of the members of the said board, or

their reasons at large for disapproving the same, together with instructions from the said board to the said court of directors in respect thereto; and that the said court of directors shall thereupon dispatch and send the letters, orders, and instructions, so approved or amended, to their servants in India, without further delay, unless, on any representation made by the said directors to the said board, the said board shall direct any alterations to be made in such letters, orders, or instructions; and no letters, orders, or instructions, until after such previous communication thereof to the said board, shall at any time be sent or dispatched by the said court of directors to the East Indies, on any account or pretence whatsoever.

XIII. . . . Be it further enacted, That whenever the court of directors of the said united company shall neglect to transmit to the said board their intended dispatches on any subject, within fourteen days after requisition made, it shall and may be lawful to and for the said board to prepare and send to the directors of the East India Company (without waiting for the receipt of the copies of dispatches intended to be sent by the said court of directors as aforesaid) any orders or instructions to any of the governments or presidencies aforesaid, concerning the civil or military government of the British territories and possessions in the East Indies; and the said directors shall . . . transmit dispatches in the usual form (pursuant to the tenor of the said orders and instructions so transmitted to them) to the respective governors and presidencies in India, unless on any representation made by the said directors to the said board, touching such orders or instructions, the said board shall direct any alteration to be made in the same, which directions the said court of directors shall in such case be bound to conform to.

XIV. And be it further enacted, That . . . it shall be lawful for the said court of directors to apply, by petition, to his Majesty in council, touching such orders and instructions; and his Majesty in council shall decide whether the same be, or be not connected with the civil or military government and revenues of the said territories and possessions in India; which decision shall be final and conclusive.

XV. Provided nevertheless, . . . That if the said board shall be of opinion that the subject matter of any of their deliberations concerning the levying of war, or making of peace, or treating or negociating with any of the native princes or states in India, shall require secrecy, it shall and may be lawful for the said board to send secret orders and instructions to the secret committee of the said court of directors for the time being, who shall thereupon, without disclosing the same, transmit their orders and dispatches in the usual form, . . . to the respective governments and presidencies in India ; and that the said governments and presidencies shall pay a faithful obedience to such orders and dispatches, and shall return their answers to the same, sealed (under cover) with their respective seals, to the said secret committee, who shall forthwith communicate such answers to the said board.

XVI. And be it enacted . . . That . . . the court of directors of the said united company . . . are hereby required . . . to appoint a secret committee, to consist of any number of the said directors for the time being, not exceeding three ; which secret committee shall, from time to time, upon the receipt of any such secret orders and instructions concerning the levying of war or making of peace, or treating or negociating with any of the native princes or states of India, from the said commissioners for the affairs of India, as are herein before mentioned, transmit to the respective governments and presidencies in India a duplicate or duplicates of such orders and instructions, together with orders in writing signed by them the members of the said secret committee, to carry the same into execution ; and to all such orders and instructions . . . the several governments and presidencies in India are hereby required to pay the same obedience as if such orders and directions had been issued and transmitted by the court of directors of the said united company.

XVII. Provided also, . . . That nothing in this act contained shall extend to give unto the said board the power of nominating or appointing any of the servants of the said united company ; anything herein contained to the contrary notwithstanding.

.   .   .   .

(XVIII. The directors not to supply the first vacancy of a counsellor at Fort William.)

XIX. . . . That the government of the several presidencies and settlements of Fort Saint George and Bombay shall, after the commencement of this act, consist of a governor or president, and three counsellors only, of whom the commander in chief in the said several settlements for the time being shall be one, having the like precedence in council as in the presidency of Fort William in Bengal, unless the commander in chief of the company's forces in India shall happen to be present in either of the said settlements ; and in such case the said commander in chief shall be one of the said counsellors, instead of the commander in chief of such settlement ; and that the said commander in chief of such settlement shall during that time have only a seat, but no voice in the said council.

XX. . . . That the court of directors of the said united company shall, within the space of one calendar month next after the passing of this act, nominate and appoint, from amongst the servants of the said company in India, or any other persons, a fit and proper person to be the governor of the said presidency or settlement of Fort Saint George, and two other fit and proper persons from amongst the said servants in India, who together with the commander in chief at Fort Saint George for the time being, shall be the council of the same presidency or settlement; and that the said court of directors shall also, in like manner, and within the time aforesaid, nominate and appoint fit and proper persons to be the governor and council of the said presidency or settlement of Bombay under the same restrictions as are herein before provided in respect to the governor or president and council of Fort Saint George.

XXI. . . . That in case the members present at any of the boards or councils of Fort William, Fort Saint George, or Bombay, shall at any time be equally divided in opinion . . . the said governor general, or the governor or president . . . shall have two voices, or the casting vote.

XXII. . . . That it shall and may be lawful to and for the King's Majesty, his heirs and successors, by any writing or instrument under his or their sign manual, countersigned by the said secretary of state, or for the court of directors of the said united company for the time being, by writing under their hands to remove or recall the present or any future governor general at Fort William at Bengal, or any of the members of the council of Fort William aforesaid, or any of the governors or presidents, and members of the council, of the presidencies or settlements of Fort Saint George and Bombay, or of any other British settlement in India, or any other person or persons holding any office, employment or commission, civil or military, under the said united company in India, for the time being; . . . Provided always, That a duplicate or copy of every such writing or instrument, under his Majesty's sign manual, attested by the said secretary of state for the time being, shall, within eight days after the same shall be signed by his Majesty, his heirs or sucessors, be transmitted or delivered by the said secretary of state, unto the chairman or deputy chairman for the time being of the said united company, to the intent that the court of directors of the said company may be apprized thereof.

XXIII. . . . That whenever any vacancy or vacancies of the office of governor general or president, or of any member of the council, shall happen . . . the court of directors of the said united company shall proceed to nominate and appoint a fit person or persons to supply such vacancy or vacancies from amongst their covenanted servants in India, except to the office of governor general, or the office of governor or president of Fort Saint George or Bombay, or of any commander in chief, to which several offices, the said court of directors shall be at liberty, . . . to nominate and appoint any other person or persons respectively.

XXIV. Provided . . . That the said commanders in chief, at each of the said presidencies respectively, shall in no case succeed to the office of governor general or president of Fort William, Fort Saint George or of Bombay, unless thereunto specially appointed by the court of directors of the said united company; but in case of the vacancy of the said offices of governor general or president respectively, when no person shall be specially appointed to succeed thereunto, the councillor next in rank to such commander in chief shall succeed to such office, and hold the same, until some other person shall be appointed thereunto by the said court of directors.

XXV. Provided always, . . . That when and so often as the court of directors shall not, within the space of two calendar months, . . . proceed to supply the same, then, . . . it shall be lawful for his Majesty, his heirs and successors, to constitute and appoint, by writing under his or their royal sign manual, (under the same restrictions and regulations as are herein before provided, . . .) such person or persons, as his Majesty, his heirs and successors, shall think proper to succeed . . . with the same powers, privileges, and authorities, as if he or they had been nominated and appointed by the said court of directors, and shall be subject to recall only by the King's Majesty, his heirs or successors; any thing herein contained to the contrary notwithstanding.

XXVI. . . . That it shall and may be lawful to and for the court of directors of the said united company, if they shall so think fit, subject to the limitations and restrictions as herein before enacted, . . . to appoint, from time to time, fit and proper persons to succeed, in case of vacancy, to the several offices of governor general or president of Fort Saint George or Bombay, or commander in chief of the company's forces at any of the said settlements, or member of any of the said councils; and such appointments respectively at their pleasure again to revoke; but that no person so

CORPUS CHRISTI BUTLER LIBRARY

appointed to succeed to any of the said offices, in case of vacancy, shall be entitled to any salary, advantage, or allowance whatsoever, by reason of such appointment, until such persons respectively shall take upon themselves the offices to which they shall so respectively have been appointed.

. . . .

(XXVII. Of the appointment of temporary counsellors.)

XXVIII. . . . That no resignation to be made of the offices of the governor general, or governor or president of any of the subordinate settlements, or commander in chief, or member of the respective councils of any of the said presidencies in India, shall be deemed or construed to be legal or valid, . . . unless the same be made by an instrument in writing under the hand of the officer or person resigning the same.

XXIX. . . . That no order or resolution of any general court of the proprietors of the said united company shall be available to revoke or rescind, or in any respect to affect, any act, order, resolution, matter or proceeding, of the said court of directors, . . . after the same shall have been approved by the said board, in the manner herein before directed; any law or usage to the contrary notwithstanding.

. . . .

(XXX. repeals part of 21 Geo. III. c. 65.)

XXXI. . . . That the governor general and council of Fort William aforesaid shall have power and authority to superintend, control, and direct the several presidencies and governments now or hereafter to be erected or established in the East Indies by the said united company, in all such points as relate to any transactions with the country powers, or to war or peace, or to the application of the revenues or forces of such presidencies and settlements in time of war, or any such other points as shall from time to time be specially referred by the court of directors of the said company to their superintendence and control.

XXXII. And, . . . Be it further enacted, That notwithstanding any doubt which may be entertained by the said presidencies or settlements to whom such orders or instructions shall be given, respecting the power of the governor general and council to give such orders, yet the said presidencies or settlements shall be bound to obey such orders and directions of the said governor general and council in all cases whatever, except only where they shall have received positive orders and instructions from the said court of directors, or from the secret committee of the said court of directors, repugnant to the orders and instructions of the said governor general and council, and not known to the said governor general and council at the time of dispatching their orders and instructions as aforesaid; and the said governor general and council shall, at the time of transmitting all such orders and instructions, transmit therewith the dates of and the times of receiving, the last dispatches, orders, and instructions, which they have received from the court of directors, or from the secret committee of the said court of directors, . . . And the said presidencies and governments, in all cases where they have received any orders . . . which they shall deem repugnant to the orders of the said governor general and council of Fort William, and which were not known to the said governor general and council at the time of dispatching their orders . . . shall forthwith transmit copies of the same, together with an account of all resolutions or orders made by them in consequence thereof, to the governor general and council of Fort William, who shall, upon receipt of the same, dispatch such further orders and instructions to the said presidencies and settlements as they may judge necessary thereupon.

.   .   .   .

(XXXIII. provides regulations for the transactions of the several boards in India.)

XXXIV. And whereas to pursue schemes of conquest and extension of dominion in India, are measures repugnant to the wish, the honour, and policy of this nation; Be it therefore further enacted . . . That it shall not be lawful for the governor general and council of Fort William aforesaid, without the express demand and authority of the said court of directors, or of the secret committee of the said court of directors, in any case (except where hostilities have actually been commenced, or preparations actually made for the commencement of hostilities, against the British nation in India, or against some of the princes or states dependent thereon, or whose territories the said united company shall be at such time engaged by any subsisting treaty to defend or guarantee), either to declare war or commence hostilities, or enter into any treaty for making war, against any of the country princes or states in India, or any treaty for guaranteeing the possessions of any country princes or states; and that in such case it shall not be lawful for the said governor general and council to declare war or commence hostilities, or enter into treaty for making war against any other prince or state than such as shall be actually committing hostilities, or making preparations as aforesaid, or to make such treaty for guaranteeing the possessions of any prince or state, but upon the consideration of such prince or state actually engaging to assist the company against such hostilities commenced, or preparations made as aforesaid; and in all cases where hostilities shall be commenced, or treaty made, the said governor general and council shall, by the most expeditious means they can devise, communicate the same unto the court of directors, together with a full state of the information and intelligence upon which they shall have commenced such hostilities, or made such treaties, and their motives and reasons for the same at large.

XXXV. . . . That it shall not be lawful for the governors or presidents and counsellors, of Fort Saint George and Bombay, or of any subordinate settlement respectively to make or issue any order for commencing hostilities, or levying war, or to negociate or conclude any treaty of peace, or other treaty, with any Indian prince or state, (except in cases of sudden emergency or imminent danger, when it shall appear dangerous to postpone such hostilities or treaty), unless in pursuance of express orders from the said governor general and council of Fort William aforesaid, or from the said court of directors, or from the secret committee of the said court of directors; and every such treaty shall, if possible, contain a clause for subjecting the same to the ratification or rejection of the governor general and council of Fort William aforesaid: And the said presidents and counsellors of the said presidencies and settlements of Fort Saint George and Bombay, or other subordinate settlement, are hereby required to yield due obedience to all such orders as they shall from time to time respectively receive from the said governor general and council of Fort William aforesaid, concerning the premises.

. . . .

(XXXVI. Of the relations of the subordinate presidents and counsellors to the governor-general.

XXXVII. The directors to consider British demands on the Nabob of Arcot; XXXVIII., and of the demands on the Rajah of Tanjore; and XXXIX., of the rajahs and zemindars.

XL. The directors to introduce "a just and laudable œconomy" in the civil and military establishments).

XLI. . . . That until the said several lists of the offices, places, and employments shall have been made . . . the said court of directors shall be, . . . prohibited from appointing or sending to India any new servant, civil or military, under the degrees of the respective counsellors and commanders in chief; and after such lists shall have been perfected and established, the said court of directors

shall in no wise appoint or send out any greater number of persons
to be cadets or writers, or in any other capacity, than will be actually
necessary, in addition to the persons on the spot, to supply and keep
up the proper complement or number of officers and servants contained in the said lists.

.   .   .   .

(XLII and XLIII. Regulations as to promotions, cadets, etc.)

XLIV. . . . That all his Majesty's subjects, as well servants of
the said united company, shall be, and are hereby declared to be,
amenable to all courts of justice (both in India and Great Britain) of
competent jurisdiction to try offences committed in India, for all acts,
injuries, wrongs, oppressions, trespasses, misdemeanours, crimes, and
offences whatsoever, by them or any of them done, or to be done or
committed, in any of the lands or territories of any native prince or
state, or against their persons or properties, or the persons or properties
of any of their subjects or people, in the same manner as if the same
had been done or committed within the territories directly subject to
and under the British government in India.

.   .   .   .

(XLV.–LXXXII. deals with prosecutions, corruption, and extortion, and
the appointment of special commissioners from the Lords and Commons.)

LXXXIII. Provided always, . . . That nothing herein contained
shall extend, . . . to prejudice or affect the rights or claims of the
public, or the said united company, respecting the said territorial
acquisitions and revenues.

LXXXIV. . . . That this act shall take place and have commencement, in Great Britain immediately after the same shall have
received his Majesty's royal assent; and shall take place and have
commencement, in the several presidencies aforesaid, and in the territories thereunto belonging, from the first day of January, one thousand
seven hundred and eighty-five.

LXXXV. . . . That this act shall, and shall be deemed and taken
to be a public act.

(See *Parlt. Hist.* xxiv. 1086 *et seq.; May*, C.H.E. iii. 381 ; *Lecky*, H.E.
v. 74 ; *Rogers*, P.L. ii. 214 ; *Ilbert*, The Government of India (esp. introduction).)

XXXIX

FOX' LIBEL ACT

32 Geo. III. Cap. 60, 1792.

An Act to remove doubts respecting the functions of Juries in Cases of Libels.

Whereas doubts have arisen whether on the trials of an indictment or information for the making or publishing any libel, where an issue or issues are joined between the king and the defendant or defendants, on the plea of Not Guilty pleaded, it be competent to the jury impanelled to try the same to give their verdict upon the whole matter in issue : Be it therefore declared and enacted . . . That, on every such trial, the jury sworn to try the issue may give a general verdict of Guilty or Not Guilty upon the whole Matter put in issue upon such indictment or information ; and shall not be required or directed, by the court or judge before whom such indictment or information shall be tried, to find the defendant or defendants guilty merely on the proof of the publication by such defendant or defendants of the paper charged to be a libel, and of the sense ascribed to the same in such indictment or information.

II. Provided always, That, on every such trial, the court or judge before whom such indictment or information shall be tried, shall, according to their or his discretion, give their or his opinion and directions to the jury on the matter in issue between the King and the defendant or defendants, in like manner as in other criminal cases.

III. Provided also, That nothing herein contained shall extend, or be construed to extend, to prevent the Jury from finding a special verdict, in their discretion, as in other criminal cases.

IV. Provided also, That in case the jury shall find the defendant or defendants guilty, it shall and may be lawful for the said defendant or defendants to move in arrest of judgement, on such ground and in such manner as by law he or they might have done before the passing of this act ; anything herein contained to the contrary notwithstanding.

(See *May*, C.H.E. ii. 256 ; *Odgers*, L. and S. (*passim*) ; *Dicey*, L.C. 234 *et seq. ; Rogers*, P.L. ii. 234 ; *Stephen*, H.C.L. ii. ch. xxiv. ; *Parlt. Hist.* xxix. 501 and 1403 *et seq.*)

XL

AN ACT FOR THE UNION WITH IRELAND

40 Geo. III. Cap. 67, 1800.

An Act for the Union of Great Britain and Ireland.

Whereas in pursuance of his Majesty's most gracious recommendation to the two houses of parliament in Great Britain and Ireland
respectively, to consider of such measures as might best tend to
strengthen and consolidate the connection between the two kingdoms,
the two houses of the parliament of Great Britain and the two houses
of the Parliament of Ireland have severally agreed and resolved,
that, in order to promote and secure the essential interests of Great
Britain and Ireland, and to consolidate the strength, power, and
resources of the British Empire, it will be advisable to concur in such
measures as may best tend to unite the two kingdoms of Great
Britain and Ireland into one kingdom, in such manner, and on such
terms and conditions, as may be established by the acts of the respective parliaments of Great Britain and Ireland.

And whereas, in furtherance of the same resolution, both houses
of the said two parliaments respectively have likewise agreed upon
certain articles for effectuating and establishing the said purposes, in
the tenor following :

ARTICLE FIRST. That it be the first article of the union of the kingdoms of Great Britain and Ireland, that the said kingdoms of Great
Britain and Ireland shall, upon the first day of January that shall be
in the year of our Lord one thousand eight hundred and one, and for
ever after, be united into one kingdom, by the name of The United
Kingdom of Great Britain and Ireland ; and that the royal style and
titles appertaining to the Imperial Crown of the said united kingdom
and its dependencies; and also the ensigns, armorial flags and banners
thereof shall be such as his Majesty, by his royal proclamation under
the great seal of the united kingdom, shall be pleased to appoint.

ARTICLE SECOND. That it be the second article of union, that the
succession to the imperial crown of the said united kingdom, and of the
dominions thereunto belonging, shall continue limited and settled,
according to the existing laws, and to the terms of union between
England and Scotland.

ARTICLE THIRD. That it be the third article of union, that the said united kingdom be represented in one and the same parliament, to be styled The Parliament of the United Kingdom of Great Britain and Ireland.

ARTICLE FOURTH. That it be the fourth article of union, that four lords spiritual of Ireland by rotation of sessions, and twenty-eight lords temporal of Ireland elected for life by the peers of Ireland shall be the number to sit and vote on the part of Ireland in the house of lords of the parliament of the United Kingdom; and 100 commoners (two for each county of Ireland, two for the city of Dublin, two for the city of Cork, one for the university of Trinity College, and one for each of the thirty-one most considerable cities, towns, and boroughs) be the number to sit and vote on the part of Ireland in the house of commons of the parliament of the united kingdom:

That such act as shall be passed in the parliament of Ireland previous to the Union to regulate the mode by which the lords spiritual and temporal, and the commons, to serve in the parliament of the united kingdom on the part of Ireland, shall be summoned and returned to the said parliament, shall be considered as forming part of the treaty of union, and shall be incorporated in the acts of the respective parliaments by which the said union shall be ratified and established:

That all questions touching the rotation or election of the lords spiritual or temporal of Ireland to sit in the parliament of the united kingdom, shall be decided by the house of lords thereof; and whenever, by reason of an equality of votes in the election of any such lords temporal a complete election shall not be made according to the true intent of this article, the names of those peers for whom such equality of votes shall be so given, shall be written on pieces of paper of a similar form, and shall be put into a glass, by the clerk of the parliaments at the table of the house of lords whilst the house is sitting; and the peer or peers whose name or names shall be first drawn out by the clerk of the parliaments, shall be deemed the peer or peers elected, as the case may be:

That any person holding any peerage in Ireland now subsisting, or hereafter to be created, shall not thereby be disqualified from being elected to serve, if he shall so think fit, for any county, city, or borough of Great Britain, in the house of commons of the united kingdom, unless he have been previously elected as above, to sit in the house of lords of the united kingdom; but that so long as such peer of Ireland shall so continue to be a member of the house of commons, he shall not be entitled to the privilege of peerage, nor be capable of being elected to serve as a peer on the part of Ireland, or of voting at any such election; and that he shall be liable to be sued, indicted, proceeded against, and tried as a commoner, for any offence with which he may be charged:

That it shall be lawful for his Majesty, his heirs, and successors, to create peers of that part of the united kingdom called Ireland, and to make promotions in the peerage thereof, after the union; provided that no new creation of any such peers shall take place after the union until three of the peerages of Ireland, which shall have been existing at the time of the union, shall have become extinct; and upon such extinction of three peerages, that it shall be lawful for his Majesty, his heirs and successors, to create one peer of that part of the united kingdom called Ireland; and in like manner so often as three peerages of that part of the united kingdom called Ireland shall become extinct, it shall be lawful for his Majesty, his heirs and successors, to create one other peer of the said part of the united kingdom; and if it shall happen that the peers of that part of the united kingdom called Ireland, shall, by extinction of peerages, or otherwise, be reduced to the number of one hundred, exclusive of all such peers of that part of the united kingdom called Ireland, as shall hold any peerage of Great Britain subsisting at the time of the union, or of the united kingdom created since the union, by which such peers shall be entitled to a hereditary seat in the house of lords of the united kingdom, then and in that case it shall and may be lawful for his Majesty, his heirs and successors, to create one peer of that part of the united kingdom called Ireland as often as any one of such hundred peerages shall fail by extinction, or as often as any one peer of that part of the United Kingdom called Ireland shall become entitled, by descent or creation, to an hereditary seat in the house of lords of the united kingdom; it being the true intent and meaning of this article, that at all times after the union it shall and may be lawful for his Majesty, his heirs and successors, to keep up the peerage of that part of the united kingdom called Ireland to the number of one hundred, over and above the number of such of the said peers as shall be entitled, by descent or creation, to an hereditary seat in the house of lords of the united kingdom:

That if any peerage shall at any time be in abeyance, such peerage shall be deemed and taken as an existing peerage; and no peerage shall be deemed extinct, unless on default of claimants to the inheritance of such peerage for the space of one year from the death of the person who shall have been last possessed thereof; and if no claim shall be made to the inheritance of such peerage, in such form and manner as may from time to time be prescribed by the house of lords of the united kingdom, before the expiration of the said period of a year, then and in that case such peerage shall be deemed extinct; provided that nothing herein shall exclude any person from afterwards putting in a claim to the peerage so deemed extinct; and if such claim shall be allowed as valid, by judgement of the house of lords of the united kingdom, reported to his Majesty, such peerage shall be considered as revived; and in case any new creation of a peerage of that part of the united kingdom called Ireland, shall have taken place in the interval, in consequence of the supposed extinction of such peerage, then no new right of creation shall accrue to his Majesty, his heirs or successors, in consequence of the next extinction which shall take place at any peerage of that part of the united kingdom called Ireland :

That all questions touching the election of members to sit on the part of Ireland in the house of commons of the united kingdom shall be heard and decided in the same manner as questions touching such elections in Great Britain now are, or at any time hereafter shall by law be heard and decided, subject nevertheless to such particular regulations in respect of Ireland as, from local circumstances, the parliament of the united kingdom may from time to time deem expedient :

That the qualifications[1] in respect of property of the members elected on the part of Ireland to sit in the house of commons of the united kingdom, shall be respectively the same as are now provided by law in the cases of elections for counties and cities and boroughs respectively in that part of the united kingdom called England, unless any other provision shall hereafter be made in that respect by act of parliament of the united kingdom :

That when his Majesty, his heirs or successors, shall declare his, her, or their pleasure for holding the first or any subsequent parliament of the united kingdom, a proclamation shall issue, under the great seal of the united kingdom, to cause the lords spiritual and temporal, and commons, who are to serve in the parliament thereof on the part of Ireland, to be returned in such manner as by any act of this present session of the parliament of Ireland shall be provided; and that the lords spiritual and temporal and commons of Great Britain shall together with the lords spiritual and temporal and commons so returned as aforesaid on the part of Ireland, constitute the two houses of the parliament of the united kingdom :

[1] Repealed 21 and 22 Vict. c. 26.

That if his Majesty,[1] on or before the first day of January one thousand eight hundred and one, on which day the union is to take place, shall declare, under the great seal of Great Britain, that it is expedient that the lords and commons of the present parliament of great Britain should be the members of the respective houses of the first parliament of the united kingdom on the part of Great Britain, then the said lords and commons of the present parliament of Great Britain shall accordingly be the members of the respective houses of the first parliament of the united kingdom on the part of Great Britain ; and they, together with the lords spiritual and temporal and commons, so summoned and returned as above on the part of Ireland, shall be the lords spiritual and temporal and commons of the first parliament of the united kingdom; and such first parliament may (in that case) if not sooner dissolved, continue to sit so long as the present parliament of Great Britain may now by law continue to sit, if not sooner dissolved : provided always, that until an act shall have passed in the parliament of the united kingdom, providing in what cases persons holding offices or places of profit under the crown in Ireland, shall be incapable of being members of the house of commons of the united kingdom, no greater number of members than twenty, holding such offices or places, as aforesaid, shall be capable of sitting in the said house of commons of the parliament of the united kingdom ; and if such a number of members shall be returned to serve in the said house as to make the whole number of members of the said house holding such offices or places as aforesaid more than twenty, then and in such cases the seat or places of such members as shall last have accepted such offices or places shall be vacated at the option of such members, so as to reduce the number of members holding such offices or places to the number of twenty ; and no person holding such office or place shall be capable of being elected or of sitting in the said house, while there are twenty persons holding such offices or places sitting in the said house; and that every one of the lords of parliament of the united kingdom, and every member of the house of commons of the united kingdom, in the first and all succeeding parliaments, shall, until the parliament of the united kingdom shall otherwise provide, take the oaths, and make and subscribe the declaration, and take and subscribe the oath now by law enjoined to be taken, made, and subscribed by the lords and commons of the parliament of Great Britain :

That the lords of parliament on the part of Ireland, in the house of lords of the united kingdom, shall at all times have the same privileges

---

[1] Repealed 34 and 35 Vict. c. 116 (S.L.R.).

M

of parliament which shall belong to the lords of parliament on the part of Great Britain ; and the lords spiritual and temporal respectively on the part of Ireland shall at all times have the same rights in respect of their sitting and voting upon the trial of peers, as the lords spiritual and temporal respectively on the part of Great Britain ; and that all lords spiritual of Ireland shall have rank and precedency next and immediately after the lords spiritual of the same rank and degree of Great Britain, and shall enjoy all privileges as fully as the lords spiritual of Great Britain do now or may hereafter enjoy the same (the right and privilege of sitting in the house of lords, and the privileges depending thereon, and particularly the right of sitting on the trial of peers, excepted) ; and that the persons holding any temporal peerages of Ireland, existing at the time of the union, shall, from and after the union, have rank and precedency next and immediately after all persons holding peerages of the like orders, and degrees in Great Britain, subsisting at the time of the union ; and that all peerages of Ireland created after the union shall have rank and precedency with the peerages of the united kingdom, so created, according to the dates of their creation, and that all peerages both of Great Britain and Ireland, now subsisting or hereafter to be created, shall in all other respects, from the date of the union, be considered as peerages of the united kingdom ; and that the peers of Ireland shall, as peers of the united kingdom, be sued and tried as peers, except as aforesaid, and shall enjoy all privileges of peers as fully as the peers of Great Britain; the right and privilege of sitting in the house of lords, and the privileges depending thereon, and the right of sitting on the trial of peers, only excepted.

ARTICLE FIFTH.[1] That it be the fifth article of union, That the churches of England and Ireland, as now by law established, be united into one protestant episcopal church, to be called, The United Church of England and Ireland ; and that the doctrine, worship, discipline, and government of the said united church shall be, and shall remain in full force for ever, as the same are now by law established for the church of England ; and the continuance and preservation of the said united church, as the established church of England and Ireland, shall be deemed and taken to be an essential and fundamental part of the union ; and that in like manner the doctrine, worship, discipline, and government of the church of Scotland, shall remain and be preserved as the same are now established

---

[1] The union of the Churches was dissolved and the Church of Ireland disestablished by 32 and 33 Vict. c. 42, the Irish Church Act, 1869.

by law, and by the acts for the union of the two kingdoms of England and Scotland.

ARTICLE SIXTH. That it be the sixth article of union, That his Majesty's subjects of Great Britain and Ireland shall, from and after the first day of January one thousand eight hundred and one, be entitled to the same privileges, and be on the same footing, as to encouragements and bounties on the like articles being the growth, produce, or manufacture of either country respectively, and generally in respect of trade and navigation in all parts and places in the united kingdom and its dependencies; and that in all treaties made by his Majesty, his heirs and successors with any foreign power, his Majesty's subjects of Ireland shall have the same privileges and be on the same footing, as his Majesty's subjects of Great Britain. . . .

(The remainder of this article is mainly concerned with duties, annexed in a schedule, repealed by 34 and 35 Vict. c. 116.)

ARTICLE SEVENTH. That it be the seventh article of union, that the charge arising from the payment of interest, and the sinking fund for the reduction of the principal, of the debt incurred in either kingdom before the union, shall continue to be separately defrayed by Great Britain and Ireland respectively, except as herein after provided: That for the space of twenty years after the union shall take place the contribution of Great Britain and Ireland respectively towards the expenditure of the United Kingdom in each year shall be defrayed in the proportion of fifteen parts for Great Britain, and two parts for Ireland; and that . . .

(The remainder of the article, providing a complicated method of determining the proportion, the interest of which is mainly financial, is omitted, the student being referred to *The Final Report of Royal Commission on the Financial Relations of Great Britain and Ireland*, 1896, Parl. Pap. C. 8262.)

ARTICLE EIGHTH. That it be the eighth article of union, That all laws in force at the time of the union, and all courts of civil and ecclesiastical jurisdiction within the respective kingdoms, shall remain as now by law established within the same, subject only to such alterations and regulations from time to time as circumstances may appear to the parliament of the united kingdom to require; provided that all writs of error and appeals, depending at the time of the union or hereafter to be brought, and which might now be finally decided by the house of lords of either kingdom, shall, from and after the union, be finally decided by the house of lords of the united kingdom; and provided, That, from and after the union, there shall remain in Ireland an instance court of admiralty, for the determination of causes, civil and maritime only, and that the appeal from sentences of the said court shall be to his Majesty's delegates in his court of chancery in that part of the united kingdom called Ireland ; and that all laws at present in force in either kingdom, which shall be contrary to any of the provisions which may be enacted by any act for carrying these articles into effect, be from and after the union repealed.

And whereas the said articles having, by address of the respective houses of parliament in Great Britain and Ireland, been humbly laid before his Majesty, his Majesty has been graciously pleased to approve the same; and to recommend it to his two houses of parliament in Great Britain and Ireland to consider of such measures as may be necessary for giving effect to the said articles : in order, therefore, to give full effect and validity to the same, be it enacted . . . That the said foregoing recited articles, each and every one of them, according to the true import and tenor thereof, be ratified, confirmed and approved, and be and they are hereby declared to be the articles of the union of Great Britain and Ireland, and the same shall be in force and have effect for ever, from the first day of January which shall be in the year of our Lord one thousand eight hundred and one ; provided that before that period an act shall have been passed by the parliament of Ireland, for carrying into effect, in the like manner, the said foregoing recited articles.

.   .   .   .

(II. recites and makes part of the Act an Act of the Irish Parliament, regulating in great detail the mode by which the representatives of Ireland in the Parliament of the United Kingdom are to be to summoned.)

III. And be it enacted, That the great seal of Ireland may, if his Majesty shall so think fit, after the union, be used in like manner as before the union, except where it is otherwise provided by the foregoing articles, within that part of the united kingdom called Ireland ; and that his Majesty may, so long as he shall think fit, continue the privy council of Ireland to be his privy council for that part of the united kingdom called Ireland.

(See *May*, C.H.E. iii. ch. xvi.; *Lecky*, H.E. viii. (*passim*); *Anson*, L.C. ii. 221 ; *Porritt*, U.H.C. ii. pt. vi.)

XLI

SUSPENSION OF THE HABEAS CORPUS
43 Geo. III. Cap. 117, 1803.

An Act for the suppression of rebellion in Ireland, and for the protection of the persons and property of his Majesty's faithful subjects there, to continue in force until six weeks after the commencement of the next session of parliament.

Whereas a treasonable and rebellious spirit of insurrection now unfortunately exists in Ireland, and hath broken out into acts of open murder and rebellion, and persons who may be guilty of acts of cruelty and outrage in furtherance and immediate prosecution of such insurrection and rebellion, and who may be taken by his Majesty's forces to be employed for the suppression of the same, may seek to avail themselves of the ordinary course of the common law to evade the punishment of such crimes committed by them, whereby it has become necessary for parliament to interpose ; be it therefore enacted . . . That from and after the passing of this act, it shall and may be lawful to and for the Lord Lieutenant, or other Chief Governor or Governors of Ireland, from time to time during the continuance of the said rebellion, whether the ordinary courts of justice shall or shall not be at such time be open, to issue his or their orders to all officers commanding his Majesty's forces in Ireland, and to all others whom he or they shall think fit to authorize in that behalf, to take the most vigorous and effectual measures for suppressing the said insurrection and rebellion in any part of Ireland, which shall appear to be necessary for the public safety, and for the safety and protection of the persons and properties of his Majesty's peaceable and loyal subjects, and to punish all persons acting, aiding, or in any manner assisting in the said rebellion, or maliciously attacking or injuring the persons or properties of his Majesty's loyal subjects, in furtherance of the same, according to martial law, either by death, or otherwise, as to them shall seem expedient for the punishment and suppression of all rebels in their several districts, and to arrest and detain in custody all persons engaged in such rebellion, or suspected thereof ; and to cause all persons so arrested and detained in custody to be brought to trial in a summary way by courts martial, to be assembled under such authority as the said Lord Lieutenant, or other Chief Governor or Governors shall from time to time direct, and to consist of commissioned officers of the line, fencible or militia regiments, or yeomanry corps, not less in number than seven, nor more than thirteen, for all offences committed in furtherance of the said insurrection and rebellion, whether such persons shall have been taken in open arms against his Majesty, or shall have been otherwise concerned in the said rebellion, or in aiding, or any manner assisting the same, and to execute the sentences of all such courts martial, whether of death or otherwise, and to do all other acts necessary for such several purposes, provided that no sentence of death shall be given against any offender by such court martial, unless the judgement shall pass by the concurrence of two thirds at least of the officers present.

II. And be it enacted, That no act which shall be done in pursuance of any order which shall be so issued as aforesaid shall be questioned in his Majesty's court of King's-bench in Ireland, or in any other court of the common law in any part of the United Kingdom: And in order to prevent any doubt which might arise, whether any act alleged to have been done in conformity to any orders so to be issued as aforesaid, was so done, it shall and may be lawful to and for the said Lord Lieutenant, or other Chief Governor or Governors, to declare such acts to have been done in conformity to such orders, and such declaration signified by any writing under the hand of such Lord Lieutenant, or other Chief Governor or Governors, shall be a sufficient discharge and indemnity to all persons concerned in any such acts, and shall, in all cases, be conclusive evidence that such acts were done in conformity to such orders.

(III. Officers and soldiers for acts so done shall be responsible to courts-martial only. IV. A sufficient return to a writ of Habeas Corpus that the party is detained by warrant of a person authorised by the lord lieutenant.)

V. Provided always, and be it declared and enacted, That nothing in this act contained shall be construed to take away, abridge, or diminish the acknowledged prerogative of his Majesty, for the public safety, to resort to the exercise of Martial Law against open enemies or traitors, or any powers by law vested in the said Lord Lieutenant or Chief Governor or Governors of Ireland, with or without the advice of his Majesty's Privy Council, or of any other person or persons whatsoever, to suppress treason or rebellion, and to do any act warranted by law for that purpose, in the same manner as if this act had never been made, or in any manner to call in question any acts heretofore done for the like purposes.

(VI. The time-limit of the Act made repealable or alterable in the present session.)

(*Dicey*, L.C. *passim*.)

XLII

THE SLAVE TRADE
47 Geo. III. Sess. 1, Cap. 36, 1807.[1]

An act for the abolition of the slave trade.

Whereas the two houses of parliament did, by their resolutions[2] of
the tenth and twenty-fourth days of June one thousand eight hundred and six, severally resolve, upon certain grounds therein mentioned, that they would, with all practicable expedition, take effectual
measures for the abolition of the African slave trade, . . . And
whereas it is fit upon all and each of the grounds mentioned in the
said resolutions, that the same should be forthwith abolished and
prohibited, and declared to be unlawful ; be it therefore enacted . . .
That from and after the first day of May one thousand eight hundred
and seven the African slave trade and all manner of dealing and
trading in the purchase, sale, barter, or transfer of slaves, or of
persons intended to be sold, or transferred, used, or dealt with as
slaves, practised or carried on in, at, to or from any part of the coast or
countries of Africa, shall be, and the same is hereby utterly abolished,
prohibited, and declared to be unlawful : And also that all manner
of dealing, either by way of purchase, sale, barter, or transfer, or
by means of any other contract or agreement whatever, relating to
any slaves, or to any persons intended to be used or dealt with as
slaves, for the purpose of such slaves or persons being removed or
transported either immediately or by transhipment at sea or otherwise, directly or indirectly from Africa, or from any island, country,
territory, or place whatever, in the West Indies, or in any other part
of America, not being in the dominion, possession, or occupation of
his Majesty, to any other island, country, territory or place whatever,
is hereby in like manner utterly abolished, prohibited, and declared
to be unlawful ; and if any of his Majesty's subjects, or any person or
persons resident within this United Kingdom, or any of the islands,
dominions, or territories thereto belonging, or in his Majesty's occupation or possession, shall from and after the day aforesaid, by him
or themselves, or by his or their factors or agents or otherwise how-
soever, deal or trade in, purchase, sell, barter, or transfer, or contract
or agree for the dealing or trading in, purchasing, selling, bartering,

---

[1] Repealed by 24 and 25 Vict. cap. 101 ; Stat. Law Revis. Act, 1861.
[2] See p. 170.

or transferring of any slave or slaves, or any person or persons intended to be sold, transferred, used or dealt with as a slave or slaves contrary to the prohibitions of this act, he or they so offending shall forfeit and pay for every such offence the sum of one hundred pounds of lawful money of Great Britain for each and every slave so purchased, sold, bartered, or transferred. . . .

II. . . . That from and after the said first day of May one thousand eight hundred and seven, it shall be unlawful for any of his Majesty's subjects, or any person or persons resident within this United Kingdom, or any of the islands, colonies, dominions, or territories thereto belonging, or in his Majesty's possession or occupation, to fit out, man, or navigate, or to procure to be fitted out . . . any ship or vessel for the purpose of assisting in, or being employed in the carrying on of the African slave trade, or in any other the dealing, trading, or concerns hereby prohibited and declared to be unlawful, and every ship or vessel which shall, from and after the day aforesaid, be fitted out, . . . for any of the purposes aforesaid, and by this act prohibited, together with all her boats, guns, tackle, apparel, and furniture, shall become forfeited, and may and shall be seized and prosecuted as herein-after is mentioned and provided.

III. . . . That from and after the said first day of May one thousand eight hundred and seven, it shall be unlawful for any of his Majesty's subjects, or any person or persons resident in this United Kingdom, or in any of the colonies, territories, or dominions thereunto belonging, or in his Majesty's possession or occupation, to carry away or remove, or knowingly and wilfully to procure, aid, or assist in the carrying away or removing, as slaves, or for the purpose of being sold, transferred, used, or dealt with as slaves, any of the subjects or inhabitants of Africa, or of any island, country, territory, or place in the West Indies or any other part of America whatsoever, not being in the dominion, possession, or occupation of his Majesty, either immediately or by transhipment at sea or otherwise, directly or indirectly from Africa, or from any such island, country, territory or place as aforesaid, to any other island, country, territory or place whatever, and that it shall also be unlawful for any of his Majesty's subjects, or any persons resident in this United Kingdom, or in any of the colonies, territories, or dominions thereunto belonging, or in his Majesty's possession or occupation, knowingly and willingly to receive, detain or confine on board, . . . any such subject or inhabitant as aforesaid, for the purpose of his or her being so carried away . . . or of his or her being sold, transferred, used, or dealt with as a slave, in any place or country whatsoever; and if any subject or inhabitant, . . . or of any island, country, territory or place in the West Indies, or America, not being in the dominion, possession, or occupation of his Majesty, shall from and after the day aforesaid, be so unlawfully carried away or removed, detained, confined, transhipped, or received on board of any ship or vessel belonging in the whole or in part to, or employed by any subject of his Majesty, or person residing in his Majesty's dominions or colonies, . . . contrary to the force and effect, true intent and meaning of the prohibitions in this act contained, every such ship or vessel, . . . together with all her boats, guns, tackle, apparel, and furniture, shall be forfeited, and all property or pretended property in any slaves or natives of Africa so unlawfully carried away or removed, . . . shall also be forfeited, and the same respectively shall and may be seized and prosecuted as hereinafter is mentioned and provided; and every subject of his Majesty, . . . who shall, as owner, part owner, freighter or shipper, factor or agent, captain, mate, supercargo, or surgeon, so unlawfully carry away, or remove, detain, confine, tranship, or receive on board, or be aiding or assisting in the carrying away, . . . for any of the unlawful purposes aforesaid, any such subject or inhabitant of Africa, or of any island, country, territory, or place, not being in the dominion, possession, or occupation of his Majesty, shall forfeit and pay for each and every slave or person so unlawfully carried away, . . . the sum of one hundred pounds. . . .

IV. . . . That if any subject or inhabitant, subjects or inhabitants of Africa, or of any island, country, territory, or place, in the West Indies or America, not being in the dominion, . . . of his Majesty, contrary to any of the prohibitions or provisions in this act contained, shall be imported or brought into any island, colony, plantation or territory, in the dominion, . . . of his Majesty, and there sold or disposed of as a slave or slaves, or placed, detained, or kept in a state of slavery, such subject . . . shall and may be seized and prosecuted, as forfeited to his Majesty. . . .

. . . .

(§§ V.–XIII. deal with insurance transactions, slaves taken as prizes of war, bounties for such captures, and the legal processes concerned.)

XIV. And be it further enacted, That all ships and vessels, slaves or natives of Africa, carried, conveyed, or dealt with as slaves, and all other goods and effects that shall or may become forfeited for any offence committed against this act, shall and may be seized by any officer of his Majesty's customs or excise, or by the commander or officers of any of his Majesty's ships or vessels of war, who . . . shall have the benefit of all the provisions . . . made for the protection of officers seizing and prosecuting for any offence against the said act or any other act of parliament relating to the trade and revenues of the British colonies or plantations in America.

XV. And be it further enacted, That all offences committed against this act may be inquired of, tried, determined, and dealt with as misdemeanours, as if the same had been respectively committed within the body of the county of Middlesex.

.   .   .   .

(§§ XVI.–XVIII. Power to make regulations for negroes after their apprenticeship, and to plead the general issue for things done in pursuance of the Act.)

(See *May*, C.H.E. ii. 35 *et seq.*; *T. F. Buxton*, The African Slave Trade.)

RESOLUTIONS

(*On which the foregoing Act was based*)

(1) [Moved by Mr. Secretary Fox]. That this House conceiving the African Slave Trade to be contrary to the principles of justice, humanity, and sound policy, will with all practicable expedition, proceed to take effectual measures for abolishing the said trade, in such manner, and at such period, as may be deemed advisable.

(2) [Moved by Mr. Wilberforce]. That an humble Address be presented to his Majesty, beseeching his Majesty to take such measures as in his wisdom he shall judge proper, for establishing by negotiation with foreign powers, a concert and agreement for abolishing the African Slave Trade : and for affording assistance mutually towards carrying into execution any regulations which may be adopted by any or all of the contracting parties for accomplishing their common purpose ; assuring his Majesty, that this house, feeling the justice and honour of the British nation to be deeply and peculiarly involved in the great object they have in view, will be ready, at all times, cheerfully to concur in giving effect to such measures as his Majesty may see fit to adopt for its attainment.

(Carried in House of Commons, June 10, 1806 ; in the House of Lords June 24, 1806. See the Journals for those dates and *Cobbett*, P.D. vi. 580–603 and 802–809.)

XLIII

THE REGENCY ACT
51 Geo. III. Cap. 1, 1811.

An act to provide for the administration of the royal authority, and for the care of his Majesty's royal person, during the continuance of his Majesty's illness; and for the resumption of the exercise of the royal authority by his Majesty.

Whereas by reason of the severe indisposition with which it hath pleased God to afflict the King's most excellent Majesty, the personal exercise of the royal authority by his Majesty is, for the present, so far interrupted, that it becomes necessary to make provision for assisting his Majesty in the administration and exercise of the royal authority, and also for the care of his royal person during the continuance of his Majesty's indisposition, and for the resumption of the exercise of the royal authority by his Majesty; Be it therefore enacted . . . That his royal Highness George Augustus Frederick, Prince of Wales shall have full power and authority, in the name and on the behalf of his Majesty, and under the style and title of "Regent of the United Kingdom of Great Britain and Ireland," to exercise and administer the royal power and authority to the crown of the United Kingdom of Great Britain and Ireland belonging, and to use, execute and perform all authorities, prerogatives, acts of government and administration of the same, which lawfully belong to the King of the said United Kingdom to use, execute and perform; subject to such limitations, exceptions, regulations and restrictions, as are hereinafter specified and contained; and all and every act and acts which shall be done by the said regent, in the name and on the behalf of his Majesty, by virtue and in pursuance of this act, and according to the powers and authorities hereby vested in him, shall have the same force and effect to all intents and purposes as the like acts would have if done by his Majesty himself, and shall to all intents and purposes be full and sufficient warrant to all persons acting under the authority thereof; and all persons shall yield obedience thereto, and carry the same into effect, in the same manner and for the same purposes as the same persons ought to yield obedience to and carry into effect the like acts done by his Majesty himself; any law, course of office, or other matter or thing to the contrary notwithstanding.

(II. lays down the form of signature of the Regent.)

III. And be it further enacted, That when his Majesty shal by the blessing of God be restored to such a state of health as to be capable of resuming the personal exercise of his royal authority and shall have declared his royal will and pleasure thereupon, a hereinafter provided, all and every the powers and authorities given by this act, for the exercise and administration of his royal powe and authority, . . . which belong to the King of the United King dom of Great Britain and Ireland to use, execute and perform, or fo the care of His Majesty's Royal Person, shall cease and determine and no act, matter, or thing, . . . shall, if done after such declara tion of his Majesty's royal will and pleasure, be thenceforth valid o effectual.

IV. Provided always, . . . That all persons holding any offices o places, or pensions during his Majesty's pleasure, at the time of sucl declaration, under any appointment or authority of the regent, or he Majesty, under the provisions of this act, shall continue to hold th same, and to use, exercise, and enjoy all the powers, authoritie privileges and emoluments thereof, notwithstanding such declaratio of the resumption of the royal authority by his Majesty, unless an until his Majesty shall declare his royal will and pleasure to the cor trary; and all orders, acts of government or administration of hi Majesty's royal authority, made, issued or done by the said regen before such declaration, shall be and remain in full force and effec until the same shall be countermanded by his Majesty.

V. Provided also, . . . That no acts of regal power . . . whic might lawfully be done or executed by the King's most exceller Majesty, personally exercising his royal authority, shall, during th continuance of the regency by this act established, be valid an effectual, unless done and executed in the name and on the behalf of his Majesty, by the authority of the said regent, according to th provisions of this act, and subject to the limitations, exception regulations and restrictions hereinafter contained.

. . . .

(VI. In what cases the acts of the Regent shall be valid.

VII. provides that the Regent on taking the oaths shall subscribe th Declaration 30 Cha. II. Stat. 2, and produce a certificate of having take the Sacrament.)

VIII. Provided always, . . . That until after the first day February one thousand eight hundred and twelve, if parliament sha be then assembled, . . . for six weeks . . . or if parliament shall l then assembled, but shall not have been so sitting for six weeks, the

until the expiration of six weeks after parliament shall have been so
assembled . . . or if parliament shall not then be assembled, then
until the expiration of six weeks after parliament shall have been
assembled . . . the regent shall not have or exercise any power or
authority to grant, in the name or on the behalf of his Majesty any
rank, title or dignity of the peerage, by letters patent, writ of
summons, or any other manner whatever, or to summon any person
to the house of lords by any title to which such person shall be the
heir apparent, or to determine the abeyance of any rank, title or
dignity of peerage, which now is or hereafter shall be in abeyance, in
favour of any of the coheirs thereof by writ of summons or otherwise.

IX. Provided also, . . . That the said regent shall not, until after
the said first day of February one thousand eight hundred and twelve,
or the expiration of such six weeks as aforesaid, have power or
authority to grant, in the name or on the behalf of his Majesty, any
office or employment whatever, in reversion, or to grant for any
longer term than during his Majesty's pleasure, any office, employment,
salary or pension whatever, except such offices and employments in
possession for the term of the natural life, or during the good behaviour of the grantee or grantees thereof respectively, as by law
must be so granted : provided always, that nothing herein contained
shall in any manner affect or extend to prevent or restrain the
granting of any pensions under the provisions of an act passed in the
thirty-ninth year of the reign of the present Majesty.[1] . . .

(The remainder of the clause cites 48 Geo. III. c. 145 ; 40 Geo. III.
(Ireland) c. 1.)

X. Provided also, . . . That nothing in this act contained, shall
in any manner affect or extend to prevent or restrain the granting of
any pensions under the provisions of an act passed in the forty-first
year of the reign of his present Majesty (*i.e.* 41 Geo. III. c. 96 ; 43
Geo. III. c. 160 ; 45 Geo. III. c. 72).

XI. And be it enacted, That nothing in this act contained shall
extend or be construed to extend to empower the said regent, in the
name and on the behalf of his Majesty, to give the royal assent to any
bill or bills in parliament, for repealing, changing, or in any respect
varying the order and course of succession to the crown of this realm,
as the same stands now established. . . .

(12 and 13 W. III. c. 2 (the Act of Settlement), 13 Cha. II. c. 4 (the Act
of Uniformity), and 5 Anne, c. 7 (Scotland) (securing the Presbyterian
Church in Scotland), are here cited.)

[1] 39 Geo. III. c. 110.

XII. Provided also, . . . That if his said Royal Highness, George Augustus Frederick Prince of Wales shall not continue to be resident in the United Kingdom of Great Britain and Ireland, or shall at any time marry a papist, then and in either of such cases, all the powers and authorities vested in his said Royal Highness by this act, shall cease and determine.

XIII. . . . Be it therefore enacted, That the care of his Majesty's royal person, and the disposing, ordering and managing of all matters and things relating thereto, shall be, and the same are hereby vested in the Queen's most excellent Majesty, during the continuance of his Majesty's indisposition. . . .

(The remainder of the article provides in detail for the Household of George III.)

.   .   .   .

(XIV., XV. provide the Queen with a Council.)

XVI. And be it further enacted, That such and every member of her Majesty's council shall, within the space of five days after his appointment by virtue of this act, or by virtue of her Majesty's nomination and appointment in manner aforesaid, take an oath before the Lord High Chancellor or Keeper of the Great Seal, or Commissioners for keeping the Great Seal of Great Britain, or the Lord President of his Majesty's Privy Council, or the Chief Justice of the Court of King's Bench, . . . or either of them, who are hereby . . . empowered to administer the same, . . . and the person administering such oath, shall give to the member of her Majesty's Council taking the same, a certificate of the same having been so taken, signed with his hand; which certificate shall be forthwith transmitted to his Majesty's Privy Council, and entered in the books of the said Privy Council. (A form of oath is here prescribed.)

.   .   .   .   .   .

(XVII., XVIII., XIX. prescribe the duties of the Council as regard the King's health and his recovery.

XX. deals with the summoning of the Privy Council should the King recover.)

XXI. And . . . That if his Majesty, by the advice of six or more of such Privy Council so assembled, shall signify his royal pleasure to resume the personal exercise of his royal authority, and to issue a proclamation declaring the same, such proclamation shall be issued accordingly, countersigned by the said six or more of the said Privy Council, and all the powers and authorities given by this act shall from thenceforth cease and determine, and the personal

exercise of the royal authority by his Majesty shall be and be
deemed to be resumed by his Majesty, and shall be exercised by his
Majesty, to all intents and purposes, as if this act had never been
made.

XXII. And . . . That if his Royal Highness George Augustus
Frederick Prince of Wales shall depart this life during the continuance of the regency by this act established, or cease to be regent
under any of the provisions thereof, the Lords of his Majesty's most
honorable Privy Council shall forthwith cause a proclamation to be
issued, in his Majesty's name, under the Great Seal of the United
Kingdom of Great Britain and Ireland, declaring the same : And if
her Majesty the Queen shall depart this life during the time that the
care of his Majesty's royal person shall be committed to her Majesty
. . the regent shall forthwith order and direct a proclamation,
under the Great Seal of the United Kingdom of Great Britain and
Ireland, to be issued and published, declaring the same : And in case
the parliament in being at the time of the issuing of any proclamation declaring the death of the regent or of her Majesty, or at the
time of the issuing of any proclamation for the resumption of the
personal exercise of the royal authority by his Majesty, shall then
be separated, by any adjournment or prorogation, such parliament
shall forthwith meet and sit.

.   .   .   .

(Articles XXIII.–XXX. (the end) deal with the dissolution of Parliament ; the death of the Queen ; the issue of money from the Civil List
to the Queen and Royal Family ; the Keeper of the Queen's Privy Purse ;
the care of the King's estates ; and with authorising the Regent to dispose
of Droits of the Crown and Admiralty.)

(A similar Bill to the above Act was introduced in 1788 on the occasion
of the first serious illness of George III., but it did not become law, as
the King recovered before, "by a fiction grotesque and dangerous," the
royal consent by Commission had been given. On the important constitutional issues involved in the whole Regency question see *Lecky*, H.E.
379–451 ; *Parlt. Hist.* xxvii. ; *Cobbett*, P.D. xviii. ; *Anson*, L. and C. ii.
-84 ; *Rogers*, P.L. ii. 226–231, 433–443 ; *May*, C.H.E. i. 168–223.)

RESOLUTIONS OF PARLIAMENT

(*On which the above Act was founded.*)

Resolved, 1, That it is the opinion of this House, that his
Majesty is prevented by his present Indisposition, from coming to
his Parliament, and from attending to public business ; and that the
personal exercise of the royal authority is thereby suspended.

2, That it is the opinion of this House, that it is the right and the duty of the Lords spiritual and temporal, and Commons of Great Britain and Ireland, now assembled, and lawfully, fully, and freely, representing all the estates of the people of this realm, to provide the means of supplying the defect of the personal exercise of the royal authority arising from his Majesty's said Indisposition, in such manner as the exigency of the case may appear to them to require.

3, That it is the opinion of this House, That for this purpose, and for maintaining entire the constitutional authority of the King, it is necessary that the said Lords Spiritual and Temporal, and commons of the United Kingdom of Great Britain and Ireland, should determine on the means whereby the Royal Assent may be given in Parliament to such Bill as may be passed by the two Houses of Parliament, respecting the exercise of the powers and authorities of the Crown, in the name and on the behalf of the King, during the continuance of his Majesty's present Indisposition.

(These resolutions, similar to those moved in 1788, were passed in both Houses of Parliament. To Resolution 3 Lord Holland moved the following amendment, which was rejected by 100 to 74.)

That his Royal Highness the Prince of Wales, being of mature age, be requested to take upon himself the exercise of the power and authorities of the Crown, in the name and on the behalf of the King, during the continuance of his Majesty's present Indisposition, and no longer. That an Address, founded on the Resolution be presented to his Royal Highness, requesting him to take upon himself the Government aforesaid, and that it be at the same time and in the same manner communicated to his Royal Highness the Prince of Wales, that it is further the opinion of this Committee that it will be expedient to abstain from the exercise of all such powers as the immediate exigencies of the state shall not call into action, until Parliament shall have passed a Bill or Bills for the future care of his Majesty's Royal Person during his Majesty present Indisposition, and the securing to his Majesty, whenever it shall please Divine Providence to restore his health, the Resumption of the Royal Authority.

THE DEBATE ON THE REGENCY IN 1788

Mr. Fox. What were they going to search for? Not precedent upon their journals, not parliamentary precedents, but precedents the history of England. He would be bold to say, nay they

knew, that the doing so would prove a loss of time, for there existed
no precedent whatever, that could bear upon the present case. The
circumstance to be provided for did not depend upon their deliberations as a house of parliament; it rested elsewhere. There was then
a person in the kingdom differing from any other person that any
existing precedents could refer to—an heir apparent of full age and
capacity to exercise the royal power. It behoved them, therefore, to
waste not a moment unnecessarily, but to proceed with all becoming
diligence to restore the sovereign power and the exercise of the royal
authority. . . .

In his firm opinion, his royal highness the Prince of Wales had as
clear, as express a right to assume the reins of government, and
exercise the power of sovereignty, during the continuance of the
illness and incapacity with which it had pleased God to afflict his
Majesty, as in the case of his Majesty's having undergone a natural
and perfect demise: and, as to this right, which he conceived the
Prince of Wales had, he was not himself to judge when he was
entitled to exercise it; but the two Houses of Parliament, as the
organs of the nation, were alone qualified to pronounce when the
Prince ought to take possession of, and exercise his right. He
thought it candid, entertaining this opinion, to come forward fairly,
and avow it at that instant; and therefore, under such an idea, he
conceived that as short a time as possible ought to intervene between
the Prince of Wales's assuming the sovereignty, and the present
moment. He justified the Prince's not making this his indubitable
claim himself, by imputing his desire of waving the open advance-
ment of it, to his having been bred in those principles which had
placed his illustrious House on the throne, and to his known reverence
and regard for those principles as the true fundamentals of our
glorious constitution, in the maintenance of which, his family had
flourished with so much prosperity and happiness, as sovereigns of
the British empire. Hence it was, that his Royal Highness chose
rather to wait the decision of Parliament, with a patient and due
deference to the constitution, than to urge a claim, that, he trusted,
a majority of that House, and of the people at large, admitted; and
which, he was persuaded, could not be reasonably disputed. But,
ought he to wait unnecessarily? Ought his Royal Highness to wait
while precedents were searched for, when it was known that none,
that bore upon the case which so nearly concerned him, existed.
Take it for granted, the House agreed to the motion, and proceeded
by their committee to search for precedents. What precedents did
the wording of the motion point to? It spoke in general and in-

N

definite language.   Possibly it might mean parliamentary precedents, referring to such contingencies as the present.   If that were its meaning, the words "parliamentary precedents" ought to have been expressed in it.   He should not oppose the motion, but he thought it his duty to say, that it was incumbent on the House to lose no time in restoring the third estate.   His Royal Highness, he was convinced, must exercise the royal prerogative during, and only during, his Majesty's illness. . . .

Mr. Pitt.   If a claim of right was intimated (even though not formally) on the part of the Prince of Wales, to assume the government, it became of the utmost consequence, to ascertain, from precedent and history, whether this claim was founded; which, if it was, precluded the House from the possibility of all deliberation on the subject.   In the meantime, he maintained, that it would appear, from every precedent and from every page of our history, that to assert such a right in the Prince of Wales, or anyone else, independent of the decision of the two Houses of Parliament, was little less than treason to the constitution of the country.   He did not mean then to enter into the discussion of that great and important point; because a fit occasion of discussing it would soon afford both the right hon. gentleman and himself an ample opportunity of stating their sentiments upon it.   In the meantime, he pledged himself to this assertion, that in the case of the interruption of the personal exercise of the royal authority, without any previous lawful provision having been made for carrying on the government, it belonged to the other branches of the legislature, on the part of the nation at large, the body they represented, to provide, according to their discretion, for the temporary exercise of the royal authority, in the name, and on the behalf of the sovereign, in such manner as they should think requisite; and that, unless by their decision, the Prince of Wales had no more right (speaking of strict right) to assume the government, than any other individual subject of the country.   What Parliament ought to determine on that subject, was a question of discretion.   However strong the arguments might be on that ground, in favour of the Prince of Wales, which he would not enter into at present, it did not affect the question of right; because, neither the whole, nor any part, of the royal authority could belong to him in the present circumstances, unless conferred by the Houses of Parliament.—As to the right hon. gentleman's repeated enforcement of the Prince of Wales's claim, he admitted that it was a claim entitled to most serious consideration; and thence, argued, that it was the more necessary to learn how the House had acted in cases of similar exigency, and what had been the opinion of Parliament on such occasions. He would not allow that no precedent analogous to an interruption of the personal exercise of the royal authority, could be found, although there might possibly not exist a precedent of an heir apparent in a state of majority, during such an occurrence, and in that case, he contended, that it devolved on the remaining branches of the legislature, on the part of the people of England, to exercise their discretion in providing a substitute. From the mode in which the right hon. gentleman had treated the subject, a new question presented itself, and that of greater magnitude even than the question which was originally before them, as matter of necessary deliberation. The question now was, the question of their own rights, and it was become a doubt, according to the right hon. gentleman's opinion, whether that House had, on this important occasion, a deliberative power. He wished, for the present, to wave the discussion of that momentous consideration; but, he declared that he would, at a fit opportunity, state his reasons for advising what step Parliament ought to take in the present critical situation of the country, contenting himself with giving his contradiction of the right hon. gentleman's bold assertion, and pledging himself to maintain the opposite ground against a doctrine so irreconcileable to the spirit and genius of the Constitution.

(*Parlt. Hist.* xxvii. pp. 706–710.)

THE PROTEST OF THE LORDS

(This protest tersely sums up the objections of the Dissentients both in 1788 and 1811.)

1st, Because we adhere to the ancient principle recognized and declared by the Act of the 13th of Charles II., that no act or ordinance, with the force and virtue of a law, can be made by either or both Houses of Parliament, without the King's assent, a principle standing as a bulwark to the people against the two Houses, as the two Houses are their security against the Crown.

2ndly, Because this principle is tacitly admitted by the third resolution, while it overthrows the practice by a simulated appearance of the Royal assent under a commission to pass Bills, a commission which would be inconsistent with the provisions of an Act of 33 Henry VIII., requiring that every commission shall be signed by his Majesty's hand.

In our present unhappy situation, that essential requisite being unattainable, we cannot condescend to give a sanction to a counterfeit representation of the Royal signature, and we dare not assume a power to dispense with the law which makes that signature essential to the validity of a commission to pass Bills.

3rdly, Because we conceive that the unquestionable rights of the people, so fallaciously represented as being upheld by these resolutions, are violently infringed by an unnecessary assumption on the part of the two Houses of powers beyond those which the nation has assigned them. Invariable practice, in all good times, and positive laws established by complete Parliaments, truly and constitutionally representing the nation, have defined these powers. And we cannot but regard with the utmost apprehension any proposal to overstep those boundaries, when the consequences of such usurpation is so fatally marked in the history of our country.

4thly, Because it was confessed in the debate, that the powers of this commission were not to be confined solely to the act of appointing a Regent; to what other purposes they may extend were not explained. State necessity, the avowed ground of the measure, may serve as the pretext for any diminution of the just prerogative of the Crown, or of the liberties of the people, that best suits the designs of ambition. Fatal experience had shown to our ancestors the boundless mischiefs of powers thus usurped under plausible appearances; and it is particularly the duty of the House of Peers to check the renewal of a practice to assume the name, without the substance of the Royal authority, by which this House was once annihilated, the monarchy overthrown, and the liberties of the people subdued.

5thly, Because these dangerous and alarming consequences of the measure adopted would have been obviated by the amendment rejected. It proposed to substitute a measure conformable to the practice of our ancestors at the glorious era of the Revolution. They seized not upon public necessity as a convenience for the usurpation of new powers, but proceeded in a plain and explicit form to the revival of the Royal authority with full efficacy, before they entered upon the exercise of their legislative functions. Pursuing a similar course, the amendment proposed the immediate nomination of the natural representative of the King, the heir apparent of the Crown, to whom alone it was universally admitted the eyes and hearts of all men were turned during the present unhappy conjuncture; that with a perfect and efficient legislature, such future provisions might be

enacted, as the preservation of the full and undiminished authority
of the Crown and the liberties of the people may require.

YORK	NORFOLK	SELKIRK	CHOLMONDELEY
CUMBERLAND	CASSILIS	CHEDWORTH	SCARBOROUGH
BEDFORD	RAWDON	FITZWILLIAM	CRAVEN
NORTHUMBERLAND	BREADALBANE	LOUGHBOROUGH	FOLEY
PONSONBY	CARDIFF	PORTLAND	PORCHESTER
CADOGAN	AUDLEY	PELHAM	HUNTINGDON
SUFFOLK AND	MALMESBURY	DEVONSHIRE	BOYLE
BERKSHIRE	HAY	WALPOLE	SOUTHAMPTON
SPENCER	CLIFTON	DERBY	LOVEL AND
CARLISLE	RODNEY	HEREFORD	HOLLAND
MAYNARD	KINNAIRD	BRISTOL	LOTHIAN
TOWNSHEND	PLYMOUTH	TEYNHAM	HERTFORD
			ABERGAVENNY
			HAMPDEN.

(L.J. xxxviii., December 29, 1788 ; *Rogers*, P.L. ii. 226.)

THE COMMISSION FOR GIVING THE ROYAL ASSENT TO THE REGENCY BILL

Resolved, "That it is expedient and necessary that Letters Patent
should pass under the Great Seal of The United Kingdom of Great
Britain and Ireland, of the tenor and in the form following :

George the Third, by the grace of God, of the United Kingdom of
Great Britain and Ireland, King, Defender of the Faith, to our right
trusty and right well beloved the Lords Spiritual and Temporal, and
to our trusty and well beloved the knights, citizens and burgesses, and
the commissioners for shires and burghs of the House of Commons,
in this present parliament assembled, greeting: . . . and whereas,
by our Letters Patent, bearing date at Westminster the 15th day of
January last past, We did give and grant unto (the Commissioners
named) . . . and any three of them, full power in our name to hold
our said Parliament, and to open and declare, and cause to be opened
and declared, the causes of holding the same, and to proceed upon
the said affairs in our said Parliament, and to do everything which,
for us, and by us, for the government of our said United Kingdom of
Great Britain and Ireland, and other our dominions thereunto belonging, should there be done : and whereas, in our said Parliament,
an Act hath been agreed and accorded on by you our loving subjects
. . . and endorsed by you, as hath been accustomed, the title and

name of which Act hereafter doth particularly ensue . . . and albeit the said Act . . . is not of force and effect in the law without our Royal Assent, given and put to the said Act : and for as much as, for divers causes and considerations, We cannot conveniently at this time be present in our Royal Person in the higher House of our said Parliament, being the place accustomed to give our Royal Assent to such Acts as have been agreed upon by our said subjects, the Lords and Commons, We have therefore caused these our Letters Patent to be made, and by the same do give and put our Royal Assent to the said Act, . . . and have fully agreed and assented to the said Act . . . from henceforth shall be of the same strength, force and effect, as if We had been personally present in the said higher House, and had openly and publicly, in the presence of you all, assented to the same : And we do by these presents declare and notify the same our Royal Assent, as well to you the Lords Spiritual and Temporal and Commons aforesaid, as to all others whom it may concern : Commanding also by these presents (the Commissioners named) . . . to declare and notify this our Royal Assent . . . and the clerk of our Parliaments to endorse the said Act with such terms and words in Our name as is requisite and hath been accustomed for the same, and also to enroll these our Letters Patent and the said Act in the Parliament Roll, and these our Letters Patent shall be to every of them a sufficient warrant in that behalf : And finally, We do declare and will, that, after this our Royal Assent given and declared by these presents and notified as aforesaid, then and immediately the said Act shall be taken, accepted and admitted a good, sufficient, and perfect Act of Parliament and law, to all intents, constructions, and purposes, and to be put in due execution accordingly, the continuance or dissolution of this our Parliament, or any other use, custom, thing or things, to the contrary thereof notwithstanding : . . . In witness whereof, We have caused these our Letters to be made Patent : Witness ourself at Westminster, the Fifth day of February, in the fifty-first year of our reign.

By the King himself, by and with the advice of the Lords Spiritual and Temporal . . . in Parliament assembled."

(Lords Journals, February 2, 1811.)

XLIV

PREROGATIVE OF PARDON
7 and 8 Geo. IV. Cap. 28, 1827.

An Act for further improving the Administration of Justice in Criminal Cases in England.

XIII. And it be it declared and enacted, That when the King's Majesty shall be pleased to extend His Royal mercy to any offenders convicted of any Felony punishable with Death or otherwise, and by Warrant under His Royal Sign Manual, countersigned by one of His principal Secretaries of State, shall grant to such offenders either a free or a conditional Pardon, the Discharge of such offenders out of Custody in the case of a free Pardon, and the Performance of the condition in the Case of a conditional Pardon, shall have the Effect of a Pardon under the Great Seal for such Offenders, as to the Felony for which such Pardon shall be so granted : Provided always, that no free Pardon, nor any such Discharge in Consequence thereof, nor any conditional Pardon, nor the Performance of the Condition thereof, in any of the Cases aforesaid, shall prevent or mitigate the Punishment to which the Offenders might otherwise be lawfully sentenced on a subsequent Conviction for any Felony committed after the granting of any such Pardon.

(By 27 Hen. VIII. c. 24, § i. the prerogative of pardon is vested solely in the Crown. All pardons passed under the Great Seal. By this Act a pardon may be granted by sign-manual warrant, countersigned by a Secretary of State ; but constructively this does not apply to treason, murder, or misdemeanour. See *Hawkins*, P.C. ii. c. 37 ; *Chitty*, Prerogative of the Crown.)

XLV

THE REPEAL OF THE TEST AND CORPORATION ACTS

9 Geo. IV. Cap. 17, 1828.[1]

An Act for repealing so much of several acts as imposes the necessity of receiving the sacrament of the Lord's Supper as a qualification for certain offices and employments.

Whereas an act[2] was passed in the thirteenth year of the reign of King Charles the Second, intituled An act for the well governing and regulating of corporations : and whereas another act[3] was passed in the twenty-fifth year of the reign of King Charles the Second, intituled An act for preventing dangers which may happen from popish recusants : And whereas another act[4] was passed in the sixteenth year of the reign of King George the Second, intituled An act to indemnify persons who have omitted to qualify themselves for offices and employments within the time limited by law, and for allowing further time for that purpose ; and also for amending so much of an Act[5] made in the twenty-fifth year of the reign of King Charles the Second, intituled, 'An act for preventing dangers which may happen from popish recusants' as relates to the time for receiving the Sacrament of the Lord's Supper now limited by the said act : and whereas it is expedient that so much of the said several acts of parliament as imposes the necessity of taking the said Sacrament of the Lord's Supper according to the rites or usage of the Church of England, for the purposes therein respectively mentioned, should be repealed : Be it therefore enacted . . . That so much and such parts of the said several acts passed in the thirteenth and twenty-fifth years of the reign of King Charles the Second, and of the said act[6] passed in the sixteenth year of the reign of King George the Second, as require the person or persons in the said acts respectively described to take or receive the Sacrament of the Lord's Supper according to the rites or usage of the Church of England, for the several purposes

---

[1] Repealed by 34 and 35 Vict. c. 48, 1871 ("The Promissory Oaths Act").
[2] 13 Cha. II. St. 2, c. 1.   [3] 25 Cha. II. c. 2.
[4] 16 Geo. II. c. 30.   [5] 25 Cha. II. c. 2.
[6] 16 Geo. II. c. 30.

therein expressed, or to deliver a certificate, or to make proof of the truth of such his or their receiving the said sacrament in manner aforesaid, or as impose upon any such person or persons any penalty, forfeiture, incapacity, or disability whatsoever for or by reason of any neglect or omission to take or receive the said Sacrament, within the respective periods and in the manner in the said acts respectively provided in that behalf, shall, from and immediately after the passing of this act, be and the same are hereby repealed.

II. And whereas the protestant episcopal Church of England and Ireland, and the doctrine, discipline, and government thereof, and the protestant presbyterian Church of Scotland, and the doctrine, discipline and government thereof, are by the laws of this realm severally established, permanently and inviolably : . . . Be it therefore enacted, That every person who shall hereafter be placed, elected, or chosen in or to any office of mayor, alderman, recorder, bailiff, town clerk, or common councilman, or in or to any office of magistracy, or place, trust, or employment relating to the government of any city, corporation, borough, or cinque port within England and Wales or the town of Berwick-upon-Tweed, shall within one calendar month next before or upon his admission into any of the aforesaid offices or trusts, make and subscribe the declaration following :

' I A. B. do solemnly and sincerely, in the presence of God, profess, testify, and declare, upon the true faith of a Christian, That I will never exercise any power, authority or influence I may possess by virtue of the office of   to injure or weaken the Protestant Church as it is by law established in England, or to disturb the said Church, or the bishops and clergy of the said Church, in the possession of any rights or privileges to which such Church, or the said bishops and clergy, are or may be by law entitled.'

III. And be it enacted, That the said declaration shall be made, as aforesaid, in the presence of such person or persons respectively, who, by the charters or usages of the said respective cities, corporations, boroughs, and cinque ports, ought to administer the oath for the due execution of the said offices or places respectively, and in default of such, in the presence of two justices of the peace of the respective counties, ridings, divisions, or franchises, wherein the said cities, corporations, boroughs, and cinque ports are ; which said declaration shall either be entered in a book, roll, or other record, to be kept for that purpose, or shall be filed amongst the records of the city, corporation, borough or cinque port.

IV. And be it enacted, That if any person placed, elected, or chosen into any of the aforesaid offices or places, shall omit or neglect to make and subscribe the said declaration in manner above mentioned, such placing, election, or choice shall be void. . . .

V. And be it further enacted, That every person who shall hereafter be admitted into any office or employment, or who shall accept from His Majesty, his heirs or successors, any patent, grant, or commission, and who by his admittance into such office or employment or place of trust, or by his acceptance of such patent, grant, or commission, or by the receipt of any pay, salary, fee, or wages by reason thereof, would, by the laws in force immediately before the passing of this act have been required to take the Sacrament of the Lord's Supper according to the rites or usage of the Church of England, shall, within six calendar months after his admission to such office, employment, or place of trust, or his acceptance of such patent, grant, or commission, make and subscribe the aforesaid declaration, or in default thereof his appointment to such office, employment or place of trust, and such patent, grant, or commission, shall be wholly void.

VI. And be it further enacted, That the aforesaid declaration shall be made and subscribed in His Majesty's High Court of Chancery, or in the Court of King's Bench, or at the Quarter Sessions of the county or place where the person so required to make the same shall reside ; and the court in which such declaration shall be so made and subscribed shall cause the same to be preserved among the records of the said court.

VII. Provided always, That no naval officer below the rank of rear admiral, and no military officer below the rank of major general in the army or colonel in the militia, shall be required to make or subscribe the said declaration, in respect of his naval or military commission ; and that no commissioner of customs, excise, stamps, or taxes, or any person holding any of the offices concerned in the collection, management, or receipt of the revenues which are subject to the said commissioners, or any of the officers concerned in the collection, management, or receipt of the revenues subject to the authority of the postmaster-general, shall be required to make or subscribe the said declaration, in respect of their said offices or appointments : Provided also, that nothing herein contained shall extend to require any naval or military officer, or other person as aforesaid, upon whom any office, place, commission, appointment, or promotion shall be conferred during his absence from England, or within three months previous to his departure from thence, to make and subscribe the said declaration until after his return to England, or within six months thereafter.

VIII. And be it further enacted, That all persons now in the actual possession of any office, command, place, trust, service, or employment, or in the receipt of any pay, salary, fee, or wages, in respect of or as a qualification for which, by virtue of or under any of the before-mentioned acts or any other act or acts, they respectively ought to have heretofore taken or ought hereafter to receive the said Sacrament of the Lord's Supper, shall be and are hereby confirmed in the possession and enjoyment of their said several offices, commands, places, trusts, services, employments, pay, salaries, fees, and wages respectively, notwithstanding their omission or neglect to take or receive the Sacrament of the Lord's Supper in manner aforesaid, and shall be and are hereby indemnified, freed, and discharged from all incapacities, disabilities, forfeitures, and penalties whatsoever, already incurred or which might hereafter be incurred in consequence of any such omission or neglect; and that no election of or act done or to be done by any such person or under his authority, and not yet avoided, shall be hereafter questioned or avoided by reason of any such omission or neglect; but that every such election and act shall be as good, valid, and effectual as if such person had duly received the Sacrament of the Lord's Supper in manner aforesaid.

IX. Provided nevertheless, That no act done in the execution of any of the corporate or other offices, places, trusts, or commissions aforesaid, by any such person omitting or neglecting as aforesaid, shall by reason thereof be void or voidable as to the rights of any other person not privy to such omission or neglect, or render such last-mentioned person liable to any action or indictment.

(*Walpole*, H.E. ii. 470 *et seq.*; *May*, C.H.E. iii. chs. xii.–xiv.)

XLVI

ROMAN CATHOLIC EMANCIPATION ACT
10 Geo. IV. Cap. 7, 1829.[1]

An Act for the relief of His Majesty's Roman Catholic subjects.

Whereas by various acts of parliament certain restraints and disabilities are imposed on the Roman Catholic subjects of His Majesty, to which other subjects of His Majesty are not liable : and whereas it is expedient that such restraints and disabilities shall be from henceforth discontinued : and whereas by various acts certain oaths and declarations, commonly called the declaration against transubstantiation, and the declaration against transubstantiation and the invocation of saints and the sacrifice of the mass, as practised in the Church of Rome, are or may be required to be taken, made, and subscribed by the subjects of His Majesty, as qualifications for sitting and voting in parliament, and for the enjoyment of certain offices, franchises, and civil rights: Be it enacted . . . That from and after the commencement of this act all such parts of the said acts as require the said declarations, . . . as a qualification for sitting and voting in parliament, or for the exercise or enjoyment of any office, franchise or civil right, be and the same are (save as hereinafter provided and excepted) hereby repealed.

II. And be it enacted, That from and after the commencement of this act it shall be lawful for any person professing the Roman Catholic religion, being a peer, or who shall after the commencement of this act be returned as a member of the House of Commons, to sit and vote in either house of parliament respectively, being in all other respects duly qualified to sit and vote therein, upon taking and subscribing the following oath, instead of the oaths of allegiance, supremacy, and abjuration.

' I A. B. do sincerely promise and swear, that I will be faithful and bear true allegiance to His Majesty King George the Fourth, and will defend him to the utmost of my power against all conspiracies and attempts whatever, which shall be made against his person, crown, or dignity; and I will do my utmost endeavour to disclose and make known to His Majesty, his heirs and successors, all treasons and

[1] Repealed in part by 34 and 35 Vict. c. 48 ; 36 and 37 Vict. c. 91 ; 53 and 54 Vict. c. 33.

traitorous conspiracies which may be formed against him or them : and I do faithfully promise to maintain, support, and defend, to the utmost of my power, the succession of the crown, which succession, by an act,[1] intituled An act for the further limitation of the crown, and better securing the rights and liberties of the subject, is and stands limited to the Princess Sophia, Electress of Hanover, and the heirs of her body, being protestants ; hereby utterly renouncing and abjuring any obedience unto any other person claiming or pretending a right to the crown of this realm : and I do further declare, that it is not an article of my faith, and that I do denounce, reject, and abjure the opinion, that princes excommunicated or deprived by the pope, or any other authority of the see of Rome, may be deposed or murdered by their subjects, or by any person whatsoever : and I do declare, that I do not believe that the pope of Rome, or any other foreign prince, prelate, person, state, or potentate, hath or ought to have any temporal or civil jurisdiction, power, superiority, or pre-eminence, directly or indirectly, within this realm. I do swear, that I will defend to the utmost of my power the settlement of property within this realm, as established by the laws : and I do hereby disclaim, disavow, and solemnly abjure, any intention to subvert the present church establishment, as settled by law within this realm : and I do solemnly swear, that I will never exercise any privilege to which I am or may become entitled, to disturb or weaken the protestant religion, or protestant government in the united kingdom : and I do solemnly, in the presence of God, profess, testify, and declare, that I do make this declaration, and every part thereof, in the plain and ordinary sense of the words of this oath, without any evasion, equivocation, or mental reservation whatever. So help me God.'

. . . .

(III. The name of the sovereign for the time being to be used in the above oath.)

IV. Provided always, . . . That no peer professing the Roman Catholic religion, and no person professing the Roman Catholic religion, who shall be returned a member of the House of Commons after the commencement of this act, shall be capable of sitting or voting in either house of parliament respectively, unless he shall first take or subscribe the oath hereinbefore appointed ; . . . and that any such person professing the Roman Catholic religion, who shall sit or vote in either house of parliament, without having first taken or subscribed, in the manner aforesaid, the oath in this act, appointed and set forth, shall be subject to the same penalties, forfeitures, and

[1] 12 and 13 W. III. c. 2.

disabilities, and the offence of so sitting and voting shall be followed and attended by and with the same consequences, as are by law enacted and provided in the case of persons sitting or voting in either house of parliament respectively, without the taking, making, and subscribing the oaths and the declaration now required by law.

V. And be it further enacted, That it shall be lawful for persons professing the Roman Catholic religion to vote at elections of members to serve in parliament for England and for Ireland, and also to vote at the elections of representative peers of Scotland and of Ireland, and to be elected such representative peers, being in all other respects duly qualified, upon taking and subscribing the oath hereinbefore appointed and set forth, . . . and instead also of such other oath or oaths as are now by law required to be taken by any of His Majesty's subjects professing the Roman Catholic religion, and upon taking also such other oath or oaths as may now be lawfully tendered to any person offering to vote at such elections.

.　　.　　.　　.　　.　　.　　.　　.　　.

(VI. Oath to be administered as former oaths. VII. Persons administering the oath at elections to take an oath to administer.)

VIII. And whereas in an Act [1] of the parliament of Scotland made in the eighth and ninth session of the first parliament of King William the Third, intituled an act for the preventing the growth of popery, a certain declaration or formula is therein contained, which it is expedient should no longer be required to be taken and subscribed: Be it therefore enacted, That such parts of any acts as authorize the said declaration or formula to be tendered, . . . shall be and the same are hereby repealed, except as to such offices, places, and rights as are hereinafter excepted; and that from and after the commencement of this act, it shall be lawful for persons professing the Roman Catholic religion to elect and be elected members to serve in parliament for Scotland, and to be enrolled as freeholders in any shire or stewartry of Scotland, and to be chosen commissioners or delegates for choosing burgesses to serve in parliament . . . such persons always taking and subscribing the oath hereinbefore appointed and set forth. . . .

IX. And be it further enacted, That no person in Holy Orders in the Church of Rome shall be capable of being elected to serve in parliament as a member of the House of Commons; and if any such person shall be elected to serve in parliament as aforesaid, such election shall be void; and if any person, being elected to serve

[1] 8 and 9 W. III. c. 3 (Scotland).

in parliament as a member of the House of Commons, shall, after his election, take or receive Holy Orders in the Church of Rome, the seat of such person shall immediately become void; and if any person shall, in any of the cases aforesaid, presume to sit or vote as a member of the House of Commons, he shall be subject to the same penalties, forfeitures, and disabilities as are enacted by an act passed in the forty-first year of the reign of King George the Third, intituled An act to remove doubts respecting the eligibility of persons in Holy Orders to sit in the House of Commons. . . .

X. And be it enacted, That it shall be lawful for any of his Majesty's subjects professing the Roman Catholic religion to hold, exercise, and enjoy all civil and military offices and places of trust or profit under His Majesty, his heirs or successors, and to exercise any other franchise or civil right, except as hereinafter excepted, upon taking and subscribing at the times and in the manner hereinafter mentioned, the oath hereinbefore appointed and set forth. . . .

XI. Provided always, . . . That nothing herein contained shall be construed to exempt any person professing the Roman Catholic religion from the necessity of taking any oath or oaths, or making any declaration, not hereinbefore mentioned, which are or may be by law required to be taken or subscribed by any person on his admission into any such office or place of trust or profit as aforesaid.

XII. Provided also, . . . That nothing herein contained shall extend or be construed to extend to enable any person or persons professing the Roman Catholic religion to hold or exercise the office of guardians and justices of the United Kingdom, or of Regent of the United Kingdom, under whatever name, style, or title such office may be constituted; nor to enable any person, otherwise than as he now by law enabled, to hold and enjoy the office of Lord High Chancellor, Lord Keeper or Lord Commissioner of the Great Seal of Great Britain or Ireland; or the office of Lord Lieutenant, or Lord Deputy, or other chief governor or governors of Ireland; or His Majesty's High Commissioner to the general assembly of the Church of Scotland.

XIII. Provided also, . . . That nothing herein contained shall be construed to affect or alter any of the provisions of an act [1] passed in the seventh year of His present Majesty's reign, intituled An act to consolidate and amend the laws which regulate the levy and application of church rates and parish cesses, and the election of churchwardens; and the maintenance of parish clerks, in Ireland. [2]

[1] 7 Geo. IV. c. 72.   [2] This section has become obsolete.

XIV. And be it enacted, That it shall be lawful for any of His Majesty's subjects professing the Roman Catholic religion to be a member of any lay body corporate, and to hold any civil office or place of trust or profit therein, and to do any corporate act, or vote in any corporate election or other proceeding, upon taking or subscribing the oath hereby appointed and set forth. . . .

XV. Provided nevertheless, . . . That nothing herein contained shall extend to authorize or empower any of His Majesty's subjects professing the Roman Catholic religion, and being a member of any lay body corporate, to give any vote at, or in any manner to join in the election, presentation, or appointment of any persons to any ecclesiastical benefice whatsoever, or any office or place belonging to or connected with the United Church of England and Ireland, or the Church of Scotland, being in the gift, patronage, or disposal of such lay corporate body.

XVI. Provided also, . . . That nothing in this act contained shall be construed to enable any persons, otherwise than as they are now by law enabled, to hold, enjoy, or exercise any office, place, or dignity of, in or belonging to the United Church of England and Ireland, or the Church of Scotland, or any place or office whatever of, in or belonging to any of the ecclesiastical courts of judicature of England and Ireland respectively, or any court of appeal from or review of the sentences of such courts, or of, in, or belonging to the commissary court of Edinburgh, or of, in, or belonging to any cathedral or collegiate or ecclesiastical establishment or foundation; or any office or place whatever, of, in or belonging to any of the universities of this realm; or any office or place whatever, and by whatever name the same may be called, of, in, or belonging to any of the colleges or halls of the said universities, or the colleges of Eton, Westminster, or Winchester or any college or school within this realm; or to repeal, abrogate, or in any manner interfere with any local statute, ordinance, or rule, which is or shall be established by a competent authority within any University, college, hall, or school, by which Roman Catholics shall be prevented from being admitted thereto, or from residing, or taking degrees therein : Provided also, that nothing herein contained shall extend or be construed to extend to enable any person, otherwise than he is now by law enabled, to exercise any right of presentation to any ecclesiastical benefice whatsoever; or to repeal, vary, or alter in any manner the law now in force in respect to the right of presentation any ecclesiastical benefice.

XVII. Provided always, . . . That where any right of presentation to any ecclesiastical benefice shall belong to any office in the gift or appointment of His Majesty, his heirs or successors, and such office shall be held by a person professing the Roman Catholic religion, the right of presentation shall devolve upon and be exercised by the Archbishop of Canterbury for the time being.

XVIII. And be it enacted, That it shall not be lawful for any person professing the Roman Catholic religion, directly or indirectly, to advise His Majesty, his heirs or successors, or any person or persons holding or exercising the office of guardians of the United Kingdom, or of Regent of the United Kingdom, under whatever name, style, or title such office may be constituted, or the Lord Lieutenant, or Lord Deputy, or other chief governor or governors of Ireland, touching or concerning the appointment to or disposal of any office or preferment in the United Church of England and Ireland, or in the Church of Scotland; and if any person shall offend in the premises, he shall, being thereof convicted by due course of law, be deemed guilty of a high misdemeanour, and disabled for ever from holding any office, civil or military, under the crown.

XIX. And be it enacted, That every person professing the Roman Catholic religion, who shall after the commencement of this act be placed, elected, or chosen in or to the office of mayor, provost, alderman, recorder, bailiff, town clerk, magistrate, councillor, or common councilman, or in or to any office of magistracy or place of trust or employment relating to the government of any city, corporation, borough, burgh, or district within the United Kingdom of Great Britain and Ireland, shall, within one calendar month next before or upon his admission into any of the same respectively, take and subscribe the oath herein-before appointed and set forth . . . which said oath shall either be entered in a book, roll, or other record to be kept for that purpose, or shall be filed amongst the records of the city, corporation, burgh, borough, or district.

XX. And be it enacted, That every person professing the Roman Catholic religion, who shall after the commencement of this act be appointed to any office or place of trust or profit under His Majesty, his heirs or successors, shall within three calendar months next before such appointment, or otherwise shall, before he presumes to exercise or enjoy or in any manner to act in such office or place, take and subscribe the oath herein-before appointed and set forth . . . and the proper officer of the court in which such oath shall be so taken and subscribed shall cause the same to be preserved

o

among the records of the court; and such officer shall make, sign, and deliver a certificate of such oath having been duly taken and subscribed, as often as the same shall be demanded of him, upon payment of two shillings and sixpence for the same; and such certificate shall be sufficient evidence of the person therein named having duly taken and subscribed such oath.

XXI. And be it enacted, That if any person professing the Roman Catholic religion shall enter upon the exercise or enjoyment of any office or place of trust or profit under His Majesty, or any other office of franchise, not having in the manner or at the times aforesaid taken and subscribed the oath herein-before appointed and set forth, then and in every such case such person shall forfeit to His Majesty the sum of two hundred pounds; and the appointment of such person to the office, place, or franchise so by him held shall become altogether void, and the office, place or franchise shall be deemed and taken to be vacant to all intents and purposes whatsoever.

XXII. Provided always, That for and notwithstanding any thing in this act contained, the oath herein-before appointed and set forth shall be taken by the officers in His Majesty's land and sea service, professing the Roman Catholic religion, at the same times and in the same manner as the oaths and declarations now required by law are directed to be taken, and not otherwise.

XXIII. And be it further enacted, That from and after the passing of this act, no oath or oaths shall be tendered to or required to be taken by His Majesty's subjects professing the Roman Catholic religion, for enabling them to hold or enjoy any real or personal property, other than such as may by law be tendered to and required to be taken by His Majesty's other subjects; and that the oath herein appointed and set forth, being taken and subscribed in any of the courts, or before any of the persons above-mentioned shall be of the same force and effect, to all intents and purposes, as, and shall stand in the place of, all oaths and declarations required or prescribed by any law now in force for the relief of his Majesty's Roman Catholic subjects from any disabilities, incapacities, or penalties. . .

XXIV. And whereas the protestant episcopal Church of England and Ireland, and the doctrine, discipline, and government thereof and likewise the protestant presbyterian Church of Scotland, and the doctrine, discipline and government thereof, are by the respective acts of union of England and Scotland, and of Great Britain and Ireland, established permanently and inviolably: and whereas the right and title of archbishops to their respective provinces of bishops to their sees, and of deans to their deaneries, as well in England as in Ireland, have been settled and established by law; Be it therefore enacted, That if any person, after the commencement of this act, other than the person thereunto authorized, by law, shall assume or use the name, style, or title of archbishop of any province, bishop of any bishoprick, or dean of any deanery, in England or Ireland, he shall for every such offence forfeit and pay the sum of one hundred pounds.

(XXV. Judicial or other officers not to attend with insignia of office at any place of worship other than Established Church.

XXVI. Penalty on Roman Catholics officiating except in their usual places of worship.

XXVII. Not to repeal 5 Geo. IV. c. 25.)

XXVIII. And ... Be it therefore enacted, That every Jesuit, and every member of any other religious order, community, or society of the Church of Rome, bound by monastic or religious vows, who at the time of the commencement of this act shall be within the United Kingdom, shall, within six calendar months after the commencement of this act, deliver to the clerk of the peace of the county or place where such person shall reside, or to his deputy, a notice or statement, in the form and containing the particulars required to be set forth in the schedule to this act annexed; which notice or statement such clerk of the peace, or his deputy, shall preserve and register amongst the records of such county or place, without any fee, and shall forthwith transmit a copy of such notice or statement to the chief secretary of the Lord Lieutenant, or other chief governor or governors of Ireland, if such person shall reside in Ireland, or if in Great Britain, to one of His Majesty's principal Secretaries of State; and in case any person shall offend in the premises, he shall forfeit and pay to His Majesty, for every calendar month during which he shall remain in the United Kingdom without having delivered such notice or statement, as is herein-before required, the sum of fifty pounds.

XXIX. And be it further enacted, that if any Jesuit, or member of any such religious order, community, or society, as aforesaid, shall, after the commencement of this act, come into this realm, he shall be deemed and taken to be guilty of a misdemeanour, and being thereof lawfully convicted, shall be sentenced and ordered to be banished from the United Kingdom for the term of his natural life.

(XXX. Natural-born subjects being Jesuits may return into the kingdom and be registered.)

XXXI. Provided also, . . . That, notwithstanding any thing herein-before contained, it shall be lawful for any one of His Majesty's principal Secretaries of State, being a protestant, by a licence in writing, signed by him, to grant permission to any Jesuit, or member of any such religious order, community, or society as aforesaid, to come into the United Kingdom, and to remain therein for such period as the said Secretary of State shall think proper, not exceeding in any case the space of six calendar months; and it shall also be lawful for any of His Majesty's principal Secretaries of State to revoke any licence so granted before the expiration of the time mentioned therein, if he shall think so fit. . . .

XXXII. And be it further enacted, That there shall annually be laid before both houses of parliament an account of all such licences as shall have been granted for the purpose herein-before mentioned within the twelve months then next preceding.

XXXIII. And be it further enacted, That in case any Jesuit, or member of any such religious order, community, or society as afore-said, shall, after the commencement of this act, within any part of the United Kingdom, admit any person to become a regular ecclesi-astic, or brother or member of any such religious order, community, or society, or be aiding or consenting thereto, or shall administer or cause to be administered, . . . any oath, vow, or engagement purporting or intending to bind the person taking the same to the rules ordinances, or ceremonies of such religious order, community, or society, every person offending in the premises in England or Ireland shall be deemed guilty of a misdemeanour, and in Scotland shall be punished by fine and imprisonment.

XXXIV. And be it further enacted, That in case any person shall after the commencement of this act, within any part of this United Kingdom, be admitted or become a Jesuit, or brother or member of any such religious order, community, or society aforesaid, such person shall be deemed and taken to be guilty of a misdemeanour, and being thereof lawfully convicted shall be sentenced and ordered to be banished from the United Kingdom for the term of his natural life

.   .   .   .

(XXXV. The party offending may be banished by the King; and XXXVI., if at large after three months, may be transported for life.)

XXXVII. Provided always, and be it enacted, That nothing herein contained shall extend or be construed to extend in any man-ner to affect any religious order, community, or establishment con-sisting of females bound by religious or monastic vows.

.   .   .   .

(XXXVIII. As to how penalties may be recovered. XXXIX. As to alterations in the present session. XL. Act to take effect ten days after it has become law.)

(*May*, C.H.E. ii. 192, iii. 162 *et seq.; Rogers*, P.L. iii. 47–63 ; *Walpole*, H.E. ii. ch. viii. ; *Lecky*, H.E. viii. 501 *et seq.; Porritt*, U.H.C. ii. 218–289.)

XLVII

THE REFORM ACT

2 Will. IV. Cap. 45, 1832.

An act to amend the representation of the people in England and Wales.

Whereas it is expedient to take effectual measures for correcting divers abuses that have long prevailed in the choice of members to serve in the commons house of parliament, to deprive many inconsiderable places of the right of returning members, to grant such privilege to large, populous, and wealthy towns, to increase the number of knights of the shire to extend the elective franchise to many of his Majesty's subjects who have not heretofore enjoyed the same, and to diminish the expense of elections ; be it therefore enacted . . . That each of the boroughs enumerated in the schedule marked (A.)[1] to this act annexed, (that is to say,) Old Sarum, Newtown, St. Michael's or Midshall, Gatton, Bramber, Bossiney, Dunwich, Ludgershall, St. Mawe's, Beeralston, West Looe, St. Germain's, Newport, Blechingley, Aldborough, Camelford, Hindon, East Looe, Corfe Castle, Great Bedwin, Yarmouth, Queenborough, Castle Rising, East Grinstead, Higham Ferrars, Wendover, Weobly, Winchelsea, Tregony, Haslemere, Saltash, Orford, Callington, Newton, Ilchester, Boroughbridge, Stockbridge, New Romney, Hedon, Plympton, Seaford, Heylesbury, Steyning, Whitchurch, Wootton Bassett, Downton, Fowey, Milbourne Port, Aldeburgh, Minehead, Bishop's Castle, Okehampton, Appleby, Lostwithiel, Brackley, and Amersham, shall from and after the end of this present parliament cease to return any member or members to serve in parliament.

II. And be it enacted that each of the boroughs enumerated in the schedule[1] marked (B.) to this act annexed, (that is to say,) Petersfield, Ashburton, Eye, Westbury, Wareham, Midhurst, Woostock, Wilton, Malmesbury, Liskeard, Reigate, Hythe, Droitwich, Lyme

[1] Schedule omitted. See p. 212.

Regis, Launceston, Shaftesbury, Thirsk, Christchurch, Horsham, Great Grimsby, Calne, Arundel, St. Ives, Rye, Clitheroe, Morpeth, Helston, North Allerton, Wallingford, and Dartmouth, shall from and after the end of this present parliament return one member and no more to serve in parliament.

III. And be it enacted, That each of the places named in the schedule marked[1] (C.) to this act annexed, (that is to say,) Manchester, Birmingham, Leeds, Greenwich, Sheffield, Sunderland, Devonport, Wolverhampton, Tower Hamlets, Finsbury, Marylebone, Lambeth, Bolton, Bradford, Blackburn, Brighton, Halifax, Macclesfield, Oldham, Stockport, Stoke-upon-Trent, and Stroud, shall for the purposes of this act be a borough, and shall as such borough include the place or places respectively which shall be comprehended within the boundaries of such borough, as such boundaries shall be settled and described by an act to be passed for that purpose in this present parliament, which act, when passed, shall be deemed and taken to be part of this act as fully and effectually as if the same were incorporated herewith ; and that each of the said boroughs named in the said schedule (C.) shall from and after the end of this present parliament return two members to serve in parliament.

IV. And be it enacted, That each of the places named in the schedule marked[1] (D.) to this act annexed, (that is to say,) Ashton-under-Lyne, Bury, Chatham, Cheltenham, Dudley, Frome, Gateshead, Huddersfield, Kidderminster, Kendal, Rochdale, Salford, South Shields, Tynemouth, Wakefield, Walsall, Warrington, Whitby, Whitehaven, and Merthyr Tydvil, shall for the purposes of this act be a borough, and shall as such borough include the place or places respectively which shall be comprehended within the boundaries of such borough, as such boundaries shall be settled and described by an act to be passed for that purpose in this present parliament, which act, when passed, shall be deemed and taken to be part of this act as fully and effectually as if the same were incorporated herewith ; and that each of the said boroughs named in the said schedule (D.) shall from and after the end of this present parliament return one member to serve in parliament.

.   .   .   .

(V. Boroughs of Shoreham, Cricklade, Aylesbury, and East Retford to include certain defined adjacent districts. VI. Weymouth and Melcomb Regis to return two members only ; Penryn to include Falmouth ; Sandwich to include Deal and Walmer. VII.–X. Settlement of Boundaries b

[1] Schedule omitted. See p. 212.

annexed schedules. XI. Description of the returning officers for the new boroughs. XII.–XVIII. Redistribution and division of certain counties by annexed schedules.)

XIX. And be it enacted, That every male person of full age, and not subject to any legal incapacity, who shall be seized at law or in equity of any lands or tenements of copyhold or any other tenure whatever except freehold, for his own life, or for the life of another, or for any lives whatsoever, or for any larger estate, of the clear yearly value of not less than ten pounds over and above all rents and charges payable out of or in respect of the same, shall be entitled to vote in the election of a knight or knights of the shire to serve in any future parliament for the county, or for the riding, parts, or division of the county, in which such lands or tenements shall be respectively situate.

XX. And be it enacted, That every male of full age, and not subject to any legal incapacity, who shall be entitled, either as lessee or assignee, to any lands or tenements, whether of freehold or any other tenure whatever, for the unexpired residue, whatever it may be, of any term originally created for a period of not less than sixty years, (whether determinable on a life, or lives, or not,) of the clear yearly value of not less than ten pounds over and above all rents and charges payable out of or in respect of the same, or for the unexpired residue, whatever it may be, of any term originally created for a period of not less than twenty years, (whether determinable on a life or lives, or not,) of the clear yearly value of not less that fifty pounds over and above all rents and charges payable out of or in respect of the same, or who shall occupy as tenant any lands or tenements for which he shall be *bona fide* liable to a yearly rent of not less than fifty pounds, shall be entitled to vote in the election of a knight or knights of the shire to serve in any future parliament for the county, or for the riding, parts, or division of the county, in which such lands or tenements shall be respectively situate ; Provided always, that no person being only a sub-lessee, or the assignee of any under-lease, shall have a right to vote in such election in respect of any such term of sixty years or twenty years as aforesaid, unless he shall be in the actual occupation of the premises.

XXI. And be it . . . enacted, That no public or parliamentary tax, nor any church rate, county rate, or parochial rate, shall be deemed to be any charge payable out of or in respect of any lands or tenements within the meaning of this act.

XXII. And be it enacted, That in order to entitle any person to vote in any election of a knight or knights of the shire or other member to serve in any future parliament, in respect of any messuages, lands, or tenements, whether freehold or otherwise, it shall not be necessary that the same shall be assessed to the land tax; any statute to the contrary notwithstanding.

XXIII. And be it enacted, That no person shall be allowed to have any vote in the election of a knight or knights of the shire for or by reason of any trust estate or mortgage, unless such trustee or mortgagee be in actual possession or receipt of the rents and profits of the same estate, but that the mortgagor or cestuique trust in possession shall and may vote for the same estate notwithstanding such mortgage or trust.

XXIV. And be it enacted, That notwithstanding anything hereinbefore contained no person shall be entitled to vote in the election of a knight or knights of the shire to serve in any future parliament in respect of his estate or interest as a freeholder in any house, warehouse, counting-house, shop, or other building occupied by himself or in any land occupied by himself together with any house, warehouse, counting-house, shop, or other building, such house, warehouse, counting-house, shop, or other building being, either separately, or jointly with the land so occupied therewith, of such value as would, according to the provisions hereinafter contained, confer on him the right of voting for any city or borough, whether he shall or shall not have actually acquired the right to vote for such city or borough in respect thereof.

XXV. And be it enacted, That notwithstanding anything hereinbefore contained no person shall be entitled to vote in the election of a knight or knights of the shire to serve in any future parliament in respect of his estate or interest as a copyholder or customary tenant, or tenant in ancient demesne, holding by copy of court roll, or as such lessee or assignee, or as such tenant and occupier as aforesaid, in any house, warehouse, counting-house, shop or other building, or in any land occupied together with a house, warehouse, counting-house, shop, or other building, such house, warehouse, counting-house, shop, or other building being, either separately, or jointly with the land so occupied therewith, of such value as would according to the provisions hereinafter contained confer on him or on any other person the right of voting for any city or borough, whether he or any other person shall or shall not have actually acquired the right to vote for any such city or borough in respect thereof.

XXVI. And be it enacted, That notwithstanding anything herein-before contained no person shall be entitled to vote in the election of a knight or knights of the shire to serve in any future parliament unless he shall have been duly registered according to the provisions hereinafter contained; and that no person shall be so registered in any year in respect of his estate or interest in any lands or tene-ments, as a freeholder, copyholder, customary tenant, or tenant in ancient demesne, unless he shall have been in the actual possession thereof, or in the receipt of the rents and profits thereof for his own use, for six calendar months at least next previous to the last day of July in such year, which said period of six calendar months shall be sufficient, any statute to the contrary notwithstanding; and that no person shall be so registered in any year, in respect of any lands or tenements held by him as such lessee or assignee, or as such occupier and tenant as aforesaid, unless he shall have been in the actual possession thereof, or in the receipts of the rents and profits thereof for his own use, as the case may require, for twelve calendar months next previous to the last day of July in such year: Provided always, that where any lands or tenements, which would otherwise entitle the owner, holder, or occupier thereof to vote in any such election, shall come to any person, at any time within such respective periods of six or twelve calendar months, by descent, succession, marriage, marriage settlement, devise, or promotion to any benefice in a church, or by promotion to any office, such person shall be entitled in respect thereof to have his name inserted as a voter in the election of a knight or knights of the shire in the lists then next to be made by virtue of this act as hereinafter mentioned, and, upon his being duly registered according to the provisions hereinafter con-tained, to vote in such election.

XXVII. And be it enacted, That in every city or borough which shall return a member or members to serve in any future parliament, every male person of full age, and not subject to any legal incapacity, who shall occupy, within such city or borough, or within any place sharing in the election for such city or borough, as owner or tenant, any house, warehouse, counting-house, shop, or other building, being, either separately, or jointly with any land within such city, borough, or place occupied therewith by him as owner, or occupied therewith by him as tenant under the same landlord, of the clear yearly value of not less than ten pounds, shall, if duly registered according to the provisions hereinafter contained, be entitled to vote in the election of a member or members to serve in any future parliament for such city or borough: Provided always, that no such person shall be so registered in any year unless he shall have occupied such premises as aforesaid for twelve calendar months next previous to the last day of July in such year, nor unless such person, where such premises are situate in any parish or township in which there shall be a rate for the relief of the poor, shall have been rated in respect of such premises to all rates for the relief of the poor in such parish or township made during the time of such his occupation so required as aforesaid, nor unless such person shall have paid, on or before the twentieth day of July in such year, all the poor's rates and assessed taxes which shall have become payable from him in respect of such premises previously to the sixth day of April then next preceding: Provided also, that no such person shall be so registered in any year unless he shall have resided for six calendar months next previous to the last day of July in such year within the city or borough, or within the place sharing in the election for the city or borough, in respect of which city, borough, or place respectively he shall be entitled to vote, or within seven statute miles thereof or of any part thereof.

XXVIII. And be it enacted, That the premises in respect of the occupation of which any person shall be entitled to be registered in any year, and to vote in the election for any city or borough as aforesaid, shall not be required to be the same premises, but may be different premises occupied in immediate succession by such person during the twelve calendar months next previous to the last day of July in such year, such person having paid, on or before the twentieth day of July in such year, all the poor's rates and assessed taxes which shall previously to the sixth day of April then next preceding have become payable from him in respect of all such premises so occupied by him in succession.

XXIX. And be it enacted, That where any premises as aforesaid, in any such city or borough, or in any place sharing in the election therewith, shall be jointly occupied by more persons than one as owners or tenants, each of such joint occupiers shall, subject to the conditions herein-before contained as to persons occupying premises in any such city, borough, or place, be entitled to vote in the election for such city or borough, in respect of the premises so jointly occupied, in case the clear yearly value of such premises, shall be of an amount which, when divided by the number of such occupiers, shall give a sum of not less than ten pounds for each and every such occupier, but not otherwise.

.   .   .   .

(XXX. Occupiers may demand to be rated.)

XXXI. And be it enacted, That in every city or town being a county of itself, in the election for which freeholders or burgage tenants, either with or without any superadded qualification, now have a right to vote, every such freeholder or burgage tenant shall be entitled to vote in the election of a member or members to serve in all future parliaments for such city or town, provided he shall be duly registered according to the provisions hereinafter contained : but that no such person shall be so registered in any year in respect of any freehold or burgage tenement, unless he shall have been in the actual possession thereof, or in receipt of the rents and profits thereof for his own use, for twelve calendar months next previous to the last day of July in such year (except where the same shall have come to him, at any time within such twelve months, by descent, succession, marriage, marriage settlement, devise, or promotion to any benefice in a church, or to any office,) nor unless he shall have resided for six calendar months next previous to the last day of July in such year within such city or town, or within seven statute miles thereof or of any part thereof : Provided always, that nothing in this enactment contained shall be deemed to vary or abridge the conditions herein-before made relative to the right of voting for any city or town, being a county of itself, in respect of any freehold for life or lives : Provided also, that every freehold or burgage tenement which may be situate without the present limits of any such city or town being a county of itself, but within the limits of such city or town, as the same shall be settled and described by the act to be passed for that purpose, as herein-before mentioned, shall confer the right of voting in the election of a member or members to serve in any future parliament for such city or town in the same manner as if such freehold or burgage tenement were situate within the present limits thereof.

.   .   .   .

(XXXII. Freemen not to vote in boroughs unless resident ; freemen created since March 1, 1831, excluded, with provisos as to the freemen of certain boroughs.)

XXXIII. And be it enacted, That no person shall be entitled to vote . . . for any City or Borough, save and except in respect of some Right conferred by this Act, or as a Burgess or Freeman . . . or as a Liveryman . . . or as a Freeholder or Burgage Tenant, as hereinbefore mentioned . . . but that no such person shall be registered unless . . . he shall have resided for six calendar months . . . within such City or Borough or within seven statute miles.

.   .   .   .

(XXXIV. Provisions as to freeholders in New Shoreham, Cricklade, Aylesbury, or East Retford.)

XXXV. Provided nevertheless, and be it enacted, That notwithstanding any thing herein-before contained no person shall be entitled to vote in the election of a member or members to serve in any future parliament for any city or borough (other than a city or town being a county of itself, in the election for which freeholders or burgage tenants have a right to vote as herein-before mentioned,) in respect of any estate or interest in any burgage tenement or freehold which shall have been acquired by such person since the first day of March one thousand eight hundred and thirty-one, unless the same shall have come to or been acquired by such person, since that day, and previously to the passing of this act, by descent, succession, marriage, marriage settlement, devise, or promotion to any benefice in a church, or by promotion to any office.

XXXVI. And be it enacted, That no person shall be entitled to be registered in any year as a voter in the election of a member or members to serve in any future parliament for any city or borough who shall within twelve calendar months next previous to the last day of July in such year have received parochial relief or other alms which by the law of parliament now disqualify from voting in the election of members to serve in parliament.

XXXVII. And whereas it is expedient to form a register of all persons entitled to vote in the election of a knight or knights of the shire to serve in any future parliament, and that for the purpose of forming such register the overseers of every parish and township should annually make out lists in the manner hereinafter mentioned; be it therefore enacted, That the overseers of the poor of every parish and township shall on the twentieth day of June in the present and every succeeding year cause to be fixed on or near the doors of all the churches and chapels within such parish or township, or if there be no church or chapel therein, then to be fixed in some public and conspicuous situation within the same respectively, a notice according to the form numbered 1, in the schedule[1] (H.) to this act annexed, requiring all persons who may be entitled to vote in the election of a knight or knights of the shire to serve in any future parliament, in respect of any property situate wholly or in part in such parish or township, to deliver or transmit to the said overseers on or before the twentieth day of July in the present and in every succeeding year a notice of their claim as such voters according to the form numbered

[1] Schedule omitted.

2, in the said schedule (H.), or to the like effect : Provided always, that after the formation of the register to be made in each year, as herein-after mentioned, no person whose name shall be upon such register for the time being shall be required thereafter to make any such claim as aforesaid, as long as he shall retain the same qualification, and continue in the same place of abode described in such register.

XXXVIII. And be it enacted, That the overseer of the poor of every parish and township shall on or before the last day of July in the present year make out or cause to be made out, according to the form numbered 3, in the said schedule (H.) an alphabetical list of all persons who shall claim as aforesaid to be inserted in such list as voters in the election of a knight or knights of the shire, to serve for the county, or for the riding, parts, or division of the county wherein such parish or township lies, in respect of any lands or tenements situate wholly or in part within such parish or township ; and that the said overseers shall on or before the last day of July in any succeeding year make out or cause to be made out a like list, containing the names of all persons who shall be upon the register for the time being as such voters, and also the names of all persons who shall claim as aforesaid to be inserted in such last-mentioned list as such voters : and in every list so to be made by the overseers as aforesaid the christian name and surname of every person shall be written at full length, together with the place of his abode, the nature of his qualification, and the local or other description of such lands or tenements, as the same are respectively set forth in his claim to vote, and the name of the occupying tenant, if stated in such claim : and the said overseers if they shall have reasonable cause to believe that any person so claiming as aforesaid, or whose name shall appear in the register for the time being, is not entitled to vote in the election of a knight or knights of the shire for the county, or for the riding, parts, or division of the county in which their parish or township is situate, shall have power to add the words " objected to " opposite the name of every such person on the margin of such list ; and the said overseers shall sign such list, and shall cause a sufficient number of copies of such list to be written or printed, and to be fixed on or near the doors of all the churches or chapels within their parish or township, or if there be no church or chapel therein, then to be fixed up in some public and conspicuous situation, within the same respectively, on the two Sundays next after such list shall have been made ; and the said overseers shall likewise keep a true copy of such list, to be perused by any person without payment of any fee, at all reasonable hours within the two first weeks after such lists shall have been made : Provided always, that every precinct or place, whether extra-parochial or otherwise, which shall have no overseers of the poor, shall for the purpose of making out such list as aforesaid be deemed to be within the parish or township adjoining thereto, such parish or township being situate within the same county, or the same riding, parts, or division of a county, as such precinct or place ; and if such precinct or place shall adjoin two or more parishes or townships, so situate as aforesaid, it shall be deemed to be within the least populous of such parishes according to the last census for the time being ; and the overseers of the poor of every such parish or township shall insert in the list for their respective parish or township the names of all persons who shall claim as aforesaid to be inserted therein as voters in the election of a knight or knights of the shire to serve for the county, or for the riding, parts, or division of the county, in which such precinct or place as aforesaid lies, in respect of any lands or tenements situate wholly or in part within such precinct or place.

·   ·   ·   ·   ·   ·   ·   ·

(XXXIX.–LIX. Provisions as to objections to names on the lists, the revision of the lists by barristers appointed by the Judges of Assize, their remuneration, the keeping of the lists, and as to the identification of voters who names appear on the lists.)

LX. Provided also, . . . That, upon petition to the House of Commons, complaining of an undue election or return of any member or members to serve in parliament, any petitioner, or any person defending such election or return, shall be at liberty to impeach the correctness of the register of voters in force at the time of such election, by proving that in consequence of the decision of the barrister who shall have revised the lists of voters from which such register shall have been formed the name of any person who voted at such election was improperly inserted or retained in such register, or the name of any person who tendered his vote at such election improperly omitted from such register ; and the select committee appointed for the trial of such petitions shall alter the poll taken at such election according to the truth of the case, and shall report their determination thereupon to the house, and the house shall thereupon carry such determination into effect, and the return shall be amended, or the election declared void, as the case may be, and the register corrected accordingly, or such other order shall be made as to the house shall seem proper.

(LXI. Sheriffs of the counties divided by the Act to fix the time of, and to preside at, the elections.)

LXII. And be it enacted, That at every contested election of a knight or knights to serve in any future parliament for any county, or for any riding, parts, or division of a county, the polling shall commence at nine o'clock in the forenoon of the next day but two after the day fixed for the election, unless such next day but two shall be Saturday or Sunday, and then on the Monday following, at the principal place of election, and also at the several places to be appointed as hereinafter directed for taking polls; and such polling shall continue for two days only, such two days being successive days; (that is to say,) for seven hours on the first day of polling, and for eight hours on the second day of polling; and no poll shall be kept open later than four o'clock in afternoon of the second day; any statute to the contrary notwithstanding.

LXIII. And be it enacted, That the respective counties in England and Wales, and the respective ridings, parts, and divisions of counties, shall be divided into convenient districts for polling, and in each district shall be appointed a convenient place for taking the poll at all elections of a knight or knights of the shire to serve in any future parliament, and such districts and places for taking the poll shall be settled and appointed by the act to be passed in this present parliament for the purpose of settling and describing the divisions of the counties enumerated in the schedule marked (F.) to this act annexed : provided that no county, nor any riding, parts, or division, of a county, shall have more than fifteen districts and respective places appointed for taking the poll for such county, riding, parts, or division.

LXIV. And be it enacted, That at every contested election for any county, or riding, parts or division of a county, the sheriff, under sheriff, or sheriff's deputy shall, if required thereto by or on behalf of any candidate, on the day fixed for the election, and if not so required may, if it shall appear to him expedient, cause to be erected a reasonable number of booths for taking the poll at the principal place of election, and also at each of the polling places so appointed as aforesaid, and shall cause to be affixed on the most conspicuous part of each of the said booths the names of the several parishes, townships, and places for which such booth is respectively allotted; and no person shall be admitted to vote at any such election in respect of any property situate in any parish, township, or place, except at the booth so allotted for such parish, township, or place, and if no booth shall be so allotted for the same, then at any of the booths for the same district; and in case any parish, township, or place shall happen not to be included in any of the districts to be appointed, the votes in respect of any property situate in any parish, township, or place so omitted shall be taken at the principal place of election for the county, or riding, parts, or division of the county, as the case may be.

. . . .

(LXV., LXVI. Provision as to sheriffs' deputies, custody of the poll books, and the final declaration of the poll in counties.)

LXVII. And be it enacted, That at every contested election of a member or members to serve in any future parliament for any city or borough in England, except the borough of Monmouth, the poll shall commence on the day fixed for the election, or on the next following, or at the latest on the third day, unless any of the said days shall be Saturday or Sunday, and then on the Monday following, the particular day for the commencement of the poll to be fixed by the returning officer; and such polling shall continue for two days only, such two days being successive days, (that is to say,) for seven hours on the first day of polling, and for eight hours on the second day of polling; and that the poll shall on no account be kept open later than four o'clock in the afternoon of the second day; any statute to the contrary notwithstanding.

LXVIII. And be it enacted, That at every contested election of a member or members to serve in any future parliament for any city or borough in England, except the borough of Monmouth, the returning officer shall, if required thereto by or on behalf of any candidate, on the day fixed for the election, and if not required may, if it shall seem to him expedient, cause to be elected for taking the poll at such election, different booths for different parishes, districts, or parts of such city or borough, which booths may be situate either in one place or in several places, and shall be so divided and allotted into compartments as to the returning officer shall seem most convenient so that no greater number than six hundred shall be required to poll at any one compartment; and the returning officer shall appoint a clerk to take the poll at each compartment, and shall cause to be fixed on the most conspicuous part of each of the said booths the names of the several parishes, districts, and parts for which such booth is respectively allotted; and no person shall be admitted to vote at any such election, except at the booth allotted for the parish district, or part wherein the property may be situate in respect of which he claims to vote, or in case he does not claim to vote in respect of property, then wherein his place of abode as described in the register may be ; but in case no booth shall happen to be provided for any particular parish, district or part as aforesaid, the votes of persons voting in respect of property situate in any parish, district, or part so omitted, or having their place of abode therein, may be taken at any of the said booths, and the votes of freemen residing out of the limits of the city or borough may be taken at any of the said booths ; and public notice of the situation, division, and allotment of the different booths shall be given two days before the commencement of the poll by the returning officer ; and in case the booths shall be situated in different places, the returning officer may appoint a deputy to preside at each place ; and at every such election the poll clerks at the close of each day's poll shall enclose and seal their several poll books, and shall publicly deliver them, so enclosed and sealed, to the returning officer or his deputy, who shall give a receipt for the same, and shall, on the commencement of the poll on the second day, deliver them back, so enclosed and sealed, to the persons from whom he shall have received the same ; and every deputy so receiving any such poll books, on the final close of the poll shall forthwith deliver or transmit the same, so enclosed and sealed, to the returning officer, who shall receive and keep all the poll books unopened until the following day, unless such day be Sunday, and then till the Monday following, when he shall openly break the seals thereon, and cast up the number of votes as they appear on the several books, and shall openly declare the state of the poll, and make proclamation of the member or members chosen, not later than two o'clock in the afternoon of the said day : Provided always, that the returning officer, or his lawful deputy may, if he think fit, declare the final state of the poll, and proceed to make the return immediately after the poll shall have been lawfully closed : Provided also, that no nomination shall be made or election holden of any member for the city or borough, in any church, chapel, or other place of public worship.

. . . .

(LXIX. Polling districts for Shoreham, Cricklade, Aylesbury, and East Retford.)

LXX. And be it enacted, That nothing in this act contained shall prevent any sheriff or other returning officer, or the lawful deputy of any returning officer, from closing the poll previous to the time fixed by this act, in any case where the same might have been lawfully

P

closed before the passing of this act; and that where the proceedings at any election shall be interrupted or obstructed by any riot or open violence, the sheriff or other returning officer, or the lawful deputy of any returning officer, shall not for such cause finally close the poll, but, in case the proceedings shall be so interrupted or obstructed at any particular polling place or places, shall adjourn the poll at such place or places only until the following day, and if necessary shall further adjourn the same until such interruption or obstruction shall have ceased, when the returning officer or his deputy shall again proceed to take the poll at such place or places; and any day whereon the poll shall have been so adjourned shall not, as to such place or places, be reckoned one of the two days of polling at such election within the meaning of this act; and whenever the poll shall have been so adjourned by any deputy of any sheriff or other returning officer, such deputy shall forthwith give notice of such adjournment to the sheriff or returning officer, who shall not finally declare the state of the poll, or make proclamation of the member or members chosen, until the poll so adjourned at such place or places as aforesaid shall have been finally closed, and delivered or transmitted to such sheriff or other returning officer; anything herein-before contained to the contrary notwithstanding.

.   .   .   .

(LXXI.-LXXVII. Detailed regulations as to the conduct of elections.)

LXXVIII. Provided always, and be it enacted, That nothing in this act contained shall extend to or in any wise affect the election of members to serve in parliament for the universities of Oxford or Cambridge, or shall entitle any person to vote in the election of members to serve in parliament for the city of Oxford or town of Cambridge in respect of the occupation of any chambers or premises in any of the colleges or halls of the universities of Oxford or Cambridge.

LXXIX. And be it enacted, That throughout this act wherever the words " city or borough," "cities or boroughs," may occur, those words shall be construed to include, except there be something in the subject or context manifestly repugnant to such construction, all towns corporate, cinque ports, districts, or places within England and Wales which shall be entitled after this act shall have passed to return a member or members to serve in parliament, other than counties at large, and ridings, parts, and divisions of counties at large, and shall also include the town of Berwick upon Tweed; and the words "returning officer" shall apply to every person or persons to whom, by virtue of his or their office, either under the present act, or under any law, custom or statute, the execution of any writ or precept doth or shall belong for the election of a member or members to serve in parliament, by whatever name or title such person or persons may be called; and the words "parish or township" shall extend to every parish, township, vill, hamlet, district, or place maintaining its own poor; and the words "overseers of the poor" shall extend to all persons who by virtue of any office or appointment shall execute the duties of overseers of the poor, by whatever name or title such persons may be called, and in whatsover manner they may be appointed, and that all matters by this act directed to be done by the overseers of a parish or township may be lawfully done by the major part of such overseers, and that when any notice is by this act required to be given to the overseers of any parish or township, it shall be sufficient if such notice shall be delivered to any one of such overseers, or shall be left at his place of abode, or at his office or other place for transacting parochial business, or shall be sent by the post, addressed by a sufficient direction, to the overseers of the particular parish or township, or to any one of them, either by their or his particular christian name and surname, or by their or his name of office; and that all provisions in this act relative to any matters to be done by or with regard to justices of the peace for counties, or sessions of the peace for counties, or clerks of the peace for counties, or treasurers of counties, shall extend to the justices, sessions, clerks of the peace, and treasurers of the several ridings of Yorkshire and parts of Lincolnshire, and that the clerk of the peace for the time being for the borough of Newport in the Isle of Wight shall for the purposes of this act be deemed and taken to be the clerk of the peace for the county of the Isle of Wight, and that all the said respective justices, sessions, and clerks of the peace shall have power to do the several matters required by this act, as well within places of exclusive jurisdiction as without; and that no misnomer or inaccurate description of any person or place named or described in any schedule to this act annexed, or in any list or register of voters, or in any notice required by this act, shall in anywise prevent or abridge the operation of this act with respect to such person or place, provided that such person or place shall be so desigated in such schedule, list, register or notice as to be commonly understood.

(LXXX. Provisions if the Boundary Act be not law by June 20, 1832.

LXXXI. Voting to take place without registration if a dissolution follows the Boundary Act before registration has been effected.

LXXXII. Regulation for counties and boroughs in the event of a dissolution preceding the passing of the Boundary Act.)

SUMMARY OF SCHEDULES ANNEXED TO THE ACT

A. Fifty-five boroughs returning two members, Higham Ferrers returning one member, disfranchised (see § 1).

B. Thirty boroughs returning two members deprived of one member (§ 2).

C. Twenty-two cities and boroughs given two members (§ 3).

D. Twenty boroughs given one member (§ 4).

E. List of places sharing in members with their shire-towns and counties.

E. 2. List of places sharing in members with places from which the seven miles are calculated.

F. Schedule of divided counties.

F. 2. Schedule of counties returning three members.

G. Schedule of cities and towns included in counties.

H.–L. Forms of lists and notices.

(See *May*, C.H.E. i. 390–458; *Hansard*, P.D. third series, xii.; *Anson*, L.C. i. 72–134; *Clarendon Press Historical Atlas*, plates 23, 24; *Spencer Walpole*, H.E. iii. 176 *et seq.*; *Porritt*, U.H.C. i. 1–117.)

PROTESTS OF THE LORDS

(The introduction and passing of the Reform Bill occasioned several lengthy and important protests from the dissentient peers. In the annexed text an attempt has been made, by eliminating the repetition of arguments common to all the protests, to reproduce the substance of the leading objections recorded. The full text and signatures will be found in the *Lords Journals* and *Rogers, op. cit.*, to which the student is referred. As to the proposed creation of peers, and the measures taken by the King, see especially *The Correspondence of William and Earl Grey*; *Anson*, L.C. i. 191 and 329; *Roebuck*, History of the Whig Ministry, 331 *et seq.*)

Because I cannot consider the changes made by this Bill in the representation of the people as founded upon the acknowledged principles of the Constitution, or tending to uphold the just right and prerogatives of the Crown, and to give security to the liberties of the people.

Because I think that this Bill cannot be a final adjustment as to the representation of the people, and that it must, by the operation of the principles upon which it is founded, lead to further dangerous changes in the Constitution, bringing into imminent hazard the monarchy and the prerogatives of the Crown, and consequently the rights and liberties of the people.

Because this Bill appears to me calculated to introduce unnecessarily into the Constitution of the House of Commons an increase of democratical influence, not called for by any increase of influence in the other branches of the Legislature. . . .

. . . Because having observed the great anxiety with which the laws and customs of the realm have for ages held sacred the rights of property and other vested rights, I cannot agree to the unqualified and unconditional destruction by this Bill of such rights.

(Signed by Lord Eldon and thirty-one Peers.)

Because the elective franchise is by this Bill unequal, and unjustly distributed. . . .

Because by this Bill the influence of the landed interest is destroyed, by its giving a majority of the members taken from those boroughs which usually supported that interest, to the great towns, and by its depriving it of the county representation, by allowing the inhabitants of represented towns to vote for knights of the shire for estates within such towns.

Because, although the preamble to the Bill states that one of its objects is to prevent abuses at elections, no provision is made for the prevention of any one abuse. . . .

(Signed by Lords Wynford and Kenyon.)

Because the Bill, changing the constituency of every county, city and borough, disfranchising with injustice, in many cases enfranchising with impolicy or partiality, leaving or creating as many incongruities as it attempts to correct, opening many new questions and settling none, contains within itself the elements of further change, and thus tends to continue an agitation destructive of the comfort of society, and fatal to the prosperity of the country.

(Signed by Lord Ellenborough and sixteen Peers.)

Because we object to the shameful mode by which a majority was obtained for the second reading and subsequent stages of the Bill; the most scandalous arts of seduction and menace having been resorted to in order to effect the purpose. . . . Because, by the proceedings enumerated, the royal authority has been extended for purposes not contemplated by law, and the King has been advised and induced to control and to coerce the free deliberations of the House of Lords, whereby the dignity and character of the House have been grievously impaired, and its rights, privileges, and independence have been alarmingly outraged, and most unconstitutionally violated. . . .

(Signed by the Duke of Newcastle, Lords Kenyon and Abingdon.)

Because the principles of this Bill are carried to an extent that will give an undue preponderance to the popular branch of the Legislature, and by thereby endangering the privileges of this House, and the legitimate power and prerogatives of the Crown, may in the end destroy that balance, on the maintenance of which depend the existence of the Constitution and of the settled institutions of the country. . . .

(Signed by Lord Melros and fourteen Peers.)

We protest against the doctrine that any individual or corporate body can be justly deprived of any rights which have been legally enjoyed . . . either delinquency must have been proved, or compensation must have been given, before the sacrifice was exacted; upon this principle Parliament proceeded in approving the purchase of the heritable jurisdictions in Scotland, and in a more recent and analogous instance, compensation was given to individuals and to corporate bodies in Ireland, for the deprivation of their right of returning members. . . .

(Signed by Lord Mansfield and twenty-four Peers.)

Because by the ancient laws and constitution of this realm the House of Peers is entitled to exercise a free and uncontrolled judgment in framing, altering and amending Bills in Parliament, before they can attain the validity of law, and because the said privilege has been invaded and rendered of none effect by the unconstitutional advice given to his Majesty (advice which is not denied by his servants) to create peers in sufficient numbers to control the decision of this House, and consequently to secure an unconstitutional majority in favour of this measure.

(Signed by Lord Salisbury and twenty-seven Peers.)

Because some of the enactments of this Bill are to be carried into execution by calling for aid (and that in not a few cases largely) of that fund which, under the denomination of poor rates, is levied for the maintenance and support of the aged, the infirm and the needy . . . and in all instances, must females, and those otherwise disqualified, be thus exposed to a partial and arbitrary tax on the property that they occupy or possess. . . .

(Signed by Lord Malmesbury and ten Peers.)

(Lords Journals, June 4, 1832; *Rogers*, P.L. iii. 84–107.)

XLVIII

THE PREROGATIVE OF MERCY
7 Will. IV. and 1 Vict. Cap. 77, 1837.

" Whereas it is expedient to assimilate the Practice of the Central Criminal Court to other Courts of Criminal Judicature within the Kingdom of England and Wales with respect to offenders liable to the punishment of Death " : Be it therefore enacted by the Queen's Most Excellent Majesty, by and with the Advice and Consent of the Lords Spiritual and Temporal, and Commons, in this present Parliament assembled, and by the authority of the same, That from and after the passing of this Act it shall not be necessary that any Report should be made to Her Majesty, Her Heirs and Successors, in the Case of any Prisoner convicted before the said Central Criminal Court, and now under Sentence of Death, or who may be hereafter convicted before such court and sentenced to the like Punishment, previously to such sentence being carried into execution : any Law, Usage, or Custom to the contrary notwithstanding. . . .

VI. Provided always, and be it enacted, That nothing in this Act contained shall affect Her Majesty's Royal Prerogative of Mercy. . . .

II

CASES

I

SKINNER v. THE EAST INDIA COMPANY
18 Charles II., 1666.

[This case, like that of *Shirley v. Fagg* (see p. 230), raised important
issues as to the royal prerogative, parliamentary privilege, and the jurisdiction of the House of Lords, and caused a violent quarrel between the
two Houses of Parliament. The facts are clearly explained in *Hallam*,
C.H. iii. 21. Significant points are : (1) the reference of the Petition of
Thomas Skinner for redress by the King in Council to the House of Lords ;
(2) the determination of the Lords to act on the reference and to exercise
an *original jurisdiction* in a civil case ; (3) the opposition of the Commons
to this claim, the counter-assertion of their privilege, and their champion-
ship of the cause of the East India Company. The sharp quarrel between
the two Houses lasted from November, 1666, to February 22, 16$\frac{6}{7}\frac{8}{8}$; and
then it threatened to block all business, was only ended by the inter-
vention of the King, who persuaded both Houses to drop the quarrel and
erase all records of it from their respective journals. It is noticeable that
in the printed journals those of the Commons give the King's Speech and
the resolution adopted, whereas those of the Lords show a blank. Further,
owing to the completeness with which the Lords obliterated the records,
their printed journals invariably represent all references to the dispute by
a row of asterisks. But with the help of the MS. Minute Book and other
papers, these have now been deciphered, and are printed in H.M.C.R. viii.
pp. pp. 107, 165–174, which should be consulted by all who desire full
information. Though the Lords technically refused to waive their original
claim as a fact, they ceased henceforward to claim or exercise an original
jurisdiction in civil cases where the parties were Commoners. See generally
Hallam, op. cit.; Pike, H.L. 272–307 ; *Hargrave*, H.J.L. (Preface) ; S.T.
710–770 ; *Hatsell*, Precedents, iii. ; *Hunter*, H.B.D. ii. ; *Macqueen*,
J.L. 1–17, 81–90. Brief notes of the debates will be found in *Grey's
Debates*, vol. i.]

I

Whereas upon the petition of Thomas Skinner merchant, setting forth his sufferings under the barbarous oppressions of the East India Company, his majesty was graciously pleased by order of the 27th of August last to defer the clearing of the matter for erecting a court to determine affairs of this nature till the second meeting of this board at Whitehall, and in regard the said Company have slighted the orders of this Board, and not complied with any references or mediations, designing to wear out the Petitioner's life in tedious attendances; he did by his Petition this day read at the board, humbly pray that the said Court may be now erected to relieve the petitioner according to justice, and put a period to his grievances: Whereupon his majesty present in Council did order, That his grace the Lord Archbishop of Canterbury, the Lord Chancellor, Lord Privy Seal, and the lord Ashley do send for the Governor and some of the Members of the East India Company, to treat with them and to induce them to give the said Mr. Skinner such reasonable satisfaction as may in some measure be answerable to the loss and damage he hath suffered under them.   (Signed) JOHN NICHOLAS.

March 23, 1866.—(S.T. vi. 711.)

II

To the Honourable the Commons of England in Parliament assembled: The humble petition of the Governor and Company of the Merchants of London, trading to the East Indies.

Humbly sheweth:

That Thomas Skinner lately exhibited a Petition to the right honourable the Lords spiritual and temporal in Parliament assembled against your Petitioners (many of which are and were member of this honourable House, when the said Petition was exhibited) for injuries pretended to be done by your Petitioners' factor in the East Indies . . . all which matters (excepting what concerns the island are matters clearly determinable in his majesty's ordinary court of law, as by the judges attending their lordships, hath been resolved and reported: And for the island the same is parcel of the dominion of a foreign prince, and so the right thereof only determinable by the laws of that prince. That though the Petitioners did humbly tender a plea to their lordships, for that the Petition was in nature of an original complaint (concerning commoners only) and not brought to their lordships by Writ of Error, or Bill of Review, or any way of Appeal, and that the matters therein were relievable in

the courts of Westminster Hall . . . yet their lordships have been
pleased not only to give a hearing in all the matters in the said
Petition contained, but have denied to grant the Petitioners a commission, or so much as time to send for their witnesses now inhabiting
upon the place, where the injuries were pretended to be done, and
without whose testimony it was impossible for the Petitioners to
make their defence. That upon the said hearing, their lordships
were further pleased to appoint a Committee to assess damages against
your Petitioners, which Committee is now proceeding thereon accordingly, whereby several members of this honourable house, who
are of the said Company as well as other your Petitioners, may be
highly detrimented. All which proceedings, as your humble Petitioners humbly submit to your honourable judgments, are against the
laws and statutes of this nation, and custom of Parliament. In
tender consideration whereof, and forasmuch as these unusual and
extraordinary proceedings of their lordships are not only grievous to
your petitioners at present, but may also be a precedent of ill consequence to all the Commons of England hereafter, and forasmuch as
your petitioners have no way of relief in this case than by making
their humble addresses to this honourable house, your Petitioners do
therefore most humbly pray, that your honours will be pleased to
take the premises into your grave consideration, and to interpose
with their lordships for your Petitioners' relief therein, in such way
and manner as to your great wisdoms shall seem meet. And your
Petitioners, as in duty bound, shall pray, etc.

Signed by the Order, and in the name of the said Governor and
Company,   ROBERT BLACKBORNE, *Sec.*

The Lords voted this Petition "to be a scandalous Libel against the
House of Peers."

III

RESOLUTIONS OF THE HOUSE OF LORDS

(1) That the House of Commons entertaining the scandalous petition
of the East India Company against the Lords House of Parliament,
and their proceedings, examinations, and votes thereupon had and
made, are a breach of the privileges of the House of Peers, and contrary to the fair correspondency which ought to be between the two
Houses of Parliament, and unexampled in former times.

(2) That the House of Peers taking cognizance of the cause of
Thomas Skinner merchant, a person highly oppressed and injured in
East India by the Governor and company of merchants of London

trading thither, and over-ruling the plea of the said Company, and adjudging £5,000 damages thereupon against the said Governor and Company, is agreeable to the laws of the land, and well warranted by the law and custom of Parliament, and justified by many parliamentary precedents, ancient and modern.

RESOLUTIONS OF THE HOUSE OF COMMONS

(1) That the proceedings of the House of Lords, upon the petition of Thomas Skinner, merchant, against the governor and company of merchants of London trading to the East Indies, Sir William Thompson, and several other members of the House of Commons, are a breach upon the privilege of the House of Commons.

(2) That the House of Lords assuming and exercising a jurisdiction, and taking cognizances of the matters set forth and complained of in the petition of Thomas Skinner, Merchant . . . and their Lordships' over-ruling of the plea of the said Governor and Company, put into the jurisdiction of the said House of Lords; the said cause coming before the House originally only upon the complaint of the said Thomas Skinner, and the matters in the said petition complained of, concerning the taking away of the said petitioner's ship and goods, and assaulting his person, being relievable in the ordinary courts of law; is contrary to the law of the land, and tends to the depriving of the subject of the benefit of the known law, and the introducing of an arbitrary way of proceeding.

(3) That the House of Lords, in the cause depending before them, upon the petition of Thomas Skinner . . . allowing of affidavits taken before masters of the Chancery, and a judge of the Admiralty, as proof in the said cause, wherein also the Governor and Company had no liberty to cross-examine the said persons making such affidavits; and the House of Lords not granting a commission to the said Governor and Company for the examination of their witnesses, the same being desired by the said Governor and Company is illegal, and a grievance to the subject.

Resolved.—That whosoever shall be aiding or assisting in putting the order or sentence of the House of Lords, in the case of Thomas Skinner against the East India Company, in execution, shall be deemed a betrayer of the rights and liberties of the Commons of England, and an infringer of the privileges of this House.

(May 9, 1669.)

(1) That it is an inherent right of every Commoner of England, to prepare and present petitions to the House of Commons, in case of grievance, and the House of Commons to receive the same.

(2) That it is the undoubted Right and Privilege of the House of Commons to judge and determine touching the nature and matter of such petitions, how far they are fit or unfit to be received.

(3) That no Court whatsoever hath power to judge or censure any petition prepared for, or presented to, the House of Commons, and received by them, unless transmitted from thence, or the matter complained of by them.

(4) Whereas a petition by the Governor and Company of Merchants trading to East India was presented to the House of Commons by Sir Samuel Barnardiston and others, complaining of grievances therein —which the Lords have censured, under the notion of a scandalous paper or libel—the said censure and proceeding of the Lords against the said Sir Samuel Barnardiston are contrary to, and in subversion of, the Rights and Privileges of the House of Commons, and Liberties of the Commons of England.

(5) That the continuance upon record of the judgment given by the Lords, and complained of by the House of Commons, in the last session of this Parliament, in the case of Thomas Skinner and the East India Company, is prejudicial to the Rights of the Commoners of England.

(December 7, 1669.)

THE KING'S SPEECH

My Lords and Gentlemen,

I did very earnestly recommend to you, the other day, that you would not suffer any differences between yourselves to be revived. ... I remember very well, that the case of *Skinner* was first sent by *me* to the Lords. I have, therefore, thought myself concerned to offer to you, what I judge the best and safest way to put an end to the difference; and, indeed, I can find no other. I will myself give present order to raze all Records and Entries of this matter, both in the Council-books and in the Exchequer; and do desire you to do the like in both Houses, that no memory may remain of this dispute between you. And then, I hope, all future apprehensions will be secured.

Resolved.—That, in obedience to His Majesty's command, in his speech, a Razure or Vacat be made, in the Journals of this House, of all the matters therein contained, relating to the business between the *East India* Company and *Skinner* which was accordingly done in the House.

(C.J. February 22, 1669.)

IV

It hath already been observed to your Lordships, that this cause is not negatively; to wit, it comes not before your Lordships as matter of evidence to the King, nor as matter of favour, but is brought to you by way of complaint, by one Commoner against another, as supposing your Lordships to be proper judges, *prima instantia*, to hear and determine the cause, as it hath been summarily, and without such legal trial as by Law ought to have been had in such a case. The Common Law is that . . . by which Justice is to be administered, and whatever is done without this Law, by way of judgment, is done against it. . . . The grand work of all which I shall farther say is expressed in the vote itself, that the suit is a common plea, it concerns not the King in his interest, nor any crime . . . and "a common person" in this matter is every person under the King, noble or ignoble . . . and it extends to ecclesiastical as well as secular jurisdictions and interests. . . . This being premised, I say, *non recurritur ad extraordinarium remedium nisi deficiente ordinario.* The Petitioner might have had his ordinary remedy in the inferior Courts . . . and therefore need not, nor ought, to fly to an unusual and extraordinary remedy. . . . By this way of proceeding, the subject loses that legal and indifferent way of trial, which the Law hath provided for him, by Jurors of his own condition, which is as much his right, yea his birth right and inheritance, as his lands are. . . . This way of trial is his fence and protection against all storms of power . . . therefore the Commons are careful (even) to jealousy, that this their liberty and buckler be not taken from them. . . . But by this way of proceeding before your Lordships all these advantages are lost, for the trial of fact and of Law, the office of the Judge and Juror, are confounded. . . . Again, in case an error be committed in the proceedings, be the same ever so unjust, whether in fact, or in Law . . . yet he is without all remedy in the way of proceeding. . . . Again; the way of proceeding summarily by *English* Petition, and without trial by Jury, is against several Statutes and Declarations in Parliament by the Lords themselves. (Here are examined at length 9 Hen. III. ch. 29, "Magna Charta"; 5 Edw. III. ch. 3, 25; 6 Edw. III. ch. 4, 42; Edw. III. ch. 2, 4; Hen. IV. ch. 23, 15, etc.) I next say, this power now claimed and used in this case by the Lords, is a lessening or "emblemissement" of the King's Royalty, to use the words of the Act, since . . . if either party hath cause to complain in Parliament of the Judgment as erroneous, he cannot do it by petition in Parliament, but must bring a writ of error in Parliament in the King's name, and under the King's seal to authorise the party's complaint, and the jurisdiction of the Lords, and of the Court. . . . This is not a formality only, but the ill inferences and consequences drawn from the neglect of it go farther than at first sight appears, viz. that the subject, on original petition to him, should have jurisdiction over the estate and person of his fellow-subject. . . . Now the question in the writ of error before the Lords is this regularly, viz. admitting all facts to be as they are alleged, whether the Law be as is adjudged in the inferior Courts, or that the proceedings have been otherwise than by Law they ought to have been. . . . It is considerable to the Lords themselves, whether this jurisdiction be not as disadvantageous to themselves as to the Commoners; let them consider whether it be not most for the interest and safety of their estates for them to be tried by Jurors sworn . . . to be tried there, where if injustice be done, redress may be had, or there where, if wrong be done, it shall be to the day of doom. . . . Last of all, it is clear that where the jurisdiction is changed, the Law is changed, as appears by all the instances of trial, appeal, proceeding, judgment, and execution, fact and law, equity and law, all blended together, and indifferent and arbitrary.

(From Serjeant Maynard's Speech, to the Lords on behalf of the Commons. C.J. Ap. 17, 1671, and *Grey's* Debates, i. 446–462.)

II

BUSHELL'S CASE
22 Charles II., 1670.

[Edward Bushell had been one of a jury who acquitted William Penn and William Mead at the Old Bailey Sessions, and had been fined by the Recorder 40 marks, and committed in default of payment to prison. The return to a writ of *habeas corpus* stated that the prisoner was committed for finding "*contra plenam et manifestam evidentiam, et contra directionem curiæ in materia legis.*" Chief Justice Vaughan, in a luminous and historic judgment, the salient passages of which are given in the excerpt, ruled that the return was insufficient and thereby established the immunity of the jury from fines for their verdict. On the importance of the case with reference to the liberty of the subject, and the various legal points arising out of it see *Hallam*, C.H. iii. 9 *et seq.*; *Broom*, C.L. 115 *et seq.*; S.T. vi. 967 *et seq.*, 999 *et seq.*; *Forsyth*, History of Trial by Jury; *Hawkins*, Pleas of the Crown, ii.]

The king's writ of Habeas Corpus, dat. 9 die Novembris, 22 Car. 2, issued out of this court directed to the then Sheriffs of London, to have the body of Edward Bushell, by them detained in Prison, together with the day and cause of his caption and detention, on Friday then next following, before this court, to do and receive as the court should consider; as also to have then the said writ in court. . . .

In the present case it is returned, That the prisoner, being a juryman, among others charged at the Sessions Court of the Old Bailey, to try the issue between the king, and Penn, and Mead, upon an indictment for assembling unlawfully and tumultuously, did "contra plenam et manifestam evidentiam," openly given in court, acquit the prisoners indicted, in contempt of the king, etc.

The court hath no knowledge by this return, whether the evidence given were full and manifest, or doubtful, lame, and dark, or, indeed, evidence at all material to the issue, because it is not returned what evidence in particular, and as it was delivered, was given. For it is not possible to judge of that rightly, which is not exposed to a man's judgment. But here the evidence given to the jury is not exposed at all to this court, but the judgment of the Court of Sessions upon that evidence is only exposed to us; who tell us it was full and manifest. But our judgment ought to be grounded upon our own inferences and understandings, and not upon theirs.

It was said by a learned judge, If the jury might be fined for finding against manifest evidence, the return was good, though it did not impress what the evidence particularly was, whereby the court might judge of it, because returning all the evidence would be too long. A strange reason: For if the law allow me remedy for wrong imprisonment, and that must be by judging whether the cause of it were good, or not, to say the cause is too long to be made known, is to say the law gives a remedy which it will not let me have, or I must be wrongfully imprisoned still, because it is too long to know that I ought to be freed? What is necessary to amend, the law allows is never too long. "Non sunt longa quibus nihil est quod demere possis," is as true as any axiom of Euclid. Besides, one manifest evidence returned had sufficed, without returning all the evidence. But the other judges were not of his mind.

If the return had been, That the jurors were committed by an order of the Court of Sessions, because they did, "minus juste" acquit the persons indicted. Or because they did, "contra legem" acquit the persons indicted. Or because they did, "contra sacramentum suum," acquit them.

The judges cannot upon the present more judge of the legal cause of their commitment, than they could if any of these causes, as general as they are, had been returned for the cause of their commitment. And the same argument may be exactly made to justify any of these returns, had they been made as to justify the present return, they being equally as legal, equally as certain, and equally as far from possessing the court with the truth of the cause : and in what condition should all men be for the just liberty of their persons, if such causes should be submitted sufficient causes to remand persons to prison. . . .

I would know whether anything be more common than for two men students, barristers or judges, to deduce contrary and opposite conclusions out of the same case in law ? And is there any difference that two men should infer distinct conclusions from the same testimony ? Is anything more known than that the same author, and place in that author, is forcibly urged to maintain contrary conclusions, and the decision hard, which is in the right ? Is anything more frequent in the controversies of religion, than to press the same text for opposite tenets ? How then comes it to pass that two persons may not apprehend with reason and honesty, what a witness, or many, say, to prove in the understanding of one plainly one thing, but in the apprehension of the other, clearly the contrary thing ? Must therefore one of these merit fine and imprisonment, because he doth that which he cannot otherwise do, preserving his oath and integrity ? And this often is the case of the judge and jury.

I conclude therefore, That this return, charging the prisoners to have acquitted Penn and Mead, against full and manifest evidence, first and next, without saying that they did know and believe that evidence to be full and manifest against the indicted persons, is no cause of fine or imprisonment.

And by the way I must here note, That the Verdict of a Jury, and the Evidence of a Witness are very different things, in the truth and falsehood of them : a witness swears but to what he hath heard or seen, generally or more largely, to what hath fallen under his senses. But a juryman swears to what he can infer and conclude from the testimony of such witnesses, by the act and force of his understanding, to be the fact inquired after, which differs nothing in the reason, though much in the punishment, from what a judge, out various cases considered by him, infers to be the law in the question before him. . . . The words, that the jury did acquit, against the direction of the court, in matter of law, literally taken, and *de uno*, are insignificant and not intelligible, for no issue can be joined of in matter of law, no jury can be charged with the trial of matter in law barely, no evidence ever was, or can be given to a jury of what is law, or not; nor no such oath can be given to, or taken by, a jury, to try matter in law; nor no attaint can lie for such a false oath . . . if the judge having heard the evidence given in court (for he knows no other) shall tell the jury, upon this evidence, The law is for the plaintiff, or for the defendant, and you are under the pain of fine and imprisonment to find accordingly, then the jury ought of duty so to do . . . for if the judge, from the evidence, shall by his own judgment first resolve upon any trial what the fact is, and so knowing the fact, shall then resolve what the law is, and order the jury penally to find accordingly, what either necessary or convenient uses can be fancied of juries, or to continue trials by them at all ? . . . And how the jury should, in any other manner, according to the course of trials used, find against the direction of the court in matter of law, is really not conceptible. . . .

But the reasons are, I conceive, most clear, that the judge could not, nor can fine and imprison the jury in such cases.

Without a fact agreed, it is as impossible for a judge, or any other, to know the law relating to that fact or direct concerning it, as to know an accident that hath no subject.

Hence it follows, that the judge can never direct what the law is in any matter controverted, without first knowing the fact; and then it follows, that without his previous knowledge of the fact, the jury cannot go against his direction in law, for he could not direct.

But the judge, *quâ* judge, cannot know the fact possibly but from the evidence which the jury have, but (as will appear) he can never know what evidence the jury have, and consequently he cannot know the matter of fact, nor punish the jury for going against their evidence, when he cannot know what their evidence is.

It is true, if the jury were to have no other evidence for the fact but what is deposed in court, the judge might know their evidence and the fact from it, equally as they, and so direct what the law were in the case, though even then the judge and jury might honestl differ in the result from the evidence, as well as two judges may which often happens. But the evidence which the jury have is much other than that : for—

(1) Being returned of the vicinage, whence the cause of action ariseth, the law supposeth them thence to have sufficient knowledg to try the matter in issue (and so they must) though no evidenc were given on either side in court, but to this evidence the judge is stranger.

(2) They may have evidence from their own personal knowledge, by which they may be assured, and sometimes are, that what is deposed in court, is absolutely false : but to this the judge is a stranger, and he knows no more of the fact than he hath learned in court, and perhaps by false depositions, and consequently knows nothing.

(3) The jury may know the witnesses to be stigmatized and infamous, which may be unknown to the parties, and consequently to the court.

(4) In many cases the jury are to have views necessarily, in many, by consent, for their better information ; as to this evidence likewise the judge is a stranger.

(5) If they do follow his direction, they may be attainted and the judgment reversed for doing that, which if they had not done, they should have been fined and imprisoned by the judge which is unreasonable.

(6) If they do not follow his direction, and be therefore fined, yet they may be attainted, and so doubly punished by distinct judicatures for the same offence, which the common law admits not.

A fine reversed in Banco Regis for infancy, per inspectionem et per testimonium del 4 fide dignorum. After upon examination of divers witnesses in chancery, the supposed infant was proved to be of age, "tempore finis levati," which testimonies were exemplified, and given in evidence after in Communi Banco in a writ of entry in the quibus there brought. And though it was the opinion of the court, that those testimonies were of no force against the judgment in the King's-Bench, yet the jury found, with the testimony in chancery, against direction of the court, upon a point in law, and their verdict after affirmed in an attaint brought, and after a writ of right was brought, and battle joined.

(7) To what end is the jury to be returned out of the vicinage, whence the cause of action ariseth ? To what end must hundredors be of the jury, whom the law supposeth to have nearer knowledge of the fact than those of the vicinage in general : To what end are they challenged so scrupulously to array and pole ? To what end must they have such a certain freehold, and be " probi et legales homines," and not of affinity with the parties concerned ? To what end must they have in many cases the view, for their exacter information chiefly ? To what end must they undergo the heavy punishment of the villainous judgment, if after all this they implicitly must give a verdict by the dictates and authority of another man, under pain of fines and imprisonment, when sworn to do it to the best of their own knowledge ?

A man cannot see by another's eye, nor hear by another's ear, no more can a man conclude or infer the thing to be resolved by another's understanding or reasoning; and though the verdict be right the jury give, yet they being not assured it is so from their own understanding, are forsworn, at least *in foro conscientiæ*.

(9) It is absurd a jury should be fined by the judge for going against their evidence, when he who fineth knows not what it is, as where a jury find without evidence, in court of either side, so if the jury find, upon their own knowledge, as the course is if the defendant plead solvit ad diem, to a bond proved, and offers no proof. The jury is directed to find for the plaintiff, unless they know payment was made of their own knowledge, according to the plea.

(After reviewing in detail the cases and objections " out of the ancient and modern books.")

The Chief Justice delivered the opinion of the court, and accordingly the prisoners were discharged.

(*Vaughan*, Reports, 135 *et seq.*   S.T. vi. 999–1260.)

III
THOMAS *v.* SORRELL
25 Charles II., 1674.

[This was a case which involved the dispensing power of the Crown. By statute (12 Charles II. c. 25 and 7 Edward VI. c. 5) to sell wine on retail without a licence was forbidden. James VI. had granted the Vintners' Company, of whom Sorrell was one, a patent with power to sell wine *non obstante* the statutes. Was the Dispensation conveyed in the letters patent valid? Lord Chief Justice Vaughan's judgment, which decided that it was, is remarkable for its learning and its ingenious and subtle reasoning, but " perhaps it was impossible to state the law in a clear and satisfactory form" (Anson). As with *Godden v. Hales* (p. 245), the matter has only a historic interest as showing the view taken by the courts in the seventeenth century, for after the Bill of Rights " the doctrine of *non obstante* . . . abdicated Westminster Hall when King James abdicated the Kingdom." See *Vaughan's* Reports, 330 *et seq.*; Anson, L.C. i. 300, ii. 31 ; *Hallam*, C.H. iii. 60.]

I observed not that any steady rule hath been drawn from the cases cited to guide a man's judgment, where the king may or may not dispense in penal laws, excepting that old rule taken from the case of 11 H. 7. "That with *malum prohibitum* by stat. the king may dispense, but not with *malum per se*." But I think that rule hath more confounded men's judgments on that subject, than rectified them. Yet I conceive that case, and the instances given in it, rightly understood, to be the best key afforded by our books to open this dark learning (as it seems to me) of Dispensations. . . . I agree that with *malum prohibitum* by stat. indefinitely understood, the king may dispense. But I deny that the king can dispense with every *malum prohibitum* by statute, though prohibited by statute only. . . . So it is generally true that *malum per se* cannot be dispensed with ; but thence to infer (as many do) that every *malum* which the king cannot dispense with is *malum per se* is not true. . . . When the suit is only the king's, but for the benefit and safety of a third person . . . the king cannot release, discharge or dispense with the suit, but by consent and agreement with of the party concerned . . . and by the same reason other penal laws, the breach of which are to men's particular damage, cannot be dispensed with. . . . And the reason why the king cannot dispense in such cases is, not only as nuisances are *contra bonum publicum*, but because if a Dispensation might make it lawful to do a nuisance . . . the person damaged would be deprived of his action. . . . No *non obstante* can dispense in these cases, and many the like, for that were to grant that a man should not have lawful actions brought against him . . . which the king cannot grant. . . . As to the second question ; admitting King James might have dispensed with particular persons for selling wine by retail . . . whether he could dispense with a Corporation ? . . . First, that the nature of the offence is such as may be dispensed with, seems clear in reason of law, and by constant practice of licensing particular persons. 2. Where the king can dispense with particular persons, he is not confined to number or place, but may license as many, and in such places, as he thinks fit. . . . I must say, as my Brother Atkins observed before, that in this case the Plaintiff's council argue against the king's Prerogative, for the extent of his Prerogative is the extent of his power, and the extent of his power is to do what he hath will to do, according to that, *ut summæ potestatis Regis est posse quantum velit sic magnitudinis est velle quantum potest ;* if therefore the king have a will to dispense with a Corporation, as it seems King James had in this case, when the patent was granted, but by law cannot, his power, and consequently his Prerogative, is less than if he could. *Malum Prohibitum* is that which is prohibited *per le statute : Per le Statute* is not intended only an act of Parliament, but any obliging law of constitution, as appears by the case.

(From Chief Justice Vaughan's Judgment, *Vaughan's* Reports, **331–359.**)

IV

SHIRLEY *v.* FAGG

27 Charles II., 1675.

[Six years after the violent quarrel between the two Houses of Parliament in the case of *Skinner v. The East India Company*, a second equally violent quarrel broke out, and, as with the previous case, the cause had its origin in a disputed claim of jurisdiction. Sir John Fagg, a member of the House of Commons, had obtained a verdict against Dr. Thomas Shirley in the Court of Chancery. Shirley, by a petition, brought the case on appeal before the House of Lords, who ordered Fagg to appear and answer at their bar. The House of Commons promptly espoused Fagg's cause, contending (1) that members of their House were exempted by privilege from legal process during the session of Parliament; (2) that the Lords had no appellate jurisdiction in Equity cases. The Lords replied with a contention (1) that an appeal to their House lay from *all* inferior courts: (2) that the claim of privilege could not bar their right to do justice. As both Houses were determined to maintain what they conceived were their privileges, the quarrel resolved itself into a sharp struggle between the two branches of the legislature to assert by arrest and counter-arrest the interpretations of their respective privileges, in which the important issue as to whether the Lords had an appellate jurisdiction in Equity cases was almost ignored. The main phases of the quarrel, illustrating the summary methods adopted to enforce the views of each House, have a historic interest, and can be followed in the excerpts given from the Journals. A series of fruitless conferences, even when aided by the efforts of the King to restore harmony, ended in a complete dead-lock. Nor did a prorogation from June 9 to October 13 lull the quarrel, for both Houses promptly renewed their conflicting claims when Parliament reassembled. The dispute only received its quietus with the prolonged prorogation from November 22, 1675, to February of 1677. As the House of Lords in *Skinner v. The East India Company* refused to admit that it was beaten, so now the Commons declined formally to abandon their claims. As a fact, however, the Lords had won. Dr. Shirley did not pursue his petition, but the Lords henceforward exercised without protest an appellate jurisdiction in Equity cases. See *Hallam*, C.H. iii. 25 *et seq.*; S.T. vi. 1122–1189; *Hatsell*, Precedents; *Hargrave*, H.J.L. ; *Pike*, H.L. 279–307 ; *Rogers*, P.L. i. 49, 52–54.]

Resolved, That a message be sent to the Lords, to acquaint them, that this House hath received information, That there is a Petition of appeal depending before them, at the suit of Thomas Shirley, Esq. against Sir John Fagg, a member of this House ; to which petition, he is, by order of the House of Lords, directed to answer on Friday next; and to desire the Lords to have a regard to the privileges of this House.

(Commons Journal, May 5, 1675.)

The House (of Lords) agreed with the Committee in this Declaration and ordered the same to be entered into the Journal-book of this House as their Declaration, viz.—

That it is the undoubted right of the Lords in judicature, to receive and determine in time of parliament, appeals from inferior courts, though a member of either House be concerned, that there may be no failure of justice in the land.

(Lords Journals, May 6, 1675.)

THE SPEAKER'S WARRANT FOR THE ARREST OF SHIRLEY

By virtue of an order, made the 12th day of May, 1675, by the Honourable the House of Commons assembled in Parliament, these are to require and authorise you forthwith to apprehend Dr. Thomas Shirley, and bring before the House, to answer his breach of privilege, in prosecuting a suit, by petition of appeal, in the House of Lords, against Sir John Fagg a member of this House : and for so doing this shall be your warrant. Given under my hand on Friday the 14th day of May in the 27th year of the reign of our Sovereign Lord King Charles the Second, etc. EDWARD SEYMOUR, *Speaker.*

Annoque Domini, 1675.

To Sir James Northfolk Knight, one of his majesty's serjeants-at-arms in ordinary now attending the hon. House of Commons, his deputy or deputies.

Resolved, That the appeal brought by Dr. Shirley in the House of Lords, against Sir John Fagg, a member of this House, and the proceedings thereupon, are a breach of the undoubted right and privileges of this House.

(Commons Journals, May 14, 1675.)

Whereas Thomas Shirley Esq., his majesty's physician in ordinary, hath a cause depending in this House, by way of appeal against Sir John Fagg, a member of the House of Commons, and, by law and course of parliament, ought to have privilege and freedom from arrest :

It is ordered, by the Lords spiritual and temporal, in parliament assembled, "That the said Thomas Shirley be, and he is hereby, privileged and protected accordingly, by the authority of this House, during the depending of his said cause in this House; and all persons whatsoever are hereby prohibited from arresting or otherwise molesting the said T. Shirley upon any pretence whatsoever, as they and every of them will answer the contrary to this House."

(Lords Journals, May 14, 1675.)

The House . . . after a serious debate, made this declaration following:

The Lords do order and declare, That it is the undoubted right of the Lords, in judicature, to receive and determine, in time of parliament, appeals from inferior courts, though a member of either House be concerned therein, that there may be no failure of justice in the land; and from this right and the exercise thereof, the Lords will not depart.

(Lords Journals, May 17, 1675.)

The matter of the Lords' answer being debated, *Resolved* "That it is the undoubted right of this House, that none of their members be summoned to attend the House of Lords during the sitting or privilege of parliament."

(Commons Journals, May 18, 1675.)

Sir Thomas Lee reports, from the Committee appointed to draw up Reasons to be offered at the Conference to be had with the Lords upon the Privileges of this House, contained in the Lords' Answer to the last Message of this House, in the case of Mr. Onslow; which Reasons were twice read, and with some alterations at the clerk's table (upon the question severally put) agreed to: which are as follow, viz.—

1. "That by the laws and usage of parliament, privilege of parliament belongs to every member of the House of Commons, in all cases, except treason, felony, and breach of the peace; which hath often been declared in parliament, without any exception of appeals before the Lords.

2. "That the reason of that privilege is, that the members of the House of Commons may freely attend the public affairs of that House, without disturbance or interruption; which doth extend as well to appeals before the House of Peers, as to proceedings in other courts.

3. "That by the constant course and usage of parliament, no member of the House of Commons can attend the House of Lords

without the especial leave of that House first obtained, much less be summoned or compelled so to do.

4. "If the Lords shall proceed to hear and determine any appeal where the party neither can, nor ought to attend, such proceedings would be contrary to the rules of justice.

5. "That the not determining of an appeal against a member of the House of Commons, is not a failure of justice, but only a suspension of proceedings in a particular case, during the continuance of that parliament, which is but temporary.

6. "That in case it were a failure of justice, it is not to be remedied by the House of Lords alone, but it may be by act of parliament."

Then sir Trevor Williams reports from the Lords, That he had attended, and desired a Conference with the Lords on the Privilege of this House, contained in the Lords' Answer to the Message to this House, in the case of Mr. Onslow : And that the Lords will return an Answer by messengers of their own.

Mr. Powle reports, from the Conference had with the Lords upon the subject matter of the former Conference, concerning the Warrant for apprehending Dr. Shirley, That the Lords had returned an Answer to the Reasons of this House, delivered at the former Conference, and are as follow :

"The Lords have appointed this Conference, upon the subject matter of the last Conference, and have commanded us to give these Answers to the Reasons and other matters then delivered by the House of Commons.

"To the first Reason the Lords conceive, that the most natural way of being informed, is by way of question ; and seeing a paper here which did reflect upon the privileges of the Lords' House, their lordships would not proceed upon it till they were assured it was owned by the House of Commons : But the Lords had no occasion at that time, nor do they now think fit to enter into the debate of the House of Commons being or not being proper judges in the case concerning the privilege of a member of that House ; their lordships' necessary consideration upon sight of that paper, being only, how far the House of Commons ordering (if that paper was theirs) the apprehension of Dr. Shirley, for prosecuting his appeal before the Lords, did entrench upon their lordships' both privilege and undoubted rights of judicature in the consequence of it, exempting all members of both Houses from the judicature of this the highest court of the kingdom ; which would cause a failure of that supreme justice, not administrable in any other court, and which their lordships will never admit.

"As to the second Reason, the Lords answer, That they do not apprehend how the matter of this message is any reflection upon the Speaker of the House of Commons.

"To the third Reason. The Lords cannot imagine how it can be apprehended in the least to reflect upon the House of Commons, for the House of Peers, upon a paper produced to their lordships, in form of a warrant of that House, whereof doubt was made among the Lords, whether any such thing had been ordered by that House, to enquire of the Commons, whether such warrant was ordered there or no? And without such liberty used by the Lords, it will be very hard for their lordships to be rightly informed, so as to preserve a good correspondence between the two Houses, which their lordships shall endeavour; or to know when warrants in the name of that House are true or pretended: And it is so ungrounded an apprehension, that their lordships intended any reflection in asking that question, and not taking notice in their Message of the complaint of the House of Commons owning that warrant, that the Lords had sent their Message concerning that paper to the House of Commons, before the Lords had received the said Commons' complaint.

"But their lordships have great cause to except against the unjust and strained reflection of that House upon their lordships, in asserting that the question in the Lords' Message could not be for information, as we affirm, but tending to interrupt the mutual correspondence between the two Houses; which we deny, and had not the least thought of.

"The Lords have further commanded us to say, That they doubt not when the House of Commons have received what we have delivered at this Conference, they will be sensible of their error, in calling our Message strange, unusual, or unparliamentary. Though we cannot but take notice, that their Answer to our Message, That they would consider of it, was the first of that kind that we can find to have come from that House."

The question being put, Whether the House be satisfied with the Reasons delivered by the Lords at the last Conference? it passed in the negative.

Resolved, That a Free Conference be desired with the Lords upon the matter delivered at the last Conference; and that the former managers do attend, and manage the Free Conference. . . .

(Commons Journals, May 20, 1675.)

Mr. Serjeant Pemberton, sir John Churchill, Mr. Serjeant Peck, and Mr. Porter, attending at the door, in obedience to the order of this house, and being severally called in; Mr. Speaker did severally acquaint them, that they were summoned to give an account to the house of their appearing as counsel at the bar of the House of Lords, in the prosecution of a cause depending upon an Appeal, wherein Mr. Dalmahay, a member of this house, is concerned; in the manifest breach of the order of this house; and giving up, as much as in them lay, the rights and privileges of the Commons of England. . . . And being withdrawn, and the matter debated. . . . Ordered, That Serjeant Pemberton, sir John Churchill, Mr. Serjeant Pecky and Charles Porter Esq. be taken into custody of the serjeant at arms attending this house, for their breach of the privilege of this house.

(Commons Journals, June 1, 1675.)

The Lord Privy Seal reported the draught of the ensuing order; which was read as followeth:

The House of Peers being made acquainted by examination of two witnesses upon oath at their bar, that the lower house of parliament had ordered into custody of their serjeant, Mr. Serjeant Peck, sir John Churchill, Mr. Serjeant Pemberton, heard at their lordships' bar, for doing their duty therein; and judging this to be a great indignity to the king's majesty in this his highest court of judicature in this kingdom, and an unexampled usurpation, and breach of privilege against the whole House of Peers, and tending to the subversion of the government of this kingdom, and a transcendent breach on the right and liberty of the subject, which is not to be impeached but by due process of law, and being by the law of the land concerned in all respects to do themselves and any oppressed subject right; do order the gentleman usher of the black-rod attending this house to repair to any place or prison within the kingdom of England where the said persons, or any of them, or Mr. Charles Porter counsellor at law, are, or shall be, detained or held in custody; and from any person or persons detaining they, or any of them, to demand delivery of them without fees; and the said usher of the black-rod is hereby empowered to call all persons necessary to his assistance herein, and to make return of this warrant to-morrow morning, by eight of the clock, to this House; and this shall be a sufficient authority on that behalf. . . .

The House approved of this Order, and ordered it to be signed by the clerk of the parliaments.

(Lords Journals, June 1, 1675.)

Mr. Vaughan reports, That the Lord Privy Seal did manage the Conference; and had delivered the occasion and intent of the Conference: Which Mr. Vaughan did report to the House, to the effect following, viz.—

"The Lords do take notice of the House of Commons their ordering into custody of their serjeant, Mr. Serjeant Peck, sir John Churchill, Mr. Serjeant Pemberton, and Mr. Charles Porter, counsellors at law, assigned by their lordships to be of counsel in an appeal, heard at their lordships' bar, in the case of sir Nicholas Crispe, against the lady Bowyer, Mr. Dalmahay, and others. The Lords in parliament, where his majesty is highest in his royal estate, and where the last resort of judging upon Writs of Error, and appeals in equity, in all causes, and over all persons, is undoubtedly fixed and permanently lodged.

It is an unexampled usurpation, and breach of privilege against the House of Peers, that their orders or judgments should be disputed, or endeavoured to be controlled, or the execution thereof destructed, by the lower house of parliament, who are no court, nor have any authority to administer an oath, or give any judgment.

"It is a transcendent invasion on the right and liberty of the subject, and against Magna Charta, the Petition of Right, and many other laws, which have provided, that no freeman shall be imprisoned, or otherwise restrained of his liberty, but by due process of law."

"This tends to the subversion of the government of this kingdom, and to the introducing of arbitrariness and disorder:

"Because it is in nature of an injunction from the lower house, who have no authority nor power of judicature over inferior subjects; much less over the King and Lords, against the orders and judgments of the supreme court."

"We are further commanded to acquaint you, That the Lords have therefore, out of that justice, which they are dispensers of, against oppression, and breach of laws, by judgment of this court, set at liberty, by the Gentleman Usher of the Black Rod, all the said serjeants and counsellors; and prohibited the lieutenant of the Tower, and all other keepers of prisons, and gaolers, and all persons whatsoever, from arresting, imprisoning, detaining, or otherwise molesting or charging the said gentlemen, or any of them, in this case: and if any person, of what degree soever, shall presume to the contrary, their lordships will exercise the authority with them intrusted, for putting the laws in execution: and we are further commanded to read to you a roll of parliament in the first year of the reign of King Hen. the fourth, whereof we have brought the original with us."

And a debate arising thereupon ;

Resolved, That a Conference be desired with the Lords, upon the subject matter of the last Conference.

Ordered, That Mr. Speaker do issue his warrant to the Serjeant at Arms attending this House, for the apprehending Charles Porter, esq. and bring him to the bar of this House, to answer the breach of privilege objected against him.

A petition of Sir John Fagg was read, submitting himself to the House, and craving their pardon for his offence, and praying, he might be released of his imprisonment.

Ordered, That Sir John Fagg [1] be released and enlarged from his imprisonment in the Tower. . . .

(Commons Journals, June 3, 1675.)

Then instead of putting the question, it was ordered, That this House will proceed upon no other business (except what shall be recommended by his majesty) till they have received full satisfaction, and vindicated themselves in this breach of their privileges. . . .

Ordered, That the humble address of this House to His Majesty . . . shewing, That whereas this House directed the Gentleman Usher of the Black-rod to demand the persons of Serjeant Peck, sir John Churchill, Serjeant Pemberton and Mr. Charles Porter . . . and in pursuance of that direction, finding them to be committed prisoners to the Tower of London by order of the House of Commons, repaired to sir John Robinson, his majesty's Lieutenant of the Tower, and demanded them of him, who refused to deliver them otherwise than by order of the House of Commons ; This House humbly desires his majesty, that he will be pleased to remove the said sir John Robinson from that trust, and to appoint some other person to be his Lieutenant of the Tower.

(Lords Journals, June 4, 1675.)

Sir Thomas Lee reports, from the committee, the reasons agreed to be offered at the Conference to be had with the Lords, upon the matters delivered at the last Conference : which were twice read ; and with some amendments made at the table, severally agreed ; and are as followeth, viz.—

---

[1] Fagg had been imprisoned in the Tower by order of the House on June 1st for "a breach of privilege" in that "without leave" he had "appeared in the Lords' House, and put in his answer to the appeal of Dr. Shirley" when the matter of his privilege was, at his instance, in question "in this House of Commons."

"Your lordships having desired the last Conference upon matters of high importance concerning the dignity of the king, and the safety of the government; the Commons did not expect to hear from your lordships at that Conference, things so contrary to, and inconsistent with, the matter upon which the said Conference was desired, as were then delivered by your lordships.

"It was much below the expectation of the Commons, that, after a representation in your lordships' message of matters of so high importance, the particular upon which the Conference was grounded, should be only the commitment of four lawyers to the custody of their own serjeant at arms, for a manifest violation of the privileges of their House.

"But the Commons were much more surprised, when your lordships had introduced the Conference, with an assurance it was in order to a good correspondency between the two Houses, that your lordships should immediately assume a power to judge the order of the House of Commons, for the imprisonment of Mr. Serjeant Peck, Sir John Churchill, Mr. Serjeant Pemberton, and Mr. Charles Porter, to be illegal and arbitrary, and the execution thereof a great indignity to the king's majesty, with many other high reflections upon the House of Commons, throughout the whole Conference; whereby your lordships hath condemned the whole House of Commons as criminal: Which is without precedent, or example, or any ground of reason so to do.

"It is not against the king's dignity for the House of Commons to punish by imprisonment a commoner, that is guilty of violating their privileges, that being according to the known laws and custom of parliament, and the right of their privileges, declared by the king's royal predecessors in former parliament; and by himself in this.

"But your lordships claiming to be the supreme court, and that his majesty is highest in his royal estate in the court of judicature, there is a diminution of the dignity of the king; who is highest in his royal estate, in full parliament; and is derogatory to the authority of the whole parliament, by appropriating it to yourselves.

"The Commons did not infringe any privileges of the House of Peers, but only defend and maintain their own; On the other side, your lordships do highly entrench upon the rights and privileges of the House of Commons, denying them to be a court, or to have any authority or power of judicature; which, if admitted, will leave them without any authority or power to preserve themselves.

"As to what your lordships call a transcendental invasion of the rights and liberty of the subject, and against Magna Charta, the

Petition of Right, and many other laws; the House of Commons presume, that your lordships know, that neither the Great Charter, the Petition of Right, nor many other laws, do take away the law and custom of parliament, or of either House of Parliament; or else your lordships have much forgotten the Great Charter, and those other laws, in the several judgments your lordships have passed upon the king's subjects, in cases of privilege.

"But the Commons cannot find, by Magna Charta, or by any other law or ancient custom of parliament, that your lordships have any jurisdiction, in cases of appeal from courts of equity.

"We are further commanded to acquaint you, that the enlargement of the said persons imprisoned by order of the House of Commons, by the Gentleman Usher of the Black Rod; and the prohibition, with threats to all officers and other persons whatsoever, not to receive or detain them, is an apparent breach of the rights and privileges of the House of Commons: and they have therefore caused them to be retaken into the custody of the Serjeant at Arms, and hath committed them to the Tower.

"As to the Parliament-Roll of 1st Hen. 4, caused to be read by your lordships at the last Conference, but not applied, the Commons apprehend it doth not concern the case in question; for that this record was made upon occasion of judgments given by the Lords to depose and imprison their lawful king; to which the Commons were unwilling to be made parties; and therefore the Commons conceived it will not be for the honour of your lordships, to make further use of that record.

"But we are commanded to read to your lordships the Parliament-Roll of the 4th of Edward the 3rd, n. 6; which if your lordships please to consider, they doubt not but your lordships will find occasion to apply it to the present purpose."

(Commons Journals, June 4, 1675.)

Resolved, *nem. con.* That as to the case of Appeal, brought against sir John Fagg in the House of Lords, sir John Fagg shall have the protection and the assistance of this House.

Resolved, *nem. con.* That if any person or persons shall be aiding or assisting in putting in execution any Sentence or Judgment that shall be given by the House of Lords, upon the Appeal brought by Dr. Shirley, against sir John Fagg, a member of this House, such person and persons shall be adjudged and taken to be betrayers of the rights and liberties of the Commons of England, and the privileges of this House; and shall be proceeded against accordingly.

(Commons Journals, June 7, 1675.)

Resolved, *nem. con.* That no commoners of England, committed by order or warrant of the House of Commons for breach of privilege or contempt of that house, ought, without order of that House, to be by any writ of Habeas Corpus, or other authority whatsoever, made to appear, and answer, and do and receive a determination in the House of Peers, during the session of parliament, wherein such person was so committed.

(Commons Journals, June 9, 1675.)

(The King prorogued Parliament from June 9 to October 13.)

"Whereas this House hath been informed of several Appeals depending in the House of Lords, from Courts of Equity, to the great violation of the Rights and Liberties of the Commons of England; it is this day Resolved and Declared, 'That whosoever shall solicit, plead, or prosecute any appeal against any commoner of England, from any Court of Equity before the House of Lords, shall be deemed and taken a betrayer of the Rights and Liberties of the Commons of England; and shall be proceeded against accordingly.'"

(Commons Journals, November 19, 1675.)

It is ordered by the Lords Spiritual and Temporal in parliament assembled, That this House will hear the said cause (Shirley *v.* Fagg), by counsel at the bar, on Monday the twenty-second instant, at ten of the clock in the forenoon. . . . And upon debate of the Commons Vote made yesterday, it was ordered, "That the Paper posted up in several places, signed by William Goldsbro, Cler. Dom. Com. against the Judicature of the House of Peers in Cases of Appeals from Courts of Equity, is illegal, unparliamentary, and tending to the dissolution of the government."

(Lords Journals, Nov. 20, 1675.)

(On November 22 the King again prorogued Parliament, which did not meet again until February, 1677.)

V

THE CASE OF BENJAMIN HARRIS
32 Charles II., 1680.

[Harris was tried for "causing to be printed and sold" a libellous pamphlet. The charge of Chief Justice Scroggs to the jury illustrates the historic features of the case, and may be compared with that of Holt in Tutchin's case (p. 267). The jury tried to find Harris guilty "only of selling the book," but under pressure from the Judge brought in a verdict of guilty, and subsequently the court inflicted a fine of £500, the pillory for one hour, and the finding of sureties for good behaviour for three years. See S.T. vii. 926–932 and authorities on *Tutchin's* case.]

Because my brother shall be satisfied with the opinion of all the judges of England, what this offence is, which they would insinuate, as if the mere selling of such a book was no offence: it is not long since, that all the judges met, by the King's command: as they did some time before too: and they both times declared unanimously, that all persons that do write, or print, or sell any pamphlet, that is either scandalous to public or private persons; such books may be seized and the person punished by law: that all books, which are scandalous to the government may be seized: and all persons so exposing them may be punished. And further, that all writers of news, though not scandalous, seditious, nor reflective upon the government or the state: yet if they are writers (as there are few others) of false news, they are indictable and punishable on that account. So that your hopes of any thing of that kind will be vain: for all the judges have declared this offence, at the common law, to be punishable in the seller, though in the way of his trade: the books may be seized, and the person punished. As for this book, in particular: you can hardly read a more low and pernicious book, to put us all into a flame. . . . Except the writer of it, there cannot be a worse man in the world . . . and, Mr. Harris, if you expect any thing in this world, of this kind of favour, you must find out the author: for he must be a rebellious, and villainous traitor. . . . You (the Jury) have nothing more to do, but to give your verdict: If there be any thing in law, let me know it because you go out.

(From the charge to the Jury of Scroggs, C.J.)

Then one of the Jury asked my lord, if they might not have the book with them, which was then in the court, and it was answered in the negative.

(S.T. 7, 930.)

R

VI

THE CASE OF HENRY CARR
32 Charles II., 1680.

[Carr was tried before Lord Chief Justice Scroggs, and the nature of the case is sufficiently explained in the charge to the jury. The jury found him guilty, and were told by the Judge and the Recorder (Jefferies) they "had done like honest men." See S.T. vii. 1111–1130.]

The present case it stands thus : Mr. Carr, here in an information brought against him for publishing a printed pamphlet called, The Pacquet of Advice from Rome . . . the question is, Whether he was the author or publisher of this. . . . If there be a known case in men's lives, certainly that should govern in offences, and especially when offences are of a nature that reflect upon the Government. As for those words, *illicite, maliciose,* unlawful : for that I must recite what Mr. Recorder (Sir Geo. Jefferies) told you of at first, what all the judges of England have declared under their hands. The words I remember are these : When, by the King's command, we were to give in our opinion what was to be done in point of the regulation of the press ; we did all subscribe, that to print or publish any news books or pamphlets of news whatsoever, is illegal : that it is a manifest intent to the breach of the peace, and they may be proceeded against by law for an illegal thing. Suppose now that this thing is not scandalous, what then ? If there had been no reflection in this book at all, yet it is *illicite,* and the author ought to be convicted for it. And that is for a public notice to all people, and especially printers and booksellers, that they ought to print no book or pamphlet of news whatsoever without authority. So as he is to be convicted for it as a thing *illicite* done, not having authority. And I will assure you, if you find any of those papers, I shall be more merciful in the consideration of their punishment, if it be inoffensive. But if so be they will undertake to print news foolishly, they ought to be punished and shall be punished if they do it without authority, though there is nothing reflecting on the government as an unlawful thing. . . Therefore this book, if it be made by him to be published, it is unlawful whether it be malicious or not. . . . If you find him guilty, and say what he is guilty of, we will judge whether the thing imports malice or not. . . . Now there only remains one thing, that is, whether or no he was the publisher of this book. . . . If you are satisfied in your conscience that you believe he is not the author, you must acquit him. If you are satisfied it is not he, you must find him Not guilty. . . .

(The Jury went from the Bar and nigh an hour after returned, and brought him in guilty.)

(From Scroggs', C.J., charge to the jury. S.T. 1126 *et seq.*)

VII

THE CASE OF THE CHARTER OF THE CITY OF LONDON

33–35 Charles II., 1681–1683.

[This important case, which "gave a pretext for the most dangerous aggression on public liberty that occurred" (Hallam) in the reign of Charles II., raised, beside the specific legal points involved, the theory and powers of the royal prerogative. An information by *Quo Warranto* was brought into the Court of King's Bench against the Corporation of London—the object being to obtain the surrender of the charter into the king's hands—on the ground (1) that the imposition of a toll on certain goods in the city markets was *extra vires;* (2) that the petition of the Common Council to the king in December, 1679, was a misdemeanour which warranted a judgment of forfeiture. Practically the following points were involved in the arguments : (1) Whether a corporation can be forfeited ; (2) whether an act of the Mayor, Aldermen, and Common Council be an act of the Corporation ; (3) whether the toll and the petition being such acts justify forfeiture. Judgment was given on all these against the Corporation. On the importance of the decision and the subsequent history of the case see *Hallam*, C.H. ii. 453 *et seq.; S.T.* viii. 1039–1358 ; *Macaulay*, H.E. ch. ii.; *Ranke*, H.E. iii. The text of the citations from the judgment has been collated with the MS. Report in the Owen Wynne MS. vol. 75, in the Codrington Library of All Souls' College.]

Saunders, C.J. But this is one thing, Mr. Pollexfen, that I would say to you upon your argument, what a grievous thing would it be, if so be, the being of a corporation might be forfeited or dissolved, because say you, it is possible that all the corporations in England may be dissolved because they have committed such things that may be forfeitures. We must put the scales equal on both sides. Let us then consider the other side, whether, if so be that it should be taken for law, that a corporation is indissoluble or cannot be dissolved for any crime whatsoever, then those two things do not follow; First, you will shut out the King's *Quo Warranto*, let him have what reason he can for it, or let them do what they will: And in the next place, you have set up so many independent commonwealths. For if a corporation may do nothing amiss whatsoever, what else does follow, for now I am not on the point, whether this corporation has done any act that is amiss, but considering your argument in general, when you make it a thing of such ill consequence that a corporation should be forfeited by any crime; but I say now, to put in the other scale the mischiefs that would follow, if so be law a corporation might not be dissolved for one fault or another: But let them do what they would, it should still remain a corporation. Then it is plain, they are so many commonwealths independent upon the king, and the king's *Quo Warranto* is quite shut out; that is mighty considerable. For a man to make an argument and to say it would be very mischievous, inconvenient, or worse to the city of London, if a judgment should be given against it, is not to govern us . . . what we are to look at principally is what the law is, for that way the law goes, we must go . . . and that the way the law has settled has the least inconvenience in it. . . .

Jones, J. We are all unanimously agreed in one and the same opinion in this whole matter. . . . First, Then as to the great preliminary point, Whether a corporation aggregate such as the city is, may be forfeited or seized into the king's hands. We are of opinion that it may, upon breach of that condition which the law annexes to it. . . . And this seems evident beyond all contradiction . . . by the statute of 28 Edward III. cap. 10. . . . And as to a forfeiture it seems to me plain, by the general act of oblivion, by which all bodies corporate and politic as well as persons natural are pardoned. . . . It is likewise plain by the very act for regulating corporations . . . and if the law should be otherwise it would erect as many independent republics in the kingdom as there are corporations aggregate, which, how fatal that might prove to the crown and the government now established, every man may easily conceive. To the Second point, we are of opinion that the assuming a power by the mayor, commonalty and citizens of London, to make by-laws, to levy money upon the subject, and the levying vast sums of money thereby is a great oppression upon the people . . . and so a just cause of forfeiture. Thirdly, We are of opinion, that the charge touching the ordering, exhibiting and printing the Petition, so scandalous to the king and government, so dangerously tending to the seduction of hi subjects, to a dislike of his person and government, and so evidently tending to sedition thereby and rebellion, is another just cause of forfeiture. Fourthly : we are of opinion, that these acts are the acts of the corporation, being so alleged by the replication, and not sufficiently answered by the rejoinder. . . . And it is the judgment of this Court : That the franchise and liberty of London be taken into the king's hands. . . . And it is the opinion of the whole Court.

VIII

GODDEN *v.* HALES

2 James II., 1686.

[Sir Edward Hales, the defendant, was a Roman Catholic and lieutenant of the Tower, who had neglected to take the oaths of supremacy and allegiance prescribed by the statute 25 Car. II. c. 2. A collusive action was brought against him by Arthur Godden with a view of establishing the prerogative power claimed by the Crown to dispense with the operation of the statute. Hales was indicted and convicted at the Rochester Assizes, and the action was brought to recover the £500 awarded by the statute to the informer. It was argued before twelve judges in the King's Bench, when Hales pleaded a royal pardon and dispensation in bar of the action. Eleven judges (Street J. alone dissenting) agreed that the plea in bar was good, *i.e.* that the Crown had the power to dispense. The case is therefore remarkable : (1) when compared with the decision in that of *The Seven Bishops ;* (2) for the arguments explicitly laid down by Lord Chief Justice Herbert, which were trenchantly dealt with in the Bill of Rights. See S.T. xi. 1166–1315 (the appendices quote contemporary pamphlets in which the judgment is minutely examined) ; *Hallam*, C.H. iii. ch. xiv.; *Macaulay*, H.E. ch. vi.; *Broom*, C.L. 492–506.]

Then the Lord chief Justice Herbert spake thus :

Chief Justice. This is a case of great consequence, but of as little difficulty as ever any case was, that raised so great an expectation : for if the king cannot dispense with this statute, he cannot dispense with any penal law whatsoever.

As to the first point, whether he shall be admitted to plead this dispensation and pardon to this action of debt : (having not pleaded it to the indictment) I think he may : for this court shall not be bound by the finding of the jury below, for he (for anything that does appear) did plead it there, and the jury might have gone against the direction of the court, yet that shall not conclude us : but if the party has good matter to discharge himself, he may shew it : as if a man be convicted of an assault and battery against the defendant, the plaintiff may give the former conviction in evidence, but yet he must also prove the battery, or else he shall not recover.

And this being an estapel, it shall not bind because the plaintiff was not a party to the first suit.

As to the second point, whether the king can dispense with the act or no, I think it a question of little difficulty. There is no law whatsoever but may be dispensed with by the supreme lawgiver; as the laws of God may be dispensed with by God himself; as it appears by God's command to Abraham, to offer up his son Isaac; So likewise the law of man may be dispensed with by the legislator, for a law may be either too wide or too narrow, and there may be many cases which may be out of the conveniencies which did induce the law to be made; for it is impossible for the wisest lawmaker to foresee all the cases which may be or are to be remedied, and therefore there must be a power somewhere, able to dispense with these laws. But as to the case of simony, that is objected by the other side, that is against the law of God, and a special offence, and therefore *malum in se*, which I do agree the king cannot dispense with. And as to the cases of usury and non-residence, those cases do come in under that rule, that the king cannot dispense with them, because the subject has a benefit by them; for in case of usury the bond is made void by the statute, and therefore if the king should dispense with it, the subject would lose the benefit of the avoiding the bond. And as to the cases of buying and selling of offices, which are objected, there is no need of resolving, whether the king could dispense with the statute or no, because the party was disabled to take any such office by the contract, and the disability was attacked by force before the office was vested, so that the king could not remove the disability; and so I do agree that it would have been in this case, if the defendant had by his neglect or refusal to take the oaths rendered himself incapable before he had taken the king's dispensation; for the king's dispensation coming before the disability attacked, it does prevent it.

The case of the sheriff is much a stronger case than this, and comes up to it in every particular, for that statute doth disable the party to take, and the king to grant; and there is also a clause in that statute, which says, that the patent shall be void, notwithstanding any Non Obstante to the contrary; and there is a penalty of £200 like to our case : and yet by the opinion of all the judges of England, the king has a power of dispensing with that statute; yet that statute does expressly say, the king shall not dispense with it by a Non Obstante : so if an act of parliament had a clause in it, that it should never be repealed, yet without question, the same power that made it may repeal it. Besides, that statute makes the patents void at the time of granting them; but by this statute the patents are good at the time of granting them, and continue so 'till the neglect to take the oaths, for doing of which the patentee has three months time. And if the case of the sheriff be law, as it hath been taken ever since Hen. 7th's time, and is cited for good law in many of our books, and never 'till now questioned; for the common cause and experience have been according to it : then I defy all the world to show me any material difference between that and this, only that this is the stronger case of the two, in many particulars. But because the case has been denied by the plaintiff's counsel, it does concern us to take the opinion of our brethren, it being a matter of so great consequence in the circuits; for if it be not law, then there are some sheriffs that be not lawful, and so have not power to return the juries, and then we have no power to try and give judgment upon any offenders; and it also concerns us who go into our countries, to take advice of it : for if that case is not law, our patents, which are Non Obstantes to 23 Hen. 8. 24, may not be good, and so we have no authorities to go the circuits; and therefore I will ask the opinion of all the judges, as well in that case as this.

On Monday the 21st of June, after having consulted with all the judges, his lordship delivered their opinions in open court, thus :

In the case of Goodwin and Hales, wherein the defendant pleads a dispensation from the king; it is doubted, whether or no the king had such a prerogative? Truly, upon the argument before us, it appeared as clear a case as ever came before this court : but because men fancy I know not what difficulty, when really there is none, we were willing to give so much countenance to the question in the case, as to take the advice of all the judges of England. They were all assembled at Serjeant's Inn, and this case was put to them; and the great case of the sheriffs was put, whether the dispensation in that case were legal? because upon that depended the execution of all the law of the nation : and I must tell you, that there were ten upon the place that clearly delivered their opinions, that the case of the sheriffs was good law; and that all the attainders grounded upon indictments found by juries returned by such sheriffs were good, and not erroneous; and consequently that men need not have any fears or scruples about that matter. And in the next place they did clearly declare, that there was no imaginable difference between that case and this; unless it were, that this were very much the clearer case of the two, and liable to the fewer exceptions.

My brother Powell said, he was inclined to be of the same opinion; but he would rather have some more time to consider of it: but he has since sent by my lord Holloway, to let us know that he does concur with us. To these eleven judges there is one dissenter, brother Street, who yet continues his opinion, That the king cannot dispense in this case: but that's the opinion of one single judge, against the opinion of eleven. We were satisfied in our judgments before, and having the concurrence of eleven out of twelve, we think we may well declare the opinion of the court to be, that the king may dispense in this case: and the judges go upon these grounds;

1. That the kings of England are sovereign princes.

2. That the laws of England are the king's laws.

3. That therefore 'tis an inseparable prerogative in the kings of England, to dispense with penal laws in particular cases, and upon particular necessary reasons.

4. That of those reasons and these necessities, the king himself is sole judge: and then, which is consequent upon all,

5. That this is not a trust invested in, or granted to the king by the people, but the ancient remains of the sovereign power and prerogative of the kings of England; which never yet was taken from them, nor can be. And therefore such a dispensation appearing upon record to come time enough to save him from the forfeiture, judgment ought to be given for the defendant.

(S.T. xi. 1195–1199.)

A Warrant of Dispensation.

James R.,

Right trusty &c. we greet you well. Whereas in the 12th Act of our current parliament, intituled "Act of Supply," there is a clause ordaining . . . to take the oath and that appointed by law, which clause we judge fit, for our service, to require you to put vigorously in execution excepting these . . . whom we have dispensed with from taking the same, and such as we shall hereafter dispense with under our royal hand. For doing whereof this shall be your warrant, and so we bid you heartily farewell. Given at our Court at Whitehall, the 7th day of November, 1685, and of our reign the first year.

By His Majesty's command,   MELFORD.

IX

THE CASE OF THE SEVEN BISHOPS
4 James II., 1688.

[Archbishop Sancroft and six bishops, St. Asaph, Ely, Peterborough, Bath and Wells, Chichester, and Bristol, petitioned the King in person against the orders to distribute and read the Declaration of Indulgence. Subsequently being informed that a criminal information for libel would be exhibited against them in the Court of King's Bench, they refused on the ground of their privileges as Peers to enter into recognisances to appear, and were committed to the Tower. On June 29, 1688, they were tried before the Lord Chief Justice and a jury, on a charge of writing and publishing a "false, feigned, malicious, pernicious, and seditious libel." The trial turned largely on two points : (1) Was the publication proved ? (2) Was the petition libellous ? It has since become a leading case on (1) the right to petition, (2) the nature of seditious libel, and (3) the legality of the power by prerogative to suspend and dispense with existing laws, as had been claimed and exercised in the Declaration of Indulgence. The extracts give (1) the Declaration of Indulgence, (2) the Order in Council, (3) the Bishop's Protest, and (4) a report of the case. On June 30 the jury found a verdict of "Not Guilty" on the whole question. See *Macaulay*, H. of E. ch. viii.; S.T. xii. 183-433 ; *Hallam*, C.H. iii. ch. xiv.; *May*, C.H.E. i. 444-451, ii. 107-117 ; *Broom*, C.L. 406-517.]

I

THE DECLARATION OF INDULGENCE, 1687.[1]

His Majesty's gracious declaration to all his loving subjects for liberty of conscience.

It having pleased God Almighty not only to bring us to the imperial crown of these kingdoms through the greatest difficulties, but to preserve us by a more than ordinary providence upon the throne of our royal ancestors, there is nothing now that we so fondly desire as to establish our government on such a foundation as may make our subjects happy, and unite us by inclination as well as duty. Which we think can be done by no means so effectually as by granting to them the free exercise of their religion for the time to come, and add that to the perfect enjoyment of their property, which has never been in any case invaded by us since our coming to the crown. Which being the two things men value most, shall ever be preserved in these kingdoms, during our reign over them, as the truest methods

---

[1] Cp. throughout with the Declaration of Charles II., p. 42.

of their peace and our glory. We cannot but heartily wish, as it will easily be believed, that all the people of our dominions were members of the Catholic Church; yet we humbly thank Almighty God, it is and has of long time been our constant sense and opinion (which upon divers occasions we have declared) that conscience ought not to be constrained nor people forced in matters of mere religion: it has ever been directly contrary to our inclination, as we think it is to the interest of government, which it destroys by spoiling trade, depopulating countries, and discouraging strangers, and finally, that it never obtained the end for which it was employed. And in this we are the more confirmed by the reflections we have made upon the conduct of the four last reigns. For after all the frequent and pressing endeavours that were used in each of them to reduce this kingdom to an exact conformity in religion, it is visible the success has not answered the design, and that the difficulty is invincible.

We therefore, out of our princely care and affection to all our loving subjects, that they may live at ease and quiet, and for the increase of trade and encouragement of strangers, have thought fit by virtue of our royal prerogative to issue forth this our declaration of indulgence, making no doubt of the concurrence of our Two Houses of Parliament when we shall think it convenient for them to meet.

In the first place, we do declare that we will protect and maintain our archbishops, bishops, and clergy, and all other our subjects of the Church of England in the free exercise of their religion as by law established, and in the quiet and full enjoyment of all their possessions, without any molestation or disturbance whatsoever.

We do likewise declare that it is our royal will and pleasure that from henceforth the execution of all and all manner of penal laws in matters ecclesiastical, for not coming to church, or not receiving the Sacrament, or for any other nonconformity to the religion established, or for or by reason of the exercise of religion in any manner whatsoever be immediately suspended; and the further execution of the said penal laws and every of them is hereby suspended.

And to the end that by the liberty hereby granted the peace and security of our government in the practice thereof may not be endangered, we have thought fit, and hereby straitly charge and command all our loving subjects, that—as we do freely give them leave to meet and serve God after their own way and manner, be it in private houses or places purposely hired or built for that use, so that they take especial care that nothing be taught or preached amongst them, which may any way tend to alienate the hearts of our people from us or our government, and that their meetings and assemblies be peaceably, openly, and publicly held, and all persons freely admitted to them, and that they do signify and make known to some one or more of the next justices of the peace what place or places, they set apart for those uses, and that all our subjects may enjoy such their religious assemblies with greater assurance and protection—we have thought it requisite, and do hereby command, that no disturbance of any kind be made or given unto them, under pain of our displeasure, and to be further proceeded against with the utmost severity.

And forasmuch as we are desirous to have the benefit of the service of all our loving subjects, which by the law of nature is inseparably annexed and inherent in our royal person, and that none of our subjects may for the future be under any discouragement or disability (who are otherwise well inclined and fit to serve us) by reason of some oaths or tests that have been usually administered on such occasions, we do hereby further declare, that it is our royal will and pleasure that the oaths commonly called "The oaths of supremacy and allegiance," and also the several tests and declarations mentioned in the Acts of Parliament made in the five-and-twentieth[1] and thirtieth years of the reign of our late royal brother, King Charles II., shall not at any time hereafter be required to be taken, declared, or subscribed by any person or persons whatsoever, who is or shall be employed in any office or place of trust, either civil or military, under us or in our government. And we do further declare it to be our pleasure and intention from time to time hereafter, to grant our royal dispensations under our great seal to all our loving subjects so to be employed, who shall not take the said oaths, or subscribe or declare the said tests or declarations in the above-mentioned Acts and every of them.

And to the end that all our loving subjects may receive and enjoy the full benefit and advantage of our gracious indulgence hereby intended, and may be acquitted and discharged from all pains, penalties, forfeitures, and disabilities by them or any of them incurred or forfeited, or which they shall or may at any time hereafter be liable to, for or by reason of their nonconformity, or the exercise of their religion, and from all suits, troubles, or disturbances for the same ; we do hereby, give our free and ample pardon unto all nonconformists, recusants, and other our loving subjects, for all crimes and things

[1] Tho Test Act, p. 39.

committed or done contrary to the penal laws, formerly made relating to religion, and the profession or exercise thereof; hereby declaring that this our royal pardon and indemnity shall be as good and effectual to all intents and purposes, as if every individual person had been therein particularly named, or had particular pardons under the great seal, which we do likewise declare shall from time to time be granted unto any person or persons desiring the same; willing and requiring our judges, justices, and other officers to take notice of and obey our royal will and pleasure hereinbefore declared.

And although the freedom and assurance we have hereby given in relation to religion and property might be sufficient to remove from the minds of our loving subjects all fears and jealousies in relation to either, yet we have thought fit further to declare that we will maintain them in all their properties and possessions, as well of church and abbey lands, as in any other their lands and properties whatsoever.

Given at our court at Whitehall the fourth day of April, 1687, in the third year of our reign.

II

ORDER IN COUNCIL

It is this day ordered by his Majesty in Council, that his Majesty's late gracious declaration, bearing date the 27th of April last, be read at the usual time of divine service, upon the 20th and 27th of this month, in all churches and chapels within the cities of London and Westminster, and ten miles thereabouts; and upon the 3rd and 10th of June next, in all other churches and chapels throughout this Kingdom. And it is hereby further ordered, that the right reverend the bishops cause the said declaration to be sent and distributed throughout their several and respective dioceses, to be read accordingly.

(London Gazette, May 7, 1688.)

III

THE BISHOP'S PROTEST

"We are not averse to the publishing of the Declaration, out of want of due tenderness towards Dissenters, with whome wee shall be willing to come to such a temper as shall be thought fitt when the matter comes to be settled and considered in parl'mt. But the Declaration being founded on such a dispensing power, as may at pleasure sett aside all law, ecclesiastical or civill, appears to us illegall,

and did soe to the parl'mt of 72, and it is a point of soe great consequence, that we cannot soe farre make o'selves p'ties to it, as the
reading of it in the churches at ye time of divine service will
amount to.   (Signed)   CANTERBURY,
 "This was delivered   ELY,
  to ye King, May 7,   PETERBOROW,
  1688, by these Bps.   &c., &c."

(Bodleian Library, Rawl. MSS. C. 798, 368b. Cited also in *Duckett*,
Penal Laws and Test Act, 1883 ; privately printed.)

IV

THE CASE

Serj. Levinz (for the defence). Now, my lord, if your lordship
pleases, the charge is a charge for a libel, and there are two things to
be considered.

First, Whether the bishops did deliver this paper to the king?
But that we leave upon the evidence that has been given ; only we
say, there has been no direct proof of that.

In the next place, supposing they did deliver this petition to the
king, Whether this be a libel upon the matter of it, the manner of
delivering it, or the persons that did it?

And with submission, my lord, this cannot be a libel, although it
be true that they did so deliver it.

First, my lord, there is little disingenuity offered to my lords the
bishops, in only setting forth part, and not the whole, in only reciting
the body, and not the prayer.

But, my lord, with your lordship's favour, taking the petitionary
part, and adding it to the other, it quite alters the nature of the
thing ; for it may be, a complaint without seeking redress might be
an ill matter ; but here taking the whole together, it appears to be a
complaint of a grievance, and a desire to be eased of it.

With your lordship's favour, the subjects have a right to petition
the king in all their grievances, so say all our books of law, and so
says the statute of the thirteenth of the late king ; they may petition,
and come and deliver their petition under the number of ten, as
heretofore they might have done, says the statute ; so that they all
times had a right so to do, and indeed if they had not it were the
most lamentable thing in the world, that men must have grievances
upon them, and yet they not to be admitted to seek relief in an
humble way.

Now, my lord, this is a petition setting forth a grievance, and praying his majesty to give relief. And what is this grievance? It is that command of his, by that order made upon my lords the bishops, to distribute the declaration and cause it to be read in the churches: and pray, my lord, let us consider what the effects and consequences of that distribution and reading is: it is to tell the people, that they need not submit to the Act of Uniformity, nor to any act of parliament made about ecclesiastical matters, for they are suspended and dispensed with. This my lords the bishops must do, if they obey this order; but your lordship sees, if they do it, they lie under an Anathema by the statute of 1 Eliz., for they are under a curse if they do not look to the preservation and observation of that act: but this command to distribute and read the declaration, whereby all these laws are dispensed with, is to let the people know, they will not do what the act requires of them.

Now, with your lordship's favour, my lords the bishops lying under this pressure, the weight of which was very grievous upon them, they by petition apply to the king to be eased of it, which they might do as subjects: besides, my lord, they are peers of the realm, and were most of them sitting as such in the last parliament, where, as you have heard, it was declared, such a dispensation could not be; and then in what a case should they have been, if they should have distributed this declaration, which was so contrary to their actings in parliament? What could they have answered for themselves, had they thus contributed to this declaration, when they had themselves before declared, that the king could not dispense.

And that this was no new thing, for it had been so declared in a parliament before in two sessions of it, in the late king's reign within a very little time one of another; and such a parliament that were so liberal in their aids to the crown, that a man would not think they should go about to deprive the crown of any of its rights. It was a parliament that did do as great services for the crown as ever any did, and therefore there is no reason to suspect, that if the king had had such a power, they would have appeared so earnest against it.

But, my lord, if your lordship pleases, these are not the beginnings of this matter; for we have shewed you from the fifteenth of Richard the Second, that there was a power granted by the parliament to the king to dispense with a particular act of parliament, which argues, that it could not be without an act of parliament: and in 1662, it is said expressly, that they could not be dispensed with but by act of parliament. It is said so again in 1672. The king was then pleased to assume to himself such a power as is pretended to in this declaration; yet upon information from his houses of parliament, the king declared himself satisfied that he had no such power, cancelled his declaration, and promised that it should not be drawn into consequence or example. And so the Commons, by their protestation, said in Richard the Second's time, that it was a novelty and should not be drawn into consequence or example.

Now, my lord, if your lordship pleases, if this matter that was commanded the bishops to do, were something which the law did not allow of, surely then my lords the bishops had all the reason in the world to apply themselves to the king, in an humble manner to acquaint him why they could not obey his commands: and to seek relief against that which lay so heavy upon them.

Truly, my lord, Mr. Attorney was very right in the opening of the cause at first, that is, That the government ought not to receive affronts, no, nor the inferior offices are not to be affronted; a justice of the peace, so low a man in office is not. For a man to say to a justice of the peace, when he is executing his office, that he does not right in it is a great crime, and Mr. Attorney said right in it: but suppose a justice of the peace were making of a warrant to a constable, to do something that was not legal for him to do, if the constable should petition this justice of the peace, and therein set forth, Sir, you are about to command me to do a thing, which, I conceive is not legal; surely that would not be a crime that he was to be punished for: for he does but seek relief, and shew his grievance in a proper way, and the distress he is under.

My lord, this is the bishop's case with submission; they are under a distress being commanded to do a thing which they take not to be legal, and they with all humility, by way of petition acquaint the king with this distress of theirs, and pray him, that he will please to give relief.

My lord, there is no law, but is either an act of parliament, or the common law; for an act of parliament there is none for such a power; all that we have of it in parliamentary proceedings is against it; and for the common law, so far as I have read it, I never did meet with anything of such a nature, as a grant or dispensation that pretended to dispense with any one whole act of parliament; I have not so much as heard of any such thing mentioned by any of the king's counsel; but here, my lord, is a dispensation that dispenses with a great many of the king's laws at once, truly I cannot take upon me to tell how many, there may be forty or above, for aught I know.

Therefore, my lord, the bishops lying under such a grievance as this, and under such a pressure, being ordered to distribute this declaration in all their churches, which was to tell the people they ought to be under no law in this case, which surely was a very great pressure, both in point of law and in conscience too, they lying under such obligations to the contrary as they did; with submission to your lordship, and you gentlemen of the jury, if they did deliver this petition (publishing of it I will not talk of, for there has been no proof of a publication, but a delivering of a petition to his majesty in the most secret and decent manner that could be imagined), my lords the bishops are not guilty of the matter charged upon them in this information. . . .

My lord, I would only mention the great case of Thomas and Sorrel in the Exchequer-chamber, upon the validity of a dispensation of the statute of Edward the 6th, touching selling of wine. There it was the opinion of every one of the judges, and they did lay it down as a settled position, that there could never be an abrogation, or a suspension (which is a temporary abrogation) of an act of parliament, but by the legislative power. That was a foundation laid down quite through the debate of that case. Indeed it was disputed how far the king might dispense with the penalties in such a particular law, as to particular persons; but it was agreed by all, that the king had no power to suspend any law; and, my lord, I dare appeal to Mr. Attorney General himself, whether, in the case of Godden and Hales, which was lately in this court, to make good that dispensation, he did not use it as an argument then, that it could not be expounded into a suspension: he admitted it not to be in the king's power to suspend a law, but he might give a dispensation to a particular person, was all that he took upon to justify him at that time.

My lord, by the law of all civilised nations, if the prince does require something to be done, which the person who is to do it takes it to be unlawful, it is not only lawful, but his duty, *rescribere principi*. This is all that is done here, and that in the most humble manner that could be thought of. Your lordship will please to observe how far it went, how careful they were that they might not any way justly offend the king; they did not interpose by giving advice, as peers; they never stirred till it was brought home to themselves. When they made their petition all they beg is, that it may not so far be insisted upon by his majesty as to oblige them to read it. Whatever they thought of it, they do not take upon them to desire the declaration to be revoked.

My lord, as to matters of fact alleged in the said petition, that they are perfectly true, we have shewn by the journals of both houses. In every one of those years which are mentioned in the petition, this power of dispensation was considered in parliament, and, upon debate, declared to be contrary to law : there could be no design to diminish the prerogative, because the king hath no such prerogative. Seditious, my lord it could not be, nor could possibly stir up sedition in the minds of the people, because it was presented to the king in private and alone : false it could not be, because the matter of it is true : there could be nothing of malice, for the occasion was not sought : the thing was pressed upon them ; and a libel it could not be, because the intent was innocent, and they kept within the bounds set by the act of parliament, that gives the subject leave to apply to his prince by petition, where he is aggrieved. . . .

FROM THE SPEECH OF THE SOLICITOR-GENERAL FOR THE CROWN.

Then, my lord, let us take this case as it is, upon the nature of the petition, and the evidence that they have given, and then consider whether it will justify all that is done : for the business of petitioning, I would distinguish and inquire, whether my lords the bishops out of parliament can present any petition to the king ? I do agree, that in parliament the lords and commons may make addresses to the king, and signify their desires, and make known their grievances there ; and there is no doubt but that is a natural and proper way of application : for in the beginning of the parliament, there are receivers of petitions appointed, and upon debates, there are committees appointed to draw up petitions and addresses ; but to come and deduce an argument, that because the lords in parliament have done thus (there being such methods of proceedings usual in parliament) therefore my lords the bishops may do it out of parliament, that is certainly a *non sequitur*, no such conclusion can be drawn, from those premises.

My lord, I shall endeavour to lay the fact before you as it really is, and then consider what is proper for the court to take notice of, as legal proof or evidence : and I take it, all those precedents that they have produced of what the lords did, and what the commons did in parliament, is no warrant for them to shelter themselves under, against the information here in question.

(Here Mr. Justice Powell spake aside to the Lord Chief Justice thus.)

Mr. Just. Powell. My Lord, this is strange doctrine ! Shall not the subject have liberty to petition the king but in parliament ? If that be law, the subject is in a miserable case.

S

L. C. J. Brother, let him go on, we will hear him out, though I approve not of his position.

Sol. Gen. The Lords may address to the king in parliament, and the commons may do it, but therefore that the bishops may do it out of parliament, does not follow. . . .

I dare say it will not be denied me that the king may by his prerogative royal, issue forth his proclamation; it is as essential a prerogative as it is to give his assent to an act of parliament to make it a law. And it is another principle, which I think cannot be denied, that the king may make constitutions and orders in matters ecclesiastical; and that these he may make out of parliament, and without the parliament. If the king may do so, and these are his prerogatives, then suppose the king do issue forth his royal proclamation (and such in effect is this declaration under the great seal) in a matter ecclesiastical, by virtue of his prerogative royal; and this declaration is read in the council, and published to the world, and then the bishops come and tell the king, Sir you have issued out an illegal proclamation or declaration, being contrary to what has been declared in parliament, when there is no declaration in parliament; is not this a diminishing the king's power and prerogative in issuing forth his proclamation or declaration, and making constitutions in matters ecclesiastical? Is not this a questioning his prerogative Do not my lords the bishops in this case raise a question between the king and the people? Do not they, as much as in them lies, stir up the people to sedition? For who shall be judge between the king and the bishops? Says the king, I have such a power and prerogative to issue forth my royal proclamation, and to make order and constitutions in matters ecclesiastical, and that without the parliament, and out of parliament. Say my lords the bishops, you have done so, but you have no warrant for it. Says the king, every prince has done it, and I have done no more than what is my prerogative to do. But this, say the bishops, is against law. How shall this be tried? Should not the bishops have had the patience to have waited until a parliament came and complained there, and sought redress. The question in this case is not whether the king may dispense with the law, but whether he may issue out his proclamation in matters ecclesiastical. . . .

Now my lord, I come to that which is very plain from the case of De Libellis Famosis, in lord Coke's Reports: if any person have slandered the government in writing, you are (*sic?* "not") to examine the truth of that fact in such writing, but the slander which it imports to the king or government; and be it never so true, y if slanderous to the king or the government, it is a libel, and to be punished: in that case, the right or wrong is not to be examined, or if what was done by the government be legal or no; but whether the party have done such an act. If the king have a power (for still I keep to that) to issue forth proclamations to his subject, and to make orders and constitutions in matters ecclesiastical, if he do issue forth his proclamation, and make an order upon the matters within his power and prerogative; and if any one would come and bring that power in question otherwise than in parliament, that the matter of that proclamation be not legal, I say that is seditious, and you are not to examine the legality or illegality of the order or proclamation, but the slander and reflexion upon the government, and that, I think, is very plain upon that case, in the fifth Report De Libellis Famosis: for it says, If a person do a thing that is libellous, you shall not examine the fact, but the consequence of it; whether it tended to stir up sedition against the public, or to stir up strife between man and man, in the case of private persons: as if a man should say of a judge, he has taken a bribe, and I will prove it; this is not to be sent in a letter, but they must take a regular way to prosecute it according to law.

If it be so in the case of an inferior magistrate, what must it be in the case of a king? To come to the king's face, and tell him, as they do here, that he has acted illegally, doth certainly sufficiently prove the matter to be libellous. What do they say to the king? They say and admit, that they have an averseness for the declaration, and they tell him from whence that averseness doth proceed: and yet they insinuate that they had an inclination to gratify the king, and embrace the dissenters, that were as averse to them as could be, with due tenderness, when it should be settled by parliament and convocation. Pray what hath their convocation to do in this matter?

L. C. J. Mr. Solicitor General, I will not interrupt you; but pray come to the business before us. Shew us that this is in diminution of the king's prerogative, or that the king ever had such a prerogative.

Sol. Gen. I will, my lord, I am observing what it is they say in his petition—They tell the king it is inconsistent with their honour, prudence and conscience, to do what he would have them to do: And if these things be not reflective upon the king and government, I know not what is. This is not in a way of judicature: possibly it might have been allowed to petition the king to put it into a course of justice, whereby it may be tried; but alas! there is no such thing in this matter.

It is not their desire to put it into any method for trial, and so it comes in the case de Libellis Famosis; for by this way they make themselves judges, which no man by law is permitted to do. My lords the bishops have gone out of the way, and all that they have offered does not come home to justify them; and therefore I take it, under favour, that we have made it a good case for the king: We have proved what they have done, and whether this be warrantable or not, is the question, gentlemen, that you are to try. The whole case appears upon record; the declaration and petition are set forth, and the order of the king and council. When the verdict is brought in, they may move anything what they please in arrest of judgement. They have had a great deal of latitude, and taken a great deal of liberty; but truly, I apprehend, not so very pertinently. But I hope we have made a very good case of it for the king, and that you, gentlemen, will give us a verdict.

Just. Holloway. Mr. Solicitor, there is one thing I would fain be satisfied in: You say the bishops have no power to petition the king.

Sol. Gen. Not out of parliament, Sir.

Just. Holloway. Pray give me leave, Sir: Then the king having made such a declaration of a general toleration and liberty of conscience, and afterwards he comes and requires the bishops to disperse this declaration; this, they say, out of a tenderness of conscience, they cannot do, because they apprehend it is contrary to law, and contrary to their function: What can they do if they may not petition?

Sol. Gen. I'll tell you what they should have done, Sir. If they were commanded to do anything against their consciences, they should have acquiesced till the meeting of the parliament. [At which some people in the court hissed.] . . .

FROM THE SUMMING UP OF THE LORD CHIEF JUSTICE, WRIGHT.

Gentlemen, thus stands the case: it is an information against my lords the bishops, his grace my lord of Canterbury, and the other six noble lords; and it is for preferring, composing, making, and publishing, and causing to be published a seditious libel: the way that the information goes is special, and it sets forth, that the king was graciously pleased, by his royal power and prerogative, to set forth a declaration of indulgence for liberty of conscience, in the third year of his reign; and afterwards upon the 27th of April, the fourth year he comes and makes another declaration; and afterwards in May, orders in council that this declaration should be published by my lords the bishops in their several dioceses; and after this was done, my lords the bishops come and present a petition to the king in which were contained the words which you have seen.

Now, gentlemen, the proofs that have been upon this you will see what they are. The two declarations are proved by the clerks of the council, and they are brought here under the great seal. A question did arise, whether the prints were the same with the original declarations, and that is proved by Hills or his man, that they were examined, and are the same. That the order of the council was proved by Sir John Nicholas, and has likewise been read to you. Then they come to prove the fact against the bishops, and first they fall to proving their hands. They began indeed a great way off, and did not come so close to it as they afterwards did; for some of their hands they could hardly prove, but my lord archbishop's hand was only proved, and some others; but there might have been some question about that proof. But afterwards it came to be proved, that my lords the bishops owned their hands; which if they had produced at first, would have made the cause something shorter that it was.

The next question that did arise was about the publishing of it, whether my lords the bishops had published it? And it was insisted upon, that nobody could prove the delivery of it to the king. It was proved, the king gave it to the council, and my lords the bishops were called in, and there they acknowledged their hands; but nobody could prove how it came to the king's hands. Upon which we were all of opinion, that it was not such a publishing as was within the information; and I was going to have directed you to find my lords the bishops not guilty : but it happened that being interrupted in my directions, by an honest, worthy, learned gentleman, the king's counsel took the advantage, and informing the court that they had further evidence for the king, we staid till my lord president came, who told us how the bishops came to him to his office at Whitehall, and after they had told him their design, that they had a mind to petition the king, they asked him the method they were to take for it, and desired him to help them to the speech of the king : and he tells them he will acquaint the king with their desire which he does; and the king giving leave, he comes down and tells the bishops, that they might go and speak with the king when they would ; and, says he, I have given direction that the door shall be opened for you as soon as you come. With that the two bishops went away, and said, they would go and fetch their other brethren, and they did bring the other four, but my lord archbishop was not there; and immediately when they came back, they went up into the chamber, and there a petition was delivered to the king. He cannot speak to that particular petition, because he did not read it, and that is all he knew of the matter; only it was all done the same day, and that was before my lords the bishops appeared at the council.

Gentlemen, after this was proved, then the defendants came to their part; and these gentlemen that were of counsel for my lords, let themselves into their defence by notable learned speeches, by telling you that my lords the bishops are guardians to the church, and great peers of the realm, and were bound in conscience to take care of the church. They have read you a clause of a statute made in Queen Elizabeth's time, by which they say, my lords the bishops were under a curse, if they did not take care of that law: then they shew you some records, one in Richard's the second's time, which they could make little of, by reason their witness could not read it; but it was, in short, a liberty given to the king, to dispense with the statute of provisors. Then they shew you some journals of parliament; first in the year 1672, where the king had granted an indulgence, and the house of commons declared it was not fit to be done, unless it were by act of parliament. Then they come to that in 1685, where the commons take notice of something about the soldiers in the army that had not taken the test, and make an address to the king about it: but in all these things (as far as I can observe) nothing can be gathered out of them one way or the other; it is nothing but discourses. Sometimes this dispensing power has been allowed, as in Richard's the 2nd's time, and sometimes it has been denied, and the king did once waive it: Mr. Solicitor tells you the reason, there was a lump of money in the case; but I wonder indeed to hear it come from him.

Sol. Gen. My lord, I never gave my vote for money, I assure you.

L. C. J. But those concessions which the king sometimes makes for the good of the people, and sometimes for the profit of the prince himself (but I would not be thought to distinguish between the profit of the prince and the good of the people, for they are both one; and what is the profit of the prince is always for the good of the people), but I say, those concessions must not be made law, for that is reserved in the king's breast, to do what he pleases in it at any time.

The truth of it is, the dispensing power is out of the case, it is only a word used in the petition; but truly, I will not take upon me to give my opinion in the question, to determine that now, for it is not before me: the only question before me is, and so it is before you, gentlemen, it being a question of fact, whether here be a certain proof of a publication? And then the next question is a question of law indeed, whether, if there be a publication proved, it be a libel.

Gentlemen, upon the point of the publication, I have summed up all the evidence to you; and if you believe that the petition which these lords presented to the king was this petition, truly, I think, that is a publication sufficient: if you do not believe it was this petition, then my lords the bishops are not guilty of what is laid to their charge in this information, and consequently there needs no inquiry whether they are guilty of a libel? but if you do believe that this was the petition they presented to the king, then we must come to inquire whether this be a libel.

Now, gentlemen, any thing that shall disturb the government, or make mischief and a stir among the people, is certainly within the case of "Libellis Famosis"; and I must in short give you my opinion, I do take it to be a libel. Now, this being a point of law, if my brothers have anything to say to it, I suppose they will deliver their opinions.

Just. Holloway. Look you, gentlemen, it is not usual for any person to say anything after the Chief Justice has summed up the evidence; it is not according to the course of the court: but this is a case of an extraordinary nature, and there being a point of law in it, it is very fit that everybody should deliver their own opinion. The question is, whether this petition of my lords the bishops be a libel or no. Gentlemen, the end and intention of every action is to be considered, and likewise, in this case, we are to consider the nature of the offence that these noble persons are charged with; it is for delivering a petition, which, according as they have made their defence, was with all the humility and decency that could be: so that if there was no ill intent, and they were not (as it is not, nor can be pretended they were) men of evil lives, or the like, to deliver a petition cannot be a fault, it being the right of every subject to petition. If you are satisfied there was an ill intention of sedition, or the like, you ought to find them guilty: but if there be nothing in the case that you find, but only that they did deliver a petition to save themselves harmless, and to free themselves from blame, by shewing the reason of their disobedience to the king's command, which they apprehended to be a grievance to them, and which they could not in conscience give obedience to, I cannot think it is a libel: it is left to you, gentlemen, but that is my opinion.

L. C. J. Look you, by the way, brother, I did not ask you to sum up the evidence (for that is not usual) but only to deliver your opinion, whether it be a libel or no.

Just. Powell. Truly, I cannot see, for my part, any thing of sedition, or any other crime, fixed upon these reverend fathers, my lords the bishops.

For, gentlemen, to make it a libel, it must be false, it must be malicious, and it must tend to sedition. As to the falsehood, I see nothing that is offered by the king's counsel, nor any thing as to the malice : It was presented with all humility and decency that became the king's subjects to approach their prince with.

Now, gentlemen, the matter of it is before you ; you are to consider of it, and it is worth your consideration. They tell his majesty, it is not out of averseness to pay all due obedience to the king, nor out of a want of tenderness to their dissenting fellow subjects, that made them not perform the command imposed upon them ; but they say because they do conceive that the thing that was commanded them was against the law of the land, therefore they do desire his majesty, that he would be pleased to forbear to insist upon it, that they should perform that which they take to be illegal.

Gentlemen, we must consider what they say is illegal in it. They say, they apprehend the declaration is illegal, because it is founded upon a dispensing power, which the king claims, to dispense with the laws concerning ecclesiastical affairs.

Gentlemen, I do not remember in any case in all our law (and I have taken some pains upon this occasion to look into it), that there is any such power in the king, and the case must turn upon that. In short, if there be no such dispensing power in the king, then that can be no libel which they presented to the king, which says, that the declaration, being founded upon such a pretended power, is illegal.

Now, gentlemen, this is a dispensation with a witness : it amounts to an abrogation, an utter repeal of all the laws ; for I can see no difference, nor know of none in law, between the king's power to dispense with laws ecclesiastical, and his power to dispense with any other laws whatever. If this be once allowed of, there will need no parliament ; all the legislature will be in the king, which is a thing worth considering, and I leave the issue to God and your consciences.

Just. Allybone. The single question that falls to my share is, to give my sense of this petition, whether it shall be in construction of law a libel in itself, or a thing of great innocence. I shall endeavour to express myself in as plain terms as I can, and as much as I can, by way of proposition.

And I think, in the first place, that no man can take upon him to write against the actual exercise of the government, unless he have leave from the government, but he makes a libel, be what he writes true or false; for if once we come to impeach the government by way of argument, it is the argument that makes it the government or not the government. So that I lay down that, in the first place, the government ought not to be impeached by argument, nor the exercise of the government shaken by argument, because I can manage a proposition in itself doubtful, with a better pen than another man: this, say I, is a libel.

Then I lay down this for my next position, that no private man can take upon him to write concerning the government at all; for what has any private man to do with the government, if his interest be not stirred or shaken? It is the business of the government to manage affairs relating to the government, it is the business of subjects to mind only their own properties and interests. If my interest is not shaken, what have I to do with matters of government? They are not within my sphere. If the government does come to shake my particular interest, the law is open for me, and I may redress myself by law: and when I intrude myself into other men's business that does not concern my particular interest, I am a libeller.

These I have laid down for plain propositions; now then, let us consider further, whether, if I will take upon me to contradict the government, any specious pretence that I shall put upon it shall dress it up in another form, and give it a better denomination? And truly I think it is the worse, because it comes in a better dress; for by that rule, every man that can put on a good vizard, may be as mischievous as he will to the government at the bottom: so that whether it be in the form of a supplication, or an address, or a petition, if it be what it ought not to be, let us call it by its true name, and give it its right denomination—it is a libel.

Then, gentlemen, consider what this petition is: this is a petition relating to something that was done and ordered by the government. Whether the reasons of the petition be true or false, I will not examine that now, nor will I examine the prerogative of the crown, but only take notice that this relates to the act of the government. The government here has published such a declaration as this that has been read, relating to matters of government; and shall, or ought anybody to come and impeach that as illegal, which the government has done? Truly, in my opinion, I do not think he should, or ought; for by this rule may every act of the government be shaken, when there is not a parliament *de facto* sitting.

I do agree, that every man may petition the government, or the king, in a matter that relates to his own private interest, but to meddle with a matter that relates to the government, I do not think my lords the bishops had any power to do more than any others.

When the house of lords and commons are in being, it is a proper way of applying to the king: there is all that openness in the world for those that are members of parliament, to make what addresses they please to the government, for the rectifying, altering, regulating, and making of what law they please; but if every private man shall come and interpose his advice, I think there can never be an end of advising the government. I think there was an instance of this in king James' time, when by a solemn resolution it was declared to be a high misdemeanour, and next to treason, to petition the king to put the penal laws in execution.

Just. Powell. Brother, I think you do mistake a little.

Just. Allybone. Brother, I dare rely upon it that I am right: it was so declared by all the judges.

Sol. Gen. The Puritans presented a petition to that purpose, and in it they said, if it would not be granted, they would come with a great number.

Just. Powell. Aye, there it is.

Just. Allybone. I tell you, Mr. Solicitor, the resolution of the judges is, That such a petition is next door to treason, a very great misdemeanour.

Just. Powell. They accompanying it with threats of the people's being discontented.

Just. Allybone. As I remember, it is in the second part of the folio 35, or 37, where the resolution of the judges is, That to frame a petition to the king, to put the penal laws in execution, is next to treason; for, say they, no man ought to intermeddle with matters of government without leave of the government.

Serj. Pemberton. That was a petition against the penal laws.

Just. Allybone. Then I am quite mistaken indeed, in case it be so.

Serj. Trinder. That is not material at all which it was.

Mr. Pollexfen. They there threatened, unless their request were granted, several thousands of the king's subjects would be discontented.

Just. Powell. That is the reason of that judgment, I affirm it.

Just. Allybone. But then I'll tell you, brother, again, what is said in that case that you hinted at, and put Mr. Solicitor in mind of; for any man to raise a report that the king will or will not permit a toleration, if either of these be disagreeable to the people, whether he may or may not, it is against law; for we are not to measure things from any truth they have in themselves, but from that aspect they have upon the government; for there may be every tittle of a libel true, and yet it may be a libel still : so that I put no stress upon that objection, that the matter of it is not false; and for sedition, it is that which every libel carries in itself; and as every trespass implies *vi and armis*, so every libel against the government carries in it sedition, and all the other epithets that are in the information. This is my opinion as to the law in general. I will not debate the prerogatives of the king, nor the privileges of the subject; but as this fact is, I think these venerable bishops did meddle with that which did not belong to them : they took upon them in a petitionary, to contradict the actual exercise of the government, which I think no particular persons, or singular body, may do.

(S.T. xii. 183–433.)

X

THE CASE OF JOHN TUTCHIN
3 Anne, 1704.

[John Tutchin was tried for writing and publishing "false, malicious and seditious libels." The passages on which the indictment was based complained of mismanagement and peculation in the navy, and accused certain government officials of being bribed by France. The jury found him guilty of "composing and publishing," but not of "writing" the alleged libel. On appeal in arrest of judgment the verdict was quashed on technical grounds, but "it was never afterwards thought proper to try him again." Chief Justice Holt's charge to the jury has a historic and constitutional interest as showing the interpretation of the law of libel by a judge whose defence of popular liberties in *Ashby v. White* proved his courage and independence. See *Broom*, C.L. 517 ; *Odgers*, L. and S. 410–422 ; *Stephen*, H.C.L. ii. 298–396 ; *Hallam*, C.H. iii. 166 ; S.T. xiv. 1095–1199.]

Gentlemen of the jury, this is an information that is preferred by the queen's attorney general against Mr. Tutchin for writing and composing, and publishing, or causing to be writ, composed or published, several libels against the queen and her government . . . So that now you have heard this evidence, you are to consider whether you are satisfied that Mr. Tutchin is guilty of writing, composing and publishing these libels. They say they are innocent papers, and no libels, and they say nothing is a libel but what reflects upon some particular person. But this is a very strange doctrine, to say, it is not a libel reflecting on the government, endeavouring to possess the people that the government is maladministered by corrupt persons, that are employed in such or such stations either in the navy or army. To say that corrupt officers are appointed to administer affairs, is certainly a reflection on the government. If people should not be called to account for possessing the people with an ill opinion of the government, no government can subsist. For it is very necessary for all governments that the people should have a good opinion of it, and nothing can be worse to any government, than to endeavour to procure animosities, as to the management of it: this has always been looked upon as a crime, and no government can be safe without it be punished. Now you are to consider, whether these words I have read to you, do not tend to beget an ill opinion of the administration of the government? To tell us, that those that are employed know nothing of the matter, and those that do know are not employed. Men are not adapted to offices, but offices to men, out of a particular regard to their interest, and not to their fitness for the places : this is the purport of these papers. . . . Gentlemen, I must leave it to you; if you are satisfied that he is guilty of composing and publishing these papers at London, you are to find him guilty.

(From Holt's, C.J., charge to the jury. S.T. xiv. 1126.)

XI

ASHBY *v.* WHITE AND OTHERS
2 Anne, 1704.

[The importance of this historic case, with which is also concerned *The Case of the Aylesbury Men*, justifies the length of the extracts. Matthew Ashby brought an action against William White, Mayor of Aylesbury, and others, for refusing his vote at an election of burgesses to Parliament, and obtained a verdict with costs and £5 damages. On a motion in the Queen's Bench in arrest of judgment before Lord Chief Justice Holt and Justices Powell, Powys, and Gould, judgment was given for the defendant on the ground that an action did not lie against the returning officers, Holt, C.J., dissenting. The case was brought on writ of error before the House of Lords, and on January 14, 1703, the judgment of the Queen's Bench was reversed on the grounds set forth in Holt's dissenting judgment in the court below (Excerpt I.). The House of Commons at once took the challenge up, and after debating it from January 17 to 25, adopted certain resolutions to protect their interpretation of their privileges (see Excerpt II., p. 271). The House of Lords also debated this question and passed counter-resolutions, and conferences between the two chambers failed to effect a reconciliation. When five other Aylesbury men, supported by the decision of the House of Lords, brought actions similar to that of Ashby's, they were promptly committed to Newgate by the House of Commons for a breach of privilege. A motion to obtain their discharge on a writ of *habeas corpus* was argued in the Queen's Bench before the same four judges who had already given a judgment in *Ashby v. White*, and with the same result. By three to one (Holt, C.J., again dissenting) the court refused to order their discharge (see Excerpt IV.). Paty, one of the five Aylesbury men, petitioned the Queen for a writ of error to bring his case before the House of Lords, as Ashby had done ; the Commons petitioned the Queen not to grant the writ, whereupon the Crown referred the question to the judges as to whether such writs were "of right" or "of grace." Ten judges answered that such writs were "of right" (*ex debito vel merito justitiae*), two that they were "of grace" (*ex gratia*). The Lords also drew up a representation to the Crown, and Anne solved the difficulty by proroguing Parliament. This freed the Aylesbury men from the restrictions of the privilege of the House of Commons, and they finally obtained verdicts against the returning officers. On the whole matter see S.T. xiv. 695–888 ; *Hallam*, C.H. iii. 274 ; *Anson*, L.C. i. 170 ; *Broom*, C.L. 841–874 ; *May*, P.P. 57–142. The extracts are: (1) from Holt's judgment in the Queen's Bench ; (2) the resolutions of the House of Commons ; (3) the counter-resolutions of the House of Lords ; (4) the judgments of the judges in the argument on the writ of *Habeas Corpus* for "the Aylesbury men" ; (5) the certificates of the judges to the question submitted by the Crown ; (6) from the representation of the Lords to the Crown with the Queen's answer.]

I

The Case is truly stated, and the only question is, whether or not, if a Burgess of a Borough that has an undoubted right to give his vote for the chusing a Burgess of Parliament for that Borough, is refused giving his vote, has any remedy in the King's Courts for this Wrong against the Wrong-doer ? All my Brothers agree that he has no Remedy ; but I differ from them, for I think the Action well maintainable, that the Plaintiff had a Right to vote, and that in consequence thereof the Law gives him a Remedy, if he is obstructed ; and this Action is the proper Remedy. By the Common Laws of England, every Commoner hath a Right not to be subjected to Laws, made without their Consent ; and because it cannot be given by every individual Man in Person by Reason of Number and Confusion, therefore that Power is lodged in the Representatives, elected by them for that purpose, who are either Knights, Citizens or Burgesses ; and the Grievance here is, that the Party not being allowed his Vote, is not represented. The Election of Knights of

Shires is by Freeholders; and a Freeholder has a Right to vote by Reason of his Freehold, and it is a real Right. . . . In Boroughs . . . they have a Right of voting *Ratione Burgagii* and *Ratione Tenurae;* and this like the Case of a Freeholder before mentioned is a real Right, annexed to the Tenure in Burgage. . . . This is a noble Franchise and Right, which entitles the subject in a Share of the Government and Legislature. And here the Plaintiff having this Right, it is apparent that the Officer did exclude him from the enjoyment of it, wherein none will say he has done well, but Wrong to the Plaintiff; and it is not at all material whether the Candidate, that he would have voted so, were chosen, or likely to be so, for the Plaintiff's Right is the same, and being hindered of that, he has Injury done him, for which he ought to have Remedy. It is a vain Thing to imagine, there should be Right without a Remedy; for Want of Right and Want of Remedy are Convertibles: If a Statute gives a Right, the Common Law will give Remedy to maintain it; and wherever there is Injury, it imposts a Damage. And there can be no Petition in this Case to the Parliament, nor can they judge of this Injury, or give Damages to the Plaintiff. And although this Matter relates to the Parliament, yet it is an injury precedaneous to the Parliament; and where Parliamentary Matters come before us, as incident to a Cause of Action concerning the Property of the Subject, which we in Duty must determine, though the Matter be Parliamentary, we must not be deterred, but are bound by our Oaths to determine it. The Law consists not in particular Instances, but in the Reason that rules them; and if where a Man is injured in one Sort of Right, he has a good Action, why shall he not have it in another? And though the House of Commons have Right to decide Elections, yet they cannot judge of the Charter originally, but secondarily in the Determination of the Election; and therefore where an Election does not come in Debate, as it doth not in this Case, they have nothing to do: and we are to exert and vindicate the Queen's Jurisdiction, and not to be frighted because it may come in Question in Parliament; and I know nothing to hinder us from judging Matters depending on Charter or Prescription. He concluded for the Plaintiff.

(Holt's Judgment. Holt's Reports (ed. 1737), pp. 525 *et seq.*)

II

RESOLUTIONS OF THE HOUSE OF COMMONS

Mr. Freeman. The question as I have it upon my Paper, is this :

"That according to the known law and usage of parliament, neither the qualification of any elector, or the right of any person elected, is cognizable or determinable elsewhere than before the Commons of England in parliament assembled, except in such cases as are specially provided for by act of parliament."

But some gentlemen are for leaving out these words, ["Neither the qualification of any elector, or,"] So that I must put a question, Whether these words shall stand part of the question ? (Members. Aye, aye.)

Then Mr. Freeman put the Question, and the Committee divided.

Teller for the Ayes, Mr. Gulston . . 215
Teller for the Noes, Mr. Wylde . . 97

So it was carried, that those words should stand part of the question.

And the main Question being put,

Resolved, 2. "That according to the known law and usage of parliament, neither the qualifications of any elector, or the right of any person elected, is cognizable or determinable elsewhere, than before the Commons of England in parliament assembled, except in such cases as are specially provided for by act of parliament."

Resolved, 3. "That the examining and determining the qualification or right of any elector, or any person elected to serve in parliament, in any court of law, or elsewhere than before the Commons of England in parliament assembled, except in such cases as are specially provided for by act of parliament, will expose all mayors, bailiffs, and other officers, who are obliged to take the poll, and make a return thereupon, to multiplicity of actions vexatious suits, and unsupportable expenses, and will subject them to different and independent jurisdictions, and inconsistent determinations in the same case, without relief."

Resolved, 4. "That Matthew Ashby having, in contempt of the jurisdiction of this House, commenced and prosecuted an action at common law against William White, and others, the constables of Aylesbury, for not receiving his Vote at an election of burgesses to serve in parliament for the said borough of Aylesbury, is guilty of a breach of the privilege of this House."

Resolved, 5. "That whoever shall presume to commence or prosecute any action, indictment, or information [at common law],[1] which shall bring the right of electors, or persons elected to serve in parliament, to the determination of any other jurisdiction than that of the House of Commons, except in cases specially provided for by act of parliament, such person and persons, and all attorneys, solicitors, counsellors, serjeants-at-law, soliciting, prosecuting or pleading in any such case, are guilty of a high breach of the privilege of this House."

Ordered, "That the said Resolutions be fixed upon Westminster-Hall Gate, signed by the Clerk."

These Resolutions, with this, (to wit,)

Resolved 1. "That according to the known laws and usage of parliament, it is the sole right of the Commons of England in parliament assembled, except in cases otherwise provided for by act of parliament to examine and determine all matters relating to the right of elections of their own members" . . . were reported to the House.

(C.J., Jan. 25, 1704.)

III

RESOLUTIONS OF THE HOUSE OF LORDS

This State of the Case being read, and approved of, the House came to the following Resolution; (videlicet,)

"It is resolved, by the Lords Spiritual and Temporal in Parliament assembled, That, by the known Laws of this Kingdom, every Freeholder, or other Person having a Right to give his Vote at the Election of Members to serve in Parliament, and being wilfully denied or hindered so to do, by the Officer who ought to receive the same, may maintain an Action in the Queen's Courts against such Officer, to assert his Right, and recover Damages for the Injury."

"It is resolved, by the Lords Spiritual and Temporal in Parliament assembled, That the asserting, that a Person, having Right to give his Vote at an Election, and being hindered so to do by the Officer who ought to take the same, is without Remedy for such Wrong by the ordinary Course of Law, is destructive of the Property of the Subject, against the Freedom of Elections, and manifestly tends to encourage Corruption and Partiality in Officers, who are to make Returns in Parliament, and to subject the Freeholder and other Electors to their arbitrary Will and Pleasure."

[1] Omitted, on amendment, next day—January 26, 1704.

"It is resolved, by the Lords Spiritual and Temporal in Parliament assembled; That the declaring *Mathew Ashby* guilty of a Breach of Privilege of the House of Commons, for prosecuting an Action against the Constables of *Aylesbury*, for not receiving his Vote at an Election, after he had, in the known and proper Methods of Law, obtained a Judgement in Parliament for Recovery of his Damages, is an unprecedented Attempt upon the Judicature of Parliament, and is, in Effect, to subject the Law of England, to the Votes of the House of Commons."

"It is Resolved, by the Lords Spiritual and Temporal in Parliament assembled, That the deterring Electors from prosecuting Actions in the ordinary Course of Law, where they are deprived of their Right of Voting, and terrifying Attornies, Solicitors, Counsellors, and Serjeants at Law, from soliciting, prosecuting, and pleading, in such Cases, by voting their so doing to be a Breach of Privilege of the House of Commons, is a manifest assuming a Power to control the Law, to hinder the Course of Justice, and subject the Property of *Englishmen* to the arbitrary Votes of the House of Commons."

(L.J. xvii. 534.)

IV

JUDGMENT ON THE HABEAS CORPUS OF THE AYLESBURY MEN

Mr. Justice Powell. That this is a case of the highest consequence, for it concerns the privileges of the House of Commons, the liberty of the subject, and the jurisdiction of this court; it is the first case of this nature, for the lord Shaftesbury was a member of the House,[1] and there may be a greater jurisdiction in some cases over their own members, than over strangers; however, they had not any authority upon the return, for they[2] are committed by another law than we proceed by: and to be committed by one law, and to judge of the commitment by another law, would be a strange thing: for the House do not commit by the authority of the common law, but by another law, 'Legem et Consuetudinem Parliamenti'; for there are in England several other laws, besides the common law, viz. the ecclesiastical law, the admiralty law, etc., and there is the law and customs of parliament, where they have particular laws and customs for their directions.

To state judicature will help to clear this case. The House of Lords have a power to judge by the common law, but not originally,

---

[1] *i.e.* of the House of Lords.   [2] The Aylesbury men.

T

but a dernier resort upon Writs of Error and Appeals; and for that reason it is provided by the constitution, for the judges to give their assistance, which they are bound to do. But they have another law, viz. 'Lex et Consuetudo Parliamenti,' which the judges are not to assist in, or give any opinion; and I dare say, the House of Lords would take it ill, should they meddle or advise therein, for they have their privileges in their own rolls and books.

That the Commons have also a judicature, not by the common law, but do judge of breaches of privileges, and contempts to their House, 'Secundum Legem et Consuetudinem Parliamenti,' 4. Inst. 23, and by this law these persons are committed, and are now brought to be discharged by the common law. The Resolution of the Commons upon the breach of privileges is a judgement, and the commitment an execution of it, which cannot be controlled; for this would be to draw it ad aliud Examen, and then the Commons would not be supreme judges of their own privileges.

That the Resolution in the House of Lords, in the case of Ashby and White, does not bind the House of Commons, nor determine their privileges; for they judged of the privileges of the Commons as an incident to the action, and one court may judge of a matter within the jurisdiction of another court, when without it they cannot determine the case before them; as this court may of admiralty, or ecclesiastical jurisdiction, if the question arises in an action depending in this court. But such a determination will not bind another court, which has an original cognizance of that matter, as in ejectment now depending in the Common Pleas, the general issue pleaded, and a special verdict; the question there is, If a Quaker's marriage be good? Now if it should be held in that court a void marriage, and the judgement should be affirmed in this court, and upon a Writ of Error in the House of Lords, it should be reversed, this would not bind the ecclesiastical court, but they might proceed there for incontinency, and if they should proceed there to excommunication finding it a void marriage and the party taken by the Excommunicato Capiendo should bring this Habeas Corpus upon the return of it, we could not discharge him. But this is a matter originally arising in Parliament.

That this court may keep other inferior courts within their jurisdictions, but not the House of Commons; for no prohibition was ever granted to that court, though they exceeded jurisdiction; so if the House of Lords do exceed, or take cognizance of matters in the first instance, no prohibition would lie; for no inferior court can prohibit a superior: and no prohibition was moved here, nor could we have granted it; for the House of Commons is superior to all ordinary Courts of law. When the House of Lords took cognizance, and proceeded upon the petition of my lord Wharton, complaining of an order of the court of Exchequer, for filing the record of a survey of the honour of Richmond, and lordship of Middleton, which the House of Commons, upon the petition of Mr. Bathhurst, complaining of this proceeding, Jan. 28, 1703, resolved to be without precedent, and unwarrantable, and tending to the subjecting all the rights and properties of the Commons of England to an illegal and arbitrary power; they also resolved then, that it is the undoubted right of all the subjects of England to make use of the record; as they ought by law to have done before the said proceeding of the House of Lords. . . .

Lord Chief Just. Holt. That this case does depend upon the vote that is recited in the Speaker's Warrant of Commitment, which was to this effect:

That it did appear to that honourable House, that John Paty of Aylesbury has been guilty of commencing and prosecuting an action at common law, against W. White and others, late constables of Aylesbury, for not allowing his vote in an election of members to serve in parliament, contrary to the declaration, in high contempt of the jurisdiction, and in breach of the known privileges of this House.

That he owned himself to lie under two disadvantages: one, That all the rest of the judges do agree with his three brethren, from whom he had the misfortune to dissent. The other, That he opposed the votes of the House of Commons, and did begin to think he might justify himself in resigning his opinion to the rest; but that he valued more the dictates of his own conscience, than anything he could suffer in this world, and by that and his judgement (though it were but weak) he would be guided.

That this was not such an imprisonment as the freemen of England ought to be bound by. And that it did highly concern the people of England, not to be bound by a declaration of the House of Commons in a matter that before was lawful.

That neither House of Parliament has a power separately to dispose of the liberty or property of the people, for that cannot be done but by the Queen, Lords, and Commons; and this is the security of our English constitution, which cannot be altered but by act of parliament.

That there is a crime charged by the vote for commencing an action; but sure that cannot be a breach of privilege; for an original may be filed against a member of parliament during the time of privilege, so that you do not molest him, and it is no breach of privilege; as it was resolved in Sir George Binion's case, 14 ch. 2; for otherwise, by lapse of time in several actions, he may be barred by the statute of limitations; so that if it be not a breach of privilege to commence an action against a member of parliament, then how can it be so to commence an action against the constable of Aylesbury.

But then the vote goes further, and says, for commencing and prosecuting an action: but prosecuting may not be a breach of privilege neither; for entering and continuing is prosecuting, which may be done without a breach of privilege.

That it does not appear, that the constable of Aylesbury has any privilege above another person, for no man is presumed to be privileged unless it be shown; and he has no privilege as constable.

That the vote goes yet further, and says, for not allowing his vote in an election of members to serve in this present parliament: but this can be no crime.

That he admitted they were judges of their own privileges; but the law must also be observed. By 2 Ric. 3, fol. 9, it appears, it was no crime by the common law, to bring an action, though never so malicious, false, or groundless, where it is adjudged, that there is no punishment for it, because it was in a method of justice; but when business began to increase, costs were given against the plaintiff by 23 Hen. 8, for bringing an action causelessly. A peer cannot have an action of Scandalum magnatum, where there is no cause for the action wherein he is charged with scandal; so much the law regarded the right of bringing actions.

That when subjects have such a right to bring actions, it cannot be stopped by privilege of parliament, for no privilege of parliament can intend so far as to destroy a man's right.

That it has been adjudged a good action by the law of the land, and that damages may be recovered for the injury, in not allowing his vote; and this action is the same as Ashby and White, which lies before us; and if we consult the records, we shall find it to be the same.

That the latter part of this vote is, That the prosecuting this action is contrary to the declaration, in high contempt of the jurisdiction, and in breach of the known privileges of this House.

That the privileges of the House of Commons are limited, for there is no privilege in case of treason, or felony, or breach of the peace; for a justice of the peace may commit a member for breach of the peace, and if he should be indicted for it, his plea of privilege would not be allowed.

That nothing can make a privilege that was not so before, (for the breach of which a man shall lose his liberty) but an act of parliament.

That each House is judge of their own privileges, because they are more conversant with the privileges of their own House; so the judges decline it; but if they come incidently before the courts of law, they must determine it there.

That suppose the House of Commons had not meddled in this matter, but the defendants in this action had pleaded to the jurisdiction of this court, that this was a matter examinable only in parliament, and the plaintiff had demurred, we must then have determined it, and be judges then of their privileges.

Coke's 1 Inst. 'Lex et Consuetudo Parliamenti ab omnibus querenda, ā multis ignota, ā paucis cognita,' and the reason it is known by so few is, because they do not seek for it. We are bound to take notice of the customs of parliament, for they are part of the law of the land; and there are the same methods of knowing it, as the law in Westminster-hall. (After quoting from Clarendon's History as to privileges of parliament, the Chief Justice proceeded) That if bringing an action is a breach of privilege, why was not Ashby laid hold on? He prosecuted to judgement and execution; but these persons are committed for commencing an action.

How can the bringing an action in one court be a contempt to another?

If a man that has a privilege in one court is sued in another, he shall have his privilege: but it is no contempt in a plaintiff that sues in another court, and there is no punishment for it; much less can it be a contempt to the House of Commons, where no action can be brought.

That he admitted, the House of Commons may commit any person, and for any crime, because they may impeach any person for any crime whatsoever; but that course is seldom taken, unless where the crime requires a strict prosecution, and much concerns the public.

That the lord Shaftesbury's case is not like this; for he was a member of the House, and it was for a contempt in the House.

The House may at any time commit a man for a contempt in the face of the House; whereas the prisoners are committed not for a breach of privilege or contempt, but because they have brought their actions which are legal, and so adjudged by the Lords in the Writ of Error.

That he did not question but that the warrant was a good warrant.

That 'lex et consuetudo parliamenti' is as much the law of the land as any other law. It is the law gives the queen her prerogative:

It is the law gives jurisdiction to the House of Lords; and it is the law limits the jurisdiction of the House of Commons.

That if the ecclesiastical court exceed their jurisdiction, a prohibition will lie; and even the king's acts, if contrary to law, are void.

He insisted that the lord Banbury's case was a great authority for him.

He petitioned the House of Lords to sit, and also to have the king's leave. The lords determined he was not a lord; yet when he was brought up on an indictment by the name of Charles Knowles, esq. he here pleaded and insisted that he was a peer; which plea was allowed and he was not tried.

Though the Lord Chief Justice was so clear in his judgement, yet the other three judges being of a contrary opinion, the majority prevailed; and the prisoners were remanded to Newgate.

v

May it please your majesty;

In obedience to your majesty's command, we have considered of the Petition hereunto annexed; and we are humbly of opinion that a Writ of Error in this case ought to be granted of right, and not of grace. But we give no opinion whether a Writ of Error does lie in the case; because it is proper to be determined in parliament, where the writ of error and record are returned and certified.

HOLT	POWIS
TREVOR	BLENCOWE
WARD	GOLD
NEVILL	TRACEY
POWELL	BURY.

May it please your majesty;

In obedience to your majesty's command, we have considered of the petition hereunto annexed; and we are humbly of opinion that your majesty is not of right and justice obliged to grant a Writ of Error in this case.   PRICE   SMITH.

The judges all attended the queen at the cabinet[1] on the 25th February, and delivered these their several resolutions to her majesty, in the presence of the prince and many of the principal members of the Council.

(S.T. xiv. 862.)

[1] The expression might be pressed as an instance of the presence of the Sovereign at a meeting of the Cabinet, in which Anne was accustomed to sit, but it is probably here used loosely for the Privy Council.

VI

(On the commitment of the five Aylesbury men, the Lords drew up an elaborate Representation and Address, March 14, 1705, the substance of which is given in the concluding paragraphs.)

We humbly beg pardon of your majesty for this long and melancholy Representation, which we could not avoid without being guilty of treachery to your majesty and to our native country. The five persons immediately concerned are but poor men; but we well know your majesty's justice and compassion extends itself to the meanest of your subjects.

The matters in dispute are of the highest consequence: Your majesty's prerogative, the reverence due to laws, and the liberties and properties of all the people of England are concerned and at stake, if these encroachments prevail.

We do not pretend to solicit your majesty to put a stop to these innovations, your own wisdom will suggest the most proper methods: We have endeavoured to do our duty by laying the whole matter before you.

We humbly beg leave as far to resume what has been said, as to present to your majesty a short view of the unhappy condition of such of your subjects, as have right of giving votes for chusing members to serve in parliament, which has hitherto been thought a great and valuable privilege: but by the late proceedings of the House of Commons, is likely to be made only a dangerous snare to them, in case they who may hereafter be chosen to serve in parliament, shall think fit to pursue the methods of this present House of Commons.

If they refrain from making use of their right in giving their Votes, they are wanting in duty to their country, by not doing their parts towards the chusing such representatives as will use their trust towards the good of the kingdom, and not for the oppression of their fellow subjects.

If the officer, who has the right of taking the suffrages, refuse to admit them to give their Votes, they must either sit down by it, and submit to be wrongfully and maliciously deprived of their rights; or if they bring their actions at law, in order to assert their rights, and recover damages for the injury (as all other injured men may do in like cases) they become liable to indefinite imprisonment, by incurring the displeasure of those who are elected.

If, being thus imprisoned, they seek their liberty by Habeas Corpus, (the known remedy of all other subjects) they do not only tie their own chains faster, but bring all their friends and agents, their solicitors and counsel, into the same misfortune with themselves.

If they think themselves to have received injury by the judgement upon the Habeas Corpus and seek relief by Writ of Error, (the known refuge of these who suffer wrong by any wrong judgement) all that assist them in that matter are likewise to lose their liberties for it, and they themselves will be removed to new prisons, in order to avoid the justice of the law.

We humbly conclude with acquainting your majesty, that we have been informed by the petition of two of the prisoners, that they have been long delayed, though they have made their applications in due manner for Writs of Error: We are under a necessary obligation, for the sake of justice, and asserting the judicature of Parliament, to make this humble Address to your majesty, that no importunity of the House of Commons, nor any other consideration whatsoever, may prevail with your majesty to suffer a stop to be put to the known course of justice, but that you will be pleased to give effectual orders for the immediate issuing of the Writs of Error.

THE QUEEN'S ANSWER

To which her majesty was pleased, the same day, to return the following most gracious answer.

"My Lords: I should have granted the Writ of Error desired in this Address: But finding an absolute necessity of putting an immediate end to this session, I am sensible there could have been no further proceeding upon that matter."

VOTE OF THANKS

Ordered by the Lords spiritual and temporal in parliament assembled, that the humble thanks of this House be presented to her majesty, for her most gracious Answer, in which she has expressed so great a regard to the judgement of this House, so much compassion to the petitioners, and such tenderness to the rights of the subject.

The same day the Queen came to the House and put an end to the session, and the lord keeper prorogued the parliament to Tuesday the 1st of May, which put an end to this affair.

XII

THE IMPEACHMENT OF HENRY SACHEVERELL
9 Anne, 1710.

[Henry Sacheverell, D.D., had preached two sermons (a) "The Communication of Sin," on August 5; (b) "The Perils of False Brethren both in Church and State," on November 15, 1709, both of which were subsequently printed and sold in large numbers; and for the sentiments expressed in these, as tending to deny the principles of the Revolution, the Whig Government with considerable reluctance decided to impeach him. Articles of impeachment were agreed on in the House of Commons on January 12, 1710. The trial commenced before the Lords on February 27, and on March 23 the Lords found him guilty (69 to 52), and the judgment was: (1) Sacheverell should be suspended from preaching for three years; (2) the two sermons in question were condemned to be burnt on March 27 by the common hangman. The proceedings in the Lords and the judgment occasioned several numerously signed protests (see *Rogers*, P.L. i. 189–198). Burke, in his *Appeal from the new to the old Whigs*, was of opinion that the trial furnished the best statement of the doctrine and counter-doctrine of the Revolution of 1688, and the extracts given are intended to illustrate this view. See *Hallam*, C.H. ch. xvi.; *Lecky*, H.E. i.; S.T. xv. 1–522; *Burke, op. cit.; Wyon*, History of Queen Anne's Reign, ii.; *Sandersom*, A Complete History of Dr. Sacheverell.]

ARTICLES OF IMPEACHMENT AGAINST HENRY SACHEVERELL

I. He, the said Henry Sacheverell, in his said Sermon, preached at St. Paul's, doth suggest and maintain, That the necessary means used to bring about the said happy Revolution, were odious and unjustifiable : That his late majesty, in his Declaration, disclaimed the least imputation of Resistance : And that to impute Resistance to the said Revolution, is to cast black and odious colours upon his late majesty and the said Revolution.

II. He, the said Henry Sacheverell, in his said Sermon preached at St. Paul's, doth suggest and maintain, That the foresaid Toleration granted by law is unreasonable, and the allowance of it unwarrantable: And asserts, That he is a false brother with relation to God, religion or the Church who defends Toleration and Liberty of Conscience; That Queen Elizabeth was deluded by archbishop Grindall, whom he scurrilously calls A False Son of the Church, and a Perfidious

Prelate, to the toleration of the Genevan discipline: And that it is the duty of superior pastors to thunder out their ecclesiastical anathemas against persons intitled to the benefit of the said Toleration, and insolently dares, or defies any power on earth to reverse such sentences.

III. He, the said Henry Sacheverell, in his said Sermon, preached at St. Paul's, doth falsely and seditiously suggest and assert, That the Church of England is in a condition of great peril and adversity under her majesty's administration; and in order to arraign and blacken the said Vote or Resolution of both Houses of Parliament, approved by her majesty as aforesaid, he, in opposition thereto, doth suggest the Church to be in Danger: and, as a parallel, mentions a Vote, That the person of king Charles the first was voted to be out of danger, at the same time that his murderers were conspiring his death; thereby wickedly and maliciously insinuating, that the members of both Houses, who passed the said vote, were then conspiring the ruin of the Church.

IV. He, the said Henry Sacheverell, in his said Sermons and Books, doth falsely and maliciously suggest, That her majesty's administration, both in ecclesiastical and civil affairs, tends to the destruction of the constitution: And that there are men of characters and stations in Church and State who are False Brethren, and do themselves weaken, undermine and betray, and do encourage, and put it in the power of others, who are professed enemies, to overturn and destroy the constitution and establishment: and chargeth her majesty, and those in authority under her, both in Church and State, with a general mal-administration: And, as a public incendiary, he persuades her majesty's subjects to keep up a distinction of factions and parties; instils groundless jealousies, foments destructive divisions among them, and excites and stirs them up to arms and violence: And that his said malicious and seditious suggestions may make the stronger impression upon the minds of her majesty's subjects, he the said Henry Sacheverell doth wickedly wrest and pervert divers texts and passages of Holy Scripture.

Attorney General (Sir J. Montague). And to shew his little liking of the great work which was begun to be wrought on that day by the arrival of his late majesty, the chief turn of his discourse is, to cry up Non-Resistance and Passive Obedience.

And to make it most evident, that what he said of Non-Resistance, was to cast black and odious colours upon the Revolution; he lays down a general position, 'That it is not lawful, upon any pretence whatsoever, to make Resistance to the supreme power'; which supreme power, by other passages, he explains to be the regal power.

And being apprehensive, that every one that heard him talking in that manner against Resistance, would see plainly he was censuring and condemning the means that brought about the Revolution, and being desirous to cast as heavy reflections as he could upon the memory of king William, he asserts, 'That the Prince of Orange, in his Declaration, utterly disclaimed all manner of Resistance.'

My lords, everybody knows, that knows anything of the Revolution, That the Prince of Orange came over with an armed force; and that in several paragraphs of his Declaration, (the Doctor speaks of) His late Majesty invites and requires all peers of the realm, both spiritual and temporal lords, all gentlemen, citizens, and other commoners, to come in and assist him, in order to the executing that design he had then undertook, against all that should endeavour to oppose him.

Therefore it must be accounted very ridiculous for the Doctor to advance such a position, if he had no further meaning in it, than to give an account of the Prince of Orange's design in coming over here into England.

And this will make it necessary for your lordships to consider what is the true meaning of this assertion : is it not plainly to make the Prince of Orange say one thing, and at the same time do directly another? And can this be done with any other design than to asperse the memory of the late king William?

Then as to his discourse concerning Passive Obedience and Non-Resistance, in such latitude as is there mentioned; what could it tend to, but to cast reflections upon that Resistance, which was the means that brought about the Revolution?

For was there any occasion at that time to be so earnest to cry down Resistance and preach up Passive Obedience?

Can any one pretend to say, there were any symptoms of discontent throughout the nation, in any parts thereof?

No : to our comfort be it spoken, no reign, no age, no history, can give a better account of the good dispositions of the people to their sovereign. Therefore, since the preaching these doctrines was needless, it does savour of some wicked design, to be talking so unreasonably of this subject.

If what the doctor very frequently asserts in this sermon be true, That all are false sons of the Church, who assisted in bringing about the Revolution, or that joined in the opposition that was made to the encroachments which were begun by evil ministers in the reign of king James 2, against our religion and liberties; let the Doctor a little consider, how far his character of a False Brother may be carried!

Everybody knows, that lived in those days that the body of the clergy of the Church of England made a noble stand against the encroachments which were then making, and appeared as active as any of the laity.

And was it not by their writings, preaching, and example, that the nobility and gentry were animated to maintain and defend their rights, religion and liberties? . . .

Mr. Lechmere. I crave leave to remind your lordships of the condition of things in both kingdoms immediately preceding the late Revolution: the case is stated and recorded, between the late king James and the subjects of both kingdoms, in the several Declarations of the Rights of both nations made by them at that time.

I shall forbear to aggravate the miscarriages of that unhappy prince, further than by saying that it is declared in the preamble to the bill passed in England, That by the assistance of evil counsellors, judges and ministers, employed by him, he did endeavour to subvert and extirpate the Protestant Religion, the laws and liberties of this kingdom, in the several instances there enumerated. And in that passed in the kingdom of Scotland, it stands declared, That, by the advice of evil counsellors, he did invade the fundamental constitution of that kingdom, and altered it from a legal limited monarchy, to an arbitrary despotic power.

Your lordships, on this occasion, will again consider the ancient legal constitution of the government of this kingdom; from which it will evidently appear to your lordships, that the subjects of this realm had not only a power and right in themselves to make that Resistance, but lay under an indispensable obligation to do it.

The nature of our constitution is that of a limited monarchy, wherein the supreme power is communicated and divided between Queen, Lords, and Commons, though the executive power and administration be wholly in the crown. The terms of such a constitution do not only suppose, but express an original contract between the crown and the people; by which that supreme power was [by mutual consent and not by accident] limited and lodged in more hands than one: and the uniform preservation of such a constitution for so many ages without any fundamental change, demonstrates to your lordships the continuance of the same contract.

The consequences of such a frame of government are obvious: that the laws are the rule to both, the common measure of the power of the crown, and of the obedience of the subject; and if the executive part endeavours the subversion, and total destruction of the government, the original contract is thereby broke, and the right of allegiance ceases : that part of the government thus fundamentally injured, hath a right to save or recover that constitution in which it had an original interest.

Nay, the nature of such an original contract of government proves, that there is not only a power in the people, who have inherited its freedom, to assert their own title to it, but they are bound in duty to transmit the same constitution to their posterity also.

It is mis-spending your lordships' time to illustrate this : it is an eternal truth, essential to the government itself and not to be defaced or destroyed by any force or device.

That the rights of the crown of England are legal rights, and its power stated and bounded by the laws of the kingdom; that the executive power and administration itself is under the strictest guard for the security of the people; and that the subjects have an inheritance in their ancient fundamental constitutions, and the laws of the land, appears from every branch of this government. It is the tenour of all antiquity; our histories and records afford innumerable proofs of it : and when your lordships look back on the history of Magna Charta alone, you cannot doubt of the sense of our ancestors, that they were masters of franchises that were truly their own, and which no earthly power had right to extort from them. Many others, of incontestable authority, are those valuable relicts which our popish ancestors have left us, as proofs of the freedom of our constitution, of the constant claims they made, both in and out of parliament, to their inheritance in their laws against the encroachment of arbitrary power; and when the last extremity called them to it, they never failed to vindicate them by the arms of Resistance.

Such was the genius of the people, whose government was built on that noble foundation, not to be bound by laws to which they did not consent : that muffled up in darkness and superstition, as our ancestors were, yet that notion seemed engraven on their minds, and the impressions so strong, that nothing could impair them.

Upon the Reformation of religion, when all foreign power was abolished, and the supremacy of the crown was restored to its height by many acts of parliament, your lordships will always find declarations at the same time made of the rights of the people; particularly that of 25th of H. 8, where it is said, That the realm of England is free from any man's laws, but such as have been devised, made and ordained within the same, for the wealth of it; or such other, as the people of the realm have taken at their free will and consent, and by long use have bound themselves to, as the ancient established laws of the realm, and none otherwise.

Your lordships will, I doubt not, consider those laws made at that time, to be fresh and remarkable declarations and ratifications of the original contract . . .

My lords, I take the liberty to acquaint your lordships, that the Commons conceive, that the laws and statutes of the realm, and the order and peace of government, necessarily enjoin it as a duty upon all private subjects, to represent their sense of the nation's grievances in a course of law and justice, and not otherwise; and whenever the oppressions become national or public, they claim it as the peculiar right of their own body, to pursue the evil instruments of them, till public vengeance be done; and at the same time the Commons assure your lordships, that they will account it their indispensable duty to her majesty and their country to assert the justice and wisdom of her administration, against the enemies of both.

I have thus stated to your lordships the nature of this cause; wherein, I persuade myself you perceive many points of the highest moment to the peace and welfare of the kingdom.

The tendency of the crimes, of which the prisoner stands accused, lies open and apparent. But yet I beg your patience, to draw the scene a little closer.

Your lordships will perceive the necessary consequence of a position meant and expounded so as to persuade the world, that the glorious work of the Revolution was the fruit of rebellion, and the work of traitors. Does it not declare the late reign to be one of continued usurpation? And under what better circumstances does it bring the present?

Is the Act of Toleration condemned with any other tendency than to weaken so great a support of the Revolution itself? And I entreat your lordships to consider the certain fatal effects of a universal dissatisfaction of the people, in things that concern them nearest, the safety of the Church of England, and the Protestant interest, and the security of themselves and their prosperity.

It is true, my lords, that, considered at a distance, there seems a repugnancy in this gentleman's system. How comes it to pass, that absolute Non-Resistance and the spirit of rebellion stand so well together, and are made so suitable, in the same discourse?

But, if your lordships should discern, in any part of his Sermon, any dark hints, or disguised opinions, of a sole Hereditary Right of Succession to the crown, that will show your lordships the true consistency of the whole; your lordships will find, that in his opinion, the duty of absolute Non-Resistance is owing to him only that has the divine commission to govern; and from thence your lordships cannot fail of knowing against what queen, what government, what establishment, he encourages the taking up the arms of Resistance. . . .

Mr. Walpole. My lords, the Commons are now making good their Charge against Doctor Henry Sacheverell contained in the first Article, wherein he is accused for suggesting and maintaining, that the necessary means used to bring about the happy Revolution were odious and unjustifiable, and that to impute Resistance to the Revolution, is to cast black and odious colours on his late Majesty and the Revolution.

By what has been already offered to your lordships, I make no doubt but you are fully convinced how injurious these positions must be to the peace and quiet of the kingdom, and how highly they deserve, and loudly call for, your lordships' speedy and exemplary justice.

The great licentiousness of the press, in censuring and reflecting upon all parts of the government, has of late given too just cause of offence; but when any pamphlets and common libels are matters of complaint; when none but mercenary scribblers, and the hackney pens of a discontented party, are employed to vent their malice, it is fit to leave them to the common course of the law, and to the ordinary proceeding of the courts below. But, my lords, when the trumpet is sounded in Sion; when the pulpit takes up the cudgels; when the cause of the enemies of our government is called the cause of God, and of the Church; when this bitter and poisonous pill is gilded over with the specious name of loyalty, and the people are taught, for their soul's and conscience's sake, to swallow these pernicious doctrines: when, instead of sound religion, divinity, and morality, factious and seditious discourses are become the constant entertainments of some congregations; the Commons cannot but think it high time to put a stop to this growing evil, and for the authority of a parliament to interpose, and exert itself, in defence of the Revolution, the present government, and the Protestant succession. All which the Commons think so materially concerned in this question, that if the doctrines advanced by Doctor Sacheverell are not criminal in the highest degree, it will follow that the necessary means used to bring about the Revolution were illegal, and consequently that the present establishment, and Protestant succession, founded upon that Revolution, are void and of no effect.

The Commons cannot but apprehend, that the just resentment and indignation they have shown upon this occasion, will meet with the general applause of all that are heartily and sincerely well affected to her majesty and her government; but for all those, whose principles and practices render them most justly suspected to have other views, they are not at all surprised to find them alarmed, and under the greatest concern at this trial.

I am very sensible, my lords, of the difficulty and nicety that attends the speaking to this point, and that whilst a loyal subject and faithful servant to the best of queens, is speaking in defence of the necessary and commendable Resistance used at the Revolution, his arguments may be misconstrued and misrepresented, as maintaining anti-monarchical schemes.

But surely, my lords, to plead for Resistance, that Resistance, I mean, which alone can be concerned in this debate, is to assert and maintain the very being of our present government and constitution; and to assert Non-Resistance in that boundless and unlimited sense in which Doctor Sacheverell presumes to assert it, is to sap and undermine the very foundations of our government, to remove the natural basis and fundamental strength of our constitution, and to leave it underset, with imaginary props and buttresses, which do, at best, but ill support a shaken foundation: and it is a most surprising assurance in the enemies of our government, that whilst they are striking at the root, and digging up the foundations, upon which our present and future settlement is built, they should hope to pass upon the world as friends to either. But so irreconcilable are the professions and practices of some men; so awkwardly do they speak well of what they do not in their hearts approve, that in vindication of his late majesty (for that is a part that sometimes they think useful to act) they declare his most glorious enterprise to save a sinking nation, utterly illegal: to recommend themselves to the queen, they condemn that Revolution, without which she had never been queen, and we a most unhappy people: to testify their zeal and affection to the Protestant succession, they invalidate all the laws that have been made for securing that blessing to posterity and lastly, to manifest their aversion, and for ever to blast all hopes of the Pretender, they advance and maintain the hereditary right, as the only true right of the crown. But what interest these opinions may at one time or another be produced to support, and in favour of whose pretensions these insinuations are easily understood to be and in favour of what settlement they can hardly be construed, I submit to your lordships' consideration.

The utter illegality of Resistance, upon any pretence whatsoever, is the general position laid down in the Sermon, which, if it be strictly, and in the most extensive manner, true, the assuming and exercising a power of dispensing with, and suspending the laws; the commitment and prosecution of the bishops; the erecting a court of commissioners for ecclesiastical causes, the levying money by pretence of prerogative; the raising and keeping a standing army without consent of parliament; the violating the freedom of elections of members to serve in parliament; and all the grievances enumerated in the Bill of Rights, were all mere pretences, and not sufficient to warrant and justify what was then done in defence of the true, ancient, and indubitable rights and liberties of the people of this kingdom; which are now again enacted, ratified and confirmed, and enjoined to be firmly and strictly holden and observed. By what evasions, or distinctions, the Doctor will explain himself off upon this head, I cannot easily foresee; unless he will be so ingenuous as now to confess, what there is too much reason to believe will be his opinion, if ever a proper time shall serve for declaring, that the acts of parliament made upon, and since the Revolution, are only the effects of a happy usurpation, and no part of the true law of the land.

Resistance is no where enacted to be legal, but subjected, by all the laws now in being, to the greatest penalties; it is what is not, cannot, nor ought ever to be described or affirmed, in any positive law, to be excusable: when, and upon what never-to-be-expected occasions it may be exercised, no man can foresee, and ought never to be thought of, but when an utter subversion of the laws of the realm threatens the whole frame of a constitution, and no redress can otherwise be hoped for: it therefore does, and ought for ever to stand, in the eye and letter of the law, as the highest offence. But because any man, or party of men, may not, out of folly or wantonness, commit treason, or make their own discontents, ill principles, or disguised affections to another interest, a pretence to resist the supreme power, will it follow from thence that the utmost necessity ought not to engage a nation in its own defence for the preservation of the whole? Or, on the other side, because the greatest and most inexpressible emergencies did sufficiently justify and warrant the Resistance of the Revolution, will it be a consequence, that therefore, upon every slight pretext or common occasion, the laws that fence against treason will be of no effect? No, my lords, I hope your just judgment in this case will convince the world, that every seditious, discontented, hot-headed, ungifted, unedifying preacher, (the Doctor

U

will pardon me for borrowing one string of epithets from him, and
for once using a little of his own language) who had no hopes of
distinguishing himself in the world, but by a matchless indiscretion,
may not advance, with impunity, doctrines destructive of the peace
and quiet of her majesty's government, and the Protestant Succession,
and prepare the minds of the people for an alteration, by giving them
ill impressions of the present establishment and its administration.

The doctrine of unlimited, unconditional Passive Obedience, was
first invented to support arbitrary and despotic power, and was never
promoted or countenanced by any government that had not designs
some time or other of making use of it : what then can be the design
of preaching this doctrine now, unasked, unsought for, in her majesty's
reign, where the law is the only rule and measure of the power of the
crown, and of the obedience of the people ? If then this doctrine
can neither be an advantage or security to her majesty, who neither
wants nor desires it, to what end and purpose must every thinking
man conclude it is now set on foot, but to unhinge the present
government, by setting aside all that has been done in opposition to
that doctrine ? and when, by these means the way is made clear to
another's title, the people are ready instructed to submit to whatever
shall be imposed upon them.

It may be expected, after I have said thus much in general, that I
should proceed to shew in what parts of the Sermon these aspersions
are contained : but, my lords, that part has been so fully and distinctly spoke to by those learned gentlemen who are more proper, and
a great deal more able to manage that province, that I will not mis-
spend your lordships' time by repeating what has been so fully and
justly made out; but so much I will venture to say, that if we
remove the rubbage, with which the Doctor has an excellent talent
at puzzling common sense, and bring together the several sentences,
that can only be relative to one another, it is impossible for the art
of man to make any inferences or constructions, so close and strong,
as the plain and general sense of the whole scope of his Sermon
must, at first view, suggest to every man's understanding. And all
that the Doctor alleges in his defence is, that in the Revolution there
was no Resistance at all ; and that the king did utterly disclaim any
such imputation. But surely, my lords, it cannot be now necessary to
prove Resistance in the Revolution; I should as well expect that your
lordships would desire me, for form's sake, to prove the sun shines at
noon-day. If then there was most undoubtedly Resistance used to

bring about the Revolution, it will follow that all the censures, which are so freely bestowed upon Resistance in general, must attend, and will be imputed to the Revolution; and if Resistance be utterly illegal, upon any pretence whatsoever; if it is a sin, which unrepented of, by the doctrine of the Church of England, carries sure and certain damnation; if, upon repentance, there is no remission of sins without a stedfast purpose to amend the evil we have done, and to make all possible restitution, or at least to do our utmost endeavours for that purpose; I beg your lordships to consider what a duty is here pressed, upon the peril of damnation, upon every man's conscience, that knows or believes that there was Resistance in the Revolution, and is conscious to himself of being any ways assisting, or even consenting to this damnable sin; and what must be the consequences if these doctrines, without any reserve or exception, are with impunity preached throughout the kingdom. All which, my lords, I hope, is sufficient to satisfy your lordships that Doctor Sacheverell is guilty of the charge exhibited against him in the First Article; and that he is an offender of that nature and malignity, that this Court only could be the proper judge of such high crimes; and from your lordships' justice, the Commons hope, That his punishment will be adequate to the heinousness of his offence. . . .

Sir Simon Harcourt, (For the Defence.) Having thus stated to your lordships the question between us, Whether such excepted cases, as the Revolution was, are not more proper to be left as implied, than to be expressed, when the general duty of obedience is taught?

I shall endeavour to satisfy your lordships, first, that the Doctor's assertion of the illegality of Resistance to the supreme power on any pretence whatsoever, in general terms, without expressing any exception, or that any exception is to be made, is warranted by the authority of the Church of England: And secondly, That his manner of expression is agreeable to the law of England. . . .

My lords, is this doctrine of Non-Resistance taught in the Homilies in general terms, in the same manner as doctor Sacheverell has asserted it, without expressing any exception? Do the articles of our religion declare the doctrine taught in the homilies to be a godly and whole-some doctrine? and will your lordships permit this gentleman to suffer for preaching it? Is it criminal in any man to preach that doctrine, which it is his duty to read? The Doctor is not only required by the 35th Article to read this doctrine diligently, and dis-tinctly, that it may be understood by the people; but to shew your lordships, the doctrine taught in the homilies did not die, nor was altered at the Revolution, I must observe to your lordships, that the rubric of the office appointed for the 6th of November, by the late queen of blessed memory, directs the clergy on that day if there be no sermon, to read one of these homilies against rebellion. Since the Doctor chose rather to preach, than to read a homily on that day, how could he better comply with the command of her late majesty, than by preaching the same doctrine as was contained in those homilies he was commanded to read on that day, if he did not preach? Does an act of parliament inserted in the Act of Union, injoin him to subscribe to this doctrine before the ordinary, and declare his unfeigned assent to it in his parish church? and shall he be condemned in parliament, for asserting the truth of it? I must admit this 35th article of our religion is not by the Toleration-act (I will give no offence by calling it by its true name) required to be subscribed by any persons dissenting from the Church of England, to entitle them to their exemption from the penalties mentioned in that act. But that act of parliament no way varies the case with respect to the clergy; so that whatever duty was incumbent on them before, is so still: and therefore I hope, your lordships will not think this gentleman has so highly offended.

As a further proof that this doctrine of Non-Resistance, as laid down by the Doctor in general terms, without making any exception, is the doctrine of the Church of England, I shall shew your lordships, that it has been so preached, maintained and avowed, and in much stronger terms than the Doctor has expressed himself, by our most orthodox and able divines from the time of the Restoration. It would be endless to offer your lordships all the authorities I might produce on this occasion; but we shall beg your lordships' patience to lay before you some passages out of the learned writings of several reverend fathers of our Church, of nine archbishops, above twenty bishops, and of several other very eminent and learned men.

That your lordships may not think this doctrine died at the Revolution, I shall humbly lay before your lordships the opinions of three archbishops, and eleven bishops, made since the Revolution which will fully shew the doctrine of Non-Resistance is still the doctrine of our Church; I would not willingly give offence in naming them; I am sure I mean no reflection, nor can it, as I think, be any reproach to them; I find no other doctrine in this case taught by them, as far as I am able to judge, than what the Apostles taught before them. With your lordships' leave, I will therefore presume to name them: archbishop Tillotson, the two present archbishops

---

[1] Dennison and Sharpe. See the case of Bishop Compton, S.T. xi. p. 1123.

bishop Stillingfleet, late bishop of Worcester, the present bishops of Rochester,[1] Salisbury,[2] Worcester,[3] Ely,[4] Bath and Wells,[5] Lincoln,[6] Exeter,[7] St. Asaph,[8] Carlisle,[9] and Chichester.[10]   If I am able to show your lordships that all these right reverend fathers of our Church have preached the same doctrine the Doctor has,[11] are the same words coming out of their mouths to be received as oracles of truth, but spoke by the Doctor, fit for articles of impeachment?   I am sure it is impossible to enter into the heart of man to conceive, that what these reverend prelates have asserted, that any general position they have laid down concerning Non-Resistance, is an affirmance that necessary means used to bring about the Revolution were odious and unjustifiable : why then is Doctor Sacheverell, by having taught the same doctrine, in the same manner as they did, to be charged for having suggested or maintained any such thing?

My lords, I dare not suppose this doctrine, thus established by so many reverend fathers of our Church to be erroneous.   If an intemperate expression of one single archbishop above a hundred years since dead, is fit to be inserted in an Article of Impeachment of High Crimes and Misdemeanours, what punishment should I deserve, could I suppose the doctrine, taught by so many archbishops and bishops, to be erroneous?   But if I might hope to be excused, if I made the supposition, that the homilies of the Church contain false doctrine, and that so many of the right reverend fathers of our Church are capable of erring, or being ignorant in the doctrine of their Church, I humbly propose it to your lordships, whether a clergyman who errs after such great examples, might not reasonably have hoped for a more moderate correction, than an impeachment !   Had this slavish doctrine of Non-Resistance been first branded with its indelible mark of infamy, and the right and indispensable duty of Resistance to princes plainly shewn ; had all the slavish notions of the common law which we find dispersed throughout our law-books, which give

[1] Sprat.   See his case, vol. 12, p. 1051.

[2] Burnet.   See his case, vol. 11, p. 1103.

[3] Lloyd, one of the seven.   See their case, vol. 12, p. 183 ; see also Proceedings against Lloyd, vol. 14, p. 545.

[4] Moore.   [5] Hooper.   [6] Wake.

[7] Blackhall, an antagonist of Hoadley, ridiculed in Powell's letter, Tatler, No. 50.

[8] Fleetwood.   [9] Nicholson.   [10] Manningham.

[11] In the case of Daniel Holt, November 23, 1793, it was decided that a defendant charged with having published a libel shall not be permitted to prove, that a paper similar to that for the publication of which he is prosecuted was published on a former occasion, by other persons who have never been prosecuted for it.   5 Term Rep. 436.

countenance to this doctrine of Non-Resistance, been first weeded out of them, and some few acts of parliament, entirely agreeable with this slavish doctrine, been first repealed; had the people been set right in the notions of their obedience, and the ministers of the Gospel been instructed by act of parliament what doctrine they ought to preach, and what not; had all these things been first done, and the Doctor had afterwards erred, your lordships might have then looked upon him as an obstinate offender. . . .

The next thing I beg leave to consider is, the law of England; whether the Doctor's assertion of the utter illegality of Resistance to the supreme power on any pretence whatsoever, in general terms, is agreeable to the law of England. . . . I mean, that as the general rule is always taught and inculcated by the Church, so it has always been declared by the legislature, without making any particular exception. . . .

(Sir Simon Harcourt then discusses 15 Edw. II. (the Act banishing the Dispensers), 25 Edw. III. c. 2 (the Treason Statute), 3 Ja. I. c. 4 (prescribing an oath of obedience), 12 Car. II. c. 30 (the Act against the Regicides), 13 and 14 Car. II. c. 3 (the Militia Act), 13 Car. II. Sess. 2, c. 1 (the Corporation Act), 13 and 14 Car. II. c. 4 (the Act of Uniformity as exemplifying the doctrine of Non-Resistance)).

My lords, I have gone through the several laws I shall lay before your lordships on this occasion; and let me once more humbly beg your lordships, that you will be pleased to compare the Doctor's assertion in his Sermon, concerning the illegality of Resistance, with them; whether it be stronger than the declaration of the undoubted and fundamental law of the kingdom, in the act against the regicides; than the declaration in the Militia Act; than the oath required to be taken by so many acts of parliament; than the declaration in the 25th of Edw. 3. All the Doctor has said is, that Resistance to the supreme power is illegal, on any pretence whatsoever. All the peers and commons of England, under the characters and employments I have mentioned, have sworn to the truth of it; the 25th of Edw. 3, declares it to be high treason; and your lordships have heard what St. Paul says.

My lords, I began this discourse, relating to the doctrine of the Church and the laws of the land, with the most sincere protestation, that it was far from my intention to offer anything inconsistent with the justice of the Revolution : I think the justice of it consistent with our laws, the exception to be made to be always implied. And surely none can shew themselves truer friends to the Revolution, than those who prove that the Revolution may stand without impeaching the doctrines of our Church, or any fundamental law of the kingdom. . . .

Mr. Lechmere (in reply). And what light doth it give to the question now before your lordships, when at your bar, in defence of a person accused by the Commons, for condemning the necessary means which brought about the Revolution, you have heard that original contract, at that time so solemnly declared to be a fundamental principle, publicly denied, ridiculed, and endeavoured (in what manner it is easy to judge) to have been exploded?

My lords, the truth of that position has its foundation in the nature and essence of the constitution of our government, and it will stand so long as this remains; and the sanction it has received from your lordships, and from that House of Commons, who had with so much wisdom and bravery asserted the rights of the kingdom in that extraordinary juncture, and who, pursuant to that Resolution, settled the crown upon her sacred majesty, ought to render it indisputable, so long at least as that establishment is preserved to us. But yet, could I think it seasonable to enter into it, to consider more particularly the nature of our government, to draw together some of the many incontestable evidences of its original freedom, to consider the nature, antiquity and history of the Coronation Oath, and the Oath of Allegiance, and the mutual obligations and consequences arising from them to the prince and people: Was I to go over the several branches that make up the ancient frame of our government, and which speak and express a consent and compact between the prince and people in their institution; and was I to observe that inseparable relation and equal security which they import between the crown and the subject, and which are so many infallible tokens of original consent stamped upon them; the truth and certainty of that position of an original contract between the king and people, might be laid down to your lordships in demonstrative terms. The gentleman that raised this observation, soon afterwards, in the same discourse, supposed, that by the original contract, the original constitution was meant; how strictly proper that manner of speaking might be found to be, I will not now determine; yet thus much may with certainty be concluded, that the denying the original contract, is not only to disavow the whole proceeding at the time of the Revolution, but to renounce the constitution itself, to disclaim those many and undeniable proofs and testimonies of it, which almost every part of our history, our records, and memorials of antiquity, will furnish: To deny the original contract of government, is to contradict and condemn the voice and tenor of all our laws, of every act of the supreme legislative power, the force and efficacy of which exists upon the consent of the Crown,

Lords and Commons, and are therefore so many lasting and unerring proofs of that, as the original foundation of that supreme power; it is not only to oppose the constant judgment of all learned men, who have understood and wrote impartially of our government, but even the sense of many of those writings which have been produced and read to you in the Doctor's defence, and more particularly that of the judicious Mr. Hooker: To deny and condemn the original contract between king and people, what other consequences could it produce, than to unhinge the government, and to destroy that excellent balance of power, which is secured by it, and by which it has been so long preserved? It must weaken the ancient and just prerogatives of the crown, subvert the foundations of your lordships' legislative and judicial powers, render the parliamentary rights of the Commons precarious and uncertain, and terminate at length, in that absurd, yet dangerous opinion, of the patriarchal right, which, when together joined with the doctrines of absolute and unlimited Non-Resistance, and unconditional obedience of the subject to their prince, completes that fatal system, which has been of late so much contended for towards the enslaving mankind.

(S.T. xv. 1–522.)

XIII

THE CASE OF DAMMAREE
9 Anne, April 19, 1710.

[Daniel Dammaree was a waterman who during the tumults and riots at the time of Sacheverell's trial put himself at the head of a party which destroyed a meeting-house of Dissenters in Drury Lane. He was indicted for High Treason, on the ground that an avowed intention to destroy all the meeting-houses of Presbyterians (which by the Toleration Act were under the protection of the law) was constructively an attempt to levy and raise war, rebellion, and insurrection against the Queen within the kingdom, and therefore brought the offence within the Treason Statute of Edward III. Dammaree was found guilty and sentenced to death; he was subsequently reprieved and finally pardoned. The case (with the similar one of *Purchase*), "the most severe ever decided upon this point," has a great historical and legal interest, and the excerpt is intended to illustrate this from Chief Justice Parker's summing up. See S.T. xv. 522 *et seq.* (the notes are very helpful); *Hallam*, C.H. iii. 150 *et seq.*; *Stephen*, H.C.L. ii. 241–298. *Wyon*, Reign of Queen Anne, ii.]

L. C. J. Parker. Give me leave to take notice what the law is in this case. For it has been insisted on by the counsel for the prisoner (and I must do them right, they have taken into consideration all the cases that relate to this matter)—They insist that this is not levying war; and on this ground, that he was not proved to be at the meeting-house in Drury-lane, but only at the fire at Dr. Burgess's; and if he was only at one place, one instance would not make it levying war. If, say they, there had been a general intention, it would have gone hard with him there was an intention the night before, and Mr. Burgess's was only mentioned; and it was not certain that there was a general design to pull down the rest. Nay, he was not there, and it was by accident he came to Lincoln's-inn-fields, and he was but at that one place; and they take notice of some cases, especially that about the bawdy-houses, and that the lord-chief-justice Hale differed from the rest of the judges.

This is a matter that has been often under consideration: the act of the 25th Edward the 3rd, which is the great law for declarations of treason, declares what shall be adjudged treason: compassing or imagining the death of the king, and levying war against the king, are two distinct species of treason. Now they say, that nothing was designed against the queen. If the levying war against the queen, was there meant only of a war against the queen's person, it would have been idle to mention it in that act, because they had before made the compassing her death to be treason.

Now he that levies war, does more than compass or imagine the king's death: therefore it has been always ruled, that where there is an actual levying of war, which concerns the person of the king, they lay the treason to be the compassing the death of the king, and give a proof of it by levying war. But there is another levying of war, which is not immediately against the person of the king, but only between some particular persons. There is a vast difference between a man's going to remove an annoyance to himself, and going to remove a public nuisance, as the case of the bawdy-houses: and the general intention to pull them down all is the treason: for if those that were concerned for them would defend them, and the others would pull them down, there would be a war immediately.

In the case of inclosures, where the people of a town have had a part of their common inclosed, though they have come with a great force to throw down that inclosure, yet that is not levying of war; but if any will go to pull down all inclosures, and make it a general thing to reform that which they think a nuisance, that necessarily makes it a war between all the lords and the tenants. A bawdy-house is a nuisance, and may be punished as such; and if it be a particular prejudice to any one, if he himself should go in an unlawful manner to redress that prejudice; it might be only a riot; but if he will set up to pull them all down in general, he has taken the queen's right out of her hand: he has made it a general thing, and when they

are once up, they may call every man's house a bawdy-house; and this
is a general thing, it affects the whole nation.

Now to come to this instance. If you believe the evidence,
Dammaree was concerned in pulling down two meeting-houses: he was
not present at Drury-lane, that is, he was not proved to be there: but
if he set others on to do it, it is his doing, and he as much pulled
down that meeting-house in Drury-lane, as if he had pulled it down
with his own hands. Besides, they tell you his declaration, that he
would have all of them pulled down. Again, these gentlemen do not
seem to deny, but if the intention were general, it would be levying
war: if it were general, where would it end? And it is taking on
them the royal authority; nay, more, for the queen cannot pull them
down till the law is altered: therefore he has here on him not only
the royal authority, but a power that no person in England has. It
concerns all that are against the meeting-houses on one side, and all
that are for them on the other, and therefore is levying war.

They said, they would desire this point to be reserved to them
on the account of the opinion of the lord chief justice Hale: But
I believe this matter has been so often settled, that it would be
strange for us to depart from such a settled rule of law; for these
are only the same arguments that were offered by the lord-chief-
justice; and he offered the same arguments that were used in queen
Elizabeth's reign; but it was then held to be treason, and has been
held so ever since. His objection made them consider it then, and
they did so; and I suppose they will not expect that it should have
more weight out of their mouths than out of his. It was then
settled, and has been taken for law at all times since, so that it is
not a matter to be now called in question. And as to the statute
of 13 Eliz. the intention to levy war is surely not an intention to
do a thing, which when it is done, is not levying war.

Thus the matter stands in point of law: I take it to be clear that
it is levying war, if you take him to be guilty of being at one of the
meeting-places, and leading them, and tempting them to another.
Whether that is true, or not, must be left to your consideration.
You have heard what has been said, and what difficulties arise in
point of time, and on the other proofs: If you are of opinion, that
he was present at Lincoln's-inn-fields, and did encourage them, and
acted any otherwise than by force; if you believe he led, or invited
them to another place, and pulled down that, then you will find him
guilty of high treason. If you think he was not there, or was under
a compulsion, then he will not be guilty.

(S.T. xv. pp. 606–610.)

XIV

WILKES AND GENERAL WARRANTS
(1763–1766)

[During the seventeenth century it had been customary for the Secretary
of State from time to time to issue General Warrants for the arrest of the
author or authors, publisher or publishers of alleged libellous papers, and
for the seizure of the papers concerned.   And the practice was continued
after 1695, when the House of Commons refused to re-enact the Licensing
Act, which had given special powers to the authorities for the arrest of
libellers and seizure of their papers.   On April 30, 1763, John Wilkes,
a member of Parliament, who had published in the famous No. 45 of
The North Briton a severe criticism of the King's Speech, was arrested by
two of the King's Messengers on a General Warrant issued by the Earl
of Halifax, Secretary of State, and committed to the Tower of London.
On the same day in the Court of Common Pleas a writ of Habeas Corpus
was moved for.   On May 2 the return to the writ by the Messengers
concerned certified that Wilkes " was not in their custody," whereupon
another writ was directed to the Constable of the Tower, the return to
which on May 3 certified as reason for his detention the warrant of
commitment of two secretaries of state in terms similar to the General
Warrant on which Wilkes had originally been arrested.   Serjeant Glynn
on behalf of Wilkes then moved the court for his discharge out of custody
without bail on these grounds : (1) that there was no evidence he was
the author or publisher of No. 45 of *The North Briton;* nor (2) that
No. 45 was a seditious libel ; (3) that Wilkes as a member of Parliament
was privileged from arrest save for treason, felony, or breach of the peace.
It is to be observed that the legality of a General Warrant was not before
the court.   Subsequently Lord Chief Justice Pratt, afterwards Lord
Camden, gave judgment (Excerpt IV.) that Wilkes must be discharged
from his imprisonment—a decision which caused "a loud huzza in Westminster Hall."   Meanwhile the matter had been discussed in both Houses
of Parliament, for accounts of which see the authorities cited below, and
it ultimately occasioned several important cases in the law courts.   See
Leach v. Three of the King's Messengers (p. 314) and *Entick v. Carrington*
(p. 316).   The excerpts here given are : (1) two specimens of General
Warrants ; (2) the resolutions of the House of Commons in 1763 and
1764 ; (3) the resolutions of the House of Lords and a protest arising
therefrom ; (4) the judgment of Pratt, C.J., in *Wilkes v. Lord Halifax;*
(5) a passage from the summing up of Pratt, C.J., in *Wilkes v. Wood;*
(6) the resolutions of the House of Commons in 1766 declaring General
Warrants illegal ; (7) a passage from Lord Mansfield's speech in the House
of Lords on January 9, 1770, concerning these resolutions.   Extracts
giving the incriminated passages of No. 45 of *The North Briton* will be
found in App. to *State Trials,* xix. 1382–1401.   See for the whole matter
S.T. xix. 982–1175 ; *Lecky,* H.E. ch. ix.; the *Letters of Junius; May,* C.H.E.
ii. ch. 7, iii. ch. 11 ; *Broom,* C.L. 521–619 ; *Fitzgerald,* Life of Wilkes ;
The North Briton, Nos. 1–46, with notes 1769.]

I

GENERAL WARRANTS

A

It is his majesty's pleasure that you take into your custody the person of Francis Smith, Stationer, for having a hand in printing and compiling dangerous books, and that you keep him close prisoned till further orders from his majesty, and for so doing this shall be your warrant. Dated at the court at Whitehall this 15th day of August, 1681.   EDWARD NICHOLAS.

To the Keeper of the Gatehouse, Westminster, or his Deputy. (S.T. 7, 946.)

B

George Montagu Dunk, Earl of Halifax, viscount Sunbury, and baron Halifax, one of the lords of his majesty's honourable privy council, lieutenant general of his majesty's forces, lord lieutenant general and general governor of the kingdom of Ireland, and principal secretary of state, etc. etc. these are in his majesty's name to authorize and require you, taking a constable to your assistance, to make strict and diligent search for John Entick, the author, or one concerned in writing of several weekly very seditious papers, intitled the Monitor or British Freeholder, No. 357, 358, 360, 373, 376, 378, 379, and 380, London, printed for J. Wilson and S. Fell in Pater Noster Row, which contains gross and scandalous reflections and invections upon his majesty's government, and upon both houses of parliament; and him having found you are to seize and apprehend, and to bring, together with his books and papers, in safe custody before me to be examined concerning the premises, and further dealt with according to law; in the due execution whereof all mayors, sheriffs, justices of the peace, constables and other his majesty's officers—civil and military, and loving subjects whom it may concern, are to be aiding and assisting to you as there shall be occasion; and for so doing this shall be your warrant.

Given at St. James's the sixth day of November 1762, in the third year of his majesty's reign,   DUNK HALIFAX.

To Nathan Carrington, James Watson, Thomas Ardran, and Robert Blackmore, four of his majesty's messengers in ordinary.

(S.T. xix. 1034.)

II

THE PROCEEDINGS IN THE COMMONS

Mr. Chancellor of the Exchequer informed the House, that he was commanded by the King to acquaint the House, that his Majesty having received Information that John Wilkes Esquire, a Member of this House, was the Author of a most seditious and dangerous Libel, published since the last Session of Parliament; He had caused the said John Wilkes Esquire to be apprehended, and secured, in order to his being tried for the same by due Course of Law: And Mr. Wilkes having been discharged out of Custody by the Court of Common Pleas, upon account of his Privilege as a Member of this House; and having, when called upon by the legal Process of the Court of King's Bench, stood out, and declined to appear, and answer to an Information which has since been exhibited against him by His Majesty's Attorney General for the same Offence: In this Situation, His Majesty being desirous to show all possible Attention to the Privileges of the House of Commons, in every Instance wherein they can be supposed to be concerned; and at the same time thinking it of the utmost Importance not to suffer the Public Justice of the Kingdom to be eluded, has chosen to direct the said Libel, and also Copies of the Examination upon which Mr. Wilkes was apprehended and secured, to be laid before this House for their consideration: And Mr. Chancellor of the Exchequer delivered the said papers in at the Table.

(a) Resolved, Nemine contradicente, That an humble Address be presented to His Majesty, to return His Majesty the Thanks of this House for His most gracious Message, and for the tender Regard therein expressed for the Privileges of this House; and to assure His Majesty that this House will forthwith take into their most serious Consideration the very important Matter communicated by His Majesty's Message. . . .

(b) Resolved, That the Paper intituled, "The North Briton No. 45" is a false, scandalous, and seditious Libel, containing Expressions of the most unexampled Insolence and Contumely towards His Majesty, the grossest Aspersions upon both Houses of Parliament, and the most audacious Defiance of the Authority of the whole Legislature; and most manifestly tending to alienate the Affections of the People from His Majesty, to withdraw them from their Obedience to the Laws of the Realm, and to excite them to traitorous Insurrections against His Majesty's Government.

Resolved, That the said Paper be burnt by the Hands of the common Hangman. . . .

(c) Resolved, That it appears to this House that the said John Wilkes Esquire is guilty of Writing and Publishing the Paper, intituled, "The North Briton, No. 45," which this House has voted to be a false, scandalous and seditious Libel, containing Expressions of the most unexampled Insolence and Contumely towards His Majesty, the grossest Aspersions upon both Houses of Parliament, and the most audacious Defiance of the Authority of the whole Legislature; and most manifestly tending to alienate the Affections of the People from His Majesty, to withdraw them from their Obedience to the Laws of the Realm, and to excite them to traitorous Insurrection against His Majesty's government.

(d) Resolved, That the said John Wilkes, Esquire be, for his said Offence, expelled this House.

(C.J. xxix. 667.)

(e) Resolved, That Privilege of Parliament does not extend to the writing and publishing Seditious libels, nor ought it to be allowed to obstruct the ordinary course of the laws, in the speedy and effectual prosecution of so heinous and dangerous an offence.

(C.J. November 24, 1763.)

III

PROCEEDINGS IN THE LORDS

And it being moved, "To agree with the Commons in the said Resolution:" (i.e. (e))

The same was objected to.

After long Debate thereupon;

The Question was put, "Whether to agree with the Commons in the said Resolution?"

It was resolved in the Affirmative.

"*Dissentient.*

1. Because we cannot hear without the utmost Concern and Astonishment, a Doctrine advanced now for the First Time in this House, which we apprehend to be new, dangerous, and unwarrantable; *videlicet*, That the Personal Privilege of both Houses of Parliament has never held, and ought not to hold, in the Case of any Criminal Prosecution whatsoever; by which, all the Records of Parliament, all History, all the authorities of the gravest and soberest Judges, are entirely rescinded; and the fundamental principles of the Constitu-

tion, with regard to the independence of Parliament, torn up, and buried under the Ruins of our most established Rights.

We are at a Loss to conceive with what View such a Sacrifice should be proposed, unless to amplify in effect the Jurisdiction of the inferior, by annihilating the ancient Immunities of this superior Court: The very Question itself proposed to us from the Commons, and now agreed to by the Lords, from the Letter and Spirit of it, contradicts this Assertion; for, whilst it only narrows Privilege in Criminal Matters, it establishes the Principle.

The Law of Privilege, touching Imprisonment of the Person of Lords of Parliament, as stated by the Two Standing Orders, declares generally, "That no Lord of Parliament, sitting the Parliament, or within the usual Times of Privilege of Parliament, is to be imprisoned or restrained without Sentence or Order of the House, unless it be for Treason or Felony, or for refusing to give Security for the Peace, and Refusal to pay Obedience to a Writ of *Habeas Corpus*."

The first of these Orders was made, after long Consideration, upon a Dispute with the King, when the Precedents of both Houses had been fully inspected, commented upon, reported, and entered in the Journals; and after the King's Counsel had been heard: It was made in sober Times, and by a House of Peers, not only loyal, but devoted to the Crown; and it was made by the unanimous Consent of all, not one dissenting. These Circumstances of Solemnity, Deliberation, and Unanimity, are so singular and extraordinary, that the like are scarce to be found in any Instance among the Records of Parliament.

When the Two Cases, of Surety for the Peace and *Habeas Corpus*, come to be well considered; it will be found that they both breathe the same Spirit, and grow out of the same Principle.

The Offences that call for Surety and *Habeas Corpus* are both Cases at present continuing Violence; the Proceedings in both have the same End, *videlicet*, to repress the Force, and disarm the offender.

The Proceeding stops, in both, when that End is attained.

The Offence is not prosecuted, nor punished in either.

The Necessity is equal in both; and, if Privilege was allowed in either so long as the Necessity lasts, a Lord of Parliament would enjoy a mightier Prerogative than the Crown itself is entitled to. Lastly they both leave the Prosecution of all Misdemeanours still under Privilege; and do not derogate from that great Fundamental, "That none shall be arrested in the Course of Prosecution for any Crime under Treason and Felony."

These Two Orders comprise the whole Law of Privilege; and are both of them Standing Orders, and consequently the fixed Laws of the House, by which we are all bound, till they are duly repealed.

The Resolution of the other House, now agreed to, is a direct Contradiction to the Rule of Parliamentary Privilege laid down in the aforesaid Standing Orders, both in Letter and Spirit. Before the Reasons are stated, it will be proper to premise two Observations.

That, in all Cases where Security of the Peace may be required, the Lord cannot be committed till that Security is refused; and consequently the Magistrate will be guilty of a Breach of Privilege, if he commits the Offender without demanding that Security.

Although the Security should be refused; yet, if the Party is committed generally, the Magistrate is guilty of a Breach of Privilege, because the Party refusing ought only to be committed till he has found Sureties: Whereas, by a general Commitment, he is held fast, even though he should give Sureties; and can only be discharged by giving Bail for his Appearance.

This being premised, The First Objection is to the Generality of this Resolution, which, as it is penned, denies the Privilege to the supposed Libeller, not only where he refuses to give Sureties, but likewise throughout the whole Prosecution from the Beginning to the End; so that, although he should submit to be bound, he may notwithstanding be afterwards arrested, tried, convicted, and punished, sitting the Parliament, and without Leave of the House; wherein the Law of Privilege is fundamentally misunderstood, by which no Commitment whatever is tolerated, but that only which is made upon the Refusal of Sureties, or in other excepted Cases, of Treason or Felony, and the *Habeas Corpus*.

If Privilege will not hold throughout in the Case of a Seditious Libel, it must be, because that Offence is such a Breach of the Peace for which Sureties may be demanded; and if that be so, it will readily be admitted, that the Case comes within the Exception; Provided always that Sureties have been refused, and that the Party is committed only till he shall give Sureties.

But this Offence is not a Breach of the Peace; it does not fall within any Definition of a Breach of the Peace, given by any of the good Writers upon that Subject; all which Breaches, from Menace to actual Wounding, either alone or with a Multitude, are described to be, Acts of Violence against the Person, Goods, or Possession, putting the Subject in ear by Blows, Threats, or Gestures: Nor is this Case of the Libeller ever enumerated in any of these Writers among the Breaches of Peace; on the contrary, it is always described as an Act tending to excite, provoke, or produce, Breaches of the Peace. And although a Secretary of State may be pleased to add the inflaming Epithets of treasonable, traitorous, or seditious, to a particular Paper; yet no Words are strong enough to alter the nature of Things. To say then that a Libel, possibly productive of such a Consequence, is the very Consequence so produced, is in other Words, to declare that the Cause and the Effect are the same Thing.

But if a Libel could possibly by any abuse of Language, or has anywhere been, called inadvertently a Breach of the Peace; there is not the least Colour to say, that the Libeller can be bound to give Sureties for the Peace, for the following Reasons:

Because none can be so bound unless he be taken in the actual commitment of a Breach of the Peace, striking, or putting some one or more of his Majesty's Subjects in Fear.

Because there is no Authority, or even ambiguous Hint, in any Law Book, that he may be so bound.

Because no Libeller, in Fact, was ever so bound.

Because no Crown Lawyer, in the most despotic Times, ever insisted he should be so bound, even in the Days when the Press swarmed with the most envenomed and virulent Libels, and when the Prosecutions raged with such uncommon Fury against this Species of Offenders; when the Law of Libels was ransacked every Term; when Loss of Ears, perpetual Imprisonment, Banishment, and Fines of Ten and Twenty Thousand Pounds, were the common Judgments in *The Star Chamber;* and when the Crown had assumed an uncontrollable Authority over the Press.

This Resolution does not only infringe the Privilege of Parliament, but points to the Restraint of the Personal Liberty of every common Subject in these Realms; seeing that it does in Effect affirm, that all men, without Exception, may be bound to the Peace for this Offence.

By this Doctrine, every Man's Liberty, privileged as well as unprivileged, is surrendered into the Hands of a Secretary of State: *He* is by this means empowered, in the first Instance, to pronounce the Paper to be a seditious Libel, a matter of such Difficulty, that some have pretended it is too high to be intrusted to a Special Jury of the First Rank and Condition: *He* is to understand and decide by himself the meaning of every *Innuendo: He* is to determine the tendency thereof, and brand it with his own Epithets: *He* is to adjudge the Party guilty, and make him Author or Publisher, as he sees good; and, lastly, *He* is to give Sentence, by Committing the Party.

x

All these Authorities are given to one single magistrate, unassisted by Counsel, Evidence, or Jury, in a Case where the Law says no Action will lie against him because he acts in the Capacity of a Judge.

From what has been observed, it appears to us, that the Exception of a seditious Libel from Privilege is neither founded on Usage or written Precedents; and therefore this Resolution is of the First Impression: Nay, it is not only a new Law narrowing the known and ancient Rule, but it is likewise a Law *ex post facto, pendente Lite, et ex Parte*, now first declared to meet with the Circumstances of a particular Case: And it must be further considered, that this House is thus called upon to give a Sanction to the Determinations of the other, who have not condescended to confer with us upon this Point, till they have prejudged it themselves.

This Method of relaxing the Rule of Privilege, Case by Case, is pregnant with this further Inconvenience, that it renders the Rule precarious and uncertain. Who can foretell where the House will stop, when they have, by One Infringement of their own Standing Orders, made a Precedent, whereon future Infringements may with equal Reason be founded? How shall the Subject be able to proceed with Safety in this perilous Business? How can the Judges decide, on these or the like Questions, if Privilege is no longer to be found in Records, and Journals, and Standing Orders? Upon any occasion, Privilege may be enlarged; no Court will venture for the future, without trembling, either to recognize or to deny it.

We manifestly see this effect of excluding by a general Resolution one Bailable Offence from Privilege To-day; that it will be a Precedent for doing so by another upon some future Occasion, till, instead of Privilege holding in every Case not excepted, it will at last come to hold in none but such as are expressly saved.

When the Case of the *Habeas Corpus* is relied upon as a Precedent to enforce the present Declaration; the Argument only shews, that the Mischief afore-mentioned has taken Place already; since one alteration, though a very just one, and not at all applicable to the present Question, is produced, to justify another that is unwarrantable.

But it is strongly objected, that, if privilege be allowed in this Case, a Lord of Parliament might endanger the Constitution, by a continual Attack of successive Libels; and, if such a Person should be suffered to escape, under the Shelter of Privilege with perpetual Impunity, all Government would be overturned; and therefore it is inexpedient to allow the Privilege now, when the Time of Privilege by Prorogations is continued for ever, without an Interval.

This Objection shall be answered in Two Ways: If Inexpediency is to destroy Personal Privilege in this Case of a seditious Libel, it is at least as inexpedient that other great misdemeanours should stand under the like Protection of Privilege: Neither is it expedient that the smaller Offences should be exempt from Prosecution in the Person of a Lord of Parliament. So that, if this argument of Inexpediency is to prevail, it must prevail throughout, and subvert, the whole Law of Privilege in Criminal Matters; in which Method of Reasoning, there is this Fault that the Argument proves too much.

If this Inconvenience be indeed grievous, the Fault is not in the Law of Privilege, but in the Change of Times, and in the Management of Prorogations by the Servants of the Crown; which are so contrived, as not to leave an Hour open for Justice. Let the Objection, nevertheless, be allowed in its utmost Extent; and then compare the Inexpediency of Stripping Parliament of all Protection from Privilege on the other: Unhappy as the Option is, the Public would rather wish to see the Prosecution for Crimes suspended, than the Parliament totally unprivileged; although, notwithstanding this pretended Inconvenience is so warmly magnified upon the present Occasion, we are not apprized that any such inconvenience has been felt, though the Privilege has been enjoyed Time immemorial.

But the Second and Best Answer, because it removes all Pretence of Grievance, is this, that this House, upon Complaint made, has the Power (which it will exert in Favour of Justice) to deliver up the Offender to Prosecution.

It is a dishonourable, and an undeserved, Imputation upon the Lords, to suppose, even in Argument, that they would nourish an impious Criminal in their Bosoms, against the Call of Offended Justice, and the Demand of their country. It is true however, and it is hoped that this House will always see (as every Magistrate ought that does not betray his Trust) that their Member is properly charged; but, when that Ground is once laid, they would be ashamed to protect the Offender One Moment. Surely this Trust (which has never yet been abused) is not too great to be reposed in the High Court of Parliament. While it is lodged there, the Public Justice is in safe Hands, and the Privilege untouched; whereas, on the contrary, if, for the Sake of coming at the Criminal at once without this Application to the House, Personal Privilege is taken away; not only the Offender, but the whole Parliament at the same Time, is delivered up to the Crown.

It is not to be conceived that our Ancestors, when they framed the Law of Privilege, would have left the Case of a Seditious Libel (as it is called) the only unprivileged Misdemeanour : Whatever else they had given up to the Crown, they would have guarded the Case of supposed Libels, above all others, with Privilege, as being most likely to be abused by outrageous and vindictive Prosecutions.

But this great Privilege had a much deeper Reach ; it was wisely planned, and hath hitherto, through all Times, been resolutely maintained.

It was not made to screen Criminals, but to preserve the very Being and Life of Parliament ; for, when our Ancestors considered, that the Law had lodged the great Powers of Arrest, Indictment, and Information, in the Crown, they saw the Parliament would be undone, if, during the Time of Privilege, the Royal Process should be admitted in any Misdemeanour whatsoever ; therefore they excepted none : Where the Abuse of Power would be fatal, the Power ought never to be given, because Redress comes too late.

A Parliament under perpetual Terror of Imprisonment can neither be free, nor bold, nor honest ; and, if this Privilege was once removed, the most important Question might be irrecoverably lost, or carried, by a sudden Irruption of Messengers, let loose against the Members Half an Hour before the Debate.

Lastly, as it has already been observed, the case of supposed Libels is of all others the most dangerous and alarming to be left open to Prosecution during the Time of Privilege.

If the Severity of the Law touching Libels, as it hath sometimes been laid down, be duly weighed, it must strike both Houses of Parliament with Terror and Dismay.

The Repetition of a Libel, the Delivery of it unread to another, is said to be a Publication ; nay the bare Possession of it has been deemed criminal, unless it is immediately destroyed, or carried to a Magistrate.

Every Lord of Parliament then, who hath done this, who is falsely accused, nay who is, though without any Information, named in the Secretary of State's Warrant, has lost his Privilege by this Resolution, and lies at the Mercy of that Enemy to Learning and Liberty *the Messenger of the Press.*

For these, and many other forcible Reasons, we hold it highly unbecoming the Dignity, Gravity, and Wisdom, of the House of Peers, as well as their Justice, thus judicially to explain away and diminish the Privilege of their Persons, founded in the Wisdom of Ages, declared with Precision in our Standing Orders, so repeatedly confirmed, and hitherto preserved inviolable, by the Spirit of our Ancestors; called to it only by the other House on a particular Occasion and to serve a particular Purpose, *ex post facto, ex Parte, et pendente Lite in the Courts below.*

TEMPLE.	ABERGAVENNY.
BOLTON.	FRED. LICH. & COV.
GRAFTON.	ASHBURNHAM.
CORNWALLIS.	FORTESCUE.
PORTLAND.	GRANTHAM.
BRISTOL.	WALPOLE.
DEVONSHIRE.	PONSONBY.
SCARBOROUGH.	FOLKESTONE."
DACRE.	

Resolved, That this House doth agree with the Commons in the said Resolution; and that the Blank be filled up with ["the Lords Spiritual and Temporal and"].

(L.J. xxx. 426, November 29, 1763.   See also *Rogers*, P.L. ii. 68 *et seq.*).

IV

WILKES *v.* LORD HALIFAX
3 George III., 1763.

L. C. J. Pratt, after stating the warrant of commitment, said; There are two objections taken to the legality of this warrant, and a third insisted on for the defendant, is privilege of parliament.

The first objection is, that it does not appear to the Court that Mr. Wilkes was charged by any evidence before the secretaries of State, that he was the author or the publisher of the North Briton No. 45. In answer to this, we are all of opinion, that it is not necessary to state in the warrant that Mr. Wilkes was charged by any evidence before the secretaries of state, and that this objection has no weight. Whether a justice of peace can, ex officio, without any evidence or information, issue a warrant for apprehending for a crime, is a different question. If a crime be done in his sight, he may commit the criminal upon the spot; but where he is not present, he ought not to commit upon discretion. Suppose a magistrate hath notice, or a particular knowledge that a person has been guilty of an offence, yet I do not think it is a sufficient ground for him to commit the criminal; but in that case he is rather a witness than a magistrate, and ought to make oath of the fact before some other magistrate, who should thereupon act the official part, by granting a warrant to apprehend the offender; it being more fit that the accuser should appear as a witness, than act as a magistrate. But that is not the question upon this warrant. The question here is, whether it is an essential part of the warrant, that the information, evidence, or grounds of the charge before the secretaries of state should be set forth in the warrant? And we think it is not. Thomas Rudyard's case, 2 Vent. 22, cannot be applied to this case, for in the case of a conviction it is otherwise. It was said that a charge by witness was the ground of a warrant; but we think it not requisite to set out more than the offence, and the particular species of it. It may be objected, if this be good, every man's liberty will be in the power of a justice of peace. But Hale, Coke and Hawkins, take no notice that a charge is necessary to be set out in the warrant. In the case of the Seven Bishops, their counsel did not take this objection, which no doubt they would have done, if they had thought there had been any weight in it. I do not rely upon the determination of the judges who then presided in the King's bench. I have been attended with many precedents of warrants returned into the King's-bench; they are almost universally like this; and in Sir William Wyndham's case, 1 Stra. 2, 3, this very point before us is determined. And Hawkins, in his 2 Pl. Coron. 120, Sect. 17, says, "It is safe to set forth that the party is charged upon oath; but this is not necessary; for it hath been resolved, that a commitment for treason, or for suspicion of it, without setting forth any particular accusation, or ground of suspicion, is good"; and cites Sir William Wyndham's case, Trin. 2 Geo. Dalt. cap. 121. Cromp. 223, v.

The second objection is, that the libel ought to be set forth in the warrant in hæc verba, or at least so much thereof as the secretaries of state deemed infamous, seditious, etc. that the Court may judge whether any such paper ever existed; or if it does exist, whether it be an infamous and seditious libel, or not. But we are all of a contrary opinion. A warrant for commitment for felony must contain the species of felony briefly, "as for felony for the death of J. S. or for burglary in breaking the house of J. S. etc. and the reason is, because it may appear to the judges upon the return of an Habeas Corpus, whether it be felony or not." The magistrate forms his judgement upon the writing, whether it be an infamous and seditious libel or not at his peril; and perhaps the paper itself may not contain the whole of the libel; innuendoes may be necessary to make the whole out. There is no other word in the law but libel whereby to express the true idea of an infamous writing. We understand the nature of a libel as well as a species of felony. It is said that the libel ought to be stated, because the court cannot judge whether it is a libel or not without it; but that is a matter for the judge and jury to determine at the trial. If the paper was here, I should not be afraid to read it. We might perhaps be able to determine that it was a libel, but we could not judge that it was not a libel because of the innuendoes, etc. It may be said, that without seeing the libel we are not able to fix the quantum of the bail; but in answer to this, the nature of the offence is known by us. It is said to be an infamous and seditious libel, it is such a misdemeanor as we should require good bail for, (moderation to be observed) and such as the party may be able to procure.

The third matter insisted upon for Mr. Wilkes is, that he is a member of parliament, (which has been admitted by the king's sergeants) and intitled to privilege to be free from arrests in all cases except treason, felony, and actual breach of the peace; and therefore ought to be discharged from imprisonment without bail; and we are all of opinion that he is intitled to that privilege, and must be discharged without bail. In the case of the Seven Bishops, the Court took notice of the privilege of parliament, and thought the bishops would have been intitled to it, if they had not judged them to have been guilty of a breach of the peace; for three of them, Wright, Holloway, and Allybone, deemed a seditious libel to be an actual breach of the peace, and therefore they were ousted of their privilege most unjustly. If Mr. Wilkes had been described as a member of parliament in the return, we must have taken notice of the law of privilege of parliament, otherwise the members would be without remedy, where they are wrongfully arrested against the law of parliament. We are bound to take notice of their privileges as being part of the law of the land. 4 Inst. 25, says, the privilege of parliament holds unless it be in three cases, viz. treason, felony, and the peace; these are the words of Coke. In the trial of the Seven Bishops, the word 'peace' in the case of privilege is explained to mean where surety of the peace is required. Privilege of parliament holds in informations for the king, unless in the cases before excepted. The case of an information against Lord Tankerville for bribery, 4 Annæ,[1] was within the privilege of parliament. See the Resolution of Lords and Commons, anno 1675. We are all of opinion that a libel is not a breach of the peace. It tends to the breach of the peace, and that is the utmost, 1 Lev. 139. But that which only tends to the breach

[1] The Tankerville case was in 1758, not "4 Annæ."

of the peace cannot be a breach of the peace. Suppose a libel to be a breach of the peace, yet I think it cannot exclude privilege; because I cannot find that a libeller is bound to find surety of the peace, in any book whatever, nor ever was, in any case, except one, viz. the case of the Seven Bishops, where three judges sáid, that surety of the peace was required in the case of a libel. Judge Powell, the only honest man of the four judges, dissented; and I am bold to be of his opinion, and to say, that case is not law. But it shews the miserable condition of the state at that time. Upon the whole, it is absurd to require surety of the peace or bail in the case of a libeller, and therefore Mr. Wilkes must be discharged from his imprisonment.

(S.T. xix. 987–990.)

V

WILKES v. WOOD
3 George III., 1763.

His lordship[1] then went upon the warrant, which he declared was a point of the greatest consequence he had ever met with in his whole practice. The defendants claimed a right, under precedents, to force persons' houses, break open escrutores, seize their papers, &c. upon a general warrant, where no inventory is made of the things thus taken away, and where no offenders' names are specified in the warrant, and therefore a discretionary power given to messengers to search wherever their suspicions may chance to fall. If such a power is truly invested in a Secretary of State, and he can delegate this power, it certainly may affect the person and property of every man in this kingdom, and is totally subversive of the liberty of the subject. And as for the precedents, will that be esteemed law in a secretary of state which is not law in any other magistrate of this kingdom? If they should be found to be legal, they are certainly of the most dangerous consequences; if not legal, must certainly aggravate damages. . . . I still continue of the same mind, that a jury have it in their power to give damages more than the injury received . . . it is my opinion the office precedents, which had been produced since the Revolution, are no justification of a practice in itself illegal, and contrary to the fundamental principles of the constitution; though its having been the constant practice of the office, might fairly be pleaded in mitigation of damages.

(S.T. xix. 1167. The jury found a general verdict for the plaintiff, Wilkes, with £1,000 damages.)

[1] Pratt, C. J. (afterwards Lord Camden).

VI

A motion was made, and the Question being proposed, That a General Warrant for seizing and apprehending any Person or Persons being illegal, is, if executed upon a member of this House, a Breach of the Privilege of this House. . . . An Amendment was proposed to be made to the Question, by inserting, after the word "illegal," these words, "except in cases provided for by Act of Parliament." And the said Amendment was, upon the Question put thereupon, agreed to by the House. . . . Then the main Question, so amended, being put;

Resolved, That a General Warrant for seizing and apprehending any Person or Persons being illegal, except in cases provided for by Act of Parliament, is, if executed upon a member of this House, a breach of the Privilege of this House.

(C.J. April 25, 1766, xxx. 771. On April 29, leave was refused to bring in a Bill founded on this Resolution; though a Bill to restrain the issuing of General Warrants in certain cases was finally read a third time, May 14. But it was rejected by the House of Lords. See Parlt. Hist. xvi. 210.)

VII

LORD MANSFIELD'S OPINION

That, in his opinion, declarations of the law made by either House of Parliament were always attended with bad effects; he had constantly opposed them whenever he had an opportunity, and in his judicial capacity thought himself bound never to pay the least regard to them.[1] That, although thoroughly convinced of the illegality of general warrants, which indeed naming no persons, were no warrants at all, he was sorry to see the House of Commons by their vote declare them to be illegal. That it looked like a legislative act, which yet had no force nor effect as law: for, supposing the House had declared them to be legal, the courts in Westminster would nevertheless have been bound to declare the contrary; and consequently to throw a disrespect on the vote of the House: but he made a wide distinction between general declarations of law, and the particular decision which might be made by either House, in their judicial capacity, on a case coming regularly before them, and properly the subject of their jurisdiction. That here they did not

---

[1] Sir Fletcher Norton, attorney-general, had said in debate that " he should regard a resolution of the members of the House of Commons no more than the oaths of so many drunken porters in Covent Garden."

act as legislators, . . . but as judges, drawing the law from the several sources from which it ought to be drawn, for their own guidance in deciding the particular question before them, and applying it strictly to the decision of that question. That, for his own part, wherever the statute law was silent, he knew not where to look for the law of parliament, or for a definition of the privileges of either House, except in the proceedings and decisions of each House respectively. That he knew of no parliamentary code to judge of questions depending on the judicial authority of parliament, but the practice of each House, moderated or extended according to the wisdom of the House, and accommodated to the cases before them.

(Lord Mansfield, in the House of Lords, Parlt. Hist. xvi. 653.)

XV

LEACH v. THREE OF THE KING'S MESSENGERS
6 George III., 1765.

[This was a case which arose out of the action of the Secretary of State against Wilkes, and the publishers and printers of No. 45 of *The North Briton*. Dryden Leach sued John Money, James Watson, and Robert Blackmore, three of the King's Messengers, for false imprisonment and trespass. Under the General Warrant issued by Lord Halifax, Leach had been apprehended on the ground that he was concerned in printing and publishing No. 45. He was released after four days, when it was clear that he was not the printer, and he then sued the Messengers for damages. The case was tried before Lord Chief Justice Pratt on December 10, 1763, and the jury found for the plaintiff with £400 damages. The case was argued before Lord Mansfield in the Court of King's Bench on June 18 and November 8, 1765, on a bill of exception, the King's Messengers asking on the ground of error that the judgment in the former trial should be reversed. The excerpt is from Lord Mansfield's judgment, and was in favour of Leach on the technical point that the warrant had not been "pursued." The important question as to the legality of general warrants was only indirectly dealt with and not formally decided in this case. Authorities as in *Wilkes v. Lord Halifax*.]

The three material Questions are—1st, "Whether a secretary of state acting as a conservator of the peace by the common law, is to be construed within the statutes of James the first, and of the last king."

The protection of the officers, if they have acted in obedience to the warrant, is consequential, in case a secretary of state is within these statutes. As to the arrest being made in obedience to the warrant, or only under colour of it and without authority from it—this question depends upon the construction of the warrant; whether it must not be construed to mean ' such persons as are under a violent suspicion of being guilty of the charge;' (for they cannot be conclusively considered as guilty, till after trial and conviction). The warrant itself imparts only suspicion; for, it says,—"to be brought before me, and examined, and dealt with according to law": and this suspicion must eventually depend upon future trial. Therefore the warrant does not seem to me, to mean conclusive guilt; but only violent suspicion. If the person apprehended should be tried and acquitted, it would shew 'that he was not guilty'; yet there might be sufficient cause of suspicion.

Mr. Dunning says, very rightly, that, 'to bring a person within 24 G. 2, the act must be done in obedience to the warrant.'

The last point is, ' whether this general warrant be good.' One part of it may be laid out of the case : for, as to what relates to the seizing his papers, that part of it was never executed; and therefore it is out of the case.

It is not material to determine, 'whether the warrant be good or bad'; except in the event of the case being within 7 J. 1, but not within 24 G. 2.

At present—as to the validity of the warrant, upon the single objection of the uncertainty of the person, being neither named nor described—the common law, in many cases, gives authority to arrest without warrant; more especially, where taken in the very act : and there are many cases where particular acts of parliament have given authority to apprehend, under general warrants; as in the case of writs of assistance, or warrants to take up loose, idle, and disorderly people. But here, it is not contended, that the common law gave the officer authority to apprehend; nor that there is any act of parliament which warrants this case.

Therefore it must stand upon principles of common law.

It is not fit, that the receiving or judging of the information should be left to the discretion of the officer. The magistrate ought to judge; and should give certain directions to the officer. This is so upon reason and convenience.

Then as to authorities—Hale and all others hold such an uncertain warrant void : and there is no case or book to the contrary.

It is said, 'that the usage hath been so; and that many such have been issued, since the Revolution, down to this time.'

But a usage, to grow into a law, ought to be a general usage, communiter usitata et approbata; and which, after a long continuance, it would be mischievous to overturn.

This is only the usage of a particular office, and contrary to the usage of all other justices and conservators of the peace.

There is the less reason for regarding this usage; because the form of the warrant probably took its rise from a positive statute, and the former precedents were inadvertently followed, after that law was expired.

Mr. Justice Wilmot declared, that he had no doubt, nor ever had, upon these warrants: he thought them illegal and void.

Neither had the two other judges, Mr. Justice Yates, and Mr. Justice Ashton, any doubt (upon this first argument) of the illegality of them: for no degree of antiquity can give sanction to a usage bad in itself. And they esteemed this usage to be so. They were clear and unanimous in opinion, that this warrant was illegal and bad. . . .

[On Nov. 8.] Lord Mansfield . . . continued of the same opinion. When the justice cannot be liable, the officer is not within the protection of the act. . . . For, here the warrant is to take up the author, printer or publisher; but they took up a person who was neither author, printer nor publisher so . . . the judgment must be affirmed. The other judges assenting, the rule of the court was, 'that the judgments be affirmed.'

(S.T. xix. 1026–1028.)

XVI

ENTICK *v.* CARRINGTON
6 Geo. III., 1765.

[This was an action of trespass brought by John Entick against Nathan Carrington and three other King's Messengers, who under a general warrant from a secretary of state forcibly entered Entick's house on Nov. 11, 1762, carried away his books and papers on the ground that he was the author of a seditious libel. The jury found a special verdict, which was subsequently twice argued at the bar. Lord Camden, L.C.J., gave judgment for the plaintiff, and the excerpt gives the salient passages of this famous decision, which finally decided the illegality of general warrants. The whole judgment is well worth careful study. Authorities as in *Wilkes v. Lord Halifax*, and for the constitutional points involved, see especially *Dicey*, L.C., and *Broom, op. cit.* Two other cases reported in *State Trials*, xix., viz. *Wilkes v. Wood* and *Wilkes v. Lord Halifax* (1769), in which Wilkes was awarded £4,000 damages, complete the cases which involve the legality of general warrants and the seizure of papers.]

This record hath set up two defences to the action, on both of which the defendants have relied.

The first arises from the facts disclosed in the special verdict; whereby the defendants put their case upon the statute of 24 Geo. 2, insisting that they have nothing to do with the legality of the warrants, but that they ought to have been acquitted as officers within the meaning of that act.

The second defence stands upon the legality of the warrants; for this being a justification at common law, the officer is answerable if the magistrate has no jurisdiction.

These two defences have drawn several points into question, upon which the public, as well as the parties, have a right to our opinion.

Under the first, it is incumbent upon the officers to shew, that they are officers within the meaning of the Act of parliament, and likewise that they have acted in obedience to the warrant.

The question, whether officers or not, involves another; whether the secretary of state, whose ministers they are, can be deemed a justice of the peace, or taken within the equity of the description; for officers and justices are here co-relative terms: therefore either both must be comprised, or both excluded.

The question leads me to an inquiry into the authority of that minister, as he stands described upon the record in two capacities, viz. secretary of state and privy counsellor. And since no statute has conferred any such jurisdiction as this before us, it must be given, if it does really exist, by the common law; and upon this ground he has been treated as a conservator of the peace.

The matter thus opened, the questions that naturally arise upon the special verdict, are;

First, whether in either of the characters, or upon any other foundation, he is a conservator of the peace.

Secondly, admitting him to be so, whether he is within the equity of the 24th Geo. 2.

These points being disposed of, the next in order is, whether the defendants have acted in obedience to the warrant.

In the last place, the great question upon the justification will be, whether the warrant to seize and carry away the plaintiff's papers is lawful.

First Question

The power of this minister, in the way wherein it has been usually exercised, is pretty singular.

If he is considered in the light of a privy counsellor, although every member of that board is equally entitled to it with himself,

yet he is the only one of that body who exerts it.   His power is so
extensive in place, that it spreads throughout the whole realm; yet
in the object it is so confined, that except in libels and some few
state crimes, as they are called, the secretary of state does not pretend
to the authority of a constable.

To consider him as a conservator. He never binds to the peace, or
good behaviour, which seems to have been the principal duty of a
conservator; at least he never does it in those cases, where the law
requires those sureties. But he commits in certain other cases, where
it is very doubtful, whether the conservator had any jurisdiction
whatever.

His warrants are chiefly exerted against libellers, whom he binds
in the first instance to their good behaviour, which no other conservator ever attempted, from the best intelligence that we can learn
from our books.

And though he doth all these things, yet it seems agreed, that
he hath no power whatsoever to administer an oath or to take
bail.

This jurisdiction, as extraordinary as I have described it, is so dark
and obscure in its origin, that the counsel have not been able to form
any certain opinion from whence it sprang.

Sometimes they annex it to the office of secretary of state, sometimes to the quality of privy counsellor; and in the last argument
it has been derived from the king's royal prerogative to commit by
his own personal command.

Whatever may have been the true source of this authority, it must
be admitted, that in this day he is in the full legal exercise of it;
because there has been not only a clear practise of it, at least since
the Revolution, confirmed by a variety of precedents; but the
authority has been recognized and confirmed by two cases in the
very point since that period: and therefore we have not a power to
unsettle or contradict it now, even though we are persuaded that
the commencement of it was erroneous. . . .

Having thus shewn, not only negatively that this power of committing was not annexed to the secretary's office, but affirmatively
likewise that he was notifier or countersigner of the king's personal
warrant acting in alio jure down to the times of the 16th of Charles
the first, and consequently to the Restoration I have but little to add
on this head. . . .

There cannot be a stronger authority than this I have now cited
for the present purpose. The whole body of the law, if I may use
the phrase, were as ignorant at that time of a privy counsellor's

right to commit in the case of a libel, as the whole body of privy counsellors are at this day.

The counsel on both sides in that cause were the ablest of their time, and few times have produced abler. They had been concerned in all the state cases during the whole reign of Charles the second, on the one side or the other; and to suppose that all these persons could be utterly ignorant of this extraordinary power, if it had been either legal or even practised, is a supposition not to be maintained.

This is the whole that I have been able to find, touching the power of one or more privy counsellors to commit, and to sum up the whole of this business in a word it stands thus:

The two cases in Leonard do presuppose some power in a privy counsellor to commit, without saying what; and the case in Anderson does plainly recognize such a power in high treason: but with respect to his jurisdiction in other offences, I do not find it was either claimed or exercised.

In consequence of all this reasoning, I am forced to deny the opinion of my lord chief justice Holt to be law, if it shall be taken to extend beyond the case of high treason. But there is no necessity to understand the book in a more general sense; nor is it fair indeed to give the words a more large construction: for as the conclusion ought always to be grounded on the premises, and the premises are grounded on the case of high treason only, the opinion should naturally conform to the cases cited, more especially as the case there before the Court was a case of high treason, and they were under no necessity to lay down the doctrine larger than the case required.—Now whereas it has been argued, that if you admit a power of committing in high treason, the power of committing in lesser offences follows à fortiori; I beg leave to deny that consequence, for I take the rule with respect to all special authorities to be directly the reverse. They are always strictly confined to the letter; and when I see therefore, that a special power in any single case only has been permitted to a person, who in no other instance is known or recorded by the common law as a magistrate, I have no right to enlarge his authority one step beyond that case. Consider how strange it would sound, if I should declare at once, that every privy counsellor without exception is invested with a power to commit in all offences without exception from high treason down to trespass, when it is clear that he is not a conservator. It might be said of me, 'he should have explained himself a little more clearly, and told us where he had found the description of so singular a magistrate, who being no conservator was yet in the nature of a conservator.'

I have now finished all I have to say upon this head; and am satisfied, that the secretary of state hath assumed this power as a transfer, I know not how, of the royal authority to himself; and that the common law of England knows no such magistrate. At the same time I declare, wherein my brothers do all agree with me, that we are bound to adhere to the determination of the Queen against Derby, and the King against Earbury; and I have no right to overturn those decisions, even though it should be admitted, that the practise, which has subsisted since the Revolution, had been erroneous in its commencement. . . .

And now give me leave to ask one question. Will the secretary of state be classed with the higher or the lower conservator? If with the higher, such as the king, the chancellor, etc. he is too much above the justice to be within the equity. If with the lower, he is too much below him. And as to the sheriff and the coroner, they cannot be within the law; because they never grant such warrants as these. So that at last, upon considering all the conservators, there is not one who does not stand most evidently excluded, unless the secretary of state himself shall be excepted.

But if there wanted arguments, to confute this pretension, the construction that has prevailed upon the seventh of James the First, would decide the point. That is an act of like kind to relieve justices of the peace, mayors, constables, and certain other officers, in troublesome actions brought against them for the legal execution of their offices; who are enabled by that act to plead the general issue. Now that law has been taken so strictly, that neither church-wardens, nor overseers, were held to be within the equity of the word 'constables,' although they were clearly officers, and acted under the justice's warrants. Why? Because that act, being made to change the course of the common law, could not be extended beyond the letter. Is then that privilege of giving the special matter in evidence upon the general issue is contrary to the common law, how much more substantially is this act an innovation of the common law, which indemnifies the officer upon the production of the warrant, and deprives the subject of his right of action?

It is impossible, that two acts of parliament can be more nearly allied or connected with one another, than that of 24 George 2, and the 7th of James 1. The objects in both are the same, and the remedies are similar in both, each of them changing the common law for the benefit of the parties concerned. The one, in truth, is the sequel or second part of the other. The first not being an adequate remedy in case of the several persons therein mentioned, the second is added to complete the work, and to make them as secure as they ought to be made, from the nature of the case. If by a contrary construction any person should be admitted into the last that are not included in that first, the person, whoever he is, will be without the privilege of pleading the general issue, and giving the special matter in evidence, which the latter would have certainly given by express words, if the parliament could have imagined he was not comprised in the first.

Upon the whole, we are all of opinion, that neither secretary of state, nor the messenger, are within the meaning of this act of parliament. . . .

I come in my last place to the point, which is made by the justification; for the defendants, having failed in the attempt made to protect themselves by the statute of the 24th of Geo. 2, are under a necessity to maintain the legality of the warrants, under which they have acted, and to shew that the secretary of state in the instance now before us, had a jurisdiction to seize the defendant's papers. If he had no such jurisdiction, the law is clear that the officers are as much responsible for the trespass as their superior.

This, though it is not the most difficult, is the most interesting question in the cause; because if this point should be determined in favour of the jurisdiction, the secret cabinets and bureaus of every subject in this kingdom will be thrown open to the search and inspection of a messenger, whenever the secretary of state shall think fit to charge, or even to suspect, a person to be the author, printer, or publisher of a seditious libel.

The messenger, under this warrant, is commanded to seize the person described, and to bring him with his papers to be examined before the secretary of state. In consequence of this, the house must be searched; the lock and doors of every room, box, or trunk must be broken open; all the papers and books without exception, if the warrant be executed according to its tenor, must be seized and carried away; for it is observable that nothing is left either to the discretion or to the humanity of the officer.

This power so assumed by the secretary of state is an execution upon all the party's papers, in the first instance. His house is rifled; his most valuable secrets are taken out of his possession, before the paper for which he is charged is found to be criminal by any competent jurisdiction, and before he is convicted either of writing, publishing or being concerned in the paper.

This power, so claimed by the secretary of state, is not supported by one single citation from any law book extant. It is claimed by

Y

no other magistrate in this kingdom but himself : the great executive
hand of criminal justice, the lord chief justice of the court of the
King's-bench, chief justice Scroggs excepted, never having assumed
this authority.

The arguments, which the defendant's counsel have thought fit to
urge in support of this practice, are of this kind.

That such warrants have issued frequently since the Revolution,
which practice has been found by the special verdict; though I must
observe, that the defendants have no right to avail themselves of
that finding, because no such practice is averred in their justification.

That the case of the warrants bears a resemblance to the case of
search for stolen goods.

They say too, that they have been executed without resistance
upon many printers, booksellers, and authors, who have quietly submitted to their authority; that no action hath hitherto been brought
to try the right; and that although they have been often read upon
the returns of Habeas Corpus, yet no court of justice has ever
declared them illegal.

And it is further insisted, that this power is essential to government, and the only means of quieting clamours and sedition.

These arguments, if they can be called arguments, shall be all
taken notice of; because upon this question I am desirous of removing
every colour or plausibility.

Before I state the question, it will be necessary to describe the
power claimed by this warrant in its full extent.

If honestly exerted, it is a power to seize that man's papers, who
is charged upon oath to be the author or publisher of a seditious
libel; if oppressively, it acts against every man, who is so described
in the warrant, although he be innocent.

It is executed against the party, before he is heard or even summoned; and the information, as well as the informers, is unknown.

It is executed by messengers with or without a constable (for it
can never be pretended, that such is necessary in point of law) in the
presence or absence of the party, as the messengers shall think fit,
and without a witness to testify what passes at the time of the
transaction; so that when the papers are gone, as the only witnesses
are the trespassers, the party injured is left without proof.

If this injury falls upon an innocent person, he is as destitute of
remedy as the guilty : and the whole transaction is so guarded against
discovery, that if the officer should be disposed to carry off a bank
bill, he may do it with impunity, since there is no man capable of
proving either the taker or the thing taken.

It must not be here forgot, that no subject whatsoever is privileged from this search; because both Houses of Parliament have resolved, that there is no privilege in the case of a seditious libel.

Nor is there pretence to say, that the word 'papers' here mentioned ought in point of law to be restrained to the libellous papers only. The word is general, and there is nothing in the warrant to confine it; nay, I am able to affirm that it has been upon a late occasion executed in its utmost latitude: for in the case of Wilkes against Wood, when the messengers hesitated about taking all the manuscripts, and sent to the secretary of state for more express orders for that purpose, the answer was, "that all must be taken, manuscripts and all." Accordingly, all was taken, and Mr. Wilkes' private pocket-book filled up the mouth of the sack.

I was likewise told in the same cause by one of the most experienced messengers, that he held himself bound by his oath to pay an implicit obedience to the commands of the secretary of state; that in common cases he was contented to seize the printed impressions of the papers mentioned in the warrant; but when he received directions to search further, or to make a more general seizure, his rule was to sweep all. The practice has been correspondent to the warrant.

Such is the power, and therefore one should naturally expect that the law to warrant it should be clear in proportion as the power is exorbitant.

If it is law it will be found in our books. If it is not to be found there, it is not law.

The great end, for which men entered into society, was to secure their property. That right is preserved sacred and incommunicable in all instances, where it has not been taken away or abridged by some public law for the good of the whole. The cases where this right of property is set aside by positive law, are various. Distresses, executions, forfeitures, taxes, etc., are all of this description, wherein every man by common consent gives up that right, for the sake of justice and the general good. By the laws of England, every invasion of private property, be it ever so minute, is a trespass. No man can set his foot upon my ground without my licence, but he is liable to an action, though the damage be nothing; which is proved by every declaration in trespass, where the defendant is called upon to answer for bruising the grass, and even treading upon the soil. If he admits the fact, he is bound to shew by way of justification, that some positive law has empowered or excused him. The justification is submitted to the judges, who are to look into the books; and if such a justification can be maintained by the text of the statute law, or by the principles of common law. If no such excuse can be found or produced, the silence of the books is an authority against the defendant, and the plaintiff must have judgement.

According to this reasoning, it is now incumbent upon the defendants to shew the law, by which this seizure is warranted. If that cannot be done, it is a trespass. . . .

What would the parliament say, if the judges should take upon themselves to mould an unlawful power into a convenient authority, by new restrictions? That would be, not judgement, but legislation.

I come now to the practice since the Revolution, which has been strongly urged, with this emphatical addition, that an usage tolerated from the æra of liberty, and continued downwards to this time through the best ages of the constitution, must necessarily have a legal commencement. Now, though that pretence can have no place in the question made by this plea, because no such practice is there alleged; yet I will permit the defendant for the present to borrow a fact from the special verdict, for the sake of giving it an answer.

If the practice began then, it began too late to be law now. If it was more ancient the Revolution is not to answer for it; and I could have wished, that upon this occasion the Revolution had not been considered as the only basis of our liberty.

The Revolution restored this constitution to its first principles. It did no more. It did not enlarge the liberty of the subject; but gave it a better security. It neither widened nor contracted the foundation, but repaired, and perhaps added a buttress or two to the fabric; and if any minister of state has since deviated from the principles at that time recognized, all that I can say is, that, so far from being sanctioned, they are condemned by the Revolution.

With respect to the practice itself, if it goes no higher, every lawyer will tell you, it is much too modern to be evidence of the common law; and if it should be added that these warrants ought to acquire some strength by the silence of those courts, which have heard them read so often upon returns without censure or animadversion, I am able to borrow my answer to that pretence from the Court of King's-bench, which lately declared with great unanimity in the Case of General Warrants, that as no objection was taken to them upon the returns, and the matter passed sub silentio, the precedents were of no weight. I most heartily concur in that opinion; and the reason is more pertinent here, because the Court had no authority in the present case to determine against the seizure of papers, which was not before them; whereas in the other they might, if they had thought fit, have declared the warrant void, and discharged the prisoner ex officio.

This is the first instance I have met with, where the ancient immemorable law of the land, in a public manner, was attempted to be proved by the practice of a private office.

The names and rights of public magistrates, their power and forms of proceeding as they are settled by law, have been long since written, and are to be found in books and records. Private customs indeed are still to be sought from private tradition. But whoever conceived a notion, that any part of the public law could be buried in the obscure practice of a particular person?

To search, seize, and carry away all the papers of the subject upon the first warrant: that such a right should have existed from the time whereof the memory of man runneth not to the contrary, and never yet have found a place in any book of law, is incredible. But if so strange a thing could be supposed, I do not see how we could declare the law upon such evidence.

But it is still insisted that there has been a general submission, and no action brought to try the right.

I answer, there has been a submission of guilt and poverty to power and the terror of punishment. But it would be strange doctrine to assert that all the people of this land are bound to acknowledge that to be universal law, which a few criminal book-sellers have been afraid to dispute. . . .

It was very evident, that the Star-Chamber, how soon after the invention of printing I know not, took to itself the jurisdiction over public libels, which soon grew to be the peculiar business of that court. Not that the courts of Westminster-hall wanted the power of holding pleas in those cases; but the Attorney-general for good reasons chose rather to proceed there; which is the reason, why we have no cases of libels in the King's-bench before the Restoration.

The Star-chamber from this jurisdiction presently usurped a general superintendance over the press, and exercised a legislative power in all matters relating to the subject. They appointed licencers; they prohibited books; they inflicted penalties; and they dignified one of their officers with the name of the messenger of the press, and among other things enacted this warrant of search.

After that court was abolished, the press became free, but enjoyed its liberty not above two or three years; for the Long Parliament thought fit to restrain it again by ordinance. Whilst the press is free, I am afraid it will always be licentious, and all governments have an aversion to libels. This parliament, therefore, did by ordinance restore the Star-Chamber practice; they recalled the licences, and sent forth again the messenger. It was against the ordinance, that Milton wrote that famous pamphlet called Areopagitica. Upon the Restoration, the press was free once more, till the 13th and 14th of Charles 2, when the Licensing Act passed, which for the first time gave the secretary of state a power to issue search warrants: but these warrants were neither so oppressive, nor so inconvenient as the present. The right to enquire into the licence was the pretence of making the searches; and if during the search any suspected libels were found, they and they only could be seized.

This act expired on the 32nd year of that reign, or thereabouts. It was revived again in the 1st year of king James 2, and remained in force till the 5th of King William, after one of his parliaments had continued it for a year beyond its expiration.

I do very much suspect, that the present warrant took its rise from these search-warrants, that I have been describing; nothing being easier to account for than this engraftment; the difference between them being no more than this that the apprehension of the person in the first was to follow the seizure of the papers, but the seizure of the papers in the latter was to follow the apprehension of the person. The same evidence would serve equally for both purposes. If it was charged for printing or publishing, that was sufficient for either of the warrants. Only this material difference must always be observed between them, that the search-warrant only carried off the criminal papers, whereas this seizes all.

When the Licensing Act expired at the close of King Charles 2's reign, the twelve judges were assembled at the king's command, to discover whether the press might not be as effectually restrained by the common law as it had been by that statute.

I cannot help observing in this place, that if the secretary of state was still invested with a power of issuing this warrant, there was no occasion for the application to the judges: for though he could not issue the general search-warrant, yet upon the least rumour of a libel he might have done more, and seized everything. But that was not thought of, and therefore the judges met and resolved:

First, that it was criminal at common law, not only to write public seditious papers and false news; but likewise to publish any new without a licence from the king, though it was true and innocent.

Secondly, that libels were seizable. This is to be found in th State Trials; and because it is a curiosity, I will recite the passag at large. . . .

(Lord Camden here quoted the judgment of Chief Justice Scroggs i the case of *Harris*, which is cited on p. 241.)

These are the opinions of all the twelve judges of England; a great and reverend authority.

Can the twelve judges extrajudicially make a thing law to bind the kingdom by a declaration that such is their opinion?—I say No. —It is a matter of impeachment for any judge to affirm it. There must be an antecedent principle or authority, from whence this opinion may be fairly collected; otherwise the opinion is null, and nothing but ignorances can excuse the judge that subscribed it. Out of this doctrine sprang the famous general search-warrant, that was condemned by the House of Commons; and it was not unreasonable to suppose, that the form of it was settled by the twelve judges that subscribed the opinion.

The deduction from the opinion to the warrant is obvious. If you can seize a libel, you may search for it: if search is legal, a warrant to authorize that search is likewise legal: if any magistrate can issue such a warrant, the chief justice of the King's-bench may clearly do it.

It falls here naturally in my way to ask, whether there be any authority besides this opinion of these twelve judges to say, that libels may be seized? If they may, I am afraid that all the inconveniences of a general seizure will follow upon a right allowed to seize a part. The search in such cases will be general, and every house will fall under the power of a secretary of state to be rummaged before proper conviction.—Consider for a while how the law of libels now stands.

Lord Chief Justice Holt and the Court of the King's-bench have resolved in the *King and Bear*, that he who writes a libel, though he neither composes it nor publishes, is criminal.

In the 5th Report, 125, lord Coke cites it in the Star Chamber, that if a libel concerns a public person, he that hath it in his custody ought immediately to deliver it to a magistrate, that the author may be found out.

In the case of *Lake and Hutton*, Hobart 252, it is observed, that a libel, though the contents are true is not to be justified; but the right way is to discover it to some magistrate or other, that they may have cognizance of the cause.

In 1st Ventrio 31, it is said, that the having a libel, and not discovering it to a magistrate, was only punishable in the Star Chamber, unless the party maliciously publish it. But the Court corrected this doctrine in the *King and Bear*, where it said, though he never published it, yet his having it in readiness for that purpose, if any occasion should happen, is highly criminal: and though he might design to keep it private, yet after his death it might fall into such hands as might be injurious to the government; and therefore men ought not to be allowed to have such evil instruments in their keeping.   Carthew 409.   In Salkeld's report of the same case, Holt chief justice says, if a libel be publicly known a written copy of it is evidence of a publication.   Salk. 418.

If all this be law, and I have no right at present to deny it, whenever a favourite libel is published (and these compositions are apt to be favourites) the whole kingdom in a month or two becomes criminal, and it would be difficult to find one innocent jury amongst so many millions of offenders.

I can find no other authority to justify the seizure of a libel, than that of Scroggs and his brethren.

If the power of search is to follow the right of seizure, everybody sees the consequence.   He that has it or has had it in his custody; he that has published, copied, or maliciously reported it, may fairly be under a reasonable suspicion of having the thing in his custody, and consequently become the object of the search-warrant.   If libels may be seized, it ought to be laid down with precision, when, where, upon what charge, against whom, by what magistrate, and in what state of the prosecution.   All these particulars must be explained and proved to be law, before this general proposition can be established.

As therefore no authority in our books can be produced to support such a doctrine, and so many Star Chamber devices, ordinances, and acts have been thought necessary to establish a power of search, I cannot be persuaded, that such a power can be justified by the common law.

I have now done with the argument, which has endeavoured to support this warrant by the practice since the Revolution.

It is then said, that it is necessary for the ends of Government to lodge such a power with a state officer; and that it is better to prevent the publication before than to punish the offender afterwards. I answer, that if the legislature be of that opinion they will revive the Licensing Act.   But if they have not done that, I conceive they are not of that opinion.   And with respect to the argument of state necessity, or a distinction which has been aimed at between state offences and others, the common law does not understand that kind of reasoning, nor do our books take notice of any such distinctions.

Sergeant Ashley was committed to the Tower in the 3rd of Charles 1st, by the House of Lords only for asserting in argument, that there was a 'law of state' different from the common law; and the Ship-Money judges were impeached for holding, first, that state-necessity would justify the raising money without consent of parliament; and secondly, that the king was judge of that necessity.

If the king himself has no power to declare when the law ought to be violated for reason of state, I am sure we his judges have no such prerogative.

Lastly, it is urged as an argument of utility, that such a search is a means of detecting offenders by discovering evidence. I wish some cases had been shown, where the law forceth evidence out of the owner's custody by process. There is no process against papers in civil causes. It has been often tried, but never prevailed. Nay, where the adversary has by force or fraud got possession of your own proper evidence, there is no way to get it back but by action.

In the criminal law such a proceeding was never heard of; and yet there are some crimes, such for instance as murder, rape, robbery, and house-breaking, to say nothing of forgery and perjury, that are more atrocious than libelling. But our law has provided no paper-search in these cases to help forward the conviction.

Whether this proceedeth from the gentleness of the law towards criminals, or from a consideration that such a power would be more pernicious to the innocent than useful to the public, I will not say.

It is very certain, that the law obligeth no man to accuse himself; because the necessary means of compelling self-accusation, falling upon the innocent as well as the guilty, would be both cruel and unjust; and it should seem that search for evidence is disallowed upon the same principle. There too the innocent would be confounded with the guilty.

Observe the wisdom as well as the mercy of the law. The strongest evidence before a trial, being only ex parte, is but suspicion; it is not proof. Weak evidence is a ground of suspicion, though in a lower degree; and if suspicion at large should be a ground of search, especially in the case of libels, whose house would be safe?

If, however, a right of search for the sake of discovering evidence ought in any case to be allowed, this crime above all others ought to be excepted, as wanting such a discovery less than any other. It is committed in open daylight, and in the face of the world; every act of publication makes new proof; and the solicitor of the treasury, if he pleases, may be the witness himself.

The messenger of the press, by the very constitution of his office, is directed to purchase every libel that comes forth, in order to be a witness.

Nay, if the vengeance of government requires a production of the author, it is hardly possible for him to escape the impeachment of the printer, who is sure to seal his own pardon by the discovery. But suppose he should happen to be obstinate, yet the publication is stopped, and the offence punished. By this means the law is satisfied, and the public secured.

Before I conclude, I desire not to be understood as an advocate for libels. All civilized governments have punished calumny with severity; and with reason; for these compositions debauch the manners of the people; they excite a spirit of disobedience, and enervate the authority of government; they provoke and excite the passions of the people against their rulers, and the rulers oftentimes against the people.

After this description, I shall hardly be considered as a favourer of these pernicious productions. I will always set my face against them, when they come before me; and shall recommend it most warmly to the jury always to convict when the proof is clear. They will do well to consider, that unjust acquittals bring an odium upon the press itself, the consequence whereof may be fatal to liberty; for if kings and great men cannot obtain justice at their hands by the ordinary course of law, they may at last be provoked to restrain that press, which the juries of their country refuse to regulate. When licentiousness is tolerated, liberty is in the utmost danger; because tyranny, bad as it is, is better than anarchy, and the worst of governments is more tolerable than no government at all.

(S.T. xix. 1044–1076.)

XVII

WILKES AND THE MIDDLESEX ELECTION
1768–9.

[In 1764 Wilkes had been condemned in the Court of King's Bench by default to outlawry for "a false, malicious, and scandalous libel." He remained abroad till February, 1768, when he returned to stand for the city of London. Defeated there, he stood for Middlesex and was elected. The sentence of outlawry was quashed on technical grounds, but on the original charge of libel he was fined £1,000 and sentenced to imprisonment for twenty-two months. In November he petitioned the House of Commons, claiming his privileges against further imprisonment. The claim was disallowed, and on February 17, 1769, he was expelled the House, and a new writ for Middlesex issued. Wilkes was elected unopposed a second time, and a second time a new writ was issued; Wilkes stood a third time and

a third time was elected.   Col. Luttrell, the ministerial candidate, who had
been defeated by 1043 to 296 votes, was then, in spite of a petition against
his return, declared to be the true member for Middlesex, and accordingly
took his seat.   In 1774 Wilkes was again returned for Middlesex and was
allowed to sit unquestioned.   Finally in 1782, under the Rockingham
Government, the resolutions of 1769 were by vote expunged from the
Commons Journals.   The excerpts give : (1) the resolutions of 1769 ; (2)
a Protest of dissentient Peers which summarises the arguments of the
opposition ; and (3) the resolution of the Commons in 1782.   For the
whole question see *The Letters of Junius; Grafton's Autobiography* (ed.
Anson) ; *Parlt. History*, xvi., especially Chatham's speech, 657 *et seq.; Lecky*,
H.E. iii. ch. x. ; *Anson*, L.C. ; 142–177; *May*, C.H.E. ii. ch. vii ; *ib.* P.P.
57–142 ; *The Annual Register* for 1769 (probably written by Burke) ; *Rogers*,
P.L. ii. 68, 99–110.]

I

Ordered, That the Deputy Clerk of the Crown do attend this
House immediately, with the Return to the Writ for electing a
Knight of the Shire to serve in this present Parliament for the
County of Middlesex, in the room of John Wilkes, Esquire, expelled
this House.

And the Deputy Clerk of the Crown attending, according to
order ;

The said Writ and Return were read.

A Motion was made, and the Question being proposed, That John
Wilkes, Esquire, having been, in this Session of Parliament, expelled
this House, was, and is, incapable of being elected a Member to serve
in this present Parliament ;

The House was moved, That the entry in the Journal of the
House, of the 6th Day of March, 1711, in relation to the Proceedings
of the House, upon the Return of a Burgess to serve in Parliament
for the Borough of King's Lynn in the County of Norfolk, in the
room of Robert Walpole, Esquire, expelled the House, might be
read.

And the same was read accordingly.

The House was also moved ; that the Resolution of the House, of
Friday the 3rd Day of this Instant February, relating to the Expulsion of John Wilkes, Esquire, then a Member of this House,
might be read.

And the same being read accordingly ;

An Amendment was proposed to be made to the Question, by
inserting after the word "House," these Words, "for having been
the Author and Publisher of what this House hath resolved to be

an insolent, scandalous, and seditious Libel; and for having been convicted in the Court of King's Bench, of having printed and published a seditious Libel, and three obscene and impious Libels; and having, by the Judgment of the said Court, been sentenced to undergo Twenty-two months Imprisonment, and being in Execution under the said Judgment."

And the Question being put, That those Words be there inserted; The House divided.

The Yeas went forth,

Tellers for the Yeas $\left\{\begin{array}{l}\text{Sir Joseph Mawbey,}\\\text{Mr. Nicholson Calvert:}\end{array}\right\}$ 102.

Tellers for the Noes $\left\{\begin{array}{l}\text{Mr. Edward Bayntun,}\\\text{Mr. Burrell.}\end{array}\right\}$ 228.

So it passed in the Negative.

Then the main Question being put, That John Wilkes, Esquire, having been, in this Session of Parliament, expelled this House, was, and is, incapable of being elected a Member to serve in this present Parliament;

The House divided.

The Yeas went forth.

Tellers for the Yeas $\left\{\begin{array}{l}\text{Lord Strange,}\\\text{Mr. Onslow:}\end{array}\right\}$ 235.

Tellers for the Noes $\left\{\begin{array}{l}\text{Lord John Cavendish,}\\\text{Mr. Hotham.}\end{array}\right\}$ 89.

So it was resolved in the Affirmative.

A Motion being made, That the late Election of a Knight of the Shire to serve in this present Parliament for the County of Middlesex, is a void Election;

A Member, in his Place, informed the House, that he was present at the last Election of a Knight of the Shire to serve in this present Parliament for the said County; that there was no other Candidate than the said Mr. Wilkes; that there was no Poll demanded for any other Person, nor any kind of Opposition to the Election of the said Mr. Wilkes.

Resolved, That the late Election of a Knight of the Shire to serve in this present Parliament for the County of Middlesex, is a void Election.

Ordered, That Mr. Speaker do issue his Warrant to the Clerk of the Crown, to make out a new Writ for the Electing a Knight of the Shire to serve in this present Parliament for the County of Middlesex, in the room of John Wilkes, Esquire, who is adjudged incapable of being elected a Member to serve in this present Parliament, and whose Election for the said County has been declared void.

(C.J. xxxii. 228.)

Then the Question being put, That *Henry Lawes Luttrell*, Esquire, ought to have been returned a Knight of the Shire to serve in this present Parliament for the County of *Middlesex:*

The House divided.
The Yeas went forth.   [The votes were 197–143.]
So it was resolved in the affirmative.

Ordered, That the Deputy Clerk of the Crown do amend the Return for the County of *Middlesex*, by rasing out the name *John Wilkes* Esquire, and inserting the name of *Henry Lawes Luttrell* Esquire, instead thereof.

And the Deputy Clerk of the Crown, attending according to order, amended the said Return accordingly.

(C.J. April 15, 1769.)

And a Motion being made, and the Question being put, That *Henry Lawes Luttrell*, Esquire, is duly Elected a Knight of the Shire to serve in this present Parliament for the County of *Middlesex;*

The House Divided.
The Noes went forth.   [Votes 221–152].
So it was resolved in the affirmative.

(C.J. May 8, 1769.)

II

THE LORDS' PROTEST

1st, Because the resolution[1] proposed was in our judgment highly necessary to lay the foundation of a proceeding which might tend to quiet the minds of the people, by doing them justice, at a time when the decision of the other House, which appears to us inconsistent with the principles of the Constitution, and irreconcileable to the law of the land, has spread so universal an alarm, and produced so general a discontent throughout the kingdom.

[1] Moved by Lord Rockingham, "that the House of Commons in the exercise of its judicature in matters of election is bound to judge according to the law of the land, and the known and established custom of Parliament which is part thereof." Negatived by 47–96. This resolution had already been moved in the Commons by Mr. Dowdeswell and practically defeated by an amendment.

2ndly, Because, although we do not deny that the determination on the right to a seat in the House of Commons is competent to the jurisdiction of that House alone, yet, when to this is added, that whatever they in the exercise of that jurisdiction think fit to declare to be law, is therefore to be considered as law, because there lies no appeal, we conceive ourselves called upon to give that proposition the strongest negative; for if admitted, the law of the land (by which all courts of judicature, without exception, are equally bound to proceed) is at once overturned, and resolved into the will and pleasure of a majority of one House of Parliament; who, in assuming it, assume a power to over-rule at pleasure the fundamental right of election, which the Constitution has placed in other hands, those of their constituents: and if ever this pretended power should come to be exercised to the full extent of the principle, the House will be no longer a representative of the people, but a separate body altogether independent of them, self-existing and self-elected.

3rdly, Because we are told that expulsion implies incapacity, and the proof insisted upon is, that the people have acquiesced in the principle by not re-electing persons who have been expelled; we equally deny the position as false, and reject the proof offered as in no way supporting the position to which it is applied. We are sure the doctrine is not to be found in any statute or lawbook, nor in the Journals of the House of Commons, Neither is it consonant with any just or known analogy of law. And as not re-electing would at most but infer a supposition of the electors' approbation of the grounds of the expulsion, and by no means their acquiescence in the conclusion of an implied incapacity, so were there not one instance of a re-election after expulsion but Mr. Woolaston's,[1] that alone demonstrates that neither did the constituents admit, nor the House of Commons maintain incapacity to be the consequence of expulsion. Even the case of Mr. Walpole[2] shews, by the first re-election, the sense of the people, that expulsion did not infer incapacity; and that precedent too, which is the only one of a declaration of incapacity, produced as it was, under the influence of party violence, in the latter days of Queen Anne, in so far as it relates to the introduction of a candidate having a minority of votes, it decides expressly against the proceedings of the House of Commons in the late Middlesex Election.

4thly, Because, as the Constitution hath been once already destroyed by the assumption and exercise of the very power which is now claimed, the day may come again when freedom of speech may be

---

[1] Expelled February 20, 1699, because he was a receiver of taxes.
[2] Expelled January 15, 1712, for "notorious corruption."

criminal in that House, and every member who shall have virtue enough to withstand the usurpations of the time, and assert the rights of the people, will for that offence be expelled by a factious and corrupt majority; and by that expulsion rendered incapable of serving the public: in which case the electors will find themselves reduced to the miserable alternative of giving up altogether their right of election, or of choosing only such as are enemies of their country, and will be passive at least, if not active, in subverting the Constitution.

5thly, Because, although it has been objected in the debate, that it is unusual or irregular in either House of Parliament to examine into the judicial proceedings of the other, whose decisions, as they cannot be drawn into question by appeal, are, it is said, to be submitted to without examination of the principles of them elsewhere; we conceive the arguments go directly to establish the exploded doctrine of passive obedience and non-resistance, which, as applied to the acts of any branch of the supreme power, we hold to be equally dangerous; and though it is generally true, that neither House ought lightly and wantonly to interpose even an opinion upon matters which the Constitution hath entrusted to the jurisdiction of the other, we conceive it to be no less true, that where under colour of a judicial proceeding, either House arrogates to itself the power of the whole legislature, and makes the law which it professes to declare; the other not only may but ought to assert its own right and those of the people; that this House has done so in former instances, particularly in the famous case of *Ashby and White*, in which the first resolution of the Lords declares, 'that neither House of Parliament hath any power by any vote or declaration to create to themselves any new privilege that is not warranted by the known laws and customs of Parliament.' We ought to interfere at this time, the rather as our silence on so important and alarming an occasion might be interpreted into an approbation of the measure, and be a means of losing that confidence with the people which is so essential to the public welfare, that this House, the hereditary guardians of their rights, should at all times endeavour to maintain.

6thly, Because, upon the whole, we deem the power, which the House of Commons have assumed to themselves, of creating an incapacity, unknown to the law, and thereby depriving, in effect, all the electors of Great Britain of their valuable right of free election, confirmed to them by so many solemn statutes, a flagrant usurpation, as highly repugnant to every essential principle of the Constitution, as the claim of ship-money by King Charles I., or that of suspending and dispensing power by King James II. This being, indeed, in our opinion, a suspending and dispensing power assumed and exercised by the House of Commons, against the ancient and fundamental liberties of the Kingdom.

TEMPLE	RADNOR	EXETER	PONSONBY
SUFFOLK AND	HUNTINGDON	GROSVENOR	CHATHAM
BERKSHIRE	THANET	TORRINGTON	HYDE
AUDLEY	ABERGAVENNY	TANKERVILLE	MONSON
AYLESFORD	LYTTELTON	EFFINGHAM	ALBEMARLE
CRAVEN	BOYLE	ARCHER	SCARBOROUGH
FITZWILLIAM	COVENTRY	FORTESCUE	
CAMDEN	BUCKINGHAM-	BOLTON	
TREVOR	SHIRE	WYCOMBE	
PORTLAND	STAMFORD	KING	
ROCKINGHAM	MILTON	MANCHESTER	
RICHMOND	BANGOR	CHEDWORTH	
BERKELEY	NORTHUMBERLAND		

(L.J. February 2, 1770 ; *Rogers*, P.L. ii. 101 *et seq.*)

III

The House was moved, That the entry in the Journal of the House, of the 17th Day of February 1769, of the Resolution, "That John Wilkes, Esquire, having been in this Session of Parliament expelled this House, was and is incapable of being elected a Member to serve in this present Parliament," might be read.

And the same being read accordingly ; A Motion was made, and the Question being put, That the said Resolution be expunged from the Journals of this House, as being subversive of the Rights of the whole Body of Electors of this Kingdom ;

The House divided.

The yeas went forth.

Tellers for the Yeas $\left\{ \begin{array}{l} \text{Sir Philip Jennings Clerke,} \\ \text{Mr. Byng :} \end{array} \right\}$ 115.

Tellers for the Noes $\left\{ \begin{array}{l} \text{Mr. John St. John,} \\ \text{Sir William Augustus Cunynghame :} \end{array} \right\}$ 47.

So it was resolved in the affirmative.

And the same was expunged, by the Clerk, at the Table accordingly.

(C.J. xxxviii. 977.)

XVIII

THE CASE OF BRASS CROSBY
11 Geo. III., 1771.

[The House of Commons previous to 1771 had repeatedly declared the publishing of debates to be a breach of privilege. In 1771, in consequence of a motion of Col. Onslow, various printers were ordered to attend at the bar of the House. One of them, Whible, refused and was ordered into custody; instead, he was collusively apprehended by a friend and brought before Wilkes as an alderman of the city of London, who promptly discharged him. Shortly after another printer, Miller, was apprehended on a warrant from the Speaker, but gave the messenger into custody for assault. The case came before the Lord Mayor (Brass Crosby) and Aldermen Wilkes and Oliver. They discharged Miller, thus defying the authority of the House of Commons and bringing the city into conflict with it. The Lord Mayor, who was a member of Parliament, was finally committed to the Tower for a breach of privilege (see Excerpt I.). The commitment caused a tremendous ferment. A writ of Habeas Corpus was moved for, thus raising the question whether the commitment by a warrant from the Speaker was legal (see Excerpt II.). By ordering the remandment of the prisoner the Court of Common Pleas decided that it was, and the extract is taken from the judgment of Chief Justice Grey, which gives the grounds of the decision. As a result of the struggle the House of Commons, though not abandoning the claim that publication of debates was a breach of privilege, practically ceased to enforce it. The case therefore marks an epoch in the history of the relations of Parliament to the public Press. See *The Chatham Correspondence*, vol. iv.; *The Letters of Junius; The Annual Register* for 1771; *May*, C.H.E. ii. 34–59; *Anson*, L.C. i. ch. v.; *Broom*, L.C. 901–964; and the analogous case of *The Sheriff of Middlesex*, p. 388.]

I

Resolved, That *Brass Crosby*, Esquire, Lord Mayor of the City of *London*, having discharged out of the custody of one of the Messengers of this House *J. Miller* (for whom the News Paper, intituled, "*The London Evening Post*, from *Thursday, March 7*, to *Saturday, March 9*, 1771," purports to be printed, and of which a Complaint was made in the House of Commons, on the 12th Day of this Instant *March*, and who, for his Contempt, in not obeying the Order of this House, for his Attendance on this House upon *Thursday* the 14th Day of this Instant March, was ordered to be taken into the custody of the Serjeant at Arms or his Deputy, attending this House, and who, by virtue of the Speaker's Warrant, issued under the said Order, had been taken into the Custody of the said

z

Messenger) and having signed a Warrant against the said Messenger, for having executed the said Warrant of the Speaker, and having held the said Messenger to Bail for the same, is guilty of a Breach of the Privileges of this House.

A motion was made, and the Question being proposed, That *Brass Crosby*, Esquire, Lord Mayor of the City of *London*, and a Member of this House, be, for his said Offence, committed to the custody of the Serjeant at Arms attending this House.

The Lord Mayor was heard in his Place.

And then he again withdrew.

Then an Amendment was proposed to be made to the Question, by leaving out the Words, "Custody of the Serjeant at Arms attending this House," and inserting the Words "Tower of *London*" instead thereof;

And the Question being put, That the Words "Custody of the Serjeant at Arms attending this House," stand Part of the Question;

It passed in the Negative.

And the Question being put, That the Words "Tower of *London*" be inserted instead thereof;

It was resolved in the Affirmative.

Then the main Question, so amended, being put, That *Brass Crosby*, Esquire, Lord Mayor of the City of *London*, and a Member of this House, be, for his said Offence, committed to the Tower of *London*;

The House divided.

The Yeas went forth.

Tellers for the Yeas, { Lord *Burgersh*, Mr. *Gascoigne*: } 202.

Tellers for the Noes, { Colonel *Jennings*, Mr. *Whitworth*: } 39.

So it was resolved in the Affirmative.

Ordered, That Mr. Speaker do issue his Warrants accordingly.

(C.J. xxxiii. 289.)

II

L. C. J. De Grey.—If either myself or any of my brothers on the bench, had any doubt in this case, we should certainly have taken some time to consider, before we had given our opinions; but the case seems so very clear to us all, that we have no reason for delay.

The writ by which the lord mayor is now brought before us, is a Habeas Corpus at common law, for it is not signed per statutum. It is called a prerogative writ for the king; or a remedial writ: and this writ was properly advised by the counsel for his lordship, because all the judges (including Holt) agreed that such a writ as the present case required, is not within the statute. This is a writ by which the subject has a right of remedy to be discharged out of custody, if he hath been committed and is detained contrary to the law; therefore the Court must consider, whether the authority committing is a legal authority. If the commitment is made by those having authority to commit, this Court cannot discharge or bail the party committed; nor can this Court admit to bail, one charged or committed in execution. Whether the authority committing the lord mayor, is a legal authority or not, must be adjudged by the return of the writ now before the Court. The return states the commitment to be made by the House of Commons, for a breach of privilege, which is also stated in the return; and this breach of privilege or contempt is, as the counsel has truly described it, three-fold; discharging a printer in custody of a messenger by order of the House of Commons; signing a warrant for the commitment of the messenger, and holding him to bail; that is, treating a messenger of the House of Commons as acting criminally in the execution of the orders of that House. In order to see whether that House has authority to commit, see Co. 4. Inst. 23. Such an assembly must certainly have such authority; and it is legal, because necessary. Lord Coke says they have a judicial power; each member has a judicial seat in the House: he speaks of matters of judicature of the House of Commons, 4 Inst. 23. The House of Commons, without doubt, have power to commit persons examined at their bar touching elections, when they prevaricate or speak falsely; so they have for breaches of privilege; so they have in many other cases. Thomas Long gave the mayor of Westbury £4 to be elected a burgess: he was elected, and the mayor was fined and imprisoned, and Long removed. Arthur Hall, a member, was sent to the Tower, for publishing the conferences of the House, 4 Inst. 23. This power of committing must be inherent in the House of Commons, from the very nature of its institution, and therefore is part of the law of the land. They certainly always could commit in many cases. In matters of elections, they can commit sheriffs, mayors, officers, witnesses, etc. and it is now agreed that they can commit generally for all contempts. All contempts are either punishable in the Court contemned, or in some higher Court. Now the parliament has no superior court; therefore the contempts against either house can only be punished by themselves. The stat. 1 Jac. 1, cap. 13. sect. 3, sufficiently proves that they have power to punish: it is in these words: viz. 'Provided always, that this Act, or anything therein contained, shall not extend to the diminishing of any punishment to be hereafter by censure in parliament inflicted upon any person which hereafter shall make, or procure to be made, any such arrest as is aforesaid.' So that it is most clear the legislature have recognized this power of the House of Commons.

In the case of the Aylesbury men, the counsel admitted, lord chief justice Holt owned, and the House of Lords acknowledged, that the House of Commons had power to commit for contempt and breach of privilege. Indeed, it seems, they must have power to commit for any crime, because they have power to impeach for any crime. When the House of Commons adjudge anything to be a contempt, or a breach of privilege, their adjudication is a conviction, and their commitment in consequence, is execution; and no court can discharge or bail a person that is in execution by the judgement of any other court. The House of Commons therefore having an authority to commit, and that commitment being an execution, the question is, what can this court do? It can do nothing when a person is in execution by the judgement of a court having a competent jurisdiction: in such case, this court is not a court of appeal.

It is objected, 1. That the House of Commons are mistaken, for they have not this power, this authority; 2. That supposing they have, yet in this case they have not used it rightly and properly; and, 3. That the execution of their orders was irregular. In order to judge, I will consider the practice of the courts in common and ordinary cases. I do not find any case where the courts have taken cognisance of such execution, or of commitments of this kind: there is no precedent of Westminster Hall interfering in such a case. . . .

How then can we do anything in the present case, when the law by which the lord mayor is committed, is different from the law by which he seeks to be relieved? He is committed by the law of parliament, and yet he would have redress from the common law. The law of parliament is only known to parliament men, by experience in the House. Lord Cope says, every man looks for it, but few can find it. The House of Commons only know how to act within their own limits. We are not a court of appeal. We do not know certainly the jurisdiction of the House of Commons. We cannot judge of the laws and privileges of the House, because we have no knowledge of those laws and privileges. We cannot judge of the contempts thereof: we cannot judge of the punishment thereof.

I wish we had some code of the law of parliament; but till we have such a code, it is impossible we should be able to judge of it.

Perhaps a contempt in the House of Commons, in the Chancery, in this court, and in the court of Durham, may be very different; therefore we cannot judge of it, but every court must be sole judge of its own contempts. Besides, as the court cannot go out of the return of this writ, how can we inquire as to the truth of the fact, as to the nature of the contempt? We have no means of trying whether the lord-mayor did right or wrong. This court cannot summon a jury to try the matter. We cannot examine into the fact. Here are no parties in litigation before the court. We cannot call in any body. We cannot hear any witnesses, or depositions of witnesses. We cannot issue any process. We are even now hearing ex parte, and without any counsel on the contrary side. Again, if we could determine upon the contempts of any other court, so might the other courts of Westminster-hall; and what confusion would then ensue! none of us knowing the law by which persons are committed by the House of Commons. If three persons are committed for the same breach of privilege, and applied severally to different courts, one court perhaps would bail, another court discharge, a third re-commit.

Two objections have been made, which I own have great weight; because they hold forth, if pursued to all possible cases, consequences of most important mischief. 1st, It is said, that if the rights and privileges of parliament are legal rights, for that very reason the Court must take notice of them, because they are legal. And 2ndly, If the law of parliament is part of the law of the land, the judges must take cognizance of one part of the law of the land, as well as of the other. But these objections will not prevail. There are two sorts of privileges which ought never to be confounded; personal privilege, and the privilege belonging to the whole collective body of that assembly. . . .

At present, when the House of Commons commits for contempt, it is very necessary to state what is the particular breach of privilege; but it would be a sufficient return, to state the breach of privilege generally. This doctrine is fortified by the opinion of all the judges, in the case of lord Shaftesbury, and I never heard this decision complained of till 1704. Though they were times of heat, the judges could have no motive in their decision, but a regard to the laws. The houses disputed about jurisdiction, but the judges were not concerned in the dispute. As for the present case, I am perfectly satisfied, that if Lord Holt himself were to have determined it, the lord-mayor would be remanded. In the case of Mr. Murray, the judges could not hesitate concerning the contempt by a man who refused to receive his sentence in a proper posture. All the judges agreed, that he must be remanded, because he was committed by a court having competent jurisdiction. Courts of justice have no cognizance of the acts of the houses of parliament, because they belong 'ad aliud examen.' I have the most perfect satisfaction in my own mind in that determination. Sir Martin Wright, who felt a generous and distinguished warmth for the liberty of the subject; Mr. Justice Denison, who was so free from connexions and ambition of every kind; and Mr. Justice Foster, who may truly be called the Magna Charta of liberty of persons, as well as fortunes; all these reverend judges concurred in this point: I am therefore clearly and with full satisfaction of opinion, that the lord-mayor must be remanded.

(S.T. xix. 1146-1152.)

XIX

SOMERSETT'S CASE

12 Geo. III., 1771-1772.

[The facts in this case are stated with sufficient clearness in the excerpt from Lord Mansfield's remarkable judgment, June 22, 1772. It affirmed the doctrine laid down in *Stanley v. Harvey* by Lord Northington. It is noticeable that Lord Mansfield delayed judgment for three terms, having failed to effect a compromise between the parties. On the question see *Broom*, C.L. 59-114; *May*, C.H.E. iii. 36. The whole of the lengthy argument of Mr. Hargrave for the negro (S.T. xx. 23-67) is full of valuable and historical matter, well worthy of study, but too long for quotation.]

I shall recite the return to the writ of Habeas Corpus, as the ground of our determination; omitting only words of form. The captain of the ship on board of which the negro was taken, makes his return to the writ in terms signifying that there have been, and still are, slaves to a great number in Africa; and that the trade in them is authorized by the laws and opinions of Virginia and Jamaica; that they are goods and chattels; and, as such, saleable and sold. That James Somersett is a negro of Africa, and long before the return of the writ was brought to be sold, and was sold to Charles Steuart, Esq., then in Jamaica, and has not been manumitted since: that Mr. Steuart, having occasion to transact business, came over hither, with an intention to return; and brought Somersett to attend and abide with him, and to carry him back as soon as the business should be transacted. That such intention has been, and still continues; and that the negro did remain till the time of his departure in the service of his master Mr. Steuart, and quitted it without his consent; and thereupon, before the return of the king's writ, the said Charles Steuart did commit the slave on board the Anne and Mary, to safe custody, to be kept till he should set sail, and then to be taken with him to Jamaica, and there sold as a slave. And this is the cause why he, captain Knowles, who was then and now is, commander of the above vessel, then and now lying in the river of Thames, did the said negro, committed to his custody, detain; and on which he now renders him to the orders of the court. We pay all attention to the opinion of Sir Philip Yorke, and lord Chancellor Talbot, whereby they pledged themselves to the British planters, for all the legal consequences of slaves coming over to this kingdom or being baptized, recognized by lord Hardwicke, sitting as Chancellor on the 19th of October, 1749, that trover would lie: that a notion prevailed, if a negro came over, or became a Christian, he was emancipated, but no ground in law; that he and lord Talbot, when attorney and solicitor general, were of opinion, that no such claim for freedom was valid;[1] that though the statute of tenures had abolished villeins regardant to a manor, yet he did not conceive but that a man might still become a villein in gross, by confessing himself such in open court. We are so well agreed that we think there is no occasion of having it argued . . . before all the judges, as is usual, for obvious reasons, on a return to a Habeas Corpus. The only question before us is, whether the cause on the return is sufficient? If it is so, the negro must be remanded; if it is not so, he must be discharged. Accordingly the return states, that the slave departed and refused to serve; whereupon he was kept, to be sold abroad. So high an act of dominion must be recognized by the law of the country where it is used. The power of a master over his slave has been extremely different, in different countries. The state of slavery is of such a nature, that it is incapable of being introduced on any reasons, moral or political, but only by positive law, which preserves its force long after the reasons, occasion, and time itself from whence it was created, is erased from memory. It is so odious that nothing can be suffered to support it, but positive law. Whatever inconveniences, therefore, may follow from this decision, I cannot say this case is allowed or approved by the law of England; and therefore the black must be discharged.

(S.T. xx. 80–82.)

[1] The opinion was "that a slave coming from the West Indies to Great Britain doth not become free."

XX

REX *v.* TUBBS

17 Geo. III., 1776.

[John Tubbs was a certificated waterman of the city of London, who was impressed for the Royal Navy by Lieutenant Tait, acting under a warrant "to impress seamen, sea-faring men, and persons whose occupations and callings were to work in vessels and boats upon rivers." Tubbs claimed that by his certificate he was exempted from such impressment. In 1743 it had already been decided (see note below) in *R. v. Broadfoot* that the Crown had the right to impress seafaring persons (S.T. xviii. 1323–1362). Mansfield's judgment in this case completes that decision, and is an important one in its bearing on the liberty of the subject and the powers of the executive. The right to impress had been claimed as far back as the reign of Richard II. See *Stubbs*, C.H. ii. 311 ; **2** Rich. II. St. i. c. 4 ; 2 Phil. and Mary, c. 16 ; **5** Eliz. c. 25 ; *Broom*, C.L. 113 ; *Prendergast*, Navy, p. 78.]

The power of pressing is founded upon immemorial usage allowed for ages; if it be so founded and allowed for ages it can have no ground to stand upon, nor can it be vindicated or justified by any reason, but the safety of the state : and the practice is deduced from that trite maxim of the constitutional law of England "that private mischief had better be submitted to, than public detriment and inconvenience should ensue." . . . Being founded on immemorial usage, there can be no doubt but there may be an exception out of it, on the same foundation—upon immemorial usage. I therefore lay out of the case all that has been said about the necessity of an act of parliament to create an exemption ; and likewise all that has been mentioned relative to the doubt stated of the power of the crown to exempt by charter. . . . The only question is, "Whether, in fact, there is evidence of such usage as a matter of right?" . . . In the first place, it does not appear from any law book, it does not appear from any history, it has not been suggested at the bar, that there is, throughout the whole kingdom, any other exemption by the *common law*. . . . Persons liable, must come purely *within the description* of seamen, sea-faring men &c. . . . The commission is not to press landsmen, or persons of any other description of life. . . . It is a very strong circumstance, therefore, that there is in fact no other exemption stated or alluded to, which rests upon the common law. There are many exemptions by statute ; but they are grounded upon considerations of public policy . . . but the exemption of those

called the watermen of the city of London, is to be found in no
statute or common law book whatever. . . . There is no instance of
any officer upon the impress service ever having paid any regard to
a water-bailiff's certificate, nor any case produced where the city has
taken it up as a matter of right, or insisted upon it as such in a court
of justice. Therefore to give my opinion upon the case as at present
stated, and upon the mere fact whether *this exemption* as *here claimed*
is, or is not, warranted by immemorial usage, I cannot say it is.

(From Lord Mansfield's judgment. Cowp. Rep. ii. 517–520.)

[NOTE.—"The only question at present is, whether mariners, persons
who have freely chosen a sea-faring life, persons whose education and
employment have fitted them for the service, and inured them to it—
whether such persons may not be legally pressed into the service of the
crown, whenever the public safety requireth, 'ne quid detrimenti republica
capiat.' For my part, I think they may. I think the crown hath a right
to command the service of these people, whenever the public safety calleth
for it. The same right that it hath to require the personal service of
every man able to bear arms, in case of a sudden invasion or formidable
insurrection. The right in both cases is founded on one and the same
principle, the necessity of the case in order to the preservation of the
whole. . . . According to my present apprehension . . . the right of im-
pressing mariners for the public service is a prerogative inherent in the
crown, grounded upon common law, and recognized by many acts of
parliament. . . . As to the point of usages in the matter of pressing, I have
met with a multitude of commissions and mandatory writs to that purpose
conceived in various forms. . . . When I consider these precedents . . .
running uniformly through a course of many ages . . . with the practice
down to the present time, I cannot conceive otherwise of the point in
question, than that the crown hath been always in possession of the
prerogative of pressing mariners for the public service. . . . But when
the prerogative hath not only this tacit approbation of all ages, the present
as well as the former, on its side, but is recognized, or evidently pre-
supposed, by many acts of Parliament, as in the present case I think it
is, I see no legal objection that can be made to it."

From the charge to the jury of the Recorder, Sir M. Foster, in
Rex v. Broadfoot, S.T. xviii. 1326–1358.]

XXI

THE CASE OF THE DEAN OF ST. ASAPH

23, 24, 25 Geo. III., 1783–1784.

[The Rev. William Davies Shipley, Dean of St. Asaph, was prosecuted for publishing a pamphlet called *A Dialogue between a Gentleman and a Farmer*, the real author of which was his brother-in-law, Sir William Jones. The subject of the pamphlet was the principles of government. The Dean's trial took place at Shrewsbury Assizes, August 6, 1784, before Mr. Justice Buller. The jury found the Dean guilty of publishing *only*. On November 8, motion was made before Lord Mansfield, L.C.J., for a new trial on the ground of misdirection by the Judge, but the motion was rejected by the court. Subsequently a motion was made in arrest of judgment, and "judgment was accordingly arrested, and no new proceedings were ever had upon the subject against the Dean or the printer." Throughout the Dean was defended by Erskine, whose speech, called by Fox "the finest argument in the English language," in moving for a new trial was one of his most famous forensic efforts; Mansfield's judgment is not less celebrated. Nine years later the law was altered by 32 Geo. III. c. 60 (Fox's Libel Act, see p. 156). See S.T. xxi. 847–1046; *Stephen*, H.C.L. ii. 316–345; *Erskine's* speeches (ed. Ridgeway), vol i. The excerpts give (1) the passage from Mr. Justice Buller's charge which was the ground of the motion for the new trial; (2) the salient passages from Mansfield's judgment.]

I

You have been addressed by the quotation of a great many cases upon libels. It seems to me that the question is so well settled, that gentlemen should not agitate it again . . . there could be but three questions;—first, whether the defendant is guilty of publishing the libel? the second whether the innuendoes or the averments made upon the record are true? the third, which is a question of law, Whether it is or is not a libel? Therefore the two first are the only question which you (the Jury), have to consider; and this, added he very rightly, is clear and undoubted law. It is adopted by me as clear and undoubted law, and it has been held so for considerably more than a century past. . . . With such a train of authorities it is really extraordinary to hear the matter now insisted on as a question which admits a doubt; and if we go further back, it will be found still clearer, for about the time of the Revolution authorities will be found which go directly to the point. . . . If one looks a little farther into the constitution, it seems to me, that without recourse to authorities, it cannot admit of a doubt. . . . The judges are sworn to administer the law faithfully and truly. The jury are not so sworn, but to give a true verdict according to the evidence. Did any man ever hear of it, or was it ever yet attempted, to give evidence of what the law was? If it were done in one instance it must hold in all. . . . It is, after the fact is found by the jury, for the Court to say whether it is an offence or not. It would undoubtedly hold in civil cases as well as criminal. . . . In a future stage of the business, if the defendant is found guilty, he will have a right to demand my opinion; and if ever that happens, it is my duty to give it, and then I will. . . . Therefore I can only say, that if you are satisfied that the defendant did publish this pamphlet, and are satisfied as to the truth of the innuendoes in point of law, you ought to find him guilty. If you are not satisfied of that, you will of course acquit him.

(From the charge of Buller, J., in the Dean of St. Asaph's case, S.T. xxi. pp. 945 and 946.)

II

The answer to these three objections is, that by the constitution the jury ought not to decide the question of law, whether such a writing, of such a meaning, published without a lawful excuse, be criminal; . . . therefore it is the duty of the judge to advise the jury to separate the question of fact from the question of law; and as they ought not to decide the law . . . the judge is not called upon necessarily to tell them his own opinion. It is almost peculiar to the form of prosecution for libel, that the question of law remains entirely for the Court *upon record* . . . so that a general verdict, "that the defendant is guilty," is equivalent to a special verdict in other cases. It finds all which belongs to the jury to find; it finds nothing as to the law. Therefore when a jury have been satisfied as to every fact within their province to find, they have been advised to find the defendant *guilty*, and in that shape they take the opinion of the Court upon the law. . . . The subject matter of these three objections has arisen upon every trial for a libel since the Revolution, which is now near one hundred years ago. . . . During all this time, as far as it can be traced, one may venture to say, that the direction of every judge has been consonant to the doctrine of Mr. Justice Buller; and no counsel has complained of it by any application to the Court . . . the formal direction of every judge (under which every lawyer for near a hundred years, has so far acquiesced as not to complain of it to the Court) seems to me, ever since the Revolution, to have been agreeable to the direction of Mr. Justice Buller. It is difficult to cite cases; the trials are not printed. . . . We must in all cases of tradition trace backwards, and presume, from the usage which is remembered, that the precedent usage was the same . . . I by accident (from memory only I speak now) recollect one where the *Craftsman* was acquitted; and I recollect it from a famous, witty, and ingenious ballad that was made at the time by Mr. Pulteney; and though it is a ballad, I will cite the stanza from it, because it will show you the idea of the able men in opposition, and the leaders of the popular party in those days. They had not an idea of assuming that the jury had a right to determine upon a question of law, but they put it upon another and much better ground. The stanza I allude to is this:

> For Sir Philip well knows,
> That his *innuendos*
> Will serve him no longer
> In verse or in prose;
> For twelve honest men have decided the cause,
> Who are judges of fact, though not judges of laws.

. . . Such a judicial practice in the precise point from the Revolution, as I think, down to the present day, is not to be shaken by arguments of general theory or popular declamation. Every species of criminal prosecution has something peculiar in the mode of prosecution; therefore general propositions, applied to all, tend only to complicate and embarrass the question. No deduction or conclusion can be drawn from what a jury *may* do, from the *form* of procedure, to what they *ought* to do upon the fundamental principles of the constitution and the reason of the thing, if they will act with integrity and good conscience. The fundamental definition of trial by jury depends upon a universal maxim that is without an exception. Though a definition or maxim in law, without an exception, it is said, is hardly to be found, yet I take this to be a maxim without an exception: *Ad quaestionem juris non respondent juratores; ad quaestionem facti non respondent judices.* . . . The constitution trusts that, under the direction of a judge, they will not usurp a jurisdiction which is not in their province. They do not know and are not presumed to know the law; they are not sworn to decide the law; they are not required to decide the law. . . . But further, upon the reason of the thing, and the eternal principles of justice, the jury ought not to assume the jurisdiction of the law. As I said before, they do not know, and are not presumed to know anything of the matter; they do not understand the language in which it is conceived, or the meaning of the terms. They have no rule to go by but their affections and wishes . . . so the jury who usurp the judicature of the law, though they happen to be right, are themselves wrong, because they are right by chance only, and have not taken the constitutional way of deciding the question. It is the duty of the judge, in all cases of general justice, to tell the jury how to do right, though they have it *in their power* to do wrong, which is a matter entirely between God and their consciences. To be free, is to live under a government by law. The liberty of the press consists in printing without any previous license, subject to the consequences of law. The licentiousness of the press is Pandora's box, the source of every evil. . . . Jealousy of leaving the law to the Court, as in other cases, so in the case of libels, is now, in the present state of things, puerile rant and declamation. The judges are totally independent of the minister that may happen to be, and of the king himself. Their temptation is rather to the popularity of the day. But I agree with the observation cited by Mr. Cowper from Mr. J. Foster, "that a *popular* judge is an odious and pernicious character." . . . In opposition to this, what is contended for? That the law shall be in every particular cause what any twelve men, who shall happen to be the jury, shall be inclined to think, liable to no review, and subject to no control, under all the prejudices of the popular cry of the day, and under all the bias of interest in this town, where thousands, more or less are concerned in the publication of newspapers, paragraphs, and pamphlets. Under such an administration of law, no man may counsel or advise, whether a paper was or was not punishable. I am glad I am not bound to subscribe to such an absurdity, such a solecism in politics. Agreeable to the *uniform* judicial practice since the Revolution warranted by the fundamental principles of the constitution, of the trial by jury, and upon the reason and fitness of the thing, we are all of opinion that this motion should be rejected, and this rule discharged.

(From Mansfield's judgment, S.T. xxi. 1034–1041.)

XXII

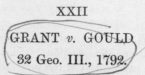

GRANT *v.* GOULD

32 Geo. III., 1792.

[The issue in this case was the power of the court at Westminster to grant a prohibition to prevent a sentence passed by a court-martial being executed. The plaintiff, having been so sentenced, pleaded that he was not liable to "martial law," and accordingly applied for a prohibition. Lord Loughborough, in a judgment frequently quoted, distinguished "martial" from "military" law, and, while pointing out that the court at Westminster claimed the right to issue such prohibitions, refused to grant it in this case on the ground that the military court had not exceeded its jurisdiction. The passages from Hale and Blackstone alluded to in the judgment are, for convenience, cited below, A and B. See *Blackstone's* (H.) Rep. ii. 69, and authorities cited in *Dicey*, L.C. app. xii. note.]

This leads me to an observation that martial law such as it is described by Hale, and such also as it is marked by Mr. Justice Blackstone, does not exist in England at all. Where martial law is established and prevails in any country, it is of a totally different nature from that, which is inaccurately called martial law, merely because the decision is by a Court Martial, but which bears no affinity to that which was formerly attempted to be exercised in this kingdom; which was contrary to the constitution, and which has been for a century totally exploded. Where martial law prevails, the authority under which it is exercised, claims a jurisdiction over all military persons, in all circumstances. Even their debts are subject to enquiry by a military authority: every species of offence, committed by any person who appertains to the army, is tried, not by a civil judicature, but by the judicature of the regiment or corps to which he belongs. It extends also to a great variety of cases, not relating to the discipline of the army, in those states which subsist by military power. Plots against the Sovereign, intelligence to the enemy, and the like, are all considered as cases within the cognizance of military authority.

In the reign of King William, there was a conspiracy against his person in Holland, and the persons guilty of that conspiracy were tried by a council of officers. There was also a conspiracy against him in England, but the conspirators were tried by the common law. And within a very recent period, the incendiaries who attempted to set fire to the Docks at Portsmouth, were tried by the common law.

In this country, all the delinquences of soldiers are not triable, as in most countries of Europe, by martial law; but where they are ordinary offences against the civil peace, they are tried by the common law courts. Therefore it is totally inaccurate, to state martial law, as having any place whatever within the realm of Great Britain. But there is by the providence and wisdom of the Legislature, an army established in this country, of which it is necessary to keep up the establishment. The army being established by the authority of the Legislature, it is an indispensable requisite of that establishment, that there should be order and discipline kept up in it, and that the persons who compose the army, for all offences in their military capacity, should be subject to a trial by their officers. That has induced the absolute necessity of a mutiny act, accompanying the army. . . .

This Court (*i.e.* a military court) being established in this country by positive law, the proceedings of it, and the relation in which it will stand to the Courts of Westminster Hall, must depend upon the same rules, with all other courts, which are instituted, and have particular powers given them, and whose acts therefore, may become the subject of application to the Courts of Westminster Hall, for a prohibition. Naval Courts Martial, Military Courts Martial, Courts of Admiralty, Courts of Prize are all liable to the controlling authority, which the Courts of Westminster Hall have, from time to time, exercised, for the purpose of preventing them from exceeding the jurisdiction given to them : the general ground of prohibition, being an excess of jurisdiction, when they assume a power to act in matters not within their cognizance.

My brother Adair justly and correctly said, that a prohibition to prevent the proceedings of a court martial, is not to be granted, without very sufficient ground and due consideration. Not that it is not to be granted, because it would be dangerous in all cases to grant prohibitions ; for it would be undoubtedly dangerous, if there was a facility in applying for prohibitions, and the sentence were to be stopped, for asking it to be further enquired into. But in such cases it is the duty of the court to consider the matter fully and deliberately, upon the motion to prohibit, and the court not without great danger, take the course in such a case which they have done in others, where there is no danger in the delay, to put the matter in prohibition, and determine it, upon the record.

A

But, secondly, as to matters of war. The constable and marshal had a double power, viz.

1. A ministerial power, as they were two great ordinary officers, anciently, in the king's army; the constable being in effect the king's general, and the marshal was employed in marshalling the king's army, and keeping the list of the officers and soldiers therein, and his certificate was the trial of those whose attendance was requisite. Vide Littleton, § 102.

Again, 2, the constable and marshal had also a judicial power, or a court wherein several matters were determinable: as first, appeals of death or murder committed beyond the sea, according to the course of the civil law. Secondly, the right of prisoners taken in war. Thirdly, the offences and miscarriages of soldiers contrary to the laws and rules of the army: for always preparatorily to an actual war, the kings of this realm, by advice of the constable, and marshal, were used to compose a book of rules and orders, for the due order and discipline of their officers and soldiers, together with certain penalties on the offenders; and this was called martial law. We have extant in the black book of the admiralty, and elsewhere, several exemplars of such military laws, and especially that of the ninth of Richard II. composed by the king, with the advice of the duke of Lancaster, and others.

But touching the business of martial law, these things are to be observed, viz.

First, that in truth and reality it is not a law, but something indulged, rather than allowed, as a law; the necessity of government, order and discipline in an army, is that only which can give those laws a countenance, quod enim necessitas cogit defendit.

Secondly, this indulged law was only to extend to members of the army, or to those of the opposite army, and never was so much indulged as intended to be executed or exercised upon others; for others who were not listed under the army, had no colour or reason to be bound by military constitutions, applicable only to the army, whereof they were not parts; but they were to be ordered and governed according to the laws to which they were subject, though it were a time of war.

Thirdly, that the exercise of martial law, whereby any person should lose his life, or member, or liberty, may not be permitted in time of peace, when the king's courts are open for all persons to receive justice, according to the laws of the land. This is in substance declared by the petition of right, 3 Car. 1. whereby such commissions and martial law were repealed, and declared to be contrary to law: and accordingly was that famous case of Edmond earl of Kent; who, being taken at Pomfret, 15 Edw. II. the king and divers lords proceeded to give sentence of death against him, as in a kind of military court by a summary proceeding, which judgement was afterwards, in 1 Edw. III. reversed in parliament.

And accordingly the judgement was reversed; for martial law, which is rather indulged than allowed, and that only in cases of necessity, in time of open war, is not permitted in time of peace, when the ordinary courts of justice are open.

In this military court, court of honour, or court martial, the civil law has been used and allowed in such things as belong to their jurisdiction, as the rule or direction of their proceedings and decisions ; so far forth as the same is not controlled by the laws of this kingdom, and those customs and usages which have obtained in England, which even in matters of honour are in some points derogatory to the civil law. But this court has long been disused upon great reasons.

(*Hale*, Hist. of the Common Law, pp. 34 and 36.)

B

For martial law, which is built upon no settled principles, but is entirely arbitrary in its decisions, is, as sir Matthew Hale observes, in truth and reality no law, but something indulged rather than allowed as a law. The necessity of order and discipline in an army is the only thing which can give it countenance; and therefore it ought not to be permitted in time of peace, when the king's courts are open for all persons to receive justice according to the laws of the land. Wherefore, Thomas earl of Lancaster being condemned at Pontefract, 15 Edw. II. by martial law, his attainder was reversed 1 Edw. III. because it was done in time of peace. And it is laid down, that if a lieutenant, or other, that hath commission of martial authority, doth in time of peace hang or otherwise execute any man by colour of martial law, this is murder ; for it is against Magna Carta. And the Petition of Right enacts, that no soldier shall be quartered on the subject without his own consent; and that no commission shall issue to proceed within this land according to martial law. And whereas, after the restoration, king Charles the second kept up about five thousand regular troops, by his own authority, for guards and garrisons ; which king James the second by degrees increased to no less than thirty thousand, all paid from his own civil list ; it was made one of the articles of the Bill of Rights, that the raising or keeping a standing army within the kingdom in time of peace, unless it be with consent of parliament, is against law.

But, as the fashion of keeping standing armies (which was first introduced by Charles VII. in France, A.D. 1445) has of late years universally prevailed over Europe (though some of its potentates, being themselves unable to maintain them, are obliged to have recourse to richer powers, and receive subsidiary pensions for that purpose) it has also for many years past been annually judged necessary by our legislature, for the safety of the kingdom, the defence of the possessions of the crown of Great Britain, and the preservation of the balance of power in Europe, to maintain even in time of peace a standing body of troops, under the command of the crown ; who are, however ipso facto disbanded at the expiration of every year, unless continued by parliament. And it was

2 A

enacted by statute 10 W. III. c. 1. that not more than twelve thousand regular forces should be kept on foot in Ireland, though paid at the charge of that kingdom : which permission is extended by statute 8 Geo. III. c. 13. to 16,235 men, in time of peace.

However expedient the most strict regulations may be in time of actual war, yet, in times of profound peace, a little relaxation of military rigour would not, one should hope, be productive of much inconvenience. And upon this principle, though by our standing laws (still remaining in force, though not attended to) desertion in time of war is made felony, without benefit of clergy, and the offence is triable by a jury and before the judges of the common law; yet, by our militia laws before-mentioned, a much lighter punishment is inflicted for desertion in time of peace. So, by the Roman law also, desertion in time of war was punished by death, but more mildly in time of tranquillity. But our Mutiny Act makes no such distinction : for any of the faults above-mentioned are, equally at all times, punishable with death itself, if a court martial shall think proper. This discretionary power of the court martial is indeed to be guided by the directions of the crown ; which, with regard to military offences, has almost an absolute legislative power. "His majesty, says the act, may form articles of war, and constitute courts martial, with power to try any crime by such articles, and inflict such penalties as the articles direct." A vast and most important truth ! an unlimited power to create crimes, and annex to them any punishments, not extending to life or limb ! These are indeed forbidden to be inflicted, except for crimes declared to be so punishable by this act ; which crimes we have just enumerated, and, among which, we may observe that any disobedience to lawful commands is one. Perhaps in some future revision of this act, which is in many respects hastily penned, it may be thought worthy the wisdom of parliament to ascertain the limits of military subjection, and to enact express articles of war for the government of the army, as is done for the government of the navy.

(*Blackstone*, Commentaries, I. 414.)

XXIII

THE CASE OF WOLFE TONE
Geo. III., 1798.

[Wolfe Tone, a subject of George III., who had taken part in French invasion of Ireland in 1798, was captured on a French man-of war and sentenced by a court-martial in Dublin to be hanged. The points at issue are very clearly explained in the excerpt. "No more splendid assertion of the supremacy of the law can be found than the protection of Wolfe Tone by the Irish Bench." *Dicey*, L.C. 290; see the whole of ch. viii. and app. xii.]

In the interval a motion was made in the Court of King's Bench by Mr. Curran, on an affidavit of Mr. Tone's father, stating that his son had been brought before a bench of officers, calling itself a court martial, and by them sentenced to death.

"I do not pretend to say," observed Mr. Curran, "that Mr. Tone is not guilty of the charges of which he was accused ;—I presume the officers were honourable men ;—but it is stated in the affidavit, as a solemn fact, that Mr. Tone had no commission under His Majesty, and therefore no court martial could have any cognizance of any crime imputed to him, while the Court of King's-bench sat in the capacity of the great criminal court of the land. In times when war was raging, when man was opposed to man in the field, courts martial might be endured ; but every law authority is with me, while I stand upon this sacred and immutable principle of the constitution—*that martial law and civil law are incompatible ;* and that the former must cease with the existence of the latter. This is not the time for arguing this momentous question. My client must appear in this court. *He is cast for death this day.* He may be ordered for execution while I address you. I call on the Court to support the law. I move for a *Habeas Corpus* to be directed to the provost marshal of the barracks of Dublin, and Major Sandys to bring up the body of Mr. Tone.

Lord Chief Justice [Kilwarden].—Have a writ instantly prepared.

Mr. Curran.—My client may die while this writ is preparing.

Lord Chief Justice.—Mr. Sheriff, proceed to the barracks, and acquaint the provost marshal that a writ is preparing to suspend Mr. Tone's execution ; and *see that he be not executed.*

[The Court awaited in a state of the utmost agitation, the return of the Sheriff.]

Mr. Sheriff.—My lords, I have been at the barracks, in pursuance of your order. The provost marshal says he must obey Major Sandys. Major Sandys says he must obey lord Cornwallis.

Mr. Curran.—Mr. Tone's father, my lords, returns, after serving the Habeas Corpus : he says General Craig will not obey it.

Lord Chief Justice.—Mr. Sheriff, take the body of Tone into your custody : Take the provost marshal and Major Sandys into custody : and show the order of this Court to General Craig.

Mr. Sheriff (who was understood to have been refused admittance to the barracks) returns.—I have been at the barracks. Mr. Tone, having cut his throat last night, is not in a condition to be removed. As to the second part of your order, I could not meet the parties.

[A French Emigrant Surgeon, whom General Craig had sent along with the Sheriff, was sworn.]

Surgeon.—I was sent to attend Mr. Tone this morning at four o'clock, his windpipe was divided. I took instant measures to secure his life, by closing the wound. There is no knowing, for four days, whether it will be mortal. His head is now kept in one position. *A sentinel is over him, to prevent his speaking.* His removal would kill him.

Mr. Curran applied for further surgical aid, and for the admission of Mr. Tone's friends to him. [Refused.]

Lord Chief Justice.—Let a rule be made for suspending the execution of Theobald Wolfe Tone; and let it be served on the proper persons.

XXIV

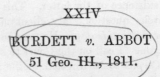

BURDETT *v.* ABBOT

51 Geo. III., 1811.

[Sir Francis Burdett, M.P., had published a letter in *Cobbett's Weekly Register* which the House of Commons pronounced to be "a libellous and scandalous paper, reflecting on the just privileges of the House," and declared the author to be "guilty of a breach of privilege." The Speaker's warrant for Burdett's arrest was executed with the assistance of soldiers, and Burdett was carried off to, and confined in, the Tower of London. He then brought an action against the Speaker for trespass, thus raising the issues : (1) whether the House of Commons had power to commit for contempt ; (2) whether in executing such a process for contempt it was justifiable to break into a house. Lord Chief Justice Ellenborough's elaborate judgment, many historical points of which are open to criticism, but with which Bayley and Grove, JJ., concurred, was subsequently confirmed on a writ of error by the Court of Exchequer Chamber and the House of Lords. See *East's Rep.* xiv. 1–163 ; *Anson*, L.C. i. 169 ; *May*, P.P. 47–142 ; and cf. with the case of *The Sheriff of Middlesex*, p. 388.]

The only points which are immediately presented by the record for our decision are, first, Whether the House of Commons has any authority by law to commit in cases of contempt as a breach of privilege ? Secondly, Whether, supposing the House to have such an authority in general, that authority has been well executed by the warrant in question ; that is, whether the warrant stated in the plea of the defendant discloses a sufficient ground of commitment in this instance? And thirdly, Whether the means which have been used for the execution of the Speaker's warrant are in law justifiable? The subject, as it seems to me, cannot properly be branched out and divided into more points. In argument it has indeed been dilated to a much wider extent here, and has been considered in much greater latitude as a question of controversy elsewhere, than is at all necessary for the decision of these which are the only points with which we have judicially any concern upon the present occasion. The citations made upon the first argument from the judgement of Sir Orlando Bridgeman rather tend to illustrate the character of that most eminent judge, by exhibiting the profundity of his learning, and the extent of his industry, than to throw any material light upon the present question. A very moderate portion of the learning there displayed by him is at all applicable to the present case. The main point decided, and properly decided, in that case was, that the privilege of Parliament, which exempted members from arrest, did not wholly suspend the right of suit against them during the entire continuance of the Parliament, at least so as to prevent the suing by original. So a great part of the learning exhibited upon Thorpe's case there cited, though properly adverted to as the case itself was, bears very little on the question immediately before us. That case, which is to be found in the rolls of Parliament, 31 H. 6. No. 26, 27, 28, decides that a suit commenced against a member might proceed to any extent in the time of the vacation of Parliament, though not in parliament time, as it is called. Thorpe's case appears to be the earliest applicable to parliamentary privilege; for the two other cases of an earlier date mentioned by Lord Coke in his 4th Institute (24), that of John de Thoresby, 10. Ed. 3. and of Bogo de Clare 18 Ed. 1., are shewn by Sir Orlando Bridgeman in his judgement, in Benyon v. Evelyn, to have no proper reference to the privileges of the members of the House of Commons: and indeed, according to this case of Thorpe, as supposed by Lord Coke, it appears that the exemption from arrest was not claimed or considered as the peculiar privilege of a member of one or of the other House of Parliament, properly as such; but as the privilege of a member of the High Court of Parliament *generally:* and the reason of such privilege, as given by the judges, is one which applies equally to the members of both Houses, viz. "that they may have their freedom and liberty freely to intende upon Parliament." Other cases have been cited, in which the right of the subject to sue in matters of parliamentary cognizance has been in part recognized by the courts. The first mentioned of these cases, however, that of Thorpe, respects merely the privileges of individual members, and the means of their individual protection, not the vindictive privileges of the House for offences done generally against the body of the House, in breach of the rights and privileges of the whole House collectively considered. The other cases next mentioned, that of Bogo de Clare, and John de Thoresby, do not apply to this question; which is, what acts the House of Commons may justifiably do; not where, or how, such acts shall be alone brought into question. As to the first point which arises in this case; has the House of Commons a right to commit for breach of privilege? It has been argued, that they are prohibited from imprisoning persons by the statute of Magna Charta, and the 28 Ed. 3. c. 3.: but the provision in Magna Charta directed against acts of unauthorized force, "that no man shall be imprisoned but by the *lawful* judgement of his peers, or *by the law of the land;*" and that of the stat. 28 Ed. 3. "that no man shall be put out of land or tenement, *nor taken or imprisoned*, nor disinherited, nor put to death, without being brought in to answer *by due process of the law;*" are satisfied as far as they relate to this subject, if the *lex et consuetudo parliamenti* be, as Lord Coke and all the writers on the law have held that it is, part of the *law of the land* in its large and extended sense: At what time the two Houses of Parliament, as at present constituted and distinguished, that is, as Lords and Commons, first ceased to sit together, as originally they did, and began to have a separate existence, is a matter more of antiquarian curiosity than of legal importance. The separation of the two Houses seems to have taken place as early as the 49 H. 3. about the time of the battle of Evesham; for I think it is at that period that the first return of of "knights, citizens, and burgesses" is to be found; and that separation was probably effected and previously sanctioned by a formal act for that purpose by the King and Parliament as originally constituted. At any rate the very first subsequent act of the parliament, acting in the two Houses conjointly with the King, operated as a formal recognition of an antecedently authorized separation of parliament into the two Houses in which they then and have since sat. The privileges which have been since enjoyed, and the functions which have been since uniformly exercised, by each branch of the legislature, with the knowledge and acquiescence of the other House and of the King, must be presumed to be the privileges and functions which then, that is, at the very period of their original separation, were statutably assigned to each. The privileges which belong to them seem at all times to have been, and necessarily must be, inherent in them, independent of any precedent: it was necessary that they should have the most complete personal security, to enable them freely to meet for the purpose of discharging their important functions, and also that they should have the right of self-protection: I do not mean merely against acts of individual wrong; for poor and impotent indeed would be the privileges of Parliament, if they could not also protect themselves against injuries and affronts offered to the aggregate body, which might prevent or impede the full and effectual exercise of their parliamentary functions. 'Tis an essential right necessarily inherent in the supreme legislature of the kingdom, and of course as necessarily inherent in the parliament assembled in two houses as in one. The right of self-protection implies, as a consequence, a right to use the necessary means for rendering such self-protection effectual. Independently, therefore, of any precedents or recognized practice on the subject, such a body must a priori be armed with a competent authority to enforce the free and independent exercise of its own proper functions, whatever those functions might be. On this ground it has been, I believe, very generally admitted in argument, that the House of Commons must be and is authorized to remove any immediate obstructions to the due course of its own proceedings. But this mere power of removing actual impediments to its proceedings would not be sufficient for the purposes of its full and efficient protection: it must also have the power of protecting itself from insult and indignity wherever offered, by punishing those who offer it. Can the High Court of Parliament, or either of the two Houses of which it consists, be deemed not to possess intrinsically that authority of punishing summarily for contempts which is acknowledged to belong, and is daily exercised as belonging, to every superior court of law, of less dignity undoubtedly than itself? And is not the degradation and disparagement of the two Houses of parliament in the estimation of the public, by contemptuous libels, as much an impediment to their efficient acting with regard to the public, as the actual obstruction of an individual member by bodily force, in his endeavour to resort to the place where parliament is holden? And what would it consist with the dignity of such bodies, or what is more, with the immediate and effectual exercise of their important functions, that they should wait the comparatively tardy result of a prosecution in the ordinary course of law, for the vindication of their privilege from wrong and insult? The necessity of the case would, therefore, upon principles of natural reason, seem to require that such bodies, constituted for such purposes, and exercising such functions as they do, should possess the powers which the history of the earliest times shews that they have in fact possessed and used. It is therefore idle to contend, as some have done, that, as the House of Commons is a body which has began to exist separately and substantively since the time of legal memory, that is, since the return of Richard the First from the Holy Land; and that, as they cannot on that account claim by prescription or immemorial custom any power of commitment, and that no act of parliament since that time has expressly given it to them; therefore, it cannot legally belong to them. I am glad that nothing of that kind has been advanced in argument upon this occasion; but it is impossible not to have heard of its having been urged elsewhere and on other occasions. And perhaps more weight has been given to the argument that seems to belong to it, from the pains that Sir Robert Atkyns (in his treatise in the form of an argument upon the information against William Williams Esq.) has taken to answer it. For he seems to suppose it necessary, "to support the power and privilege of the House of Commons, as being an essential part of the parliament, to make out against these innovators, (as he calls them,) that the House of Commons has ever been part of the parliament, and that it was so long before the 49 H. 3.;" which, as already mentioned, is the date of the first writ of summons for knights, citizens, and burgesses now extant: admitting, "that, where the beginning of a thing is known, there can be nothing belonging to it by *prescription.*" But Selden, I observe, (Priv. of Parl. 713) acknowledges that there had been a great change in the constitution of Parliament, but supposes it to have happened long before 49 H. 3. namely, in the time of that king's father, King John; (still placing it however in the time of legal memory;) and he supposes it was done *by a law*, though the *law be lost;* as *many Rolls of Parliament were: wherein those laws were entered*. But supposing the separate existence of the House of Commons to have began only in the 49 H. 3., or at some other period within the time of legal memory; the answer to the objection is that some statute or act of supreme national authority, whatever it was, by which the House then began to exist and act, and has since acted, separately, as a distinct branch of the legislature from the Lords, and conjointly with the Lords and the King, as a Parliament, invested them, as such House, with the antecedent essential privileges which belonged to the aggregate body of Parliament, at least to the extent in which they have been ever since enjoyed by that House, and of which the subsequent enjoyment is evidence: and it would only vary the form of prescribing, if any prescription were in such case necessary, to such an one as the following; namely that from time whereof the memory of man is not to the contrary until the 49 H. 3. all the members of Parliament, by their then name of Proceres Nobiles et Magnates, and since the 49 H. 3. by their several names of Lords spiritual and temporal and of Knights, Citizens, and Burgesses, in parliament assembled, have had and used, and now still of right ought to have and use such and such privileges. So that if the *Parliament itself*, in any *anterior form* of its existence, be of prescriptive antiquity, about which no reasonable doubt can be entertained, the same privileges which were in such anterior form then enjoyed by it may still (if necessary so to consider it) be even technically prescribed for by Parliament in the very form into which it has since resolved itself and now subsists : unless, indeed, it can be contended with effect, that the legislature itself is incompetent to vary the precise form in which, in time beyond memory, it appears to have existed and acted; a point which, I presume, few persons will be hardy enough to contend for. There is no pretence, therefore, for treating the privileges of the House of Commons, as some persons have treated them, as things of a novel origin and constitution, beginning within time of legal memory, and standing upon no authority of prescription or statute.

These privileges appear to have been claimed, exercised and recognized in numerous precedents almost as early as we can distinctly trace the House acting in its separate parliamentary capacity. Without referring more at large to Thorpe's case, the personal privileges of Parliament are stated in it in these terms : "If any person that is a member of this High Court of Parliament be arrested in such case as be not for treason or felony, or surety of the peace, or for a condemnation had before the parliament, it is used that all such persons shall be released of such arrests, and make an attorney, so that they may have their freedom and liberty freely to intende upon the Parliament." I am aware that this authority in terms relates only to privileges of personal freedom from arrest, and not to the vindictive privilege of committing for *contempts against the whole House*. But on this latter point, not to incumber the case unnecessarily with a vast variety and quantity of matter, I would refer only generally to the case of Ferrers, (very fully reported in Crompton's Jurisdiction of Courts;) Trewinnard's case in Dy. 59; William Thranwis' case in 1529, who was committed to the custody of the Sergeant at Arms for a contempt in words against the dignity of the House ; John Wentworth's case, of the same kind, in 1575, in D'Ewes' Journal 244 ; and the case of Hall, a member of the

House of Commons, in 1580, which is also in D'Ewes' Journal, from page 291 to 298, and which is the first instance of a libel punished by the House. In that case Arthur Hall was punished for a libel on the dignity of the House, by being committed and expelled; and he was also *fined:* in respect to which species of punishment, that of fining, the House exercised in that instance a power which they have not since been in the *habit* of exercising; but certainly that precedent, as far as it goes to the expulsion and imprisonment of a member, is fully sustained by more modern usage. He was committed for six months, and to be further imprisoned till a revocation and retraction under his hand of the slander contained in his book. That might perhaps be considered as an access of jurisdiction, as contrary to the general principles of English law: for the courts of law cannot commit a person *till* he retracts or makes personal submission for his offence: but as far as the mere infliction of imprisonment goes, it shews at least that the House were in the habit of committing for contempts. And the sort of libel for which he was punished, as it appeared in D'Ewes' Journal, was not a libel upon individual members, but upon the whole parliament.

Without resting any longer, however upon these precedents, I come with more satisfaction to an authority which cannot be gainsayed or questioned; to the legislative recognition of a power in either House of Parliament to punish by imprisonment; for that, I think, is virtually to be understood from the stat. 1 Jac. 1. c. 13. But before I observe upon that statute, I will shortly advert to a prior act of the 4th H. 8. made in the case of a Mr. Strode, who was imprisoned for something he had done in parliament; and by which it was enacted, that "all suits, accusements, condemnations, executions, fines, amerciaments, punishments, corrections, grants, charges, or impositions put or had, or hereafter to be put or had unto or upon the said R. Strode, and to every other person or persons afore specified in that parliament, *or that* of any parliament that *shall be,* for any bill speaking, reasoning, or declaring of any matter concerning the parliament to be commenced and treated, should be utterly void and of none effect." I own I agree with the cogent reasons given by Sir Robert Atkyns, (p. 56) that this is to be considered as a general act, notwithstanding the opinion given to the contrary in the case of Mr. Holles 3 Char. 1. This act, however, only relates to the personal immunity and protection of the members themselves, for acts done in Parliament or concerning the same. Then comes the stat. 1 Jac. 1. c. 13. which, after reciting, that "heretofore doubt had been made if any person, being arrested in execution, and by *privilege* of either of the *Houses of Parliament set at liberty*, whether the party at whose suit such execution was pursued, be forever after barred and disabled to sue forth a new writ of execution in that case : " (which shews very clearly, that Parliament had been in the habit of setting aside or superseding such executions ;) for avoiding all further doubt and trouble which in like cases may hereafter ensue ; *enacts*, " that the party at whose suit such writ of execution was pursued, his executors, etc. *after such time as the privilege* of *that session of parliament*, in which such privilege shall be so granted, *shall cease*, may sue forth and execute a *new* writ or writs of execution," etc. Is not this an ample recognition of the prior exercise of an authority by the Houses of Parliament to liberate persons entitled to privilege, who were in execution : this statute enacting however, at the same time, that it should not be an answer to the further charging him in execution by his creditor, that he had once been taken in execution. The statute then provides, that from thenceforth no sheriff, bailiff, or other officer, from whose arrest or custody any such *person* so arrested in execution *shall be delivered by any such privilege*, shall be charged or chargeable with or by any action whatsoever, for delivering out of execution any such *privileged person so as is aforesaid by such privilege of Parliament set at liberty ;* any law, custom, or privilege heretofore to the contrary notwithstanding." And then follows this proviso, which is very material to the present purpose : " Provided always, that this act, or anything therein contained, shall not extend to the *diminishing* of any *punishment* to be hereafter *by censure in parliament inflicted* upon any person which shall hereafter make or procure to be made any such arrest as aforesaid." Now by *inflicting censure*, the power of doing which was thus saved to the Houses of Parliament, as they had been before accustomed to exercise it, must be meant, not a mere crimination or reproof in *words only*, but the substantial *infliction* of positive *punishment* by Parliament upon the offender. This act, indeed, applies in terms only to the particular case of arrests ; but no one can reason so weakly as to suppose, or argue so narrowly as to say, that the power of the Houses of Parliament to inflict punishment existed and had been exercised only in that particular case. I have mentioned this instance, not from the necessity of the thing in so plain a case, but because it has been thrown out very confidently, that the privilege of the House of Commons stood upon no parliamentary recognition or authority whatsoever : here, however, is a direct parliamentary recognition of their right to inflict punishment by censure in parliament in the one case that is specially mentioned, and it virtually ratifies what had been antecedently done by the House in the way of punishment, of which the usual mode appears to have been by imprisonment.

Having stated thus much of the earlier precedents and authorities in respect to the Parliament itself, and their own practice of committing for contempts, I come now to a period nearer to our own times, and more within our own immediate contemplation and view, where the materials for our judgement are more abundant, and the sources from which they are drawn are in some respects more satisfactory. If any person more than another could be supposed to doubt the power of the House of Commons to commit for contempt; if any person whoever sat in this place was, more than another, jealous of any supposed encroachment upon the rights of the people, either on the part of the Crown, or of either House of Parliament, or less favourable in general to claims of parliamentary privilege, it was my Lord Holt. . . .

(The account of the points in Ashby v. White is here omitted. See p. 268.)

It is impossible for anything to be more full, explicit, and unqualified, than this language of Lord Holt, in which he recognizes a power of commitment in the House of Commons for a breach of the privileges of their House : and what is said of the House of Commons may be understood as said also of the House of Lords ; for they are one and the same in this respect : they are but the grand council of the realm divided into two different parts, each carrying with it this essential power and privilege to protect itself, which each has exercised ever since (and therefore must be presumed collectively to have exercised before) their separation.

Prior to Ashby v. White, in point of time, was the Earl of Shaftesbury's case, which was a commitment by the House of Lords "for a high contempt (stated to have been) committed against this House." Two of the judges there thought it was a material ingredient in that case, that the sessions during which the commitment was made was then continuing. The Chief Justice Rainsford thought, that the Court of K.B. had no jurisdiction of the cause ; and Twisden J., who was absent, communicated by Jones J. his opinion, that Lord Shaftesbury should be remanded. No distinction was taken in that case between the authority of the Lords and that of the Commons to commit. And notwithstanding the generality of the commitment, which was for a high contempt without saying when, where, or how committed, it was sustained by this court, and Lord Shaftesbury was remanded. This case has been referred to by judges in later times as an authority upon the point. And in Alexander Murray's case, the commitment which was by the House of Commons for an offence against them was in the same terms, "for a high contempt of this House." Mr. Justice Wright says in that case, "that it was agreed on all hands that they (the House of Commons) have power to judge of their own privileges. It need not appear to us what the contempt was; for if it did appear, we could not judge thereof"; And then he cites Lord Shaftesbury's case. Mr. Justice Dennison says, "They need not tell us what the contempt was, because we cannot judge of it." Mr. Justice Foster says, "The law of Parliament is part of the law of the land, and there would be an end of all law, if the House of Commons could not commit for a contempt: all courts of record, even the lowest, may commit for a contempt: and Lord Holt, though he differed with the other judges, yet agreed that the House might commit for a contempt in the face of the House." That statement of Mr. Justice Foster certainly represents Lord Holt as having narrowed his admission far beyond what he appears to have done by Lord Raymond's report. The power of committing for contempts is not there limited by Lord Holt to contempts committed in the face of the House. I do not know how those words got into Wilson's report; but the report of Lord Holt's own words, as made by Lord Raymond, who heard them, is more likely to be correct. Upon this case I would observe, that I agree with Wright and Dennison, Justices, in thinking, that it *need* not appear what the contempt was; but I am not prepared to say with them, that we could in *no case* judge of it, or that there might not appear such a cause of commitment as, coming collaterally before the Court in the way of a justification pleaded to an action of trespass, the Court might not be obliged to consider and to pronounce to be defective: but it might be a more doubtful question whether, coming directly before us, as on a return to a habeas corpus, we could relieve the subject from the commitment of the House in any case whatever. . . .

(The account of Brass Crosby's case is omitted. See p. 337.)

Now to what extent it may be warrantable to inquire into the cause of commitment, it is not necessary to pronounce: the commitment must always be by a Court of competent jurisdiction; and the competence of the House of Commons to commit for a contempt and breach of privilege cannot be questioned. A competence to commit for all matters and in all cases has never been asserted or pretended to on the part of either House of Parliament: the House of Commons does not pretend to a general criminal jurisdiction. But if the judges before whom those applications were made on writs of habeas corpus had felt that the House had no pretence of power to commit, or had seen upon the face of the returns that they had exercised it in those cases extravagantly, and beyond all bounds of reason and law, would they not have been wanting in their duty if they had not looked into the causes of commitment stated? . . . Upon this subject I will only say that if a commitment appeared to be for a *contempt* of the House of Commons *generally*, I would neither in the case of that Court, or of any other of the superior Courts, inquire further: but if it did not *profess* to commit *for a contempt* of the Court committing, but a ground of commitment palpably and evidently arbitrary, unjust, and contrary to every principle of positive law, or national justice; I say, that in the case of such commitment, (if it ever should occur, but which I cannot possibly anticipate as ever likely to occur,) we must look at it and act upon it as justice may require from whatever Court it may profess to have proceeded. . . .

Thus the matter stands upon the authority of precedents in parliament, upon the recognition by statute, upon the continued recognition of all the judges, and particularly of Lord Holt, who was one of the greatest favourers of the liberties of the people, and as strict an advocate for the authority of the common law against the privileges of parliament as ever existed. . . . What is there against it? Is it inexpedient that they should have such a power? . . . I have already said that a priori, if there were no precedents upon the subject, no legislative recognition, no practice or opinions in the Courts of law recognizing such an authority, it would still be essentially necessary for the Houses of Parliament to have it; indeed that they would sink into utter contempt and inefficiency without it. Could it be expected that they should stand high in the estimation and reverence of the people, if, whenever they were insulted, they were obliged to await the comparatively slow proceedings of the ordinary course of law for their redress? That the Speaker with his mace should be under the necessity of going before a grand jury to prefer a bill of indictment for the insult offered to the House? They certainly must have the power of self-vindication and self-protection in their own hands; and if there be any authenticity in the recorded precedents of Parliament, any force in the recognition of the legislature, and in the decisions of the Courts of law, they have such power.

Assuming then that the House has the power of commitment, the next point is whether it has been well exercised by the warrant

in question. . . . But if it be clear, as it is, that this was a matter
which the House were competent to decide both as to the fact and
the effect of the publication; then by analogy to the judgement
of a Court of law, (and the judgements of either House of Parliament
cannot with propriety be put upon a footing less authoritative than
those of the ordinary Courts of law,) the House must be considered
as having decided both, as far as respects any question thereupon
which may arise in other Courts. . . .

Supposing then a power of commitment for breach of privilege to
exist in the House, and that the warrant itself discloses a sufficient
ground of commitment, and an order to their officer to execute it,
the justification for the persons acting under it is made out, unless
any unjustifiable means appear to have been afterwards used to carry
the warrant into execution. And that brings me to the last point
to be considered, whether the means which appear to have been used
on this occasion for the execution of the Speaker's warrant were
justifiable? And that depends upon the single question, Whether,
after notice given by the Sergeant at Arms of the purpose of his
coming to the plaintiff's house, and the nature of the warrant he
came to execute, and after a request, made by him, that the outer
door might be opened to him, which was not complied with, he was
authorized to break into the House for the purpose of arresting the
plaintiff, and carrying the warrant into full execution? . . . Therefore upon authorities the most unquestionable this point also has
been settled, that where an injury to the public has been committed
in the shape of an insult to any of the Courts of justice, on which
process of contempt is issued, the officer charged with the execution
of such process may break open doors if necessary in order to
execute it. And therefore, upon these authorities, I conceive myself
justified in saying, that all the points essential to be maintained in
order to sustain the defendant's justification upon this record are
made out. First, it is made out that the power of the House of
Commons to commit for contempt stands upon the ground of reason
and necessity independent of any positive authorities on the subject:
but it is also made out by the evidence of usage and practice, by
legislative sanction and recognition, and by the judgements of the
Courts of law, in a long course of well-established precedents and
authorities. 2dly, That the resolution of the House, that the
plaintiff had been guilty of a breach of its privileges, and that the
order made for his commitment for that offence, were in conformity
to their power: that the warrant issued by the Speaker in this case,
which warrant itself embraces the resolution and order of the House,

was made in the due execution of their order: and that the mode of executing that warrant in this case, by breaking the house, after due notification and demand of admittance without effect, is justifiable, upon the ground of its being an execution for a process of contempt, to which the personal privilege of the individual in respect to his door must give way for the public good. Under these circumstances, without the least particle of doubt upon my mind, I am clearly of opinion that there must be a judgement for the defendant.

(From Lord Ellenborough's judgment, East's Reports, xiv. 132 *et seq.*)

XXV

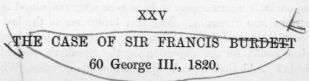

THE CASE OF SIR FRANCIS BURDETT
60 George III., 1820.

[This was a trial for seditious libel. On August 22, 1819, Sir F. Burdett, M.P., addressed a letter from Leicestershire to the electors of Westminster, whom he represented in Parliament, commenting with great severity on the conduct of the authorities in dispersing a meeting held on August 19, in S. Peter's Field, Manchester, and the government prosecuted him for the expressions used in that letter. The case was tried at the Spring Assizes at Leicester before Best, J., on March 20, 1820, when the jury found Burdett guilty. Subsequently a motion was made in the King's Bench before Abbot, C.J., and Best, Holroyd, and Bayley, JJ., for a new trial, but the court, after elaborate judgments, refused to grant it, and Burdett was sentenced to a fine of £2,000 and imprisonment for three months. The excerpts are intended to illustrate the interpretation of seditious libel given by the judges, particularly with reference to "Fox' Libel Act." See for the whole trial S.T. (N.S.) i. 1–170.]

The question is not, nor ever can be (if the liberty of the press is to be supported), whether that which has been written be true or false; because then a man meaning honestly might be convicted for stating an untruth. It is not the truth or falsehood that makes a libel, but the temper with which it is published; and another ground on which the truth or falsehood cannot be inquired into is this: because whether it be true or false no man ought to charge another with crime. That would make the liberty of the press inconsistent with another liberty equally dear to an Englishman—his character. No man's character is to be taken from him by attacks in newspapers or any publication whatever. If they do what is wrong, you were properly told by the learned counsel in the outset, the courts of justice are open to bring them to punishment. It is on these grounds I refused the evidence,[1] because according to the law of the land it is not admissible. Gentlemen, there is another point touched on, and that is the question of intention. Gentlemen, intention is undoubtedly a matter of importance in the inquiry; but whether a man intends to publish a libel or not is not to be collected from declarations and acts of another time, but from the paper itself, unless the defendant is in a condition to repel by evidence the inference immediately arising from the paper. The defendant has given you in his speech his notions of how that might be done. Suppose the paper libellous; yet if he had shown after he had written it he endeavoured to stop the publication, that would repel the libellous intention. Or suppose, as in the other case, the case of the Seven Bishops, where it was charged to be a malicious libel, the defendant could prove it was not published by a man intruding his opinions upon the public, but it was a petition addressed by him to his Sovereign on a subject on which he was called on to advise. This is the way intention is to be inquired into. It is to be collected from facts connected with the publication, and not by what the defendant is proved to have said at another time. . . .

Gentlemen, with respect to Locke I quite agree with the observation that has been made; and if when you come by-and-by to attend to this libel, you think this paper was written with the same pure spirit and intention with which the invaluable and immortal works of that writer were written, it is no libel, because they are protected by the true liberty of the press, which is nothing more than this— it is said without the liberty of the press a free Government cannot be supported—the liberty of the press is this, that you may communicate any information that you think proper to communicate by print; that you may point out to the Government their errors, and endeavour to convince them their system of policy is wrong, and attended with disadvantage to the country, and that another system of politics would be attended with benefit. It is from such writings that the religion of this country has been purified; it is by writings of that spirit the Constitution has been brought to the perfection it now has. And, therefore, God forbid that I should utter a sentence to show that a man, speaking with that respect which he ought to speak with of established institutions, may not show some reform may be necessary, or that the military ought not to be used in the manner in which they are. . . .

[1] *i.e.* relating to what had taken place at the Manchester meeting.

2 B

Gentlemen, here (in a passage quoted from the alleged libel) there is nothing directly charged, but there is a great deal insinuated.

" 'Tis true James could not inflict the torture on his soldiers—could not tear the living flesh from their bones with a cat-o'-nine-tails—could not flay them alive."

Insinuating, undoubtedly, that it may and can be done now. Will any man tell me that is temperate discussion ? Will any man tell me that a thing more pregnant with mischief could be published ? Do not suppose I think the Government rests on the army,—it rests on the affections of the people. And I believe it will be a long time before any set of persons can so far detach the people from the Government as to render it insecure. But, although the Government is secure, when insurrections take place, the soldiers are wanted to assist the magistrates. Therefore, at a moment like this, to put them in mind of circumstances likely to paralyse them in the discharge of their duty, is the most dangerous libel that could be circulated. It was published—it would find its way into the hands of the soldiers as well as into the hands of gentlemen; and to-day we are told that the same soldiers that fought for Cæsar abroad destroyed the liberties of their country. They fought abroad to establish a domination in a foreign land. The British army has been used for no such purpose. It has fought for the establishment of our nation, and on all these occasions it is known that the discipline which exists in that army has not destroyed its spirit. It is, thank God, what it was, still; and they will meet again with the same spirit when called on on a future occasion, and I hope and trust, whether men mean it or not, no man will be able to render a British soldier other than he is, one of the most respectable. The passage concludes with a profanation of the words used by Nelson immediately before the battle of Trafalgar, "Be this as it may, our duty is to meet, and England expects every man to do his duty." Gentlemen, I have no hesitation in declaring this a libel. Is it a calm appeal to the judgement of the people, or a most inflammatory paper addressed to the passions of those whose passions are most likely to be acted upon ?

(From the charge of Best, J., to the jury in the first trial.)

Another point on which the motion for a new trial was made was, that I took upon myself to lay down the law to the jury as to the libel, and that since the statute 32 Geo. 3. c. 60.[1] I was not warranted in so doing. I told the jury that they were to consider

[1] "Fox' Libel Act" (see p. 156).

whether the paper was published with the intent charged in the information; and that if they thought it was published with that intent, I was of opinion that it was a libel. I, however, added that they were to decide whether they would adopt my opinion. In forming their opinion on the question of libel, I told the jury that they were to consider whether the paper contained a sober address to the reason of mankind, or whether it was an appeal to their passions, calculated to incite them to acts of violence and outrage. If it was of the former description, it was not a libel; if of the latter description, it was. It must not be supposed that the statute of George the Third made the question of libel a question of fact. If it had, instead of removing an anomaly it would have created one. Libel is a question of law, and the judge is the judge of the law in libel as in all other cases, the jury having the power of acting agreeably to his statement of the law or not. All that the statute does is to prevent the question from being left to the jury in the narrow way in which it was left before that time. The jury were then only to find the fact of the publication, and the truth of the innuendoes; for the judges used to tell them that the intent was an inference of law, to be drawn from the paper, with which the jury had nothing to do. The Legislature has said that that is not so, but that the whole case is to be left to the jury. But the judges are in express terms directed to lay down the law as in other cases. In all cases the jury may find a general verdict; they do so in cases of murder and treason, but there the judge tells them what is the law, though they may find against him; unless they are satisfied with his opinion. And this is plain from the words of the statute.[1] . . .

My opinion of the liberty of the press is, that every man ought to be permitted to instruct his fellow subjects; that every man may fearlessly advance any new doctrines, provided he does so with proper respect to the religion and Government of the country; that he may point out errors in the measures of public men; but he must not impute criminal conduct to them. The liberty of the press cannot be carried to this extent without violating another equally sacred right, namely, the right of character. This right can only be attacked in a court of justice, where the party attacked has a fair opportunity of defending himself. Where vituperation begins, the liberty of the press ends. This maxim was acted upon by the greatest states of antiquity. In our country, the liberty of the press allows us to persuade men to use their constitutional influence over their representatives to obtain in the regular parliamentary manner a redress of real

[1] "Fox' Libel Act" (see p. 156).

or supposed grievances. But this must be done with temper and moderation, otherwise instead of setting the Government in motion for the people, the people may be set in motion against the Government. . . .

(From the judgment of Best, J., in the application for a new trial.)

With respect to the objection of the learned Judge's refusing to receive evidence of the truth of the facts alleged, or rather assumed in the libel, there is, I think, not the least doubt upon the point. Although the objection was made, it was not even attempted to be supported by argument at the trial. Whatever might be the result of a due inquiry into those facts elsewhere, it is clear that that was not the proper place or occasion for inquiring into them, nor would the writing be otherwise than in law a libel. It assumes as true a statement most highly calumnious on individuals, and on the Government, merely from a statement in a public newspaper, and without the knowledge, whether it were true or not, to any or to what extent, and indulges in the highest strain of invective, for the purpose of inflaming the public, and raising in their minds the greatest discontent, disaffection, and alarm. That is, in itself, a seditious libel, and the question for the jury was, whether what the defendant had written and published, with the intent stated in the information, was a libel or not, and not to what extent it was so; even supposing that the result of that inquiry would have any palliation of the libel. With respect to the objections taken to the learned Judge's having given his opinion and directions to the jury upon the question, whether the writing was a libel or not, it seems to me that he left it to them to consider, whether they would adopt his opinion in that respect or not; and he is expressly directed, by the statute of the 32d of the late King, according to his discretion, to give his opinion and directions to the jury on the matter in issue, in like manner as in other criminal cases. And with respect to the objections to his summing up, I do not, upon an attentive consideration of it, find any reason to disagree with his observations in that respect.

(From the judgment of Holroyd, J., in the application for a new trial.)

I also entirely agree that the learned judge did right in intimating to the jury his opinion on the question, whether this was or was not a libel, and in telling them that they were to take the law from him, unless they were satisfied he was wrong. The old rule of law is, ad quæstionem juris respondent judices, ad quæstionem facti respondent juratores; and I take it to be the bounden duty of the judge to lay down the law as it strikes him, and that of the jury to accede to it, unless they have superior knowledge on the subject : and the direction in this case did not take away from the jury the power of acting on their own judgement. Besides, if the judge be mistaken in his view of the law, his mistake may be set right by a motion for a new trial ; but if the jury are wrong in their view of it, it is not so easy to rectify their mistake. . . .

(From the judgment of Bayley, J.)

Another ground for the motion was, that the learned Judge gave his own opinion to the jury upon the character of the publication in question, expressing himself at the same time somewhat to this effect : You are to say whether you will adopt this opinion or not ; and unless you are satisfied that I am wrong, you will take the law from me. This was supposed to be contrary to, or at least beyond, the duty of the Judge, as prescribed by the statute to which I have just alluded ; it was, however, in my opinion, not only not contrary to, or beyond, the duty of the Judge, as prescribed by that statute, but in strict conformity to it. The clauses of the statute have been referred to. If the Judge is to give his opinion to the jury, it must be not only competent but proper for him to tell the jury, if the case will so warrant that in his opinion the publication before them is of the character and tendency attributed to it by the indictment ; and that, if it be so in their opinion, the publication is an offence against the law. This has been repeatedly done by different Judges within my experience, and I am not aware of any instance in which it has been omitted. The contrary has sometimes occurred, in cases where the Judge has thought that the matter of the publication was innocent ; but those cases also are instances of an opinion given, and not of silence on the part of the Judge, as to the law of the case. The statute was not intended to confine the matter in issue exclusively to the jury without hearing the opinion of the Judge, but to declare that they should be at liberty to exercise their own judgement upon the whole matter in issue, after receiving thereupon the opinions and directions of the Judge. For these reasons I am of opinion that the rule ought to be discharged.

(From the judgment of Abbot, C.J.)

Best, J. : I entirely agree with my Lord Chief Justice and my brother Holroyd in the opinion that, if a libel be written in one county and published in another, the libeller may be prosecuted in either.

XXVI

THE CASES OF THE BRISTOL RIOTS, 1831-2.

[On October 29, 30, 31, 1831, there had been riots at Bristol, and a special Commission was sent down to try the prisoners concerned in these riots. The various trials furnished some very important rulings from the Bench on the nature of Riot, and the legal relations of the subject to the executive. See S.T. (N.S.) iii. 2-567; *Broom*, C.L. 521-795; *Dicey*, L.C. *passim*.]

I

The law of England hath, accordingly, in proportion to the danger which it attaches to riotous and disorderly meetings of the people, made an ample provision for preventing such offences, and for the prompt and effectual suppression of them when they arise. . . . In the first place by the common law, every private person may lawfully endeavour, of his own authority, and without any warrant or sanction of the magistrate to suppress a riot by every means in his power. He may disperse, or assist in dispersing, those who are assembled; he may stay those who are engaged in it from executing their purpose; he may stop and prevent others whom he shall see coming up with the rest; and not only has he the authority, but it is his bounden duty, as a good subject of the King to perform this to the utmost of his ability. If the riot be general and dangerous, he may arm himself against the evildoers, to keep the peace. Such was the opinion of all the judges of England in the time of Queen Elizabeth, in a case called 'the Case of Armes,' (Popham's Rep. 121) although the judges add that it would be more discreet for everyone in such a case to attend and be assistant to the justices, sheriffs, or other ministers of the King, in the doing of it.

It would undoubtedly be more advisable so to do; for the presence and authority of the magistrate would restrain the proceedings to such extremities, until the danger was sufficiently immediate, or until some felony was either committed, or could not be prevented without recourse to arms; and at all events, the assistance given by men who act in subordination and concert with the civil magistrate, will be more effectual to attain the object proposed, than any efforts, however well intended, of separated and disunited individuals. But if the occasion demands immediate action, and no opportunity is given for procuring the advice or sanction of the magistrate, it is the duty of every subject to act for himself, and upon his own responsibility.

in suppressing a riotous and tumultuous assembly; and he may be assured that whatever is honestly done by him in the execution of that object will be supported and justified by the Common Law. And whilst I am stating the obligation imposed by the law on every subject of the realm, I wish to observe that the law acknowledges no distinction in this respect between the soldier and the private citizen. The soldier is still a citizen, lying under the same obligation, and invested with the same authority, to preserve the peace of the King, as any other subject. If the one is bound to attend the call of the civil magistrate, so also is the other; if the one may interfere for that purpose, when the occasion demands it, without the requisition of the magistrate, so may the other too; if the one may employ arms for that purpose, when arms are necessary, the soldier may do the same. Undoubtedly, the same exercise of discretion which requires the private subject to act in subordination to, and in aid of, the magistrate ought to operate in a still stronger degree with a military force. But where the danger is pressing and immediate, where a felony has actually been committed, or cannot otherwise be prevented, and from the circumstances of the case no opportunity is offered of obtaining a requisition from the proper authorities, the military subjects of the King, like his civil subjects, not only may, but are bound, to do their utmost, of their own authority, to prevent the perpetration of outrage, to put down riot and tumult, and to preserve the lives and property of the people. . . . Gentlemen, still further, by the Common Law, not only is each subject bound to exert himself to the utmost, but every sheriff, constable, and other peace officer is called upon to do all that in them lies for the suppression of riot, and each has authority to command all other subjects of the King to assist them in the undertaking. By an early statute, which is still in force (the 13 Hen. 4. c. 7), any two justices, together with the sheriff or under-sheriff of the county, shall come with the power of the county, if need be, to arrest any rioters, and shall arrest them; and they have power to record that which they see done in their presence against the law, by which record the offenders shall be convicted, and may afterwards be brought to punishment. And here I most distinctly observe that it is not left to the choice or will of the subject, as some have erroneously supposed, to attend or not to attend to the call of the magistrate, as they think proper; but every man is bound, when called upon, under pain of fine or imprisonment, to yield a ready and implicit obedience to the call of the magistrate, and to do his utmost in assisting him to suppress any tumultuous assembly; for in the succeeding reign another statute was passed, which enacts that the King's liege people, being sufficient to travel in the counties where such routs, assemblies, or riots be, shall be assistant to the justices, commissioners, sheriffs, and other officers upon reasonable warning . . . to ride with them in aid to resist such riots, routs, and assemblies, on pain of imprisonment, and to make fine and ransom to the king (2 Hen. V. st. 1. c. 8). . . . In later times the course has been for the magistrate, on occasion of actual riot and confusion, to call in the aid of such persons as he thought necessary, and to swear them as special constables. And in order to prevent any doubt, if doubt could exist, as to his power to command their assistance by way of precaution, the statute 1 Geo. 4. c. 37, and since that has been repealed by the still more recent Act of 1 and 2 Will. 4. c. 41, the statute last referred to has invested the magistrate with that power in direct and express terms, when tumult, riot, or felony, was only likely to take place, or might reasonably be apprehended. Again, that this call of the magistrate is compulsory, and not left to the choice of the party to obey or not, appears from the express enactment in the latter Act, that, if he disobeys, unless legally exempted, he is liable to the penalties and punishments therein specified.

But the most important provision of the law for the suppression of riots is to be found in the statute 1 Geo. 3. st. 2. c. 5. by which it is enacted. (Here follow the main clauses of "the Riot Act."[1])

. . . Such are the different provisions of the law of England for the putting down of tumultuary meetings; and it is not too much to affirm that if the means provided by the law are promptly and judicially enforced by the magistrate, and honestly seconded by the co-operation of his fellow-subjects, very few and rare would be the instances in which tumultuous assemblages of the people would be able to hold defiance to the laws.

(From the charge of Tindal, C.J., head of the Special Commission, to the grand jury, S.T. (N.S.), iii. 4–7.)

II

You will take into consideration the circumstances in which a man is placed. He is bound to hit the exact line between an excess and what is sufficient . . . in point of law he is bound to do it . . . the law requires that, whether a man seeks an office or is compelled to accept it, he should do his best. . . . A man is bound by law to do his duty, and you are to consider whether he has done his duty or

[1] See p. 113.

not. . . . Has the defendant done all that he knew was in his power to suppress the riots, that could reasonably be expected from a man of honesty, and ordinary prudence and activity, under the circumstances in which he was placed ? . . . Did he use those means that the law requires to assemble a sufficient force to prevent the mischief that an honest man ought to have done, by his own personal exertion? . . . I lay down to you as the general duty of justices as to riots; they are to keep the peace and to pursue and arrest rioters; and to enable them to do that they are empowered to call upon the King's subjects to aid them in suppressing riots when they shall be reasonably required. Therefore in the case of riot, the Common Law obligation upon a justice is to call upon the King's subjects to aid him in suppressing the riot. . . . You will have to consider whether that has been done upon this occasion. . . .

(From the charge of Littledale, J., to the jury in *Rex v. Pinney* (the Mayor of Bristol). Pinney, it should be noted, was charged with wilful neglect of his duty as magistrate, to suppress, or aid in suppressing, the riot in question. The trial took place in the Court of King's Bench, October 25, 1832, and the jury brought in a verdict of Not Guilty.)

III

It appears from the evidence of Mr. Stallwood that the proclamation contained in the Riot Act was not read. Now, a riot is not the less a riot nor an illegal meeting the less an illegal meeting because the proclamation of the Riot Act has not been read, the effect of that proclamation being to make the parties guilty of a capital offence, if they do not disperse within an hour; but, if that proclamation be not read, the common law offence remains, and it is a misdemeanour, and all magistrates, constables and even private individuals are justified in dispersing the offenders; and if they cannot otherwise succeed in doing so, they may use force. . . .

(From the charge to the jury of Gaselee, J., in *Rex v. Fursey*, July 4, 1833. S.T. (N.S.), iii. pp. 565, 566.)

IV

(As a supplement to the rulings in the cases arising out of the Bristol Riots, the salient passages from the Report on the Featherstone Riots in 1893 are here cited, because they express with great clearness and force the law relating to the subject.)

We pass next to the consideration of the all-important question whether the conduct of the troops in firing on the crowd was justifiable; and it becomes essential for the sake of clearness to state succinctly what is the law which bears upon the subject. By the law of this country everyone is bound to aid in the suppression of riotous assemblies. The degree of force however which may be lawfully used in their suppression depends on the nature of each riot, for the force used must always be moderated and proportioned to the circumstances of the case and to the end to be attained.

The taking of life can only be justified by the necessity for protecting persons or property against various forms of violent crime, or by the necessity of dispersing a riotous crowd which is dangerous unless dispersed, or in the case of persons whose conduct has become felonious through disobedience to the provisions of the Riot Act, and who resist the attempt to disperse or apprehend them. . . . The necessary prevention of such outrage on person or property justifies the guardians of the peace in the employment against a riotous crowd of even deadly weapons. Officers and soldiers are under no special privileges and subject to no special responsibilities as regards this principle of the law. A soldier for the purpose of establishing civil order is only a citizen armed in a particular manner. He cannot because he is a soldier excuse himself if without necessity he takes human life. The duty of magistrates and peace officers to summon or to abstain from summoning the assistance of the military depends in like manner on the necessities of the case. A soldier can only act by using his arms. The weapons he carries are deadly. They cannot be employed at all without danger to life and limb, and in these days of improved rifles and perfected ammunition without some danger of injuring distant and possibly innocent bystanders. To call for assistance against rioters from those who can only interpose under such grave conditions ought, of course, to be the last expedient of the civil authorities. But when the call for help is made, and a necessity for assistance from the military has arisen, to refuse such assistance is in law a misdemeanour.

The whole action of the military when called in ought, from first to last, to be based on the principle of doing, and doing without fear, that which is absolutely necessary to prevent serious crime, and of exercising all care and skill with regard to what is done. No set of rules exists which governs every instance or defines beforehand every contingency that may arise. One salutary practice is that a magistrate should accompany the troops. The presence of a magistrate on such occasions, though not a legal obligation, is a matter of the highest importance. The military come, it may be, from a distance. They know nothing, probably of the locality, or of the special circumstances. They find themselves introduced suddenly on a field of action, and they need the council of the local justice, who is presumably familiar with the details of the case. But, although the magistrate's presence is of the highest value and importance, his absence does not alter the duty of the soldier, nor ought it to paralyse his conduct, but only to render him doubly careful as to the proper steps to be taken. No officer is justified by English law in standing by and allowing felonious outrage to be committed merely because of a magistrate's absence.

The question whether, on any occasion, the moment has come for firing upon a mob of rioters, depends, as we have said, on the necessities of the case. Such firing to be lawful, must . . . be necessary to stop or prevent such serious and violent crime as we have alluded to ; and it must be conducted without recklessness or negligence. When the need is clear, the soldier's duty is to fire with all reasonable caution, so as to produce no further injury than what is absolutely wanted for the purpose of protecting person or property. An order from the magistrate who is present is required by military regulations, and wisdom and discretion are entirely in favour of the observance of such a practice. But the order of the magistrate has at law no legal effect. Its presence does not justify the firing if the magistrate is wrong. Its absence does not excuse the officer for declining to fire when the necessity exists.

With the above doctrines of English law the Riot Act does not interfere. Its effect is only to make the failure of a crowd to disperse for a whole hour after the proclamation has been read a felony ; and on this ground to afford statutory justification for dispersing a felonious assemblage, even at the risk of taking life. In the case of the Ackton Hall Colliery, an hour had not elapsed after what is popularly called the reading of the Riot Act, before the military fired. No justification for their firing can therefore be rested upon the provisions of the Riot Act itself, the further consideration of which may indeed be here dismissed from the case. But the fact that an hour had not expired since its reading did not incapacitate the troops from acting when an outrage had to be prevented. All their common law duty as citizens and soldiers remained in full force. The justification of captain Barker and his men must stand or fall entirely by the common law. Was what they did necessary, and no more than was necessary, to put a stop to or prevent felonious crime ? In doing it did they exercise all ordinary skill and caution, so as to do no more harm than could be reasonably avoided ? If these two conditions are made out, the fact that innocent people have suffered does not involve the troops in legal responsibility. A guilty ringleader who under such conditions is shot dead, dies by justifiable homicide. An innocent person killed under such conditions, the where no negligence has occurred, dies by an accidental death. The legal reason is not that the innocent person has to thank himself for what has happened, for it is conceivable (though not often likely) that he may have been unconscious of any danger and innocent of all imprudence. The reason is that the soldier who fired has done nothing except what was his strict legal duty.

The Report was signed by

(Lord Justice) BOWEN
ALBERT K. ROLLIT
R. B. HALDANE.

(Parliamentary Papers, c. 7234, December 6, 1893.)

XXVII

STOCKDALE v. HANSARD

2 Victoria, 1839.

[This was an action, or series of actions, in which the plaintiff, John Joseph Stockdale, sued Messrs. Hansard, the printers to the House of Commons, for libels contained in Parliamentary Papers, viz. "Reports of the Inspector of Prisons of Great Britain." The defendant, represented by the Attorney-General at the request of the House, pleaded the previous authority and order of the House of Commons for the publication, and a resolution of the House (after action brought) declaring its power to authorise the publication of such of its reports, notes, and proceedings as it should deem necessary or conducive to the public interest. The action for libel was tried before Lord Denman, C.J., and a special jury on February 7, 1837, and resulted in a verdict for the plaintiff. The second action arose out of a demurrer which was argued before Lord Denman, C.J., and Justices Littledale, Paterson, and Coleridge on April 23, 24, 25, May 28 and 31, and judgment was given on May 31, 1837. The court held that: (1) it had jurisdiction to inquire into the existence and extent of the privilege or power alleged in the plea; (2) the resolution and declaration of the House of Commons did not prevent the court from such inquiry; (3) the privileges of the House did not include the power to authorise the publication of the libel to the general public as distinguished from the members of the House; (4) declarations of the House of its own privileges ought to be treated with all possible respect as authorities, but were not conclusive. Judgment was accordingly given for the plaintiff, Stockdale. The extracts given are (a) the resolutions of the House of Commons in question; and (b) passages from the

Judge's decision illustrative of the view taken by the court. The other three actions which arose out of this are of purely technical interest. A full report of all five actions will be found in State Trials (New Series), iii. pp. 723 *et seq*. As a result of the judicial decisions an Act of Parliament was passed (3 and 4 Vict. c. 9), in virtue of which in respect of publications ordered by either House of Parliament any person may produce before a court of law a certificate from the Lord Chancellor or the Speaker of the House of Commons that the publication was under the authority of the House of Lords or House of Commons, and such court shall then stay all proceedings. For the whole question see *Anson*, L.C. i. pp. 169-177 ; *Erskine May*, C.H. ii. ; *Porritt*, U.H.C. i. 584-596 ; *Broom*, C.L. 875-983.]

RESOLUTIONS OF THE HOUSE OF COMMONS

Resolved, That the power of publishing such of its reports, notes and proceedings as it shall deem necessary or conducive to the public interests is an essential incident to the constitutional function of Parliament, more especially of this House, as the representative portion of it.

Resolved, That by the law and privilege of Parliament, this House has the sole and exclusive jurisdiction to determine upon the existence and extent of its privileges ; and that the institution or prosecution of any action, suit, or other proceeding, for the purpose of bringing them into discussion or decision, before any court or tribunal elsewhere than in Parliament is a high breach of such privilege, and renders all parties concerned therein amenable to its just displeasure and to the punishment consequent thereon.

Resolved, That for any court or tribunal to assume to decide upon matters of privilege inconsistent with the determination of either House of Parliament thereon is contrary to the law of Parliament, and is a breach and contempt of the privileges of Parliament.

(C.J. May 31, 1837, xcii. 419.)

Lord Denman, C.J. : This was an action for a publication defaming the plaintiff's character, by imputing that he had published an obscene libel. The plea was that the inspectors of prisons made a report to the Secretary of State, in which improper books were said to be permitted in the prison of Newgate ; that the Court of Aldermen wrote an answer to that part of the report, and the inspectors replied repeating the statements, and adding that the improper books were published by the plaintiff. That all these documents were printed by and under orders from the House of Commons, who had come to a resolution to publish and sell all the papers they should print for the use of the Members, and who also resolved, declared, and adjudged that the power of publishing such of their reports, votes, and proceeding as they thought conducive to the public interest, is an essential incident to the due performance of the functions of Parliament, more especially, etc. The plea, it is contended, establishes a good defence to the action on various grounds.

1. The grievance complained of appears to be an act done by order of the House of Commons, a court superior to any court of law, and none of whose proceedings are to be questioned in any way. This principle the learned counsel for the defendant repeatedly avowed in his long and laboured argument; but it does not appear to be put forward in its simple terms in the report that was published by a former House of Commons.

It is a claim for an arbitrary power to authorise the commission for any act whatever on behalf of a body which in the same argument is admitted not to be the supreme power in the State.

The supremacy of Parliament, the foundation upon which the claim is made to rest, appears to me to completely overturn it, because the House of Commons is not the Parliament, but only a co-ordinate and component part of the Parliament. That sovereign power can make or unmake the laws; but the concurrence of the three legislative estates is necessary : the resolution of any one of them cannot alter the law or place anyone beyond its control. The proposition, is, therefore, wholly untenable, and abhorrent to the first principles of the constitution of England.

2. The next defence involved in this plea is that the defendant committed the grievance by order of the House of Commons in a case of privilege, and that each House of Parliament is the sole judge of its own privileges. This last proposition requires to be first considered. For, if the *Attorney General* was right in contending, as he did more than once in express terms, that the House of Commons, by claiming anything as its privilege thereby makes it a matter of privilege, and also that its own decision upon its own claim is binding and conclusive, then plainly this court cannot proceed in any inquiry into the matter, and has nothing else to do but declare the claim well founded because it has been made.

This is the form in which I understand the committee of a late House of Commons to have asserted the privileges of both Houses of Parliament, and we are informed that a large majority of that House adopted the assertion. It is not without the utmost respect and deference that I proceed to examine what has been promulgated by such high authority : most willingly would I decline to enter upon an enquiry which may lead to my differing from that great and powerful assembly. But when one of my fellow subjects presents himself before me in this Court demanding justice for an injury, it is not at my option to grant or withhold redress ; I am bound to afford it if the law declares him entitled to it. I must then ascertain how the law stands, and, whatever defence may be made for the wrongdoer, I must examine its validity. The learned counsel for the defendant contends for his legal right to be protected against all consequences of acting under an order issued by the House of Commons in conformity with what that House asserts to be its privilege : nor can I avoid then the question whether the defendant possesses that legal right or not.

Parliament is said to be supreme ; I must fully acknowledge its supremacy. It follows, then, as before observed, that neither branch of it is supreme when acting by itself. It is also said that the privilege of each House is the privilege of the whole Parliament. For one sense I agree to this, because whatever impedes the proper action of either impedes those functions which are necessary for the performance of their joint duties. All the essential parts of a machine must be in order before it can work at all. But it by no means follows that the opinion that either House may entertain of the extent of its own privileges is correct, or its declaration of them binding. In the course of the argument the privileges of the Commons were said to belong to them for their protection against encroachment by the Lords. The fact of an attempt at encroaching may then be imagined, and we must also suppose that the Commons would resist it. In such a case the claims set up by the two Houses being inconsistent both could not be well founded, and an instance would occur of adverse opinions and declarations, while the real privilege, whenever it is ascertained, would certainly be the inherent right of Parliament itself. . . .

But it is said that the courts of law must be excluded from all interference from transactions in which the name of privilege has been mentioned, because they have no means of informing themselves what these privileges are. They are well known, it seems, to the two Houses, and to every member of them, as long as he continues a member ; but the knowledge is as incommunicable as the privileges to all beyond that pale. It might be presumption to ask how this knowledge may be obtained, had not the *Attorney General* read to us all he had to urge on the subject from works accessible to all, and familiar to every man of education. The argument here seems to run in a circle. The courts cannot be trusted with any matter connected with privilege, because they know nothing about privilege; and this ignorance must be perpetual, because the law has taken such matters out of their cognizance. The old text writers, indeed, affirm the law and custom of parliament, although a part of the *lex terræ*, to be, "*ab omnibus quæsita, a multis ignorata.*" This and other phrases, repeated in the law books, have thrown a kind of mystery over the subject, which has kept aloof the application of reason and common sense. Lord Holt, in terms denied this presumption of ignorance, and asserted the right and duty of the courts to know the law of Parliament, because the law of the land on which they are bound to decide. Other judges, without directly asserting the proposition, have constantly acted upon it; and it was distinctly admitted by the *Attorney General* in the course of his argument. I do not know to whom he alluded as disputing the existence of any parliamentary privilege; no such opinion has come under my notice. That Parliament enjoys privileges of the most important character, no person capable of the least reflection can doubt for a moment. Some are common to both Houses, some peculiar to each; all are essential to the discharge of their functions. If they were not the fruit of deliberation in *aulâ regiâ*, they rest on the stronger ground of a necessity which became apparent at least as soon as the two Houses took their present position in the State. . . .

The privilege of committing for contempt is inherent in every deliberative body invested with authority by the constitution. But, however flagrant the contempt, the House of Commons can only commit till the close of the existing session. Their privilege to commit is not better known than this limitation of it. Though the party should deserve the severest penalties, yet, his offence being committed the day before a prorogation, if the House ordered his imprisonment but for a week, every court in Westminster Hall and every judge of all the courts would be bound to discharge him by *habeas corpus.* . . .

3. I come at length to consider whether this privilege of publication exists. The plea states the resolution of the House that all parliamentary reports printed for the use of the House should be sold to the public, and that these several papers were ordered to be printed, not however stating that they were printed for the use of the House. It then sets forth the resolution and adjudication before set out. We know, by looking at the documents before referred to at the bar, that this resolution and adjudication could not justify the libel complained of, because it was not in fact passed till after action brought. But, passing over all minor objections, I assume that the

defendant has properly pleaded a claim, on the part of the House, to authorise the indiscriminate publication and sale of all such papers as the House may order to be printed for the use of its members.

The *Attorney General* would preclude us from commencing this inquiry. He protests against our taking any other step than that of recording the judgment already given in the superior court, and registering the edict which *Mr. Hansard* brings to our knowledge. But, having convinced myself that the mere order of the House will not justify an act otherwise illegal, and that the simple declaration that that order is made in exercise of a privilege does not prove the privilege, it is no longer optional with me to decline or accept the office of deciding whether this privilege exist in law. If it does, the defendant's prayer must be granted and judgment awarded in his favour; or, if it does not, the plaintiff, under whatever disadvantages he may appear before us, has a right to obtain at our hands, as an English subject, the establishment of his lawful rights and the means of enforcing them. . . .

It is said the House of Commons is the sole judge of its own privileges: and so I admit so far as the proceedings in the House and some other things are concerned; but I do not think it follows that they have a power to declare what their privileges are, so as to preclude inquiry whether what they declare are part of their privileges. The *Attorney General* admits that they have not the power to create new privileges; but they declare this to be their privilege. But how are we to know that this is part of their privileges, without inquiring into it, when no such privilege was ever declared before? We must therefore be enabled to determine whether it be part of their privileges or not. . . .

The privileges of Parliament appear to me to be confined to the walls of Parliament, for what is necessary for the transaction of business there, to protect individual members so as that they may always be able to attend their duties, and to punish persons who are guilty of contempts to the House, or against the orders and proceedings or other matters relating to the House, or to individual members in discharge of their duties to the House, and to such other matters and things as are necessary to carry on their parliamentary functions; and to print documents for the use of the members. But a publication sent out to the world, though founded on and in pursuance of an order of the House, in my opinion, becomes separated from the House; it is no longer any matter of the House, but of the agents they employ to distribute the papers; those agents are not the House,

2 c

but, in my opinion they are individuals acting on their own responsibility as other publishers of papers.

I admit that, if my opinion be correct, the same question may be agitated in the inferior courts, such as the quarter sessions and county and borough courts; that, however, results from the law: if the law be so, they have the right to inquire into it.

I therefore, upon the whole of this case, again point out what Lord *Ellenborough* very much relied on in his judgment in Burdett v. Abbot,[1] when he said that—

"It is made out that the power of the House of Commons to commit for contempt stands upon the ground of reason and necessity independent of any positive authorities on the subject; but it is also made out by the evidence of usage and practice, by legislative sanction and recognition, in the courts of law, in a long course of well-established precedents and authorities."

But in the case now before the Court I think that the power of the House of Commons to order the publication of papers containing defamatory matter does not stand upon the ground of reason and necessity, independent of any positive authorities on the subject. And I also think that it is not made out by the evidence of usage and practice, by legislative sanction and recognition in the courts of law, in a long course of well-established precedents and authorities. . . .

Three questions appear to arise on this record.

First, whether an action at law will lie in any case for any act whatever admitted to have been done by the order and authority of the House of Commons.

Secondly, whether a resolution of the House of Commons, declaring that it had power to do the act complained of, precludes this court from inquiring into the legality of that act.

Thirdly, if such resolution does not preclude this Court from inquiring, then whether the act complained of be legal or not.

With respect to the first question, it has not been contended in argument that either House of Parliament can authorise any person to commit with impunity a known and undoubted breach of the law. Extravagant questions have been sometimes put, illustrating the impossibility of maintaining such a proposition. . . .

Upon the whole the true doctrine appears to me to be this, that every court in which an action is brought upon a subject-matter generally and *prima facie* within its jurisdiction, and in which, by the course of the proceedings in that action, the powers and privileges and jurisdiction of another court come into question, must

[1] See p. 356.

of necessity determine as to the extent of those powers, privileges
and jurisdiction : that the decisions of that court, whose powers,
privileges, and jurisdiction are so brought into question, as to their
extent, are authorities, and if I may say so, evidences in law upon
the subject, but not conclusive.   In the present case, therefore, both
upon principle and authority, I conceive that this Court is not precluded by the resolution of the House of Commons of May 31,
1837 from inquiring into the legality of the act complained of,
although we are bound to treat that resolution with all possible
respect, and not by any means to come to a decision contrary to that
resolution unless we find ourselves compelled to do so by the law
of the land, gathered from the principles of the common law, so far
as they are applicable to the case, and from the authority of decided
cases, and the judgments of our predecessors, if any be found which
bear upon the question. . . .

Where, then is the necessity for this power ? Privileges, that is
immunities and safeguards, are necessary for the protection of the
House of Commons, in the exercise of its high functions. All
the subjects of this realm have derived, are deriving, and I trust
and believe will continue to derive, the greatest benefits from the
exercise of those functions. All persons ought to be very tender in
preserving to the House all privileges which may be necessary for
their exercise, and to place the most implicit confidence in their
representatives as to the due exercise of those privileges. But power,
and especially the power of invading the rights of others, is a very
different thing : it is to be regarded not with tenderness but with
jealousy ; and, unless the legality of it be most clearly established,
those who act under it must be answerable for the consequences.
The onus of showing the existence and legality of the power now
claimed lies upon the defendants ; it appears to me, after a full and
anxious consideration of the reasons and authorities adduced by the
Attorney General in his learned argument, and after much reflection
upon the subject, that they have entirely failed to do so ; and I am
therefore of opinion that the plaintiff is entitled to our judgment in
his favour. . . .

But it is said that this and all other courts of law are inferior in
dignity to the House of Commons, and that, therefore, it is impossible
for us to review its decisions. This argument appears to me founded
on a misunderstanding of several particulars ; first, in what sense it is
that this court is inferior to the House of Commons ; next, in what
sense the House is a court at all ; and, lastly, in what sense we are
now assuming to meddle with any of its decisions. Vastly inferior

as this Court is to the House of Commons, considered as a body in the State, and amenable as its members may be for ill conduct in their office to its animadversions, and certainly are to its impeachment before the Lords, yet, as a court of law, we know no superior but those courts which may revise our judgments for error; and in this respect there is no common term of comparison between this Court and the House. In truth, the House is not a court of law at all, in the sense in which that term can alone be properly applied here; neither originally, nor by appeal, can it decide a matter in litigation between two parties; it has no means of doing so; it claims no such power; powers of inquiry and of accusation it has, but it decides nothing judicially, except where it is itself a party, in the case of contempts. As to them, no question of degree arises between courts; and, in the only sense, therefore, in which this argument would be of weight, it does not apply. In any other sense the argument is of no force. Considered merely as resolutions or acts, I have yet to learn that this Court is to be restrained by the dignity or the power of anybody, however exalted, from fearlessly, though respectfully, examining their reasonableness and justice, where the rights of third persons, in litigation before us, depend upon their validity. But I deny that this inquiry tends to the reversal of any decision of the House; the general resolution and the *res judicanda* are not identical; the House of Commons has never decided upon the fact on which the plaintiff tendered an issue; that argument will be found by-and-by to apply to the cases of committal for contempt, but it has no place in the consideration immediately before me.

XXVIII

THE CASE OF THE SHERIFF OF MIDDLESEX
3 Victoria, 1840.

[This was a case arising out of that of Stockdale *v.* Hansard. William Evans and John Wheelton, Sheriff of Middlesex, had been committed to the custody of the Serjeant-at-Arms, having been adjudged guilty of a contempt and breach of privilege of the House of Commons, in executing a writ issued after the judgment given in Stockdale *v.* Hansard. On January 23, 1840, R. V. Richards moved for a writ of habeas corpus. The Serjeant-at-Arms was directed by the House of Commons to make a return, stating that he "held the bodies" of W. Evans and John Wheelton, " by virtue of a warrant under the hand of Mr. Speaker for a contempt and a breach of the privilege of the House" (Com. Journ. xcv. 25); and on January 27, 1840, before Denman, C.J., and Justices Littledale, Williams, and Coleridge, it was moved that the prisoners be discharged on the ground that the return to the writ was bad. The court held that (a) a warrant for commitment by order of the House of Commons for contempt of the House need not specify the grounds of the order; (b) it would take judicial notice of the office of the Speaker of the House and his authority to give effect to its order. Judgment accordingly that the prisoners be remanded, not discharged. Wheelton was discharged out of custody on February 11, because confinement endangered his life ; but in order to maintain the claim of the House of Commons, Evans was not discharged until April 15, the royal assent to 3 and 4 Vict. c. 9, which altered the law, having been given on April 14. The extracts are quotations from the Judge's decision. For authorities see those under Stockdale v. Hansard.]

There is something in the nature of the Houses themselves which carries with it the authority that has been claimed ; though, in discussing such questions, the last important decision is always referred to. Instances have been pointed out in which the Crown has exerted its prerogative in a manner now considered illegal, and the Courts have acquiesced : but the cases are not analagous. The Crown has no rights which it can exercise other than by process of law and through amenable officers, but representative bodies must necessarily vindicate their authority by means of their own, and those means lie in the process of committal for contempt. This applies not to the Houses of Parliament only, but, as was observed in *Burdett v. Abbot*, to the courts of justice, which, as well as the Houses, must be liable to continual obstruction and insult if they were not intrusted with such powers. It is unnecessary to discuss the question whether each House of Parliament be or be not a court ; it is clear that they cannot exercise their proper functions without the power of protecting themselves against interference. The test of the authority of the House of Commons in this respect, submitted by Lord *Eldon* to the judges in *Burdett v. Abbot*, was whether, if the Court of Common Pleas had adjudged an act to be a contempt of court, and committed for it, stating the adjudication generally, the Court of King's Bench on a *habeas corpus* setting forth the warrant, would discharge the prisoner because the facts and circumstances of the contempt were not stated, A negative answer being given, Lord *Eldon*, with the concurrence of Lord *Erskine* (who had before been adverse to the exercise of jurisdiction), and without a dissentient voice from the House, affirmed the judgement below. And we must presume that what any court, much more, what either House of Parliament, acting on great legal authority, takes upon it to pronounce a contempt is so.

It was urged that, this not being a criminal matter, the Court was bound by stat. 56 Geo. 3. c. 100. s. 3 to inquire into the case on affidavit, but I think the provision cited is not applicable. On the motion for a *habeas corpus*, there must be an affidavit from the party applying, but the return, if it discloses a sufficient answer, puts an end to the case, and I think the production of a good warrant is a sufficient answer. Seeing that, we cannot go into the question of contempt on affidavit, nor discuss the motives which may be alleged. indeed (as the courts have said in some of the cases) it would be unseemly to suspect that a body, acting under such sanctions as a House of Parliament, would in making its warrant suppress facts which, if discussed, might entitle the person committed to his liberty. If they ever did so act I am persuaded that on further consideration they would repudiate such a course of proceeding. What injustice might not have been committed by the ordinary courts in past times if such a course had been recognised, as, for instance, if the Recorder of London in Bushell's case, had in the warrant of commitment suppressed the fact that the jurymen were imprisoned for returning a verdict of acquittal. I am certain that such will never become the practice of any body of men amenable to public opinion.

In the present case, I am obliged to say that I find no authority under which we are entitled to discharge these gentlemen from their imprisonment.

XXIX
THE QUEEN *v.* NELSON AND BRAND
31 Vict., 1867.

[During the Jamaica riots, George William Gordon, a civilian, was tried by court-martial for high treason and complicity in the rebellion, sentenced and put to death. The court-martial was ordered by Col. Nelson, and presided over by Lieut. Brand ; the sentence was approved of by Col. Nelson and Governor Eyre. Subsequently Nelson and Brand were indicted for murder mainly on two grounds : (1) that those who ordered and took part in the trial of Gordon had no jurisdiction ; (2) that if they had jurisdiction it was corruptly exercised. Lord Chief Justice Cockburn, in an elaborate charge to the grand jury, reviewed the evidence and stated his view of the law. The salient passages of this charge are here excerpted. The jury found "no true Bill," but made a formal presentment strongly recommending that "martial law" should be clearly defined by legislative enactment, with which recommendation the Lord Chief Justice concurred, adding a "solemn and emphatic protest" against "the exercise of martial law in the form in which it has lately been enforced." See authorities for *Phillips v. Eyre*, and add Journal for Soc. of Comp. Leg., April, 1900 ; L.Q.R. xviii.]

The first question, therefore, is whether the Governor had authority to proclaim martial law—a question obviously of infinite importance, not only in this case, but in any other similar case which may arise hereafter. Now one thing is quite clear—namely, that the power of a Governor to declare martial law can proceed only from one of two sources. It must either be derived from the commission which he has received from the Crown, or from some statute, either of imperial or local legislation. It can be derived from no other source. A Governor, simply as such, would have no power to declare martial law ; but, if the terms of his commission are large enough to invest him with such authority as the Crown possesses, and the Crown has, by virtue of the prerogative inherent in it, the power to proclaim martial law, the Governor would have that power. So, again, if, by virtue of any imperial or local legislation, authority to declare and exercise martial law has been conferred upon him, he would be entitled, on the necessity arising, to act upon that authority. We have, therefore, to inquire, on the present occasion, whether by virtue of his commission or by virtue of any legislative enactment the Governor of Jamaica was invested with such power. . . .

This being so, it follows that the Governor, assuming, as I do for the present purpose, that his commission confers on him all the executive power of the Crown in the government of the island, can have no further power to declare martial law, as derived from his commission, than that which the Sovereign would have. We are, therefore, brought face to face, with this great constitutional question —Has the Sovereign, by virtue of the prerogative of the Crown, in the event of rebellion, the power of establishing and exercising martial law within the realm of England ? . . .

We need not trouble ourselves with the consideration of whether there ought to be such a thing as martial law or not : the question for us is whether there is such a thing, and whether the Crown has the power, and whether the representives of the Crown in our colonies abroad have the power, to call it into action. And if martial law can thus be called into existence, then arises this all-important question, what this martial law is. . . .

So far as I have been able to discover, no such thing as martial law has ever been put in force in this country against civilians, for the purpose of putting down rebellion. I own, therefore, that I am a little astonished when I find persons, in authority and out of authority, talking and writing about martial law in the easy familiar way in which they do talk about it, as one of the settled prerogatives of the Crown in this country, and as a thing perfectly ascertained and understood, when, so far as I can find it never has been resorted to or exercised in England for such a purpose at all. . . .

Assuming the existence of the power to put martial law in force, whether as inherent in the prerogative or as derived from statutory enactment, a question of vital importance presents itself, namely, What is this martial law which is thus to supersede the common law of England? . . .

In like manner, if a mutiny breaks out on board ship, immediate force may be resorted to; you may quell the mutiny if necessary by killing those engaged in it. So, if a regiment in an army, or a company in a regiment, breaks out into mutiny, you may put it down at once by the immediate application of force. You may order other troops to fire on them, or put them to the sword, if they refuse to submit. But this is not what can properly be called martial law. It is part and parcel of the law of England—or perhaps I should say it is a right paramount to all law, and which the law of every civilised country recognises—that life may be protected or crime prevented by the immediate application of any amount of force which, under the circumstances, may be necessary. But that is not what we are dealing now with. What we are considering is whether, for the suppression of a rebellion, you may subject persons not actively engaged in it, and whom you therefore cannot kill on the spot, to an anomalous and exceptional law, and try them for their lives without the safeguards which the law ought to afford. . . .

Now, if such be the law as applied to the soldier, why should it not be the law applicable to the civilian? Why are we to be told that when you come to deal with a civilian by martial law, it is to be something different from the martial law which is applied to the soldier? I confess myself at a loss for any reason that can be given for that assertion, and certainly before I adopt the doctrine that a law, if it may be called a law, of the uncertain and arbitrary character which martial law is said to be, can be administered in this country, and that Englishmen can be tried for their lives under it, I shall require something more than assertion unsupported by authority—of this I am perfectly sure—namely, that in those repertories of the law of England which have been compiled by the sages and fathers of the law, and which have been handed down to us with the sanction of their great names, to inform us, and those who are to come after us in future ages, what the law of England was and is, no authority for anything of the sort can be found.   On the contrary, when Coke, and Hale, and Blackstone speak of martial law, it is plain they are speaking of the law applicable to the soldier, or what in modern phrase is called military law.   It is plain that they knew of no other; and the fact that when speaking, and clearly speaking, about the law applicable to soldiers, such men as Lord Hale and Sir William Blackstone, with their accuracy of statement, call it martial law and do not point out any distinction between martial law and military law as it is spoken of now, goes far indeed to show that they knew of no such difference, and that the distinction now supposed to exist is a thing that has come into the minds of men certainly much later than when these eminent luminaries of the law of England wrote their celebrated treatises.

On the other hand, let us see what authority there is which justifies the assertion that, if martial law can be legally exercised, it can be exercised in the arbitrary and despotic form which some persons contend for, as being something that has no limit, except for the particular exigency, or, I might almost say, the convenience of the moment.   I will bring before you all that I have been able to discover.   In the first place, I find this distinction taken in the works upon military courts-martial, written mostly by military men, as I think, from an entire misconception of the meaning of Lord Hale, and especially of that of Sir William Blackstone in his commentaries—a work probably more ready to their hands, and the language of which is certainly ambiguous and calculated to mislead until you carefully look to see what is the subject-matter of which he is treating, upon which all difficulty vanishes.   But military writers upon courts-martial certainly do make this distinction, and there is also the Authority of two distinguished members of the legal profession, though not of judicial position.   Mr. Headlam, certainly a gentleman of great learning and judgement, being called upon, when Judge-Advocate-General, to afford information to the commissioners at that time appointed under a Royal Commission to inquire into the defences of the United Kingdom, makes the following statement. He writes :—

"I have to observe, with a view of preventing any misunderstanding on the subject, that there is a broad distinction between the martial law called into existence and the law administered by courts-martial for the ordinary government of the army, which for distinction and accuracy may be called 'military law.'   The latter, namely, military law, is applicable only to the army and such persons connected with it as are made amenable to it by the Mutiny Act. Martial law, according to the Duke of Wellington, is 'neither more nor less than the will of the general who commands the army; in fact, martial law means no law at all.   Therefore the general who declares martial law, and commands that it shall be carried into execution, is bound to lay down the rules, regulations, and limits, according to which his will is to be carried out.'"

The opinion thus cited by Mr. Headlam was that of a very great man, and as to what may be done in an enemy's country, in time of war, may be perfectly sound—on that I pronounce no opinion—but I cannot accept the opinion even of so great a man as authority on a question of law, and I certainly should not recommend anybody to act upon it in case martial law should be proclaimed in our own country, or to rely on it as a protection if called upon to answer for his conduct in a court of justice for any injury inflicted on a fellow-subject in the exercise of martial law. Mr. Headlam goes on to say—

"The effect of a proclamation of martial law in a district of England is a notice to the inhabitants that the executive government has taken upon itself the responsibility of superseding the jurisdiction of all the ordinary tribunals, for the protection of life, person, and property, and has authorised the military authorities to do whatever they think expedient for the public safety."

All this may be true, but I should like to know on what authority the statement rests.   I can only say that I have not been able to find it, and I hope I shall give no offence when I say that, in a matter of such importance, before such doctrines as these, involving such serious consequences if carried into effect, are enunciated in this positive and unqualified manner, and spoken of as though of ordinary occurrence, some judicial decision or some high legal authority should be cited, or at all events instances adduced of the exercise of such a power. . . .

Gentlemen, it may be that all I have said upon the subject of the law will have left you, as I own candidly it still leaves me, not having the advantage of judical opinion to guide me, nor of forensic argument and disputation to enlighten and instruct me, in some degree of doubt. Let me, therefore, add that if you are of opinion, upon the whole, that the jurisdiction to exercise martial law is not satisfactorily made out, and that it is a matter which ought to be submitted to further consideration on the trial of the accused before a competent court where all the questions of law incident to the discussion and decision of the case may be fully raised and authoritatively and definitely considered and decided, I must say that I think that the safer course will be to let this matter go forward.   If there was a power to put martial law in force, and consequently jurisdiction to try persons under it, that will be safely ascertained and firmly established by judicial decision; if there was none, it follows that there has been a miscarriage of justice which calls for inquiry, and as to which further inquiry ought to take place. If, however, upon the review of the authorities to which I have called your attention, and of the enactments of the Jamaica statutes, and the recognition and reservation of the power of the Crown in the Acts of Parliament, you think the accused ought not further to be harassed by criminal proceedings, and that the case against them ought not to be submitted to the consideration of a jury, you will say so by ignoring this indictment; upon this you must exercise your own judgement. Again on the second branch of the case, in which we take the legality of martial law for granted, if you think that although there may have been a mistake, and a most grievous mistake, in condemning and sending this man to death, yet that the proceedings were done honestly and faithfully, and in what was believed to be the due course of the administration of justice, again I say you ought not to harass the accused persons by sending them to trial to another tribunal. If, on the other hand, you think there is a case which, at all events, calls for further inquiry and for an answer on the part of those who stand charged with this most serious offence, then you will find a true bill.

(Charge of Cockburn to the grand jury in R. *v.* Nelson and Brand, ed. by F. Cockburn, 2nd ed., 1867.)

XXX

WASON *v.* WALTER

32 Vict., 1868.

[Wason, the defendant, brought an action for libel against Walter, one of the proprietors of *The Times*, for a report of a debate in the House of Lords, in which it was contended that statements had been made affecting the character of the plaintiff. The statements made in debate were, of course, privileged; but it was argued that the privilege did not extend to a report not published under the authority of Parliament; see *Stockdale v. Hansard*, p. 380. The jury found for the defendant, and on argument for a new trial Cockburn, C.J., for reasons set forth in the excerpt, gave the judgment of the court discharging the rule, *i.e.* confirming the verdict in the first trial. See *Broom*, C.L. 843 *et seq.*; *Anson*, L.C. i. 136; *Odgers*, L. and S. 295.]

Cockburn, C. J. This case was argued a few days since before my Brothers Lush, Hannen, and Hayes, and myself, and we took time, not to consider what our judgment should be, for as to that our minds were made up at the close of the argument, but because, owing to the importance and novelty of the point involved, we thought it desirable that our judgment should be reduced to writing before it was delivered.

The main question for our decision is, whether a faithful report in a public newspaper of a debate in either House of Parliament, containing matter disparaging to the character of an individual, as having been spoken in the course of the debate, is actionable at the suit of the party whose character has thus been called in question. We are of opinion that it is not.

Important as the question is, it comes now for the first time before a court of law for decision. Numerous as are the instances in which the conduct and character of individuals have been called in question in Parliament during the many years that parliamentary debates have been reported in the public journals, this is the first instance in which an action of libel founded on a report of a parliamentary debate has come before a court of law. There is, therefore, a total absence of direct authority to guide us. There are, indeed, dicta of learned judges having reference to the point in question, but they are conflicting and inconclusive, and having been unnecessary to the decision of the cases in which they were pronounced, may be said to be extrajudicial. In the case of Rex v. Wright, Lawrence, J., placed the reports of parliamentary debates on the same footing with respect to privilege as is accorded to reports of proceedings in courts of justice, and expressed an opinion that the former were as much entitled to protection as the latter. But it is to be observed that in that case the question related to the publication by the defendant of a copy of a report of a committee of the House of Commons, which report the House had ordered to be printed, not to the publication of a debate unauthorized by the House. Again, in Davis v. Duncan, Wightman, J., seems disposed to treat the reports of proceedings in Parliament as entitled to the same privilege as reports of proceedings in courts of justice. But here again the question before the Court had reference to a report, not of a proceeding in Parliament, but of proceedings at a public meeting of improvement commissioners of a particular locality, in which the conduct of an individual had been assailed, and which report the Court held not to be privileged, without being in any way called upon to determine how far the privilege would have extended to a report of proceedings in parliament. On the other hand, in Stockdale v. Hansard, Littledale, J., and Patteson, J., use language from which it may be safely inferred that they would have deemed the report of a parliamentary debate, if containing an attack on character, as not entitled to be held privileged in an action for libel. But here again the question was not how far the publication of parliamentary debates was privileged but solely whether an order of the House of Commons directing a paper, forming no part of the proceedings of the House, and containing libellous matter, to be printed and sold to the public, and a resolution of the House that such an order was within its privileges, protected the publisher of the paper from an action of libel. Any opinion expressed on the subject of the report of parliamentary debate was therefore beyond the scope of the inquiry, and must be considered as more or less extrajudicial.

Several cases were cited in the course of the argument before us, but they turned for the most part on the question of parliamentary privilege, and therefore appear to us very wide of the present question. The case of Rex v. Wright approaches nearest to the one before us. In that case a committee of the House of Commons having made a report imputing to Horne Tooke seditious and revolutionary designs after his acquittal on a trial for high treason, and the House having ordered the report to be printed for the use of its members, the defendant, a bookseller and publisher, printed and published copies of the report. On an application for a criminal information the Court refused the rule, apparently on the ground that the report of a committee of the House of Commons, approved of by the House, being part of the proceedings of parliament, could not possibly be libellous. Lord Kenyon, C.J., says, "This report was first made by a committee of the House of Commons, then approved by the House at large, and then communicated to the other House, and it is now sub judice; and yet it is said that this is a libel on the prosecutor. It is impossible for us to admit that the proceeding of either of the houses of parliament is a libel; and yet that is to be taken as the foundation of this application." Lord Kenyon and his colleagues appear to have thought that a paper, though containing matter reflecting on the character of an individual, if it formed part of the proceedings of the House of Commons, would be so divested of all libellous character as that a party publishing it, even without the authority of the House, would not be responsible at law for the defamatory matter it contained. If this doctrine could be upheld, it would have a manifest bearing on the present question, for as no speech made by a member of either house, however strongly it may

assail the character and conduct of others, can be held to be libellous,
it would follow, such a speech being a parliamentary proceeding, that
the publication of it would not be actionable. But this is directly
contrary to the decision in Rex v. Lord Abingdon, and Rex v.
Creevey, in which the publication of speeches made in parliament
reflecting on the character of individuals was held to be actionable.
And it must be admitted that the authority of the case of Rex v.
Wright is much shaken, not only by the decision of Rex v. Creevey,
but also by the observations made by Lord Ellenborough in his
judgement in the latter case.

Beyond, however, impugning the authority of Rex v. Wright,
the two last-mentioned cases afford little assistance towards the solution of the present question. There is obviously a very material
difference between the publication of a speech made in parliament
for the express purpose of attacking the conduct or character of a
person, and afterwards published with a like purpose or effect, and
the faithful publication of parliamentary debates in their entirety,
with a view to afford information to the public, and with a total
absence of hostile intention or malicious motive towards any one.

The case of Lake v. King, which was cited in the argument before
us, has no application to the present case. There a petition having
been presented to the House of Commons by the defendant, impugning the conduct of the plaintiff, copies of the petition had been
printed and circulated among the members of the house, and it was
held that, the printing and circulating petitions being according to
the course and usage of parliament, no action would lie.

The case of Stockdale v. Hansard, which was much pressed upon
us by the counsel for the defendant, is in like manner beside the
question. . . .

To the decision of this Court in that memorable case we give our
unhesitating and unqualified adhesion. But the decision in that case
has no application to the present. The position that an order of the
House of Commons cannot render lawful that which is contrary to
law, still less that a resolution of the House can supersede the
jurisdiction of a court of law by clothing an unwarranted exercise
of power with the garb of privilege, can have no application where
the question is, not whether the act complained of being unlawful at
law, is rendered lawful by the order of the House or protected by
the assertion of its privilege, but whether it is, independently of such
order or assertion of privilege, in itself privileged and lawful.

Decided cases thus leaving us without authority on which to
proceed in the present instance, we must have some recourse to

principle in order to arrive at a solution of the question before us, and fortunately we have not far to seek before we find principles in our opinion applicable to the case, and which will afford a safe and sure foundation for our judgement.

It is now well established that faithful and fair reports of the proceedings of courts of justice, though the character of individuals may incidently suffer, are privileged, and that for the publication of such reports the publishers are neither criminally nor civilly responsible. . . .

We entirely concur with Lawrence, J., in Rex v. Wright, that the same reasons which apply to the reports of the proceedings in courts of justice apply also to proceedings in parliament. It seems to us impossible to doubt that it is of paramount public and national importance that the proceedings of the houses of parliament shall be communicated to the public, who have the deepest interest in knowing what passes within their walls, seeing that on what is there said and done, the welfare of the community depends. Where would be our confidence in the government of the country or in the legislature by which our laws are framed, and to whose charge the greatest interests of our country are committed,—where would be our attachment to the constitution under which we live, if the proceedings of the great council of the realm were shrouded in secrecy and concealed from the knowledge of the nation? How could the communications between the representatives of the people and their constituents, which are so essential to the working of the representative system, be usefully carried on, if the constituencies were kept in ignorance of what their representatives are doing? What would become of the right of petitioning on all measures pending in parliament, the undoubted right of the subject, if the people are to be kept in ignorance of what is passing in either house? Can any man bring himself to doubt that the publicity given in modern times to what passes in parliament is essential to the maintenance of the relations subsisting between the government, the legislature, and the country at large. It may, no doubt, be said that, while it may be necessary as a matter of national interest that the proceedings of parliament should in general be made public, yet that debates in which the character of individuals is brought into question ought to be suppressed. But to this, in addition to the difficulties in which parties publishing parliamentary reports would be placed, if this distinction were to be enforced and every debate had to be critically scanned to see whether it contained defamatory matter, it may be further answered that there is perhaps no subject in which the public have a deeper interest than in all that relates to the conduct of public servants of the state,—no subject of parliamentary discussion which more requires to be made known than an inquiry relating to it. Of this no better illustration could possibly be given than is afforded by the case before us. A distinguished counsel, whose qualification for the judicial bench had been abundantly tested by a long career of forensic eminence, is promoted to a high judicial office, and the profession and the public are satisfied that in a most important post the services of a most competent and valuable public servant have been secured. An individual comes forward and calls upon the House of Lords to take measures for removing the judge, in all other respects so well qualified for his office, by reason that on an important occasion he had exhibited so total a disregard of truth as to render him unfit to fill an office for which a sense of the solemn obligations of truth and honour is an essential qualification. Can it be said that such a subject is not one in which the public has a deep interest and as to which it ought not to be informed of what passes in debate? Lastly, what greater anomaly or more flagrant injustice could present itself than that, while from a sense of the importance of giving publicity to their proceedings, the houses of parliament not only sanction the reporting of their debates, but also take measures for giving facility to those who report them, while every member of the educated portion of the community from the highest to the lowest looks with eager interest at the debates of either house, and considers it a part of the duty of the public journals to furnish an account of what passes there, we were to hold that a party publishing a parliamentary debate is to be held liable to legal proceedings because the conduct of a particular individual may happen to be called in question? . . .

We however are glad to think that, on closer inquiry, the law turns out not to be as on some occasions it has been assumed to be. To us it seems clear that the principles on which the publication of reports of the proceedings of courts of justice have been held to be privileged apply to the reports of parliamentary proceedings. The analogy between the two cases is in every respect complete. If the rule has never been applied to the reports of parliamentary proceedings till now, we must assume that it is only because the occasion has never before arisen. If the principles which are the foundation of the privilege in the one case are applicable to the other, we must not hesitate to apply them, more especially when by so doing we avoid the glaring anomaly and injustice to which we have before adverted. Whatever disadvantages attach to a system of unwritten law, and of these we are fully sensible, it has at least this advantage, that its elasticity enables those who administer it to adapt it to the varying conditions of society, and to the requirements and habits of the age in which we live, so as to avoid the inconsistencies and injustice which arise when the law is no longer in harmony with the wants and usages and interests of the generation to which it is immediately applied. Our law of libel has, in many respects, only gradually developed itself into anything like a satisfactory and settled form. The full liberty of public writers to comment on the conduct and motives of public men has only in very recent times been recognized. Comments on government, on ministers and officers of state, on members of both houses of parliament, on judges and other public functionaries, are now made every day, which half a century ago would have been the subject of actions or ex officio informations, and would have brought down fine and imprisonment on publishers and authors. Yet who can doubt that the public are gainers by the change, and that, though injustice may often be done, and though public men may often have to smart under the keen sense of wrong inflicted by hostile criticism, the nation profits by public opinion being thus freely brought to bear on the discharge of public duties? Again, the recognition of the right to publish the proceedings of courts of justice has been of modern growth. Till a comparatively recent time the sanction of the judges was thought necessary even for the publication of the decisions of the courts upon points of law. Even in quite recent days judges, in holding publication of the proceedings of courts of justice lawful, have thought it necessary to distinguish what are called ex parte proceedings as a probable exception from an operation of the rule. Yet ex parte proceedings before magistrates, and even before this Court, as, for instance, on application of criminal informations, are published every day, but such a thing as an action or indictment founded on a report of such an ex parte proceeding is unheard of, and if any such action or indictment should be brought, it would probably be held that the true criterion of the privilege is, not whether the report was or was not ex parte, but whether it was a fair and honest report of what had taken place, published simply with a view to the information of the public and innocent of all intention to do injury to the reputation of the party affected.

It is to be observed that the analogy between the case of reports of proceedings of courts of justice and those of proceedings in parliament being complete, all the limitations placed on the one to prevent injustice to individuals will necessarily attach on the other : a garbled

2 D

or partial report, or of detached parts of proceedings, published with intent to injure individuals, will equally be disentitled to protection. Our judgement will in no way interfere with the decisions that the publication of a single speech for the purpose or with the effect of injuring an individual will be unlawful, as was held in the cases of Rex v. Lord Abingdon, and Rex v. Creevey. At the same time it may be as well to observe that we are disposed to agree with what was said in Davison v. Duncan, as to such a speech being privileged if bonâ fide by a member for the information of his constituents. But whatever would deprive a report of the proceedings in a court of justice of immunity will equally apply to a report of proceedings in parliament.

It only remains to advert to an argument urged against the legality of the publication of parliamentary proceedings, namely, that such publication is illegal as being in contravention of the standing orders of both houses of parliament. The fact, no doubt, is, that each house of parliament does, by its standing orders, prohibit the publication of its debates. But practically, each house not only permits, but also sanctions and encourages, the publication of its proceedings, and actually gives every facility to those who report them. Individual members correct their speeches for publication in Hansard or the public journals, and in every debate reports of former speeches contained therein are constantly referred to. Collectively, as well as individually, the members of both houses would deplore as a national misfortune the withholding their debates from the country at large. Practically speaking, therefore, it is idle to say that the publication of parliamentary proceedings is prohibited by parliament. The standing orders which prohibit it are obviously maintained only to give to each house the control over the publication of its proceedings, and the power of preventing or correcting any abuse of the facility afforded. Independently of the orders of the houses, there is nothing unlawful in publishing reports of parliamentary proceedings. Practically such publication is sanctioned by parliament; it is essential to the working of our parliamentary system, and to the welfare of the nation. Any argument founded on its alleged illegality appears to us, therefore, entirely to fail. Should either house of parliament ever be so ill-advised as to prevent its proceedings from being made known to the country—which certainly never will be the case—any publication of its debates made in contravention of its orders would be a matter between the house and the publisher. For the present purpose, we must treat such publication as in every respect lawful, and hold that, while honestly and faithfully carried on, those who publish them will be free from legal responsibility, though the character of individuals may incidentally be injuriously affected.

So much for the great question involved in this case. We pass on to the second branch of this rule, which has reference to alleged misdirection in respect of the second count of the declaration, which is founded on the article in the Times commenting on the debate in the House of Lords and the conduct of the plaintiff in preferring the petition which gave rise to it. We are of the opinion that the direction given to the jury was perfectly correct. The publication of the debate having been justifiable, the jury were properly told the subject was, for the reasons we have already adverted to, pre-eminently one of public interest, and therefore one on which public comment and observation might properly be made, and that consequently the occasion was privileged in the absence of malice. As to the latter the jury were told that they must be satisfied that the article was an honest and fair comment on the facts,—in other words, that, in the first place, they must be satisfied that the comments had been made with an honest belief in their justice, but that this was not enough, inasmuch as such belief might originate in the blindness of party zeal, or in personal or political aversion, that a person taking upon himself publicly to criticise and condemn the conduct or motives of another, must bring to the task, not only an honest sense of justice, but also a reasonable degree of judgement and moderation, so that the result may be what a jury shall deem, under the circumstances of the case, a fair and legitimate criticism on the conduct and motives of the party who is the object of censure.

Considering the direction thus given to have been perfectly correct, we are of opinion that in respect of the alleged misdirection as also on the former point, the ruling at nisi prius was right, and that consequently this rule must be discharged.

Rule discharged.

(L.R. ; iv. Q.B.D. lxxxii. *et seq.*)

XXXI

PHILLIPS *v.* EYRE

34 Vict., 1870.

[This was an action brought against Eyre, Governor of Jamaica, for false imprisonment and other injuries, committed during a rebellion in the island. The defendant pleaded that (1) the Colonial Legislature had passed an Act of Indemnity ; (2) that the acts complained of were *bona fide* done to put an end to the rebellion, and so were included in the Indemnity. The case was tried before Cockburn, C.J., Lush and Hayes, JJ., in the Queen's Bench, January, 1869 (see L.R.Q.B.D. iv. 225–244), when judgment was given for the defendant. The case was brought on appeal before the court of Court of Exchequer Chamber (Kelly, C.B. ; Martin, Channell, Pigott, and Charley, BB. ; Willes and Brett, JJ.), and the judgment, delivered by Willes, J., affirmed the decision of the Court of Queen's Bench. See L.R.Q.B.D. vi. 1–31 ; *Broom,* C.L. 622 *et seq. ; Clode,* Military Forces of the Crown, ii. xviii. ; *Finlason,* History of the Jamaica Case (and other works by the same author on the same subject) ; *Dicey,* L.C. 282 and app. xii.]

Willes, J. . . . It may be convenient to consider generally the condition of the governor of a colony and other subjects of Her Majesty there in case of open rebellion. To a certain extent their duty is clear to do their best and utmost in suppressing the rebellion. Even as to tumultuous assemblies and riots of a dangerous character, though not approaching to actual Rebellion, Tindal, C.J., in his charge to the Bristol grand jury on the special commission upon the occasion of the riots in 1832, there, in accordance with many authorities, stated the law as to private citizens. . . .

(Passage from Tindal's (C.J.) Charge to the Bristol grand jury here quoted. See p. 374.)

This perillous duty, shared by the governor with all the Queen's subjects, whether civil or military, is in a special degree incumbent upon him as being entrusted with the powers of government for preserving the lives and property of the people and the authority of the Crown ; and if such duty exist as to tumultuous assemblies of a dangerous character, the duty and responsibility in case of open rebellion are heightened by the consideration that the existence of the law itself is threatened by force of arms and a state of war against the Crown established for the time. To act under such circumstances within the precise limits of the law of ordinary peace is a difficult and may be an impossible task, and to hesitate or temporize may entail disastrous consequences. Whether the proper, as distinguished from the legal course has been pursued by the governor in so great a crisis, it is not within the province of a court of law to pronounce. Nor are we called upon to offer any judicial opinion as to the lawfulness or propriety of what was done in the present case, apart from the validity and legalizing effect of the colonial Act. It is manifest, however, that there may be occasions in which the necessity of the case demands prompt and speedy action for the maintenance of law and order at whatever risk, and where the governor may be compelled, unless he shrinks from the discharge of paramount duty, to exercise de facto powers which the legislature would assuredly have confided to him if the emergency could have been foreseen, trusting that whatever he has honestly done for the safety of the state will be ratified by an Act of indemnity and oblivion. There may not be time to appeal to the legislature for special powers. The governor may have, upon his own responsibility, acting upon the best advice and information he can procure at the moment, to arm loyal subjects, to seize or secure arms, to intercept munitions of war, to cut off communication between the disaffected, to detain suspected persons, and even to meet armed force by armed force in the open field. If he hesitates, the opportunity may be lost of checking the first outbreak of insurrection, whilst by vigorous action the consequences of allowing the insurgents to take the field in force may be averted. In resorting to strong measures he may have saved life and property out of all proportion to the mistakes he may honestly commit under information which turns out to have been erroneous or treacherous. The very efficiency of his measures may diminish the estimate of the danger with which he had to cope, and the danger once past, every measure he has adopted may be challenged as violent and oppressive, and he and everyone who advised him, or acted under his authority, may be called upon, in actions at the suit of individuals dissatisfied with his conduct, to establish the necessity or regularity of every act in detail by evidence which it may be against public policy to disclose. The bare litigation to which he and those who acted under his authority may be exposed, even if defeated by proving the lawfulness of what was done, may be harassing and ruinous. Under these and like circumstances it seems to be plainly within the competence of the legislature, which could have authorized by antecedent legislation the acts done as necessary or proper for preserving the public peace, upon a due consideration of the circumstances to adopt and ratify like acts when done, or, in the language of the law under consideration, to enact that they shall be "made and declared lawful and confirmed." Such is the effect of the Act of Indemnity in question, which follows the example of similar legislation in the mother-country and in other dominions and colonies of the Crown. . . .

We have thus discussed the validity of the defence upon the only question argued by counsel, touching the effect of the Colonial Act, but we are not to be understood as thereby intimating any opinion that the plea might not be sustained upon more general grounds as shewing that the acts complained of were incident to the enforcement of martial law. It is, however, unnecessary to discuss this further question, because we are of opinion with the Court below that the Colonial Act of Indemnity, even upon the assumption that the acts complained of were originally actionable, furnishes an answer to the action.

The judgement of the Court of Queen's Bench for the defendant was right, and is affirmed.

(L.R.Q.B.D. vi. 1–31.)

XXXII
BRADLAUGH v. GOSSETT
46 & 47 Vict., 1883–84.

[In May, 1883, Mr. Bradlaugh, duly elected burgess for Northampton, required the Speaker to call him to the table to take the oath. The Speaker did not do so. On July 9 the House resolved to exclude Mr. Bradlaugh until he engaged not to disturb their proceedings. Accordingly, in an action brought against Gossett, the Sergeant-at-Arms, he claimed (1) that the declaration of July 9 should be made void ; (2) an order restraining the Sergeant-at-Arms from excluding him ; (3) such other relief as he was entitled to. The case on December 7, 1883, was argued on demurrer to the statement of claim before Lord Coleridge, C.J., and Justices Mathew and Stephen. Judgment was delivered on February 9, 1884. See *Broom*, C.L. 975 ; *Anson*, i. 175 ; *May*, P.P. 134.]

Lord Coleridge, C.J. In this as in so many matters of practical concern difficulties are created by the laying down of principles in terms so wide and general, that, although logic may justify them, the sense and feeling of men imposes upon them in fact limitations which are said not altogether untruly to be sometimes inconsistent with the principle they are supposed to admit. For example, it seems to be conceded that a resolution of the House of Commons only (and what is true of one House of Parliament is true of the other) cannot change the law of the land. Sir John Patteson and Sir John Coleridge,—the former especially,—put this point with great force in their judgements in Stockdale v. Hansard: and yet, if the House of Commons is,—as for certain purposes and in relation to certain persons it certainly is, and is on all hands admitted to be,—the absolute judge of its own privileges, it is obvious that it can, at least for these purposes, and in relation to those persons, practically change or practically supersede the law.

Again, there can be no doubt, that in an action between party and party brought in a court of law, if the legality of a resolution of the House of Commons arises incidentally, and it becomes necessary to determine whether it be legal or no for the purpose of doing justice between the parties to the action, in such a case the Courts must entertain and must determine that question. Lord Ellenborough expressly says so in Burdett v. Abbot; and Bayley, J., seems to assume it at p. 161. All the four judges who gave judgement in Stockdale v. Hansard assert this in the strongest terms. That case, indeed, was an illustration of this necessity. The Attorney-General, Sir John Campbell, could undoubtedly have succeeded at nisi prius upon the facts of the case, without raising the question of privilege upon which the arguments and judgements were delivered. But, for reasons perfectly well understood at the time, he forced Lord Denham (who tried the cause) to give the ruling which he was determined to question. It is perhaps not to be regretted that he did so, when the arguments and judgements which were the result are remembered: but I see no answer to the statements of the judges, at pp. 193 and 243, that, when a question is raised before the Court, the Court must give judgement on it according to its notions of the law, and not according to a resolution of either House of Parliament. Cases may be put, cases have been put, in which, did they ever arise, it would be the plain duty of the Court, at all hazards to declare a resolution illegal and no protection to those who acted under it. Such cases might by possibility occasion unseemly conflicts between the Courts and the Houses. But, while I do not deny that as matter of reasoning such things might happen, it is consoling to reflect that they have scarce ever happened in the long centuries of our history, and that in the present state of things it is but barely possible that they should ever happen again.

Alongside, however, of these propositions, for the soundness of which I should be prepared most earnestly to contend, there is another proposition equally true, equally well established, which seems to me decisive of the case before us. What is said or done within the walls of Parliament cannot be inquired into in a court of law. On this point all the judges in the two great cases which exhaust the learning on the subject, Burdett v. Abbot and Stockdale v. Hansard;—are agreed, and are emphatic. The jurisdiction of the Houses over their own members, their right to impose discipline within their walls, is absolute and exclusive. To use the words of Lord Ellenborough, "They would sink into utter contempt and inefficiency without it."

Whether in all cases and under all circumstances the Houses are the sole judges of their own privileges, in the sense that a resolution of either House on the subject has the same effect for a court of law as an Act of Parliament, is a question which it is not now necessary to determine. No doubt, to allow any review of parliamentary privilege by a court of law may lead, has led, to very grave complications, and might in many supposable cases end in the privileges of the Commons being determined by the Lords. But, to hold the resolutions of either House absolutely beyond inquiry in a court of law may land us in conclusions not free from grave complications too. It is enough for me to say that it seems to me that in theory the question is extremely hard to solve; in practice it is not very important, and at any rate does not now arise.

On the question that does arise, if cases are required there is a remarkable one to be quoted regarding each House,—the case of the Earl of Shaftesbury, in which the Court of King's Bench altogether declined jurisdiction to inquire as to what had passed in the House of Lords; and the case of Sir John Eliot and his fellows, reported fully at the end of Cro. Car. That was a very remarkable case; for, no doubt, Sir John Eliot, Mr. Valentine, and Mr. Hollis had held the Speaker in the chair by main force, to prevent his adjourning the House before a motion had been made. They were sued in the King's Bench: they pleaded by demurrer to the jurisdiction that the offences (if any) had been committed in Parliament, and ought to be there examined and punished, and not elsewhere. The demurrer was overruled, and they were heavily fined and imprisoned. Sir John Eliot was killed by the rigours of his imprisonment: Mr. Valentine died; but Mr. Hollis survived; and in 1668 the judgement of the King's Bench was reversed by the House of Lords, on the ground that it was an illegal judgement and against the freedom and privilege of Parliament. These cases seem direct in point; and we could not give judgement for the plaintiff in this action without overruling them.

I need not discuss at any length the fact that the defendant in this case is the Sergeant-at-arms. The Houses of Parliament cannot act by themselves in a body; they must act by officers; and the Sergeant-at-arms is the legal and recognized officer of the House of Commons to execute its orders. I entertain no doubt that the House had a right to decide on the subject-matter, have decided it, and have ordered their officer to give effect to their decision. He is protected by their decision. They have ordered him to do what they have a right to order, and he has obeyed them.

It is said that in this case the House of Commons has exceeded its legal powers, because it has resolved that the plaintiff shall not take an oath which he has a right to take, and the threatened force is force to be used in compelling obedience to a resolution in itself illegal. But there is nothing before me upon which I should be justified in arriving at such a conclusion in point of fact. Consistently with all the statements in the claim, it may be that the plaintiff insisted on taking the oath in a manner and under circumstances which the House had a clear right to object to or prevent. Sitting in this seat I cannot know one way or the other. But, even if the fact be as the plaintiff contends, it is not a matter into which this Court can examine. If injustice has been done, it is injustice for which the courts of law afford no remedy. On this point I agree with and desire to adopt the language of my Brother Stephen. The history of England, and the resolutions of the House of Commons itself, shew that now and then injustice has been done by the House to individual members of it. But the remedy, if remedy it be, lies, not in actions in the courts of law (see on this subject the observations of Lord Ellenborough and Bayley, J., in Burdett v. Abbot, 14 East, 150, 151, and 160, 161), but by an appeal to the constituencies whom the House of Commons represents.

It follows that this action is against principle and is unsupported by authority, and that therefore the demurrer must be allowed, and that there must be judgement for the defendant.

Stephen, J. The legal question which this statement of the case appears to me to raise for our decision is this:—Suppose that the House of Commons forbids one of its members to do that which an Act of Parliament requires him to do, and in order to enforce its prohibition, directs its executive officer to exclude him from the House by force if necessary, is such an order one which we can declare to be void and restrain the executive officer of the House from carrying out. In my opinion we have no such power. I think that the House of Commons is not subject to the control of Her

Majesty's Courts in its administration of that part of the statute-law which has relation to its own internal proceedings, and that the use of such actual force as may be necessary to carry into effect such a resolution as the one before us is justifiable.

Many authorities might be cited for this principle; but I will quote two only. The number might be enlarged with ease by reference to several well-known cases. Blackstone says: "The whole of the law and custom of Parliament has its original from this one maxim, 'that whatever matter arises concerning either House of Parliament ought to be examined, discussed, and adjudged in that House to which it relates, and not elsewhere.'" This principle is re-stated nearly in Blackstone's words by each of the judges in the case of Stockdale v. Hansard. As the principal result of that case is to assert in the strongest way the right of the Queen's Bench to ascertain in case of need the extent of the privileges of the House, and to deny emphatically that the Court is bound by a resolution of the House declaring any particular matter to fall within their privilege, these declarations are of the highest authority. Lord Denman says: "Whatever is done within the walls of either assembly must pass without question in any other place." Littledale, J., says: "It is said the House of Commons is the sole judge of its own privileges; and so I admit as far as the proceedings in the House and some other things are concerned." Patteson, J., says: "Beyond all dispute, it is necessary that the proceedings of each House of Parliament should be entirely free and unshackled, that whatever is said or done in either House should not be liable to examination elsewhere." And Coleridge, J., said: "That the House should have exclusive jurisdiction to regulate the course of its own proceedings, and animadvert upon any conduct there in violation of its rules or derogation from its dignity stands upon the clearest grounds of necessity."

Apply the principle thus stated to the present case. We are asked to declare an order of the House of Commons to be void, and to prevent its execution in the only way in which it can be executed, on the ground that it constitutes an infringement of the Parliamentary Oaths Act. This Act requires the plaintiff to take a certain oath. The House of Commons have resolved that he shall not be permitted to take it. Grant, for the purposes of argument, that the resolution of the House and the Parliamentary Oaths Act contradict each other; how can we interfere without violating the principle just referred to? Surely the right of the plaintiff to take the oath in question is "a matter arising concerning the House of Commons," to use the words of Blackstone. The resolution to exclude him from the House is a thing " done within the walls of the House," to use Lord Denman's words. It is one of those " proceedings in the House of which the House of Commons is the sole judge," to use the words of Littledale, J. It is a " proceeding of the House of Commons in the House," and must therefore in the words of Patteson, J., " be entirely free and unshackled." It is " part of the course of its own proceedings," to use the words of Coleridge, J., and is therefore " subject to its exclusive jurisdiction." These authorities are so strong and simple that there may be some risk of weakening them in adding to them. Nevertheless, the importance of the case may excuse some further exposition of the principle on which it seems to me to depend.

A resolution of the House permitting Mr. Bradlaugh to take his seat on making a statutory declaration would certainly never have been interfered with by this Court. If we had been moved to declare it void and to restrain Mr. Bradlaugh from taking his seat until he had taken the oath, we should undoubtedly have refused to do so. On the other hand, if the House had resolved ever so decidedly that Mr. Bradlaugh was entitled to make the statutory declaration instead of taking the oath, and had attempted by resolution or otherwise to protect him against an action for penalties, it would have been our duty to disregard such resolutions, and, if an action for penalties were brought, to hear and determine it according to our own interpretation of the statute. Suppose, again, that the House had taken the view of the statute ultimately arrived at by this Court, that it did not enable Mr. Bradlaugh to make the statutory promise, we should certainly not have entertained an application to declare their resolution to be void. We should have said that, for the purpose of determining on a right to be exercised within the House itself, and in particular the right of sitting and voting, the House and the House only could interpret the statute; but that, as regarded rights to be exercised out of and independently of the House, such as the right of suing for a penalty for having sat and voted, the statute must be interpreted by this Court independently of the House.

This view of the subject is perhaps most simply and completely illustrated by the 4th section; but it seems to me to apply equally well to the 3rd, and I therefore think that we ought not to make the declaration asked for. I may observe, in conclusion, that, apart from these considerations, I should in any case whatever feel a reluctance almost invincible to declaring a resolution of the House of Commons to be beyond the powers of the House, and to be void. Such a declaration would in almost every imaginable case be unnecessary and disrespectful. I will not say that extraordinary circumstances might not require it, because it is impossible to foresee every event which may happen. It is enough to say that the circumstances which would justify such a declaration must be extraordinary indeed, and that, even if relief had to be given in this case, I should think it sufficient to restrain the Sergeant-at-arms from acting on the order of the House. I do not dwell upon this, however, as I wish to put my judgement on the plain and broad ground already stated. . . .

Before leaving this part of the subject, I may observe that in my judgement the case before us differs widely from a possible case suggested in argument in Burdett v. Abbot, as to the effect of an order by the House of Commons to put a member to death or to inflict upon him bodily harm. Of such a case it is enough to say, as Lord Ellenborough said, that it will be time to decide it when it arises. The only force which comes in question in this case is, such force as any private man might employ to prevent a trespass on his own land. I know of no authority for the proposition that an ordinary crime committed in the House of Commons would be withdrawn from the ordinary course of criminal justice. One of the leading authorities on the privilege of parliament contains matter on the point which shews how careful parliament has been to avoid even the appearance of countenancing such a doctrine. This is the case of Sir John Eliot, Denzil Hollis, and Others, of which a complete history is given in 3 Howell's State Trials, pp. 294–336. In this case the defendants were convicted in 1629 on an information before the Court of King's Bench for seditious speeches in parliament and also for an assault on the Speaker in the chair. They pleaded to the jurisdiction that these matters should be inquired into in Parliament and not elsewhere; and their plea was overruled. In 1666 this judgement was reversed upon writ of error; one error assigned being that the speaking of the seditious words and the assault on the Speaker were made the subject of one judgement; whereas the seditious speech, if made in parliament, could not be inquired into out of parliament, even if the assault upon the Speaker could be tried in the Court of King's Bench: hence there should have been two separate judgements. This case is the great leading authority, memorable on many grounds, for the proposition that nothing said in parliament by a member as such, can be treated as an offence by the ordinary Courts. . . . But the House of Lords carefully avoided deciding the question whether the Court of King's Bench could try a member for an assault on the Speaker in the House.

The plaintiff argued his own case before us at length. It is due to him to state the reasons why his arguments do not convince me. He referred to a great number of authorities; but his argument was in substance short and simple. He said that the resolution of the House of Commons was illegal, as the House had no power to alter the law of the land by resolution; and, admitting that the House has power to regulate its own procedure, he contended that in preventing him from taking his seat, the House went beyond matter of internal regulation and procedure, as they deprived both him and the electors of Northampton of a right recognized by law, which ought to be protected by the law; and so inflicted upon him and them wrongs which would be without a remedy if we failed to apply one. I think that each part of this argument requires a plain, direct answer.

It is certainly true that a resolution of the House of Commons cannot alter the law. If it were ever necessary to do so, this Court would assert this doctrine to the full extent to which it was asserted in Stockdale v. Hansard. The statement that the resolution of the House of Commons was illegal must, I think, be assumed to be true, for the purposes of the present case. The demurrer for those purposes admits it. We decide nothing unless we decide that, even if it is illegal in the sense of being opposed to the Parliamentary Oaths Act, it does not entitle the plaintiff to the relief sought. This admission, however, must be regarded as being made for the purposes of argument only. It would, as I have already said, be wrong for us to suggest or assume that the House acted otherwise than in accordance with its own view of the law; and, as we know not what that view is, nor by what arguments it is supported, we can give no opinion upon it. I do not say that the resolution of the House is the judgement of a Court not subject to our revision; but it has much in common with such a judgement. The House of Commons is not a Court of Justice; but the effect of its privilege to regulate its own internal concerns practically invests it with a judicial character when it has to apply to particular cases the provisions of Acts of Parliament. We must presume that it discharges this function properly and with due regard to the laws, in the making of which it has so great a share. If its determination is not in accordance with law, this resembles the case of an error by a judge whose decision is not subject to appeal. There is nothing startling in the recognition of the fact that such an error is possible. If, for instance, a jury in a criminal case give a perverse verdict, the law has provided no remedy. The maxim that there is no wrong without a remedy does not mean, as it is sometimes supposed, that there is a legal remedy for every moral or political wrong. If this were its meaning, it would be manifestly untrue. There is no legal remedy for the breach of a solemn promise not under seal and made without consideration; nor for many kinds of verbal slander, though each may involve utter ruin; nor for oppressive legislation, though it may reduce men practically to slavery; nor for the worst damage to person and property inflicted by the most unjust and cruel war. The maxim means only that legal wrong and legal remedy are correlative terms; and it would be more intelligibly and correctly stated, if it were reversed, so as to stand, "Where there is no legal remedy there is no legal wrong."

The assertion that the resolution of the House goes beyond matter of procedure, and that it does in effect deprive both Mr. Bradlaugh himself and his constituents of legal rights of great value, is undoubtedly true if the word "procedure" is construed in the sense in which we speak of civil procedure and criminal procedure, by way of opposition to the substantive law which systems of procedure apply to particular cases. No doubt, the right of the burgesses of Northampton to be represented in parliament, and the right of their duly elected representative to sit and vote in parliament and to enjoy the other rights incidental to his position upon the terms provided by law are in the most emphatic sense legal rights of the highest importance, and in the strictest sense of the words. Some of these rights are to be exercised out of Parliament, others within the walls of the House of Commons. Those which are to be exercised out of Parliament are under the protection of this Court, which, as has been shown in many cases, will apply proper remedies if they are in any way invaded, and will in so doing be bound, not by resolutions of either House of Parliament, but by its own judgement as to the law of the land, of which the privileges of Parliament form a part. Others must be exercised, if at all, within the walls of the House of Commons; and it seems to me that, from the nature of the case, such rights must be dependent upon the resolution of the House. In my opinion the House stands with relation to such rights, in precisely the same relation as we the judges of this Court stand in to the laws which regulate the rights of which we are the guardians, and to the judgements which apply them to particular cases; that is to say, they are bound by the most solemn obligations which can bind men to any course of conduct whatever, to guide their conduct by the law as they understand it. If they understand it, or (I apologize for the supposition) wilfully disregard it, they resemble mistaken or unjust judges; but in either case there is in my judgement no appeal from their decision. The law of the land gives no such appeal; no precedent has been or can be produced in which any Court has ever interfered with the internal affairs of either House of Parliament, though the cases are no doubt numerous in which the Courts have declared the limits of their powers outside of their respective Houses. This is enough to justify the conclusion at which I arrive.

We ought not to try to make new laws, under the pretence of declaring the existing law.   But I must add that this is not a case in which I at least feel tempted to do so.   It seems to me that, if we were to attempt to erect ourselves into a Court of Appeal from the House of Commons, we should consult neither the public interest, nor the interests of parliament and the constitution, nor our own dignity. We should provoke a conflict between the House of Commons and this Court, which in itself would be a great evil; and even upon the most improbable supposition of their acquiescence in our adverse decision; an appeal would lie from that decision to the Court of Appeal, and thence to the House of Lords, which would thus become the judge in the last result of the powers and privileges of the House of Commons.

For these reasons I am of opinion that there must be judgement for the defendant.

(L.R. 12 Q.B.D. 273 *et seq.*)

APPENDIX (GENERAL)

I. IMPEACHMENTS

A.

ARTICLES OF TREASON EXHIBITED IN PARLIAMENT AGAINST EDWARD EARL OF CLARENDON.

I. That the earl of Clarendon hath designed a standing army to be raised, and to govern the kingdom thereby ; advising the king to dissolve the present parliament ; to lay aside all thoughts of parliaments for the future ; to govern by military power, and to maintain the same by free quarter and contribution.

II. That he hath, in hearing of many of his majesty's subjects falsely and seditiously said, the king was in his heart a Papist, Popishly affected, or words to that effect.

III. That he hath received great sums of money for passing the Canary Patent, and other illegal patents ; and granting several injunctions to stop proceedings at law against them and other illegal Patents formerly granted.

IV. That he hath advised and procured divers of his majesty's subjects to be imprisoned against law, in remote islands, garrisons, and other places thereby to prevent them from the benefit of the law ; and to introduce precedents for imprisoning of other of his majesty's subjects in like manner.

V. That he hath corruptly sold several offices, contrary to law.

VI. That he hath procured his majesty's customs to be farmed at under rates, knowing the same ; and great pretended debts to be paid by his majesty, to the payment whereof his majesty was not in strictness bound. And hath received great sums of money for procuring the same.

VII. That he hath received great sums of money from the company of vintners, or some of them, or their agents, for enhancing the prices of wine, and for freeing them from the payment of legal penalties which they had incurred.

VIII. That he hath in a short time gained to himself a far greater estate than can be imagined to be lawfully gained in so short a time : And contrary to his oath, hath procured several grants under the great seal from his majesty, to himself and relations, of several of his majesty's lands, hereditaments, and leases, to the dis-profit of his majesty.

2 E

IX. That he introduced an arbitrary government in his majesty's foreign plantations; and hath caused such as complained thereof, before his majesty and council, to be long imprisoned for so doing.

X. That he did reject and frustrate a proposal and undertaking, approved by his majesty, for the preservation of Nevis and St. Christopher's, and reducing the French plantations to his majesty's obedience, after the commissions were drawn for that purpose; which was the occasion of such great losses and damages in those parts.

XI. That he advised and effected the sale of Dunkirk to the French king, being part of his majesty's dominions, together with the ammunition, artillery, and all sorts of stores there, and for no greater value than the said ammunition, artillery, and stores were worth.

XII. That the said earl did unduly cause his majesty's letters patent under the Great Seal of England (to one Dr. Crowther) to be altered, and the inrollment thereof to be unduly razed.

XIII. That he hath, in an arbitrary way, examined and drawn into question divers of his majesty's subjects concerning their lands, tenements, goods and chattels, and properties; determined thereof at the council-table, and stopped proceedings at law; and threatened some that pleaded the Statute of 17 Car. 1.

XIV. That he had caused Quo Warrantos to be issued out against most of the corporations of England by act of parliament, to the intent he might receive great sums of money from them for renewing their charters; which when they complied withal, he caused the said Quo Warrantos to be discharged, and prosecution thereon to cease.

XV. That he procured the bills of settlement for Ireland, and received great sums of money for the same in a most corrupt and unlawful manner.

XVI. That he hath deluded his majesty and the nation, in all foreign treaties and negotiations relating to the late war.

XVII. That he was a principal author of that fatal counsel of dividing the fleet, about June 1666.

(S.T. vi. 397.)

B.

ARTICLES OF IMPEACHMENT OF HIGH TREASON, AND OTHER HIGH CRIMES AND MISDEMEANOURS, AND OFFENCES, AGAINST THOMAS EARL OF DANBY, LORD HIGH TREASURER OF ENGLAND.

I. That he hath traitorously encroached to himself Regal Power, by treating of Matters of Peace and War with Foreign Princes and Ambassadors, and giving Instructions to his Majesty's Ambassadors abroad, without communicating the same to the Secretaries of State, and the rest of his Majesty's Council; and against the express Declaration of his Majesty and his Parliament; thereby intending to defeat and overthrow the Provisions which had been deliberately made by his Majesty and his Parliament for the Safety and Preservation of his Majesty's Kingdoms and Dominions.

II. That he hath traitorously endeavoured to subvert the ancient and well established Form of Government in this Kingdom; and instead thereof to introduce an arbitrary and tyrannical Way of Government. And the better to effect this his Purpose, he did design the raising of an Army, upon Pretence of a War against the French King; and then to continue the same as a Standing Army within this Kingdom: And an Army being so raised, and no War ensuing, an Act of Parliament having passed to pay off and disband the same, and a great Sum of Money being granted for that End, he did continue this Army contrary to the said Act, and misemployed the said Money, given for disbanding, to the continuance thereof; and issued out of his Majesty's Revenue divers great Sums of Money for the said Purpose; and wilfully neglected to take Security from the Paymaster of the Army, as the said Act required; whereby the said Law is eluded, and the Army is yet continued to the great Danger and unnecessary Charge of his Majesty and the whole Kingdom.

III. That he, traitorously intending and designing to alienate the Hearts and Affections of his Majesty's good Subjects from his Royal Person and Government, and to hinder the Meeting of Parliaments, and to deprive his Sacred Majesty of their safe and wholesome Councils, and thereby to alter the Constitution of the Government of this Kingdom, did propose and negotiate a Peace for the French King, upon Terms disadvantageous to the Interests of his Majesty and his Kingdoms: For the Doing whereof he did endeavour to procure a great Sum of Money from the French King, for Enabling of him to carry on and maintain his said traitorous Designs and Purposes, to the Hazard of his Majesty's Person and Government.

IV. That he is popishly affected; and hath traitorously concealed, after he had Notice, the late horrid and bloody Plot and Conspiracy contrived by the Papists, against his Majesty's Person and Government, and hath suppressed the Evidence, and reproachfully discountenanced the King's Witnesses in the Discovery of it, in Favour of Popery; immediately tending to the Destruction of the King's Sacred Person, and the Subversion of the Protestant Religion.

V. That he hath wasted the King's Treasure, by issuing out of his Majesty's Exchequer, and several Branches of his Revenue, for unnecessary Pensions and secret Services, to the Value of Two hundred Thirty-one thousand Six hundred and Two Pounds, within Two Years: And that he hath wholly diverted, out of the known Method and Government of the Exchequer, One whole Branch of his Majesty's Revenue to private Uses, without any Account to be made of it to his Majesty in the Exchequer, contrary to the Express Act of Parliament which granted the same: And he hath removed Two of his Majesty's Commissioners of that Part of the Revenue, for refusing to consent to such his unwarrantable Actings therein, and to advance Money upon that Branch of the Revenue, for private Uses.

VI. That he hath by indirect Means procured from his Majesty for imself, divers considerable Gifts and Grants of Inheritance of the ancient Revenue of the Crown, even contrary to Acts of Parliament.

(C.J. ix. 561.)

RESOLUTION OF THE COMMONS, MAY 5, 1679.

Resolved, Nemine Contradicente, That it is the opinion of this House, That the Pardon pleaded by the Earl of Danby is illegal and void ; and ought not to be allowed in Bar of the Impeachment of the Commons of England.

Resolved, Nemine Contradicente, That the whole House will go up to the Lords Bar, and demand their Judgment against the Earl of Danby ; for that the Pardon by him pleaded is illegal and invalid ; and ought not to bar or preclude the Commons from having Justice upon their Impeachment. . . .

(The form of words drawn up by the Committee and adopted by the House.)

My Lords,

The Knights, Citizens, and Burgesses, in Parliament assembled, are come up to demand Judgment in their own Names, and the Names of all the Commons of England, against Thomas, Earl of Danby, who stands impeached by them before Your Lordships of High Treason, and divers High Crimes and Misdemeanors, to which he has pleaded a Pardon : which Pardon the Commons conceive to be illegal and void ; and therefore they do demand Judgment of Your Lordships accordingly. [See p. 91.]

(C.J. ix. 612.)

C.

RESOLUTIONS OF THE COMMONS IN THE CASE OF FITZHARRIS, 1681.

The House being informed, That the Lords had refused to proceed upon the Impeachment of the Commons against *Edward Fitzharris;* and had directed That he should be proceeded against at the Common Law ;

And a Debate arising in the House thereupon :

Resolved, That it is the Undoubted Right of the Commons in Parliament assembled, to impeach, before the Lords in Parliament, any Peer or Commoner for Treason, or any other Crime or Misdemeanor ; And that the Refusal of the Lords to proceed in Parliament upon such Impeachment is a Denial of Justice, and a Violation of the Constitution of Parliaments.

Resolved, That in the Case of *Edward Fitzharris,* who, by the Commons had been impeached for High Treason before the Lords, with a Declaration, that in convenient time they would bring up the Articles against him ; for the Lords to resolve, That the said *Edward Fitzharris* should be proceeded with according to the Course of Common Law, and not by way of Impeachment in Parliament, at this time ; is a Denial of Justice, and a Violation of the Constitution of Parliaments, and an Obstruction to the further Discovery of the Popish Plot, and of great Danger to his Majesty' Person, and the Protestant Religion.

Resolved, That for any inferior Court to proceed against *Edward Fitz-harris,* or any other person, lying under an Impeachment in Parliament for the same Crimes for which he or they stand impeached, is a high Breach of the Privilege of Parliament.

(C.J., March 26, 1681.)

(Note.—Edward Fitzharris, a Commoner, had been impeached by the Commons ; but the Lords had voted he should be proceeded against at Common Law. On the importance of the Constitutional question involved see *Hallam,* C.H. ii. 447 ; *Hatsell,* Precedents, iv. 54 ; S.T. viii. 236 ; and for precedents, *Stubbs,* C.H. ii. 593, iii. 273 ; *Pike,* H.L. 209–234.)

II. TAXATION AND SUPPLY

1.

THE LORDS RESOLUTION.

The Question was put, " Whether it shall be ordered and declared, That the annexing any Clause or Clauses to a Bill of Aid or Supply, the Matter of which is foreign to, and different from, the Matter of the said Bill of Aid or Supply, is Unparliamentary, and tends to the Destruction of the Constitution of this Government ? "

It was resolved in the Affirmative.

It is Ordered and Declared, by the Lords Spiritual and Temporal in Parliament assembled, That the annexing any Clause or Clauses to a Bill of Aid or Supply, the Matter of which is foreign to, and different from, the Matter of the said Bill of Aid or Supply, is Unparliamentary, and tends to the Destruction of the Government.

It is Ordered, by the Lords Spiritual and Temporal in Parliament assembled, That this Order and Declaration be added to the Roll of Standing Orders.

(L.J. xvii. 135.)

2.

A. RESOLUTION OF THE COMMONS OF 1661.

And the House observing, that the said Bill (a Passing Bill) was to alter the course of Law in Part, and to lay a Charge upon the People ; and conceiving that it is a privilege inherent to this House, that Bills of that Nature ought to be first considered here ;

Ordered, That the said Bill be laid aside ; And that the Lords be acquainted therewith, and with the reasons inducing this House thereunto ; and the Lords are to be desired, for that Cause, not to suffer any Mention of the said Bill to remain in the Journals of their House. . . .

(C.J. viii. 311.)

B. The Resolution of the Commons, 1671.

The House then proceeded to the Reading the Amendments and Clauses, sent from the Lords to the Bill for an Imposition upon foreign Commodities : Which were once read :

And the first Amendments, sent from the Lords, being for changing the proportion of the Impositions on white Sugars from One Penny per Pound, to Halfpenny half Farthing, was read the second Time ; and debated.

Resolved, etc. Nemine contradicente, That, in all Aids given to the King, by the Commons, the Rate or Tax ought not to be altered by the Lords.

(C.J. ix. 235.)

C. Resolution of the Commons, 1678.

Mr. Solicitor General reports from the Committee to whom it was, amongst other things referred, to prepare and draw up a State of Rights of the Commons, in Granting of Money, a Vote agreed by the Committee : Which he read at his Place, and afterwards delivered the same in at the Clerk's Table : Where the same was read; and, upon the Question, agreed; and is as followeth ; viz.

Resolved, etc. That all Aids and Supplies, and Aids to his Majesty in Parliament, are the sole Gift of the Commons : And that it is the un-doubted and sole right of the Commons, to direct, limit, and appoint, in such Bills, the Ends, Purposes, Considerations, Conditions, Limitations, and Qualifications of such Grants ; which ought not to be changed, or altered by the House of Lords.

(C.J. ix. 509.)

D. Resolutions of the Commons of 1860.

(1) That the right of granting Aids and Supplies to the Crown is in the Commons alone, as an essential part of their Constitution ; and the limita-tion of all such Grants, as to matter, manner, measure, and time, is only in them.

(2) That, although the Lords have exercised the power of rejecting Bills of several descriptions relating to Taxation by negativing the whole, yet the exercise of that power by them has not been frequent, and is justly re-garded by this House with peculiar jealousy, as affecting the right of the Commons to grant the Supplies and to provide the Ways and Means for the Services of the year.

(3) That, to guard for the future against an undue exercise of that power by the Lords, and to secure to the Commons their rightful control over Taxation and Supply, this House has in its own hands the power so to im-pose and remit Taxes, and to frame Bills of Supply, that the right of the Commons as to the matter, manner, measure and time may be maintained inviolate.

(Hansard, P.D., Third Series, clix. 1384–1606.)

3.

STANDING ORDERS OF THE COMMONS.

57. [11th June, 1713 ; 25th June, 1852 ; 20th March, 1866.] That this House will receive no petition for any sum relating to public service, or proceed upon any motion for a grant or charge upon the public revenue, whether payable out of the Consolidated Fund or out of moneys to be provided by Parliament, unless recommended from the Crown.

58. [29 March, 1707.] That this House will not proceed upon any petition, motion, or Bill, for granting any money, or for releasing or compounding any sum of money owing to the Crown, but in a Committee of the whole house.

60. [22nd February, 1821.] That this House will not proceed upon any motion for an address to the Crown, praying that any money may be issued, or that any expense may be incurred, but in a Committee of the whole house.

61. [21st July, 1856.] That this House will not receive any petition, or proceed upon any motion for a charge upon the revenues of India, but what is recommended by the Crown.

62. [20th March, 1866.] That if any motion be made in the House for any aid, grant or charge upon the public revenue, whether payable out of the Consolidated Fund, or out of moneys to be provided by Parliament, or for any charge upon the people, the consideration and debate thereof shall not be presently entered upon, but shall be adjourned till such further days as the House shall think fit to appoint, and then it shall be referred to a Committee of the whole House before any resolution, or vote of the House do pass therein.

(See *Hallam, passim ; Porritt,* U.H.C. i. 545–564 ; *Anson,* L.C. i. 252, ii. 303 ; *Pike,* H.L. 334–344.)

III. THE EXCLUSION BILL, 1680.

Whereas James Duke of York is notoriously known to have been perverted from the Protestant to the Popish Religion, whereby not only great encouragement hath been given to the Popish party to enter into and carry on most devilish and horrid plots and conspiracies for the destruction of His Majesty's sacred person and government, and for the extirpation of the true Protestant Religion, but also, if the said Duke should succeed to the Imperial Crown of this Realm, nothing is more manifest than that a total change of Religion within these kingdoms would ensue ; For the prevention whereof, Be it therefore enacted . . . That the said James, Duke of York shall be, and is, by authority of this present Parliament, excluded and made for ever incapable to inherit, possess and enjoy the Imperial Crown of this Realm and of the Kingdom of Ireland and the

Dominions and Territories to them or either of them belonging, or to have, exercise, or enjoy any Dominion, Power, Jurisdiction, or Authority within the same Kingdoms, Dominions, or any of them. And be it further enacted . . . That if the said James, Duke of York, shall at any time hereafter challenge, claim or attempt to possess or enjoy or shall take upon him to use or exercise any dominion, power, authority, or jurisdiction within the said kingdoms, dominions, or any of them, as King or Chief Magistrate of the same, That then he the said James Duke of York, for every such offence shall be deemed and adjudged guilty of high treason, and shall suffer the pains, penalties and forfeitures as in cases of high treason ; And further, That if any person . . . whatsoever shall assist, aid, maintain, abet or willingly adhere unto the said James, Duke of York in such his challenge . . . or shall of themselves attempt . . . to bring the said James, Duke of York, into the possession or exercise of any regal power . . . or shall by writing . . . declare that he hath any right . . . to exercise the office of King. . . . That then every such person . . . shall undergo the pains, penalties, and forfeitures aforesaid ; And . . . That if the said James Duke of York, shall . . . come into or within any of the kingdoms or dominions aforesaid, That then shall he . . . suffer the pains, penalties and forfeitures as in cases of high treason . . . And be it further enacted . . . That the said James, Duke of York, or any other person being guilty of any of the treasons aforesaid shall not be capable of . . . any pardon otherwise than by Act of Parliament . . . And that it shall and may be lawful to and for all magistrates . . . and other subjects . . . to apprehend and secure the said James Duke of York, and every other person offending any of the premises . . . for all which actings and for so doing they are . . . by virtue of this Act saved harmless and indemnified. Provided . . . That nothing in this Act contained shall be construed . . . to disable any person from inheriting . . . the Imperial Crown of the Realms and Dominions aforesaid . . . but that in case the said James Duke of York shall survive his now Majesty . . . the said Imperial Crown shall descend to . . . such persons successively . . . as should have inherited . . . the same in case the said James, Duke of York were naturally dead. . . . And that during the life of the said James, Duke of York this Act shall be given in charge at every Assizes and General Sessions of the Peace . . . and also shall be openly read in every Cathedral, Collegiate Church, parish Church and Chapel . . . by the several and respective parsons . . . who are hereby required immediately after Divine Service in the forenoon to read the same twice in every year . . . during the life of the said James, Duke of York.

(The text of the above is given from the version found in the Papers of the House of Lords and printed in H.M.C.R. xi. app. pt. ii. 283, pp. 195–197. It is headed, "Common's Engrossment of an Act," etc. On the first reading after four days' debate the Bill was rejected by 63 votes to 30. The version printed in A. and S.S.D. is taken from Cobbett's Parlt. Hist. iv. 1136, and differs throughout from that given above, which is probably the original text.)

IV. SUPPLEMENTAL (Summaries Mainly)

I. THE FRANCHISE.

A. The Reform Act of 1867 (30 and 31 Vict. Cap. 102).

An Act further to amend the Laws relating to the Representation of the People in England and Wales.

Whereas it is expedient to amend the laws relating to the representation of the people in England and Wales, Be it enacted. . . . (The Act not to affect Scotland, Ireland, nor the representation of the Universities of Oxford and Cambridge.)

3. Every man shall . . . be entitled to be registered as a voter and to vote . . . for a member . . . to serve in parliament for a borough who is qualified as follows ;

(1) Is of full age, and not subject to any legal incapacity ;

(2) Is on the last day of July in any year, and has during the whole of the preceding twelve calendar months been, an inhabitant occupier, as owner or tenant, of any dwelling house within the borough ;

(3) Has . : . been rated as an ordinary occupier . . . to all rates made for the relief of the poor. . . .

(4) Has . . . bona fide paid an equal amount in the pound to that payable by other ordinary occupiers in respect of all poor rates. . . . Provided that no man shall . . . be entitled to be registered by reason of his being a joint occupier of any dwelling house.

4. Every man . . . shall also be entitled . . . to vote for a borough . . . who. . . .

(1) Is of full age and not subject to any legal incapacity ;

(2) As a lodger has occupied . . . separately and as sole tenant for the twelve months preceding the last day of July in any year the same lodgings, such lodgings being part of one and the same dwelling house and of a clear yearly value, if let unfurnished, of ten pounds or upwards ;

(3) Has resided in such lodgings for the twelve months . . . and has claimed to be registered. . . .

5. Every man shall . . . be entitled to be registered as a voter and . . . to vote . . . for a member or members to serve in parliament for a county who is qualified as follows ;

(1) Is of full age, and not subject to any legal incapacity, and is seised at law or in equity of any lands or tenements of freehold, copyhold, or any other tenure whatever, for his own life, or for the life of another, . . . or for any larger estate of the clear yearly value of not less than five pounds over and above all rents and charges payable out of or in respect of the same, or who is entitled, either as lessee or assignee, to any lands, or tenements of freehold or any other tenure whatever for the unexpired residue . . . of any term originally created for a period of not less than sixty years . . . of the clear yearly value of not less than five pounds. . . . Provided that every voter complies with 2 William 4. c. 45.)

6. Every man shall be also entitled to . . . vote who. . . .

(1) Is of full age, etc.

(2) Is on the last day of July in any year, and has during the twelve months immediately preceding been, the occupier . . . of lands or tenants within the county of the rateable value of twelve pounds or upwards ;

(3) Has . . . been rated . . . to all rates made for the relief of the poor. . . .

(4) Has . . . paid all poor rates. . . .

9. At a contested Election for any County or Borough represented by Three Members no Person shall vote for more than Two Candidates.

24. In all future parliaments the university of London shall return one member to serve in Parliament.

25. Every man whose name is for the time being on the register of graduates constituting the convocation of the university of London shall, if of full age, and not subject to any legal incapacity, be entitled to vote in the election of a member to serve in any future parliament for the said university. . . .

30. The overseers of every parish or township shall make out . . . a list of all persons on whom a right to vote for a county . . . is conferred by this Act . . . subject to the same regulations . . . in and subject to which to the overseers of parishes and townships in boroughs are required by the registration acts to make out . . . a list of all persons entitled to vote . . . for a borough in respect of the occupation of premises of a clear yearly value of not less than ten pounds. . . .

51. . . . That the parliament in being at any future demise of the crown shall not be determined or dissolved by such demise, but shall continue so long as it would have continued but for such demise, unless it should be sooner prorogued or dissolved by the crown (*i.e.* repeals 6 Anne, c. 7).

52. . . . That where a person has been returned as a member to serve in parliament since the acceptance by him from the crown of any office described in schedule (H) . . . the subsequent acceptance by him from the crown of any other office or offices described in such schedule in lieu of and in immediate succession the one to the other shall not vacate his seat. . . .

Analysis of Schedules (specifying §§ 17–24).

A. List of 38 Boroughs to return only one member in future Parliaments.

B. List of 9 *New* Boroughs to return 1 member ; Chelsea (a new borough) to return 2.

C. The Tower Hamlet Borough to be divided into 2 parts, each returning 2 members (*i.e.* 4 as against 2).

D. List of 13 Counties hitherto returning 2 members each (26 in all), now divided into 35 divisions, each returning 2 members (70 in all).

§ 18. City of Manchester, Borough of Liverpool, Birmingham, Leeds to return 3 not 2 members.

§ 21. Merthyr Tydvil, Salford to return 2 members, not 1.

(*Rogers*, P.L. iii. 468.)

B. The Reform Act, 1884 (48 Vict. Cap. 3).

An Act to amend the Law relating to the Representation of the People of the United Kingdom.

Be it enacted . . . that. . . .

2. A uniform household and a uniform lodger franchise at elections shall be established in all counties and boroughs throughout the united kingdom, and every man possessed of a household qualification or a lodger qualification shall, if the qualifying premises be situate in a county in England or Scotland, be entitled to be registered as a voter, and when registered to vote at an election for such county; and if the qualifying premises be situate in a county or borough in Ireland, be entitled to be registered as a voter, and when registered to vote at an election for such county or borough.

3. Where a man himself inhabits any dwelling house by virtue of any office, service or employment, and the dwelling house is not inhabited by any person under whom such man serves in such office, employment or service, he shall be deemed for the purposes of this Act and of the representation of the people acts to be an inhabitant occupier of such dwelling house as a tenant. . . .

4. (Restriction on Fagot votes.)

5. Occupation qualification of a clear annual value of not less than £10 made the same for both Boroughs and Counties.

6. The occupation of property in a borough entitling to a vote shall not entitle to a vote for the county.

7. "The household qualification" and "the lodger qualification" to be interpreted as defined in the Reform Act of 1867 and as amended or defined for England, Scotland, Ireland by subsequent Acts ; (particularly by the Registration Acts "to assimilate the Law," 48 Vict. c. 15, 16, 17, 1885).

C. Analysis of the Redistribution of Seats Act (48 & 49 Vict. C. 23), 1885.

§ 2. 103 Boroughs in the United Kingdom (Schedule i. 1) to cease to return any member. 5 Counties of Cities and Towns to be included in the county at large for representation (i. 2).

§ 3. Macclesfield, Sandwich disfranchised for corruption (i. 3).

§ 4. The City of London to return only 2 members.

Schedule ii. of 36 English, 3 Irish Boroughs to return 1 member, not 2 members.

§ 5. Schedule iii. of Boroughs to have additional members—14 English returning 63 members, 3 Scottish returning 13, 2 Irish returning 8.

§ 6. Schedule iv. New Boroughs created with their representation, viz. :—33 in England returning 56 members.

§ 7. Schedule v. defining areas and boundaries of Boroughs with altered boundaries.

§ 8. Schedule vi. The Divisions of Boroughs, each returning 1 member.

§ 9. Schedule vii. List of Counties at large divided into the number of divisions corresponding to the representation, *i.e.* 2 members, 2 divisions, 4 members, 4 divisions, etc. Each division therefore is treated "as a separate county."

The Changes of the Reform Acts in Diagram.

	Before 1832				1832				1867				1885			
	C	B	U	Total	C	B	U	Total	C	B	U	Total	C	B	U	T
ENGLAND AND WALES	94	415	4	513	159	336	4	499	186	302	5	493	253	237	5	
SCOTLAND	30	15	–	45	30	23	1	54	33	25	2	60	39	31	2	
IRELAND	62	35	1	100	64	39	2	105	64	39	2	105	85	16	2	
TOTAL	188	465	5	658	253	398	7	658	283	366	9	658	377	284	9	

C = COUNTIES ; B = BOROUGHS ; U = UNIVERSITIES.

II. POOR LAW.
A. 13 & 14 CHARLES II. CAP. 12, 1662.
An Act for the better relief of the poor of this Kingdom.

Be it enacted . . . That whereas by reason of some defects in the law, poor people are not restrained from going from one parish to another, and therefore do endeavour to settle themselves in those parishes where there is the best stock . . . and when they have consumed it then to another parish, and at last become rogues and vagabonds . . . that it shall be lawful . . . within forty days after any such person or persons coming so to settle as aforesaid, in any tenement under the yearly value of ten pounds, for any two justices of the peace, whereof one to be of the quorum . . . by their warrant to remove and convey such person or persons to such parish where he or they were last legally settled, either as a native, householder, sojourner, apprentice or servant, for the space of forty days at least, unless he or they give sufficient security for the discharge of the said parish, to be showed by the said justices. . . .

4. And for the further redress of the mischiefs . . . That from henceforth there . . . shall be, one or more corporation or corporations, workhouse or workhouses within the cities of London and Westminster, and within the boroughs, towns and places of the county of Middlesex and Surrey. . . .

6. That it shall be lawful to and for the said president and governors of the said corporation . . . to apprehend . . . any rogues, vagrants, sturdy beggars, or idle and disorderly persons within the said cities . . . and to cause them to be kept and set to work in the several and respective corporations or work-houses. . . .

19. That it shall be lawful for the churchwardens and overseers for the poor of such parish when any bastard child shall be born, to take and

seize so much of the goods and chattels . . . of such putative father or lewd mother, for or towards the discharge of the parish, to be confirmed at the sessions, for the bringing up and providing for such bastard child. . . .

B. (GILBERT'S ACT.) 22 GEO. III. C. 83, 1782.

Be it enacted . . . (2) that it shall . . . be lawful for . . . the visitors and guardians . . . of any parish . . . to make agreement . . . for the diet or clothing of such poor persons who shall be sent to the house or house or houses provided under this act . . . (3) with the consent of two-thirds of the rate payers at a public meeting and with the approval of two justices of the peace, 3 salaried guardians and 3 governors "of the poor house" may be appointed. (4) Two or more parishes may be united with the approval of two justices to carry out and benefit by this Act. (6) The voters at the public meeting to be owners or occupiers of property rated to the poor rate, not less than £5. (7) The Justices to appoint a guardian of the poor for every parish who except as regards making and collecting poor rate shall have the statutory powers of an overseer. (8) The church-wardens or overseers to receive the poor rate. (a) The Justices to appoint a paid governor of the poor house "who shall have the care, management and employment of the poor." (9) The guardians and justices to appoint a visitor to inspect and superintend the management of the poor house and control the Governor. (17, 18) The Guardians of the poor shall provide and fit up a poor house or poor houses situate within the parish or united parishes, at the expense of the parish. (21) The visitor and Guardians are "declared to be one body politic and corporate." (24) The poor to be maintained at the expense of the parish, the Guardians to have a monthly meeting for the transaction of all necessary business. (29) "That no person shall be sent to such poor house . . . except such as are become indigent by old age, sickness or infirmities, and are unable to acquire a maintenance by their labour : and except such orphan children as shall be sent thither by order of the guardians with the approbation of the visitor." (30) The Guardians are empowered to apprentice, or put out to service or trade, orphan children. (31) Idle and disorderly persons, able but unwilling to work, may be prosecuted by the Guardians. (32) The Guardians are empowered to provide work for the poor, able and willing to work, but who cannot get employment, and to maintain, or help in maintaining such persons until they are provided for. (35) A Justice of the peace when the Guardians have refused relief may order some weekly or other relief for such poor person or send him to the poor house, or order the Guardians to provide him with employment as provided by § 32. (39) "Nothing herein contained shall . . . extend to alter or affect the settlement of any person . . . or to give any illegitimate child (born in a work-house) a settlement in the parish . . . but every such child shall be considered as settled in the parish . . . to which the mother belongs. . . ."

C. THE POOR LAW AMENDMENT ACT.
4 & 5 WILLIAM IV. C. 76, 1834.

An act for the Amendment and better administration of the Laws relating to the Poor in England and Wales.

. . . Be it therefore enacted . . . that it shall be lawful for his majesty . . . to appoint three fit Commissioners to carry this Act into execution. . . .

II. That the said Commissioners shall be styled "The Poor Law Commissioners for England and Wales" (to sit as a Board, with power to examine witnesses and call for papers, on oath).

VII. The said Commissioners . . . are hereby empowered . . . to appoint such persons as they may think fit to be Assistant Commissioners. . .

XV. That . . . the administration of relief to the poor throughout England and Wales according to the existing laws . . . shall be subject to the direction and control of the said Commissioners . . . and they are . . . hereby required . . . to issue all such rules, orders and regulations for the management of the poor, for the government of workhouses . . . and for the guidance and control of all guardians, vestries and parish officers. . . .

XXIII. That it shall be lawful for the said Commissioners . . . with the consent of a majority of the guardians of any union . . . to direct the overseers or guardians of any parish . . . to build a workhouse. . . .

XXVI. It shall be lawful for the said Commissioners . . . to declare so many parishes as they may think fit to be united for the administration of the laws for the relief of the poor, and such parishes shall thereupon be deemed a union. . . .

XXVII. It shall be lawful for any two of his Majesty's Justices of the peace . . . to direct . . . that relief shall be given to any adult person . . . unable to work, without requiring that such person shall reside in any workhouse. . . .

XXXVIII. That . . . a board of Guardians of the poor for such union shall be constituted . . . and the workhouse or workhouses shall be governed, and the relief of the poor . . . be administered, by such board of guardians : and the said guardians shall be elected by the ratepayers . . . and every justice of the peace residing in any such parish . . . shall be an ex officio guardian of such united or common workhouses. . . .

(XXXIX. A similar board for single parishes.)

XL. No person shall be deemed a ratepayer, or be entitled to vote . . . unless he shall have been rated to the relief of the poor for the whole year immediately preceding . . . and shall have paid the parochial rates. . . .

XLIII. It shall be lawful . . . for any justice of the peace acting in and for the county . . . to visit, inspect and examine such workhouse . . . for the purpose of ascertaining whether such rules . . . have been duly observed. . . .

XLVII. That all overseers . . . having the collection, receipt or distribution of monies . . . assessed for the relief of the poor . . . shall, once in every quarter . . . make and render to the guardians . . . a full and distinct account in writing of all monies . . . committed to their charge. . . .

LII. That it shall be lawful . . . for the said Commissioners . . . to declare to what extent . . . relief to be given to able-bodied persons or their families . . . may be administered out of the workhouse . . . and all relief . . . contrary to such orders . . . shall be . . . unlawful. . . . (But overseers may delay the operation of such regulations under special circumstances.)

LIV. That . . . the giving of all relief to the poor . . . shall appertain and belong exclusively to such guardians of the poor or select vestry . . . and it shall not be lawful for any overseer to give any further . . . relief . . . than such as shall be ordered by such guardians. . . . (Except in specified cases of urgent necessity.)

LV. The master of every workhouse . . . shall . . . register in a book to be provided at the expense of the parish . . . the name of every person . . . in the receipt of relief at or in such workhouse . . . and in like manner . . . the overseer of the poor shall . . . register in a book . . . the name of every person then in the receipt of relief in such parish out of the workhouse (and in both cases particulars as to family, settlement, previous employment are to be added as required). . . .

LXIV. No settlement shall be acquired . . . (by hiring, service, occupation, except by paying poor rate for one year, apprenticeship in the sea service, by possession of an estate within a parish except during residence within 10 miles).

(LXIX. repeals the Acts imposing liability and punishment of the putative father and punishment of the mother of illegitimate children.)

LXXI. Every child which shall be born a bastard shall . . . follow the settlement of the mother . . . until such child shall attain the age of sixteen or shall acquire a settlement in its own right . . . and such mother, so long as she is unmarried or a widow shall be bound to maintain such child as a part of her family (until it is 16) . . . provided that such liability . . . shall cease on the marriage of such child, if a female.

(The remainder of the Act deals with the duties of officials, jurisdiction, appeals, penalties for contravening the Act, prohibition of introducing alcoholic liquors into workhouses, forfeitures, etc.)

(See *Fowle*, P.L. *passim;* *Redlich* and *Hirst*, E.L.G. i. 98–134, ii. 203–319 ; *Gneist*, E.C. 723–748 ; *Rogers*, P.L. iii. 145–152.)

III. LOCAL GOVERNMENT.

A. (MUNICIPAL CORPORATIONS) 5 & 6 WILLIAM IV. CAP. 76, 1835.[1]

An act to provide for the Regulation of Municipal Corporations in England and Wales.

I. Be it therefore enacted . . . that [all laws, customs and charters inconsistent with the act repealed]. . . .

II. That every person who now is or hereafter may be an inhabitant of any borough . . . and any freeman or burgess . . . shall have and enjoy the same share and benefit of the lands . . . of any borough . . . as he or she might . . . have enjoyed in case this Act had not been passed. . . .

III. That no person . . . shall be . . . made a burgess or freeman of any borough by gift or purchase. . . .

IV. That every person . . . who . . . would have enjoyed . . . the right of voting in the election of a member to serve in Parliament . . . shall enjoy . . . such right for the future. . . .

VI. That . . . in any borough the body . . . corporate . . . shall take . . . the name of the mayor, aldermen and burgesses of such borough. . . .

IX. That every such person of full age . . . who shall have occupied any house . . . or shop within any borough during that year and the whole of each of the two preceding years and . . . shall have been an inhabitant householder . . . shall . . . be a burgess of such borough . . . provided always . . . that he shall have been rated . . . to all rates made for the relief of the poor. . . .

XI. That . . . in every borough it shall be lawful for any person occupying any house . . . or shop to claim to be rated to the relief of the poor in respect of such premises. . . .

XIII. That . . . no person shall be enrolled a burgess . . . in respect of any title other than by occupancy and payment of rates. . . .

(XIV.–XXIV. Provisions for drawing up and revising "The Burgess List".)

XXV. That in every borough shall be elected . . . one fit person who shall be . . . "the mayor" . . . and a certain number of fit persons who shall be . . . "aldermen" . . . and a certain number of other fit persons who shall be . . . "the councillors" . . . and such mayor, aldermen and councillors shall be . . . "the council of such borough." . . .

(XXVI.–XXVIII. Qualifications of aldermen.)

XXIX. Every burgess . . . shall be entitled to vote in the election of councillors. . . .

(XXX.–XLVIII. The mode and time of election of councillors, auditors and assessors. The boroughs scheduled in the Act to be divided into wards, each ward to elect councillors as arranged.)

---

[1] Repealed in part 6 & 7 Will. IV. c. 103 ; 16 & 17 Vict. c. 79 ; 35 & 36 Vict. c. 33 ; Stat. Law Rev. Act, 1874.

XLIX. On the ninth day of November in every year the Council of the borough shall elect out of the aldermen or councillors of such borough a fit person to be the mayor of such borough.

LI. That every person . . . who shall be elected to the office of alderman, councillor, auditor, or assessor, and every councillor who shall be elected to the office of mayor for any borough shall accept such office . . . or shall in lieu thereof pay . . . such fine . . . as the Council of such borough . . . shall declare. . . .

LVII. That the mayor for the time being . . . shall be a justice of the peace of and for such a borough . . . and in boroughs which return a member . . . to serve in parliament . . . shall be the returning officer at all such elections. . . .

LVIII. That the Council of every borough . . . shall appoint a fit person, not being a member of the Council, to be the town-clerk of such borough. . . .

(LX.–LXXIII. As to Coroners, removal of officers, and meetings of the Council, compensation, charitable trusts, etc.)

LXXVI. That the Council shall . . . appoint . . . a sufficient number of their own body who, together with the mayor . . . shall be . . . the watch committee of such borough . . . and such watch committee shall . . . appoint a sufficient number of fit men who shall be sworn in before some justice of the peace . . . to act as constables for preserving the peace day and night. . . .

(LXXVII.–LXXXVI. Duties of Constables, penalties for assaults, etc.)
(LXXXVII.–LXXXIX. Powers for regulating lighting.)

XC. That it shall be lawful for the Council of any borough to make such bye-laws as to them shall meet for the good rule and government of the borough. . . .

(XCI.–XCVII. Finance, leases, watch rate, etc.)

XCVIII. That it shall be lawful for his majesty . . . to assign to so many persons as he shall think proper his majesty's commission to act as justices of the peace in and for each borough. . . .

(XCIX.–CXXXIV. Regulations as to Justices, separate Quarter Sessions, Recorders, jurisdiction of Borough courts, jurors, etc.)

The remainder (CXXXV.–CXIII.) deals with exemptions from the Act *e.g.* the Cinque Ports, the universities of Oxford and Cambridge, etc. Schedules are appended giving lists:—A. Boroughs to have a Commission of the Peace. B. Boroughs to have such Commission on Petition and grant. And various forms for complying with the Regulations of the Act.

(See *Redlich* and *Hirst*, E.L.G. i. 98–419 ; *Gneist*, E.C. 723–748 ; *Rogers*, P.L. iii. 153–163 ; *Somers Vine*, The English Municipal Code.)

2 F

B. (County Councils) 51 & 52 Vict. Cap. 41, 1888.

An Act to amend the Laws relating to Local Government in England and Wales.

1. A Council shall be established in every administrative County, with the management of administrative and financial business, and consist of a chairman, aldermen, and councillors.

2. The Council shall be constituted and elected as the Council of a Borough divided into wards, with the exception of certain specified points as regards the councillors, their numbers, etc. The voters shall be, in a borough, burgesses as defined by 45 & 46 Vict. c. 50 (Municipal Corporation Act, 1882) and elsewhere as defined by this Act. The chairman to be so called, and to be ex officio a justice of the peace.

3. The administrative business of the justices in Quarter Sessions shall be transferred to the County Council, particularly the levying of all rates, borrowing of money, power over county buildings, licensing of music, dancing places, licensing of race-courses, asylums for pauper lunatics, reformatory schools, bridges and roads, county officials, salaries, etc.

4. The Local Government Board may transfer additional local powers.

5. The County Council shall appoint Coroners.

7. Certain powers of the Justices out of sessions (licensing of theatres, etc.) are transferred.

9. The powers of quarter sessions and of justices out of sessions with regard to the police to be vested jointly in Quarter Sessions and the County Council.

10. The Local Government Board may transfer powers of certain Government Departments.

11. The County Council shall maintain the roads.

14, 17, 18, 19. The County Council to have certain powers as a sanitary authority, and appoint and act on reports of officers of health.

15. Power to oppose Bills in Parliament.

16. Power to make bye-laws.

§§ 20–27 define the Financial relations between the National Exchequer and the County, and the contributions by the County for the cost of Union officers.

28. Power to delegate business to a Committee of the County or District Council, or of the justices in petty sessions.

30. A standing joint Committee of quarter sessions and the County Council for police, clerk of the peace, officers, etc.

31. Certain large boroughs named in a schedule (with a population of not less than 50,000) are made administrative counties and called county boroughs.

32–34. The financial and administrative relations of the county boroughs to the counties in which they are situated are defined.

35. The Act is applied as regards certain provisions to "quarter sessions boroughs" (not in the schedule of § 31, but having a population of not less than 10,000).

40. The Act is applied in transfer of powers, duties, and liabilities to the Metropolis, which is to be an administrative County ; but the County of the city of London for jurisdiction and other non-administrative purposes is reserved as a separate County, unless the mayor and citizens thereof desire the contrary. And for the administrative County of London the number of councillors shall be double the number of members of Parliament for the area defined.

42. On petition from the Council the Crown may appoint a paid chairman of quarter sessions for the County of London.

43. The London County Council shall make certain payments to Poor Law Unions within the County.

44, 45. The London County Council shall take over the duties of Metropolitan asylum managers and other duties.

§§ 46–63 deal with application of the Act to Special Counties, Liberties, definition of areas, boundaries, districts, etc.

§ 64–73 define the financial powers, the power to acquire lands, borrow money, audit accounts, the annual budget, etc., of the County Council.

§§ 75–78 define the procedure and machinery of elections, etc.

§§ 79–82 define the procedure of business at meetings.

§ 82 provides for the appointment of a clerk of the peace and of the County Council, but in the administrative County of London they are to be two distinct officials.

§§ 85–126 are supplemental and contain a great number of "Transitory Provisions."

The Third schedule catalogues the name of 61 Boroughs under § 31 which are to be County Boroughs.

Note : The qualification and registration of County electors are defined in the County Electors Act, 1888 (51 & 52 Vict. c. 10), viz.

1. The burgess qualification of the Municipal Corporations Act, 1882 (45 & 46 Vict. c. 50, § 9). Full age, 12 months' occupation of a house, shop, or other building, residence in or within 7 miles of the borough, rating for, and payment of rates of, the qualifying property unless disqualified as an alien, by parochial relief, or by a statutory disentitlement.

2. Occupation of land of the value of £10.

(See *Redlich* and *Hirst*, E.L.G. i. 104 ; *Chalmers*, L.G., and *Odgers*, L.G. ; *Gneist*, S.G.; *Macmorran* and *Dill*, The Local Government Act of 1888, 3rd ed.)

C. (Parish Councils) 56 & 57 Vict. Cap. 73, 1894.

An Act to make further provision for Local Government in England and Wales.

Part I.

1. There shall be a parish meeting for every rural parish, and there shall be a parish Council for every rural parish which has a population of three hundred or upwards ; but the County Council may (a) establish on petition from a parish meeting a parish Council in parishes with a popula-

tion of 100 or more, entitled under (1) only to a parish meeting ; (b) group with their consent parishes under a common parish Council, but each parish shall retain its separate parish meeting.

2. The parish meeting shall consist of "parochial electors," *i.e.* persons registered as electors in the local government or parliamentary registers.

3. The Parish Council shall be elected for one year from the parochial electors and consist of a chairman and councillors, not less than 5 and not more than 15. No disqualification by sex or marriage. The Parish Council shall be a body corporate.

5, 6. The Parish Council to have powers to appoint overseers of the poor, and additional overseers in the place of the churchwardens, and take over the powers, duties, and liabilities of the vestry except "so far as relates to the affairs of the church or ecclesiastical charities," the powers of overseers and churchwardens in respect to poor and county rate, and statutory powers with regard to the Housing of the Working Classes Act of 1890, and the Allotment Acts of 1887 and 1890.

7. Power conferred to adopt statutory powers conferred by "the adoptive Acts," *e.g.* Lighting (1833), Baths and Washhouses (1846–1882), Burial (1832–1885), Public Improvements (1860), Public Libraries (1892), etc.

8, 9, 10. Additional powers conferred to acquire buildings, lands, water, control sewage, rights of way, hiring of lands for allotments, etc.

11. But no financial liability may be incurred without the consent of a parish meeting which involves a rate exceeding 3d. in the Pound or a loan without the approval of the County Council.

12. The powers of a Parish Council to borrow are defined and limited ; (*i.e.* mainly subject to the approval of the Local Government Board and County Council).

14. Powers as regards public property and charities defined and limited.

Part II.

20. As regards Boards of Guardians, ex officio and nominated Guardians to cease ; for the future Guardians to be parochial electors for a parish in the union, elected by parochial electors for 3 years. No disqualification by sex or marriage.

21. (a) Urban sanitary authorities to be called Urban District Councils ; (b) rural sanitary districts to have a Rural District Council.

22. The chairman of a District Council, unless a woman, to be a justice of the peace for the County.

23. Every Urban District, not a borough, to have a District Council of councillors, *all* of whom are to be elected by parochial electors for three years, such councillors themselves being qualified as parochial electors. No disqualification by sex or marriage.

24. Rural District Councils to consist of a chairman and councillors elected by the parishes or other areas for electing guardians in the district.

25, 26, 27. Definition of the powers of District Councils in sanitary, highway matters, and powers transferred from the powers of justices out of session.

30. The provisions of the Act respecting guardians to apply to the administrative County of London and every County borough.

(Part III., 36–42, deals with areas and boundaries.)

(Part IV., 43–77, deals mainly with parish meetings and elections, place of meeting, procedure, registration, definition of the relations of these newly constituted bodies to each other, to the County Council and the Central Authority, the Local Government Board.)

Note § 43. No woman to be disqualified by marriage from being registered as an elector, provided husband and wife are not qualified in respect of the same property.

§ 66. " Nothing in this act shall affect the trusteeship, management or control of any elementary school " (*i.e.* as within the meaning of the Elementary Education Act, 1870).

§ 76. " This Act shall not extend to Scotland or Ireland."

(Part V., 78–89, are "Transitory Provisions.")

(See *Redlich* and *Hirst*, E.L.G. ii. 117–232.)

IV. THE REORGANIZATION OF THE CENTRAL AND COUNTY COURT OF JUSTICE

(Owing to the length, complexity, and technical character of these Acts, a summary rather than a reproduction of the text is given. But so far as possible in important matter the phraseology of the Acts is preserved.)

A. THE JUDICIAL COMMITTEE OF THE PRIVY COUNCIL (3 & 4 WILLIAM IV. CAP. 41, 1833).

An Act for the better administration of Justice in His Majesty's Privy Council.

The preamble refers to 2 & 3 Will. IV. c. 92 ("transferring the powers of the High Court of Delegates in ecclesiastical and maritime causes, to His Majesty in Council "), 25 Hen. VIII. c. 19 ("the submission of the clergy and restraint of appeals "), and 8 Eliz. c. 5 (permitting suit to the Crown in Council), and enacts that (the President of the Privy Council, the Lord Chancellor, Lord Keeper of the Great Seal, Lord Chief Justices of King's Bench and Common Pleas, Master of the Rolls, Vice-chancellor, Lord Chief Baron of the Exchequer, etc., together with all members of the Council who have filled these offices, together with any two other privy councillors specially appointed) shall form a Committee and shall be styled "The Judicial Committee of the Privy Council " to hear and report to the Crown on all appeals (to the Crown in Council).

II., III. Appeals shall lie from Ecclesiastical Courts, Admiralty Courts abroad, and Courts "in the plantations in America" or elsewhere, together with any appeals as either by this Act or by previous Statute or custom have lain to the Crown in Council, as well as such additional matters as are referred to it by the Crown. The report of the Committee to the Crown on these appeals to be read in open court.

V., VI. The decision to be by a majority of those present. The Crown may summon other members of the Council or any other judge of King's Bench, Common Pleas, or Exchequer.

VII.-XIII. Evidence to be taken either *vivâ voce* on oath, or upon written depositions. New trials may be ordered.

XVI. The decrees of the Crown in Council to be enrolled.

XVIII. The Crown is empowered to appoint "a registrar of the said privy council" and to define his duties.

XXI. The order and decree of the Crown in Council on appeal from any court, whether in the East Indies or "other his Majesty's dominions abroad," shall be carried into effect as the Crown in Council shall direct, provided that "the powers, jurisdiction, or authority," "the constitution and duties" of the Privy Council (as a whole) are not "impeached or abridged" except where expressly altered by this Act.

XXII. Appeals permitted from the Superior Court in the East Indies.

XXVIII. Power to enforce throughout the dominions of the Crown the decrees of the Crown in Council and of punishing contempts.

XXX. Two retired Indian or colonial judges, being members of the Privy Council, shall be appointed by the Crown to attend the Judicial Committee and shall be paid for their services.

XXXI. The rights under treaties made with foreign powers, for appeals from Admiralty Courts "in causes of prize" are safe-guarded.

(See *Selborne*, Judicial Procedure in the Privy Council; *Holdsworth*, H.E.L. i. 292–402; *Pike*, H.L. 279–307.)

B. THE COUNTY COURTS (9 & 10 VICT. CAP. 95), 1846.

An Act for the more easy recovery of Small Debts and Demands in England.

. . . And whereas the County Court is a Court of ancient Jurisdiction having cognizance of all Pleas of Personal actions to any amount by virtue of a Writ of Justices issued in that behalf ; and whereas the proceedings in the County Court are dilatory and expensive . . . and that the Courts established . . . should be holden . . . as branches of the County Court under the provisions of this Act . . . be it enacted. . . .

II. The Counties (including Counties of Cities and Towns) to be divided into districts, the County Court to be holden shall be holden for the recovery of Debts and Demands in each of such districts. The City of London excepted.

III. Every Court so holden to have the Jurisdiction and Powers of the County Court, to be a Court of Records, with a Judge "created under this Act" for each district.

IV. The Lord Chancellor to "appoint as many fit persons as are needed to be Judges of the County Court, each of whom shall be a Barrister at

Law of seven years standing" (or practised for seven years as a Barrister and Special Pleader).

XIV. "The lord of any Hundred, Manor, or Liberty having any Court in which Debts or Demands may be recovered" may "surrender the right of holding such a Court" with consent of persons interested.

XVIII. The Lord Chancellor (or in the Duchy of Lancaster the Chancellor of the Duchy) may remove a County Court Judge for Inability or Misbehaviour.

XXI. Every County Court Judge who shall be in the Commission of the Peace may act as a Justice of the Peace.

XXXI. Every Court to have one or more High Bailiffs, appointed and removable by the Judge.

XXXII. The High Bailiffs to serve all summonses and orders and execute all Warrants and Writs.

LVI. The Court to be held in such Place as is appointed by the Crown.

LVIII. Jurisdiction limited to debt or damages not exceeding £20. (This jurisdiction has been widely extended by subsequent Acts, particularly 51 & 52 Vict. c. 43.)

LXX. "When the amount claimed shall exceed" £5 the action may be tried by a Jury when the Parties require it.

CXIII. The County Court Judge has power to commit for contempt.

CXXIV. Judges, Clerks, and Bailiffs not liable to actions for proceedings taken.

CXL., CXLI. The Rights of the Universities of Oxford and Cambridge, and the Courts of the Wardens of the Stannaries exempted from the operation of the Act.

(The greater portion of this long Act is occupied with minute provisions regulating the procedure of the Courts created.)

(See *Holdsworth*, H.E.L. i. 418–421 ; *Redlich and Hirst*, E.L.G. ii. *passim*.)

C. The Judicature Act of 1873 (36 & 37 Vict. Cap. 66).

An Act for the constitution of a Supreme Court and for other purposes relating to the better Administration of Justice in England. (The operation of the Act was deferred to November 1, 1875.)

§ 3. The High Court of Chancery, the Court of Queen's Bench, the Court of Common Pleas, the Court of Exchequer, the High Court of Admiralty, the Court of Probate, the Court for Divorce and Matrimonial Causes "shall be united and consolidated together and shall constitute one Supreme Court of Judicature in England."

§ 4. This Supreme Court "shall consist of two permanent Divisions"— (1) "Her Majesty's High Court of Justice," with original jurisdiction (and appeals from inferior courts as determined) ; (2) "Her Majesty's Court of Appeal," with appellate jurisdiction.

§ 5. The first Judges to be the Lord Chancellor, the Master of the Rolls, the Lord Chief Justice of England (and all other judges of the courts specified in § 1). New Judges to be appointed by letters patent of the

Crown. All the Judges to have "equal power, authority, and jurisdiction." The president in the absence of the Lord Chancellor to be the Lord Chief Justice of England.

§ 9. The Judges to hold office for life; (38 & 39 Vict. c. 77, § 5, substitute "during good behaviour" for "for life" and except the Lord Chancellor) subject to removal by the Crown on an address from both Houses of Parliament. No Judge to be capable of sitting in the House of Commons.

§ 16. The High Court of Justice to be a Superior Court of Record and to exercise the jurisdiction of the High Court of Chancery, Queen's Bench, Common Pleas, Exchequer, Admiralty, Probate, Divorce, Common Pleas at Lancaster, Durham, and jurisdictions by Commissions of Assize, oyer and terminer, Gaol Delivery, or any such Commissions.

§ 18. The Court of Appeal to exercise the jurisdiction of the Chancery Court of Appeal, of the Chancery Appeal Court of Lancaster as a County Palatine, of the Warden of the Stannaries, of the Court of Exchequer Chamber, and of appeals to the Crown in Council from the High Court of Admiralty.

§ 19. The Court of Appeal to have jurisdiction in appeals from "Her Majesty's High Court of Justice" as enacted by § 4 (save when expressly stated to the contrary).

§ 24. Law and Equity to be administered in the High Court of Justice and the Court of Appeal, according to the rules prescribed, and in cases of conflict "the rules of Equity shall prevail."

§ 29. The Crown is empowered to issue Commissions of Assize and the like to the Judges of the High Court of Justice.

§ 31. The High Court of Justice is divided into five divisions—(1) the Chancery; (2) the Queen's Bench; (3) Common Pleas; (4) Exchequer; (5) Probate, Divorce, and Admiralty. Any Judge, if required, may sit in any division or be transferred from one to the other.

§§ 40–44 provide for the constitution of Divisional Courts apart and distinct from the Five Divisions defined in § 31.

§ 45. Appeals from Petty or Quarter Sessions, a County or other inferior court to be determined by the Divisional Courts.

§ 47. The Jurisdiction "in relation to questions of law reserved in criminal trials," *i.e.* "Crown Cases Reserved," is vested in the Judges of the High Court of Justice, or at least five of them, of whom the Lord Chief Justice of England must be one.

(The remainder of the Act is occupied with procedure, and other purely technical or legal points.)

D. The Judicature Act of 1875 (38 & 39 Vict. Cap. 77).

§ 4. The Court of Appeal to consist of five ex officio Judges (Lord Chancellor, Lord Chief Justice, Master of the Rolls, Lord Chief Justice of Common Pleas, Lord Chief Baron of the Exchequer) and not more than three ordinary Judges, the first of whom shall be the existing Lords Justices of Appeal in Chancery. These ordinary Judges to be styled

Justices of Appeal. An additional Judge from the High Court of Justice may serve temporarily on the request of the Lord Chancellor.

§ 6. The Lord Chancellor shall be President of the Court of Appeal.

§ 23. Her Majesty empowered to regulate all circuits of assizes by order in Council laid before each House of Parliament, and such Orders may be annulled on address from either House.

E. The Appellate Jurisdiction Act (39 & 40 Vict. Cap. 59), 1876.

An Act for amending the Appellate Jurisdiction of the House of Lords, and for other purposes.

§ 3. Appeals to the House of Lords to lie from (1) the Court of Appeal in England ; (2) the Courts in Scotland from which appeals had previously lain ; (3) from the Courts in Ireland in the same way. (But by § 12 Appeals from Scotch and Irish Courts not hitherto by law or practice reviewed by the House of Lords are excluded.)

§ 4. Appeals are to be by way of petition to the House of Lords for the matter to be reviewed before the Crown in Court of Parliament to determine what of right ought to be done according to the law and custom of the realm.

§ 5. Not less than three of the following must be present at the hearing of the Appeal, *i.e.* (1) the Lord Chancellor ; (2) the Lords of Appeal in ordinary ; (3) Peers of Parliament "who have held high judicial office."

§ 6. The Crown is empowered to create by letters patent two Lords of Appeal in ordinary, qualified either by (1) high judicial office, or (2) fifteen years as a practising Barrister in England, Scotland, or Ireland, to hold office during good behaviour, but removable on address of both Houses of Parliament, with an annual salary of £6,000 (paid out of the Consolidated Fund § 7), entitled to a writ of summons to attend, sit, and vote in the House of Lords, "but his dignity as a Lord of Parliament shall not descend to his heirs." If the Lord of Appeal is a Privy Councillor he shall also be a member of the Judicial Committee of the Privy Council.

§ 14. By 34 & 35 Vict. c. 91, the Crown had been empowered to appoint four paid members of the Judicial Committee of the Privy Council, but had not power to fill vacancies by death ; the Crown is therefore empowered to fill two of these four paid places by creating two additional Lords of Appeal in ordinary (*i.e.* with the two in § 6, making four in all). The Crown may on the advice of the Privy Council summon, by order in Council, Archbishops and Bishops to sit as assessors of the Judicial Committee for "the hearing of Ecclesiastical Cases." Such order shall be laid before both Houses of Parliament, and may be annulled by the Crown on address from either House.

§ 25. "High Judicial Office" means "any of the following offices, that is to say : The office of Lord Chancellor of Great Britain and Ireland, or of paid Judge of the Judicial Committee of the Privy Council, or of Judge of one of her Majesty's Superior Courts of Great Britain and Ireland."

"Superior Courts" means (1) for England, "Her Majesty's High Court of Justice and Her Majesty's Court of Appeal and the Superior Courts of law and equity in England as they existed before the constitution of Her Majesty's High Court of Justice"; (2) for Ireland, "The Superior Courts of law and equity at Dublin"; (3) for Scotland, "The Court of Session."

(See *Holdsworth*, H.E.L. 402–417; *Wilson*, The Judicature Acts, ed. Chalmers and Mackenzie; *Rogers*, P.L. iii. 485–492.)

V. THE GOVERNMENT OF INDIA.
21 & 22 Vict. Cap. 106, 1858.

An Act for the better Government of India.

Whereas (by the Government of India Act, 1853[1]) the territories in the possession or under the Government of the East India Company were continued under such Government, in trust for her Majesty, until Parliament should otherwise provide, ... And whereas it is expedient that the said territories should be governed by and in the name of Her Majesty : be it therefore enacted . . . as follows : that is to say,

Transfer of the Government of India to Her Majesty.

1. The government of the territories now in possession or under the Government of the East India Company, and all powers in relation to government vested in or exercised by the said Company in trust for her Majesty, shall cease to be vested in or exercised by the said Company; and all territories in the possession or under the Government of the said Company, and all rights vested in or which if this Act had not been passed might have been exercised by the said Company in relation to any territories, shall become vested in Her Majesty and be exercised in her name; and . . . India shall mean the territories vested in Her Majesty as aforesaid, and all territories which may become vested in Her Majesty. . . .

2. India shall be governed by and in the name of Her Majesty; and all rights in relation to any territories which might have been exercised by the said Company . . . shall and may be exercised by and in the name of Her Majesty as rights incidental to the Government of India ; and all the territorial and other revenues of or arising in India, and all tributes and other payments . . . shall be received for and in the name of Her Majesty, and shall be applied and disposed of for the purposes of the Government of India alone, subject to the provisions of this Act.

3. Save as herein otherwise provided, one of Her Majesty's principal Secretaries of State shall have and perform all such or the like powers and duties in anywise relating to the Government or revenues of India, and all such and the like powers over all officers appointed or continued under this

[1] 16 & 17 Vict. c. 95.   See also 24 Geo. III. Sess. 2, c. 25, p. 145.

Act, as might or should have been exercised and performed by the East India Company, or by the Court of Directors or Court of Proprietors of the said Company, either alone or by the direction or with the sanction or approbation of the Commissioners for the affairs of India in relation to such government or revenues, and the officers and servants of the said Company respectively, and also all such powers as might have been exercised by the said Commissioners alone. . . .

(Warrants under 17 & 18 Vict. c. 77 to be countersigned by one of the Principal Secretaries of State.)

4. Any four of Her Majesty's Principal Secretaries of State for the time being, and any four of the Under-Secretaries for the time being to Her Majesty's Principal Secretaries of State, may sit and vote as members of the House of Commons ; but not more than four such Principal Secretaries and not more than four such Under-Secretaries shall sit and vote as members of the House of Commons at the same time.

5. In case the Person who . . . is the President of the Commissioners for the Affairs of India be appointed, . . . one of Her Majesty's Principal Secretaries of State, and be . . . a member of the House of Commons, he shall not by reason of such appointment vacate his seat in Parliament.

6. In case Her Majesty be pleased to appoint a fifth Principal Secretary of State, there shall be paid out of the revenues of India to such Principal Secretary of State and to his Under-Secretaries respectively the like yearly salaries as may for the time being be paid to any other of such Secretaries of State and his Under-Secretaries respectively.

Council of India.

7. For the purposes of this Act a Council shall be estabished, to consist of Fifteen members, and to be styled the Council of India ; and henceforth the Council in India now bearing that name shall be styled the Council of the Governor General of India.

(8. Regulations as to first members of the Council.)

9. Every vacancy . . . among the members of the Council appointed by Her Majesty, . . . shall be filled up by Her Majesty, by Warrant under Her Royal Sign Manual, and every other Vacancy shall be filled up by the by Council Election made at a Meeting to be held for that purpose.

10. The major part of the persons to be elected by the Court of Directors, and the major part of the persons to be first appointed by Her Majesty . . . to be members of the Council, shall be persons who have served or resided in India for ten years at the least, and . . . shall not have last left India more than ten years next preceding the date of their appointment ; and no person other than a person so qualified shall be appointed . . . unless . . . nine at the least of the continuing members of the Council be persons qualified as aforesaid.

11. Every member of the Council . . . shall hold his office during good behaviour ; provided, that it shall be lawful for Her Majesty to remove any such member from his office upon an address of both Houses of Parliament.

12. No member of the Council . . . shall be capable of sitting or voting in Parliament.

13. There shall be paid to each member of the Council the yearly salary of one thousand two hundred pounds, out of the revenues of India.

(14. As to retiring Pensions. 15. The formation of a permanent Home Establishment. 16. As to removal of officers. 17. Compensation to officers not retained. 18. As to Superannuation.)

Duties and Procedure of the Council.

19. The Council shall, under direction of the Secretary of State, and subject to the provisions of this Act, conduct the business transacted in the United Kingdom in relation to the Government of India and the correspondence with India ; but every order or communication sent to India shall be signed by one of the Principal Secretaries of State ; and, save as expressly provided by this Act, every order in the United Kingdom in relation to the Government of India under this Act shall be signed by such Secretary of State ; and all despatches from governments and presidencies in India, and other despatches from India, . . . shall be addressed to such Secretary of State.

20. It shall be lawful for the Secretary of State to divide the Council into committees for the more convenient transaction of business. . . .

21. The Secretary of State shall be the President of the Council, with power to vote. . . .

(22. As to meetings of the Council.)

23. At any meeting of the Council at which the Secretary of State is present, if there be a difference of opinion . . . the determination of the Secretary of State shall be final ; and in case of an equality of votes at any meeting of the Council, the Secretary of State, if present, and, in his absence, the Vice-President, or presiding member, shall have a casting-vote ; and all acts done at any meeting of the Council in the absence of the Secretary of State, except the election of a member of the Council, shall require the sanction or approval in writing of the Secretary of State; and . . . the Secretary of State may require that his opinion, and the reasons for the same, be entered in the minutes of the proceedings, and any member of the Council who may have been present at the meeting may require that his opinion, and any reasons for the same that he may have stated at the meeting, be entered in like manner.

(24. Orders to be open to members of Council who may record their opinions.)

25. If a majority of the Council record as aforesaid their opinions . . . the Secretary of State shall, . . . record his reasons for acting in opposition thereto.

26. Provided, . . . that the despatch of any communication, . . . is urgently required, the communication may be sent or order given notwithstanding the same may not have been submitted to a meeting of the Council, . . . the urgent reasons for sending or making the same being recorded by the Secretary of State, and notice thereof being given

to every member of the Council, except in the cases herein-after mentioned.

(28. As to Secret Orders and Despatches.)

Appointments and Patronage.

29. The appointments of Governor General of India . . . and Governors of Presidencies in India, . . . and the appointments of Advocate General for the several Presidencies, . . . shall be made by Her Majesty by warrant under Her Royal Sign Manual ; . . . the appointments of Lieutenant Governors of provinces or territories shall be made by the Governor General of India, subject to the approbation of Her Majesty. . . .

30. . . . The Secretary of State in Council, with the concurrence of a majority of members present at a meeting, shall have the like power to make regulations for the division and distribution of patronage and power of nomination among the several authorities in India, and the like power of restoring to their stations, offices, or employments, officers and servants suspended or removed by any authority in India as might have been exercised by the said Court of Directors. . . .

(31 repeals §§ 37–42 of 16 & 17 Vict. c. 95.

32–38. Regulations as to Civil Service, Cadetships, etc.)

Transfer of Property.

39. All lands and hereditaments, monies, stores, goods, chattels, and other real and personal estate of the said Company, subject to the debts and liabilities affecting the same respectively, and the benefit of all contracts, covenants, and engagements, and all rights to fines, penalties, and forfeitures, and all other emoluments, which the said Company shall be seized or possessed of or entitled to at the time of the commencement of this Act, except the capital stock of the said Company, and the dividend thereon, shall become vested in Her Majesty, to be applied and disposed of, subject to the provisions of this Act, for the purposes of the Government of India.

40. The Secretary of State in Council, with the concurrence of a majority of votes at a meeting, shall have full power to sell or dispose of all real and personal estate . . . vested in Her Majesty . . . or to raise money on any such real estate by way of mortgage, . . . and to purchase and acquire any land or hereditaments, or any interests therein, stores, goods, chattels, and other property, and to enter into any contracts whatsoever, . . . for the purposes of this Act ; and all property so acquired shall vest in Her Majesty for the service of the Government of India. . . .

Revenues.

41. The expenditure of the Revenues of India, both in India and elsewhere, shall be subject to the control of the Secretary of State in Council ; and no grant or appropriation of any part of such revenues, or of any other property coming into possession of the Secretary of State in Council by

virtue of this Act, shall be made without the concurrence of a majority of votes at a meeting of the Council.

(42–52. Detailed regulations as to Finance, and providing for Audit.)

53. The Secretary of State in Council shall, within the first fourteen days during which Parliament may be sitting next after the first day of May in every year, lay before both Houses of Parliament an account for the financial year preceding . . . of the annual produce of the revenues of India, . . . together with the latest estimate of the same for the last financial year, and also the amount of the debts chargeable on the revenues of India, with the rates of interest they respectively carry, and the annual amount of such interest, . . . and also a list of the Establishment of the Secretary of State in Council, and the Salaries and Allowances payable in respect thereof ; . . . and such account shall be accompanied by a statement prepared from detailed reports from each presidency and district in India in such form as shall best exhibit the moral and material progress and condition of India in each such presidency.

54. When any Order is sent to India directing the actual commencement of hostilities by Her Majesty's forces in India, the fact of such order having been sent shall be communicated to both Houses of Parliament within three months after the sending of such order, if Parliament be sitting, . . . and if Parliament be not sitting at the end of such three months, then within one month after the next meeting of Parliament.

55. Except for preventing or repelling actual invasion of Her Majesty's Indian possessions, or under other sudden or urgent necessity, the revenues of India shall not, without the consent of both Houses of Parliament, be applicable to defray the expenses of any military operation carried on beyond the external frontiers of such possessions by Her Majesty's Forces charged upon such Revenues.

Existing Establishments.

56. The military and naval forces of the East India Company shall be deemed to be the Indian military and naval forces of Her Majesty, and shall be under the same obligations to serve Her Majesty as they would have been under to serve the said Company, and shall be liable to serve within the same territorial limits only, for the same terms only, and be entitled to the like pay, pensions, allowances, and privileges, and the like advantages as regards promotions and otherwise, as if they had continued in the service of the said Company : Such forces, and all persons hereafter enlisting in or entering the same, shall continue and be subject to all Acts of Parliament, Laws of the Governor General of India in Council, and Articles of War, and all other Laws, Regulations, and Provisions relating to the East India Company's military and naval forces respectively, as if Her Majesty's Indian military and naval forces respectively had throughout such acts, laws, articles, regulations and provisions been mentioned to or referred to, instead of such forces of the said Company ; and the pay and expenses of and incident to Her Majesty's Indian military and naval forces shall be defrayed out of the Revenues of India.

57. Provided, That it shall be lawful for Her Majesty from time to time by order in Council to alter or regulate the terms and conditions of service under which persons hereafter entering Her Majesty's Indian forces shall be commissioned, enlisted, or entered to serve, . . . Provided, that every such order in Council shall be laid before both Houses of Parliament within fourteen days after the making thereof, if Parliament be sitting, and if Parliament be not sitting, then within fourteen days within the next meeting thereof.

(58–61. As to officers now in the service of the Company and the orders of Directors before the Act is operative.

62. The Records and Archives of the Company to be delivered to the Secretary of State.

63. The Governor General may exercise his powers before he takes his seat in Council.)

Continuance of Existing Enactments.

64. All Acts and provisions now in force under charter or otherwise concerning India shall, subject to the provisions of this Act, continue in force, and be construed as referring to the Secretary of State in Council in the place of the said Company and the Court of Directors and Court of Proprietors thereof, . . . of this Act.

Actions and Contracts.

65. The Secretary of State in Council shall and may sue and be sued as well in India as in England by the name of the Secretary of State in Council as a body corporate ; and all persons and bodies politic shall and may have and take the same suits, remedies, and proceedings, legal and equitable, against the Secretary of State in Council of India as they could have done against the said Company ; and the property and effects hereby vested in Her Majesty for the purposes of the Government of India, or acquired for the said purposes, shall be subject and liable to the same judgements and executions as they would while vested in the said Company have been liable to respect of debts and liabilities lawfully contracted and incurred by the said Company.

(66. The Secretary of State to represent the Company in pending suits.)

67. All treaties made by the said Company shall be binding on Her Majesty, and all contracts, covenants, liabilities, and engagements of the said Company made, incurred, or entered into before the commencement of this Act may be enforced by and against the Secretary of State in Council. . . .

(68. Members of Council not to be personally liable.

69.–73. Regulations for winding up and settling the Company's affairs.

74.–75. Provisions for bringing the Act into force.)

(See *Hansard*, P.D., third series, clix. ; *Walpole*, H.E. v. 428 ; *Ilbert*, G.I. ; *Anson*, L.C. ii.; *Rogers*, P.L. iii. 432.)

INDEX

See also Table of Contents at the beginning, referred to in the Index as T. of C.
Items printed in italics are cases cited or referred to otherwise than in the Table
of Contents.

J. after a name signifies Mr. Justice . . .

2 G

CORPUS CHRISTI BUTLER LIBRARY COLLEGE

PLYMOUTH
WILLIAM BRENDON AND SON, PRINTERS

A CATALOGUE OF BOOKS PUBLISHED BY METHUEN AND COMPANY: LONDON 36 ESSEX STREET W.C.

CONTENTS

NOVEMBER 1907

A CATALOGUE OF

MESSRS. METHUEN'S

PUBLICATIONS

Colonial Editions are published of all Messrs. METHUEN'S Novels issued at a price above 2s. 6d., and similar editions are published of some works of General Literature. These are marked in the Catalogue. Colonial editions are only for circulation in the British Colonies and India.

I.P.L. represents Illustrated Pocket Library.

PART I.—GENERAL LITERATURE

Abbott (J. H. M.). Author of 'Tommy Cornstalk.' AN OUTLANDER IN ENGLAND: BEING SOME IMPRESSIONS OF AN AUSTRALIAN ABROAD. *Second Edition. Cr. 8vo. 6s.*
A Colonial Edition is also published.

Acatos (M. J.). See Junior School Books.

Adams (Frank). JACK SPRATT. With 24 Coloured Pictures. *Super Royal 16mo. 2s.*

Adeney (W. F.), M.A. See Bennett and Adeney.

Æschylus. See Classical Translations.

Æsop. See I.P.L.

Ainsworth (W. Harrison). See I.P.L.

Alderson (J. P.). MR. ASQUITH. With Portraits and Illustrations. *Demy 8vo. 7s. 6d. net.*

Aldis (Janet). MADAME GEOFFRIN, HER SALON, AND HER TIMES. With many Portraits and Illustrations. *Second Edition. Demy 8vo. 10s. 6d. net.*
A Colonial Edition is also published.

Alexander (William), D.D., Archbishop of Armagh. THOUGHTS AND COUNSELS OF MANY YEARS. *Demy 16mo. 2s. 6d.*

Alken (Henry). THE NATIONAL SPORTS OF GREAT BRITAIN. With descriptions in English and French. With 51 Coloured Plates. *Royal Folio. Five Guineas net.* The Plates can be had separately in a Portfolio. *£3, 3s. net.*
See also I.P.L.

Allen (C. C.) See Textbooks of Technology.

Allen (Jessie). See Little Books on Art.

Allen (J. Romilly), F.S.A. See Antiquary's Books.

Almack (E.). See Little Books on Art.

Amherst (Lady). A SKETCH OF EGYPTIAN HISTORY FROM THE EARLIEST TIMES TO THE PRESENT DAY. With many Illustrations. *Demy 8vo. 7s. 6d. net.*

Anderson (F. M.). THE STORY OF THE BRITISH EMPIRE FOR CHILDREN. With many Illustrations. *Cr. 8vo. 2s.*

Anderson (J. G.), B.A., Examiner to London University, NOUVELLE GRAMMAIRE FRANÇAISE. *Cr. 8vo. 2s.*
EXERCICES DE GRAMMAIRE FRANÇAISE. *Cr. 8vo. 1s. 6d.*

Andrewes (Bishop). PRECES PRIVATAE. Edited, with Notes, by F. E. BRIGHTMAN, M.A., of Pusey House, Oxford. *Cr. 8vo. 6s.*

Anglo-Australian. AFTER-GLOW MEMORIES. *Cr. 8vo. 6s.*
A Colonial Edition is also published.

Anon. FELISSA; OR, THE LIFE AND OPINIONS OF A KITTEN OF SENTIMENT. With 12 Coloured Plates. *Post 16mo. 2s. 6d. net.*

Aristotle. THE NICOMACHEAN ETHICS. Edited, with an Introduction and Notes, by JOHN BURNET, M.A., Professor of Greek at St. Andrews. *Cheaper issue. Demy 8vo. 10s. 6d. net.*

Atkins (H. G.). See Oxford Biographies.

Atkinson (C. M.). JEREMY BENTHAM. *Demy 8vo. 5s. net.*

Atkinson (T. D.). A SHORT HISTORY OF ENGLISH ARCHITECTURE. With over 200 Illustrations. *Second Edition. Fcap. 8vo. 3s. 6d. net.*
A GLOSSARY OF TERMS USED IN ENGLISH ARCHITECTURE. Illustrated. *Second Ed. Fcap. 8vo. 3s. 6d. net.*

Auden (T.), M.A., F.S.A. See Ancient Cities.

Aurelius (Marcus) and **Epictetus.** WORDS OF THE ANCIENT WISE: Thoughts from. Edited by W. H. D. ROUSE, M.A., Litt.D. *Fcap. 8vo. 3s. 6d. net.* See also Standard Library.

Austen (Jane). See Little Library and Standard Library.

Bacon (Francis). See Little Library and Standard Library.

Baden-Powell (R. S. S.), Major-General. THE DOWNFALL OF PREMPEH. A Diary of Life in Ashanti 1895. Illustrated. *Third Edition. Large Cr. 8vo. 6s.*
A Colonial Edition is also published.

THE MATABELE CAMPAIGN, 1896. With nearly 100 Illustrations. *Fourth Edition. Large Cr. 8vo. 6s.*
A Colonial Edition is also published.

Bailey (J. C.), M.A. See Cowper.

Baker (W. G.), M.A. See Junior Examination Series.

Baker (Julian L.), F.I.C., F.C.S. See Books on Business.

Balfour (Graham). THE LIFE OF ROBERT LOUIS STEVENSON. *Third and Cheaper Edition, Revised. Cr. 8vo. 6s.*
A Colonial Edition is also published.

Ballard (A.), B.A., LL.B. See Antiquary's Books.

Bally (S. E.). See Commercial Series.

Banks (Elizabeth L.). THE AUTO-BIOGRAPHY OF A 'NEWSPAPER GIRL.' *Second Edition. Cr. 8vo. 6s.*
A Colonial Edition is also published.

Barham (R. H.). See Little Library.

Baring (The Hon. Maurice). WITH THE RUSSIANS IN MANCHURIA. *Third Edition. Demy 8vo. 7s. 6d. net.*
A Colonial Edition is also published.

A YEAR IN RUSSIA. *Second Edition. Demy 8vo. 7s. 6d.*

Baring-Gould (S.). THE LIFE OF NAPOLEON BONAPARTE. With over 150 Illustrations in the Text, and a Photogravure Frontispiece. *Royal 8vo. 10s. 6d. net.*

THE TRAGEDY OF THE CÆSARS. With numerous Illustrations from Busts, Gems, Cameos, etc. *Sixth Edition. Royal 8vo. 10s. 6d. net.*

A BOOK OF FAIRY TALES. With numerous Illustrations by A. J. GASKIN. *Third Edition. Cr. 8vo. Buckram. 6s.*

OLD ENGLISH FAIRY TALES. With numerous Illustrations by F. D. BEDFORD. *Third Edition. Cr. 8vo. Buckram. 6s.*

THE VICAR OF MORWENSTOW. Revised Edition. With a Portrait. *Third Edition. Cr. 8vo. 3s. 6d.*

A BOOK OF DARTMOOR: A Descriptive and Historical Sketch. With Plans and numerous Illustrations. *Second Edition. Cr. 8vo. 6s.*

A BOOK OF DEVON. Illustrated. *Second Edition. Cr. 8vo. 6s.*

A BOOK OF CORNWALL. Illustrated. *Second Edition. Cr. 8vo. 6s.*

A BOOK OF NORTH WALES. Illustrated. *Cr. 8vo. 6s.*

A BOOK OF SOUTH WALES. Illustrated. *Cr. 8vo. 6s.*

A BOOK OF BRITTANY. Illustrated. *Cr. 8vo. 6s.*

A BOOK OF THE RIVIERA. Illustrated. *Cr. 8vo. 6s.*
A Colonial Edition is also published.

A BOOK OF THE RHINE: From Cleve to Mainz. Illustrated. *Second Edition. Crown 8vo. 6s.*
A Colonial Edition is also published.

A BOOK OF THE PYRENEES. With 24 Illustrations. *Crown 8vo. 6s.*
A Colonial Edition is also published.

A BOOK OF GHOSTS. With 8 Illustrations by D. MURRAY SMITH. *Second Edition. Cr. 8vo. 6s.*

OLD COUNTRY LIFE. With 67 Illustrations. *Fifth Edition. Large Cr. 8vo. 6s.*

A GARLAND OF COUNTRY SONG: English Folk Songs with their Traditional Melodies. Collected and arranged by S. BARING-GOULD and H. F. SHEPPARD. *Demy 4to. 6s.*

SONGS OF THE WEST: Folk Songs of Devon and Cornwall. Collected from the Mouths of the People. By S. BARING-GOULD, M.A., and H. FLEETWOOD SHEPPARD, M.A. New and Revised Edition, under the musical editorship of CECIL J. SHARP, Principal of the Hampstead Conservatoire. *Large Imperial 8vo. 5s. net.*

A BOOK OF NURSERY SONGS AND RHYMES. Edited by S. BARING-GOULD, and Illustrated by the Birmigham Art School. *A New Edition. Long Cr. 8vo. 2s. 6d. net.*

STRANGE SURVIVALS AND SUPERSTITIONS. *Third Edition. Cr. 8vo. 2s. 6d. net.*

YORKSHIRE ODDITIES AND STRANGE EVENTS. *New and Revised Edition. Cr. 8vo. 2s. 6d. net.*
See also Little Guides.

Barker (Aldred F.). See Textbooks of Technology.

Barker (E.), M.A. (Late) Fellow of Merton College, Oxford. THE POLITICAL THOUGHT OF PLATO AND ARISTOTLE. *Demy 8vo. 10s. 6d. net.*

Barnes (W. E.), D.D. See Churchman's Bible.

Barnett (Mrs. P. A.). See Little Library.

Baron (R. R. N.), M.A. FRENCH PROSE COMPOSITION. *Second Edition. Cr. 8vo. 2s. 6d. Key, 3s. net.*
See also Junior School Books.

Barron (H. M.), M.A., Wadham College, Oxford. TEXTS FOR SERMONS. With a Preface by Canon SCOTT HOLLAND. *Cr. 8vo. 3s. 6d.*

Bartholomew (J. G.), F.R.S.E. See C. G. Robertson.

Bastable (C. F.), M.A. THE COMMERCE OF NATIONS. *Fourth Ed. Cr. 8vo. 2s. 6d.*

Bastian (H. Charlton), M.D., F.R.S. THE EVOLUTION OF LIFE. Illustrated. *Demy 8vo. 7s. 6d. net.*

Batson (Mrs. Stephen). A CONCISE HANDBOOK OF GARDEN FLOWERS. *Fcap. 8vo. 3s. 6d.*

Batten (Loring W.), Ph.D., S.T.D. THE HEBREW PROPHET. *Cr. 8vo. 3s. 6d. net.*

Bayley (R. Child). THE COMPLETE PHOTOGRAPHER. With over 100 Illustrations. *Second Edition. Demy 8vo. 10s. 6d. net.*

Beard (W. S.). EASY EXERCISES IN ALGEBRA. *Cr. 8vo. 1s. 6d.* See Junior Examination Series and Beginner's Books.

Beckford (Peter). THOUGHTS ON HUNTING. Edited by J. OTHO PAGET, and Illustrated by G. H. JALLAND. *Second Edition. Demy 8vo. 6s.*

Beckford (William). See Little Library.

Beeching (H. C.), M.A., Canon of Westminster. See Library of Devotion.

Begbie (Harold). MASTER WORKERS. Illustrated. *Demy 8vo. 7s. 6d. net.*

Behmen (Jacob). DIALOGUES ON THE SUPERSENSUAL LIFE. Edited by BERNARD HOLLAND. *Fcap. 8vo. 3s. 6d.*

Bell (Mrs. A.). THE SKIRTS OF THE GREAT CITY. *Second Ed. Cr. 8vo. 6s.*

Belloc (Hilaire), M.P. PARIS. With Maps and Illustrations. *Second Edition, Revised. Cr. 8vo. 6s.*

HILLS AND THE SEA. *Second Edition. Crown 8vo. 6s.*

Bellot (H. H. L.), M.A. THE INNER AND MIDDLE TEMPLE. With numerous Illustrations. *Crown 8vo. 6s. net.*

Bennett (W. H.), M.A. A PRIMER OF THE BIBLE. *Fourth Ed. Cr. 8vo. 2s. 6d.*

Bennett (W. H.) and Adeney (W. F.). A BIBLICAL INTRODUCTION. *Fourth Edition. Cr. 8vo. 7s. 6d.*

Benson (Archbishop) GOD'S BOARD : Communion Addresses. *Fcap. 8vo. 3s. 6d. net.*

Benson (A. C.), M.A. See Oxford Biographies.

Benson (R. M.). THE WAY OF HOLINESS : a Devotional Commentary on the 119th Psalm. *Cr. 8vo. 5s.*

Bernard (E. R.), M.A., Canon of Salisbury. THE ENGLISH SUNDAY. *Fcap. 8vo. 1s. 6d.*

Bertouch (Baroness de). THE LIFE OF FATHER IGNATIUS. Illustrated. *Demy 8vo. 10s. 6d. net.*

Beruete (A. de). See Classics of Art.

Betham-Edwards (M.). HOME LIFE IN FRANCE. Illustrated. *Fourth and Cheaper Edition. Crown 8vo. 6s.*
A Colonial Edition is also published.

Bethune-Baker (J. F.), M.A. See Handbooks of Theology.

Bidez (M.). See Byzantine Texts.

Biggs (C. R. D.), D.D. See Churchman's Bible.

Bindley (T. Herbert), B.D. THE OECUMENICAL DOCUMENTS OF THE FAITH. With Introductions and Notes. *Second Edition. Cr. 8vo. 6s. net.*

Binns (H. B.). THE LIFE OF WALT WHITMAN. Illustrated. *Demy 8vo. 10s. 6d. net.*
A Colonial Edition is also published.

Binyon (Lawrence). THE DEATH OF ADAM, AND OTHER POEMS. *Cr. 8vo. 3s. 6d. net.*
See also W. Blake.

Birnstingl (Ethel). See Little Books on Art.

Blair (Robert). See I.P.L.

Blake (William). THE LETTERS OF WILLIAM BLAKE, TOGETHER WITH A LIFE BY FREDERICK TATHAM. Edited from the Original Manuscripts, with an Introduction and Notes, by ARCHIBALD G. B. RUSSELL. With 12 Illustrations. *Demy 8vo. 7s. 6d. net.*

ILLUSTRATIONS OF THE BOOK OF JOB. With a General Introduction by LAWRENCE BINYON. *Quarto. 21s. net.*
See also I.P.L. and Little Library.

Blaxland (B.), M.A. See Library of Devotion.

Bloom (J. Harvey), M.A. SHAKESPEARE'S GARDEN. Illustrated. *Fcap. 8vo. 3s. 6d. ; leather, 4s. 6d. net.*
See also Antiquary's Books.

Blouet (Henri). See Beginner's Books.

Boardman (T. H.), M.A. See Textbooks of Science.

Bodley (J. E. C.), Author of ' France.' THE CORONATION OF EDWARD VII. *Demy 8vo. 21s. net.* By Command of the King.

Body (George), D.D. THE SOUL'S PILGRIMAGE : Devotional Readings from his writings. Selected by J. H. BURN, B.D., F.R.S.E. *Demy 16mo. 2s. 6d.*

Bona (Cardinal). See Library of Devotion.

Boon (F. C.). See Commercial Series.

Borrow (George). See Little Library.

Bos (J. Ritzema). AGRICULTURAL ZOOLOGY. Translated by J. R. AINSWORTH DAVIS, M.A. With 155 Illustrations. *Cr. 8vo. Third Edition. 3s. 6d.*

Botting (C. G.), B.A. EASY GREEK EXERCISES. *Cr. 8vo. 2s.* See also Junior Examination Series.

Boulting (W.) TASSO AND HIS TIMES. With 24 Illustrations. *Demy 8vo. 10s. 6d. net.*

Boulton (E. S.), M.A. GEOMETRY ON MODERN LINES. *Cr. 8vo. 2s.*

Boulton (William B.). THOMAS GAINSBOROUGH With 40 Illustrations. *Demy 8vo. 7s. 6d. net.*

SIR JOSHUA REYNOLDS, P.R.A. With 49 Illustrations. *Demy 8vo. 7s. 6d. net.*

Bowden (E. M.). THE IMITATION OF BUDDHA : Being Quotations from Buddhist Literature for each Day in the Year. *Fifth Edition. Cr. 16mo. 2s. 6d.*

Boyd-Carpenter (Margaret). THE CHILD IN ART. Illustrated. *Second Edition. Large Crown 8vo. 6s.*

Boyle (W.). CHRISTMAS AT THE ZOO. With Verses by W. BOYLE and 24 Coloured Pictures by H. B. NEILSON. *Super Royal 16mo. 2s.*

Brabant (F. G.), M.A. See Little Guides.

Bradley (A. G.) ROUND ABOUT WILTSHIRE. With 30 Illustrations of which 14 are in colour by T. C. GOTCH. *Second Ed. Cr. 8vo. 6s.*

Bradley (J. W.). See Little Books on Art.

Braid (James) and Others. GREAT GOLFERS IN THE MAKING. By Thirty-Four Famous Players. Edited, with an Introduction, by HENRY LEACH. With 34 Portraits. *Demy 8vo. 7s. 6d. net.*
A Colonial Edition is also published.

Brailsford (H. N.). MACEDONIA: ITS RACES AND ITS FUTURE. Illustrated. *Demy 8vo.* 12s. 6d. net.

Brodrick (Mary) and **Morton (Anderson).** A CONCISE HANDBOOK OF EGYPTIAN ARCHÆOLOGY. Illustrated. *Cr. 8vo.* 3s. 6d.

Brooks (E. E.), B.Sc. See Textbooks of Technology.

Brooks (E. W.). See Byzantine Texts.

Brown (P. H.), LL.D., Fraser Professor of Ancient (Scottish) History at the University of Edinburgh. SCOTLAND IN THE TIME OF QUEEN MARY. *Demy 8vo.* 7s. 6d. net.

Brown (S. E.), M.A., Camb., B.A., B.Sc., London; Senior Science Master at Uppingham School. A PRACTICAL CHEMISTRY NOTE-BOOK FOR MATRICULATION AND ARMY CANDIDATES: EASIER EXPERIMENTS ON THE COMMONER SUBSTANCES. *Cr. 4to.* 1s. 6d. net.

Browne (Sir Thomas). See Standard Library.

Brownell (C. L.). THE HEART OF JAPAN. Illustrated. *Third Edition. Cr. 8vo.* 6s.; also *Demy 8vo.* 6d.

Browning (Robert). See Little Library.

Buckland (Francis T.). CURIOSITIES OF NATURAL HISTORY. Illustrated by H. B. NEILSON. *Cr. 8vo.* 3s. 6d.

Buckton (A. M.) THE BURDEN OF ENGELA: a Ballad-Epic. *Second Edition. Cr. 8vo.* 3s. 6d. net.
KINGS IN BABYLON. A Drama. *Crown 8vo.* 1s. net.
EAGER HEART: A Mystery Play. *Fifth Edition. Cr. 8vo.* 1s. net.

Budge (E. A. Wallis). THE GODS OF THE EGYPTIANS. With over 100 Coloured Plates and many Illustrations. *Two Volumes. Royal 8vo.* £3, 3s. net.

Buist (H. Massac). THE MOTOR YEAR BOOK AND AUTOMOBILISTS' ANNUAL FOR 1906. *Demy 8vo.* 7s. 6d. net.

Bull (Paul), Army Chaplain. GOD AND OUR SOLDIERS. *Second Edition. Cr. 8vo.* 6s.

Bulley (Miss). See Lady Dilke.

Bunyan (John). THE PILGRIM'S PROGRESS. Edited, with an Introduction, by C. H. FIRTH, M.A. With 39 Illustrations by R. ANNING BELL. *Cr. 8vo.* 6s.
See also Library of Devotion and Standard Library.

Burch (G. J.), M.A., F.R.S. A MANUAL OF ELECTRICAL SCIENCE. Illustrated. *Cr. 8vo.* 3s.

Burgess (Gelett). GOOPS AND HOW TO BE THEM. Illustrated. *Small 4to.* 6s.

Burke (Edmund). See Standard Library.

Burn (A. E.), D.D., Rector of Handsworth and Prebendary of Lichfield.
See Handbooks of Theology.

Burn (J. H.), B.D. THE CHURCHMAN'S TREASURY OF SONG. Selected and Edited by. *Fcap 8vo.* 3s. 6d. net. See also Library of Devotion.

Burnand (Sir F. C.). RECORDS AND REMINISCENCES. With a Portrait by H. v. HERKOMER. *Cr. 8vo. Fourth and Cheaper Edition.* 6s.
A Colonial Edition is also published.

Burns (Robert), THE POEMS OF. Edited by ANDREW LANG and W. A. CRAIGIE. With Portrait. *Third Edition. Demy 8vo, gilt top.* 6s.

Burnside (W. F.), M.A. OLD TESTAMENT HISTORY FOR USE IN SCHOOLS. *Third Edition. Cr. 8vo.* 3s. 6d.

Burton (Alfred). See I.P.L.

Bussell (F. W.), D.D., Fellow and Vice Principal of Brasenose College, Oxford. CHRISTIAN THEOLOGY AND SOCIAL PROGRESS: The Bampton Lectures for 1905. *Demy 8vo.* 10s. 6d. net.

Butler (Joseph). See Standard Library.

Caldecott (Alfred), D.D. See Handbooks of Theology.

Calderwood (D. S.), Headmaster of the Normal School, Edinburgh. TEST CARDS IN EUCLID AND ALGEBRA. In three packets of 40, with Answers. 1s. each. Or in three Books, price 2d., 2d., and 3d.

Cambridge (Ada) [**Mrs. Cross**]. THIRTY YEARS IN AUSTRALIA. *Demy 8vo.* 7s. 6d.

Canning (George). See Little Library.

Capey (E. F. H.). See Oxford Biographies.

Careless (John). See I.P.L.

Carlyle (Thomas). THE FRENCH REVOLUTION. Edited by C. R. L. FLETCHER, Fellow of Magdalen College, Oxford. *Three Volumes. Cr. 8vo.* 18s.
THE LIFE AND LETTERS OF OLIVER CROMWELL. With an Introduction by C. H. FIRTH, M.A., and Notes and Appendices by Mrs. S. C. LOMAS. *Three Volumes. Demy 8vo.* 18s. net.

Carlyle (R. M. and A. J.), M.A. See Leaders of Religion.

Channer (C. C.) and **Roberts (M. E.).** LACEMAKING IN THE MIDLANDS, PAST AND PRESENT. With 16 full-page Illustrations. *Cr. 8vo.* 2s. 6d.

Chapman (S. J.). See Books on Business.

Chatterton (Thomas). See Standard Library.

Chesterfield (Lord), THE LETTERS OF, TO HIS SON. Edited, with an Introduction by C. STRACHEY, and Notes by A. CALTHROP. *Two Volumes. Cr. 8vo.* 12s.

Chesterton (G. K.). CHARLES DICKENS. With two Portraits in photogravure. *Fourth Edition. Demy 8vo.* 7s. 6d. net.
A Colonial Edition is also published.

Childe (Charles P.), B.A., F.R.C.S. THE CONTROL OF A SCOURGE: OR, How CANCER IS CURABLE. *Demy 8vo.* 7s. 6d. net.

Christian (F. W.). THE CAROLINE ISLANDS. With many Illustrations and Maps. *Demy 8vo. 12s. 6d. net.*

Cicero. See Classical Translations.

Clarke (F. A.), M.A. See Leaders of Religion.

Clausen (George), A.R.A., R.W.S. AIMS AND IDEALS IN ART : Eight Lectures delivered to the Students of the Royal Academy of Arts. With 32 Illustrations. *Second Edition. Large Post 8vo. 5s. net.*
SIX LECTURES ON PAINTING. *First Series.* With 19 Illustrations. *Third Edition, Large Post 8vo. 3s. 6d. net.*

Cleather (A. L.). See Wagner.

Clinch (G.). See Little Guides.

Clough (W. T.). See Junior School Books and Textbooks of Science.

Clouston (T. S.), M.D., C.C.D., F.R.S.E., Lecturer on Mental Diseases in the University of Edinburgh. THE HYGIENE OF MIND. With 10 Illustrations. *Fourth Edition. Demy 8vo. 7s. 6d. net.*

Coast (W. G.), B.A. EXAMINATION PAPERS IN VERGIL. *Cr. 8vo. 2s.*

Cobb (W. F.), M.A. THE BOOK OF PSALMS : with a Commentary. *Demy 8vo. 10s. 6d. net.*

Coleridge (S. T.). POEMS OF. Selected and Arranged by ARTHUR SYMONS. With a photogravure Frontispiece. *Fcap. 8vo. 2s. 6d. net.*

Collingwood (W. G.), M.A. THE LIFE OF JOHN RUSKIN. With Portraits. *Sixth Edition. Cr. 8vo. 2s. 6d. net.*

Collins (W. E.), M.A. See Churchman's Library.

Colonna. HYPNEROTOMACHIA POLIPHILI UBI HUMANA OMNIA NON NISI SOMNIUM ESSE DOCET ATQUE OBITER PLURIMA SCITU SANE QUAM DIGNA COMMEMORAT. An edition limited to 350 copies on handmade paper. *Folio. £3, 3s. net.*

Combe (William). See I.P.L.

Conrad (Joseph). THE MIRROR OF THE SEA : Memories and Impressions. *Third Edition. Cr. 8vo. 6s.*

Cook (A. M.), M.A., and **Marchant (C. E.),** M.A. PASSAGES FOR UNSEEN TRANSLATION. Selected from Greek and Latin Literature. *Third Ed. Cr. 8vo. 3s. 6d.*
LATIN PASSAGES FOR UNSEEN TRANSLATION. *Third Ed. Cr. 8vo. 1s. 6d.*

Cooke-Taylor (R. W.). THE FACTORY SYSTEM. *Cr. 8vo. 2s. 6d.*

Corelli (Marie). THE PASSING OF THE GREAT QUEEN. *Second Ed. Fcap. 4to. 1s.*
A CHRISTMAS GREETING. *Cr. 4to. 1s.*

Corkran (Alice). See Little Books on Art.

Cotes (Everard). SIGNS AND PORTENTS IN THE FAR EAST. With 24 Illustrations. *Second Edition. Demy 8vo. 7s. 6d. net.*

Cotes (Rosemary). DANTE'S GARDEN. With a Frontispiece. *Second Edition. Fcap. 8vo. 2s. 6d.; leather, 3s. 6d. net.*
BIBLE FLOWERS. With a Frontispiece and Plan. *Fcap. 8vo. 2s. 6d. net.*

Cowley (Abraham). See Little Library.

Cowper (William), THE POEMS OF. Edited with an Introduction and Notes by J. C. BAILEY, M.A. Illustrated, including two unpublished designs by WILLIAM BLAKE. *Demy 8vo. 10s. 6d. net.*

Cox (J. Charles), LL.D., F.S.A. See Little Guides, The Antiquary's Books, and Ancient Cities.

Cox (Harold), B.A., M.P. LAND NATIONALISATION AND LAND TAXATION. *Second Edition revised. Cr. 8vo. 3s. 6d. net.*

Crabbe (George). See Little Library.

Craigie (W. A.). A PRIMER OF BURNS. *Cr. 8vo. 2s. 6d.*

Craik (Mrs.). See Little Library.

Crane (Capt. C. P.). See Little Guides.

Crane (Walter). AN ARTIST'S REMINISCENCES. *Second Edition.*

Crashaw (Richard). See Little Library.

Crawford (F. G.). See Mary C. Danson.

Crofts (T. R. N.), M.A. See Simplified French Texts.

Cross (J. A.), M.A. THE FAITH OF THE BIBLE. *Fcap. 8vo. 2s. 6d. net.*

Cruikshank (G.). THE LOVING BALLAD OF LORD BATEMAN. With 11 Plates. *Cr. 16mo. 1s. 6d. net.*

Crump (B.). See Wagner.

Cunliffe (Sir F. H. E.), Fellow of All Souls' College, Oxford. THE HISTORY OF THE BOER WAR. With many Illustrations, Plans, and Portraits. *In 2 vols. Quarto. 15s. each.*

Cunynghame (H. H.), C.B. See Connoisseur's Library.

Cutts (E. L.), D.D. See Leaders of Religion.

Daniell (G. W.), M.A. See Leaders of Religion.

Danson (Mary C.) and Crawford (F. G.). FATHERS IN THE FAITH. *Fcap. 8vo. 1s. 6d.*

Dante. LA COMMEDIA DI DANTE. The Italian Text edited by PAGET TOYNBEE, M.A., D.Litt. *Cr. 8vo. 6s.*
THE PURGATORIO OF DANTE. Translated into Spenserian Prose by C. GORDON WRIGHT. With the Italian text. *Fcap. 8vo. 2s. 6d. net.*
See also Paget Toynbee, Little Library, Standard Library, and Warren-Vernon.

Darley (George). See Little Library.

D'Arcy (R. F.), M.A. A NEW TRIGONOMETRY FOR BEGINNERS. With numerous diagrams. *Cr. 8vo. 2s. 6d.*

Davenport (Cyril). See Connoisseur's Library and Little Books on Art.

Davey (Richard). THE PAGEANT OF LONDON. With 40 Illustrations in Colour by JOHN FULLEYLOVE, R.I. *In Two Volumes. Demy 8vo. 15s. net.*

Davis (H. W. C.), M.A., Fellow and Tutor of Balliol College, Author of 'Charlemagne.' ENGLAND UNDER THE NORMANS AND ANGEVINS : 1066-1272. With Maps and Illustrations. *Demy 8vo. 10s. 6d. net.*

Dawson (Nelson). See Connoisseur's Library.

Dawson (Mrs. N.). See Little Books on Art.

Deane (A. C.). See Little Library.

Dearmer (Mabel). A CHILD'S LIFE OF CHRIST. With 8 Illustrations in Colour by E. FORTESCUE-BRICKDALE. *Large Cr. 8vo. 6s.*

Delbos (Leon). THE METRIC SYSTEM. *Cr. 8vo. 2s.*

Demosthenes. AGAINST CONON AND CALLICLES. Edited by F. DARWIN SWIFT, M.A. *Second Edition. Fcap. 8vo. 2s.*

Dickens (Charles). See Little Library, I.P.L., and Chesterton.

Dickinson (Emily). POEMS. *Cr. 8vo. 4s. 6d. net.*

Dickinson (G. L.), M.A., Fellow of King's College, Cambridge. THE GREEK VIEW OF LIFE. *Sixth Edition. Cr. 8vo. 2s. 6d.*

Dilke (Lady), Bulley (Miss), and **Whitley (Miss).** WOMEN'S WORK. *Cr. 8vo. 2s. 6d.*

Dillon (Edward). See Connoisseur's Library and Little Books on Art.

Ditchfield (P. H.), M.A., F.S.A. THE STORY OF OUR ENGLISH TOWNS. With an Introduction by AUGUSTUS JESSOPP, D.D. *Second Edition. Cr. 8vo. 6s.*
OLD ENGLISH CUSTOMS: Extant at the Present Time. *Cr. 8vo. 6s.*
ENGLISH VILLAGES. Illustrated. *Second Edition. Cr. 8vo. 2s. 6d. net.*
THE PARISH CLERK. With 31 Illustrations. *Third Edition. Demy 8vo. 7s. 6d. net.*

Dixon (W. M.), M.A. A PRIMER OF TENNYSON. *Second Edition. Cr. 8vo. 2s. 6d.*
ENGLISH POETRY FROM BLAKE TO BROWNING. *Second Edition. Cr. 8vo. 2s. 6d*

Doney (May). SONGS OF THE REAL. *Cr. 8vo. 3s. 6d. net.*
A volume of poems.

Douglas (James). THE MAN IN THE PULPIT. *Cr. 8vo. 2s. 6d. net.*

Dowden (J.), D.D., Lord Bishop of Edinburgh. See Churchman's Library.

Drage (G.). See Books on Business.

Driver (S. R.), D.D., D.C.L., Canon of Christ Church, Regius Professor of Hebrew in the University of Oxford. SERMONS ON SUBJECTS CONNECTED WITH THE OLD TESTAMENT. *Cr. 8vo. 6s.*
See also Westminster Commentaries.

Dry (Wakeling). See Little Guides.

Dryhurst (A. R.). See Little Books on Art.

Du Buisson (J. C.), M.A. See Churchman's Bible.

Duguid (Charles). See Books on Business.

Dumas (Alexander). MY MEMOIRS. Translated by E. M. WALLER. With Portraits. *In Six Volumes. Cr. 8vo. 6s. each.* Volume I.

Dunn (J. T.), D.Sc., **and Mundella (V. A.).** GENERAL ELEMENTARY SCIENCE. With 114 Illustrations. *Second Edition. Cr. 8vo. 3s. 6d.*

Dunstan (A. E.), B.Sc. See Junior School Books and Textbooks of Science.

Durham (The Earl of). A REPORT ON CANADA. With an Introductory Note. *Demy 8vo. 4s. 6d. net.*

Dutt (W. A.). THE NORFOLK BROADS. With coloured Illustrations by FRANK SOUTHGATE. *Cr. 8vo. 6s.*
WILD LIFE IN EAST ANGLIA. With 16 Illustrations in colour by FRANK SOUTHGATE, R.B.A. *Second Edition. Demy 8vo. 7s. 6d. net.*
See also Little Guides.

Earle (John), Bishop of Salisbury. MICRO-COSMOGRAPHIE, OR A PIECE OF THE WORLD DISCOVERED. *Post 16mo. 2s net.*

Edmonds (Major J. E.). See W. B. Wood.

Edwards (Clement), M.P. RAILWAY NATIONALIZATION. *Second Edition Revised. Crown 8vo. 2s. 6d. net.*

Edwards (W. Douglas). See Commercial Series.

Egan (Pierce). See I.P.L.

Egerton (H. E.), M.A. A HISTORY OF BRITISH COLONIAL POLICY. New and Cheaper Issue. *Demy 8vo. 7s. 6d. net.*
A Colonial Edition is also published.

Ellaby (C. G.). See Little Guides.

Ellerton (F. G.). See S. J. Stone.

Ellwood (Thomas), THE HISTORY OF THE LIFE OF. Edited by C. G. CRUMP, M.A. *Cr. 8vo. 6s.*

Epictetus. See Aurelius.

Erasmus. A Book called in Latin EN-CHIRIDION MILITIS CHRISTIANI, and in English the Manual of the Christian Knight.
From the edition printed by Wynken de Worde, 1533. *Fcap. 8vo. 3s. 6d. net.*

Fairbrother (W. H.), M.A. THE PHILO-SOPHY OF T. H. GREEN. *Second Edition. Cr. 8vo. 3s. 6d.*

Farrer (Reginald). THE GARDEN OF ASIA. *Second Edition. Cr. 8vo. 6s.*

Fea (Allan). SOME BEAUTIES OF THE SEVENTEENTH CENTURY. With 82 Illustrations. *Second Edition. Demy 8vo. 12s. 6d. net.*

Ferrier (Susan). See Little Library.

Fidler (T. Claxton), M.Inst. C.E. See Books on Business.

Fielding (Henry). See Standard Library.

Finn (S. W.), M.A. See Junior Examination Series.

Firth (J. B.). See Little Guides.

Firth (C. H.), M.A. CROMWELL'S ARMY: A History of the English Soldier during the Civil Wars, the Commonwealth, and the Protectorate. *Cr. 8vo. 6s.*

Fisher (G. W.), M.A. ANNALS OF SHREWSBURY SCHOOL. Illustrated. *Demy 8vo.* 10s. 6d.

FitzGerald (Edward). THE RUBÁIYÁT OF OMAR KHAYYÁM. Printed from the Fifth and last Edition. With a Commentary by Mrs. STEPHEN BATSON, and a Biography of Omar by E. D. ROSS. *Cr. 8vo. 6s.* See also Miniature Library.

FitzGerald (H. P.). A CONCISE HANDBOOK OF CLIMBERS, TWINERS, AND WALL SHRUBS. Illustrated. *Fcap. 8vo. 3s. 6d. net.*

Fitzpatrick (S. A. O.). See Ancient Cities.

Flecker (W. H.), M.A., D.C.L., Headmaster of the Dean Close School, Cheltenham. THE STUDENT'S PRAYER BOOK. THE TEXT OF MORNING AND EVENING PRAYER AND LITANY. With an Introduction and Notes. *Cr. 8vo. 2s. 6d.*

Flux (A. W.), M.A., William Dow Professor of Political Economy in M'Gill University, Montreal. ECONOMIC PRINCIPLES. *Demy 8vo. 7s. 6d. net.*

Fortescue (Mrs. G.). See Little Books on Art.

Fraser (David). A MODERN CAMPAIGN; OR, WAR AND WIRELESS TELEGRAPHY IN THE FAR EAST. Illustrated. *Cr. 8vo. 6s.*
A Colonial Edition is also published.

Fraser (J. F.). ROUND THE WORLD ON A WHEEL. With 100 Illustrations. *Fifth Edition Cr. 8vo. 6s.*

French (W.), M.A. See Textbooks of Science.

Freudenreich (Ed. von). DAIRY BACTERIOLOGY. A Short Manual for the Use of Students. Translated by J. R. AINSWORTH DAVIS, M.A. *Second Edition. Revised. Cr. 8vo. 2s. 6d.*

Fulford (H. W.), M.A. See Churchman's Bible.

Gallaher (D.) and Stead (W. J.). THE COMPLETE RUGBY FOOTBALLER, ON THE NEW ZEALAND SYSTEM. With an Account of the Tour of the New Zealanders in England. With 35 Illustrations. *Demy 8vo. 10s. 6d. net.*

Gallichan (W. M.). See Little Guides.

Gambado (Geoffrey, Esq.). See I.P.L.

Gaskell (Mrs.). See Little Library and Standard Library.

Gasquet, the Right Rev. Abbot, O.S.B. See Antiquary's Books.

George (H. B.), M.A., Fellow of New College, Oxford. BATTLES OF ENGLISH HISTORY. With numerous Plans. *Fourth Edition.* Revised, with a new Chapter including the South African War. *Cr. 8vo. 3s. 6d.*

A HISTORICAL GEOGRAPHY OF THE BRITISH EMPIRE. *Second Edition. Cr. 8vo. 3s. 6d.*

Gibbins (H. de B.), Litt.D., M.A. INDUSTRY IN ENGLAND: HISTORICAL OUTLINES. With 5 Maps. *Fifth Edition. Demy 8vo. 10s. 6d.*

THE INDUSTRIAL HISTORY OF ENGLAND. *Thirteenth Edition.* Revised. With Maps and Plans. *Cr. 8vo. 3s.*

ENGLISH SOCIAL REFORMERS. *Second Edition. Cr. 8vo. 2s. 6d.*
See also Commercial Series and R. A. Hadfield.

Gibbon (Edward). THE DECLINE AND FALL OF THE ROMAN EMPIRE. Edited with Notes, Appendices, and Maps, by J. B. BURY, M.A., Litt.D., Regius Professor of Greek at Cambridge. *In Seven Volumes. Demy 8vo. Gilt top, 8s.6d. each. Also, Cr. 8vo. 6s. each.*

MEMOIRS OF MY LIFE AND WRITINGS. Edited by G. BIRKBECK HILL, LL.D *Cr. 8vo. 6s.*
See also Standard Library.

Gibson (E. C. S.), D.D., Lord Bishop of Gloucester. See Westminster Commentaries, Handbooks of Theology, and Oxford Biographies.

Gilbert (A. R.). See Little Books on Art.

Gloag (M. R.) and Wyatt (Kate M.). A BOOK OF ENGLISH GARDENS. With 24 Illustrations in Colour. *Demy 8vo. 10s. 6d. net.*

Godfrey (Elizabeth). A BOOK OF REMEMBRANCE. Edited by. *Fcap. 8vo. 2s. 6d. net.*

Godley (A. D.), M.A., Fellow of Magdalen College, Oxford. LYRA FRIVOLA. *Third Edition. Fcap. 8vo. 2s. 6d.*

VERSES TO ORDER. *Second Edition. Fcap. 8vo. 2s. 6d.*

SECOND STRINGS. *Fcap. 8vo. 2s. 6d.*

Goldsmith (Oliver). THE VICAR OF WAKEFIELD. *Fcap. 32mo.* With 10 Plates in Photogravure by Tony Johannot. *Leather, 2s. 6d. net.*
See also I.P.L. and Standard Library.

Goodrich-Freer (A.). IN A SYRIAN SADDLE. *Demy 8vo. 7s. 6d. net.*
A Colonial Edition is also published.

Gorst (Rt. Hon. Sir John). THE CHILDREN OF THE NATION. *Second Edition. Demy 8vo. 7s. 6d. net.*

Goudge (H. L.), M.A., Principal of Wells Theological College. See Westminster Commentaries.

Graham (P. Anderson). THE RURAL EXODUS. *Cr. 8vo. 2s. 6d.*

Granger (F. S.), M.A., Litt.D. PSYCHOLOGY. *Third Edition. Cr. 8vo. 2s. 6d.*

THE SOUL OF A CHRISTIAN. *Cr. 8vo. 6s.*

Gray (E. M'Queen). GERMAN PASSAGES FOR UNSEEN TRANSLATION. *Cr. 8vo. 2s. 6d.*

Gray (P. L.), B.Sc. THE PRINCIPLES OF MAGNETISM AND ELECTRICITY: an Elementary Text-Book. With 181 Diagrams. *Cr. 8vo. 3s. 6d.*

Green (G. Buckland), M.A., late Fellow of St. John's College, Oxon. NOTES ON GREEK AND LATIN SYNTAX. *Second Edition. Crown 8vo. 3s. 6d.*

Green (E. T.), M.A. See Churchman's Library.

Greenidge (A. H. J.), M.A. A HISTORY OF ROME: From 133-104 B.C. *Demy 8vo.* 10s. 6d. net.

Greenwell (Dora). See Miniature Library.

Gregory (R. A.). THE VAULT OF HEAVEN. A Popular Introduction to Astronomy. Illustrated. *Cr. 8vo.* 2s. 6d.

Gregory (Miss E. C.). See Library of Devotion.

Grubb (H. C.). See Textbooks of Technology.

Gwynn (M. L.). A BIRTHDAY BOOK. New and cheaper issue. *Royal 8vo.* 5s. net.

Haddon (A. C.), Sc.D., F.R.S. HEAD-HUNTERS BLACK, WHITE, AND BROWN. With many Illustrations and a Map. *Demy 8vo.* 15s.

Hadfield (R. A.) and Gibbins (H. de B.). A SHORTER WORKING DAY. *Cr. 8vo.* 2s. 6d.

Hall (R. N.) and Neal (W. G.). THE ANCIENT RUINS OF RHODESIA. Illustrated. *Second Edition, revised. Demy 8vo.* 10s. 6d. net.

Hall (R. N.). GREAT ZIMBABWE. With numerous Plans and Illustrations. *Second Edition. Royal 8vo.* 10s. 6d. net.

Hamilton (F. J.), D.D. See Byzantine Texts.

Hammond (J. L.). CHARLES JAMES FOX. *Demy 8vo.* 10s. 6d.

Hannay (D.). A SHORT HISTORY OF THE ROYAL NAVY, 1200-1688. Illustrated. *Demy 8vo.* 7s. 6d. each.

Hannay (James O.), M.A. THE SPIRIT AND ORIGIN OF CHRISTIAN MONASTICISM. *Cr. 8vo.* 6s. THE WISDOM OF THE DESERT. *Fcap. 8vo.* 3s. 6d. net.

Hardie (Martin). See Connoisseur's Library.

Hare (A. T.), M.A. THE CONSTRUCTION OF LARGE INDUCTION COILS. With numerous Diagrams. *Demy 8vo.* 6s.

Harrison (Clifford). READING AND READERS. *Fcap. 8vo.* 2s. 6d.

Harvey (Alfred), M.B. See Ancient Cities.

Hawthorne (Nathaniel). See Little Library. HEALTH, WEALTH AND WISDOM. *Cr. 8vo.* 1s. net.

Heath (Frank R.). See Little Guides.

Heath (Dudley). See Connoisseur's Library.

Hello (Ernest). STUDIES IN SAINTSHIP. Translated from the French by V. M. CRAWFORD. *Fcap 8vo.* 3s. 6d.

Henderson (B. W.), Fellow of Exeter College, Oxford. THE LIFE AND PRINCIPATE OF THE EMPEROR NERO. Illustrated. *New and cheaper issue. Demy 8vo.* 7s. 6d. net. AT INTERVALS. *Fcap 8vo.* 2s. 6d. net.

Henderson (T. F.). See Little Library and Oxford Biographies.

Henderson (T. F.), and Watt (Francis). SCOTLAND OF TO-DAY. With many Illustrations, some of which are in colour. *Cr. 8vo.* 6s.

Henley (W. E.). ENGLISH LYRICS. *Second Edition. Cr. 8vo.* 2s. 6d. net.

Henley (W. E.) and Whibley (C.) A BOOK OF ENGLISH PROSE. *Cr. 8vo.* 2s. 6d. net.

Henson (H. H.), B.D., Canon of Westminster. APOSTOLIC CHRISTIANITY: As Illustrated by the Epistles of St. Paul to the Corinthians. *Cr. 8vo.* 6s. LIGHT AND LEAVEN: HISTORICAL AND SOCIAL SERMONS. *Cr. 8vo.* 6s.

Herbert (George). See Library of Devotion.

Herbert of Cherbury (Lord). See Miniature Library.

Hewins (W. A. S.), B.A. ENGLISH TRADE AND FINANCE IN THE SEVENTEENTH CENTURY. *Cr. 8vo.* 2s. 6d.

Hewitt (Ethel M.) A GOLDEN DIAL. A Day Book of Prose and Verse. *Fcap. 8vo.* 2s. 6d. net.

Heywood (W.). PALIO AND PONTE: A Book of Tuscan Games. Illustrated. *Royal 8vo.* 21s. net. See also St. Francis of Assisi.

Hill (Clare). See Textbooks of Technology.

Hill (Henry), B.A., Headmaster of the Boy's High School, Worcester, Cape Colony. A SOUTH AFRICAN ARITHMETIC. *Cr. 8vo.* 3s. 6d.

Hind (C. Lewis). DAYS IN CORNWALL. With 16 Illustrations in Colour by WILLIAM PASCOE, and 20 Photographs. *Second Edition. Cr. 8vo.* 6s. A Colonial Edition is also published.

Hirst (F. W.) See Books on Business.

Hoare (J. Douglas). ARCTIC EXPLORATION. With 18 Illustrations and Maps. *Demy 8vo,* 7s. 6d. net.

Hobhouse (L. T.), Fellow of C.C.C., Oxford. THE THEORY OF KNOWLEDGE. *Demy 8vo.* 10s. 6d. net.

Hobson (J. A.), M.A. INTERNATIONAL TRADE: A Study of Economic Principles. *Cr. 8vo.* 2s. 6d. net. PROBLEMS OF POVERTY. *Sixth Edition. Cr. 8vo.* 2s. 6d. THE PROBLEM OF THE UNEMPLOYED. *Third Edition. Cr. 8vo.* 2s. 6d.

Hodgkin (T.), D.C.L. See Leaders of Religion.

Hodgson (Mrs. W.) HOW TO IDENTIFY OLD CHINESE PORCELAIN. *Second Edition. Post 8vo.* 6s.

Hogg (Thomas Jefferson). SHELLEY AT OXFORD. With an Introduction by R. A. STREATFEILD. *Fcap. 8vo.* 2s. net.

Holden-Stone (G. de). See Books on Business.

Holdich (Sir T. H.), K.C.I.E. THE INDIAN BORDERLAND: being a Personal Record of Twenty Years. Illustrated. *Demy 8vo.* 10s. 6d. net. A Colonial Edition is also published.

A 2

Holdsworth (W. S.), M.A. A HISTORY OF ENGLISH LAW. *In Two Volumes. Vol. I. Demy 8vo. 10s. 6d. net.*

Holland (H. Scott), Canon of St. Paul's See Library of Devotion.

Holt (Emily). THE SECRET OF POPULARITY : How to Achieve Social Success. *Cr. 8vo. 3s. 6d. net.*
A Colonial Edition is also published.

Holyoake (G. J.). THE CO-OPERATIVE MOVEMENT TO-DAY. *Fourth Edition. Cr. 8vo. 2s. 6d.*

Hone (Nathaniel J.). See Antiquary's Books.

Hoppner. See Little Galleries.

Horace. See Classical Translations.

Horsburgh (E. L. S.), M.A. WATERLOO : A Narrative and Criticism. With Plans. *Second Edition. Cr. 8vo. 5s.*
See also Oxford Biographies.

Horth (A. C.). See Textbooks of Technology.

Horton (R. F.), D.D. See Leaders of Religion.

Hosie (Alexander). MANCHURIA. With Illustrations and a Map. *Second Edition. Demy 8vo. 7s. 6d. net.*
A Colonial Edition is also published.

How (F. D.). SIX GREAT SCHOOLMASTERS. With Portraits and Illustrations. *Second Edition. Demy 8vo. 7s. 6d.*

Howell (A. G. Ferrers). FRANCISCAN DAYS. Translated and arranged by. *Cr. 8vo. 3s. 6d. net.*

Howell (G.). TRADE UNIONISM—New and Old. *Fourth Edition. Cr. 8vo. 2s. 6d.*

Hudson (Robert). MEMORIALS OF A WARWICKSHIRE PARISH. Illustrated. *Demy 8vo. 15s. net.*

Huggins (Sir William), K.C.B., O.M., D.C.L., F.R.S. THE ROYAL SOCIETY ; OR, SCIENCE IN THE STATE AND IN THE SCHOOLS. With 25 Illustrations. *Wide Royal 8vo. 4s. 6d. net.*

Hughes (C. E.). THE PRAISE OF SHAKESPEARE. An English Anthology. With a Preface by SIDNEY LEE. *Demy 8vo. 3s. 6d. net.*

Hughes (Thomas). TOM BROWN'S SCHOOLDAYS. With an Introduction and Notes by VERNON RENDALL. *Leather. Royal 32mo. 2s. 6d. net.*

Hutchinson (Horace G.) THE NEW FOREST. Illustrated in colour with 50 Pictures by WALTER TYNDALE and 4 by LUCY KEMP-WELCH. *Third Edition. Cr. 8vo. 6s.*

Hutton (A. W.), M.A. See Leaders of Religion and Library of Devotion.

Hutton (Edward). THE CITIES OF UMBRIA. With many Illustrations, of which 20 are in Colour, by A. PISA. *Second Edition. Cr. 8vo. 6s.*
A Colonial Edition is also published.
THE CITIES OF SPAIN. *Second Edition.* With many Illustrations, of which 24 are in Colour, by A. W. RIMINGTON. *Demy 8vo. 7s. 6d. net.*

FLORENCE AND NORTHERN TUSCANY. With Coloured Illustrations by WILLIAM PARKINSON. *Cr. 8vo. 6s.*
A Colonial Edition is also published.

ENGLISH LOVE POEMS. Edited with an Introduction. *Fcap. 8vo. 3s. 6d. net.*

Hutton (R. H.). See Leaders of Religion.

Hutton (W. H.), M.A. THE LIFE OF SIR THOMAS MORE. With Portraits. *Second Edition. Cr. 8vo. 5s.*
See also Leaders of Religion.

Hyde (A. G.) GEORGE HERBERT AND HIS TIMES. With 32 Illustrations. *Demy 8vo. 10s. 6d. net.*

Hyett (F. A.). A SHORT HISTORY OF FLORENCE. *Demy 8vo. 7s. 6d. net.*

Ibsen (Henrik). BRAND. A Drama. Translated by WILLIAM WILSON. *Third Edition. Cr. 8vo. 3s. 6d.*

Inge (W. R.), M.A., Fellow and Tutor of Hertford College, Oxford. CHRISTIAN MYSTICISM. The Bampton Lectures for 1899. *Demy 8vo. 12s. 6d. net.* See also Library of Devotion.

Innes (A. D.), M.A. A HISTORY OF THE BRITISH IN INDIA. With Maps and Plans. *Cr. 8vo. 6s.*
ENGLAND UNDER THE TUDORS. With Maps. *Demy 8vo. 10s. 6d. net.*

Jackson (C. E.), B.A. See Textbooks of Science.

Jackson (S.), M.A. See Commercial Series.

Jackson (F. Hamilton). See Little Guides.

Jacob (F.), M.A. See Junior Examination Series.

James (W. H. N.), A.R.C.S., A.I.E.E. See Textbooks of Technology.

Jeans (J. Stephen). TRUSTS, POOLS, AND CORNERS. *Cr. 8vo. 2s. 6d.*
See also Books on Business.

Jeffreys (D. Gwyn). DOLLY'S THEATRICALS. Described and Illustrated with 24 Coloured Pictures. *Super Royal 16mo. 2s. 6d.*

Jenks (E.), M.A., Reader of Law in the University of Oxford. ENGLISH LOCAL GOVERNMENT. *Second Edition. Cr. 8vo. 2s. 6d.*

Jenner (Mrs. H.). See Little Books on Art.

Jennings (Oscar), M.D., Member of the Bibliographical Society. EARLY WOODCUT INITIALS, containing over thirteen hundred Reproductions of Pictorial Letters of the Fifteenth and Sixteenth Centuries. *Demy 4to. 21s. net.*

Jessopp (Augustus), D.D. See Leaders of Religion.

Jevons (F. B.), M.A., Litt.D., Principal of Bishop Hatfield's Hall, Durham. RELIGION IN EVOLUTION. *Cr. 8vo 3s. 6d. net.*
See also Churchman's Library and Handbooks of Theology.

Johnson (Mrs. Barham). WILLIAM BODHAM DONNE AND HIS FRIENDS. Illustrated. *Demy 8vo. 10s. 6d. net.*

Johnston (Sir H. H.), K.C.B. BRITISH CENTRAL AFRICA. With nearly 200 Illustrations and Six Maps. *Third Edition.* *Cr. 4to.* 18s. net.
  A Colonial Edition is also published.
Jones (R. Crompton), M.A. POEMS OF THE INNER LIFE. Selected by. *Thirteenth Edition. Fcap. 8vo.* 2s. 6d. net.
Jones (H.). See Commercial Series.
Jones (H. F.). See Textbooks of Science.
Jones (L. A. Atherley), K.C., M.P. THE MINERS' GUIDE TO THE COAL MINES REGULATION ACTS. *Cr. 8vo.* 2s. 6d. net.
COMMERCE IN WAR. *Royal 8vo.* 21s. net.
Jonson (Ben). See Standard Library.
Juliana (Lady) of Norwich. REVELATIONS OF DIVINE LOVE. Ed. by GRACE WARRACK. *Second Edit. Cr. 8vo.* 3s. 6d.
Juvenal. See Classical Translations.
'Kappa.' LET YOUTH BUT KNOW: A Plea for Reason in Education. *Cr. 8vo.* 3s. 6d. net.
Kaufmann (M.). SOCIALISM AND MODERN THOUGHT. *Second Edition.* *Cr. 8vo.* 2s. 6d. net.
Keating (J. F.), D.D. THE AGAPE AND THE EUCHARIST. *Cr. 8vo.* 3s. 6d.
Keats (John). THE POEMS OF. Edited with Introduction and Notes by E. de Selincourt, M.A. *Second Edition. Demy 8vo.* 7s. 6d. net.
REALMS OF GOLD. Selections from the Works of. *Fcap. 8vo.* 3s. 6d. net.
  See also Little Library and Standard Library.
Keble (John). THE CHRISTIAN YEAR. With an Introduction and Notes by W. LOCK, D.D., Warden of Keble College. Illustrated by R. ANNING BELL. *Third Edition. Fcap. 8vo.* 3s. 6d.; *padded morocco,* 5s.
  See also Library of Devotion.
Kelynack (T. N.), M.D., M.R.C.P., Hon. Secretary of the Society for the Study of Inebriety. THE DRINK PROBLEM IN ITS MEDICO-SOCIOLOGICAL ASPECT. Edited by. With 2 Diagrams. *Demy 8vo.* 7s. 6d. net.
Kempis (Thomas à). THE IMITATION OF CHRIST. With an Introduction by DEAN FARRAR. Illustrated by C. M. GERE. *Third Edition. Fcap. 8vo.* 3s. 6d.; *padded morocco.* 5s.
  Also Translated by C. BIGG, D.D. *Cr. 8vo.* 3s. 6d. See also Library of Devotion and Standard Library.
Kennedy (Bart.). THE GREEN SPHINX. *Cr. 8vo.* 3s. 6d. net.
  A Colonial Edition is also published.
Kennedy (James Houghton), D.D., Assistant Lecturer in Divinity in the University of Dublin. ST. PAUL'S SECOND AND THIRD EPISTLES TO THE CORINTHIANS. With Introduction, Dissertations and Notes. *Cr. 8vo.* 6s.
Kimmins (C. W.), M.A. THE CHEMISTRY OF LIFE AND HEALTH. Illustrated. *Cr. 8vo.* 2s. 6d.

Kinglake (A. W.). See Little Library.
Kipling (Rudyard). BARRACK-ROOM BALLADS. 80th Thousand. *Twenty-second Edition. Cr. 8vo.* 6s.
  A Colonial Edition is also published.
THE SEVEN SEAS. 63rd Thousand. *Eleventh Edition. Cr. 8vo.* 6s.
  A Colonial Edition is also published.
THE FIVE NATIONS. 41st Thousand. *Second Edition. Cr. 8vo.* 6s.
  A Colonial Edition is also published.
DEPARTMENTAL DITTIES. *Sixteenth Edition. Cr. 8vo.* 6s.
  A Colonial Edition is also published.
Knight (Albert E.). THE COMPLETE CRICKETER. Illus. *Demy 8vo.* 7s. 6d. net.
  A Colonial Edition is also published.
Knight (H. J. C.), M.A. See Churchman's Bible.
Knowling (R. J.), M.A., Professor of New Testament Exegesis at King's College, London. See Westminster Commentaries.
Lamb (Charles and Mary), THE WORKS OF. Edited by E. V. LUCAS. Illustrated *In Seven Volumes. Demy 8vo.* 7s. 6d. each.
  See also Little Library and E. V. Lucas.
Lambert (F. A. H.). See Little Guides.
Lambros (Professor). See Byzantine Texts.
Lane-Poole (Stanley). A HISTORY OF EGYPT IN THE MIDDLE AGES. Fully Illustrated. *Cr. 8vo.* 6s.
Langbridge (F.), M.A. BALLADS OF THE BRAVE: Poems of Chivalry, Enterprise, Courage, and Constancy. *Third Edition.* *Cr. 8vo.* 2s. 6d.
Law (William). See Library of Devotion and Standard Library.
Leach (Henry). THE DUKE OF DEVONSHIRE. A Biography. With 12 Illustrations. *Demy 8vo.* 12s. 6d. net.
  See also James Braid.
GREAT GOLFERS IN THE MAKING. With 34 Portraits. *Demy 8vo.* 7s. 6d. net.
Le Braz (Anatole). THE LAND OF PARDONS. Translated by FRANCES M. GOSTLING. Illustrated in colour. *Second Edition. Demy 8vo.* 7s. 6d. net.
Lee (Captain L. Melville). A HISTORY OF POLICE IN ENGLAND. *Cr. 8vo.* 3s. 6d. net.
Leigh (Percival). THE COMIC ENGLISH GRAMMAR. Embellished with upwards of 50 characteristic Illustrations by JOHN LEECH. *Post 16mo.* 2s. 6d. net.
Lewes (V. B.), M.A. AIR AND WATER. Illustrated. *Cr. 8vo.* 2s. 6d.
Lewis (Mrs. Gwyn). A CONCISE HANDBOOK OF GARDEN SHRUBS. Illustrated. *Fcap. 8vo.* 3s. 6d. net.
Lisle (Fortunéede). See Little Books on Art.
Littlehales (H.). See Antiquary's Books.
Lock (Walter), D.D., Warden of Keble College. ST. PAUL, THE MASTER-BUILDER. *Second Ed. Cr. 8vo.* 3s. 6d.
THE BIBLE AND CHRISTIAN LIFE. *Cr. 8vo.* 6s.
  See also Leaders of Religion and Library of Devotion.

Locker (F.). See Little Library.

Lodge (Sir Oliver), F.R.S. THE SUBSTANCE OF FAITH ALLIED WITH SCIENCE: A Catechism for Parents and Teachers. *Eighth Ed. Cr. 8vo. 2s. net.*

Lofthouse (W. F.), M.A. ETHICS AND ATONEMENT. With a Frontispiece. *Demy 8vo. 5s. net.*

Longfellow (H. W.). See Little Library.

Lorimer (George Horace). LETTERS FROM A SELF-MADE MERCHANT TO HIS SON. *Sixteenth Edition. Cr. 8vo. 3s. 6d.*
A Colonial Edition is also published.

OLD GORGON GRAHAM. *Second Edition. Cr. 8vo. 6s.*
A Colonial Edition is also published.

Lover (Samuel). See I. P. L.

E. V. L. and C. L. G. ENGLAND DAY BY DAY: Or, The Englishman's Handbook to Efficiency. Illustrated by GEORGE MORROW. *Fourth Edition. Fcap. 4to. 1s. net.*

Lucas (E. V.). THE LIFE OF CHARLES LAMB. With 25 Illustrations. *Third Edition. Demy 8vo. 7s. 6d. net.*
A Colonial Edition is also published.

A WANDERER IN HOLLAND. With many Illustrations, of which 20 are in Colour by HERBERT MARSHALL. *Seventh Edition. Cr. 8vo. 6s.*
A Colonial Edition is also published.

A WANDERER IN LONDON. With 16 Illustrations in Colour by NELSON DAWSON, and 36 other Illustrations. *Fifth Edition. Cr. 8vo. 6s.*
A Colonial Edition is also published.

FIRESIDE AND SUNSHINE. *Third Edition. Fcap. 8vo. 5s.*

THE OPEN ROAD: a Little Book for Wayfarers. *Eleventh Edition. Fcap. 8vo. 5s.; India Paper, 7s. 6d.*

THE FRIENDLY TOWN: a Little Book for the Urbane. *Third Edition. Fcap. 8vo. 5s.; India Paper, 7s. 6d.*

CHARACTER AND COMEDY. *Second Edition.*

Lucian. See Classical Translations.

Lyde (L. W.), M.A. See Commercial Series.

Lydon (Noel S.). See Junior School Books.

Lyttelton (Hon. Mrs. A.). WOMEN AND THEIR WORK. *Cr. 8vo. 2s. 6d.*

Macaulay (Lord). CRITICAL AND HISTORICAL ESSAYS. Edited by F. C. MONTAGUE, M.A. *Three Volumes. Cr. 8vo. 18s.*
The only edition of this book completely annotated.

M'Allen (J. E. B.), M.A. See Commercial Series.

MacCulloch (J. A.). See Churchman's Library.

MacCunn (Florence A.). MARY STUART. With over 60 Illustrations, including a Frontispiece in Photogravure. *Second and Cheaper Edition. Cr. 8vo. 6s.*
See also Leaders of Religion.

McDermott (E. R.). See Books on Business.

M'Dowall (A. S.). See Oxford Biographies.

Mackay (A. M.). See Churchman's Library.

Macklin (Herbert W.), M.A. See Antiquary's Books.

Mackenzie (W. Leslie), M.A., M.D., D.P.H., etc. THE HEALTH OF THE SCHOOL CHILD. *Cr. 8vo. 2s. 6d.*

Mdlle Mori (Author of). ST. CATHERINE OF SIENA AND HER TIMES. With 28 Illustrations. *Demy 8vo. 7s. 6d. net.*

Magnus (Laurie), M.A. A PRIMER OF WORDSWORTH. *Cr. 8vo. 2s. 6d.*

Mahaffy (J. P.), Litt.D. A HISTORY OF THE EGYPT OF THE PTOLEMIES. Fully Illustrated. *Cr. 8vo. 6s.*

Maitland (F. W.), LL.D., Downing Professor of the Laws of England in the University of Cambridge. CANON LAW IN ENGLAND. *Royal 8vo. 7s. 6d.*

Malden (H. E.), M.A. ENGLISH RECORDS. A Companion to the History of England. *Cr. 8vo. 3s. 6d.*

THE ENGLISH CITIZEN: HIS RIGHTS AND DUTIES. *Seventh Edition. Cr. 8vo. 1s. 6d.*
See also School Histories.

Marchant (E. C.), M.A., Fellow of Peterhouse, Cambridge. A GREEK ANTHOLOGY. *Second Edition. Cr. 8vo. 3s. 6d.*
See also A. M. Cook.

Marr (J. E.), F.R.S., Fellow of St John's College, Cambridge. THE SCIENTIFIC STUDY OF SCENERY. *Second Edition.* Illustrated. *Cr. 8vo. 6s.*

AGRICULTURAL GEOLOGY. Illustrated. *Cr. 8vo. 6s.*

Marriott (J. A. R.). FALKLAND AND HIS TIMES. With 20 Illustrations. *Second Ed. Demy 8vo. 7s. 6d. net.*
A Colonial Edition is also published.

Marvell (Andrew). See Little Library.

Masefield (John). SEA LIFE IN NELSON'S TIME. Illustrated. *Cr. 8vo. 3s. 6d. net.*

ON THE SPANISH MAIN. With 22 Illustrations and a Map. *Demy 8vo. 10s. 6d. net.*

A SAILOR'S GARLAND. Edited and Selected by. *Cr. 8vo. 3s. 6d. net.*

Maskell (A.). See Connoisseur's Library.

Mason (A. J.), D.D. See Leaders of Religion.

Massee (George). THE EVOLUTION OF PLANT LIFE: Lower Forms. Illustrated. *Cr. 8vo. 2s. 6d.*

Masterman (C. F. G.), M.A., M.P. TENNYSON AS A RELIGIOUS TEACHER. *Cr. 8vo. 6s.*

Matheson (Mrs. E. F.). COUNSELS OF LIFE. *Fcap. 8vo. 2s. 6d. net.*

May (Phil). THE PHIL MAY ALBUM. *Second Edition. 4to. 1s. net.*

Mellows (Emma S.). A SHORT STORY OF ENGLISH LITERATURE. *Cr. 8vo. 3s. 6d.*

Methuen (A. M. S.). THE TRAGEDY OF SOUTH AFRICA. *Cr. 8vo. 2s. net. Also Cr. 8vo. 3d. net.*
A revised and enlarged edition of the author's 'Peace or War in South Africa.'

ENGLAND'S RUIN: DISCUSSED IN SIX-TEEN LETTERS TO THE RIGHT HON. JOSEPH CHAMBERLAIN, M.P. *Seventh Edition. Cr. 8vo. 3d. net.*

Miles (Eustace), M.A. LIFE AFTER LIFE, OR, THE THEORY OF REIN-CARNATION. *Cr. 8vo. 2s. 6d. net.*

Millais (J. G.). THE LIFE AND LET-TERS OF SIR JOHN EVERETT MILLAIS, President of the Royal Academy. With many Illustrations, of which 2 are in Photogravure. *New Edition. Demy 8vo. 7s. 6d. net.*
See also Little Galleries.

Millin (G. F.). PICTORIAL GARDEN-ING. Illustrated. *Cr. 8vo. 3s. 6d. net.*

Millis (C. T.), M.I.M.E. See Textbooks of Technology.

Milne (J. G.), M.A. A HISTORY OF ROMAN EGYPT. Fully Illus. *Cr. 8vo. 6s.*

Milton (John). A DAY BOOK OF. Edited by R. F. Towndrow. *Fcap. 8vo. 3s. 6d. net.*
See also Little Library and Standard Library.

Minchin (H. C.), M.A. See R. Peel.

Mitchell (P. Chalmers), M.A. OUTLINES OF BIOLOGY. Illustrated. *Second Edition. Cr. 8vo. 6s.*

Mitton (G. E.). JANE AUSTEN AND HER TIMES. With many Portraits and Illustrations. *Second and Cheaper Edition. Cr. 8vo. 6s.*
A Colonial Edition is also published.

Moffat (Mary M.). QUEEN LOUISA OF PRUSSIA. With 20 Illustrations. *Fourth Edition. Demy 8vo. 7s. 6d. net.*

'Moil (A.).' See Books on Business.

Moir (D. M.). See Little Library.

Molinos (Dr. Michael de). See Library of Devotion.

Money (L. G. Chiozza), M.P. RICHES AND POVERTY. *Third Edition. Demy 8vo. 5s. net.*

Montagu (Henry), Earl of Manchester. See Library of Devotion.

Montaigne. A DAY BOOK OF. Edited by C. F. POND. *Fcap. 8vo. 3s. 6d. net.*

Montmorency (J. E. G. de), B.A., LL.B. THOMAS À KEMPIS, HIS AGE AND BOOK. With 22 Illustrations. *Second Edition. Demy 8vo. 7s. 6d. net.*

Moore (H. E.). BACK TO THE LAND. An Inquiry into Rural Depopulation. *Cr. 8vo. 2s. 6d.*

Moorhouse (E. Hallam). NELSON'S LADY HAMILTON. With 51 Portraits. *Second Edition. Demy 8vo. 7s. 6d. net.*
A Colonial Edition is also published.

Moran (Clarence G.). See Books on Business.

More (Sir Thomas). See Standard Library.

Morfill (W. R.), Oriel College, Oxford. A HISTORY OF RUSSIA FROM PETER THE GREAT TO ALEXANDER II. With Maps and Plans. *Cr. 8vo. 3s. 6d.*

Morich (R. J.), late of Clifton College. See School Examination Series.

Morris (J.). THE MAKERS OF JAPAN. With 24 Illustrations. *Demy 8vo. 12s. 6d. net.*
A Colonial Edition is also published.

Morris (J. E.). See Little Guides.

Morton (Miss Anderson). See Miss Brod-rick.

Moule (H. C. G.), D.D., Lord Bishop of Dur-ham. See Leaders of Religion.

Muir (M. M. Pattison), M.A. THE CHEMISTRY OF FIRE. Illustrated. *Cr. 8vo. 2s. 6d.*

Mundella (V. A.), M.A. See J. T. Dunn.

Munro (R.), LL.D. See Antiquary's Books.

Naval Officer (A). See I. P. L.

Neal (W. G.). See R. N. Hall.

Newman (Ernest). HUGO WOLF. *Demy 8vo. 6s.*

Newman (George), M.D., D.P.H., F.R.S.E., Lecturer on Public Health at St. Bartholo-mew's Hospital, and Medical Officer of Health of the Metropolitan Borough of Finsbury. INFANT MORTALITY, A SOCIAL PROBLEM. With 16 Diagrams. *Demy 8vo. 7s. 6d. net.*

Newman (J. H.) and others. See Library of Devotion.

Nichols (J. B. B.). See Little Library.

Nicklin (T.), M.A. EXAMINATION PAPERS IN THUCYDIDES. *Cr. 8vo. 2s.*

Nimrod. See I. P. L.

Norgate (G. Le Grys). THE LIFE OF SIR WALTER SCOTT. Illustrated. *Demy 8vo. 7s. 6d. net.*

Norregaard (B. W.). THE GREAT SIEGE: The Investment and Fall of Port Arthur. Illustrated. *Demy 8vo. 10s. 6d. net.*

Norway (A. H.). NAPLES. With 25 Col-oured Illustrations by MAURICE GREIFFEN-HAGEN. *Second Edition. Cr. 8vo. 6s.*

Novalis. THE DISCIPLES AT SAIS AND OTHER FRAGMENTS. Edited by Miss UNA BIRCH. *Fcap. 8vo. 3s. 6d.*

Oldfield (W. J.), M.A., Prebendary of Lincoln. A PRIMER OF RELIGION. BASED ON THE CATECHISM OF THE CHURCH OF ENGLAND. *Fcap. 8vo. 2s. 6d.*

Oldham (F. M.), B.A. See Textbooks of Science.

Oliphant (Mrs.). See Leaders of Religion.

Oman (C. W. C.), M.A., Fellow of All Souls', Oxford. A HISTORY OF THE ART OF WAR. The Middle Ages, from the Fourth to the Fourteenth Century. Illus-trated. *Demy 8vo. 10s. 6d. net.*

Ottley (R. L.), D.D. See Handbooks of Theology and Leaders of Religion.

Overton (J. H.). See Leaders of Religion.

Owen (Douglas). See Books on Business.

Oxford (M. N.), of Guy's Hospital. A HAND-BOOK OF NURSING. *Fourth Edition. Cr. 8vo. 3s. 6d.*

Pakes (W. C. C.). THE SCIENCE OF HYGIENE. Illustrated. *Demy 8vo. 15s.*

Palmer (Frederick). WITH KUROKI IN MANCHURIA. Illustrated. *Third Edition. Demy 8vo. 7s. 6d. net.*

Parker (Gilbert). A LOVER'S DIARY. *Fcap. 8vo. 5s.*

Parkes (A. K.). SMALL LESSONS ON GREAT TRUTHS. *Fcap. 8vo. 1s. 6d.*

Parkinson (John). PARADISI IN SOLE PARADISUS TERRESTRIS, OR A GARDEN OF ALL SORTS OF PLEASANT FLOWERS. *Folio. £3, 3s. net.*

Parmenter (John). HELIO-TROPES, OR NEW POSIES FOR SUNDIALS, 1625. Edited by PERCIVAL LANDON. *Quarto. 3s. 6d. net.*

Parmentier (Prof. Leon). See Byzantine Texts.

Parsons (Mrs. Clement). GARRICK AND HIS CIRCLE. With 36 Illustrations. *Second Edition. Demy 8vo. 12s. 6d. net.*
A Colonial Edition is also published.

Pascal. See Library of Devotion.

Paston (George). SOCIAL CARICATURE IN THE EIGHTEENTH CENTURY. With over 200 Illustrations. *Imperial Quarto. £2, 12s. 6d. net.*
See also Little Books on Art and I.P.L.

LADY MARY WORTLEY MONTAGU. With 24 Portraits and Illustrations. *Second Edition. Demy 8vo. 15s. net.*
A Colonial Edition is also published.

Paterson (W. R.)(Benjamin Swift). LIFE'S QUESTIONINGS. *Cr. 8vo. 3s. 6d. net.*

Patterson (A. H.). NOTES OF AN EAST COAST NATURALIST. Illustrated in Colour by F. SOUTHGATE. *Second Edition. Cr. 8vo. 6s.*

NATURE IN EASTERN NORFOLK. A series of observations on the Birds, Fishes, Mammals, Reptiles, and Stalk-eyed Crustaceans found in that neighbourhood, with a list of the species. With 12 Illustrations in colour, by FRANK SOUTHGATE. *Second Edition. Cr. 8vo. 6s.*

Peacock (N.). See Little Books on Art.

Peake (C. M. A.), F.R.H.S. A CONCISE HANDBOOK OF GARDEN ANNUAL AND BIENNIAL PLANTS. With 24 Illustrations. *Fcap. 8vo. 3s. 6d. net.*

Peel (Robert), and **Minchin (H. C.),** M.A. OXFORD. With 100 Illustrations in Colour. *Cr. 8vo. 6s.*

Peel (Sidney), late Fellow of Trinity College, Oxford, and Secretary to the Royal Commission on the Licensing Laws. PRACTICAL LICENSING REFORM. *Second Edition. Cr. 8vo. 1s. 6d.*

Petrie (W. M. Flinders), D.C.L., LL.D., Professor of Egyptology at University College. A HISTORY OF EGYPT, FROM THE EARLIEST TIMES TO THE PRESENT DAY. Fully Illustrated. *In six volumes. Cr. 8vo. 6s. each.*

VOL. I. PREHISTORIC TIMES TO XVITH DYNASTY. *Sixth Edition.*

VOL. II. THE XVIITH AND XVIIITH DYNASTIES. *Fourth Edition.*

VOL. III. XIXTH TO XXXTH DYNASTIES.

VOL. IV. THE EGYPT OF THE PTOLEMIES. J. P. MAHAFFY, Litt. D.

VOL. V. ROMAN EGYPT. J. G. MILNE, M.A.

VOL. VI. EGYPT IN THE MIDDLE AGES. STANLEY LANE-POOLE, M.A.

RELIGION AND CONSCIENCE IN ANCIENT EGYPT. Illustrated. *Cr. 8vo. 2s. 6d.*

SYRIA AND EGYPT, FROM THE TELL EL AMARNA TABLETS. *Cr. 8vo. 2s. 6d.*

EGYPTIAN TALES. Illustrated by TRISTRAM ELLIS. *In Two Volumes. Cr. 8vo. 3s. 6d. each.*

EGYPTIAN DECORATIVE ART. With 120 Illustrations. *Cr. 8vo. 3s. 6d.*

Phillips (W. A.). See Oxford Biographies.

Phillpotts (Eden). MY DEVON YEAR. With 38 Illustrations by J. LEY PETHYBRIDGE. *Second and Cheaper Edition. Large Cr. 8vo. 6s.*

UP ALONG AND DOWN ALONG. Illustrated by CLAUDE SHEPPERSON. *Cr. 4to. 5s. net.*
A volume of poems.

Plarr (Victor G.). See School Histories.

Plato. See Standard Library.

Plautus. THE CAPTIVI. Edited, with an Introduction, Textual Notes, and a Commentary, by W. M. LINDSAY, Fellow of Jesus College, Oxford. *Demy 8vo. 10s. 6d. net.*

Plowden-Wardlaw (J. T.), B.A., King's College, Cambridge. See School Examination Series.

Podmore (Frank). MODERN SPIRITUALISM. *Two Volumes. Demy 8vo. 21s. net.*
A History and a Criticism.

Poer (J. Patrick Le). A MODERN LEGIONARY. *Cr. 8vo. 6s.*

Pollard (Alice). See Little Books on Art.

Pollard (A. W.). OLD PICTURE BOOKS. Illustrated. *Demy 8vo. 7s. 6d. net.*

Pollard (Eliza F.). See Little Books on Art.

Pollock (David), M.I.N.A. See Books on Business.

Potter (M. C.), M.A., F.L.S. A TEXT-BOOK OF AGRICULTURAL BOTANY. Illustrated. *Second Edition. Cr. 8vo. 4s. 6d.*

Power (J. O'Connor). THE MAKING OF AN ORATOR. *Cr. 8vo. 6s.*

Prance (G.). See R. Wyon.

Prescott (O. L.). ABOUT MUSIC, AND WHAT IT IS MADE OF. *Cr. 8vo. 3s. 6d. net.*

Price (L. L.), M.A., Fellow of Oriel College, Oxon. A HISTORY OF ENGLISH POLITICAL ECONOMY. *Fourth Edition. Cr. 8vo. 2s. 6d.*

Primrose (Deborah). A MODERN BŒOTIA. *Cr. 8vo. 6s.*

Protheroe (Ernest). THE DOMINION OF MAN. GEOGRAPHY IN ITS HUMAN ASPECT. With 32 full-page Illustrations. *Cr. 8vo. 2s.*

Pugin and **Rowlandson**. THE MICRO-COSM OF LONDON, OR LONDON IN MINIATURE. With 104 Illustrations in colour. *In Three Volumes. Small 4to. £3, 3s. net.*

'Q' (A. T. Quiller Couch). THE GOLDEN POMP. A PROCESSION OF ENGLISH LYRICS. *Second Edition. Cr. 8vo. 2s. 6d. net.*

Quevedo Villegas. See Miniature Library.

G.R. and **E.S.** THE WOODHOUSE COR-RESPONDENCE. *Cr. 8vo. 6s.*

A Colonial Edition is also published.

Rackham (R. B.), M.A. See Westminster Commentaries.

Ragg (Laura M.). THE WOMEN-ART-ISTS OF BOLOGNA. With 20 Illus-trations. *Demy 8vo. 7s. 6d. net.*

Ragg (Lonsdale). B.D., Oxon. DANTE AND HIS ITALY. With 32 Illustra-tions largely from contemporary Frescoes and Documents. *Demy 8vo. 12s. 6d. net.*

Rahtz (F. J.), M.A., B.Sc., Lecturer in English at Merchant Venturers' Technical College, Bristol. HIGHER ENGLISH. *Second Edition. Cr. 8vo. 3s. 6d.*

Randolph (B. W.), D.D. See Library of Devotion.

Rannie (D. W.), M.A. A STUDENT'S HISTORY OF SCOTLAND. *Cr. 8vo. 3s. 6d.*

Rashdall (Hastings), M.A., Fellow and Tutor of New College, Oxford. DOC-TRINE AND DEVELOPMENT. *Cr. 8vo. 6s.*

Raven (J. J.), D.D. See Antiquary's Books.

Rawstorne (Lawrence, Esq.). See I.P.L.

Raymond (Walter). See School Histories.

A Real Paddy. See I.P.L.

Reason (W.), M.A. UNIVERSITY AND SOCIAL SETTLEMENTS. *Cr. 8vo. 2s. 6d.*

Redpath (H. A.), M.A. See Westminster Commentaries.

Reynolds. See Little Galleries.

Rhoades (J.F.). See Simplified French Texts.

Rhodes (W. E.). See School Histories.

Rieu (H.), M.A. See Simplified French Texts.

Roberts (M. E.). See C. C. Channer.

Robertson (A.), D.D., Lord Bishop of Exeter. REGNUM DEI. The Bampton Lectures of 1901. *Demy 8vo. 7s. 6d. net.*

Robertson (C. Grant). M.A., Fellow of All Souls' College, Oxford, Examiner in the Honours School of Modern History, Oxford, 1901-1904. SELECT STATUTES, CASES, AND CONSTITUTIONAL DOCU-MENTS, 1660-1832. *Demy 8vo. 10s. 6d. net.*

Robertson (C. Grant) and **Bartholomew (J. G.),** F.R.S.E., F.R.G.S. A HIS-TORICAL AND MODERN ATLAS OF THE BRITISH EMPIRE. *Demy Quarto. 4s. 6d. net.*

Robertson (Sir G. S.), K.C.S.I. CHITRAL: THE STORY OF A MINOR SIEGE. *Third Edition. Illustrated. Cr. 8vo. 2s. 6d. net.*

Robinson (A. W.), M.A. See Churchman's Bible.

Robinson (Cecilia). THE MINISTRY OF DEACONESSES. With an Introduc-tion by the late Archbishop of Canterbury. *Cr. 8vo. 3s. 6d.*

Robinson (F. S.). See Connoisseur's Library.

Rochefoucauld (La). See Little Library.

Rodwell (G.), B.A. NEW TESTAMENT GREEK. A Course for Beginners. With a Preface by WALTER LOCK, D.D., Warden of Keble College. *Fcap. 8vo. 3s. 6d.*

Roe (Fred). OLD OAK FURNITURE. With many Illustrations by the Author, including a frontispiece in colour. *Demy 8vo. 10s. 6d. net.*

Rogers (A. G. L.), M.A. See Books on Business.

Romney. See Little Galleries.

Roscoe (E. S.). See Little Guides.

Rose (Edward). THE ROSE READER. Illustrated. *Cr. 8vo. 2s. 6d. Also in 4 Parts. Parts I. and II. 6d. each; Part III. 8d.; Part IV. 10d.*

Rowntree (Joshua). THE IMPERIAL DRUG TRADE. A RE-STATEMENT OF THE OPIUM QUESTION. *Second and Cheaper Edition. Cr. 8vo. 2s. net.*

Royde-Smith (N. G.). THE PILLOW BOOK: A GARNER OF MANY MOODS. *Second Edition. Cr. 8vo. 4s. 6d. net.*

Rubie (A. E.), D.D. See Junior School Books.

Russell (W. Clark). THE LIFE OF ADMIRAL LORD COLLINGWOOD. With Illustrations by F. BRANGWYN. *Fourth Edition. Cr. 8vo. 6s.*

Sainsbury (Harrington), M.D., F.R.C.P. PRINCIPIA THERAPEUTICA. *Demy 8vo. 7s. 6d. net.*

St. Anselm. See Library of Devotion.

St. Augustine. See Library of Devotion.

St. Bernard. See Library of Devotion.

Sales (St. Francis de). See Library of Devotion.

St. Cyres (Viscount). See Oxford Bio-graphies.

St. Francis of Assisi. THE LITTLE FLOWERS OF THE GLORIOUS MESSER ST. FRANCIS AND HIS FRIARS. Newly translated by WILLIAM HEYWOOD. With an Introduction by A. G. F. HOWELL, and 40 Illustrations from Italian Painters. *Demy 8vo. 5s. net.*

See also Standard Library and Library of Devotion.

'Saki' (H. Munro). REGINALD. *Second Edition. Fcap. 8vo. 2s. 6d. net.*

Salmon (A. L.). See Little Guides.

Sargeaunt (J.), M.A. ANNALS OF WESTMINSTER SCHOOL. Illustrated. *Demy 8vo. 7s. 6d.*

Sathas (C.). See Byzantine Texts.

Schmitt (John). See Byzantine Texts.

Scott (A. M.). WINSTON SPENCER CHURCHILL. With Portraits and Illus-trations. *Cr. 8vo. 3s. 6d.*

Scudamore (Cyril). See Little Guides.

Sells (V. P.), M.A. THE MECHANICS OF DAILY LIFE. Illustrated. *Cr. 8vo.* 2s. 6d.

Selous (Edmund). TOMMY SMITH'S ANIMALS. Illustrated by G. W. ORD. *Ninth Edition. Fcap. 8vo.* 2s. 6d. *School Edition*, 1s. 6d.

TOMMY SMITH'S OTHER ANIMALS. With 12 Illustrations by AUGUSTA GUEST. *Third Edition. Fcap. 8vo.* 2s. 6d.

Settle (J. H.). ANECDOTES OF SOLDIERS. *Cr. 8vo.* 3s. 6d. net.

Shakespeare (William).
THE FOUR FOLIOS, 1623 ; 1632 ; 1664 ; 1685. Each £4, 4s. net, or a complete set, £12, 12s. net.
Folios 3 and 4 are ready.
Folio 2 is nearly ready.
See also Arden, Standard Library and Little Quarto Shakespeare.

Sharp (A.). VICTORIAN POETS. *Cr. 8vo.* 2s. 6d.

Sharp (Cecil). See S. Baring-Gould.

Sharp (Mrs. E. A.). See Little Books on Art.

Shedlock (J. S.) THE PIANOFORTE SONATA. *Cr. 8vo.* 5s.

Shelley (Percy B.). ADONAIS; an Elegy on the death of John Keats, Author of 'Endymion,' etc. Pisa. From the types of Didot, 1821. 2s. net.

Sheppard (H. F.), M.A. See S. Baring-Gould.

Sherwell (Arthur), M.A. LIFE IN WEST LONDON. *Third Edition. Cr. 8vo.* 2s. 6d.

Shipley (Mary E.). AN ENGLISH CHURCH HISTORY FOR CHILDREN. A.D. 597-1066. With a Preface by the Bishop of Gibraltar. With Maps and Illustrations. *Cr. 8vo.* 2s. 6d. net.

Sime (J.). See Little Books on Art.

Simonson (G. A.). FRANCESCO GUARDI. With 41 Plates. *Imperial 4to.* £2, 2s. net.

Sketchley (R. E. D.). See Little Books on Art.

Skipton (H. P. K.). See Little Books on Art.

Sladen (Douglas). SICILY : The New Winter Resort. With over 200 Illustrations. *Second Edition. Cr. 8vo.* 5s. net.

Small (Evan), M.A. THE EARTH. An Introduction to Physiography. Illustrated. *Cr. 8vo.* 2s. 6d.

Smallwood (M. G.). See Little Books on Art.

Smedley (F. E.). See I.P.L.

Smith (Adam). THE WEALTH OF NATIONS. Edited with an Introduction and numerous Notes by EDWIN CANNAN, M.A. *Two volumes. Demy 8vo.* 21s. net.

Smith (Horace and James). See Little Library.

Smith (H. Bompas), M.A. A NEW JUNIOR ARITHMETIC. *Crown 8vo.* 2s. With Answers, 2s. 6d.

Smith (R. Mudie). THOUGHTS FOR THE DAY. Edited by. *Fcap. 8vo.* 3s. 6d. net.

Smith (Nowell C.). See W. Wordsworth.

Smith (John Thomas). A BOOK FOR A RAINY DAY : Or, Recollections of the Events of the Years 1766-1833. Edited by WILFRED WHITTEN. Illustrated. *Wide Demy 8vo.* 12s. 6d. net.

Snell (F. J.). A BOOK OF EXMOOR. Illustrated. *Cr. 8vo.* 6s.

Snowden (C. E.). A HANDY DIGEST OF BRITISH HISTORY. *Demy 8vo.* 4s. 6d.

Sophocles. See Classical Translations.

Sornet (L. A.). See Junior School Books.

South (E. Wilton), M.A. See Junior School Books.

Southey (R.). ENGLISH SEAMEN. Edited by DAVID HANNAY.
Vol. I. (Howard, Clifford, Hawkins, Drake, Cavendish). *Second Edition. Cr. 8vo.* 6s.
Vol. II. (Richard Hawkins, Grenville, Essex, and Raleigh). *Cr. 8vo.* 6s.
See also Standard Library.

Spence (C. H.), M.A. See School Examination Series.

Spicer (A. D.). THE PAPER TRADE. With Maps and Diagrams. *Demy 8vo.* 12s. 6d. net.

Spooner (W. A.), M.A. See Leaders of Religion.

Staley (Edgcumbe). THE GUILDS OF FLORENCE. Illustrated. *Second Edition. Royal 8vo.* 16s. net.

Stanbridge (J. W.), B.D. See Library of Devotion.

'Stancliffe.' GOLF DO'S AND DONT'S. *Second Edition. Fcap. 8vo.* 1s.

Stead (W. J.). See D. Gallaher.

Stedman (A. M. M.), M.A.
INITIA LATINA : Easy Lessons on Elementary Accidence. *Tenth Edition. Fcap. 8vo.* 1s.

FIRST LATIN LESSONS. *Tenth Edition. Cr. 8vo.* 2s.

FIRST LATIN READER. With Notes adapted to the Shorter Latin Primer and Vocabulary. *Seventh Ed. revised.* 18mo. 1s. 6d.

EASY SELECTIONS FROM CÆSAR. The Helvetian War. *Third Edition.* 18mo. 1s.

EASY SELECTIONS FROM LIVY. The Kings of Rome. 18mo. *Third Edition.* 1s. 6d.

EASY LATIN PASSAGES FOR UNSEEN TRANSLATION. *Eleventh Ed. Fcap. 8vo.* 1s. 6d.

EXEMPLA LATINA. First Exercises in Latin Accidence. With Vocabulary. *Third Edition. Cr. 8vo.* 1s.

EASY LATIN EXERCISES ON THE SYNTAX OF THE SHORTER AND REVISED LATIN PRIMER. With Vocabulary. *Eleventh and Cheaper Edition, re-written. Cr. 8vo. 1s. 6d. Original Edition. 2s. 6d.* KEY, *3s. net.*

THE LATIN COMPOUND SENTENCE : Rules and Exercises. *Second Edition. Cr. 8vo. 1s. 6d.* With Vocabulary. *2s.*

NOTANDA QUAEDAM : Miscellaneous Latin Exercises on Common Rules and Idioms. *Fifth Edition. Fcap. 8vo. 1s. 6d.* With Vocabulary. *2s.* Key, *2s. net.*

LATIN VOCABULARIES FOR REPETITION : Arranged according to Subjects. *Fourteenth Edition. Fcap. 8vo. 1s. 6d.*

A VOCABULARY OF LATIN IDIOMS. *18mo. Fourth Edition. 1s.*

STEPS TO GREEK. *Third Edition, revised. 18mo. 1s.*

A SHORTER GREEK PRIMER. *Second Edition. Cr. 8vo. 1s. 6d.*

EASY GREEK PASSAGES FOR UNSEEN TRANSLATION. *Fourth Edition, revised. Fcap. 8vo. 1s. 6d.*

GREEK VOCABULARIES FOR REPETITION. Arranged according to Subjects. *Fourth Edition. Fcap. 8vo. 1s 6d.*

GREEK TESTAMENT SELECTIONS. For the use of Schools. With Introduction, Notes, and Vocabulary. *Fourth Edition. Fcap. 8vo. 2s. 6d.*

STEPS TO FRENCH. *Eighth Edition. 18mo. 8d.*

FIRST FRENCH LESSONS. *Eighth Edition, revised. Cr. 8vo. 1s.*

EASY FRENCH PASSAGES FOR UNSEEN TRANSLATION. *Sixth Edition, revised. Fcap. 8vo. 1s. 6d.*

EASY FRENCH EXERCISES ON ELEMENTARY SYNTAX. With Vocabulary. *Fourth Edition. Cr. 8vo. 2s. 6d.* KEY. *3s. net.*

FRENCH VOCABULARIES FOR REPETITION : Arranged according to Subjects. *Thirteenth Edition. Fcap. 8vo. 1s.* See also School Examination Series.

Steel (R. Elliott), M.A., F.C.S. THE WORLD OF SCIENCE. With 147 Illustrations. *Second Edition. Cr. 8vo. 2s. 6d.* See also School Examination Series.

Stephenson (C.), of the Technical College, Bradford, and **Suddards (F.)** of the Yorkshire College, Leeds. ORNAMENTAL DESIGN FOR WOVEN FABRICS. Illustrated. *Demy 8vo. Third Edition. 7s. 6d.*

Stephenson (J.), M.A. THE CHIEF TRUTHS OF THE CHRISTIAN FAITH. *Cr. 8vo. 3s. 6d.*

Sterne (Laurence). See Little Library.

Sterry (W.), M.A. ANNALS OF ETON COLLEGE. Illustrated. *Demy 8vo. 7s. 6d.*

Steuart (Katherine). BY ALLAN WATER. *Second Edition. Cr. 8vo. 6s.*

Stevenson (R. L.) THE LETTERS OF ROBERT LOUIS STEVENSON TO HIS FAMILY AND FRIENDS. Selected and Edited by SIDNEY COLVIN. *Third Edition. Cr. 8vo. 12s.* LIBRARY EDITION. *Demy 8vo. 2 vols. 25s. net.* A Colonial Edition is also published.

VAILIMA LETTERS. With an Etched Portrait by WILLIAM STRANG. *Sixth Edition. Cr. 8vo. Buckram. 6s.* A Colonial Edition is also published.

THE LIFE OF R. L. STEVENSON. See G. Balfour.

Stevenson (M. I.). FROM SARANAC TO THE MARQUESAS. Being Letters written by Mrs. M. I. STEVENSON during 1887-8. *Cr. 8vo. 6s. net.*

LETTERS FROM SAMOA, 1891-95. Edited and arranged by M. C. BALFOUR. With many Illustrations. *Second Edition Cr. 8vo. 6s. net.*

Stoddart (Anna M.). See Oxford Biographies.

Stokes (F. G.), B.A. HOURS WITH RABELAIS. From the translation of SIR T. URQUHART and P. A. MOTTEUX. With a Portrait in Photogravure. *Cr. 8vo. 3s. 6d. net.*

Stone (S. J.). POEMS AND HYMNS. With a Memoir by F. G. ELLERTON, M.A. With Portrait. *Cr. 8vo. 6s.*

Storr (Vernon F.), M.A., Lecturer in the Philosophy of Religion in Cambridge University ; Examining Chaplain to the Archbishop of Canterbury; formerly Fellow of University College, Oxford. DEVELOPMENT AND DIVINE PURPOSE *Cr. 8vo. 5s. net.*

Straker (F.). See Books on Business.

Streane (A. W.), D.D. See Churchman's Bible.

Streatfeild (R. A.). MODERN MUSIC AND MUSICIANS. With 24 Illustrations. *Second Edition. Demy 8vo. 7s. 6d. net.*

Stroud (H.), D.Sc., M.A. PRACTICAL PHYSICS. With many Diagrams. *Second Edition. 3s. net.*

Strutt (Joseph). THE SPORTS AND PASTIMES OF THE PEOPLE OF ENGLAND. Illustrated by many Engravings. Revised by J. CHARLES COX, LL.D., F.S.A. *Quarto. 21s. net.*

Stuart (Capt. Donald). THE STRUGGLE FOR PERSIA With a Map. *Cr. 8vo. 6s.*

Sturch (F.)., Staff Instructor to the Surrey County Council. MANUAL TRAINING DRAWING (WOODWORK). Its Principles and Application, with Solutions to Examination Questions, 1892-1905, Orthographic, Isometric and Oblique Projection. With 50 Plates and 140 Figures. *Foolscap. 5s. net.*

Suddards (F.). See C. Stephenson.

Surtees (R. S.). See I.P.L.

Symes (J. E.), M.A. THE FRENCH REVOLUTION. *Second Edition. Cr. 8vo. 2s. 6d.*

Sympson (E. M.), M.A., M.D. See Ancient Cities.

A 3

Tacitus. AGRICOLA. With Introduction Notes, Map, etc., by R. F. DAVIS, M.A., *Fcap. 8vo.* 2s.

GERMANIA. By the same Editor. *Fcap. 8vo.* 2s. See also Classical Translations.

Tallack (W.). HOWARD LETTERS AND MEMORIES. *Demy 8vo.* 10s. 6d. net.

Tauler (J.). See Library of Devotion.

Taylor (A. E.). THE ELEMENTS OF METAPHYSICS. *Demy 8vo.* 10s. 6d. net.

Taylor (F. G.), M.A. See Commercial Series.

Taylor (I. A.). See Oxford Biographies.

Taylor (John W.). THE COMING OF THE SAINTS : Imagination and Studies in Early Church History and Tradition. With 26 Illustrations. *Demy 8vo.* 7s. 6d. net.

Taylor T. M.), M.A., Fellow of Gonville and Caius College, Cambridge. A CONSTITUTIONAL AND POLITICAL HISTORY OF ROME. *Cr. 8vo.* 7s. 6d.

Teasdale-Buckell (G. T.). THE COMPLETE SHOT. Illustrated. *Second Ed.*

Tennyson (Alfred, Lord). THE EARLY POEMS OF. Edited, with Notes and an Introduction, by J. CHURTON COLLINS, M.A. *Cr. 8vo.* 6s.

IN MEMORIAM, MAUD, AND THE PRINCESS. Edited by J. CHURTON COLLINS, M.A. *Cr. 8vo.* 6s. See also Little Library.

Terry (C. S.). See Oxford Biographies.

Thackeray (W. M.). See Little Library.

Theobald (F. V.), M.A. INSECT LIFE. Illustrated. *Second Edition Revised. Cr. 8vo.* 2s. 6d.

Thompson (A. H.). See Little Guides.

Tileston (Mary W.). DAILY STRENGTH FOR DAILY NEEDS. *Fourteenth Edition. Medium 16mo.* 2s. 6d. net. Also an edition in superior binding, 6s.

Tompkins (H. W.), F.R.H.S. See Little Guides.

Townley (Lady Susan). MY CHINESE NOTE-BOOK With 16 Illustrations and 2 Maps. *Third Ed. Demy 8vo.* 10s. 6d. net

Toynbee (Paget), M.A., D.Litt. See Oxford Biographies.

Trench (Herbert). DEIRDRE WEDDED AND OTHER POEMS. *Cr. 8vo.* 5s.
An episode of Thirty hours delivered by the three voices. It deals with the love of Deirdre for Naris and is founded on a Gaelic Version of the Tragical Tale of the Sons of Usnach.

Trevelyan (G. M.), Fellow of Trinity College, Cambridge. ENGLAND UNDER THE STUARTS. With Maps and Plans. *Second Edition. Demy 8vo.* 10s. 6d. net.

Troutbeck (G. E.). See Little Guides.

Tyler (E. A.), B.A., F.C.S. See Junior School Books.

Tyrrell-Gill (Frances). See Little Books on Art.

Vardon (Harry). THE COMPLETE GOLFER. Illustrated. *Eighth Edition. Demy 8vo.* 10s. 6d. net.
A Colonial Edition is also published.

Vaughan (Henry). See Little Library.

Vaughan (Herbert M.), B.A. (Oxon.). THE LAST OF THE ROYAL STUARTS, HENRY STUART, CARDINAL, DUKE OF YORK. With 20 Illustrations. *Second Edition. Demy 8vo.* 10s. 6d. net.

THE NAPLES RIVERIA. With 25 Illustrations in Colour by MAURICE GREIFFENHAGEN. *Cr. 8vo.* 6s.
A Colonial Edition is also published.

Voegelin (A.), M.A. See Junior Examination Series.

Waddell (Col. L. A.), LL.D., C.B. LHASA AND ITS MYSTERIES. With a Record of the Expedition of 1903-1904. With 155 Illustrations and Maps. *Third and Cheaper Edition. Demy 8vo.* 7s. 6d. net.

Wade (G. W.), D.D. OLD TESTAMENT HISTORY. With Maps. *Fifth Edition. Cr. 8vo.* 6s.

Wagner (Richard). MUSIC DRAMAS : Interpretations, embodying Wagner's own explanations. By A. L. CLEATHER and B. CRUMP. *In Four Volumes. Fcap 8vo.* 2s. 6d. each.
VOL. I.—THE RING OF THE NIBELUNG. *Third Edition.*
VOL. II.—PARSIFAL, LOHENGRIN, and THE HOLY GRAIL.
VOL. III.—TRISTAN AND ISOLDE.

Wall (J. C.). DEVILS. Illustrated by the Author and from photographs. *Demy 8vo.* 4s. 6d. net. See also Antiquary's Books.

Walters (H. B.). See Little Books on Art and Classics of Art.

Walton (F. W.). See School Histories.

Walton (Izaac) and **Cotton (Charles).** See I.P.L., Standard Library, and Little Library.

Warren-Vernon (Hon. William), M.A. READINGS ON THE INFERNO OF DANTE, based on the Commentary of BENVENUTO DA IMOLA and other authorities. With an Introduction by the Rev. Dr. MOORE. In Two Volumes. *Second Edition,* entirely re-written. *Cr. 8vo.* 15s. net.

Waterhouse (Mrs. Alfred). WITH THE SIMPLE-HEARTED : Little Homilies to Women in Country Places. *Second Edition. Small Pott 8vo.* 2s. net.
See also Little Library.

Watt (Francis). See T. F. Henderson.

Weatherhead (T. C.), M.A. EXAMINATION PAPERS IN HORACE. *Cr. 8vo.* 2s. See also Junior Examination Series.

Webber (F. C.). See Textbooks of Technology.

Weir (Archibald), M.A. AN INTRODUCTION TO THE HISTORY OF MODERN EUROPE. *Cr. 8vo.* 6s.

Wells (Sidney H.) See Textbooks of Science.

Wells (J.), M.A., Fellow and Tutor of Wadham College. OXFORD AND OXFORD LIFE. *Third Edition. Cr .8vo.* 3s. 6d.
A SHORT HISTORY OF ROME. *Eighth Edition.* With 3 Maps. *Cr. 8vo.* 3s. 6d.
See also Little Guides.

Wheldon (F. W.). A LITTLE BROTHER TO THE BIRDS. With 15 Illustrations,

7 of which are by A. H. BUCKLAND. *Large Cr. 8vo. 6s.*

Whibley (C). See W. E. Henley.

Whibley (L.), M.A., Fellow of Pembroke College, Cambridge. GREEK OLIGARCHIES: THEIR ORGANISATION AND CHARACTER. *Cr. 8vo. 6s.*

Whitaker (G. H.), M.A. See Churchman's Bible.

White (Gilbert). THE NATURAL HISTORY OF SELBORNE. Edited by L. C. MIALL, F.R.S., assisted by W. WARDE FOWLER, M.A. *Cr. 8vo. 6s.*
See also Standard Library.

Whitfield (E. E.). See Commercial Series.

Whitehead (A. W.). GASPARD DE COLIGNY. Illustrated. *Demy 8vo. 12s. 6d. net.*

Whiteley (R. Lloyd), F.I.C., Principal of the Municipal Science School, West Bromwich. AN ELEMENTARY TEXTBOOK OF INORGANIC CHEMISTRY. *Cr. 8vo. 2s. 6d.*

Whitley (Miss). See Lady Dilke.

Whitten (W.). See John Thomas Smith.

Whyte (A. G.), B.Sc. See Books on Business.

Wilberforce (Wilfrid). See Little Books on Art.

Wilde (Oscar). DE PROFUNDIS. *Tenth Edition. Cr. 8vo. 5s. net.*
A Colonial Edition is also published.
THE DUCHESS OF PADUA. *Demy 8vo. 12s. 6d. net.*
POEMS. *Demy 8vo. 12s. 6d. net.*
INTENTIONS. *Demy 8vo. 12s. 6d. net.*
SALOME, AND OTHER PLAYS. *Demy 8vo. 12s. 6d. net.*
LADY WINDERMERE'S FAN. *Demy 8vo. 12s. 6d. net.*
A WOMAN OF NO IMPORTANCE. *Demy 8vo. 12s. 6d. net.*
AN IDEAL HUSBAND. *Demy 8vo. 12s. 6d. net.*
THE IMPORTANCE OF BEING EARNEST. *Demy 8vo. 12s. 6d. net.*
A HOUSE OF POMEGRANATES and THE HAPPY PRINCE. *Demy 8vo. 12s. 6d. net.*
LORD ARTHUR SAVILE'S CRIME and OTHER PROSE PIECES. *Demy 8vo. 12s. 6d. net.*

Wilkins (W. H.), B.A. THE ALIEN INVASION. *Cr. 8vo. 2s. 6d.*

Williams (A.). PETROL PETER: or Pretty Stories and Funny Pictures. Illustrated in Colour by A. W. MILLS. *Demy 4to. 3s. 6d. net.*

Williamson (M. G.). See Ancient Cities.

Williamson (W.). THE BRITISH GARDENER. Illustrated. *Demy 8vo. 10s. 6d.*

Williamson (W.), B.A. See Junior Examination Series, Junior School Books, and Beginner's Books.

Willson (Beckles). LORD STRATHCONA: the Story of his Life. Illustrated. *Demy 8vo. 7s. 6d.*
A Colonial Edition is also published.

Wilmot=Buxton (E. M.). MAKERS OF EUROPE. *Cr. 8vo. Eighth Ed. 3s. 6d.*
A Text-book of European History for Middle Forms.
THE ANCIENT WORLD. With Maps and Illustrations. *Cr. 8vo. 3s. 6d.*
See also Beginner's Books.

Wilson (Bishop.). See Library of Devotion.

Wilson (A. J.). See Books on Business.

Wilson (H. A.). See Books on Business.

Wilson (J. A.). See Simplified French Texts.

Wilton (Richard), M.A. LYRA PASTORALIS: Songs of Nature, Church, and Home. *Pott 8vo. 2s. 6d.*

Winbolt (S. E.), M.A. EXERCISES IN LATIN ACCIDENCE. *Cr. 8vo. 1s. 6d.*
LATIN HEXAMETER VERSE: An Aid to Composition. *Cr. 8vo. 3s. 6d.* KEY, *5s. net.*

Windle (B. C. A.), F.R.S., F.S.A. See Antiquary's Books, Little Guides, Ancient Cities, and School Histories.

Winterbotham (Canon), M.A., B.Sc., LL.B. See Churchman's Library.

Wood (Sir Evelyn), F.M., V.C., G.C.B., G.C.M.G. FROM MIDSHIPMAN TO FIELD-MARSHAL. With 24 Illustrations and Maps. *Two Volumes. Fifth Edition. Demy 8vo. 25s. net.*
A Colonial Edition is also published.

Wood (J. A. E.). See Textbooks of Technology.

Wood (J. Hickory). DAN LENO. Illustrated. *Third Edition. Cr. 8vo. 6s.*
A Colonial Edition is also published.

Wood (W. Birkbeck), M.A., late Scholar of Worcester College, Oxford, and **Edmonds (Major J. E.),** R.E., D.A.Q.-M.G. A HISTORY OF THE CIVIL WAR IN THE UNITED STATES. With an Introduction by H. SPENSER WILKINSON. With 24 Maps and Plans. *Demy 8vo. 12s. 6d. net.*

Wordsworth (Christopher). See Antiquary's Books.

Wordsworth (W.). POEMS BY. Selected by STOPFORD A. BROOKE. With 40 Illustrations by· EDMUND H. NEW. With a Frontispiece in Photogravure. *Demy 8vo. 7s. 6d. net.*
A Colonial Edition is also published.

Wordsworth (W.) and Coleridge (S. T.). See Little Library.

Wright (Arthur), D.D., Fellow of Queen's College, Cambridge. See Churchman's Library.

Wright (C. Gordon). See Dante.

Wright (J. C.). TO-DAY. *Demy 16mo. 1s. 6d. net.*

Wright (Sophie). GERMAN VOCABULARIES FOR REPETITION. *Fcap. 8vo. 1s. 6d.*

Wrong (George M.), Professor of History in the University of Toronto. THE EARL OF ELGIN. Illustrated. *Demy 8vo. 7s. 6d. net.*
A Colonial Edition is also published.

Wyatt (Kate M.). See M. R. Gloag.

Wylde (A. B.). MODERN ABYSSINIA. With a Map and a Portrait. *Demy 8vo.* 15s. net.
A Colonial Edition is also published.

Wyndham (Rt. Hon. George). M.P. THE POEMS OF WILLIAM SHAKE-SPEARE. With an Introduction and Notes. *Demy 8vo. Buckram, gilt top.* 10s. 6d.

Wyon (R.) and Prance (G.). THE LAND OF THE BLACK MOUNTAIN. Being a Description of Montenegro. With 40 Illustrations. *Cr. 8vo.* 2s. 6d. net.

Yeats (W. B.). A BOOK OF IRISH VERSE. Selected from Modern Writers.

Revised and Enlarged Edition. Cr. 8vo. 3s. 6d.

Young (Filson). THE COMPLETE MOTORIST. With 138 Illustrations. *Seventh Edition. Demy 8vo.* 12s. 6d. net.
A Colonial Edition is also published.

THE JOY OF THE ROAD: An Appreciation of the Motor Car. *Small Demy 8vo.* 5s. net.

Young (T. M.). THE AMERICAN COTTON INDUSTRY: A Study of Work and Workers. *Cr. 8vo. Cloth,* 2s. 6d. ; *paper boards,* 1s. 6d.

Zimmern (Antonia). WHAT DO WE KNOW CONCERNING ELECTRI-CITY? *Fcap. 8vo.* 1s. 6d. net.

Ancient Cities

General Editor, B. C. A. WINDLE, D.Sc., F.R.S.

Cr. 8vo. 4s. 6d. net.

CHESTER. By B. C. A. Windle, D.Sc. F.R.S. Illustrated by E. H. New.

SHREWSBURY. By T. Auden, M.A., F.S.A. Illustrated.

CANTERBURY. By J. C. Cox, LL.D., F.S.A. Illustrated.

EDINBURGH. By M. G. Williamson, M.A. Illustrated by Herbert Railton.

LINCOLN. By E. Mansel Sympson, M.A., M.D. Illustrated by E. H. New.

BRISTOL. By Alfred Harvey. Illustrated by E. H. New.

DUBLIN. By S. A. O. Fitzpatrick. Illustrated by W. C. Green.

The Antiquary's Books

General Editor, J. CHARLES COX, LL.D., F.S.A.

Demy 8vo. 7s. 6d. net.

ENGLISH MONASTIC LIFE. By the Right Rev. Abbot Gasquet, O.S.B. Illustrated. *Third Edition.*

REMAINS OF THE PREHISTORIC AGE IN ENGLAND. By B. C. A. Windle, D.Sc., F.R.S. With numerous Illustrations and Plans.

OLD SERVICE BOOKS OF THE ENGLISH CHURCH. By Christopher Wordsworth, M.A., and Henry Littlehales. With Coloured and other Illustrations.

CELTIC ART. By J. Romilly Allen, F.S.A. With numerous Illustrations and Plans.

ARCHÆOLOGY AND FALSE ANTIQUITIES. By R. Munro, LL.D. Illustrated.

SHRINES OF BRITISH SAINTS. By J. C. Wall. With numerous Illustrations and Plans.

THE ROYAL FORESTS OF ENGLAND. By J. C. Cox, LL.D., F.S.A. Illustrated.

THE MANOR AND MANORIAL RECORDS. By Nathaniel J. Hone. Illustrated.

ENGLISH SEALS. By J. Harvey Bloom. Illustrated.

THE DOMESDAY INQUEST. By Adolphus Ballard, B.A., LL.B. With 27 Illustrations.

THE BRASSES OF ENGLAND. By Herbert W. Macklin, M.A. With many Illustrations. *Second Edition.*

PARISH LIFE IN MEDIÆVAL ENGLAND. By the Right Rev. Abbott Gasquet, O.S.B. With many Illustrations. *Second Edition.*

THE BELLS OF ENGLAND. By Canon J. J. Raven, D.D., F.S.A. With Illustrations. *Second Edition.*

The Arden Shakespeare

Demy 8vo. 2s. 6d. net each volume.

General Editor, W. J. CRAIG.

An edition of Shakespeare in single Plays. Edited with a full Introduction, Textual Notes, and a Commentary at the foot of the page.

HAMLET. Edited by Edward Dowden.

ROMEO AND JULIET. Edited by Edward Dowden.

KING LEAR. Edited by W. J. Craig.

JULIUS CAESAR. Edited by M. Macmillan.

THE TEMPEST. Edited by Moreton Luce.

[Continued

ARDEN SHAKESPEARE—*continued*.

OTHELLO. Edited by H. C. Hart.
TITUS ANDRONICUS. Edited by H. B. Baildon.
CYMBELINE. Edited by Edward Dowden.
THE MERRY WIVES OF WINDSOR. Edited by H. C. Hart.
A MIDSUMMER NIGHT'S DREAM. Edited by H. Cuningham.
KING HENRY V. Edited by H. A. Evans.
ALL'S WELL THAT ENDS WELL. Edited by W. O. Brigstocke.
THE TAMING OF THE SHREW. Edited by R. Warwick Bond.
TIMON OF ATHENS. Edited by K. Deighton.
MEASURE FOR MEASURE. Edited by H. C. Hart.
TWELFTH NIGHT. Edited by Moreton Luce.

THE MERCHANT OF VENICE. Edited by C. Knox Pooler.
TROILUS AND CRESSIDA. Edited by K. Deighton.
ANTONY AND CLEOPATRA. Edited by R. H. Case.
LOVE'S LABOUR'S LOST. Edited by H. C. Hart.
THE TWO GENTLEMAN OF VERONA. R, Warwick Bond.
PERICLES. Edited by K. Deighton.
THE COMEDY OF ERRORS. Edited by H. Cuningham.
KING RICHARD III. Edited by A. H. Thompson.
KING JOHN. Edited by Ivor B. John.

The Beginner's Books
Edited by W. WILLIAMSON, B.A.

EASY FRENCH RHYMES. By Henri Blouet. *Second Edition.* Illustrated. *Fcap. 8vo.* 1s.

EASY STORIES FROM ENGLISH HISTORY. By E. M. Wilmot-Buxton, Author of 'Makers of Europe.' *Third Edition. Cr. 8vo.* 1s.

EASY EXERCISES IN ARITHMETIC. Arranged by W. S. Beard. *Second Edition. Fcap.*

8vo. Without Answers, 1s. With Answers. 1s. 3d.

EASY DICTATION AND SPELLING. By W. Williamson, B.A. *Fifth Ed. Fcap. 8vo.* 1s.

AN EASY POETRY BOOK. Selected and arranged by W. Williamson, B.A., Author of 'Dictation Passages.' *Second Edition. Cr. 8vo.* 1s.

Books on Business
Cr. 8vo. 2s. 6d. *net.*

PORTS AND DOCKS. By Douglas Owen.
RAILWAYS. By E. R. McDermott.
THE STOCK EXCHANGE. By Chas. Duguid. *Second Edition.*
THE BUSINESS OF INSURANCE. By A. J. Wilson.
THE ELECTRICAL INDUSTRY: LIGHTING, TRACTION, AND POWER. By A. G. Whyte, B.Sc.
THE SHIPBUILDING INDUSTRY: Its History, Science, Practice, and Finance. By David Pollock, M.I.N.A.
THE MONEY MARKET. By F. Straker.
THE BUSINESS SIDE OF AGRICULTURE. By A. G. L. Rogers, M.A.
LAW IN BUSINESS. By H. A. Wilson.
THE BREWING INDUSTRY. By Julian L. Baker, F.I.C., F.C.S.

THE AUTOMOBILE INDUSTRY. By G. de H. Stone.
MINING AND MINING INVESTMENTS. By 'A. Moil.'
THE BUSINESS OF ADVERTISING. By Clarence G. Moran, Barrister-at-Law. Illustrated.
TRADE UNIONS. By G. Drage.
CIVIL ENGINEERING. By T. Claxton Fidler, M.Inst. C.E. Illustrated.
THE IRON TRADE OF GREAT BRITAIN. By J. Stephen Jeans. Illustrated.
MONOPOLIES, TRUSTS, AND KARTELLS. By F. W. Hirst.
THE COTTON INDUSTRY AND TRADE. By Prof. S. J. Chapman, Dean of the Faculty of Commerce in the University of Manchester. Illustrated.

Byzantine Texts
Edited by J. B. BURY, M.A., Litt.D.

A series of texts of Byzantine Historians, edited by English and foreign scholars.

ZACHARIAH OF MITYLENE. Translated by F. J. Hamilton, D.D., and E. W. Brooks. *Demy 8vo.* 12s. 6d. *net.*

EVAGRIUS. Edited by Léon Parmentier and M. Bidez. *Demy 8vo.* 10s. 6d. *net.*

THE HISTORY OF PSELLUS. Edited by C. Sathas. *Demy 8vo.* 15s *net.*
ECTHESIS CHRONICA. Edited by Professor Lambros. *Demy 8vo.* 7s. 6d. *net.*
THE CHRONICLE OF MOREA. Edited by John Schmitt. *Demy 8vo.* 15s. *net.*

The Churchman's Bible

General Editor, J. H. BURN, B.D., F.R.S.E.

Fcap. 8vo.   1s. 6d. net each.

A series of Expositions on the Books of the Bible, which will be of service to the general reader in the practical and devotional study of the Sacred Text.

Each Book is provided with a full and clear Introductory Section, in which is stated what is known or conjectured respecting the date and occasion of the composition of the Book, and any other particulars that may help to elucidate its meaning as a whole.   The Exposition is divided into sections of a convenient length, corresponding as far as possible with the divisions of the Church Lectionary.   The Translation of the Authorised Version is printed in full, such corrections as are deemed necessary being placed in footnotes.

THE EPISTLE OF ST. PAUL THE APOSTLE TO THE GALATIANS.   Edited by A. W. Robinson, M.A.   *Second Edition.*

ECCLESIASTES.   Edited by A. W. Streane, D.D.

THE EPISTLE OF ST. PAUL THE APOSTLE TO THE PHILIPPIANS.   Edited by C. R, D. Biggs, D.D.   *Second Edition.*

THE EPISTLE OF ST. JAMES.   Edited by H. W. Fulford M.A.

ISAIAH.   Edited by W. E. Barnes, D.D.   *Two Volumes.*   With Map.   *2s. net each.*

THE EPISTLE OF ST. PAUL THE APOSTLE TO THE EPHESIANS. Edited by G. H. Whitaker, M.A.

THE GOSPEL ACCORDING TO ST. MARK. Edited by J. C. Du Buisson, M.A.   *2s. 6d. net.*

ST. PAUL'S EPISTLES TO THE COLOSSIANS AND PHILEMON. Edited by H. J. C. Knight, M.A.   *2s. net.*

The Churchman's Library

General Editor, J. H. BURN, B.D., F.R.S.E.

Crown 8vo.   3s. 6d. each.

THE BEGINNINGS OF ENGLISH CHRISTIANITY. By W. E. Collins, M.A.   With Map.

THE KINGDOM OF HEAVEN HERE AND HEREAFTER.   By Canon Winterbotham, M.A., B.Sc., LL.B.

THE WORKMANSHIP OF THE PRAYER BOOK : Its Literary and Liturgical Aspects.   By J. Dowden, D.D.   *Second Edition.*

EVOLUTION.   By F. B. Jevons, M.A., Litt.D.

SOME NEW TESTAMENT PROBLEMS.   By Arthur Wright, D.D.   *6s.*

THE CHURCHMAN'S INTRODUCTION TO THE OLD TESTAMENT.   By A. M. Mackay, B.A.

THE CHURCH OF CHRIST.   By E. T. Green, M.A.   *6s.*

COMPARATIVE THEOLOGY.   By J. A. Mac-Culloch.   *6s.*

Classical Translations

Edited by H. F. FOX, M.A., Fellow and Tutor of Brasenose College, Oxford.

Crown 8vo.

A series of Translations from the Greek and Latin Classics, distinguished by literary excellence as well as by scholarly accuracy.

ÆSCHYLUS—Agamemnon Choephoroe, Eumenides.   Translated by Lewis Campbell, LL.D.   *5s.*

CICERO—De Oratore I.   Translated by E. N. P. Moor, M.A.   *3s. 6d.*

CICERO—Select Orations (Pro Milone, Pro Mureno, Philippic II., in Catilinam).   Translated by H. E. D. Blakiston, M.A.   *5s.*

CICERO—De Natura Deorum.   Translated by F. Brooks, M.A.   *3s. 6d.*

CICERO—De Officiis.   Translated by G. B. Gardiner, M.A.   *2s. 6d.*

HORACE—The Odes and Epodes.   Translated by A. D. Godley, M.A.   *2s.*

LUCIAN—Six Dialogues (Nigrinus, Icaro-Menippus, The Cock, The Ship, The Parasite, The Lover of Falsehood)   Translated by S. T. Irwin, M.A.   *3s. 6d.*

SOPHOCLES—Electra and Ajax.   Translated by E. D. A. Morshead, M.A.   *2s. 6d.*

TACITUS—Agricola and Germania.   Translated by R. B. Townshend.   *2s. 6d.*

THE SATIRES OF JUVENAL.   Translated by S. G. Owen.   *2s. 6d.*

Classics of Art

Edited by DR. J. H. W. LAING

THE ART OF THE GREEKS. By H. B. Walters. With 112 Plates and 18 Illustrations in the Text. *Wide Royal 8vo.* 12s. 6d. *net.*

VELAZQUEZ. By A. de Beruete. With 94 Plates. *Wide Royal 8vo.* 10s. 6d. *net.*

Commercial Series

Edited by H. DE B. GIBBINS, Litt.D., M.A.

Crown 8vo.

COMMERCIAL EDUCATION IN THEORY AND PRACTICE. By E. E. Whitfield, M.A. 5s.
An introduction to Methuen's Commercial Series treating the question of Commercial Education fully from both the point of view of the teacher and of the parent.

BRITISH COMMERCE AND COLONIES FROM ELIZABETH TO VICTORIA. By H. de B. Gibbins, Litt.D., M.A. *Third Edition.* 2s.

COMMERCIAL EXAMINATION PAPERS. By H. de B. Gibbins, Litt.D., M.A. 1s. 6d.

THE ECONOMICS OF COMMERCE, By H. de B. Gibbins, Litt.D., M.A. *Second Edition.* 1s. 6d.

A GERMAN COMMERCIAL READER. By S. E. Bally. With Vocabulary. 2s.

A COMMERCIAL GEOGRAPHY OF THE BRITISH EMPIRE. By L. W. Lyde, M.A. *Sixth Edition.* 2s.

A COMMERCIAL GEOGRAPHY OF FOREIGN NATIONS. By F. C. Boon, B.A. 2s.

A PRIMER OF BUSINESS. By S. Jackson, M.A. *Third Edition.* 1s. 6d.

COMMERCIAL ARITHMETIC. By F. G. Taylor, M.A. *Fourth Edition.* 1s. 6d.

FRENCH COMMERCIAL CORRESPONDENCE. By S. E. Bally. With Vocabulary. *Third Edition.* 2s.

GERMAN COMMERCIAL CORRESPONDENCE. By S. E. Bally. With Vocabulary. *Second Edition.* 2s. 6d.

A FRENCH COMMERCIAL READER. By S. E. Bally. With Vocabulary. *Second Edition.* 2s.

PRECIS WRITING AND OFFICE CORRESPONDENCE. By E. E. Whitfield, M.A. *Second Edition.* 2s.

A GUIDE TO PROFESSIONS AND BUSINESS. By H. Jones. 1s. 6d.

THE PRINCIPLES OF BOOK-KEEPING BY DOUBLE ENTRY. By J. E. B. M'Allen, M.A. 2s.

COMMERCIAL LAW. By W. Douglas Edwards. *Second Edition.* 2s.

The Connoisseur's Library

Wide Royal 8vo. 25s. *net.*

A sumptuous series of 20 books on art, written by experts for collectors, superbly illustrated in photogravure, collotype, and colour. The technical side of the art is duly treated. The first volumes are—

MEZZOTINTS. By Cyril Davenport. With 40 Plates in Photogravure.

PORCELAIN. By Edward Dillon. With 19 Plates in Colour, 20 in Collotype, and 5 in Photogravure.

MINIATURES. By Dudley Heath. With 9 Plates in Colour, 15 in Collotype, and 15 in Photogravure.

IVORIES. By A. Maskell. With 80 Plates in Collotype and Photogravure.

ENGLISH FURNITURE. By F. S. Robinson. With 160 Plates in Collotype and one in Photogravure. *Second Edition.*

EUROPEAN ENAMELS. By Henry H. Cunynghame, C.B. With 54 Plates in Collotype and Half-tone and 4 Plates in Colour.

GOLDSMITHS' AND SILVERSMITHS' WORK. By Nelson Dawson. With many Plates in Collotype and a Frontispiece in Photogravure. *Second Edition.*

ENGLISH COLOURED BOOKS. By Martin Hardie. With 28 Illustrations in Colour and Collotype.

GLASS. By Edward Dillon. With 37 Illustrations in Collotype and 12 in Colour.

The Library of Devotion

With Introductions and (where necessary) Notes.

Small Pott 8vo, cloth, 2s. ; *leather,* 2s. 6d. *net.*

THE CONFESSIONS OF ST. AUGUSTINE. Edited by C. Bigg, D.D. *Sixth Edition.*

THE CHRISTIAN YEAR. Edited by Walter Lock, D.D. *Third Edition.*

THE IMITATION OF CHRIST. Edited by C. Bigg, D.D. *Fourth Edition.*

A BOOK OF DEVOTIONS. Edited by J. W. Stanbridge. B.D. *Second Edition.*

[Continued.

THE LIBRARY OF DEVOTION—*continued.*

LYRA INNOCENTIUM. Edited by Walter Lock, D.D.

A SERIOUS CALL TO A DEVOUT AND HOLY LIFE. Edited by C. Bigg, D.D. *Fourth Edition.*

THE TEMPLE. Edited by E. C. S. Gibson, D.D. *Second Edition.*

A GUIDE TO ETERNITY. Edited by J. W. Stanbridge, B.D.

THE PSALMS OF DAVID. Edited by B. W. Randolph, D.D.

LYRA APOSTOLICA. By Cardinal Newman and others. Edited by Canon Scott Holland and Canon H. C. Beeching, M.A.

THE INNER WAY. By J. Tauler. Edited by A. W. Hutton, M.A.

THE THOUGHTS OF PASCAL. Edited by C. S. Jerram, M.A.

ON THE LOVE OF GOD. By St. Francis de Sales. Edited by W. J. Knox-Little, M.A.

A MANUAL OF CONSOLATION FROM THE SAINTS AND FATHERS. Edited by J. H. Burn, B.D.

THE SONG OF SONGS. Edited by B. Blaxland, M.A.

THE DEVOTIONS OF ST. ANSELM. Edited by C. C. J. Webb, M.A.

GRACE ABOUNDING. By John Bunyan. Edited by S. C. Freer, M.A.

BISHOP WILSON'S SACRA PRIVATA. Edited by A. E. Burn, B.D.

LYRA SACRA : A Book of Sacred Verse. Edited by H. C. Beeching, M.A., Canon of Westminster.

A DAY BOOK FROM THE SAINTS AND FATHERS. Edited by J. H. Burn, B.D.

HEAVENLY WISDOM. A Selection from the English Mystics. Edited by E. C. Gregory.

LIGHT, LIFE, and LOVE. A Selection from the German Mystics. Edited by W. R. Inge, M.A.

AN INTRODUCTION TO THE DEVOUT LIFE. By St. Francis de Sales. Translated and Edited by T. Barns, M.A.

MANCHESTER AL MONDO : a Contemplation of Death and Immortality. By Henry Montagu, Earl of Manchester. With an Introduction by Elizabeth Waterhouse, Editor of ' A Little Book of Life and Death.'

THE LITTLE FLOWERS OF THE GLORIOUS MESSER ST. FRANCIS AND OF HIS FRIARS. Done into English by W. Heywood. With an Introduction by A. G. Ferrers Howell.

THE SPIRITUAL GUIDE, which Disentangles the Soul and brings it by the Inward Way to the Fruition of Perfect Contemplation, and the Rich Treasure of Internal Peace. Written by Dr. Michael de Molinos, Priest. Translated from the Italian copy, printed at Venice, 1685. Edited with an Introduction by Kathleen Lyttelton. With a Preface by Canon Scott Holland.

The Illustrated Pocket Library of Plain and Coloured Books

Fcap 8*vo.* 3*s.* 6*d. net each volume.*

A series, in small form, of some of the famous illustrated books of fiction and general literature. These are faithfully reprinted from the first or best editions without introduction or notes. The Illustrations are chiefly in colour.

COLOURED BOOKS

OLD COLOURED BOOKS. By George Paston. With 16 Coloured Plates. *Fcap. 8vo. 2s. net.*

THE LIFE AND DEATH OF JOHN MYTTON, ESQ. By Nimrod. With 18 Coloured Plates by Henry Alken and T. J. Rawlins. *Fourth Edition.*

THE LIFE OF A SPORTSMAN. By Nimrod. With 35 Coloured Plates by Henry Alken.

HANDLEY CROSS. By R. S. Surtees. With 17 Coloured Plates and 100 Woodcuts in the Text by John Leech. *Second Edition.*

MR. SPONGE'S SPORTING TOUR. By R. S. Surtees. With 13 Coloured Plates and 90 Woodcuts in the Text by John Leech.

JORROCKS' JAUNTS AND JOLLITIES. By R. S. Surtees. With 15 Coloured Plates by H. Alken. *Second Edition.*

This volume is reprinted from the extremely rare and costly edition of 1843, which contains Alken's very fine illustrations instead of the usual ones by Phiz.

ASK MAMMA. By R. S. Surtees. With 13 Coloured Plates and 70 Woodcuts in the Text by John Leech.

THE ANALYSIS OF THE HUNTING FIELD. By R. S. Surtees. With 7 Coloured Plates by Henry Alken, and 43 Illustrations on Wood.

THE TOUR OF DR. SYNTAX IN SEARCH OF THE PICTURESQUE. By William Combe. With 30 Coloured Plates by T. Rowlandson.

THE TOUR OF DOCTOR SYNTAX IN SEARCH OF CONSOLATION. By William Combe. With 24 Coloured Plates by T. Rowlandson.

THE THIRD TOUR OF DOCTOR SYNTAX IN SEARCH OF A WIFE. By William Combe. With 24 Coloured Plates by T. Rowlandson.

THE HISTORY OF JOHNNY QUAE GENUS : the Little Foundling of the late Dr. Syntax. By the Author of ' The Three Tours.' With 24 Coloured Plates by Rowlandson.

THE ENGLISH DANCE OF DEATH, from the Designs of T. Rowlandson, with Metrical Illustrations by the Author of ' Doctor Syntax.' *Two Volumes.*

This book contains 76 Coloured Plates.

THE DANCE OF LIFE : A Poem. By the Author of ' Doctor Syntax.' Illustrated with 26 Coloured Engravings by T. Rowlandson.

[*Continued.*

ILLUSTRATED POCKET LIBRARY OF PLAIN AND COLOURED BOOKS—*continued*.

LIFE IN LONDON: or, the Day and Night Scenes of Jerry Hawthorn, Esq., and his Elegant Friend, Corinthian Tom. By Pierce Egan. With 36 Coloured Plates by I. R. and G. Cruikshank. With numerous Designs on Wood.

REAL LIFE IN LONDON: or, the Rambles and Adventures of Bob Tallyho, Esq., and his Cousin, The Hon. Tom Dashall. By an Amateur (Pierce Egan). With 31 Coloured Plates by Alken and Rowlandson, etc. *Two Volumes*.

THE LIFE OF AN ACTOR. By Pierce Egan. With 27 Coloured Plates by Theodore Lane, and several Designs on Wood.

THE VICAR OF WAKEFIELD. By Oliver Goldsmith. With 24 Coloured Plates by T. Rowlandson.

THE MILITARY ADVENTURES OF JOHNNY NEWCOME. By an Officer. With 15 Coloured Plates by T. Rowlandson.

THE NATIONAL SPORTS OF GREAT BRITAIN. With Descriptions and 51 Coloured Plates by Henry Alken.

This book is completely different from the large folio edition of 'National Sports' by the same artist, and none of the plates are similar.

THE ADVENTURES OF A POST CAPTAIN. By A Naval Officer. With 24 Coloured Plates by Mr. Williams.

GAMONIA: or, the Art of Preserving Game; and an Improved Method of making Plantations and Covers, explained and illustrated by Lawrence Rawstorne, Esq. With 15 Coloured Plates by T. Rawlins.

AN ACADEMY FOR GROWN HORSEMEN: Containing the completest Instructions for Walking, Trotting, Cantering, Galloping, Stumbling, and Tumbling. Illustrated with 27 Coloured Plates, and adorned with a Portrait of the Author. By Geoffrey Gambado, Esq.

REAL LIFE IN IRELAND, or, the Day and Night Scenes of Brian Boru, Esq., and his Elegant Friend, Sir Shawn O'Dogherty. By a Real Paddy. With 19 Coloured Plates by Heath, Marks, etc.

THE ADVENTURES OF JOHNNY NEWCOME IN THE NAVY. By Alfred Burton. With 16 Coloured Plates by T. Rowlandson.

THE OLD ENGLISH SQUIRE: A Poem. By John Careless, Esq. With 20 Coloured Plates after the style of T. Rowlandson.

PLAIN BOOKS

THE GRAVE: A Poem. By Robert Blair. Illustrated by 12 Etchings executed by Louis Schiavonetti from the original Inventions of William Blake. With an Engraved Title Page and a Portrait of Blake by T. Phillips, R.A.

The illustrations are reproduced in photogravure.

ILLUSTRATIONS OF THE BOOK OF JOB. Invented and engraved by William Blake.

These famous Illustrations—21 in number—are reproduced in photogravure.

ÆSOP'S FABLES. With 380 Woodcuts by Thomas Bewick.

WINDSOR CASTLE. By W. Harrison Ainsworth. With 22 Plates and 87 Woodcuts in the Text by George Cruikshank.

THE TOWER OF LONDON. By W. Harrison Ainsworth. With 40 Plates and 58 Woodcuts in the Text by George Cruikshank.

FRANK FAIRLEGH. By F. E. Smedley. With 30 Plates by George Cruikshank.

HANDY ANDY. By Samuel Lover. With 24 Illustrations by the Author.

THE COMPLEAT ANGLER. By Izaak Walton and Charles Cotton. With 14 Plates and 77 Woodcuts in the Text.

This volume is reproduced from the beautiful edition of John Major of 1824.

THE PICKWICK PAPERS. By Charles Dickens. With the 43 Illustrations by Seymour and Phiz, the two Buss Plates, and the 32 Contemporary Onwhyn Plates.

Junior Examination Series

Edited by A. M. M. STEDMAN, M.A. *Fcap. 8vo.* 1s.

JUNIOR FRENCH EXAMINATION PAPERS. By F. Jacob, M.A. *Second Edition*.

JUNIOR LATIN EXAMINATION PAPERS. By C. G. Botting, B.A. *Fourth Edition*.

JUNIOR ENGLISH EXAMINATION PAPERS. By W. Williamson, B.A.

JUNIOR ARITHMETIC EXAMINATION PAPERS. By W. S. Beard. *Fourth Edition*.

JUNIOR ALGEBRA EXAMINATION PAPERS. By S. W. Finn, M.A.

JUNIOR GREEK EXAMINATION PAPERS. By T. C. Weatherhead, M.A.

JUNIOR GENERAL INFORMATION EXAMINATION PAPERS. By W. S. Beard.

A KEY TO THE ABOVE. 3s. 6d. *net*.

JUNIOR GEOGRAPHY EXAMINATION PAPERS. By W. G. Baker, M.A.

JUNIOR GERMAN EXAMINATION PAPERS. By A. Voegelin, M.A.

Junior School-Books

Edited by O. D. INSKIP, LL.D., and W. WILLIAMSON, B.A.

A CLASS-BOOK OF DICTATION PASSAGES. By W. Williamson, B.A. *Thirteenth Edition. Cr. 8vo. 1s. 6d.*

THE GOSPEL ACCORDING TO ST. MATTHEW. Edited by E. Wilton South, M.A. With Three Maps. *Cr. 8vo. 1s. 6d.*

THE GOSPEL ACCORDING TO ST. MARK. Edited by A. E. Rubie, D.D. With Three Maps. *Cr. 8vo. 1s. 6d.*

A JUNIOR ENGLISH GRAMMAR. By W. Williamson, B.A. With numerous passages for parsing and analysis, and a chapter on Essay Writing. *Third Edition. Cr. 8vo. 2s.*

A JUNIOR CHEMISTRY. By E. A. Tyler, B.A., F.C.S. With 78 Illustrations. *Fourth Edition. Cr. 8vo. 2s. 6d.*

THE ACTS OF THE APOSTLES. Edited by A. E. Rubie, D.D. *Cr. 8vo. 2s.*

A JUNIOR FRENCH GRAMMAR. By L. A. Sornet and M. J. Acatos. *Second Edition. Cr. 8vo. 2s.*

ELEMENTARY EXPERIMENTAL SCIENCE. PHYSICS by W. T. Clough, A.R.C.S. CHEMISTRY by A. E. Dunstan, B.Sc. With 2 Plates and 154 Diagrams. *Fifth Edition. Cr. 8vo. 2s. 6d.*

A JUNIOR GEOMETRY. By Noel S. Lydon. With 276 Diagrams. *Fifth Edition. Cr. 8vo. 2s.*

ELEMENTARY EXPERIMENTAL CHEMISTRY. By A. E. Dunstan, B.Sc. With 4 Plates and 109 Diagrams. *Second Edition. Cr. 8vo. 2s.*

A JUNIOR FRENCH PROSE. By R. R. N. Baron, M.A. *Second Edition. Cr. 8vo. 2s.*

THE GOSPEL ACCORDING TO ST. LUKE. With an Introduction and Notes by William Williamson, B.A. With Three Maps. *Cr. 8vo. 2s.*

THE FIRST BOOK OF KINGS. Edited by A. E. RUBIE, D.D. With Maps. *Cr. 8vo. 2s.*

Leaders of Religion

Edited by H. C. BEECHING, M.A., Canon of Westminster. *With Portraits.*

Cr. 8vo. 2s. net.

CARDINAL NEWMAN. By R. H. Hutton.

JOHN WESLEY. By J. H. Overton, M.A.

BISHOP WILBERFORCE. By G. W. Daniell, M.A.

CARDINAL MANNING. By A. W. Hutton, M.A.

CHARLES SIMEON. By H. C. G. Moule, D.D.

JOHN KEBLE. By Walter Lock, D.D.

THOMAS CHALMERS. By Mrs. Oliphant.

LANCELOT ANDREWES. By R. L. Ottley, D.D. *Second Edition.*

AUGUSTINE OF CANTERBURY. By E. L. Cutts, D.D.

WILLIAM LAUD. By W. H. Hutton, M.A. *Third Edition.*

JOHN KNOX. By F. MacCunn. *Second Edition.*

JOHN HOWE. By R. F. Horton, D.D.

BISHOP KEN. By F. A. Clarke, M.A.

GEORGE FOX, THE QUAKER. By T. Hodgkin, D.C.L. *Third Edition.*

JOHN DONNE. By Augustus Jessopp, D.D.

THOMAS CRANMER. By A. J. Mason, D.D.

BISHOP LATIMER. By R. M. Carlyle and A. J. Carlyle, M.A.

BISHOP BUTLER. By W. A. Spooner, M.A.

Little Books on Art

With many Illustrations. Demy 16mo. 2s. 6d. net.

A series of monographs in miniature, containing the complete outline of the subject under treatment and rejecting minute details. These books are produced with the greatest care. Each volume consists of about 200 pages, and contains from 30 to 40 illustrations, including a frontispiece in photogravure.

GREEK ART. H. B. Walters. *Third Edition.*

BOOKPLATES. E. Almack.

REYNOLDS. J. Sime. *Second Edition.*

ROMNEY. George Paston.

GREUZE AND BOUCHER. Eliza F. Pollard.

VANDYCK. M. G. Smallwood.

TURNER. Frances Tyrrell-Gill.

DÜRER. Jessie Allen.

HOPPNER. H. P. K. Skipton.

HOLBEIN. Mrs. G. Fortescue.

WATTS. R. E. D. Sketchley.

LEIGHTON. Alice Corkran.

VELASQUEZ. Wilfrid Wilberforce and A. R. Gilbert.

COROT. Alice Pollard and Ethel Birnstingl.

RAPHAEL. A. R. Dryhurst.

MILLET. Netta Peacock.

ILLUMINATED MSS. J. W. Bradley.

CHRIST IN ART. Mrs. Henry Jenner.

JEWELLERY. Cyril Davenport.

[Continued.

The Little Galleries

Demy 16mo. 2s. 6d. net.

A series of little books containing examples of the best work of the great painters. Each volume contains 20 plates in photogravure, together with a short outline of the life and work of the master to whom the book is devoted.

The Little Guides

With many Illustrations by E. H. NEW and other artists, and from photographs.

Small Pott 8vo, cloth, 2s. 6d. net.; leather, 3s. 6d. net.

Messrs. METHUEN are publishing a small series of books under the general title of THE LITTLE GUIDES. The main features of these books are (1) a handy and charming form, (2) artistic Illustrations by E. H. NEW and others, (3) good plans and maps, (4) an adequate but compact presentation of everything that is interesting in the natural features, history, archæology, and architecture of the town or district treated.

The Little Library

With Introductions, Notes, and Photogravure Frontispieces.

Small Pott 8vo. Each Volume, cloth, 1s. 6d. net; leather, 2s. 6d. net.

[Continued.

THE LITTLE LIBRARY—continued.

Barham (R. H.). THE INGOLDSBY LEGENDS. Edited by J. B. ATLAY. *Two Volumes.*

Barnett (Mrs. P. A.). A LITTLE BOOK OF ENGLISH PROSE.

Beckford (William). THE HISTORY OF THE CALIPH VATHEK. Edited by E. DENISON ROSS.

Blake (William). SELECTIONS FROM WILLIAM BLAKE. Edited by M. PERUGINI.

Borrow (George). LAVENGRO. Edited by F. HINDES GROOME. *Two Volumes.*

THE ROMANY RYE. Edited by JOHN SAMPSON.

Browning (Robert). SELECTIONS FROM THE EARLY POEMS OF ROBERT BROWNING. Edited by W. HALL GRIFFIN, M.A.

Canning (George). SELECTIONS FROM THE ANTI-JACOBIN: with GEORGE CANNING's additional Poems. Edited by LLOYD SANDERS.

Cowley (Abraham). THE ESSAYS OF ABRAHAM COWLEY. Edited by H. C. MINCHIN.

Crabbe (George). SELECTIONS FROM GEORGE CRABBE. Edited by A. C. DEANE.

Craik (Mrs.). JOHN HALIFAX, GENTLEMAN. Edited by ANNE MATHESON. *Two Volumes.*

Crashaw (Richard). THE ENGLISH POEMS OF RICHARD CRASHAW. Edited by EDWARD HUTTON.

Dante (Alighieri). THE INFERNO OF DANTE. Translated by H. F. CARY. Edited by PAGET TOYNBEE, M.A., D.Litt.

THE PURGATORIO OF DANTE. Translated by H. F. CARY. Edited by PAGET TOYNBEE, M.A., D.Litt.

THE PARADISO OF DANTE. Translated by H. F. CARY. Edited by PAGET TOYNBEE, M.A., D.Litt.

Darley (George). SELECTIONS FROM THE POEMS OF GEORGE DARLEY. Edited by R. A. STREATFEILD.

Deane (A. C.). A LITTLE BOOK OF LIGHT VERSE.

Dickens (Charles). CHRISTMAS BOOKS. *Two Volumes.*

Ferrier (Susan). MARRIAGE. Edited by A. GOODRICH - FREER and LORD IDDESLEIGH. *Two Volumes.*

THE INHERITANCE. *Two Volumes.*

Gaskell (Mrs.). CRANFORD. Edited by E. V. LUCAS. *Second Edition.*

Hawthorne (Nathaniel). THE SCARLET LETTER. Edited by PERCY DEARMER.

Henderson (T. F.). A LITTLE BOOK OF SCOTTISH VERSE.

Keats (John). POEMS. With an Introduction by L. BINYON, and Notes by J. MASEFIELD.

Kinglake (A. W.). EOTHEN. With an Introduction and Notes. *Second Edition.*

Lamb (Charles). ELIA, AND THE LAST ESSAYS OF ELIA. Edited by E. V. LUCAS.

Locker (F.). LONDON LYRICS. Edited by A. D. GODLEY, M.A. A reprint of the First Edition.

Longfellow (H. W.). SELECTIONS FROM LONGFELLOW. Edited by L. M. FAITHFULL.

Marvell (Andrew). THE POEMS OF ANDREW MARVELL. Edited by E. WRIGHT.

Milton (John). THE MINOR POEMS OF JOHN MILTON. Edited by H. C. BEECHING, M.A., Canon of Westminster.

Moir (D. M.). MANSIE WAUCH. Edited by T. F. HENDERSON.

Nichols (J. B. B.). A LITTLE BOOK OF ENGLISH SONNETS.

Rochefoucauld (La). THE MAXIMS OF LA ROCHEFOUCAULD. Translated by Dean STANHOPE. Edited by G. H. POWELL.

Smith (Horace and James). REJECTED ADDRESSES. Edited by A. D. GODLEY, M.A.

Sterne (Laurence). A SENTIMENTAL JOURNEY. Edited by H. W. PAUL.

Tennyson (Alfred, Lord). THE EARLY POEMS OF ALFRED, LORD TENNYSON. Edited by J. CHURTON COLLINS, M.A.

IN MEMORIAM. Edited by H. C. BEECHING, M.A.

THE PRINCESS. Edited by ELIZABETH WORDSWORTH.

MAUD. Edited by ELIZABETH WORDSWORTH.

Thackeray (W. M.). VANITY FAIR. Edited by S. GWYNN. *Three Volumes.*

PENDENNIS. Edited by S. GWYNN. *Three Volumes.*

ESMOND. Edited by S. GWYNN.

CHRISTMAS BOOKS. Edited by S. GWYNN.

Vaughan (Henry). THE POEMS OF HENRY VAUGHAN. Edited by EDWARD HUTTON.

Walton (Izaak). THE COMPLEAT ANGLER. Edited by J. BUCHAN.

Waterhouse (Mrs. Alfred). A LITTLE BOOK OF LIFE AND DEATH. Edited by. *Tenth Edition.*
    Also on Japanese Paper. *Leather.* 5s. net.

Wordsworth (W.). SELECTIONS FROM WORDSWORTH. Edited by NOWELL C. SMITH.

Wordsworth (W.) and Coleridge (S. T.). LYRICAL BALLADS. Edited by GEORGE SAMPSON.

The Little Quarto Shakespeare

Edited by W. J. CRAIG. With Introductions and Notes

*Pott 16mo. In 40 Volumes. Leather, price 1s. net each volume.
Mahogany Revolving Book Case. 10s. net.*

Miniature Library

Reprints in miniature of a few interesting books which have qualities of
humanity, devotion, or literary genius.

EUPHRANOR: A Dialogue on Youth. By
Edward FitzGerald. From the edition published by W. Pickering in 1851. *Demy
32mo. Leather, 2s. net.*

POLONIUS: or Wise Saws and Modern Instances. By Edward FitzGerald. From
the edition published by W. Pickering in
1852. *Demy 32mo. Leather, 2s. net.*

THE RUBÁIYÁT OF OMAR KHAYYÁM. By
Edward FitzGerald. From the 1st edition
of 1859, *Fourth Edition. Leather, 1s. net.*

THE LIFE OF EDWARD, LORD HERBERT OF
CHERBURY. Written by himself. From the
edition printed at Strawberry Hill in the
year 1764. *Demy 32mo. Leather, 2s. net.*

THE VISIONS OF DOM FRANCISCO QUEVEDO
VILLEGAS, Knight of the Order of St.
James. Made English by R. L. From the
edition printed for H. Herringman, 1668.
Leather. 2s. net.

POEMS. By Dora Greenwell. From the edition of 1848. *Leather, 2s. net.*

Oxford Biographies

Fcap. 8vo. Each volume, cloth, 2s. 6d. net ; leather, 3s. 6d. net.

DANTE ALIGHIERI. By Paget Toynbee, M.A.,
D.Litt. With 12 Illustrations. *Second
Edition.*

SAVONAROLA. By E. L. S. Horsburgh, M.A.
With 12 Illustrations. *Second Edition.*

JOHN HOWARD. By E. C. S. Gibson, D.D.,
Bishop of Gloucester. With 12 Illustrations.

TENNYSON. By A. C. BENSON, M.A. With
9 Illustrations.

WALTER RALEIGH. By I. A. Taylor. With
12 Illustrations.

ERASMUS. By E. F. H. Capey. With 12
Illustrations.

THE YOUNG PRETENDER. By C. S. Terry.
With 12 Illustrations.

ROBERT BURNS. By T. F. Henderson.
With 12 Illustrations.

CHATHAM. By A. S. M'Dowall. With 12
Illustrations.

ST. FRANCIS OF ASSISI. By Anna M. Stoddart. With 16 Illustrations.

CANNING. By W. Alison Phillips. With 12
Illustrations.

BEACONSFIELD. By Walter Sichel. With 12
Illustrations.

GOETHE. By H. G. Atkins. With 12 Illustrations.

FENELON. By Viscount St Cyres. With
12 Illustrations.

School Examination Series

Edited by A. M. M. STEDMAN, M.A. *Cr. 8vo. 2s. 6d.*

FRENCH EXAMINATION PAPERS. By A. M.
M. Stedman, M.A. *Fourteenth Edition.*
A KEY, issued to Tutors and Private
Students only to be had on application
to the Publishers. *Fifth Edition.
Crown 8vo. 6s. net.*

LATIN EXAMINATION PAPERS. By A. M. M.
Stedman, M.A. *Thirteenth Edition.*
KEY (*Sixth Edition*) issued as above.
6s. net.

GREEK EXAMINATION PAPERS. By A. M. M.
Stedman, M.A. *Ninth Edition.*
KEY (*Fourth Edition*) issued as above.
6s. net.

GERMAN EXAMINATION PAPERS. By R. J.
Morich. *Sixth Edition.*

KEY (*Third Edition*) issued as above
6s. net.

HISTORY AND GEOGRAPHY EXAMINATION
PAPERS. By C. H. Spence, M.A. *Third
Edition.*

PHYSICS EXAMINATION PAPERS. By R. E.
Steel, M.A., F.C.S.

GENERAL KNOWLEDGE EXAMINATION
PAPERS. By A. M. M. Stedman, M.A.
Sixth Edition.
KEY (*Fourth Edition*) issued as above.
7s. net.

EXAMINATION PAPERS IN ENGLISH HISTORY.
By J. Tait Plowden-Wardlaw, B.A.

School Histories

Illustrated.   Crown 8vo.   1s. 6d.

A SCHOOL HISTORY OF WARWICKSHIRE. By B. C. A. Windle, D.Sc., F.R.S.

A SCHOOL HISTORY OF SOMERSET. By Walter Raymond. *Second Edition.*

A SCHOOL HISTORY OF LANCASHIRE. by W. E. Rhodes.

A SCHOOL HISTORY OF SURREY. By H. E. Malden, M.A.

A SCHOOL HISTORY OF MIDDLESEX. By V. G. Plarr and F. W. Walton.

Textbooks of Science

Edited by G. F. GOODCHILD, M.A., B.Sc., and G. R. MILLS, M.A.

PRACTICAL MECHANICS. By Sidney H. Wells. *Fourth Edition. Cr. 8vo.* 3s. 6d.

PRACTICAL CHEMISTRY. Part I. By W. French, M.A. *Cr. 8vo. Fourth Edition.* 1s. 6d. Part II. By W. French, M.A., and T. H. Boardman, M.A. *Cr. 8vo.* 1s. 6d.

TECHNICAL ARITHMETIC AND GEOMETRY. By C. T. Millis, M.I.M.E. *Cr. 8vo.* 3s. 6d.

EXAMPLES IN PHYSICS. By C. E. Jackson, B.A. *Cr. 8vo.* 2s. 6d.

PLANT LIFE, Studies in Garden and School. By Horace F. Jones, F.C.S. With 320 Diagrams. *Cr. 8vo.* 3s. 6d.

THE COMPLETE SCHOOL CHEMISTRY. By F. M. Oldham, B.A. With 126 Illustrations. *Cr. 8vo.*

AN ORGANIC CHEMISTRY FOR SCHOOLS AND TECHNICAL INSTITUTES. By A. E. Dunstan, B.Sc. (Lond.), F.C.S. Illustrated. *Cr. 8vo.*

ELEMENTARY SCIENCE FOR PUPIL TEACHERS. PHYSICS SECTION. By W. T. Clough, A.R.C.S. (Lond.), F.C.S. CHEMISTRY SECTION. By A. E. Dunstan, B.Sc. (Lond.), F.C.S. With 2 Plates and 10 Diagrams. *Cr. 8vo.* 2s.

Methuen's Simplified French Texts

Edited by T. R. N. CROFTS, M.A.

One Shilling each.

L'HISTOIRE D'UNE TULIPE. Adapted by T. R. N. Crofts, M.A. *Second Edition.*

ABDALLAH. Adapted by J. A. Wilson.

LA CHANSON DE ROLAND. Adapted by H. Rieu, M.A.

MÉMOIRES DE CADICHON. Adapted by J. F. Rhoades.

Methuen's Standard Library

In Sixpenny Volumes.

THE STANDARD LIBRARY is a new series of volumes containing the great classics of the world, and particularly the finest works of English literature. All the great masters will be represented, either in complete works or in selections. It is the ambition of the publishers to place the best books of the Anglo-Saxon race within the reach of every reader, so that the series may represent something of the diversity and splendour of our English tongue. The characteristics of THE STANDARD LIBRARY are four :—1. SOUNDNESS OF TEXT. 2. CHEAPNESS. 3. CLEARNESS OF TYPE. 4. SIMPLICITY. The books are well printed on good paper at a price which on the whole is without parallel in the history of publishing. Each volume contains from 100 to 250 pages, and is issued in paper covers, Crown 8vo, at Sixpence net, or in cloth gilt at One Shilling net. In a few cases long books are issued as Double Volumes or as Treble Volumes.

THE MEDITATIONS OF MARCUS AURELIUS. The translation is by R. Graves.

SENSE AND SENSIBILITY. By Jane Austen.

ESSAYS AND COUNSELS and THE NEW ATLANTIS. By Francis Bacon, Lord Verulam.

RELIGIO MEDICI and URN BURIAL. By Sir Thomas Browne. The text has been collated by A. R. Waller.

THE PILGRIM'S PROGRESS. By John Bunyan.

REFLECTIONS ON THE FRENCH REVOLUTION. By Edmund Burke.

THE POEMS AND SONGS OF ROBERT BURNS. Double Volume.

THE ANALOGY OF RELIGION, NATURAL AND REVEALED. By Joseph Butler, D.D.

THE POEMS OF THOMAS CHATTERTON. In 2 volumes. Vol. I.—Miscellaneous Poems.

[*Continued.*

METHUEN'S STANDARD LIBRARY—*continued.*

Vol. II.—The Rowley Poems.

THE NEW LIFE AND SONNETS. By Dante. Translated into English by D. G. Rossetti.

TOM JONES. By Henry Fielding. Treble Vol.

CRANFORD. By Mrs. Gaskell.

THE HISTORY OF THE DECLINE AND FALL OF THE ROMAN EMPIRE. By Edward Gibbon. In 7 double volumes.

The Text and Notes have been revised by J. B. Bury, Litt.D., but the Appendices of the more expensive edition are not given.

THE VICAR OF WAKEFIELD. By Oliver Goldsmith.

THE POEMS AND PLAYS OF OLIVER GOLDSMITH.

THE WORKS OF BEN JONSON.

Vol. I.—The Case is Altered. Every Man in His Humour. Every Man out of His Humour.

Vol. II.—Cynthia's Revels; The Poetaster. The text has been collated by H. C. Hart.

THE POEMS OF JOHN KEATS. Double volume. The Text has been collated by E. de Selincourt.

ON THE IMITATION OF CHRIST. By Thomas à Kempis.

The translation is by C. Bigg, DD., Canon of Christ Church.

A SERIOUS CALL TO A DEVOUT AND HOLY LIFE. By William Law.

PARADISE LOST. By John Milton.

EIKONOKLASTES AND THE TENURE OF KINGS AND MAGISTRATES. By John Milton.

UTOPIA AND POEMS. By Sir Thomas More.

THE REPUBLIC OF PLATO. Translated by Sydenham and Taylor. Double Volume. The translation has been revised by W. H. D. Rouse.

THE LITTLE FLOWERS OF ST. FRANCIS. Translated by W. Heywood.

THE WORKS OF WILLIAM SHAKESPEARE. In 10 volumes.

Vol. I.—The Tempest; The Two Gentlemen of Verona; The Merry Wives of Windsor; Measure for Measure; The Comedy of Errors.

Vol. II.—Much Ado About Nothing; Love's Labour's Lost; A Midsummer Night's Dream; The Merchant of Venice; As You Like It.

Vol. III.—The Taming of the Shrew; All's Well that Ends Well; Twelfth Night; The Winter's Tale.

Vol. IV.—The Life and Death of King John; The Tragedy of King Richard the Second; The First Part of King Henry IV.; The Second Part of King Henry IV.

Vol. V.—The Life of King Henry V.; The First Part of King Henry VI.; The Second Part of King Henry VI.

Vol. VI.—The Third Part of King Henry VI.; The Tragedy of King Richard III.; The Famous History of the Life of King Henry VIII.

THE POEMS OF PERCY BYSSHE SHELLEY. In 4 volumes.

Vol. I.—Alastor; The Dæmon of the World; The Revolt of Islam, etc.

The Text has been revised by C. D. Locock.

THE LIFE OF NELSON. By Robert Southey.

THE NATURAL HISTORY AND ANTIQUITIES OF SELBORNE. By Gilbert White.

Textbooks of Technology

Edited by G. F. GOODCHILD, M.A., B.Sc., and G. R. MILLS, M.A.

Fully Illustrated.

HOW TO MAKE A DRESS. By J. A. E. Wood. *Fourth Edition. Cr. 8vo. 1s. 6d.*

CARPENTRY AND JOINERY. By F. C. Webber. *Fifth Edition. Cr. 8vo. 3s. 6d.*

MILLINERY, THEORETICAL AND PRACTICAL. By Clare Hill. *Third Edition. Cr. 8vo. 2s.*

AN INTRODUCTION TO THE STUDY OF TEXTILE DESIGN. By Aldred F. Barker. *Demy 8vo. 7s. 6d.*

BUILDERS' QUANTITIES. By H. C. Grubb. *Cr. 8vo. 4s. 6d.*

RÉPOUSSÉ METAL WORK. By A. C. Horth. *Cr. 8vo. 2s. 6d.*

ELECTRIC LIGHT AND POWER: An Introduction to the Study of Electrical Engineering. By E. E. Brooks, B.Sc. (Lond.) Second Master and Instructor of Physics and Electrical Engineering, Leicester Technical School, and W. H. N. James, A.R.C.S., A.I.E.E., Assistant Instructor of Electrical Engineering, Manchester Municipal Technical School. *Cr. 8vo. 4s. 6d.*

ENGINEERING WORKSHOP PRACTICE. By C. C. Allen, Lecturer on Engineering, Municipal Technical Institute, Coventry. With many Diagrams. *Cr. 8vo. 2s.*

Handbooks of Theology

Edited by R. L. OTTLEY, D.D., Professor of Pastoral Theology at Oxford, and Canon of Christ Church, Oxford.

The series is intended, in part, to furnish the clergy and teachers or students of Theology with trustworthy Textbooks, adequately representing the present position of the questions dealt with; in part, to make accessible to the reading public an accurate and concise statement of facts and principles in all questions bearing on Theology and Religion.

THE XXXIX. ARTICLES OF THE CHURCH OF ENGLAND. Edited by E. C. S. Gibson, D.D. *Fifth and Cheaper Edition in one Volume. Demy 8vo. 12s. 6d.*

AN INTRODUCTION TO THE HISTORY OF RELIGION. By F. B. Jevons. M.A., Litt.D. *Third Edition. Demy 8vo. 10s. 6d.*

THE DOCTRINE OF THE INCARNATION. By R. L. Ottley, D.D. *Second and Cheaper Edition. Demy 8vo. 12s. 6d.*

AN INTRODUCTION TO THE HISTORY OF THE CREEDS. By A. E. Burn, D.D. *Demy 8vo. 10s. 6d.*

THE PHILOSOPHY OF RELIGION IN ENGLAND AND AMERICA. By Alfred Caldecott, D.D. *Demy 8vo. 10s. 6d.*

A HISTORY OF EARLY CHRISTIAN DOCTRINE. By J. F. Bethune-Baker, M.A. *Demy 8vo. 10s. 6d.*

The Westminster Commentaries

General Editor, WALTER LOCK, D.D., Warden of Keble College,
Dean Ireland's Professor of Exegesis in the University of Oxford.

The object of each commentary is primarily exegetical, to interpret the author's meaning to the present generation. The editors will not deal, except very subordinately, with questions of textual criticism or philology; but, taking the English text in the Revised Version as their basis, they will try to combine a hearty acceptance of critical principles with loyalty to the Catholic Faith.

THE BOOK OF GENESIS. Edited with Introduction and Notes by S. R. Driver, D.D. *Sixth Edition Demy 8vo. 10s. 6d.*

THE BOOK OF JOB. Edited by E. C. S. Gibson, D.D. *Second Edition. Demy 8vo. 6s.*

THE ACTS OF THE APOSTLES. Edited by R. B. Rackham, M.A. *Demy 8vo. Third Edition. 10s. 6d.*

THE FIRST EPISTLE OF PAUL THE APOSTLE TO THE CORINTHIANS. Edited by H. L. Goudge, M.A. *Demy 8vo. 6s.*

THE EPISTLE OF ST. JAMES. Edited with Introduction and Notes by R. J. Knowling, D.D. *Demy 8vo. 6s.*

THE BOOK OF EZEKIEL. Edited H. A. Redpath, M.A., D.Litt. *Demy 8vo. 10s. 6d.*

PART II.—FICTION

Adderley (Hon. and Rev. James), Author of 'Stephen Remarx.' BEHOLD THE DAYS COME. *Second Edition. Cr. 8vo. 3s. 6d.*

Albanesi (E. Maria). SUSANNAH AND ONE OTHER. *Fourth Edition. Cr. 8vo. 6s.*

THE BLUNDER OF AN INNOCENT. *Second Edition. Cr. 8vo. 6s.*

CAPRICIOUS CAROLINE. *Second Edition. Cr. 8vo. 6s.*

LOVE AND LOUISA. *Second Edition. Cr. 8vo. 6s.*

PETER, A PARASITE. *Cr. 8vo. 6s.*

THE BROWN EYES OF MARY. *Third Edition. Cr. 8vo. 6s.*

I KNOW A MAIDEN. *Third Edition. Cr. 8vo. 6s.*

Anstey (F.). Author of 'Vice Versâ.' A BAYARD FROM BENGAL. Illustrated by BERNARD PARTRIDGE. *Third Edition. Cr. 8vo. 3s. 6d.*

Bagot (Richard). A ROMAN MYSTERY. *Third Edition. Cr. 8vo. 6s.*

THE PASSPORT. *Fourth Edition. Cr. 8vo 6s.*

TEMPTATION. *Fifth Edition. Cr. 8vo. 6s.*

CASTING OF NETS. *Twelfth Edition. Cr. 8vo. 6s.*

DONNA DIANA. *A New Edition. Cr. 8vo. 6s.*

LOVE'S PROXY. *A New Edition. Cr. 8vo. 6s.*

Baring-Gould (S.). ARMINELL. *Fifth Edition. Cr. 8vo. 6s.*

URITH. *Fifth Edition. Cr. 8vo. 6s.*

IN THE ROAR OF THE SEA. *Seventh Edition. Cr. 8vo. 6s.*

CHEAP JACK ZITA. *Fourth Edition. Cr. 8vo. 6s.*

MARGERY OF QUETHER. *Third Edition. Cr. 8vo. 6s.*

THE QUEEN OF LOVE. *Fifth Edition. Cr. 8vo. 6s.*

JACQUETTA. *Third Edition. Cr. 8vo. 6s.*

KITTY ALONE. *Fifth Edition. Cr. 8vo. 6s.*

NOÉMI. Illustrated. *Fourth Edition. Cr. 8vo. 6s.*

THE BROOM-SQUIRE. Illustrated. *Fifth Edition. Cr. 8vo. 6s.*

DARTMOOR IDYLLS. *Cr. 8vo. 6s.*

THE PENNYCOMEQUICKS. *Third Edition. Cr. 8vo. 6s.*

GUAVAS THE TINNER. Illustrated. *Second Edition. Cr. 8vo. 6s.*

BLADYS OF THE STEWPONEY. Illustrated. *Second Edition. Cr. 8vo. 6s.*
PABO THE PRIEST. *Cr. 8vo. 6s.*
WINEFRED. Illustrated. *Second Edition. Cr. 8vo. 6s.*
ROYAL GEORGIE. Illustrated. *Cr. 8vo. 6s.*
MISS QUILLET. Illustrated. *Cr. 8vo. 6s.*
CHRIS OF ALL SORTS. *Cr. 8vo. 6s.*
IN DEWISLAND. *Second Ed. Cr. 8vo. 6s.*
LITTLE TU'PENNY. *A New Edition. 6d.*
See also Shilling Novels.

Barnett (Edith A.). A WILDERNESS WINNER. *Second Edition. Cr. 8vo. 6s.*

Barr (James). LAUGHING THROUGH A WILDERNESS. *Cr. 8vo. 6s.*

Barr (Robert). IN THE MIDST OF ALARMS. *Third Edition. Cr. 8vo. 6s.*
THE STRONG ARM. *Second Edition. Cr. 8vo. 6s.*
THE MUTABLE MANY. *Third Edition. Cr. 8vo. 6s.*
THE COUNTESS TEKLA. *Fourth Edition. Cr. 8vo. 6s.*
THE LADY ELECTRA. *Second Edition. Cr. 8vo. 6s.*
THE TEMPESTUOUS PETTICOAT. Illustrated. *Third Edition. Cr. 8vo. 6s.*
See also Shilling Novels and S. Crane.

Begbie (Harold). THE ADVENTURES OF SIR JOHN SPARROW. *Cr. 8vo. 6s.*

Belloc(Hilaire). EMMANUEL BURDEN, MERCHANT. With 36 Illustrations by G. K. CHESTERTON. *Second Ed. Cr. 8vo. 6s.*

Benson (E. F.) DODO. *Fifteenth Edition. Cr. 8vo. 6s.*
See also Shilling Novels.
THE CAPSINA. *Second Edit. Cr. 8vo. 6s.*

Benson (Margaret). SUBJECT TO VANITY. *Cr. 8vo. 3s. 6d.*

Bretherton (Ralph). THE MILL. *Cr. 8vo. 6s.*

Burke (Barbara). BARBARA GOES TO OXFORD. *Second Edition.*

Burton (J. Bloundelle). THE FATE OF VALSEC. *Cr. 8vo. 6s.*
See also Shilling Novels.

Capes (Bernard), Author of 'The Lake of Wine.' THE EXTRAORDINARY CONFESSIONS OF DIANA PLEASE. *Third Edition. Cr. 8vo. 6s.*
A JAY OF ITALY. *Fourth Ed. Cr. 8vo. 6s.*
LOAVES AND FISHES. *Second Edition. Cr. 8vo. 6s.*
A ROGUE'S TRAGEDY. *Second Edition. Cr. 8vo. 6s.*
THE GREAT SKENE MYSTERY. *Second Edition. Cr. 8vo. 6s.*

Charlton (Randall). MAVE. *Second Edition. Cr. 8vo. 6s.*

Carey (Wymond). LOVE THE JUDGE. *Second Edition. Cr. 8vo. 6s.*

Chesney (Weatherby). THE TRAGEDY OF THE GREAT EMERALD *Cr. 8vo. 6s.*
THE MYSTERY OF A BUNGALOW. *Second Edition. Cr. 8vo. 6s.*
See also Shilling Novels.

Conrad (Joseph). THE SECRET AGENT. *Second Edition. Cr. 8vo. 6s.*

Corelli (Marie). A ROMANCE OF TWO WORLDS. *Twenty-Eighth Ed. Cr. 8vo. 6s.*
VENDETTA. *Twenty-Fifth Edition. Cr. 8vo. 6s.*
THELMA. *Thirty-Seventh Ed. Cr. 8vo. 6s.*
ARDATH : THE STORY OF A DEAD SELF. *Eighteenth Edition. Cr. 8vo. 6s.*
THE SOUL OF LILITH. *Fifteenth Edition. Cr. 8vo. 6s.*
WORMWOOD. *Fifteenth Ed. Cr. 8vo. 6s.*
BARABBAS : A DREAM OF THE WORLD'S TRAGEDY. *Forty-second Edition. Cr. 8vo. 6s.*
THE SORROWS OF SATAN. *Fifty-second Edition. Cr. 8vo. 6s.*
THE MASTER CHRISTIAN. *Tenth Edition. Cr. 8vo. 6s.*
TEMPORAL POWER : A STUDY IN SUPREMACY. *150th Thousand. Cr. 8vo. 6s.*
GOD'S GOOD MAN : A SIMPLE LOVE STORY. *Twelfth Edition. Cr. 8vo. 6s.*
THE MIGHTY ATOM. *Twenty-sixth Edition. Cr. 8vo. 6s.*
BOY : a Sketch. *Tenth Edition. Cr. 8vo. 6s.*
CAMEOS *Twelfth Edition. Cr. 8vo. 6s.*

Cotes (Mrs. Everard). See Sara Jeannette Duncan.

Cotterell (Constance). THE VIRGIN AND THE SCALES. Illustrated. *Second Edition. Cr. 8vo. 6s.*

Crane (Stephen) and **Barr (Robert).** THE O'RUDDY. *Cr. 8vo. 6s.*

Crockett (S. R.), Author of 'The Raiders,' etc. LOCHINVAR. Illustrated. *Third Edition. Cr. 8vo. 6s.*
THE STANDARD BEARER. *Cr. 8vo. 6s.*

Croker (B. M.). THE OLD CANTONMENT. *Cr. 8vo. 6s.*
JOHANNA. *Second Edition. Cr. 8vo. 6s.*
THE HAPPY VALLEY. *Third Edition. Cr. 8vo. 6s.*
A NINE DAYS' WONDER. *Third Edition. Cr. 8vo. 6s.*
PEGGY OF THE BARTONS. *Sixth Edition. Cr. 8vo. 6s.*
ANGEL. *Fourth Edition. Cr. 8vo. 6s.*
A STATE SECRET. *Third Edition. Cr. 8vo. 3s. 6d.*

Crosbie (Mary). DISCIPLES. *Second Ed. Cr. 8vo. 6s.*

Dawson (A. J.) DANIEL WHYTE. *Cr. 8vo. 3s. 6d.*

Deane (Mary). THE OTHER PAWN. *Cr. 8vo. 6s.*

Doyle (A. Conan), Author of 'Sherlock Holmes,' 'The White Company,' etc. ROUND THE RED LAMP. *Tenth Edition. Cr. 8vo. 6s.*

Duncan (Sara Jeannette) (Mrs. Everard Cotes). THOSE DELIGHTFUL AMERICANS. Illustrated. *Third Edition. Cr. 8vo. 6s.* See also Shilling Novels.

Findlater (J. H.). THE GREEN GRAVES OF BALGOWRIE. *Fifth Edition. Cr. 8vo. 6s.*

THE LADDER TO THE STARS. *Second Edition. Cr. 8vo. 6s.*
See also Shilling Novels.

Findlater (Mary). A NARROW WAY. *Third Edition. Cr. 8vo.. 6s.*
THE ROSE OF JOY. *Third Edition. Cr. 8vo. 6s.*
A BLIND BIRD'S NEST. With 8 Illustrations. *Second Edition. Cr. 8vo. 6s.*
See also Shilling Novels.

Fitzpatrick (K.) THE WEANS AT ROWALLAN. Illustrated. *Second Edition. Cr. 8vo. 6s.*

Francis (M. E.). STEPPING WESTWARD. *Second Edition. Cr. 8vo. 6s.*
MARGERY O' THE MILL. *Second Edition. Cr. 8vo. 6s.*

Fraser (Mrs. Hugh), Author of 'The Stolen Emperor.' THE SLAKING OF THE SWORD. *Cr. 8vo. 6s.*
IN THE SHADOW OF THE LORD. *Third Edition. Crown 8vo. 6s.*

Fry (B. and C. B.). A MOTHER'S SON. *Fourth Edition. Cr. 8vo. 6s.*

Fuller=Maitland (Ella), Author of 'The Day Book of Bethia Hardacre.' BLANCHE ESMEAD. *Second Edition. Cr. 8vo. 6s.*

Gates (Eleanor), Author of 'The Biography of a Prairie Girl.' THE PLOW-WOMAN. *Cr. 8vo. 6s.*

Gerard (Dorothea), Author of 'Lady Baby.' HOLY MATRIMONY. *Second Edition. Cr. 8vo. 6s.*
MADE OF MONEY. *Cr. 8vo. 6s.*
THE BRIDGE OF LIFE. *Cr. 8vo. 6s.*
THE IMPROBABLE IDYL. *Third Edition. Cr. 8vo. 6s.*
See also Shilling Novels.

Gissing (George), Author of 'Demos,' 'In the Year of Jubilee,' etc. THE TOWN TRAVELLER. *Second Ed. Cr. 8vo. 6s.*
THE CROWN OF LIFE. *Cr. 8vo. 6s.*

Gleig (Charles). BUNTER'S CRUISE. Illustrated. *Cr. 8vo. 3s. 6d.*

Hamilton (M.), Author of 'Cut Laurels.' THE FIRST CLAIM. *Second Edition. Cr. 8vo. 6s.*

Harraden (Beatrice). IN VARYING MOODS. *Fourteenth Edition. Cr. 8vo. 6s.*
HILDA STRAFFORD and THE REMITTANCE MAN. *Twelfth Ed. Cr. 8vo. 6s.*
THE SCHOLAR'S DAUGHTER. *Fourth Edition. Cr. 8vo. 6s.*

Harrod (F.) (Frances Forbes Robertson). THE TAMING OF THE BRUTE. *Cr. 8vo. 6s.*

Herbertson (Agnes G.). PATIENCE DEAN. *Cr. 8vo. 6s.*

Hichens (Robert). THE PROPHET OF BERKELEY SQUARE. *Second Edition. Cr. 8vo. 6s.*
TONGUES OF CONSCIENCE. *Third Edition. Cr. 8vo. 6s.*
FELIX. *Fifth Edition. Cr. 8vo. 6s.*
THE WOMAN WITH THE FAN. *Sixth Edition. Cr. 8vo. 6s.*
BYEWAYS. *Cr. 8vo. 6s.*

THE GARDEN OF ALLAH. *Sixteenth Edition. Cr. 8vo. 6s.*
THE BLACK SPANIEL. *Cr. 8vo. 6s.*
THE CALL OF THE BLOOD. *Seventh Edition. Cr. 8vo. 6s.*

Hope (Anthony). THE GOD IN THE CAR. *Tenth Edition. Cr. 8vo. 6s.*
A CHANGE OF AIR. *Sixth Ed. Cr. 8vo. 6s.*
A MAN OF MARK. *Fifth Ed. Cr. 8vo. 6s.*
THE CHRONICLES OF COUNT ANTONIO. *Sixth Edition. Cr. 8vo. 6s.*
PHROSO. Illustrated by H. R. MILLAR. *Sixth Edition. Cr. 8vo. 6s.*
SIMON DALE. Illustrated. *Seventh Edition. Cr. 8vo. 6s.*
THE KING'S MIRROR. *Fourth Edition. Cr. 8vo. 6s.*
QUISANTE. *Fourth Edition. Cr. 8vo. 6s.*
THE DOLLY DIALOGUES. *Cr. 8vo. 6s.*
A SERVANT OF THE PUBLIC. Illustrated. *Fourth Edition. Cr. 8vo. 6s.*
TALES OF TWO PEOPLE. *Second Ed. Cr. 8vo. 6s.*

Hope (Graham), Author of 'A Cardinal and his Conscience,' etc., etc. THE LADY OF LYTE. *Second Edition. Cr. 8vo. 6s.*

Housman (Clemence). THE LIFE OF SIR AGLOVALE DE GALIS. *Cr. 8vo. 6s.*

Hueffer (Ford Madox). AN ENGLISH GIRL. *Second Edition. Cr. 8vo. 6s.*

Hyne (C. J. Cutcliffe), Author of 'Captain Kettle.' MR. HORROCKS, PURSER. *Fourth Edition. Cr. 8vo. 6s.*
PRINCE RUPERT, THE BUCCANEER. Illustrated. *Third Edition. Cr. 8vo. 6s.*

Jacobs (W. W.). MANY CARGOES. *Twenty-Ninth Edition. Cr. 8vo. 3s. 6d.*
SEA URCHINS. *Fourteenth Edition.. Cr. 8vo. 3s. 6d.*
A MASTER OF CRAFT. Illustrated. *Seventh Edition. Cr. 8vo. 3s. 6d.*
LIGHT FREIGHTS. Illustrated. *Sixth Edition. Cr. 8vo. 3s. 6d.*
THE SKIPPER'S WOOING. *Eighth Edition. Cr. 8vo. 3s. 6d.*
DIALSTONE LANE. Illustrated. *Seventh Edition. Cr. 8vo. 3s. 6d.*
ODD CRAFT. Illustrated. *Seventh Edition. Cr. 8vo. 3s. 6d.*
AT SUNWICH PORT. Illustrated. *Seventh Edition. Cr. 8vo. 3s. 6d.*

James (Henry). THE SOFT SIDE. *Second Edition. Cr. 8vo. 6s.*
THE BETTER SORT. *Cr. 8vo. 6s.*
THE AMBASSADORS. *Second Edition. Cr. 8vo. 6s.*
THE GOLDEN BOWL. *Third Edition. Cr. 8vo. 6s.*

Keays (H. A. Mitchell). HE THAT EATETH BREAD WITH ME. *Cr. 8vo. 6s.*

Kester (Vaughan). THE FORTUNES OF THE LANDRAYS. *Cr. 8vo. 6s.*

Lawless (Hon. Emily). WITH ESSEX IN IRELAND. *Cr. 8vo. 6s.*
See also Shilling Novels.

Le Queux (W.). THE HUNCHBACK OF WESTMINSTER. *Third Ed. Cr. 8vo. 6s.*
THE CLOSED BOOK. *Third Ed. Cr. 8vo. 6s.*

THE VALLEY OF THE SHADOW.
Illustrated. *Third Edition. Cr. 8vo. 6s.*
BEHIND THE THRONE. *Third Edition.
Cr. 8vo. 6s.*
Levett-Yeats (S.). ORRAIN. *Second
Edition. Cr. 8vo. 6s.*
London (Jack), Author of 'The Call of the
Wild,' 'The Sea Wolf,' etc. WHITE
FANG. *Fourth Edition. Cr. 8vo. 6s.*
Lucas (E. V.). LISTENER'S LURE: An
Oblique Narration. *Crown 8vo. Fourth
Edition. Cr. 8vo. 6s.*
Lyall (Edna). DERRICK VAUGHAN,
NOVELIST. *42nd Thousand. Cr. 8vo.
3s. 6d.*
M'Carthy (Justin H.), Author of 'If I were
King.' THE LADY OF LOYALTY
HOUSE. Illustrated. *Third Edition. Cr.
8vo. 6s.*
THE DRYAD. *Second Edition. Cr. 8vo. 6s.*
Macdonald (Ronald). THE SEA MAID.
Second Edition. Cr. 8vo. 6s.
A HUMAN TRINITY. *Second Edition.
Cr. 8vo. 6s.*
Macnaughtan (S.). THE FORTUNE OF
CHRISTINA MACNAB. *Fourth Edition.
Cr. 8vo. 6s.*
Malet (Lucas). COLONEL ENDERBY'S
WIFE. *Fourth Edition. Cr. 8vo. 6s.*
A COUNSEL OF PERFECTION. *New
Edition. Cr. 8vo. 6s.*
THE WAGES OF SIN. *Fifteenth Edition.
Cr. 8vo. 6s.*
THE CARISSIMA. *Fifth Ed. Cr. 8vo. 6s.*
THE GATELESS BARRIER. *Fourth Edi-
tion. Cr. 8vo. 6s.*
THE HISTORY OF SIR RICHARD
CALMADY. *Seventh Edition. Cr. 8vo. 6s.*
See also Books for Boys and Girls.
Mann (Mrs. M. E.). OLIVIA'S SUMMER.
Second Edition. Cr. 8vo. 6s.
A LOST ESTATE. *A New Ed. Cr. 8vo. 6s.*
THE PARISH OF HILBY. *A New Edition.
Cr. 8vo. 6s.*
THE PARISH NURSE. *Fourth Edition.
Cr. 8vo. 6s.*
GRAN'MA'S JANE. *Cr. 8vo. 6s.*
MRS. PETER HOWARD. *Cr. 8vo. 6s.*
A WINTER'S TALE. *A New Edition.
Cr. 8vo. 6s.*
ONE ANOTHER'S BURDENS. *A New
Edition. Cr. 8vo. 6s.*
ROSE AT HONEYPOT. *Third Ed. Cr.
8vo. 6s.* See also Books for Boys and Girls.
THE MEMORIES OF RONALD LOVE.
Cr. 8vo. 6s.
THE EGLAMORE PORTRAITS. *Third
Edition. Cr. 8vo. 6s.*
THE SHEEP AND THE GOATS. *Second
Edition. Cr. 8vo. 6s.*
Marriott (Charles), Author of 'The
Column.' GENEVRA. *Second Edition.
Cr. 8vo. 6s.*
Marsh (Richard). THE TWICKENHAM
PEERAGE. *Second Edition. Cr. 8vo. 6s.*
THE MARQUIS OF PUTNEY. *Second
Edition. Cr. 8vo. 6s.*
A DUEL. *Cr 8vo. 6s.*

IN THE SERVICE OF LOVE. *Third
Edition. Cr. 8vo. 6s.*
THE GIRL AND THE MIRACLE.
Second Edition. Cr. 8vo. 6s.
See also Shilling Novels.
Mason (A. E. W.), Author of 'The Four
Feathers,' etc. CLEMENTINA. Illus-
trated. *Second Edition. Cr. 8vo. 6s.*
Mathers (Helen), Author of 'Comin' thro' the
Rye.' HONEY. *Fourth Ed. Cr. 8vo. 6s.*
GRIFF OF GRIFFITHSCOURT. *Cr. 8vo.
6s.*
THE FERRYMAN. *Second Edition. Cr.
8vo. 6s.*
TALLY-HO! *Fourth Edition. Cr. 8vo. 6s.*
Maxwell (W. B.), Author of 'The Ragged
Messenger.' VIVIEN. *Ninth Edition.
Cr. 8vo. 6s.*
THE RAGGED MESSENGER. *Third
Edition. Cr. 8vo. 6s.*
FABULOUS FANCIES. *Cr. 8vo. 6s.*
THE GUARDED FLAME. *Seventh Edi-
tion. Cr. 8vo. 6s.*
THE COUNTESS OF MAYBURY. *Fourth
Edition. Cr. 8vo. 6s.*
ODD LENGTHS. *Second Ed. Cr. 8vo. 6s.*
Meade (L. T.). DRIFT. *Second Edition.
Cr. 8vo. 6s.*
RESURGAM. *Cr. 8vo. 6s.*
VICTORY. *Cr. 8vo. 6s.*
See also Books for Boys and Girls.
Melton (R.). CÆSAR'S WIFE. *Second
Edition. Cr. 8vo. 6s.*
Meredith (Ellis). HEART OF MY
HEART. *Cr. 8vo. 6s.*
Miller (Esther). LIVING LIES. *Third
Edition. Cr. 8vo. 6s.*
'Miss Molly' (The Author of). THE
GREAT RECONCILER. *Cr. 8vo. 6s.*
Mitford (Bertram). THE SIGN OF THE
SPIDER. Illustrated. *Sixth Edition.
Cr. 8vo. 3s. 6d.*
IN THE WHIRL OF THE RISING.
Third Edition. Cr. 8vo. 6s.
THE RED DERELICT. *Second Edition.
Cr. 8vo. 6s.*
Montresor (F. F.), Author of 'Into the
Highways and Hedges.' THE ALIEN.
Third Edition. Cr. 8vo. 6s.
Morrison (Arthur). TALES OF MEAN
STREETS. *Seventh Edition. Cr. 8vo. 6s.*
A CHILD OF THE JAGO. *Fifth Edition.
Cr. 8vo. 6s.*
TO LONDON TOWN. *Second Edition.
Cr. 8vo. 6s.*
CUNNING MURRELL. *Cr. 8vo. 6s.*
THE HOLE IN THE WALL. *Fourth Edi-
tion. Cr. 8vo. 6s.*
DIVERS VANITIES. *Cr. 8vo. 6s.*
Nesbit (E.). (Mrs. E. Bland). THE RED
HOUSE. Illustrated. *Fourth Edition
Cr. 8vo. 6s.*
See also Shilling Novels.
Norris (W. E.), HARRY AND URSULA.
Second Edition. Cr. 8vo. 6s.
Ollivant (Alfred). OWD BOB, THE
GREY DOG OF KENMUIR. *Tenth
Edition. Cr. 8vo. 6s.*

Oppenheim (E. Phillips). MASTER OF MEN. *Fourth Edition. Cr. 8vo. 6s.*

Oxenham (John), Author of 'Barbe of Grand Bayou.' A WEAVER OF WEBS. *Second Edition. Cr. 8vo. 6s.*

THE GATE OF THE DESERT. *Fifth Edition. Cr. 8vo. 6s.*

PROFIT AND LOSS. With a Frontispiece in photogravure by HAROLD COPPING. *Fourth Edition. Cr. 8vo. 6s.*

THE LONG ROAD. With a Frontispiece by HAROLD COPPING. *Fourth Edition. Cr. 8vo. 6s.*

Pain (Barry). LINDLEY KAYS. *Third Edition. Cr. 8vo. 6s.*

Parker (Gilbert). PIERRE AND HIS PEOPLE. *Sixth Edition. Cr. 8vo. 6s.*

MRS. FALCHION. *Fifth Edition. Cr. 8vo. 6s.*

THE TRANSLATION OF A SAVAGE. *Third Edition. Cr. 8vo. 6s.*

THE TRAIL OF THE SWORD. Illustrated. *Ninth Edition. Cr. 8vo. 6s.*

WHEN VALMOND CAME TO PONTIAC: The Story of a Lost Napoleon. *Sixth Edition. Cr. 8vo. 6s.*

AN ADVENTURER OF THE NORTH. The Last Adventures of 'Pretty Pierre.' *Third Edition. Cr. 8vo. 6s.*

THE SEATS OF THE MIGHTY. Illustrated. *Fifteenth Edition. Cr. 8vo. 6s.*

THE BATTLE OF THE STRONG: a Romance of Two Kingdoms. Illustrated. *Fifth Edition. Cr. 8vo. 6s.*

THE POMP OF THE LAVILETTES. *Second Edition. Cr. 8vo. 3s. 6d.*

Pemberton (Max). THE FOOTSTEPS OF A THRONE. Illustrated. *Third Edition. Cr. 8vo. 6s.*

I CROWN THEE KING. With Illustrations by Frank Dadd and A. Forrestier. *Cr. 8vo. 6s.*

Phillpotts (Eden). LYING PROPHETS. *Third Edition. Cr. 8vo. 6s.*

CHILDREN OF THE MIST. *Fifth Edition. Cr. 8vo. 6s.*

THE HUMAN BOY. With a Frontispiece. *Fourth Edition. Cr. 8vo. 6s.*

SONS OF THE MORNING. *Second Edition. Cr. 8vo. 6s.*

THE RIVER. *Third Edition. Cr. 8vo. 6s.*

THE AMERICAN PRISONER. *Fourth Edition. Cr. 8vo. 6s.*

THE SECRET WOMAN. *Fourth Edition. Cr. 8vo. 6s.*

KNOCK AT A VENTURE. With a Frontispiece. *Third Edition. Cr. 8vo. 6s.*

THE PORTREEVE. *Fourth Ed. Cr. 8vo. 6s.*

THE POACHER'S WIFE. *Second Edition. Cr. 8vo. 6s.*

See also Shilling Novels.

Pickthall (Marmaduke). SAÏD THE FISHERMAN. *Sixth Ed. Cr. 8vo. 6s.*

BRENDLE. *Second Edition. Cr. 8vo. 6s.*

THE HOUSE OF ISLAM. *Third Edition. Cr. 8vo. 6s.*

'Q,' Author of 'Dead Man's Rock.' THE WHITE WOLF. *Second Ed. Cr. 8vo. 6s,*

THE MAYOR OF TROY. *Fourth Edition. Cr. 8vo. 6s.*

MERRY GARDEN AND OTHER STORIES. *Cr. 8vo. 6s.*

MAJOR VIGOUREUX. *Second Edition. Cr. 8vo. 6s.*

Rawson (Maud Stepney), Author of 'A Lady of the Regency.' 'The Labourer's Comedy,' etc. THE ENCHANTED GARDEN. *Second Edition. Cr. 8vo. 6s.*

Rhys (Grace). THE WOOING OF SHEILA. *Second Edition. Cr. 8vo. 6s.*

Ridge (W. Pett). LOST PROPERTY. *Second Edition. Cr. 8vo. 6s.*

ERB. *Second Edition. Cr. 8vo. 6s.*

A SON OF THE STATE. *Second Edition. Cr. 8vo. 3s. 6d.*

A BREAKER OF LAWS. *A New Edition. Cr. 8vo. 3s. 6d.*

MRS. GALER'S BUSINESS. Illustrated. *Second Edition. Cr. 8vo. 6s.*

SECRETARY TO BAYNE, M.P. *Cr. 8vo. 3s. 6d.*

THE WICKHAMSES. *Fourth Edition. Cr. 8vo. 6s.*

NAME OF GARLAND. *Third Edition. Cr. 8vo. 6s.*

Roberts (C. G. D.). THE HEART OF THE ANCIENT WOOD. *Cr. 8vo. 3s. 6d.*

Russell (W. Clark). MY DANISH SWEETHEART. Illustrated. *Fifth Edition. Cr. 8vo. 6s.*

HIS ISLAND PRINCESS. Illustrated. *Second Edition. Cr. 6vo. 6s.*

ABANDONED. *Second Edition. Cr. 8vo. 6s.*

See also Books for Boys and Girls.

Sergeant (Adeline). BARBARA'S MONEY. *Cr. 8vo. 6s.*

THE PROGRESS OF RACHAEL. *Cr. 8vo. 6s.*

THE MYSTERY OF THE MOAT. *Second Edition. Cr. 8vo. 6s.*

THE COMING OF THE RANDOLPHS. *Cr. 8vo. 6s.*

See also Shilling Novels.

Shannon. (W.F. THE MESS DECK. *Cr. 8vo. 3s. 6d.*

See also Shilling Novels.

Shelley (Bertha). ENDERBY. *Third Ed. Cr. 8vo. 6s.*

Sidgwick (Mrs. Alfred), Author of 'Cynthia's Way.' THE KINSMAN. With 8 Illustrations by C. E. BROCK. *Third Ed. Cr. 8vo. 6s.*

Sonnichsen (Albert). DEEP-SEA VAGABONDS. *Cr. 8vo. 6s.*

Sunbury (George). THE HA'PENNY MILLIONAIRE. *Cr. 8vo. 3s. 6d.*

Urquhart (M.), A TRAGEDY IN COMMONPLACE. *Second Ed. Cr. 8vo. 6s.*

Waineman (Paul). THE SONG OF THE FOREST. *Cr. 8vo. 6s.*

THE BAY OF LILACS. *Second Edition. Cr. 8vo. 6s.*

See also Shilling Novels.

Waltz (E. C.). THE ANCIENT LAND MARK: A Kentucky Romance. *Cr. 8vo. 6s.*

Watson (H. B. Marriott). ALARUMS AND EXCURSIONS. *Cr. 8vo. 6s.*
CAPTAIN FORTUNE. *Third Edition. Cr. 8vo. 6s.*
TWISTED EGLANTINE. With 8 Illustrations by FRANK CRAIG. *Third Edition. Cr. 8vo. 6s.*
THE HIGH TOBY. With a Frontispiece. *Third Edition. Cr. 8vo. 6s.*
A MIDSUMMER DAY'S DREAM. *Third Edition. Crown 8vo. 6s.*
See also Shilling Novels.

Wells (H. G.). THE SEA LADY. *Cr. 8vo. 6s.*

Weyman (Stanley), Author of 'A Gentleman of France.' UNDER THE RED ROBE. With Illustrations by R. C. WOODVILLE. *Twenty-first Edition. Cr. 8vo. 6s.*

White (Stewart E.), Author of 'The Blazed Trail.' CONJUROR'S HOUSE. A Romance of the Free Trail. *Second Edition. Cr. 8vo. 6s.*

White (Percy). THE SYSTEM. *Third Edition. Cr. 8vo. 6s.*
THE PATIENT MAN. *Second Edition. Cr. 8vo. 6s.*

Williams (Margery). THE BAR. *Cr. 8vo. 6s.*

Williamson (Mrs. C. N.), Author of 'The Barnstormers.' THE ADVENTURE OF PRINCESS SYLVIA. *Second Edition. Cr. 8vo. 6s.*
THE WOMAN WHO DARED. *Cr. 8vo. 6s.*
THE SEA COULD TELL. *Second Edition. Cr. 8vo. 6s.*
THE CASTLE OF THE SHADOWS. *Third Edition. Cr. 8vo. 6s.*
PAPA. *Cr. 8vo. 6s.*

Williamson (C. N. and A. M.). THE LIGHTNING CONDUCTOR : Being the Romance of a Motor Car. Illustrated. *Sixteenth Edition. Cr. 8vo. 6s.*
THE PRINCESS PASSES. Illustrated. *Eighth Edition. Cr. 8vo. 6s.*
MY FRIEND THE CHAUFFEUR. With 16 Illustrations. *Ninth Ed. Cr. 8vo. 6s.*
THE CAR OF DESTINY AND ITS ERRAND IN SPAIN. *Fourth Edition.* Illustrated.
LADY BETTY ACROSS THE WATER. *Ninth Edition. Cr. 8vo. 6s.*
THE BOTOR CHAPERON. *Fourth Ed. Cr. 8vo. 6s.*

Wyllarde (Dolf), Author of 'Uriah the Hittite.' THE PATHWAY OF THE PIONEER (Nous Autres). *Fourth Edition. Cr. 8vo. 6s.*

Methuen's Shilling Novels

Cr. 8vo. Cloth, 1s. net.

Author of 'Miss Molly.' THE GREAT RECONCILER.

Balfour (Andrew). VENGEANCE IS MINE.
TO ARMS.

Baring-Gould (S.). MRS. CURGENVEN OF CURGENVEN.
DOMITIA.
THE FROBISHERS.
CHRIS OF ALL SORTS.
DARTMOOR IDYLLS.

Barlow (Jane), Author of 'Irish Idylls.' FROM THE EAST UNTO THE WEST.
A CREEL OF IRISH STORIES.
THE FOUNDING OF FORTUNES.
THE LAND OF THE SHAMROCK.

Barr (Robert). THE VICTORS.

Bartram (George). THIRTEEN EVENINGS.

Benson (E. F.), Author of 'Dodo.' THE CAPSINA.

Bowles (G. Stewart). A STRETCH OFF THE LAND.

Brooke (Emma). THE POET'S CHILD.

Bullock (Shan F.). THE BARRYS.
THE CHARMER.
THE SQUIREEN.
THE RED LEAGUERS.

Burton (J. Bloundelle). THE CLASH OF ARMS.
DENOUNCED.
FORTUNE'S MY FOE.
A BRANDED NAME.

Capes (Bernard). AT A WINTER'S FIRE.

Chesney (Weatherby). THE BAPTIST RING.
THE BRANDED PRINCE.
THE FOUNDERED GALLEON.
JOHN TOPP.
THE MYSTERY OF A BUNGALOW.

Clifford (Mrs. W. K.). A FLASH OF SUMMER.

Cobb, Thomas. A CHANGE OF FACE.

Collingwood (Harry). THE DOCTOR OF THE 'JULIET.'

Cornford (L. Cope). SONS OF ADVERSITY.

Cotterell (Constance). THE VIRGIN AND THE SCALES.

Crane (Stephen). WOUNDS IN THE RAIN.

Denny (C. E.). THE ROMANCE OF UPFOLD MANOR.

Dickinson (Evelyn). THE SIN OF ANGELS.

Dickson (Harris). THE BLACK WOLF'S BREED.

Duncan (Sara J.). THE POOL IN THE DESERT.
A VOYAGE OF CONSOLATION. Illustrated.

Embree (C. F.). A HEART OF FLAME. Illustrated.

Fenn (G. Manville). AN ELECTRIC SPARK.
A DOUBLE KNOT.

Findlater (Jane H.). A DAUGHTER OF STRIFE.

Fitzstephen (G.). MORE KIN THAN KIND.

Fletcher (J. S.). DAVID MARCH.
LUCIAN THE DREAMER.

Forrest (R. E.). THE SWORD OF AZRAEL.

Francis (M. E.). MISS ERIN.

Gallon (Tom). RICKERBY'S FOLLY.

Gerard (Dorothea). THINGS THAT HAVE HAPPENED.
THE CONQUEST OF LONDON.
THE SUPREME CRIME.

Gilchrist (R. Murray). WILLOWBRAKE.

Glanville (Ernest). THE DESPATCH RIDER.
THE KLOOF BRIDE.
THE INCA'S TREASURE.

Gordon (Julien). MRS. CLYDE.
WORLD'S PEOPLE.

Goss (C. F.). THE REDEMPTION OF DAVID CORSON.

Gray (E. M'Queen). MY STEWARD-SHIP.

Hales (A. G.). JAIR THE APOSTATE.

Hamilton (Lord Ernest). MARY HAMILTON.

Harrison (Mrs. Burton). A PRINCESS OF THE HILLS. Illustrated.

Hooper (I.). THE SINGER OF MARLY.

Hough (Emerson). THE MISSISSIPPI BUBBLE.

'Iota' (Mrs. Caffyn). ANNE MAULEVERER.

Jepson (Edgar). THE KEEPERS OF THE PEOPLE.

Keary (C. F.). THE JOURNALIST.

Kelly (Florence Finch). WITH HOOPS OF STEEL.

Langbridge (V.) and Bourne (C. H.). THE VALLEY OF INHERITANCE.

Linden (Annie). A WOMAN OF SENTIMENT.

Lorimer (Norma). JOSIAH'S WIFE.

Lush (Charles K.). THE AUTOCRATS.

Macdonell (Anne). THE STORY OF TERESA.

Macgrath (Harold). THE PUPPET CROWN.

Mackie (Pauline Bradford). THE VOICE IN THE DESERT.

Marsh (Richard). THE SEEN AND THE UNSEEN.
GARNERED.
A METAMORPHOSIS.
MARVELS AND MYSTERIES.
BOTH SIDES OF THE VEIL.

Mayall (J. W.). THE CYNIC AND THE SYREN.

Meade (L. T.). RESURGAM.

Monkhouse (Allan). LOVE IN A LIFE.

Moore (Arthur). THE KNIGHT PUNCTILIOUS.

Nesbit, E. (Mrs. Bland). THE LITERARY SENSE.

Norris (W. E.). AN OCTAVE.
MATTHEW AUSTIN.
THE DESPOTIC LADY.

Oliphant (Mrs.). THE LADY'S WALK.
SIR ROBERT'S FORTUNE.
THE TWO MARY'S.

Pendered (M. L.). AN ENGLISHMAN.

Penny (Mrs. Frank). A MIXED MARAGE.

Phillpotts (Eden). THE STRIKING HOURS.
FANCY FREE.

Pryce (Richard). TIME AND THE WOMAN.

Randall (John). AUNT BETHIA'S BUTTON.

Raymond (Walter). FORTUNE'S DARLING.

Rayner (Olive Pratt). ROSALBA.

Rhys (Grace). THE DIVERTED VILLAGE.

Rickert (Edith). OUT OF THE CYPRESS SWAMP.

Roberton (M. H.). A GALLANT QUAKER.

Russell, (W. Clark). ABANDONED.

Saunders (Marshall). ROSE À CHARLITTE.

Sergeant (Adeline). ACCUSED AND ACCUSER.
BARBARA'S MONEY.
THE ENTHUSIAST.
A GREAT LADY.
THE LOVE THAT OVERCAME.
THE MASTER OF BEECHWOOD.
UNDER SUSPICION.
THE YELLOW DIAMOND.
THE MYSTERY OF THE MOAT.

Shannon (W. F.). JIM TWELVES.

Stephens (R. N.). AN ENEMY OF THE KING.

Strain (E. H.). ELMSLIE'S DRAG NET.

Stringer (Arthur). THE SILVER POPPY.

Stuart (Esmè). CHRISTALLA.
A WOMAN OF FORTY.

Sutherland (Duchess of). ONE HOUR AND THE NEXT.

Swan (Annie). LOVE GROWN COLD.

Swift (Benjamin). SORDON.
SIREN CITY.

Tanqueray (Mrs. B. M.). THE ROYAL QUAKER.

Thompson (Vance). SPINNERS OF LIFE.

Trafford-Taunton (Mrs. E. W.). SILENT DOMINION.

Upward (Allen). ATHELSTANE FORD.

Waineman (Paul). A HEROINE FROM FINLAND.
BY A FINNISH LAKE.

Watson (H. B. Marriott). THE SKIRTS OF HAPPY CHANCE.

'Zack.' TALES OF DUNSTABLE WEIR.

Books for Boys and Girls
Illustrated. Crown 8vo. 3s. 6d.

THE GETTING WELL OF DOROTHY. By Mrs. W. K. Clifford. *Second Edition.*

ONLY A GUARD-ROOM DOG. By Edith E. Cuthell.

THE DOCTOR OF THE JULIET. By Harry Collingwood.

LITTLE PETER. By Lucas Malet. *Second Edition.*

MASTER ROCKAFELLAR'S VOYAGE. By W. Clark Russell. *Third Edition.*

THE SECRET OF MADAME DE MONLUC. By the Author of "Mdlle. Mori."

SYD BELTON : Or, the Boy who would not go to Sea. By G. Manville Fenn.

THE RED GRANGE. By Mrs. Molesworth.

A GIRL OF THE PEOPLE. By L. T. Meade. *Second Edition.*

HEPSY GIPSY. By L. T. Meade. 2s. 6d.

THE HONOURABLE MISS. By L. T. Meade. *Second Edition.*

THERE WAS ONCE A PRINCE. By Mrs. M. E. Mann.

WHEN ARNOLD COMES HOME. By Mrs. M. E. Mann.

The Novels of Alexandre Dumas
Price 6d. Double Volumes, 1s.

ACTÉ.

THE ADVENTURES OF CAPTAIN PAMPHILE.

AMAURY.

THE BIRD OF FATE.

THE BLACK TULIP.

THE CASTLE OF EPPSTEIN.

CATHERINE BLUM.

CECILE.

THE CHEVALIER D'HARMENTAL. Double volume.

CHICOT THE JESTER. Being the first part of The Lady of Monsoreau.

CONSCIENCE.

THE CONVICT'S SON.

THE CORSICAN BROTHERS ; and OTHO THE ARCHER.

CROP-EARED JACQUOT.

THE FENCING MASTER.

FERNANDE.

GABRIEL LAMBERT.

GEORGES.

THE GREAT MASSACRE. Being the first part of Queen Margot.

HENRI DE NAVARRE. Being the second part of Queen Margot.

HÉLÈNE DE CHAVERNY. Being the first part of the Regent's Daughter.

LOUISE DE LA VALLIÈRE. Being the first part of THE VICOMTE DE BRAGELONNE. Double Volume.

MAÎTRE ADAM.

THE MAN IN THE IRON MASK. Being the second part of THE VICOMTE DE BRAGELONNE. Double volume.

THE MOUTH OF HELL.

NANON. Double volume.

PAULINE ; PASCAL BRUNO ; and BONTEKOE.

PÈRE LA RUINE.

THE PRINCE OF THIEVES.

THE REMINISCENCES OF ANTONY.

ROBIN HOOD.

THE SNOWBALL and SULTANETTA.

SYLVANDIRE.

TALES OF THE SUPERNATURAL.

THE THREE MUSKETEERS. With a long Introduction by Andrew Lang. Double volume.

TWENTY YEARS AFTER. Double volume.

THE WILD DUCK SHOOTER.

THE WOLF-LEADER.

Methuen's Sixpenny Books

Albanesi (E. M.). LOVE AND LOUISA.

Austen (Jane). PRIDE AND PREJUDICE.

Bagot (Richard). A ROMAN MYSTERY.

Balfour (Andrew). BY STROKE OF SWORD.

Baring-Gould (S.). FURZE BLOOM.

CHEAP JACK ZITA.

KITTY ALONE.

URITH.

THE BROOM SQUIRE.

IN THE ROAR OF THE SEA.

NOÉMI.

A BOOK OF FAIRY TALES. Illustrated.

LITTLE TU'PENNY.

THE FROBISHERS.

WINEFRED.

Barr (Robert). JENNIE BAXTER, JOURNALIST.

IN THE MIDST OF ALARMS.

THE COUNTESS TEKLA.

THE MUTABLE MANY.

Benson (E. F.). DODO.

Brontë (Charlotte). SHIRLEY.

Brownell (C. L.). THE HEART OF JAPAN.

Burton (J. Bloundelle). ACROSS THE SALT SEAS.

Caffyn (Mrs)., ('Iota'). ANNE MAULEVERER.

Capes (Bernard). THE LAKE OF WINE.

Clifford (Mrs. W. K.). A FLASH OF SUMMER.

MRS. KEITH'S CRIME.

Corbett (Julian). A BUSINESS IN GREAT WATERS.

Croker (Mrs. B. M.). PEGGY OF THE BARTONS.

A STATE SECRET.

ANGEL.
JOHANNA.
Dante (Alighieri). THE VISION OF DANTE (Cary).
Doyle (A. Conan). ROUND THE RED LAMP.
Duncan (Sara Jeannette). A VOYAGE OF CONSOLATION.
THOSE DELIGHTFUL AMERICANS.
Eliot (George). THE MILL ON THE FLOSS.
Findlater (Jane H.). THE GREEN GRAVES OF BALGOWRIE.
Gallon (Tom). RICKERBY'S FOLLY.
Gaskell (Mrs.). CRANFORD.
MARY BARTON.
NORTH AND SOUTH.
Gerard (Dorothea). HOLY MATRIMONY.
THE CONQUEST OF LONDON.
MADE OF MONEY.
Gissing (George). THE TOWN TRAVELLER.
THE CROWN OF LIFE.
Glanville (Ernest). THE INCA'S TREASURE.
THE KLOOF BRIDE.
Gleig (Charles). BUNTER'S CRUISE.
Grimm (The Brothers). GRIMM'S FAIRY TALES. Illustrated.
Hope (Anthony). A MAN OF MARK.
A CHANGE OF AIR.
THE CHRONICLES OF COUNT ANTONIO.
PHROSO.
THE DOLLY DIALOGUES.
Hornung (E. W.). DEAD MEN TELL NO TALES.
Ingraham (J. H.). THE THRONE OF DAVID.
Le Queux (W.). THE HUNCHBACK OF WESTMINSTER.
Levett-Yeats (S. K.). THE TRAITOR'S WAY.
Linton (E. Lynn). THE TRUE HISTORY OF JOSHUA DAVIDSON.
Lyall (Edna). DERRICK VAUGHAN.
Malet (Lucas). THE CARISSIMA.
A COUNSEL OF PERFECTION.
Mann (Mrs. M. E.). MRS. PETER HOWARD.
A LOST ESTATE.
THE CEDAR STAR.
ONE ANOTHER'S BURDENS.
Marchmont (A. W.). MISER HOADLEY'S SECRET.
A MOMENT'S ERROR.
Marryat (Captain). PETER SIMPLE.
JACOB FAITHFUL.
Marsh (Richard). THE TWICKENHAM PEERAGE.
THE GODDESS.

THE JOSS,
A METAMORPHOSIS.
Mason (A. E. W.). CLEMENTINA.
Mathers (Helen). HONEY.
GRIFF OF GRIFFITHSCOURT.
SAM'S SWEETHEART.
Meade (Mrs. L. T.). DRIFT.
Mitford (Bertram). THE SIGN OF THE SPIDER.
Montresor (F. F.). THE ALIEN.
Morrison (Arthur). THE HOLE IN THE WALL.
Nesbit (E.). THE RED HOUSE.
Norris (W. E.). HIS GRACE.
GILES INGILBY.
THE CREDIT OF THE COUNTY.
LORD LEONARD.
MATTHEW AUSTIN.
CLARISSA FURICSA.
Oliphant (Mrs.). THE LADY'S WALK.
SIR ROBERT'S FORTUNE.
THE PRODIGALS.
Oppenheim (E. Phillips). MASTER OF MEN.
Parker (Gilbert). THE POMP OF THE LAVILETTES.
WHEN VALMOND CAME TO PONTIAC.
THE TRAIL OF THE SWORD.
Pemberton (Max). THE FOOTSTEPS OF A THRONE.
I CROWN THEE KING.
Phillpotts (Eden). THE HUMAN BOY.
CHILDREN OF THE MIST.
'Q.' THE WHITE WOLF.
Ridge (W. Pett). A SON OF THE STATE.
LOST PROPERTY.
GEORGE AND THE GENERAL.
Russell (W. Clark). A MARRIAGE AT SEA.
ABANDONED.
MY DANISH SWEETHEART.
HIS ISLAND PRINCESS.
Sergeant (Adeline). THE MASTER OF BEECHWOOD.
BARBARA'S MONEY.
THE YELLOW DIAMOND.
THE LOVE THAT OVERCAME.
Surtees (R. S.). HANDLEY CROSS. Illustrated.
MR. SPONGE'S SPORTING TOUR. Illustrated.
ASK MAMMA. Illustrated.
Walford (Mrs. L. B.). MR. SMITH.
COUSINS.
THE BABY'S GRANDMOTHER.
Wallace (General Lew). BEN-HUR.
THE FAIR GOD.
Watson (H. B. Marriot). THE ADVENTURERS.
Weekes (A. B.). PRISONERS OF WAR.
White (Percy). A PASSIONATE PILGRIM.